Victory in Vietnam

Victory in Vietnam

The Official History of the People's Army of Vietnam, 1954–1975

The Military History Institute of Vietnam
Translated by Merle L. Pribbenow
Foreword by William J. Duiker

 University Press of Kansas

Published by the University Press of Kansas (Lawrence, Kansas 66049), which was organized by the Kansas Board of Regents and is operated and funded by Emporia State University, Fort Hays State University, Kansas State University, Pittsburg State University, the University of Kansas, and Wichita State University.

First published in Hanoi, Vietnam, in 1988, and then in a revised edition in 1994, under the title *History of the People's Army of Vietnam, Volume II* [Lich su Quan doi Nhan dan Viet Nam, Tap II]: *The Maturation of the People's Army of Vietnam during the Resistance War against the Americans to Save the Nation (1954–1975)* [Thoi Ky Truong Thanh cua Quan Doi Nhan Dan Viet Nam trong cuoc Khang Chien Chong My, Cuu Nuoc (1954–1975)] for the Military History Institute of Vietnam, Ministry of Defense, by the People's Army Publishing House.

Edited by Senior General Hoang Van Thai, former Deputy Minister of Defense, and Colonel General Tran Van Quang, former Deputy Minister of Defense. Authors: Senior Colonel Phan Dinh (Part I), Senior Colonel Hoang Co Quang (Part II), Senior Colonel Nguyen Duc Thong (Part III), Senior Colonel Ho Huu Vinh (Part IV), Colonel Nguyen Quoc Dung (Parts I–V), Lieutenant General Hoang Phuong (conclusion).

Library of Congress Cataloging-in-Publication Data

Victory in Vietnam : the official history of the people's army of Vietnam, 1954–1975 : the Military History Institute of Vietnam / translated by Merle L. Pribbenow ; foreword by William J. Duiker.
    p. cm. — (Modern war studies)
Includes index.
ISBN 0-7006-1175-4 (cloth : alk. paper)
    1. Vietnamese Conflict, 1961–1975—Vietnam (Democratic Republic). 2. Vietnamese Conflict, 1961–1975—Campaigns. 3. Vietnam (Democratic Republic). Qu˘an dòãoi—History. I. Series.
    DS558.5.V47 2002
    959.704'3—dc21
              2001006344

British Library Cataloguing in Publication Data is available.

Printed in the United States of America

10 9 8 7 6 5 4 3

Contents

Foreword: The History of the People's Army

William J. Duiker

In the quarter of a century that has elapsed since the fall of Saigon, the performance of the U.S. armed forces in the Vietnam War has been exposed to exhaustive, and often critical, analysis. Relatively little attention has been paid, at least in the United States, to the victors. Although a few scholarly studies have focused on the origins and the buildup of the North Vietnamese army (formally known as the People's Army of Vietnam, or PAVN), a full-scale analysis of its own performance in the South has not yet appeared. Several books on the PAVN have been published in Hanoi, but until now, none has been translated into the English language. This is unfortunate, because the role of the PAVN in the South and the nature of its relationship with the local insurgent forces (known popularly as the Viet Cong) has never been properly explored.

With the publication of this book, ably translated from the original Vietnamese by Merle Pribbenow, the University Press of Kansas thus fills a yawning gap in the growing literature on the Vietnam War. Published in a second edition in 1994, it was written by a committee of senior Vietnamese military officers under the general direction of the Military History Institute in the Ministry of Defense in Hanoi. There are, of course, some inherent limitations with this approach, since institutions have a natural tendency to laud their own performance and cover up mistakes. This drawback is undoubtedly even more pronounced after a military victory, when it is tempting for senior military commanders to gloss over errors that have been committed and bask in the aura of success.

Such shortcomings are fully visible here. A heavy dose of triumphalism permeates the text, as well as a sense of moral superiority that the forces of good have inevitably been victorious over the ranks of global imperialism. Still, the authors are not entirely unwilling to admit errors in the drafting and execution of policy, and on occasion they display a refreshing sense of candor in admitting instances of defeatism and hubris within the ranks. It is for these reasons that this book will be useful to specialists and general readers alike who wish to explore the view from the other side of the Vietnam War.

The second of two volumes on the history of the PAVN, the book opens in 1954, a moment of considerable significance in the history of modern Vietnam. In July of that year, the Geneva Conference had brought an end to the First Indochina War, which had been fought between military forces led by the veteran Communist Ho Chi Minh and the French. Reflecting the fact that neither side had attained a decisive victory in that conflict, the Geneva Agreement had temporarily divided the country into two separate regroupment zones—Ho Chi Minh's Democratic Republic of Vietnam (DRV) in the North, and a non-Communist administration (eventually to be known as the Republic of Vietnam, or RVN) in the South. A Political Declaration drafted at the conference contained an appeal for national reunification elections to be held in 1956, but the appeal was nonbinding and had not been approved by two key delegations at Geneva, the new Vietnamese administration in the South and the United States.

It was at this point that the United States first became directly involved in Vietnam. As French forces withdrew in accordance with the Geneva Agreement, the Eisenhower administration decided to sponsor the new anti-Communist regime in South Vietnam, with its capital in Saigon. This volume thus focuses on the period leading up to and including the Second Indochina War (what is usually described in Vietnam today as "the American war"), a conflict that first began to gain momentum in the late 1950s and concluded almost two decades later with the occupation of Saigon by North Vietnamese military forces in the spring of 1975.

It is important for American readers to note, therefore, that by the time this book opens, the PAVN had already amassed considerable experience in developing its military capabilities as the vanguard of the revolution. The first units were formed during World War II, at a time when Indochina was temporarily occupied by Japanese military forces. The commander of these first units—known as Armed Propaganda Brigades because their function was as much political as military—was Ho Chi Minh's talented young colleague Vo Nguyen Giap. Giap would eventually develop as the movement's chief military strategist in the war against the French.

In preparing to make their bid for national independence at the end of the Pacific War, Communist leaders recognized that they lacked the capacity to defeat the Japanese or the French by force of arms alone. In both size and weaponry, their forces were inferior to both adversaries. They therefore sought to rely on what they perceived to be their political advantage (support for the cause of national independence from the local population), as well as on other familiar devices applied by the weak against the strong, such as guerrilla tactics and an astute use of diplomacy. This strategy led the Communist Party to victory in August 1945, when its fledgling forces (popularly known as the Vietminh) seized power in Hanoi and declared the formation of an independent Democratic Republic of Vietnam.

But the French were unwilling to abandon their "balcony on the Pacific," and after abortive negotiations during the summer of 1946, the First Indochina

War broke out in December. Although their armed forces were still no match for the French in a head-to-head confrontation, General Giap and his colleagues calculated that a protracted struggle, characterized by the military and political mobilization of the local population, could undermine enemy morale and eventually force the French to withdraw. The possibility of an outright military triumph appeared increasingly probable after Mao Zedong's Communist Party came to power in China in 1949, a stunning shift in the regional balance of power that provided the Vietminh with a powerful new ally.

By then, however, the conflict in Indochina had become a factor in the Cold War. The United States intervened on the side of the French to avert the alleged threat of a spread of the Red tide throughout Southeast Asia. After an offensive on French positions in early 1951 was driven back with heavy losses, Vietminh forces reverted to guerrilla tactics in a bid to extend the war and undermine support for the war in France. In the early spring of 1954, Vietminh troops won a major psychological victory by seizing the isolated French military base at Dien Bien Phu, located in the far northwestern part of the country. With public opinion in France increasingly tired of the "dirty war" in far-off Indochina, French leaders signed a compromise peace agreement at Geneva.

The Geneva Conference thus opened a new phase in the history of modern Vietnam, as Ho Chi Minh and his colleagues returned to Hanoi as the leaders of a de facto government with administrative control over more than 10 million people. Although the Geneva Agreement had called for national elections in 1956, it soon became clear that the new government in Saigon, led by the feisty anti-Communist Ngo Dinh Diem, had no intention of holding them. Instead, he sought to suppress the remnants of the Vietminh movement that had been left in the South after the signing of the cease-fire.

The new situation created a dilemma for DRV leaders in Hanoi, who now faced the task of bringing about recovery from the war and laying the foundations of a socialist society in North Vietnam. As a stopgap measure, the new regime authorized its followers in the South to undertake measures for their own self-defense and launched an intensive program to modernize the North Vietnamese armed forces in case armed struggle should resume. The authors provide us with some useful information about that program, but they make no reference to the bitter internal debate that took place in Hanoi over the respective priorities to be assigned to domestic reconstruction and national reunification. In fact, differences over the policy to be applied in the South became quite sharp, and threatened to undermine relations with Hanoi's allies as well as the policy of consensus that Ho Chi Minh had carefully crafted since the end of World War II.

This period of hesitation came to an end in 1959, when Ngo Dinh Diem's campaign to "eradicate the Communists" decimated the ranks of the Party's clandestine apparatus in South Vietnam. At a fateful meeting of the Central Committee held in January, Party leaders decided to return to revolutionary war. How that program would be carried out, however, was left unresolved. What was certain, as this book makes clear, was that the DRV would, if necessary, play a direct and guiding role in the process. The first priority was thus to establish supply routes for transporting equipment and personnel to the South. When completed, the land route consisted of paths and trails that crossed the Demilitarized Zone (DMZ) and snaked through the forests of southern Laos. A second maritime route was scheduled to follow the coastline of the South China Sea.

Infiltration began slowly, with only about 500 "regroupees" (southerners who had been sent north for training after the Geneva Conference) being sent down the Trail during the first year of operation. They were assigned positions of leadership for the emerging revolutionary movement in the South. But as the war heated up in the early 1960s, the rate of infiltration increased substantially. By the end of 1963, over 40,000 soldiers and cadres, mostly native southerners, moved down what would soon become known as the Ho Chi Minh Trail. That number represented about one-half of the full-time troops operating under Party command in the South, and 80 percent of the movement's technical personnel.

In the authors' own words, the infiltration of personnel and supplies became a major factor in changing the balance of forces in South Vietnam in favor of the insurgent forces. Whereas the ratio between the Viet Cong (formally labeled the People's Liberation Armed Forces, or PLAF) and the Saigon government's armed forces (the Army of the Republic of Vietnam, or ARVN) was about one to ten in 1961, it had been reduced to one to five a year later. Not surprisingly, the movement gained considerable momentum and vastly improved capabilities in confronting their adversary. By the time John F. Kennedy entered the White House in January 1961, the situation in South Vietnam had become a major issue in the Cold War.

One of the strategies applied by the Kennedy administration to counter the growing insurgent movement was the so-called "strategic hamlet"—fortified villages designed to keep the guerrillas from obtaining access to the Vietnamese population in the countryside. The authors concede that at first, the program proved to be highly effective in isolating the guerrillas from their chief source of recruits and supplies. During much of 1962, the Saigon regime managed to create the new organizations faster than the PLAF could destroy them, resulting in a perceptible decline in morale within the movement. Insurgent units also encountered serious problems in coping with ARVN's increasing mobility, as the latter could now be transported quickly by helicopter to trouble spots throughout South Vietnam. Such conditions aroused a temporary mood of optimism in Washington, and may have been a factor in persuading the administration to draft plans to reduce the size of the U.S. presence in the RVN.

But prescient observers in Washington and Saigon, noting the haste with which the strategic hamlets were built and their unpopularity among the local population, tempered their optimism. By the spring of 1963, the guerrillas had figured out how to cope with the strategic hamlets, as well as with ARVN's new mobility. At the battle of Ap Bac in January, PLAF units showed that they could defeat South Vietnamese troops even when the latter were supported by the latest in U.S. military technology.

While the strategic hamlets were being steadily attacked and destroyed in rural areas, tensions between the Diem regime and local Buddhist activists erupted in the major cities. Saigon's harsh suppression of dissident monks soured relations with the United States, and in early November a military coup, launched with tacit approval from the White House, overthrew the Diem regime. As the authors make clear, at first Party leaders were uncertain how to respond, but they soon decided that the coup in Saigon presented a major opportunity to achieve a breakthrough in the South. At a meeting of the Central Committee in December, they approved a plan to increase infiltration and intensify the level of fighting in a bid to overthrow the new government in Saigon. Although the authors are silent on the issue, the decision aroused bitter debate in Hanoi and soured relations with Moscow, where Nikita Khrushchev was opposed to measures that could threaten his policy of peaceful coexistence with the West. But Party leaders in Hanoi, urged on by the militant new First Secretary Le Duan, were obdurate. Senior civilian and military officials opposed to the decision were purged from their positions.

Beginning in 1964, the role of the North in the conflict in South Vietnam steadily increased. The Ho Chi Minh Trail was expanded to permit the dispatch of PAVN main force units to the South. The process accelerated after the Tonkin Gulf Incident in August, which Hanoi interpreted as a sign that Washington was determined to prevent a Communist victory. By the winter of 1964–1965, the Saigon regime was on the verge of collapse.

Lyndon Johnson's decision to dispatch U.S. combat troops to South Vietnam in the spring of 1965 was a major setback to policy planners in Hanoi, who had hoped to keep Washington from intervening directly in the conflict. By mid-summer, the growing U.S. military presence made it clear that victory would come only after a protracted and bitter struggle. Still, Hanoi did not flinch. Convinced that the enemy was faced with serious political weaknesses, Party leaders decided to challenge U.S. troops on the battlefield. The size of the PLAF was expanded to over 175,000 guerrillas (apparently not including 80,000 paramilitary forces), and a new DRV draft law doubled the size of the PAVN to over 400,000 by the end of the year. Of the 50,000 troops sent to the South in 1965, a growing percentage were native northerners.

It was now up to General Nguyen Chi Thanh, Hanoi's new commander in the South, to prove they could win. A charismatic military leader with a fervent belief in the Maoist doctrine that spirit could overcome superior firepower, Thanh had apparently been selected for the assignment because Le Duan now viewed Vo Nguyen Giap as excessively cautious. Expressing confidence that the PAVN could defeat the technologically superior Americans on the battlefield, Thanh lured U.S. troops to Ia Drang Valley, a mountainous region along the Cambodian border, to test his assumptions. In the bitter battle that ensued, both sides claimed victory in the first direct confrontation between North Vietnamese and American combat forces.

Nguyen Chi Thanh's ambitious strategy resulted in high casualties on both sides. For a time, Hanoi apparently made every effort to provide him with the necessary manpower. By the end of 1966, the size of the PAVN had reached

700,000, with two-thirds stationed in the North and the remainder in the South. The total number of full-time troops operating in South Vietnam was up one-third compared with the previous year.

Still, the sheer weight of the growing U.S. military presence was taking its toll. Although the authors are somewhat circumspect about the issue, they tacitly concede that Thanh's aggressive strategy was arousing second thoughts in Hanoi. As U.S. troop levels continued to increase in 1966 and 1967, Vietnamese casualties increased dramatically, with predictable consequences. Morale within the movement began to suffer, leading to passivity, lack of discipline, and high rates of desertion. U.S. military intelligence sources took such evidence as an indication that the tide was slowly beginning to turn in Saigon's favor.

By the spring of 1967, DRV leaders were faced with a difficult choice. The Saigon regime, under a series of post-Diem political and military leaders, was still quite fragile and had not been able to win the "hearts and minds" of the local population. The Johnson administration was faced with a growing antiwar movement in the United States and around the globe. Still, Hanoi had been unable to turn such advantages to good use at the conference table or on the battlefield. It was now deemed vital to bring about a change in the situation that could have a dramatic effect in the United States, where presidential elections were scheduled to take place in the fall of 1968.

Plans for the famous Tet Offensive were first drafted during the spring of 1967. Hanoi's goal was to lure U.S. troops to outlying areas around the country so as to permit its own forces to concentrate on the more vulnerable ARVN units in the highly populated lowlands. Frontal assaults on enemy positions in the countryside would be combined with general uprisings in Saigon and other major cities. North Vietnamese war planners hoped for an outright victory, but were prepared for a lesser result that would lead to the formation of a coalition government and a negotiated withdrawal of all U.S. troops from the RVN.

The authors, repeating official claims in Hanoi, declare that the Tet Offensive, launched at the end of January 1968, was a "great strategic victory," and in fact the first reports suggested that the insurgents had achieved great gains in the countryside. At the same time, suicide attacks against U.S. and GVN installations in Saigon had a massive psychological impact on public opinion in the United States. Shaken by such reports, the White House agreed to make key concessions in an effort to bring about peace talks. After Tet, it would no longer be possible for the United States to increase its military presence in South Vietnam.

Still, Hanoi's claims of victory were overstated. Internal documents indicate that Party leaders were somewhat disappointed at the results of the offensive, and the authors concede that DRV war planners had underestimated the military capabilities of the enemy and overestimated the level of support for the insurgent forces in the urban areas. They thus tacitly confirm claims by the Pentagon that the attacking forces had suffered heavy casualties in the fighting, and would be unable to retain their gains in the countyside.

The price for Hanoi's excessive optimism was paid in 1969. The insurgent forces in the South (PLAF units had been especially decimated) were unable to hold on to their territorial gains, and Saigon managed to regain control over many areas that it had lost during the offensive. In the meantime, U.S. troops managed to drive PAVN troops back to isolated areas of the country, such as the U Minh Forest in the Ca Mau Peninsula, the Plain of Reeds near the Cambodian border, and parts of the Central Highlands. Supplies of food and military equipment for the insurgents were severely affected, and pessimism about future prospects rose to dangerous levels within the ranks.

By 1970, however, the situation once again began to improve. The coup d'état that overthrew Prince Norodom Sihanouk in Cambodia helped to revitalize the revolutionary movement there, and Saigon's ill-fated attempt to cut the Ho Chi Minh Trail in southern Laos showed the ineffectiveness of ARVN troops when operating without full U.S. air support. Perhaps more important, North Vietnamese leaders took full advantage of the U.S. bombing halt announced in the autumn of 1968 to improve and expand infiltration routes into the South. The Ho Chi Minh Trail now reached a total length of over 6,000 kilometers, and a new pipeline to ship fuel to the front was under construction. Hanoi's planners could now place corps-sized main force units on the battlefield to confront the increasingly demoralized South Vietnamese forces.

In March 1972, Hanoi launched its Easter Offensive to coincide with the presidential campaign in the United States. Attacks by PAVN units were concentrated in the northern provinces of the country, where the proximity to the DRV offered the possibility of reinforcements and logistical support. The authors follow official sources in heralding the campaign as another great success, but they concede that U.S. air cover and the lack of logistical capacity prevented a greater victory. The ambiguous results were fully reflected in the compromise peace agreement that was signed in Paris the following January. All U.S. troops were to be withdrawn from South Vietnam; all Vietnamese units on both sides were permitted to remain in place. In return, the DRV formally recognized the legitimacy of the Saigon regime under its president, Nguyen Van Thieu, pending reunification elections to be held at some time in the future. There was no mention of the presence of North Vietnamese troops in the South, but Article 7 declared that no additional troops or matériel were to be introduced into the RVN.

As it turned out, neither side lived up to the terms of the Paris Agreement. The Thieu regime ignored the cease-fire and launched intensive attacks on enemy-held areas in the country. Although insurgent units at first sought to avoid confrontations with ARVN troops, the DRV took full advantage of the situation to strengthen its forces in the South. By late 1974, Party leaders recognized that a more aggressive approach was needed, and plans were drawn up to launch a military offensive aimed at achieving total victory within two years. As it turned out, the Thieu regime panicked, opening the door to Hanoi's victorious Ho Chi Minh Campaign, which brought an end to the war in the spring of 1975.

The authors have little to say about the final offensive that has not been said before, but they confirm the widespread impression that it was almost entirely a northern operation, with leadership over the operation in the hands of senior strategists sent down from Hanoi and trainloads of troops and weapons moving south from the DRV for transit over the Ho Chi Minh Trail to the battlefield.

How do the authors explain North Vietnam's stunning victory in the Vietnam War? To the seasoned observer, their answers are hardly surprising: occupation of the moral high ground, a decade of experience in fighting the French, strong Party leadership, and the support of the Vietnamese people. What is most conspicuous by its absence is any reference to the assistance provided by Hanoi's chief allies. Beginning in 1965, the Soviet Union provided significant amounts of advanced military weaponry to help the DRV defend its skies from U.S. bombing raids. Over a period of two decades, China not only sent billions of dollars in military and economic aid, but also dispatched half a million technicians, advisers, and combat troops to assist the DRV in its struggle. China also provided a major deterrent to any potential U.S. decision to invade North Vietnam. It is difficult to imagine Hanoi's stunning victory without the firm support of its fraternal allies, who will not be pleased at the lack of gratitude expressed here.

As we have seen, the authors also fail to provide sufficient insight into the strategic debates that periodically erupted within the Party leadership over the course of the war. At times, these controversies apparently became quite bitter and involved relations with Hanoi's allies as well. Also unmentioned were the occasional tensions that strained the relationship between Party strategists in the North and their representatives operating in the South. To what degree were PLAF commanders able to influence major policy decisions reached in the North? Such questions are entirely ignored in this account, which leaves the misleading impression that decisionmaking in Hanoi was a simple affair, reached by unanimous consent and carried out unquestionably by the insurgent forces in the field.

This book, then, is by no means the full story. In fact, it would undoubtedly be unrealistic to expect the current regime in Hanoi, which relies partly on its aura of victory to legitimize its rule in contemporary Vietnam, to provide a completely forthcoming assessment of its performance during the Vietnam War. Still, the authors have offered some significant revelations of their own—including the cardinal importance of the Ho Chi Minh Trail and the key role played by North Vietnam in guiding the struggle in the South—that should offer new insights to the reader interested in exploring the view from the other side. A number of key questions remain unanswered, but one of the more pernicious myths about the Vietnam War—that the insurgent movement in South Vietnam was essentially an autonomous one that possessed only limited ties to the regime in the North—has been definitively dispelled.

Translator's Preface

In 1968, faced with the prospect of a two-year commitment to a new job as a file clerk deep in the bowels of the CIA Headquarters Building at Langley, I volunteered for the only assignment with sufficient priority to free me from my desperately boring existence: training as a Vietnamese-language interpreter/ translator for assignment to Saigon Station. After more than a year of language and collateral training, I arrived in Saigon in the spring of 1970 and promptly fell in love with the country. The scenery was lushly exotic, the work exciting, the culture fascinating, the women beautiful, and the people (like me at five feet seven inches) were *short*—for the first time in my life I could stand in the middle of a crowd and actually see what was happening.

I immediately and naively informed my new boss that I intended to stay in Vietnam until someone forced me out at gunpoint. Five years later, on 29 April 1975, someone did just that. I left Saigon aboard a Marine CH-46 helicopter, dazed and confused at the rapid collapse of the largest and most expensive U.S. military effort since World War II.

Despite the shock and disappointment that attended my departure, my love for the country and its people never faded. During the next twenty years, I continued to work for the agency as a translator specializing in Indochina affairs. With an insatiable appetite, I also devoured every book I could find on the Vietnam War, in an effort to come to terms with my own experience and better understand what had gone wrong (for everyone, not just the Americans) and why. It was my great frustration, however, to find very little on the war written from anything other than an American perspective. I felt strongly that many of the answers I was seeking would come only when there was greater access to the views of the victorious Vietnamese. As the years passed, my frustrations grew, even as I accumulated a deepening understanding of the American involvement in Vietnam.

Then, in 1994, an old friend who knew of my obsession returned from Hanoi with a gift for me: a copy of the newly published *History of the People's Army of Vietnam,* the official overall history of the Vietnam War compiled by the Vietnamese Ministry of Defense's Military History Institute. Not surprisingly, given my decades-long quest, I became immediately and deeply fascinated by the book, reading and rereading it again and again. Despite the obvious (and unsurprising) Communist rhetoric, as well as the victors' understandable exaggerations and bravado, I did indeed find answers—very believable answers—to many of my questions. In effect, my reading of this tome confirmed much of what I'd only surmised previously—that many of the accepted "truths" contained in some of our most notable histories were, quite simply, wrong.

I initially translated several excerpts from the book as a favor to a friend who was compiling an official history of U.S. efforts in Vietnam. After my retirement, I wrote a related article for the magazine *Vietnam* that focused on North Vietnamese operations in the early 1960s. That article led Dr. Lewis Sorley to ask me for translations of the sections of *History of the People's Army of Vietnam* that dealt with the latter stages of the American War in Vietnam, which he incorporated into his much-praised book *A Better War.* Intrigued as I was by some of the book's revelations, Sorley encouraged me to translate the entire book for publication in this country and introduced me to Michael Briggs at the University Press of Kansas, which had published Sorley's highly regarded biography of Harold K. Johnson, LBJ's army chief of staff. Meanwhile, other authors approached me for translations of other sections of the book and, before I knew it, the entire book had been translated.

About the translation itself: I have tried very hard to render the original as accurately as possible and to preserve the "voice" of the PAVN authors. As William Duiker himself notes in the Foreword, this necessarily means that the work has some "inherent limitations . . . since institutions have a natural tendency to laud their own performance and cover up mistakes." I have made no effort to exclude or hide such "limitations," which, in any case, will be readily apparent (as well as ripe for debate) for the readers of this translation. After all, much of the point of making this translation available is to allow American readers to have unfiltered access to the Vietnamese viewpoint, however flawed some might consider it. We Americans have our own blind spots and special views with which other nations and peoples take issue. My hope here is to help further the dialogue and debate on the war by, in effect, opening a direct channel to the "other side."

It should also be noted that the Vietnamese-language edition—because the Vietnamese consider it a continuation of the previous volume—begins with Chapter 9 followed by Chapters 10, 11, 12, and 13. Each of those "chapters" are subdivided into "sections." American readers, however, will readily see that what the Vietnamese classify as chapters and sections are here more comfortably and conveniently designated as parts and chapters, respectively. In addition— because I treat this translation as a self-contained volume—I begin the book with

Chapter 1 of Part I and then number the remaining chapters and parts sequentially throughout the rest of the book—that is, no chapter or part number is repeated. Information enclosed in brackets has been added to provide additional explanatory information on terms or locations. In some cases I have provided the original Vietnamese term, also enclosed in brackets [ ], for additional clarity.

I must admit that getting to this point has not been an easy affair. Once the translation was completed, I still needed to clarify the status of the work's copyright, a concept still evolving in postwar Vietnam. Finally, after a protracted effort, in keeping with the requirements of the 1998 copyright agreement between the United States and Vietnam, and with the gracious cooperation of the Vietnam–USA Society and the People's Army Publishing House, copyright approval was obtained and the project was allowed to move forward.

In conclusion, I would like to thank Dr. Sorley for his pivotal encouragement and support, Michael Briggs for his tireless efforts, and my wife and family for their patience and understanding during the long hours this translation entailed. I hope scholars and military history devotees find this book as interesting and informative as I have.

—*Merle L. Pribbenow*

Courtesy U.S. Army Center of Military History

Terminology

A-12: Single-shot 140mm rocket launcher (modified from BM-14 launcher)

A-72: Shoulder-fired SAM-7 anti-aircraft missile launcher

Americal Division: The 23rd Division's name, the "Americal Division," is derived from the division's original formation during World War II on the island of New Caledonia in the South Pacific. The "Ameri-" in the name comes from "American" and the "cal" comes from "Caledonia."

Annamite Mountains (Truong Son): The mountain range running from the Central Highlands of South Vietnam up the spine of the Indochina Peninsula to China. The Vietnamese term means the "long mountains."

B: Communist code designation for South Vietnam

B-40: Soviet-designed shoulder-fired anti-tank rocket launcher RPG-2

B-41: Soviet RPG-7 anti-tank rocket launcher (upgraded RPG-2)

B-72: Soviet AT-3 (Sagger) anti-tank guided missile

B2: Military designation of the military front controlling the portion of South Vietnam including Cochin China and the extreme southern provinces of Central Vietnam. B2 was under the direct control of COSVN.

B3: The Central Highlands Front

B4: The Tri-Thien Front

B5: The Northern Quang Tri–Route 9 Front

C: Communist code designation for Laos

Cochin China (Nam Bo): The southern portion of South Vietnam from the southern end of the Central Highlands through the Mekong Delta to the Gulf of Thailand, approximately the South Vietnamese Army's Military Regions 3 and 4. (I have used the French colonial term for this area to make it more accessible to American readers who may have trouble dealing with the foreign sound of the Vietnamese term "Nam Bo.")

Central Cochin China: The northern half of the Mekong Delta, including the Plain of Reeds (Dong Thap)

Central Highlands: The mountainous high plateau in the central portion of South Vietnam—includes the provinces of Darlac (Ban Me Thuot), Pleiku (Gia Rai), Kontum, and Phu Bon

Central Military Party Committee (Quan Uy Truong Uong): The Communist Party Central Committee organ responsible for directing all military affairs. General Vo Nguyen Giap was Secretary of the Central Military Party Committee.

Commandos (bo doi biet dong): A subcategory of sappers specializing in operations inside enemy cities, including terrorist attacks and intelligence-gathering

COSVN: The Central Office for South Vietnam (Truong Uong Cuc Mien Nam), the organ of the Communist Party Central Committee responsible for South Vietnam

COSVN Military Command (Bo Tu Lenh Mien): COSVN's highest military command organization. Often translated as "Regional Command for South Vietnam," but translated here as COSVN Military Command to avoid confusion with Region 5 (Khu 5) and the various military regions (quan khu), which were lower-level and usually subordinate to COSVN Military Command.

DKB: Single-tube 122mm rocket launcher, modified from Soviet BM-21 multiple rocket launchers

DKZ: Recoilless rifles, also includes unguided rocket launchers such as the DKB

Demilitarized Zone (DMZ): The temporary demarcation line between North and South Vietnam established by the 1954 Geneva Peace Agreement. Located at approximately the 17th parallel, the DMZ follows the Ben Hai River to the sea.

Eastern Cochin China: The area from the southern end of the Central Highlands down to the Mekong Delta, approximately equivalent to the South Vietnamese Army's Military Region 3 (3rd Corps)

Extreme southern Central Vietnam: The provinces lying between Cochin China (Nam Bo) and the Central Highlands/Region 5—Quang Duc, Tuyen Duc, Lam Dong, Binh Thuan, Ninh Thuan

General Military Party Committee (Tong Quan Uy): The predecessor organization of the Central Military Party Committee

General Political Department (Tong Cuc Chinh Tri): The Party, propaganda, and political element of the People's Army and one of the three (later four) main administrative subdivisions of the People's Army

General Rear Services Department (Tong Cuc Hau Can): The People's Army's logistics and support element and one of the main administrative subdivisions of the People's Army

General Staff (Bo Tong Tham Muu): The People's Army's highest staff organization and one of the three (later four) main administrative subdivisions of the People's Army. General Van Tien Dung was the Chief of Staff of the General Staff.

General Technical Department (Tong Cuc Ky Thuat): The People's Army's technical support component, formed in 1974 from the technical elements of the General Rear Services Department

H-12: 107mm multiple rocket launcher

High Command (Bo Tong Tu Lenh): The People's Army's supreme military command organization. General Vo Nguyen Giap was the People's Army commander-in-chief and Commander of the High Command.

K: Communist code designation for Cambodia (Kampuchea)

K-20: Covert Vietnamese People's Army logisitics element operating under civilian business cover in Cambodia, supplying Communist units in South Vietnam with goods shipped through the port of Sihanoukville or purchased locally in Cambodia

MAAG: Military Assistance and Advisory Group

MACV: Military Assistance Command, Vietnam

Massed (or concentrated) combat (danh tap trung): Conventional (as opposed to guerrilla) combat operations

Massed (or concentrated) troops (bo doi tap trung): Full-time soldiers operating in military units. The "massed troops" are the main force and the local force soldiers, not the guerrilla militia.

Military Region 4: The "panhandle" area of North Vietnam, immediately north of the Demilitarized Zone (DMZ)

Mobile combat (danh van dong): Combat tactics involving maneuver, as opposed to defensive or siege tactics

Plain of Jars (Canh Dong Chum): The strategically important highland plateau in Laos north of the capital city of Vientianne

Region 5: The area of South Vietnam from the Central Highlands north to the Demilitarized Zone (DMZ)

Sappers (bo doi dac cong): People's Army special operations personnel, trained in explosives, infiltration, combat assaults, and reconnaissance. A cross between frontline combat engineers, Rangers, LRRPs, and special forces.

"The three kinds of troops": Main force troops (bo doi chu luc), local force troops (bo doi dia phuong), and militia (dan quan) (either guerrilla militia—dan quan du kich—or self-defense militia—dan quan tu ve). Main force troops were subordinate to military regions or higher-level organizations; local force troops operated on the provincial and district level; and militia and guerrillas operated at the village and hamlet level.

"The three-pronged attack" (ba mui giap cong): Military action, political action, military proselytizing

"The three strategic zones": The mountain jungles, the rural lowlands, and the urban areas

Tri-Thien: The provinces of Quang Tri and Thua Thien
Western Cochin China: The southern half of the Mekong Delta, from the Mekong
    River south to the Gulf of Thailand

Introduction

Following the 1974 publication of *History of the People's Army of Vietnam,* Volume I, Volume II of *History of the People's Army of Vietnam* was presented to our readers on the 45th anniversary of the formation of the People's Army and the 100th birthday of Chairman Ho Chi Minh. Because it was so thick, in this initial printing Volume II of *History of the People's Army of Vietnam* was published as two books.

Although containing a number of mistakes, because of inadequate research or because of the limitations of the writers, during the past few years *History of the People's Army of Vietnam,* Volumes I and II, have been used by the people's armed forces as documents for study, historical education, and to pass on our traditions. They have served as a useful research tool for staff agencies and research cadre, especially for historians both within and outside the armed forces.

The Military History Institute of Vietnam has received many opinions and criticisms of these two volumes. After absorbing these opinions and criticisms, and in response to our needs for research and study, the Military History Institute of Vietnam and the People's Army Publishing House has arranged to republish (with corrections and additions) both volumes of *History of the People's Army of Vietnam.* This is a work that will be of value for historical science in general and for military history in particular.

The Military History Institute of Vietnam and the People's Army Publishing House wish to sincerely thank the Ministry of Culture and Information, the Ministry of Finance, the Government Pricing Committee, and the Finance Department of the Ministry of Defense for their financial assistance. We would also like to thank all readers, staff agencies, military units, and scientists both inside and outside the armed forces for their enthusiastic response and their active contributions that enabled *History of the People's Army of Vietnam* to be reprinted on the occasion of the 50th anniversary of the founding of the People's Army of Vietnam (22 December 1944–22 December 1994).

Military History Institute of Vietnam,
People's Army Publishing House

PART I

Building the People's Army into a
Regular, Modern Armed Force:
Maintaining and Developing Revolutionary
Armed Forces in the South, 1954–1960

1
Urgently Reorganizing Our Forces: Preparations to Deal with a New Enemy

A NEW STRUGGLE BEGINS

Our victory in the resistance war against the French colonialists and the intervention of the United States marked the beginning of a new phase in the development of the Vietnamese Revolution.

On 21 July 1954, the Geneva Conference on Indochina ended. The nations participating in the conference solemnly pledged to respect the independence, sovereignty, unity, and territorial integrity of Vietnam, Cambodia, and Laos. Foreign troops were required to withdraw from Indochina. A free general election would be held to unify Vietnam two years from the day the Geneva Conference ended.

While awaiting the general election, the cease-fire agreement provided that, in Vietnam, the 17th parallel would become a temporary military boundary. The forces of the People's Army of Vietnam would regroup north of the boundary, and the forces of the army of the "French Alliance" would regroup south of the boundary. The military boundary was to be temporary and under no conditions was to be considered a political or territorial border.

To implement the agreement the High Command of the People's Army of Vietnam ordered a nationwide cease-fire for our armed forces effective 0000 hour, 22 July 1954.

The war was over. Peace had been reestablished throughout Vietnam. On 13 May 1955, the last colonial aggressor soldier withdrew from the Hai Phong assembly area. The Northern portion of our nation, now completely liberated, began an era of the building of socialism. Meanwhile, in the South our people still suffered under the yoke of the imperialists and their puppets.

Our people's mission of liberating the nation was not yet finished.

Although the United States had directly assisted the French during the Indochina war of aggression (1945–1954) and was a participant in the Geneva

3

Conference, President Eisenhower announced that "the U.S. is not bound by the terms of this agreement."[1]

"Seizing the opportunity"[2] provided by France's defeat and its forced withdrawal from Indochina, and concerned that "failure in Vietnam will lead to the expansion of communism in Southeast Asia and the western Pacific,"[3] the United States carried out a vigorous program designed to push the French out and, using a new type of colonialism, to commit aggression against us by taking control over our nation and turning South Vietnam into an American military base. The American objectives were to maintain the division of our nation, to block and push back the tide of the people's revolutionary movement in Asia and throughout the world, and to threaten the socialist nations.

In June 1954 the Americans brought Ngo Dinh Diem back from the United States to establish a puppet government in South Vietnam. A U.S. military mission (the Special Military Mission) was established in Saigon. The U.S. National Security Council approved an "emergency program" of economic and military assistance and replaced the French advisors with American advisors to Diem. The United States gathered a number of imperialist nations and U.S. satellite nations to form SEATO, a Southeast Asian military alliance. In September 1954, South Vietnam, Laos, and Cambodia were placed under the "umbrella of protection" of this Southeast Asian military group.

The Party Central Committee and Chairman Ho Chi Minh correctly assessed the aggressive nature of the American imperialists and closely monitored their schemes and actions. In mid-July 1954, even before the Geneva Conference had ended, Ho Chi Minh clearly stated that "the U.S. is not only the enemy of the people of the world, it has now become the principal, direct enemy of the people of Vietnam, Laos, and Cambodia."[4] Uncle Ho said our policy was to "concentrate our forces to oppose the American imperialists."[5]

This statement marked the dawn of a new era in the history of our nation, the era of opposing the Americans to save our nation.

Our people and our army now faced a new enemy, an aggressor, the strongest economic and military power in the imperialist camp, the largest and most dangerous counterrevolutionary power of our era. The resistance war against the Americans to save our nation would be a historic confrontation between socialism and capitalism, between the forces of the national liberation revolution and forces planning aggression and seeking to enslave all nations of the world under a new form of colonialism.

On 5 September 1954, the Politburo of the Party Central Committee met and issued a resolution to discuss "the new situation, new duties, and new policies of the Party." The Politburo made an in-depth analysis of the new elements in our nation's situation as we switched over from war to peace, from a situation in which our forces were dispersed to one in which our forces were concentrated and unified. The resolution placed special emphasis on two facts: that our nation had been divided into two zones with two different systems of social organization and that a new enemy had appeared—imperialist America.

The Politburo assessment declared that the American imperialists, the French colonialists, and their puppets would never leave us in peace to allow us to reconstruct North Vietnam. They would not allow us to unify our nation in a manner favorable to our side. The entire Party, the entire army, and the entire population would have to be vigilant and stand ready to deal with any possible development.

The immediate task facing our soldiers and civilians in both the North and the South was to struggle to implement the Geneva Agreement, to strive to consolidate the North, and to firmly maintain and expand the political struggle movement of the people of the South in order to consolidate peace, achieve national unification, and complete our mission of achieving independence and democracy for the entire nation.

During this new revolutionary phase, the People's Army would be the "pillar on which we would rely for the protection of the Fatherland and the preservation of peace." The Politburo decided to build the People's Army into a regular, modern, revolutionary army. This would be a long-term, complicated task in which the most constant and important factor would be the need for training, and especially for the training of cadres.

Under the collective, unified leadership of the Party Central Committee, our soldiers and civilians in both the North and the South urgently consolidated and reorganized our forces to prepare to enter a new struggle.

CONSOLIDATING PARTY CONTROL IN THE NORTH

In the North, because of the long rule of the imperialists and the feudalists and because of the ravages of war, we were confronted with many difficult and complex social and economic problems. Agriculture was decentralized and farming methods were backward. Industry was small and crippled. Many businesses, water control projects, transportation routes, railroad yards, and port facilities had been destroyed during the war. Before withdrawing its forces to the South, the enemy either dismantled and shipped out or sabotaged many pieces of machinery and large quantities of supplies, creating additional difficulties for us as we began the process of restoring production. In those areas that had previously been temporarily under enemy control, tens of thousands of hectares of farmland had been left to go to seed and villages and hamlets were left in shambles and desolate. Starvation appeared in many provinces. In the large cities and the province capitals over 100,000 people were unemployed. Almost 1 million people were now illiterate. Bandit gangs still operated in a number of our northern border areas. Over 1 million people, the majority of them Catholics, had been seduced, tricked, or forced to emigrate to the South.

With our nation temporarily divided into two halves, the Central Committee of the Party affirmed that the North was the revolutionary base area of the entire nation. The firm consolidation of the North was now our most basic duty. This duty was intimately connected with our struggle for complete independence, democracy, and the future development of our nation. "No matter what, the North must be consolidated. We must move the North forward gradually, firmly, advancing toward socialism on a step by step basis."[6]

For the immediate future, the Party Central Committee and the Government established a policy of rapidly completing the work of land reform and implementing a three-year (1955–1957) economic recovery plan. This plan focused on the restoration and development of agriculture, handicrafts, fishing, and salt production; on the restoration of transportation routes and postal services; on providing employment and stability for people's lives; and on strengthening security and national defense.

As the tool of the people's government, our armed forces began to carry out new roles and new duties: to protect the work of rebuilding our nation, to actively participate in production, to participate in labor and contribute to restoring the economy, and to bind up the wounds of war.

As we transferred our forces to regroupment sites and took control of newly liberated areas, our army fought and defeated many enemy plots and actions designed to sabotage the cease-fire agreement. In the cities and large towns, our troops joined the workers in struggles against factory owners and reactionaries to protect machinery and supplies and ensure that the factories could continue to operate as usual. Division-sized Units [dai doan] 320 and 308 and units from South Vietnam that had regrouped in the areas of Nghe An, Thanh Hoa, Ninh Binh, Nam Dinh, etc., formed numerous operational teams to proselytize the people and combat enemy efforts to seduce or force our Catholic brethren to emigrate to the South. Cadre and soldiers visited each family, patiently explaining the policies of the Party and of Chairman Ho Chi Minh and exposing the insidious plots of the enemy. Even though the reactionaries used all kinds of tricks and devices to obstruct these efforts, in those areas our troops were able to reach in time, our Catholic brethren stayed behind and contributed to the rebuilding of our homeland and the building of a new life.

The High Command ordered the 148th Regiment in the Northwest [Tay Bac] Region and the 238th and 246th Regiments in the Viet Bac Interzone to work with local troops, guerrilla militia, and the civilian population of the border provinces to eliminate banditry. Our troops visited every ethnic minority tribal village, spreading the policies of the Party and the Government. They divided and isolated the reactionaries and clearly exposed their crimes. Our troops helped the local population restore production, rebuild villages, and consolidate people's governmental structures. The work of our cadres and soldiers had a powerful effect on the masses and won over those people who had previously followed the wrong path. The ranks of the bandits disintegrated, and most of them turned in their guns and returned home to resume normal lives. Security in the border areas of the provinces of Lao Cai, Yen Bai, Lai Chau, etc., was firmly maintained. We had crushed the enemy's plots to sow division and commit sabotage and we had strengthened the solidarity of peoples of all ethnic groups.

With regard to our efforts to rebuild the economy, our army reclaimed and cleared 64,000 hectares of farmland and helped the population in areas where military units were stationed by contributing tens of thousands of man-days of labor, plowing, harrowing, transplanting, harvesting, etc.[7] The regular mobile divisions subordinate to the High Command and the armed forces of the Left Bank and Right Bank Military Regions contributed more than 200,000 man-days of labor, digging 500,000 cubic meters of earth and achieving high efficiency during the construction of the Bac-Hung-Hai agricultural irrigation project.[8] In early 1955 North Vietnam experienced a severe drought. Units stationed in the lowlands contributed more than 6 million man-days of labor, dredging hundreds of kilometers of irrigation ditches, digging thousands of wells, and working with the farmers to fight the drought and save the harvest. During the autumn of 1955 the North was struck by a major typhoon. The High Command immediately dispatched a number of divisions and regiments to help save our dike systems and combat floods. In many locations our troops slogged through water day and night, using their bodies as barriers against the floodwaters so that dirt could be shoveled in to shore up the dikes. In Haiphong, soldier Pham Minh Duc (of the 350th Division) died a hero's death while trying to rescue civilians. The National Assembly and the Government awarded Pham Minh Duc the title of Hero of the People's Armed Forces.

On these new combat fronts our army once again demonstrated its revolutionary character and its combat spirit of sacrifice for the sake of the people. The people in areas formerly occupied by the enemy grew to love "Uncle Ho's soldiers" even more.

In 1956 our Party uncovered errors in the implementation of the land reform program and the program to revamp our organizations. In October 1956 the 10th Central Committee Session put forward timely, appropriate, and resolute corrective measures. During this same period in the South, Diem and the Americans publicly tore up the Geneva Accords and savagely suppressed the struggle movement of the masses. On the world stage there were a number of incidents of counterrevolutionary violence. Exploiting this situation, a number of reactionary elements in the North who had not been reeducated raised their ugly heads, spreading suspicion and criticizing the leadership of the Party.

In the face of these national problems, our army demonstrated its boundless loyalty to our revolutionary cause and proved itself worthy of the trust the Party and the people placed in it. The Party sent almost 10,000 cadre and soldiers to the rural areas to work with local cadre and with our peasant brethren to correct the errors in land reform and in revamping organizations. In areas where military units were stationed our cadre and soldiers went out among the masses, disseminating the policies and goals of the Party, contributing to the work of stabilizing the situation, and helping the people increase production and build a new life.

Through the efforts of the entire Party, the entire armed forces, and the entire population, the economic and social situation in the North gradually stabilized.

Law and order were firmly maintained. The land reform campaign of 1956 focused on the right of farmers to own their own land and distributed 334,000 hectares of land to the farmers, thereby completely eliminating the landlord class and erasing the last vestiges of feudalism in the North. By the end of the three-year economic recovery program, the level of educational development and agricultural, industrial, and handicraft production in the North had been restored to pre–World War II levels.[9] Starvation and disease had been pushed back. Illiteracy had been eliminated. We had taken a step forward in improving the people's standard of living. The North had been consolidated and turned into the revolutionary base area for the entire nation, a firm foundation on which our army could build and expand.

BUILDING A PROFESSIONAL, REGULAR ARMY

In May 1955 the units of the People's Army operating in the South completed their transfer to regroupment areas in the North. The Vietnamese volunteer units operating in Laos and Cambodia completed their international mission and returned home. From an army dispersed throughout the nation and performing international duties in Laos and Cambodia, our army was now concentrated in the North. Speaking to army units preparing for a parade on 1 January 1955 to greet the return of the Party Central Committee and the Government to the capital city of Hanoi, Chairman Ho Chi Minh said, "Previously in the North we had only northern troops. Now we have troops from throughout our nation. Northern, Central, Southern—they are all here, and we even have our volunteer troops returning from service in friendly countries. We must sincerely be united, we must love each other, we must help each other make progress."[10] Uncle Ho stated clearly,

> The current duty of the armed forces is to strive to become a regular army. This is a new mission. You must not neglect your studies just because there is now peace. . . . You must study politics to have a firm grasp of the policies of the Party and the Government. You must study technical matters because, as technology is constantly advancing, we also must study in order to make progress. If we want our soldiers to be powerful, we must study politics and technology to progress toward becoming a regular army.[11]

After ten years of building up our forces and fighting and defeating the French colonialist aggressors, our army had been tempered like steel and had matured in many areas. It had gained a great deal of experience in building a revolutionary army in a country with an underdeveloped economy and had gained combat experience against an imperialist army with modern equipment. Of special importance, our army had developed a corps of cadre capable of responding to any requirement or duty. This was a very important basis upon which to continue the development of the armed forces during this new revolutionary period.

With a total of 330,000 full-time troops as of mid-1954, however, our army was still exclusively an infantry army. Its table of organization, equipment, and weapons had not been standardized and the technical and combat capabilities and levels of administration and command of each unit were different.

Our main force troops in North Vietnam (including Interzone 4) had been organized into division-sized units [dai doan] and regiments and had participated in many campaigns and large-scale massed combat actions. Because of the differing conditions of the battlefields there, our main force troops in Cochin China and Interzone 5 and our volunteer troops operating in Laos and Cambodia had been organized only up to the battalion and regimental levels. Our local force soldiers subordinate to the provinces and districts throughout our nation were organized into platoons, companies, and battalions. In mid-1954, the infantry forces of our army included six division-sized units and eight independent regiments, all subordinate to the High Command or to the interzones,[12] 54 main force and provincial battalions, and 258 companies and 175 platoons of district-level local force troops. The specialty branch units of the High Command included one engineer-artillery division-sized unit and a number of battalions and companies of anti-aircraft artillery, signal, reconnaissance, and transportation troops.[13]

The majority of our weapons and equipment were infantry weapons, which were not uniform in quantity or type and were of poor quality. Many of these weapons were unserviceable, and they were technically obsolete when compared to equipment used by other armies around the world.

Note: At that time our army possessed:
- 105,526 rifles (57 percent of which were serviceable) of four different types: Remington rifles and carbines produced during the Second World War, French MAS rifles produced during the period 1949–1950, and 7.9mm rifles produced by the Chinese Nationalists. In addition we had a number of Russian Modin rifles, Japanese Arinaka rifles, and French "Mut-co-tong" [*sic*] rifles produced during the First World War.
- 44,836 submachine guns (95 percent of which were serviceable) of five types: Thompson, Sten, "Tuyn" [*sic*], and MAS produced by the United States, England, and France, and K-50 submachine guns produced in China based on a Russian design.
- Light machine guns totaled 6,509 weapons (72 percent of which were serviceable) of the following types: Bren, Bren-no [*sic*], Hotchkiss, etc. . . .
- Heavy machine guns totaled 1,175 weapons (67 percent of which were serviceable), including Maxim machine guns produced during the time of the Russian Czars.
- Ammunition for the types of weapons we had captured from the enemy totaled only 200 rounds per weapon for rifles, 1,500 rounds per weapon for light machine guns, and 4,500 rounds per weapon for heavy machine guns.

- Artillery directly subordinate to the High Command consisted of two battalions of 105mm howitzers, three battalions of 75mm mountain guns, and seven batteries of 82mm and 120mm mortars.
- Transportation trucks totaled over 1,000.
- Signal equipment included telephones, 2-watt voice radios, and 15-watt radios.
- Engineering equipment was primarily hoes and shovels.

Almost 70 percent of our weapons and equipment had been captured from the enemy, 10 percent had been produced by our forces domestically, and 20 percent had been provided as aid by friendly countries between 1950 and mid-1954.

Our army's technical support facilities were very poor. Our entire armed forces had only five repair facilities to repair weapons and machinery and six factories producing medicines and military gear. Each of the facilities had only a few hundred workers.

Immediately after the end of the war the General Military Party Committee focused on directing all units to fulfill their responsibilities of transferring troops to regroupment sites and of urgently taking the first step in our reorganization, establishing table of organization and equipment standards and upgrading our equipment to guarantee that our forces would be ready for combat and prepared to progress toward building a regular, modern armed force.

Senior General Vo Nguyen Giap, Politburo member, Secretary of the General Military Party Committee, and Minister of Defense, and Comrades Van Tien Dung, member of the Central Committee and Chief of Staff, Nguyen Chi Thanh, Politburo member and Director of the General Political Department, and Tran Dang Ninh, member of the Central Committee and Director of the General Rear Services Department, personally went out to inspect and encourage our units as they regrouped and began to carry out their new duties.

The General Training Department, headed by Major General Hoang Van Thai, and the General Cadre Department, headed by Comrade Nguyen Chanh, were established to assist the General Political Department and the High Command in providing stronger guidance for the work of building an army under conditions of peace.

Our division-sized units [dai doan], the 308th, 304th, 312th, 316th, 320th, and 325th, were all uniformly redesignated as infantry divisions [su doan bo binh] as part of our effort to form combined-arms units and military specialty branches [binh chung]. Each division's table of organization included three infantry regiments, a composite artillery regiment,[14] an engineer battalion, a signal battalion, a military medical battalion, and a truck transportation company. A division's firepower was two or three times that which division-sized units had during the war against the French. The General Military Party Committee transferred many cadre with experience in massed combat operations from these divisions to assist in organizing a number of new divisions.

The regrouped units from the South, volunteer troops from Laos and Cambodia, and a number of Northern main force and provincial and district local force troops were gathered together to form eight new infantry divisions and five new independent infantry regiments. Each unit was given the combat traditions of one battlefield or one locality.

A number of main force and local force battalions and regiments of the Viet Bac Interzone and Interzone 3 were combined to form three new infantry divisions. The 350th Division was formed in September 1954 and the 328th and 332nd Divisions were formed in June 1955. The main force 148th and 246th Regiments of the Viet Bac Interzone were transformed into independent infantry regiments directly subordinate to the High Command.

Regrouped soldiers from Interzone 5 were organized into two infantry divisions and one independent infantry regiment. The 305th Division, formed in September 1954 at the Binh Dinh regroupment area, was made up of units that had fought in the northern Central Highlands and in the central part of Central Vietnam. The 324th Division, formed in June 1955, was made up of regiments, battalions, and companies that had been formed and had matured on the battlefields of southern Central Vietnam and in the southern part of the Central Highlands. The 120th Regiment, formed in June 1955, was made up of cadre and soldiers from the ethnic minority tribes of the Central Highlands and the mountains of Interzone 5.

Regrouped soldiers from Cochin China were organized into two divisions. The 330th Division, formed in January 1955, was made up of units that had grown up on the battlefields of eastern and central Cochin China. The 338th Division, formed in December 1956, was made up of units that had been born and matured on the battlefields of western Cochin China [the lower Mekong Delta].

Vietnamese volunteer troops from Laos and Cambodia were gathered to form the 335th Division and the independent 640th Infantry Regiment, both formed in June 1955.

A number of main force regiments and local force battalions from the coastal areas were combined to form the coastal defense forces. Interzone 4 was given the 269th and 271st Regiments and the independent 500th Battalion; the Left Bank Region got the 244th and 713th Regiments; and the Northeastern Region got the 248th Regiment.

A number of local force battalions and companies from provinces along the Lao border were converted into ten battalions of border defense troops.

The remaining local force troops of the provinces of Quang Binh, Ha Tinh, Ninh Binh, Bac Giang, Thai Nguyen, Tuyen Quang, Hai Ninh, Lang Son, Cao Bang, Ha Giang, Lao Cai, and Lai Chau were converted into internal defense troops.[15]

Our artillery forces, consisting of two regiments from the 351st Engineer-Artillery Division-Sized Unit and a number of artillery units from the various battlefields, were combined to form three artillery divisions, the 675th, 45th, and 349th Divisions, directly subordinate to the Artillery Command, and the organic artillery battalions and regiments of our infantry divisions. Major General Le Thiet Hung was appointed Commander of the Artillery Branch.

Anti-aircraft forces, consisting of six anti-aircraft artillery battalions subordinate to the High Command and a number of anti-aircraft machine-gun units from the various battlefields, were combined to form the 367th Anti-Aircraft Division and the organic anti-aircraft battalions and companies of our infantry divisions. The Headquarters of the 367th Division was assigned responsibility for providing guidance to the anti-aircraft forces of the entire armed forces.

Engineer forces, consisting of the engineer regiment from the 351st Engineer-Artillery Division-Sized Unit and the engineer battalions and companies from the various battlefields, were collected to form four engineer regiments, the 333rd, 444th, 555th, and 506th Regiments, subordinate to the Engineer Department and the organic engineer battalions and companies of our infantry divisions.

The signal forces of the armed forces were gathered together to form three battalions, the 132nd, 133rd, and 134th Battalions, directly subordinate to the Signal and Communications Department and the signal battalions and companies subordinate to the divisions and specialty branches.

The Transportation Department of the General Rear Services Department was dissolved. Military transportation forces were organized into two truck regiments, the 225th and 235th Regiments, subordinate to the General Rear Services Department and the Military Communications Office of the General Staff and the transportation companies of the divisions and specialty branches.

On 3 March 1955 the Airfield Research Section, directly subordinate to the General Staff, was formed, and on 7 May 1955 the Coastal Defense Department, subordinate to the Ministry of Defense and the High Command, was established.

The weapons and equipment of all units were cataloged and classified. A number of weapons supplied to us by the Soviet Union and other socialist countries after the signing of the Geneva Agreement were issued to the mobile divisions of the High Command and to units defending the temporary military demarcation boundary [the Demilitarized Zone], the border areas, coastal areas, and the offshore islands. Repair facilities for weapons and machinery, medical clinics, hospitals, and weapons and quartermaster warehouses were pulled together to establish production factories, repair factories, and large warehouse facilities and hospitals, which were then deployed to the appropriate areas to support the buildup of the armed forces and preparations for combat.

Under the leadership of the General Military Party Committee and the guidance of the General Political Department, all units conducted many study programs aimed at fully understanding the resolutions of the Party Central Committee and the Politburo regarding the current situation, revolutionary duties, and duties and formulas for the task of army building in this new period. Units of regrouped Southerners and volunteer troops which, unlike units in the

North, had not yet had an opportunity to study our land reform policy, were brought together for study sessions aimed at increasing their class consciousness. High- and mid-level cadre throughout the armed forces studied historical materialism. This was the first time our cadre had an opportunity to study basic Marxist-Leninist theory in one uniform study program. Educational study sessions were organized for all units. The study atmosphere was enthusiastic, especially among cadre from staff agencies and the technical specialty branches. Military schools began to hold primary and supplemental training classes in military and political subjects. Party chapters now openly provided leadership to their units, elevating the leadership role of the Party, raising the spirit of responsibility and understanding of their vanguard roles among Party members, and increasing their active involvement in building Party organizations among the masses. A system of Party activities days was implemented. This had a positive effect on the education of Party members and increased the quality of leadership provided by the Party chapters.

After many years of savage and difficult fighting, the number of wounded and disabled soldiers in our army had grown to 36,914 troops, of whom 41 percent were severely disabled. Tens of thousands of cadre and troops were suffering from disease, and of these 50 percent had serious illnesses requiring long-term treatment. In areas where troops were stationed, military units were provided with food by the local government and population, and they received skillful care for their physical and spiritual needs. The General Rear Services Department directed all units to expand their economic production programs and to build their own bases and headquarters facilities using bamboo supplied by the local population. Hundreds of State treatment facilities and hospitals and military recuperation groups, clinics, and hospitals restored our wounded and ill soldiers to health. In accordance with the requirements for national reconstruction, many healthy cadre and soldiers with specialized skills were transferred out of the army to work for State agencies and to work in political, economic, educational, or social areas. Those cadre and soldiers who no longer met the physical requirements for service in the army were sent back to their local areas to recuperate. There local Party committees, local government, and the civilian population arranged jobs for them and helped them find a new livelihood. In their new locations our cadre and soldiers demonstrated the excellent quality of our armed forces, increasing the trust and esteem in which our army was held by the local population.

Implementing the directives of the Party and the State, in all localities Party committees, local governments, and the civilian population solemnly collected the remains of soldiers of the People's Army, village guerrilla militia members, and civilians and Party members who had given their lives during the resistance war, taking them for burial in martyrs' graveyards.

On 20 December 1954 our army launched the first military training program to be implemented during peacetime.

From the Demilitarized Zone to the northern border, from the mountain jungles to the lowlands, the coastal regions, and the offshore islands, from the cities to the countryside, the atmosphere seethed with enthusiasm for study, for building our army into a regular, modern force, and for increasing vigilance and combat readiness.

The General Staff and the military regional and divisional headquarters held many short-term classes, providing supplemental training to company and battalion-level cadre and supplying basic training lessons and training methods for technical affairs and tactics at the subunit level. Training sites suited to the terrain and to unit training programs were constructed in areas where troops were stationed. Internal regulations, disciplinary regulations, garrison regulations, and unit regulations began to be drafted. Under the direct supervision of the General Military Party Committee, the staff agencies of the Ministry of Defense urgently studied and drafted the first five-year plan (1955–1960) for building a regular, modern, revolutionary army.

By the end of 1956, the program to revamp the table of organization and equipment of the armed forces had been basically completed. From an exclusively infantry force operating on a dispersed basis throughout the battlefields of the three nations of Indochina, our army had been concentrated into 14 infantry divisions and five independent infantry regiments, four artillery and anti-aircraft divisions, and a number of regiments and battalions of engineers, signal troops, and transportation troops with a relatively uniform table of organization and equipment. The organizational changes and the initial military training classes during the two years of 1955 and 1956 were suited to the immediate requirements of our army for administration, command, and combat readiness, and were at the same time preparatory steps for the work of building the armed forces in the directions laid out by the General Military Political Committee.

THE BEGINNING OF THE STRUGGLE IN THE SOUTH

In the South, during the course of the regroupment process and taking advantage of this period when the enemy had not yet established his governmental apparatus throughout the country, many localities continued to give the people temporary ownership of land that had belonged to French colonialists and local feudal landlords. Local areas also issued Government medals and commendations and Ho Chi Minh emblems to people who had been of service during the resistance war against the French and to religious officials and local elders. All areas held meetings for people from all ethnic backgrounds and religions to celebrate our victory in the resistance war against the French and to publicize the terms of the Geneva Accords.

Implementing the September 1954 Resolution of the Politburo of the Central Committee, the people of South Vietnam quickly shifted from armed struggle to political struggle. The Cochin China Party Committee, the Interzone 5 Party Committee, the Party Cadre Affairs Department for the provinces of extreme southern Central Vietnam, and provincial Party committees directed all cadre and Party members to remain in their areas of operation, to continue to recruit political assets among the masses, to maintain a number of bases in the jungles and mountains, to select and leave behind in each local area a number of military cadre, and to secretly cache a number of weapons. Party and labor youth group organizations at all levels withdrew into the shadows and began to operate in secret. Peasant associations, women's associations, etc., were disbanded. Mass organizations operating openly and legally, religious associations, production associations, mutual assistance and relief associations, sports and exercise associations, cultural and literary associations, etc., were established in all villages, hamlets, and cities. A number of cadre, Party members, and revolutionary civilians were selected and dispatched by the Party to secretly infiltrate the puppet government and the puppet army.

In November 1954 President Eisenhower sent General Collins to Saigon. A plan of aggression aimed at imposing the yoke of American neocolonialist rule in South Vietnam was drawn up under the name of the "Collins Plan." The contents of this plan were the following: The United States would provide direct support to the puppet Ngo Dinh Diem regime rather than providing assistance through the French; a "national assembly" would be established to legitimize the Diem regime; a puppet army would be established using U.S.-supplied equipment and training and operating under U.S. command; a new group of puppets would be quickly trained; and a number of economic and social programs would be implemented, such as resettlement of the population, "land reform," changing the tax laws, etc. These programs would benefit the capitalist and landlord classes and would allow U.S. capitalists to invest in South Vietnam. This was the first American plan of aggression in South Vietnam. It was to be implemented through a puppet regime and puppet army and was an extremely dangerous form of disguised, covert colonialism on the part of the imperialists.

Relying on his American masters, Ngo Dinh Diem attempted to raise the banner of "national independence" and to employ false slogans about "democratic freedoms." He spread propaganda for the reactionary "Can Lao Nhan Vi" ideology, forced the people to join reactionary associations set up by his regime, and gathered all his lackeys together to create a new social order that would serve Diem's plot to oppose the revolution.

With an ever-growing network of spies and traitors and an expanding system of guard posts and outposts, Diem and the Americans began to establish puppet governmental machinery at the local level, organizing village and hamlet leaders and interfamily groups. They forced individuals who had participated in the revolution to turn themselves in. Those who had husbands or children who had followed the revolution were forced to "disown" them. In many localities, when confronted with mass struggle movements for peace, they terrorized patriots who had participated in the resistance war against the French. The U.S.-Diem clique forcefully suppressed the population, conducting bloody massacres in Huong

Dien (Quang Tri province), Vinh Trinh and Cho Duoc (Quang Nam province), Mo Cay (Ben Tre province), etc. The population of South Vietnam did not enjoy a single day of peace after the Geneva Agreement was signed. From the very beginning the battle against this new enemy was a vicious struggle.

In June 1955, in accordance with an agreement reached between France and the United States, the French expeditionary army completed its withdrawal from South Vietnam. The puppet army that had been built by the French was now reorganized by the Americans into a puppet army subservient to the United States and designed to serve as a tool for the implementation of aggressive U.S. policies and to support the neocolonialist rule of the Americans. Most of the puppet officers trained by the French now became puppets of the Americans. As for the armed forces of the Binh Xuyen and of the Hoa Hao and Cao Dai religious sects that France had organized and equipped, Diem and the Americans bribed them and tried to entice them to join with Diem. Clashes between the U.S.-Diem forces and the armed forces of the religious sects broke out in many provinces in Cochin China and Central Vietnam.

To exploit these divisions within the enemy's ranks, the Cochin China Party Committee and the interprovincial Party committees dispatched many military cadre to armed units of the Binh Xuyen, the Cao Dai, and the Hoa Hao with the goal of guiding these forces into opposing the oppressive actions of the U.S.-Diem clique. At the same time our cadre also strove to limit the acts of banditry that these forces were committing against the civilian population. Because they did not have a cause worth fighting for and because they were undisciplined and unorganized, after a short time these armed forces disintegrated and surrendered to the U.S.-Diem clique. A small element of the Binh Xuyen armed forces joined the revolution and were led by our military cadre to War Zone D in eastern Cochin China, where they were reorganized by us.

Cadre and Party members who were being terrorized by the enemy in the lowlands fled to our old resistance bases and were reorganized by the interprovincial Party committees of eastern, central, and western Cochin China into armed teams and armed groups. A number of our units disguised themselves as armed units of the Binh Xuyen and of the Hoa Hao and Cao Dai religious sects in order to deceive the enemy.

In western Cochin China the Ca Mau Province Party Committee organized two armed units that called themselves the "Ngo Van So Company" and the "Dinh Tien Hoang Company." Each unit had a strength of about 100 soldiers, all Party members, and each was equipped with a few dozen guns. The province committees of Rach Gia, Vinh Long, Can Tho, and Soc Trang provinces organized a number of armed units, each unit having between 20 and 40 soldiers. The provincial committees dispersed the cadre and soldiers of these armed units to villages and hamlets surrounding our base areas to recruit local people to build up our organizations, to assist the local population with economic production, and to guide the people in struggling against the enemy. These units held regular meetings and study sessions at night according to a fixed schedule. Each unit could gather or disperse quickly under orders from the provincial committee.

In the Plain of Reeds base area the Interprovincial Party Committee of central Cochin China collected 150 cadre and Party members who had been operating within the ranks of the Binh Xuyen, recruited an additional group of local youths, and combined them to form two armed units that were called the 2nd and 4th Binh Xuyen Battalions. The provinces of Long An and Chau Doc also organized provincial armed teams bearing such names as the "Phuoc Du Battalion," the "Du Quang Battalion," the "Dinh Bo Linh Battalion," etc. Some of these units had almost 100 soldiers armed with several dozen guns. These armed units operated in a dispersed fashion and recruited political agents among the local population in the provinces of Kien Phong and Kien Tuong. A number of units expanded their areas of operation to the area north of Route 4 and My Tho province.

In the base areas of eastern Cochin China the provincial committees of Tay Ninh, Bien Hoa, Ba Ria, Thu Dau Mot, and Gia Dinh provinces organized a number of revolutionary armed teams, each team having around 50 soldiers. These teams established production and logging areas in Trang Bang, Long Thanh, Long Nguyen, Hat Dich, Suoi Linh, Ma Da, etc., to support their own personnel. In mid-1956, acting on orders from the Eastern Cochin China Interprovincial Committee, the Party chapter in the Bien Hoa prison organized a prison breakout in which 600 cadre and patriotic civilians being held in the prison escaped. A number of these escapees were assigned to our armed teams in War Zone D and in the Long Thanh, Hat Dich, etc., base areas.

In our former resistance bases in the Central Highlands and in the mountain jungles of the western portions of the provinces of Central Vietnam, many cadre and Party members worked with our ethnic minority compatriots, taking advantage of the tribal traditions of these people who carried weapons to protect their own villages and lands to provide armed self-defense personnel to defend our political struggle movement. They maintained control of such areas as Tra Bong and Ba To in Quang Ngai province; Vinh Thanh, An Lao, and Van Canh in Binh Dinh province; Tho Do and Ma Du in Phu Yen province; Hon Ron and Cay Dau in Khanh Hoa province; Tan Tuc, Tung Bung, Doan, Soap, and Dac Uy in Kontum province; and Bac Ai in Ninh Thuan province.

The armed teams that were maintained in our resistance bases during these years when the South Vietnamese revolution shifted from armed struggle to political struggle were the first organizations we used to restore and rebuild our revolutionary armed forces in South Vietnam in later years.

RESOLUTION TO CONTINUE THE STRUGGLE

In March 1955, the Party Central Committee (2nd Session) held its seventh plenary session in the capital city of Hanoi. Chairman Ho Chi Minh and Comrade

Truong Chinh, General Secretary of the Party, presided over the session. Shortly thereafter, in August 1955 the Central Committee held its eighth plenary session. Based on the developments within our nation following the signing of the Geneva Accords, the Party Central Committee once more affirmed that the immediate, most concrete, and most dangerous enemies of our people are the American imperialists and their lackeys. "The immediate struggle objectives for the entire Party, the entire armed forces, and the entire population of both North and South Vietnam are peace, unification, independence, and democracy. Our struggle will be prolonged and difficult, but we will surely be victorious."[16]

"If we wish to fulfill this great duty, we must have forces. In order to have forces, we must strive to consolidate the North and move the North forward step by step toward socialism. We must also maintain and expand the political struggle in South Vietnam."[17]

The Central Committee emphasized that "building a powerful People's Army, consolidating our national defense during peacetime, is one of the key tasks required for us to strengthen our revolutionary forces."[18]

In April 1956, during his closing speech to the 9th Plenum of the Party Central Committee, Chairman Ho Chi Minh stated clearly that,

When assessing the prospects for achieving unification of Vietnam through peaceful means, we must always remember that the enemies of our people, the American imperialists and their lackeys, still occupy one-half of our country, and that they are now preparing for war. Therefore, we must always raise high the flag of peace, but we must at the same time also raise high our defenses and our vigilance.[19]

Uncle Ho confirmed the decisive position of North Vietnam in this new struggle of our nation:

If you want to build a good house, you must build a truly solid FOUNDATION. If a tree is to be strong, its leaves green, its flowers beautiful, its fruit firm, then you must care for and build up the ROOTS of the tree. North Vietnam is the FOUNDATION, the ROOTS of the struggle to complete the liberation of our people and the unification of our nation. Therefore everything we do in the North must be aimed at strengthening our forces in the North and the South.[20]

The revolutionary struggle of our people in both the North and the South moved into a new phase. The Resolutions of the 6th, 7th, and 8th Plenums of the Party Central Committee and the instructions of Chairman Ho Chi Minh clearly pointed out our new enemies and laid out basic issues regarding the directions and duties of the revolution. These resolutions and instructions served as guidelines toward which the entire Party, the entire armed forces, and the entire population would strive.

During the two-year period of 1955 and 1956 our army properly carried out its "duties as a combat army and a working army,"[21] at the same time completing the task of reorganizing its forces. From an army operating on a dispersed basis and carrying out its combat duties throughout the battlefields of the three Indochinese nations, our armed forces had taken their first step toward concentrating our forces and achieving uniformity in organization, command, and equipment. These were very important foundations upon which our army could build to advance toward developing a regular, modern army under peacetime conditions in the North, at the same time standing ready to respond to any new requirements and missions for the revolution.

2

The People's Army Begins to Build a Modern, Regular Army: Maintaining Our Armed Teams in South Vietnam

NEW DIRECTIONS FOR THE DEVELOPMENT OF THE ARMY IN THE NORTH

Beginning in 1957, the revolutionary struggles of our people in the North and the South underwent a number of changes. In the North work on the economic recovery plan had been basically completed. Our work to correct errors made in the implementation of the land reform program had produced good results. The social situation and the lives of the people had been stabilized. The national defense had been strengthened to a significant extent. In 1958 the people of the North began a three-year plan for economic reform and cultural development (1958–1960).

In the South, after establishing a governing apparatus from the national level down to the grass roots, the U.S.-Diem clique openly tore up the Geneva Accords, refusing to meet with the Government of the Democratic Republic of Vietnam to discuss holding general elections to unify the nation. In March 1956 Diem's puppet government held elections to try to legitimize the puppet government. South Vietnam was placed under the umbrella of protection of the Southeast Asian military bloc (SEATO). The U.S.-Diem clique made "denouncing Communists and eliminating Communists" their national policy and they savagely terrorized Party members, patriots who had participated in the resistance against the French, people sympathetic toward the revolution, and anyone who did not agree with their policy of selling out the nation, serving as lackeys of the American imperialists, and dividing the nation and the Vietnamese race.

This situation posed new requirements for the work of building and strengthening the combat power of the armed forces.

In March 1957 the 12th Plenary Session (expanded) of the Party Central Committee was held in Hanoi. Senior General Vo Nguyen Giap, Politburo member and Minister of Defense, presented a Politburo report entitled "Actively building the armed forces and consolidating national defense" to this Party Plenum.

The Central Committee set forward the following missions for the People's Army during this new phase: Protect the building of socialism in North Vietnam; stand ready to crush any imperialist (meaning primarily the U.S. imperialists and their lackeys) schemes of aggression; implement national unification and complete the achievement of independence and democracy throughout the country.

To carry out these missions it would be necessary to "actively build a powerful people's army and gradually, step by step, regularize and modernize our armed forces."[1]

The Central Committee declared this work to be a great task directly related to the security of the nation, the independence and sovereignty of the Fatherland, the peace and happiness of the citizenry, and the future progress of the revolution. All Party chapters, all governmental agencies, and all popular organizations had to fully comprehend the importance and urgency of the work of building the army and consolidating national defense and to affirm that these missions were shared by the entire Party and the entire population.

The armed forces would be required to educate and increase the revolutionary vigilance of our troops so every cadre, every soldier thoroughly understood the missions of the revolution and of the armed forces during this new phase and so they clearly understood that the goals toward which our Party and our people were working were not solely independence, unification, and democracy, but that these goals also included building socialism.

With regard to building a regular, modern army, the Central Committee specified that

- We would carry out regularization in order to achieve uniformity of the armed forces in every aspect, with our main focus being on achieving uniformity in command, table of organization, training, regulations, and discipline in order to adapt our armed forces to the requirements of modern warfare.
- We would carry out modernization with the objective of systematically equipping our armed forces with modern weapons and equipment; conducting training to provide our personnel with a thorough understanding of modern technology and science; and moving our army forward from its present condition, that of an exclusively infantry army, to an army made up of a number of service branches and specialty branches.
- Because our nation was still economically underdeveloped, to a significant extent the modernization of our armed forces would rely on assistance provided by the Soviet Union, China, and other fraternal socialist countries.

The Central Committee emphasized the need to increase the combat readiness of our army so that the army, no matter what its stage of development and no matter what the situation, would always be ready for battle.

During this new stage in the development of our nation and of our army, the Central Committee of the Party advocated the development of a strong standing army of high quality and with an appropriate strength level, and the building of a powerful reserve force built on the entire population, the foundation of which would be the implementation of a system of universal military service.

Analyzing our situation and our revolutionary and military duties during this new phase, the Central Committee of the Party clearly stated two requirements: Building a revolutionary, regular, modern army must be closely linked with the need to consolidate and develop our rear area [North Vietnam], and consolidation of our national defense must be closely linked with economic development.

Based on an assessment of the limitations of our armed forces, on the state of our economy, on our nation's specific terrain and weather characteristics, and based on our revolutionary duties, on the responsibilities of the armed forces, and on the ability of friendly countries to provide us with assistance, the Central Committee laid out the formula: "Actively develop the armed forces in a gradual, systematic basis to move toward becoming a regular, modern army." While implementing this program, the Central Committee said, we must oppose impatient ideas that were divorced from the realities of our situation. We must, however, also make a maximum effort to save time because the schemes of the enemy are very dangerous, the requirements of the situation are very pressing, and the task of building up our army is very urgent and very demanding.

These basic concepts for building our armed forces and consolidating national defense during this new phase of the revolution, as set forward by the 12th Plenary Session of the Central Committee, marked a new level of maturity in our Party's military theory in general and in its theories for the building of revolutionary armed forces in particular. These ideas represented a step forward in improving the theories on building a people's army and consolidating a national defense based on the utilization of the entire population, which had been set forward in the Resolution on Self-Defense Units of the 1st Party Congress in 1935, the Resolution of the 1945 Military Conference of North Vietnam, and our Party's military resolutions during the resistance war against the French imperialists and the American interventionists (1945–1954).

The Resolution of the 12th Plenum of the Central Committee clearly laid out directions and targets for our army to use in developing and increasing its combat strength and combat readiness during the years North Vietnam still enjoyed peace, at the same time realistically preparing our army for a large-scale war of national salvation against the Americans.

THE 1955–1959 FIVE-YEAR MILITARY PLAN

During the 12th Plenary Session (March 1957), the Party Central Committee also approved a five-year (1955–1959) plan to build the army and consolidate national defense. This plan had previously been drafted by the General Staff and the General Departments of the armed forces in 1955 under the direct guidance of the General Party Military Committee and approved in principle by the Politburo in early 1956.

The plan set forward the following duties for building our armed forces during the five years from 1955 to 1960:

- to build a regular and relatively modern Army;
- to establish the initial basic organizational structures for Navy and Air Force Service branches;
- to create conditions that would enable us, when we began our next plan, to modernize the armed forces to an ever greater extent.

The plan spelled out the following specific requirements:

1. Reorganize the structure of the army to provide a standing force level that met the needs of the revolution and was at the same time appropriate to the size of our nation's population and to the budgetary capacity of our government.
2. Improve our weapons and equipment to strengthen our firepower and technical resources, implement rather basic changes in the equipment of our infantry divisions, and equip the specialty branches we were in the process of creating. Devote attention to the training of technical personnel, to building warehouses and supply and repair facilities, and to the instruction of cadre and soldiers in maintaining and utilizing our new weapons and equipment.
3. Expand regular training in military subjects, political subjects, cultural subjects, and physical fitness. This was a central, long-term, and continuous task necessary for building our armed forces during peacetime.
4. Cadre training was designated as the key element in the work of training our troops. Together with on-the-job training, we would send command cadre at all levels of all service branches and specialty branches to receive training in supplementary training schools and send a number of cadre to full-fledged training schools in order to enable our leaders and commanders to fully carry out their responsibilities.
5. Implement a system of regulations for the armed forces, including military regulations, security regulations, internal regulations, and disciplinary regulations. Study and draft combat regulations and regulations for political activities, staff operations, and rear services [logistics] operations. Implement four major systems within the armed forces: compulsory military service, service requirements for officers, a salary system, and a system for awards and commendations.
6. Strengthen staff agencies at all levels, especially at the General Staff level and at the Military Region and Division level. Develop staff agencies capable of organizing, training, and commanding an army made up of combined arms specialty branches.

7. Develop and expand the matériel support facilities of the armed forces to the level required for a regular and relatively modern army. Directly link the strengthening of rear service staff agencies at all levels with ensuring the provision of full matériel support to our plans to build our armed forces and prepare for combat.
8. Strengthen the leadership role of the Party and increase political activities. This was one of the most important subject areas and would play a decisive role in building a regular, modern army. Emphasize the development of basic-level Party organizations. Implement a system of delegation of responsibility under the collective and united leadership of the Party committee. Political activities must be aimed at increasing socialist awareness, increasing the combat spirit of the armed forces, developing unanimity throughout the armed forces on theories and actions for the implementation of our plan for building our armed forces and consolidating national defense and combat readiness. Political activities must delve deeply into tactical and technical matters and into the implementation of all regulations, the fulfillment of responsibilities, and specialized matters.

The first five-year military plan (1955–1959) also set forward specific tasks aimed at strengthening our defenses and combat readiness. These included increasing the combat readiness of units serving in border areas, along the Demilitarized Zone, in coastal areas (Line 1), and of air defense units. Other tasks included intelligence operations, building national defense projects and railroads, repairing airfields, studying the construction of naval bases, developing a military command communications network, etc.

The Party Central Committee approved both the national defense budget for the 1955–1959 five-year plan and the plan for distributing and utilizing that budget.

More than two years after the liberation of North Vietnam, the Party Central Committee had met and passed a special resolution regarding the work of building our army and consolidating national defense and had passed a five-year plan for building our armed forces. This was a major event, demonstrating the Party's tight control and leadership over the army. With respect to our army, this was the first time since its establishment that the army would be built in accordance with a long-term plan and under peacetime conditions. The plan set forward basic, overall issues, laying out a concrete program for our army's first step down the road toward becoming a regular, modern army. This was a new problem for our Party, our people, and our soldiers. "This is not just a political problem, it is also a political, economic, and scientific problem. It demands a continuous and vigorous effort by the entire army and the entire population."[2]

In May 1957 our army began a program of political meetings to study the Resolution of the 12th Plenum of the Party Central Committee on army building and consolidating national defense.

The program of political activities had this goal:

Based on the consolidation of the Party's leadership role in the armed forces, take a step forward in our entire army's understanding of the Party's revolutionary duties and policies during this new phase. In concrete terms, this means understanding both our policy of building North Vietnam during the transitional period as we advance toward socialism and our policy regarding national unification. Our army must at the same time take another step forward in its understanding of the tasks and formulas needed for building up the armed forces and strengthening education in policies and in current events throughout the armed forces.[3]

During this period, "because of the effects of the errors in implementing the land reform program and in revamping organizations, when considering various problems some cadre and soldiers often have been found deficient in their ability to correctly distinguish between truth and error, between right and wrong. The internal struggle to clearly distinguish between truth and error has also been overly cautious and weak."[4] A number of cadre and soldiers

do not yet clearly and definitively understand that although the work of completing the people's democratic national revolution in South Vietnam will be a difficult, protracted revolutionary struggle; this is a struggle we are certain to win. They do not yet clearly understand that the task of systematically building North Vietnam into a socialist system is a great revolutionary transformation that will require continuous and vigorous efforts. They do not yet fully realize the difficulties we must overcome. With regard to the work of building our army into a regular, modern force, there have been scattered instances of laxity and a lack of organization and discipline. Mechanical, dogmatic, and reactionary phenomena have surfaced among our ranks. These types of thinking and understanding have affected the spirit of solidarity and the enthusiasm of our troops.[5]

ARMED FORCES POLITICAL EDUCATION AND TRAINING

The first study seminar for high-level cadre from the entire army and for midlevel cadre from the staff agencies of the Ministry of Defense was held in Hanoi under the direct supervision of the General Military Party Committee. Senior General Vo Nguyen Giap, member of the Politburo of the Party Central Committee, Secretary of the General Military Party Committee, and Minister of Defense, personally read aloud to this seminar the Resolution of the 12th Plenum of the Party Central Committee on the tasks and formulas for army building during this new phase. Comrade Nguyen Chi Thanh, member of the Politburo of the Party Central Committee, Deputy Secretary of the General Military Party Committee, and Director of the General Political Department, presented a document entitled "Increasing Socialist Awareness, Opposing Individualism," which stressed the outstanding revolutionary character and traditions of the army, criticized the effects of capitalist thinking and the appearance of petit bourgeois thoughts, and emphasized the need to guard against and overcome pacifism, the weakening of our combat spirit, individualistic thinking, and arrogance and officiousness.

At the conclusion of the seminar our cadre were honored by a visit from Uncle Ho. Uncle Ho told the seminar,

> Your just-concluded studies are in unanimous agreement with the Resolution of the 12th Plenum of the Party Central Committee. That is a very good thing. During this conference, the General Military Party Committee undertook sincere self-criticism, and cadre conducted excellent criticism and made a good first step in self-criticism. You evaluated and distinguished clearly between truth and error, reviewed strengths and deficiencies in our major tasks, clearly saw your own correct thoughts and erroneous thoughts, and more clearly understood the work of building our army. You have strengthened your ideological positions, strengthened solidarity and unanimity from the top to the bottom and from the bottom to the top. These are achievements upon which you must build.[6]

Uncle Ho appealed to military cadre to "work to help the Party, the Government, and the army resolve problems and exploit advantages, increase our sense of responsibility and our efforts to complete the work of army building, our first and most immediate task being the successful completion of our program of political activity for low-level cadre and soldiers."[7]

During the summer and fall of 1957, mid- and low-level cadre and soldiers of the entire armed forces began a program of political study of the Resolution of the 12th Plenum of the Party Central Committee. "Through this study, our cadre and soldiers took their first step forward in socialist awareness. Proletarian thinking made an all-out counterattack, totally destroying capitalist thinking and erasing feudalistic thinking. A number of cadre who had fallen into error came to their senses. Those who were opportunists or harbored thoughts antagonistic to the Party gradually were exposed."[8] During this turning point for the revolution and the armed forces, the army firmly maintained its ideology. The entire armed forces united around the Party Central Committee and resolutely fought to protect the Party and defend those principles necessary to build the army.

Following the great success of the 1957 political activity program, in 1958 and 1959 our army conducted many study programs aimed at continuing to increase socialist awareness and at understanding the military and political policies and duties of the Party. Basic Marxist-Leninist theoretical subjects, such as philosophy, political economics, and scientific socialism, were incorporated into the study programs of all army schools. Cadre from the platoon level up received on-the-job training in historical materialism. Through a proper understanding of theory and methods of thinking, the political awareness of the army's cadre took a clear step forward.

BUILDING SOCIALISM AND AMENDING THE FIVE-YEAR PLAN

In December 1957, at the 13th Plenary Session of the Party Central Committee, Chairman Ho Chi Minh read an important report. For the first time Uncle Ho set out two revolutionary strategies and explained the close relationship between two revolutionary duties. He said:

> We are now implementing two revolutionary strategies: the popular democratic nationalist revolution and the socialist revolution. Both these revolutionary duties are important, and to disregard either one would be a mistake. However, the duty of consolidating the North and moving it systematically toward socialism will be of decisive importance for the total victory of the revolution during this new phase. Only if the North is consolidated and advances toward socialism will we have a firm foundation to ensure victory in the struggle to reunify the nation. On the other hand, the preservation and growth of our revolutionary forces in the South is the factor that will directly determine the success of the revolutionary struggle in South Vietnam. At the same time, this factor will also provide strong support to the task of preserving peace and consolidating North Vietnam.[9]

Correctly applying Marxism-Leninism to the specific conditions of our nation in this new situation, the Party Central Committee and Chairman Ho Chi Minh laid out a policy of simultaneously advancing the cause of socialism in the North and advancing the cause of the popular democratic national revolution in the South, thereby raising both the banners of national independence and socialism. This was the combat objective of our army and guided the entire process of army building and combat operations of our armed forces during this new phase.

In 1958 North Vietnam began a period of reform and building socialism, achieving the deepest and most profound revolutionary transformation in all history. The system of exploitation of man by man was basically eliminated. New production relationships in two forms, state ownership and collective ownership, were established. The technical and material structures of socialism began to be established. The Party sent thousands of military cadre and soldiers to our rural areas to explain our policy of collectivization of agriculture. Some units spent their money to help increase production and many cadre and soldiers contributed their own personal savings to purchase agricultural tools to support the cooperatives. The date of the establishment of agricultural cooperatives became a great holiday in the rural areas of North Vietnam.

During mid-March 1958 the General Military Party Committee decided to amend the plan for army building, increasing the time frame for the completion of the plan by one year (until 1960) in order to match it to the three-year (1958–1960) State Plan for reform and economic and cultural development, and speeding up the pace of army building in all areas. The major elements included in the amendment to the plan included:

1. Reducing our total troop strength, improving weapons and equipment, developing specialty branch units, and finalizing army administrative systems to turn the armed forces into regulars with the goal of completing the building of a regular, relatively modern Army by 1960. At the same time the full capacity of the armed forces would be utilized for the task of economic development.
2. Continuing the work of training cadre and building military schools.
3. Increasing training and the study of military science.

This plan laid out concrete measures aimed at strengthening the defenses of North Vietnam, preparing for war, building base areas in the Northwest and in the western portion of Region 4, and actively developing a reserve force.

On 20 March 1958, the General Military Party Committee held a conference of high-level cadre from the entire armed forces. During this conference the amendments to the plan for building the army were disseminated. Chairman Ho Chi Minh addressed the conference. He instructed the army on two immediate tasks:

One: Build an ever more powerful and more combat-ready army to maintain peace, defend the nation, protect the building of socialism in North Vietnam, and support the struggle to unify our nation. This task includes building a standing army and developing a reserve force.

Two: Actively participate in production to contribute to our economic development and to the building and consolidation of our rear area.

These two tasks are both important, are in total agreement with one another, and are closely linked, because both are aimed at making our army ever more powerful and North Vietnam ever more secure.[10]

On 21 March 1958, the Ministry of Defense issued a directive setting tables of organization and equipment for the specialty branches of the Army and for the first units of the Air Force and Navy.

The Army [Luc Quan] was to consist of the following specialty branches: Infantry, Anti-Aircraft, Artillery, Engineers, and Signal, plus a number of

Armored, Transportation, and Chemical Defense Branch units. The Army would be the primary service branch of our armed forces and would be the decisive force in securing victory on the battlefield.

Within the Army, the Infantry was the primary specialty branch. It was organized into seven divisions, six brigades, and 12 independent regiments, and would have a total of 93,000 soldiers.[11]

The table of organization strength of an infantry brigade was set at 3,500 soldiers organized into four infantry battalions, one artillery battalion, one anti-aircraft artillery battalion, and smaller units of signal, engineer, chemical defense, reconnaissance, transportation, and military medical troops.

The table of organization strength of an infantry division was set at 8,689 soldiers organized into three infantry regiments, one artillery regiment, and a number of support units.[12] Two-thirds of the infantry's weapons were modernized by replacing older weapons with SKS rifles, AK submachine guns, RPD light machine guns, and "Cooc-ni-lop" [sic] medium machine guns, all firing the same caliber bullet, and with the "Bazooka 40" [B-40, the Russian RPG-2]. All these weapons were made in the Soviet Union, China, and other fraternal socialist countries. The firepower of an infantry division in 1960 was equal to the firepower of our entire army at Dien Bien Phu in 1954. With vastly increased combat power, our infantry divisions and brigades were our army's tactical combat units.

The Artillery Branch, the principal fire support element of our army, had under the direct control of the Artillery Command a table of organization strength of 17,500 troops. These forces were organized into four 122mm howitzer brigades (the 364th, 368th, 374th, and 378th), four regiments (the 82nd, 14th, 204th, and 208th) of long-barreled 85mm and 122mm cannon, and four regiments (the 214th, 218th, 224th, and 228th) of 88mm and 57mm anti-aircraft guns. Besides these mobile reserve artillery units under the High Command, the branch also included the artillery regiments and anti-aircraft battalions organic to our military regions and infantry divisions. Although their primary weapons had previously been shoulder-fired artillery pieces, now our artillery troops were equipped with numerous long-range, powerful field artillery pieces, signaling a tremendous leap forward in the quantity and quality of our artillery forces.[13]

Anti-aircraft troops (the principal ground-to-air firepower of our Army) under the direction of the Anti-Aircraft Command and directly subordinate to the Ministry of Defense and the High Command, had a table of organization strength of 7,500 soldiers organized into six anti-aircraft regiments (the 210th, 220th, 230th, 240th, 250th, and 280th) equipped with 75mm, 90mm, and 100mm anti-aircraft guns, and two radar regiments (the 260th and 290th) equipped with P-8 radars. On 1 March 1959, for the first time our radars sent out their signals, defending the skies of the Fatherland. 01 March was designated as the official birthday of the Radar Branch.

Our Armored troops were established on 5 October 1959 with the formation of the initial regiment, made up of 202 cadre and soldiers and designated the

202nd Regiment. The regiment was equipped with 35 T-34 tanks and 16 CAY-76 76mm self-propelled guns produced by the Soviet Union. The birth of our armored troops was a new step forward for our army in increasing its assault power.

Our Engineer troops, the combat support force of our army, were under the command of the Engineer Department and had a table of organization strength of 4,500 troops organized into two construction regiments (the 229th and 239th) and two bridge and river-crossing regiments (the 219th and 249th) equipped with 200 specialized vehicles and a number of portable bridges and ferries. In addition, our engineer force also included the engineer battalions and companies of our military regions, infantry divisions, and brigades. The growth of the Engineer Branch provided a significant increase in the mobility of the branches of the Army.

Our Signal troops, the force that supported our army's command coordination in combat, were under the command of the Signal and Liaison Department. They had a table of organization strength of 3,000 troops organized into the 303rd Regiment,[14] which had three battalions (wireless, telephone, and cable construction). In addition to these troops were the signal battalions and companies and the general signal stations of our military regions and divisions. The birth of our first signal regiment marked a new stage in the development of our military signal and communications branch.

Our Chemical Defense troops had a table of organization strength of 600 troops organized into one independent battalion directly subordinate to the General Staff and eight chemical defense units subordinate to the infantry divisions. Our chemical troops were equipped with a number of flamethrowers, 214 specialized vehicles, and more than 4,000 gas masks and chemical protective suits. These were the first units of our Chemical Defense Branch, the branch responsible, together with our other armed forces and the civilian population, for defending against the enemy's chemical weapons of mass destruction.

Our Transportation troops had a table of organization strength of 2,000 soldiers organized into three truck transportation companies (the 225th, 235th, and 245th), subordinate to the General Department of Rear Services and equipped with 1,600 vehicles, and one river transportation unit equipped with boats. In addition to these troops were the transportation companies and battalions subordinate to our military regions and infantry divisions and brigades.

Air Force troops had a table of organization strength of 2,000 soldiers organized into the 919th Air Transport Regiment, equipped with 39 Soviet-made IL-14 and AN-2 aircraft, and a number of cadre and enlisted framework units for our first air combat regiment, which was then in training abroad. In January 1959 the Air Force Department of the General Staff was established to provide an organization to exert command over Air Force facilities and to administer our airfields. This was the initial component that formed the foundation for building the Air Force into a modern Service Branch.

Our Navy had a table of organization strength of 1,300 sailors organized into two coastal patrol boat groups (the 130th and 135th) equipped with four 50-ton patrol craft and 24 79-ton patrol craft. These boats were armed with 20mm and 40mm guns and were equipped with radar. In January 1959, the Navy Department of the General Staff was established to provide command over naval units and to administer navy port facilities.

In this manner, during the implementation of our first five-year plan to build our army and consolidate national defense (1955–1960), our armed forces took a step forward in developing specialty branches and significantly increased the firepower, assault power, and mobility of the Army. By 1960 troops of the technical specialty branches made up 49 percent of the total strength of the armed forces.

In April 1959 a number of security troop units and provincial local force troops, totaling 8,000 soldiers, were transformed into People's Armed Public Security forces whose administration, command, and training was provided by the Ministry of the Interior.

Security troops [bo doi bao ve] totaled 4,500 soldiers organized into ten battalions under the command of the General Staff and the military regions.

Based on our need to divide up the battlefields in accordance with our overall strategic deployment and the requirements of overseeing the work of army building, the Party Central Committee and the Government decided to divide North Vietnam into six military regions: The Viet Bac Military Region, the Northeast Military Region, the Northwest Military Region, the Right Bank Military Region, the Left Bank Military Region, and Military Region 4. During peacetime the military regions would oversee all activities related to combat readiness (including building of national defense fortifications), troop training, and the maintenance of security and public order in their areas. The Military Region Headquarters was the highest-level military organization in each strategic area. These headquarters were responsible for implementing the military policies and missions laid down by the Central Committee, the General Military Party Committee, and the Ministry of Defense; for guiding and leading national defense operations and building military capabilities during peacetime; and for providing guidance and command to armed forces located in the military region during time of war.[15]

Local military organizations at the province, district, and village level were all uniformly designated as provincial units, district units, and village units.

The General Staff, the General Political Department, the General Rear Services Department, and the headquarters of the military regions and the specialty branches were all reorganized in accordance with new tables of organization in order to effectively provide guidance and command to an army made up of many specialty branches. The General Cadre Department was reorganized into the Cadre Department of the General Political Department. The General Military Training Department was reorganized into the Military Training Department of the General Staff.

The implementation of this new table of organization structure was the target of a continuous effort by our army lasting for three years, from 1958 to 1960. With a new overall troop strength (160,000 soldiers) appropriate to the situation and a rationalized organizational structure and modernized equipment, the combat strength of our army was increased to a significant extent in response to the needs and responsibilities of the immediate situation. At the same time we established the organizational structure of an army made up of many combined-arms specialty branches.

To implement our policy of reducing the number of soldiers in our standing army and providing additional personnel for the work of economic development, tens of thousands of cadre and soldiers were transferred to state governmental agencies and state enterprises.[16] Older soldiers and those whose health would not permit long-term service in the armed services were demobilized or transferred to other areas. Military regions, divisions, brigades, and independent regiments also established their own units to build headquarters facilities and to build national defense construction projects. These units became national defense worker teams that built a large percentage of the offices, residences, garages and armories, training schools, rehabilitation clinics and hospitals, warehouses, etc., of our army. [Note: A "national defense worker" (cong nhan quoc phong) is a civilian employee of the Ministry of Defense.]

Troops that were declared in excess of the new tables of organization of a number of units[17] were organized into regiments and battalions under the administrative control of the Ministry of Defense. These new units built a strategic road network in the Northwest, participated in the construction of the Viet Tri and Thai Nguyen Industrial Zones, and built 35 state farms in Dien Bien Phu, Moc Chau, Yen Bai, Phu Tho, Son Tay, Hoa Binh, Phat Diem, and the western portions of Nghe An, Ha Tinh, and Quang Binh provinces. Working on this new battlefront, these units displayed the outstanding traditions of the armed forces, maintained tight organization and control over labor resources, and achieved a high level of economic efficiency. The 98th, 85th, and 83rd Regiments, working in the Northwest, became excellent bridge-building units. The cadre and soldiers who built our state farms became socialist agricultural workers, at the same time serving as reserve troops for our army. Many of the state farms built by our armed forces later became locations where troops were stationed, and some state farms later served as the foundations for the construction of the troop and supply transit stations of our strategic supply corridor during the war against the Americans to save the nation. However, because we did not correctly foresee how the situation would develop, when we transferred part of the army to the civilian sector to work on economic development duties we did not retain a sufficient number of cadre and troops familiar with the battlefields in South Vietnam to enable our army to adequately respond to developments in the revolutionary war in the South.

STRENGTHENING PARTY CONTROL AND CADRE TRAINING

To strengthen the Party's leadership over the army, with the approval of the Polit-buro and the Secretariat of the Party Central Committee, the General Military Party Committee issued a number of regulations regarding the duties, authority, and relationships between the staff agencies of the Ministry of Defense and the staff agencies of the Party Central Committee and of the Government. Military Region Party Committees under the direct leadership of the General Military Party Committee were established. The responsibilities, authority, and relation-ships between the military regions and provincial units and the local Party com-mittees and local governmental authorities were also clearly spelled out.

Campaigns for "raising socialist awareness and honing the proletarian posi-tions and beliefs of Party members" and "building strong Party chapters" were carried out throughout the army. Party members studied documents entitled "Becoming a Good Party Member" and "The Duties and Authority of Party Members." The Party system of collective democracy and Party development activities were carried out in a vigorous, uniform manner in accordance with a careful formula that placed primary emphasis on quality. Between 1954 and 1958 military Party chapters inducted 35,000 new Party members. After transferring a large number of cadre and Party members to State governmental agencies and enterprises or to local areas, Party members still made up between 30 to 40 per-cent of the total troop strength of our armed forces. In 1957 we began to conduct Party chapter congresses from the battalion up to the division level. This was a wide-ranging political program aimed at implementing the system of collective democracy, strengthening the all-encompassing leadership of Party committees at all levels, increasing criticism and self-criticism, and strengthening Party and political activities. The Vietnam Labor Youth Group was established within the army. By 1958 the entire armed forces had 3,000 Youth Group chapters and Youth Group members made up 51 percent of all cadre and soldiers in the age groups eligible for membership. After education to increase their political knowl-edge and their understanding of the importance of organization and discipline and after practicing propaganda campaigns among the masses, our Youth Group chapters became our assault units in the army-building and combat operations of all basic [low-level] units of our army.

In November 1958 the General Military Party Committee convened a confer-ence of all political commissars and political directors from the entire armed forces to disseminate a draft of proposed regulations for political activities within the People's Army of Vietnam. These regulations laid out the nature, duties, and prin-cipal content of all political activities in order to strengthen the Party's leadership over the army, set forward the duties and authority of political staff organizations, and to serve as the basis for all Party and political activities within the army.

In 1958, under the direct guidance of Comrade Nguyen Chi Thanh, the Gen-eral Political Department completed a review of the army's Party and political activities during the resistance war against the French.[18] This review laid out the history of the force-building and combat activities of our army, focusing on the history of the Party's leadership role in the army. The building, maturation, and victory of our army was directly related to the unceasing consolidation and strengthening of Party and political activities within the army. The total, un-contested leadership of the Party in political, ideological, and organizational matters was of decisive importance in enabling our armed forces to achieve maturity and gain victory. Party leadership was implemented through political and military policies and through a Party organizational network within the army and a tightly controlled system of Party and political activities.

> Use centralized democracy as the system and collective leadership as the highest principle for the Party's leadership. During periods of savage warfare as well as during this period of peace in which we are building our army into a regular, modern force, this principle must be absolutely respected. Practical experience has proven that through the strict implementation of this principle we have been able to maintain internal solidarity within the Party and, on that basis, have maintained solidarity within the army. Also through this principle we have been able to exploit the intellect of the Party and of the masses, reducing subjectivism and narrow-mindedness within the leadership and avoiding and preventing the vices of individualistic exercising of power, arbitrariness, and anarchy.[19]

It was therefore necessary to carefully build a strong, honest system of Party organization within the army; to unceasingly work to strengthen the working-class character and the revolutionary traditions of the army; to keep the army loyal to the Fatherland, to maintain a flesh-and-blood connection with the workers; to provide unquestioning support to the Party's leadership; and to fulfill the army's role as the reliable, sharp tool of the proletarian dictatorship of the State. Political work within the army took education in Marxism-Leninism and in the policies and directions of the Party as its basic responsibility. Political work also did an excellent job in persuading cadre and soldiers to strictly adhere to discipline and rules and regulations, delved deeply into technical and tactical subjects, and contributed to caring for the material and spiritual needs of the troops.

The completion of the review of Party and political activities and the dissemination of draft regulations for political work were important events that contributed to maintaining our principles for developing a revolutionary army as we moved toward building a regular, modern force. These two events helped to raise the level of political awareness of our cadre and soldiers, to implement our system of collective leadership, to stimulate democracy, and to respond to the requirements and responsibilities of our army in pursuing the cause of socialist revolution and the struggle to unify our nation.

With regard to the need to build up the cadre ranks of our army, the 12th Plenum of the Party Central Committee declared that we must "develop our cadre ranks to provide them a basic understanding of Marxism-Leninism, a certain level of cultural, scientific, and technical education, school them in modern tactics, and give them a firm grasp of modern military tactics and technology."[20] This was one of our most important responsibilities in the work of building our army and was the central component of our peacetime training program.

During the resistance war against the French colonialists, our army had developed a corps of cadre who were absolutely loyal to the Party, were aware of the ideals of the revolution, and were experienced in combat. Because our combat requirements were continuous and urgent, however, our cadre did not receive basic training in the art and science of modern warfare and their educational level was still low.[21]

As we moved into this new phase, the General Military Party Committee issued the following directive on cadre operations: "While firmly maintaining both our moral and skills standards, we must be extremely aggressive in promoting cadre from the worker and peasant classes while appropriately promoting cadre from other classes who have been tested and have demonstrated a progressive attitude and loyalty to the revolution."[22] In accordance with the spirit of this directive, during a six-year period (from 1955 through 1960) our army promoted 32,636 cadre one or two grade levels. Some problems appeared during the implementation of this directive, such as emphasizing only the above standards and disregarding the need to provide supplementary education to cadre from the worker and peasant classes. There were also problems with an excessive emphasis on ideology and continued prejudice and narrow-mindedness toward cadre who came from other backgrounds. Because our Party had correct cadre policies and regulations, and thanks to timely adjustments instituted by the General Military Party Committee, these mistaken tendencies were limited and finally overcome.

Having received both on-the-job and school training, platoon, company, and battalion-level cadre all were able to draw up unit training plans and programs for each separate phase of activity. They knew how to organize and conduct troop training in the style of a regular army. Mid- and high-level cadre underwent a yearly training program in theory, politics, and military affairs. Basic education was an element of training activities. Many collective basic education classes were organized at the unit level. The Military Cultural [Basic Education] School was established. The number of professionally trained education teachers within the armed forces grew to more than 1,000.

In April 1956, the Army Officers School of Vietnam, commanded by Comrade Le Trong Tan and Political Commissar Le Quang Hoa, began training its 10th Class in Hanoi. Almost 4,000 political and military cadets, both infantry and specialty branch students, received training and supplementary education in accordance with a basic, long-term study program. This was our largest cadre class, and most of the units of our army were represented within its ranks. Comrade Pham Van Dong, member of the Politburo of the Central Committee and Prime Minister, and Senior General Vo Nguyen Giap, member of the Politburo of the Central Committee, Deputy Prime Minister, and concurrently Minister of Defense, attended the opening ceremony for this class.

On 6 April 1958, after two years of study, the school held a graduation ceremony. The cadre and soldiers assigned to the school and the school's students were extremely honored to greet Uncle Ho, who attended the ceremony. Discussing the duties of the students after their return to their units, Uncle Ho emphasized that "you must aggressively apply those things you have learned here, but you must apply them in a practical way, appropriate to our current situation. Do not try to apply them in a dogmatic, mechanical manner."

Based on the ever-increasing requirements of our specialty branches, on 18 February 1958 the artillery training curriculum was detached from the Army Officers School and the Artillery Officers School was established. On 30 March 1959 the engineering curriculum was taken out of the Army Officers School and the Engineer Officers School was established.

The Rear Services Cadre School[23] expanded its training and supplementary education of cadre to include specialized quartermaster, weapons, ordnance, vehicle administration, transportation, and POL [petroleum, oil, and lubricants] training. The Military Medical School became the Medical Officers School, which began training military medical cadre at the university level.

Both the Mid- and High-Level Political Supplementary Training School and the Mid- and High-Level Military Supplementary Training School were established in May 1955, based on the Mid- and High-Level Political-Military School that was established during the resistance war against the French. These two schools continued to hold supplementary training classes in military and political subjects. The basic topics of these training classes were basic Marxist-Leninist theory; the military and revolutionary policies of the Party; strategic, campaign-level, and tactical problems in modern warfare; command, Party, and political operations; and rear service–technical operations within the armed forces. Although they were still small and their facilities and equipment were limited, our regular military schools systematically increased the quality of their instruction and played an important role in the training of a corps of cadres with a good basic, general level of knowledge, which responded to our requirements for building and developing our army.[24]

By 1960, of the total number of cadre from platoon level up in our army (34,856 individuals), 15,564 cadre (including infantry and specialty branch cadre, military, political, and rear services cadre) had received either basic or supplementary training at the military training schools within our nation. In addition, 2,400 cadre of all ranks had been sent abroad to more than 40 military institutes and training schools in the Soviet Union, China, and other fraternal socialist nations. This was a major achievement in the work of building the cadre ranks of our army. This achievement ensured that our army would be able to fulfill its immediate duties of army building and combat readiness and provided an excellent foundation for further progress within the army in the future.

ORGANIZATIONAL CHANGES AND ADMINISTRATIVE REGULATIONS

On 20 December 1958, Chairman Ho Chi Minh signed a decree that promulgated a system of service for officers, a salary system, and an awards and commendations system for the People's Army of Vietnam. The entire army was enthusiastic about receiving rank insignia reflecting the level of duties being performed and about receiving medals and victory commendations acknowledging their achievements in the nation's sacred resistance war. The salary system reflected the deep concern of the Party and the State for our army. The standard of living of our cadre took a step forward.

The entire nation was gratified by the honor and maturity of our army and applauded the concern and care shown by our Party and our State for the armed forces. At the ceremony bestowing rank insignia on our high-level cadre,[25] Chairman Ho Chi Minh gave the following lesson: "No matter what your position, you comrades must always serve as examples, you must always show yourselves worthy of being the loyal, complete servants of the people."

The implementation of a system of universal military service was a major reform in the work of developing the armed forces of our nation and was intimately related to the lives and the ideological thinking of the population and the army. For our army, the implementation of universal military service created conditions that enabled us to reduce the size of our standing army; implement the standards and systems for transforming our forces into a regular army; build up reserve forces; and strengthen forces devoted to the work of economic development. Universal military service was an appropriate measure to support our needs and responsibilities for army building in this new phase.

In 1958, the provinces of Vinh Phuc, Phu Tho, Nghe An, and a number of other local areas began, on a trial basis, to call youths into the army in accordance with the new system of universal military service. In August 1958, the General Staff convened a conference on building up our reserve forces in North Vietnam. The conference decided that, along with the induction of troops under a system of universal military service, we would also implement a program to register and administer all cadre and soldiers of the People's Army under the age of 45 who had been discharged or transferred to civilian jobs, and to register and administer all youths between the ages of 18 and 25 and all technical personnel employed by State agencies who met the physical standards and other requirements for service in the reserves. The conference decided to provide military training to reserve troops for a period of between ten and 15 days each year, to provide military training to students at universities and at technical high schools, and to expand the national defense physical education and sports movement for workers.

In April 1960, Chairman Ho Chi Minh signed an order implementing the national universal military service law.

Soldiers who had volunteered for service during the resistance war against the French colonialists and who had been discharged or transferred to work in

State enterprises or agencies were registered for service in the reserve forces of the army. A class of youth who had just reached the age of service under the new system, who met the physical and educational requirements, and who clearly understood their duties to the Fatherland and to the people of our nation were mobilized into the army for a three-year term of service. The army became a giant school for an entire generation of our youth.

By 1960, alongside our standing army, which was step-by-step being transformed into a regular, modern force, North Vietnam had organized a powerful reserve force totaling 780,000 soldiers, of whom 750,000 were youths from 18 to 25 years of age and 30,000 were veterans who had been discharged. Of the total number of reservists registered for service, 130,000 were Category 1 reserves. This group was held under tight administrative control and received excellent military training so that, whenever the order was given, they could be rapidly sent to reinforce units of our standing army.

Together with the implementation of systems for military ranks, salaries, awards and commendations, and compulsory military service, in 1956 our army began to study and implement the system of general army regulations consisting of internal regulations, unit regulations, disciplinary regulations, and guard regulations.

The draft internal regulations set forward the responsibilities of our soldiers, command relationships within the army, and internal systems and rules.[26] Unit relations, disciplinary regulations, and draft security regulations covered the administration of troop activities, discipline, troop conduct, and provided guidance for soldiers to carry out their duties while engaged in regular activities, training, and in combat.

In all units, from the barracks to the training fields, everything was carried out strictly in accordance with regulations. Daily life was strictly regulated and orderly. Patrols and guard duty, orderly duties, and combat alerts were all tightly organized. Understanding of the importance of adherence to orders and regulations was high. All cadre and soldiers studied and developed a thorough understanding of the requirements of these regulations. There was uniformity in basic combat procedures. Troops were trained to act seriously and swiftly and to always be vigilant and ready for combat. This was a long, patient struggle aimed at overcoming old habits from guerrilla and dispersed times and habits based on the individualistic and haphazard nature of a small-scale production economy. We developed a workers' attitude directly linked to the requirements of modern industry and inculcated in our soldiers the serious self-discipline of a revolutionary army. Although a few units still displayed manifestations of emphasizing only the mechanical and external implementation of regulations, and there were occasions when misunderstandings and mistakes occurred and when the regulations themselves were seen as the most important factor, in general the implementation of these regular army regulations produced good results and marked a new level of maturity in the organization and discipline of our army from 1954 to 1960.

COMBAT TRAINING

With regard to military training, the 12th Plenary Session of the Party Central Committee clearly stated that training was the central requirement for the completion of the work of building an army in peacetime. Working from a foundation of uniform organizational and unit structures, troop assignments were rather stable, material support facilities were strengthened, and training activities systematically began to turn the army into a regular force.

All platoon and company-level cadre and 50 percent of all cadre from the battalion level on up received instruction and training that was uniform both in content and methods.

Soldiers studied weapons theory and were trained in shooting techniques, the use of bayonets, grenade throwing, and breaching and overcoming obstacles. In addition to basic weapons training, practical fire and night firing lessons were incorporated into the training program. Training in physical fitness and sports was considered a part of the technical training program.

With regard to tactics, all units were trained from the squad up to the battalion level in offensive and defensive combat in regular terrain, and steps were taken to study and begin training in combat methods for use in mountain jungle terrain, in swampy rice fields, in river crossings, and night combat operations.

Yearly military training conferences were held both at the basic unit level and for the entire army. Infantry and artillery troops made clear progress in their firing techniques. Armored, engineer, signal, reconnaissance, etc., troops began to understand and properly utilize the technical equipment of their specialty branches.

After three years of basic-level training (from 1955 to 1957), individual and small-unit combat capabilities, technical knowledge, and tactical skills were raised to a high level. This was a very important factor that enabled us to begin training in combined-arms combat at the regimental and division level and to increase studies in the implementation of various forms of tactics.

In May 1957 the General Staff held a tactical exercise involving a regimental attack on enemy forces occupying prepared defensive positions. The objective of this exercise was to review the application of basic-level tactics in actual terrain conditions and to use the table of organization, weapons, and equipment levels on which our army was then based. The force conducting this exercise was the 88th Regiment of the 308th Division, reinforced by a number of the division's military specialty subunits. Chairman Ho Chi Minh himself came to the exercise range to observe the soldiers during this live fire exercise.

The success of this exercise marked a new step forward for our army in its ability to conduct massed regimental-level combat operations supported by specialty branch units. At the same time, the exercise revealed certain deficiencies in the application of modern combat principles to the actual conditions of our nation and our army and revealed that combat coordination between the three types of troops had not yet been truly achieved.

Speaking to the cadre and soldiers of the 308th Division and to representatives of units from all parts of our armed forces who participated in the exercise, Uncle Ho directed that combat by our main force troops must be closely coordinated with guerrilla warfare conducted by our entire population. It was necessary, he said, to draw on the experiences and build on the excellent traditions of the division during the resistance war against the French to carry out the tasks of training and development of the unit.[27]

During 1958, the General Staff directed the 324th and 325th Divisions in conducting defensive combat exercises in the Military Region 4 area and directed the 320th Division during an exercise in which they attacked an enemy force conducting an amphibious landing in low-lying rice-field terrain on the right bank of the Red River. The Mid- and High-Level Military School directed the 335th Brigade in an exercise involving combat against an enemy airborne landing in mountain jungle terrain in the Northwest. During 1958 we also carried out 48 command-post exercises at the division and regimental levels of various units. Along with "shooting congresses" and reviews at the end of training cycles, these combat exercises represented an important method for increasing the combat power and the combat readiness of our army during peacetime.

In March 1959, the General Staff held a conference to review combat training activities during the past four years (1955–1958). The conference affirmed that the formulas, principles, and content of our training program were fundamentally correct and that it was essential that the lessons must be properly absorbed by the troops. The results of the training courses conducted during the 1954–1959 period had "increased the command abilities and our cadres' and soldiers' basic understanding of modern warfare and provided a foundation for the study and development of our tactics."

The conference criticized "the appearance of instances of mechanistic actions and responses to situations based solely on the strictures of our regulations without studying and employing fighting methods appropriate to the actual equipment and weaponry of our army and to the special characteristics of the battlefields of our nation. In these instances, attention was being paid only to basic training, and there was a failure to apply training to our actual combat responsibilities."[28]

The General Staff decreed that by 1960 preliminary conclusions should be drawn up regarding the primary tactical problems facing our army. The General Staff assigned to the military regions, divisions, and brigades the responsibility of studying a number of different types of tactics. To implement the Resolution of the 12th Plenary Session of the Party Central Committee and the instructions of Chairman Ho Chi Minh, the General Military Party Committee decided to immediately conduct a review of our combat and army-building experiences during the resistance war against the French, to elevate these experiences to a new level of importance, and to apply them in the development and training of our army.

In an atmosphere of enthusiasm, as the rural areas of North Vietnam underwent agricultural collectivization, a new emulation movement arose among the
people's armed forces—a movement to advance military science, to expand
training activities, and to build the army into a regular, modern force.

The 364th Artillery Brigade began a study program to train its troops to
become "fully qualified artillerymen."[29] The 1st Battalion of the 305th Infantry
Brigade launched a movement to "take the lead." The 2nd Company of the Left
Bank Military Region came in first in the physical fitness program and was
awarded the title "Fast-as-the-Wind Company." The General Political Department compiled and disseminated the experiences gained in these programs and
publicized exemplary units and individuals. In November 1958 the General Military Party Committee launched an emulation campaign to "advance rapidly to
complete and overfulfill the army-building plan."

Following in the footsteps of the "Train Troops to Accomplish Feats of Valor"
movement and the other emulation movements during the resistance war against
the French colonialists, these were "socialist patriotic emulation movements, for
the cause of the struggle for unification, to build the army and consolidate national
defense. In truth, they were movements reflecting the consciousness of the
masses, with education and leadership provided by the Party."[30]

These training and army-building movements were strengthened by our
hatred for the United States and Diem. On 1 December 1958 the enemy viciously
poisoned and murdered hundreds of cadre and patriotic citizens being held in the
Phu Loi prison. The fascist actions of the U.S.-Diem clique created a wave of bit-
terness among all classes of the population of North Vietnam. Millions of people
in North Vietnam attended meetings and demonstrations demanding revenge for
our brothers in the South. Thinking about the South, producing and working for
the sake of the South, became a great movement among all classes of the population of North Vietnam. Training geared for the Southern battlefields and readiness to march to the South to fight became a requirement for and the sincere goal
of all units and of every single cadre and soldier in our army in the North.

The 324th Infantry Division and the 305th Infantry Brigade expanded training in troop movement operations, in moving vehicles and artillery through jungle mountains and lowland terrain cut by many rivers and creeks, in coordinating
infantry with sappers and infantry with artillery to destroy fortified "enemy"
strong points. A number of units of the 305th Brigade began airborne training to
become paratroopers.

The 330th Infantry Division trained for combat in low-lying terrain with
many villages and hamlets, rivers, streams, and water-covered fields. They
trained to attack "enemy troops" while the enemy was moving or to temporarily
shift over to the defensive.

The 335th Infantry Brigade studied and trained in offensive and defensive
combat operations in jungle mountain terrain to prepare themselves to return to
the battlefields of Laos to carry out their international duties.

The mobile divisions, brigades, and regiments of the High Command studied and trained in combat operations supported by artillery and armor provided by higher levels. They practiced long-range marches and prepared to carry out their assignments on any battlefield whenever the order was given.

Military Region 4 began to study and train in methods for organizing and supporting our troops to enable them to conduct field marches and field operations while they were on the road to the battlefield.

In 1960, all the developmental tasks of the first five-year military plan had been accomplished by our armed forces. Following the period of combat and army building during the resistance war against the French, our armed forces had developed and matured to a new level, a transition level in the quality of our combat power, thereby laying the foundation for the development of our army into an increasingly modern and increasingly regular force ready to respond to the new tasks and responsibilities of the revolution in both North and South Vietnam.

SITUATION IN THE SOUTH AND
THE DEBATE ABOUT ARMED STRUGGLE

In South Vietnam, after two years of consolidating their ruling apparatus, the United States and Diem had built up a reactionary armed force with modern equipment totaling 150,000 regular soldiers and 100,000 Regional Force, militia, and police troops. The enemy concentrated this entire force to implement their policy of "denouncing and eliminating Communists," savagely oppressing our revolutionary forces and our revolutionary movement.

As they were being terrorized by the enemy, the people of South Vietnam were filled with hatred and longed to use weapons to fight the enemy. In a number of localities, however, there was still confusion over what kinds of activities and struggle methods should be used. For this reason our revolutionary forces suffered losses and our struggle movement encountered new difficulties. The policy and methods to advance the revolutionary cause in the South became the subject of vigorous study by our Party.

In June 1956 the Politburo issued a resolution regarding the responsibilities of the revolution in the South for the immediate future. The Politburo stated clearly that "our struggle method throughout the country is presently political struggle, not armed struggle. To say this does not mean, however, that we will never employ self-defense measures in limited situations."[31] The policy laid out by the Politburo was to "once again develop armed forces up to a specified level, . . . to organize self-defense measures among the masses aimed at defending our struggle movements and rescuing our cadres when necessary."[32] To achieve this goal "we must consolidate the armed and paramilitary forces we presently possess and build bases for use as rest and fallback areas. We must also build strong mass organizations that will enable us to maintain and build armed forces."[33]

On 18 August 1956 the Politburo sent a letter to the Cochin China Party Committee setting forward more clearly a number of concrete tasks to be implemented in South Vietnam:

> In the current situation, we must organize self-defense units in the villages and hamlets and in factories, city blocks, and schools. The duties of these self-defense units will be to maintain order and defend the mass struggle movements, to provide communications and warnings, to guard cadre meetings, and to rescue cadre when the need arises. . . . Unit members must be Labor Youth members or Party members and should be organized into teams and units with an assigned unit commander and unit deputy commander.[34]

These were correct, timely policies that would have a significant effect on the maintenance and development of our self-defense armed forces in the South. Because communications were difficult, however, many localities in South Vietnam never received the June 1956 Politburo resolution.

In August 1956, Comrade Le Duan, a member of the Politburo of the Central Committee who had been ordered by Chairman Ho Chi Minh and the Politburo to remain behind to lead the revolutionary movement in South Vietnam, wrote the "Tenets of the Revolution in South Vietnam." This document affirmed that the road to advance the revolution in South Vietnam was the road of revolutionary violence.

After fully studying the resolution of the Politburo, in December 1956 the Cochin China Party Committee held an expanded meeting, including a number of secretaries of interprovincial Party committees and secretaries of provincial Party committees in Cochin China. Comrade Le Duan, Politburo member, and Comrade Nguyen Van Linh, Acting Secretary of the Cochin China Party Committee, presided over this meeting. This conference passed a resolution on the organization and operating procedures for self-defense armed forces. The resolution had been drafted by Nguyen Minh Duong, Secretary of the Central Cochin China Interprovincial Party Committee.

The resolution affirmed that

> at the present time, when the entire South is conducting a political struggle, it is not yet time to launch guerrilla warfare. Instead our policy should be to conduct armed propaganda operations. Armed propaganda units are armed operations units. Propaganda team members and cadre will reveal the true face of the enemy to the people. They will encourage hatred, develop revolutionary organizations among the masses, suppress enemy thugs and intelligence agents, win the support of enemy troops, proselytize puppet troops and governmental personnel to support our mass struggle movements, and limit any combat with the enemy that might reveal our forces. In organizational terms, we will establish separate squads and platoons. These units will be dispersed into cells and squads for purposes of living, traveling, and oper-

ations, but they must be organized into platoons with a command section to administer the unit, carry out political operations, and train the unit's troops. Their equipment must be light. Training for these units should include propaganda operations, education in inciting the masses, persuading enemy troops, and increasing understanding of the Party and knowledge of a number of military technical areas.[35]

Through the resolution of the Politburo and the resolution of the Cochin China Party Committee, our Party once again affirmed that the road to the development of the revolution in the South was the road of revolutionary violence.

With a full understanding of the guidance from the Party Central Committee, in response to the wishes of the masses and applying the guiding thoughts of Chairman Ho Chi Minh and their own experience with armed propaganda prior to the August Revolution to the new historical conditions in which they found themselves, the Cochin China Party Committee and the local Party committees in South Vietnam set forward appropriate policies and operational procedures that played a decisive role in the maintenance and development of our armed self-defense forces in the South and gradually seized the initiative in developing the revolutionary struggle and countering the new strategic measures being implemented by the United States and the Diem regime.

Beginning as early as 1957, to implement their "Communist denunciation, Communist elimination" policy, the United States and Diem mobilized a large portion of their regular troops as well as local armed forces and the puppet local governmental apparatus to increase acts of terror and oppression against the people. They began to concentrate the population, establish "new farming land" areas and "population concentration" areas, and carry out stringent population-control measures aimed at separating the people from the forces of the revolution. They established prisons all the way down to the village and local group level, and they tortured and murdered cadre, Party members, and citizens sympathetic to the revolution. They suppressed demonstrations and strikes by workers and the laboring classes in the cities. In 1957 they promulgated "Decree 57," which declared that land the revolution had distributed to the peasants had been illegally seized and forced the peasants to sign contracts, pay tribute, and return the land to the landlords.

White terror gripped the rural areas and cities of South Vietnam. In 1955, after our soldiers regrouped to the North, many provinces in South Vietnam still had several thousand cadre and Party members, and every village had a village Party chapter. By 1958–1959 many villages had no Party chapter, and many Party chapters numbered only two or three members. Only 5,000 Party members were left in all of Cochin China.[36] In Central Vietnam 70 percent of all Party chapter members, 60 percent of all district Party committee members, and 40 percent of all provincial Party committee members had been arrested or killed. A number of lowland districts had no Party organization left at all. In Cochin China

75,000 hectares of land that had been granted to the peasants by the revolution during the resistance war against the French were taken back by the Diem puppet regime. "The masses are filled with hate for the enemy but they are being savagely oppressed. They are being forced virtually to their knees and are unable to stand up against this."[37]

While all looked with longing toward Uncle Ho and North Vietnam, the revolutionary base area of the entire nation, the Party members and people of South Vietnam displayed a firm resolve not to buckle under to their vicious enemy. Even when viciously tortured to death, our cadre, Party members, and revolutionary citizens maintained their spirit, refusing to surrender, betray, or abandon the revolution.

There were continual struggles by workers and laborers in the cities demanding their rights and demanding democracy, fierce battles by the peasants to combat relocation and land-grabbing activities, and armed defensive struggles by ethnic minority peoples of the mountainous areas to protect their ancestral lands. In many locations our citizens dug up the weapons that had been cached in 1954, seized weapons from the enemy, beat their scythes into halberds and spears, or even used peasant scarves to secretly eliminate traitors, spies, informers, and police thugs.

Implementing the Party's policies concerning political struggle supported by armed self-defense, our local areas organized and developed hard-core organizations from Party members down through loyal civilians to the masses of the population to recruit and maintain contact with our agents within the traitor associations, self-defense forces, and even in a number of regular units of the puppet army. Self-defense units to protect the staff organizations of our province and district Party committees and secret armed squads and platoons were organized in many provinces. In Saigon and Cho Lon our self-defense forces grew out of the movement fighting against Diem's efforts to evict citizens and seize their property, and then remained in existence disguised under such names as volunteer fire prevention and fire-fighting associations, antirobbery associations, etc. In the villages and hamlets of the rural lowlands "secret action" cells and units were established. Faced with the demands of the masses and the need to protect our revolutionary organizations, a number of provincial and district Party committees ordered these cells and units into action to eliminate the most dangerous and vicious traitors, spies, and hooligans in local areas. In Rach Gia, Ca Mau, Kien Phong, Kien Tuong, Ben Tre, and many other locations the killing of such traitors, spies, and police thugs raised the morale of the people, caused divisions in the enemy's ranks, and reduced acts of terrorism by the enemy.

In the U Minh Forest in western Cochin China and the Plain of Reeds in central Cochin China, armed units operating under the guise of armed forces of the Binh Xuyen and of the Cao Dai and Hoa Hao religious sects were consolidated and reorganized by provincial Party committees into a number of armed propaganda units. These included the "Ngo Van So Battalion" and the "Dinh Tien Hoang Battalion" in Ca Mau province, the "U Minh Battalion" in Rach Gia, the

"502nd Battalion" in Kien Phong, the "504th Battalion" in Kien Tuong, the "506th Battalion" in Long An, and the "512th Battalion" in An Giang. In the base areas of eastern Cochin China, the Cochin China Party Committee gathered together a number of armed units and groups and, bringing in two companies and two platoons from western and central Cochin China, reorganized these units to form six armed companies (the 59th, 60th, 70th, 80th, 200th, and 300th Companies). A number of provinces established their own full-time armed units, such as the 250th Company in Bien Hoa province, the 40th Company in Ba Ria province, and the Thu Dau Mot Provincial Company. Although they were called companies and battalions, in actuality each unit had only around 50 soldiers each and was equipped with a small number of guns. Each unit operated under the guidance and leadership of the interprovincial Party committees or the provincial Party committees.

The responsibilities of these units were to conduct armed propaganda, eliminate enemy thugs, organize and proselytize the population, consolidate our forces, protect our base areas, and protect the leadership organs of the Party. In order to carry out these duties, every unit devoted a great deal of time to political and military studies. Their political study documents included the "Tenets of the Revolution in South Vietnam" by Comrade Le Duan and the resolution of the Cochin China Party Committee on the organization and operations of armed propaganda units, mass propaganda operations, and proselytizing operations against enemy troops. A review by the Central Cochin China Interprovincial Party Committee of all armed propaganda units in its area of operations in 1958 revealed that 70 percent of the cadre and soldiers of these units were able to properly present the policies and directions of the Party to the masses and could properly perform their mass proselytizing duties.

With regard to military affairs, command-level cadre relied on their experiences with training and combat during the resistance war against the French to draft training documents and to organize training for troops in firing weapons and in ambush and assault tactics.

To support their activities all units relied on the local population, at the same time actively working to increase production themselves. Soldiers operating in the outskirts of the U Minh Forest lived and worked with the local population in the villages and hamlets. Some years each soldier was able to collect 300 kilograms of paddy [rice]. In the Plain of Reeds, because the terrain was swampy and very sparsely populated, our soldiers and cadre usually had to live in bushes and thickets, using two "ca rem" boards to shield themselves from the sun and the rain, cutting reeds and wild grass[38] and harvesting untransplanted rice to support themselves. In eastern Cochin China every unit established its own production area and built bases and roads up to Binh Long and Phuoc Long to link up with the southern end of the Central Highlands. Here, in wild, sparsely populated mountain forests, our units had to move regularly to avoid enemy sweeps and their lives were filled with hardship. Sometimes they had to dig roots to eat instead of rice. In order to remedy their lack of food and weapons, a number of units organized small ambushes against enemy vehicles transporting food and money, such as the battle of Minh Thanh in Thu Dau Mot province on 10 August 1957; the battle of Trai Be in Bien Hoa province on 18 September 1957; and the battle of Dau Tieng in Thu Dau Mot province on 10 October 1958.

Beginning in 1956 the Diem puppet regime launched many large military sweep operations aimed at destroying our revolutionary armed groups in the base areas and at supporting the "Communist denunciation" and "Communist elimination" campaigns. In his "Thai Ngoc Hau" military campaign the enemy used two divisions of regular troops, many local regional force battalions, and four Navy groups to sweep through 18 provinces in the lowlands of Cochin China. In the enemy's "Truong Tan Buu" campaign he used three divisions of regulars, two regional force regiments, and one naval group to conduct sweeps in the provinces of eastern Cochin China. Enemy forces penetrated deep into our bases in the Plain of Reeds, War Zone D, and the Duong Minh Chau War Zone.

To deal with the enemy's military sweep operations the Central Cochin China Interprovincial Party Committee rapidly withdrew its leadership organs deep into the Plain of Reeds base area and ordered its armed units to avoid the enemy spearheads to preserve our forces. At the same time the Interprovincial Committee dispersed a portion of its forces out into the local villages and hamlets to help the people counter the enemy's acts of terror against them. A number of units went down to Duc Hoa and Ben Luc in Long An province to conduct armed propaganda operations, threaten the enemy's spies, thugs, and traitors, and expand our political organizations. The Interprovincial Committee of eastern Cochin China directed its armed units to withdraw to Ly Lich and Bu Chap in the north and to the northwestern portion of War Zone D in order to establish new base areas and preserve their forces.

In Interzone 5, because of the enemy's terrorist activities and because local Party chapters "did not clearly recognize the individual characteristics of each different portion of the region so that appropriate struggle methods could be applied in each different area,"[39] the struggle movement among the local population in the lowlands suffered serious setbacks. In early 1958 Comrade Le Duan, member of the Politburo of the Central Committee, met with a number of the leading cadre of Interzone 5. Le Duan pointed out to them that Interzone 5 encompassed three main areas: the cities, the lowlands, and the Central Highlands. He said the Central Highlands was a region of great political and military significance and value. Le Duan said that, building from a firm political foundation, we must rapidly organize armed forces at the squad level, or at most at the platoon level, to conduct independent operations to protect the villages and farmlands of the highlands. When the situation permits, he said, we must expand our activities to launch a guerrilla movement combined with flexible sapper-style attacks. We must urgently build up relatively secure areas to serve as base areas for our movement. On another front, he said, we must expand the political struggle in the lowlands and the cities.

Carrying out Comrade Le Duan's instructions, during the summer of 1958 the Interzone 5 Party Committee met to review the situation and lay out new policies and responsibilities. Comrade Tran Luong, Secretary of the Interzone Party Committee, presided over the meeting. The Interzone Party Committee decided to "expand the building of base areas in the Central Highlands and the western portions of the provinces of Central Vietnam. Establish production organizations, store rice and salt, mobilize the people to work 'revolutionary slash-and-burn fields.' Take the first step toward the creation of paramilitary forces. Form a number of full-time platoons and organize self-defense units in tribal communities and in villages to protect mass struggle movements, rescue cadre who have been captured by the enemy, eliminate enemy tyrants, and revive and expand our political organization."[40] These were correct and timely policies that were of decisive importance in reviving and expanding the armed forces of Interzone 5.

Implementing the policies of the Interzone Party Committee, the cadre and Party members who had remained behind in the Central Highlands and the western districts of Central Vietnam, together with a number of cadre and Party members who had fled to those areas from the lowlands, established facilities for producing food and for repairing weapons. Our people went into areas belonging to our ethnic minority brethren, worked the fields with them, lived with the population, and built up political and armed organizations. A number of full-time armed platoons were formed. In the contested areas in the lowlands and the mountains, revolutionary organizations among the population were gradually rebuilt. Some villages and hamlets were able to organize self-defense elements to kill local tyrants and to support the struggle movements of the masses that fought against the enemy's reign of terror.

By the end of 1958 many base areas had been formed at Hien (Quang Nam province); Tra Bong, Son Ha, and Ba To (Quang Ngai province); Vinh Thanh (Binh Dinh province); Tho Lo and Ma Du (Phu Yen province); Districts 2 and 7 (Gia Lai province); Tung Bung, Co Xya, Tan Tuc, Dac Min, Doan village, and Hien village (Kontum province); Dlay Ya (Darlac province); Bac Ai (Ninh Thuan province), etc.

After being revived and built from the political forces of the masses and after surviving a very fierce, difficult struggle by the masses to preserve and develop our revolutionary forces, by 1959 our armed self-defense forces in all South Vietnam totaled 139 platoons in Cochin China, 34 platoons in the mountainous areas of Interzone 5, and hundreds of secret self-defense teams and units at the village and hamlet level. This was a very important achievement of the South Vietnamese revolution during the years of political struggle between 1954 and 1959 and was one of the factors ensuring that the people of South Vietnam could move forward to carry out armed uprisings after the passage of the Resolution of the 15th Plenum of the Party Central Committee. At the same time this achievement provided the basis for the rapid expansion of our local armed forces in South Vietnam during the succeeding years.

3

The Development of Our Armed Forces during the General Uprising Movement: The Birth of Transportation Group 559

THE DECISION TO "LIBERATE" THE SOUTH

Faced with the steadily growing strength of the people's struggle movement in South Vietnam, in March 1959 Ngo Dinh Diem's puppet regime proclaimed that a state of war existed in South Vietnam. The regime switched part of its regular armed forces from mobile reserve duties to "territorial security" duties and ordered regular regiments and divisions to work with local forces in conducting sweeps in every region. In May 1959, Ngo Dinh Diem promulgated Law No. 10/59. According to this law, anyone guilty of an act of "opposition to the regime" could be punished instantly by execution "on the spot" by guillotine without a trial.

Hatred for the United States and Diem reached a peak throughout South Vietnam. "Where before in a single village a few hundred people had wanted to pour out of their homes to fight to the death against the enemy, now the masses had no other option than to rise up in a life-and-death struggle against the U.S.-Diem clique."[1] The elimination of the American neocolonial yoke of oppression on South Vietnam, the overthrow of Ngo Dinh Diem's brutal fascist regime, and the achievement of national liberation became vital requirements of the revolution. After almost five years (1954–1958) of savage struggle and although they had suffered losses, our revolutionary forces in South Vietnam survived and were again growing. The people of South Vietnam "have a high spirit of patriotism which I instilled in them during the resistance war against the French, during the revolution."[2] Although the world situation was experiencing a number of complicated developments during these years, through the use of appropriate struggle methods we now had the possibility of advancing the cause of the revolution in South Vietnam.

In January 1959 the 15th Plenary Session (expanded) of the Party Central Committee, chaired by Chairman Ho Chi Minh, was held in Hanoi. Representatives of the Cochin China Party Committee, the Interzone 5 Party Committee, and the Cadre Affairs Section of the provinces of extreme southern Central Vietnam participated in the session.

During this session the Central Committee decided "to liberate South Vietnam from the yoke of oppression imposed by the imperialists and the feudalists; to secure national independence and grant land to the farmers; to complete the people's national democratic revolution in South Vietnam, and to build a peaceful, unified, independent, democratic, and prosperous Vietnamese nation."[3] The revolutionary methods to be used to accomplish these goals were "to utilize the strength of the masses, relying primarily on the political forces of the masses (operating in conjunction with large or small armed forces, depending on the situation) to overthrow the imperialist and feudalist rulers and establish a revolutionary regime belonging to the people."[4] "In order to achieve this goal, we must make vigorous preparations aimed at launching a popular uprising to overthrow the U.S.-Diem regime."[5]

In its resolution the Central Committee also foresaw that "it is possible the popular uprising of South Vietnam may become a protracted armed struggle between ourselves and the enemy. Our Party must plan for this possibility and make adequate and vigorous preparations for any eventuality."[6]

Summarizing the conclusions of the Central Committee session, Chairman Ho Chi Minh declared, "The responsibility for saving our nation belongs to the entire Party, to the entire population. . . . We must include South Vietnam in the general revolution of our entire nation and include our nation's revolution in the world revolution. . . . We will hold high the banner of peace because this is very much to our advantage. Peace does not mean, however, that our forces will not be ready. . . . If we organize our political forces properly, when weapons are needed we will have no problems."[7]

The Resolution of the 15th Plenum of the Party Central Committee demonstrated the offensive revolutionary thinking of our Party and once again confirmed that the road to the liberation of South Vietnam was the road of revolutionary violence. Foreseeing the direction in which the revolution in the South would develop, the resolution laid out guidelines for the developmental and combat operations of our armed forces in both North and South Vietnam. The resolution also gave our army additional time to make ready and actively prepared us to respond to all requirements for the expansion of the revolution.

In February 1959, immediately after the 15th Plenary Session of the Party Central Committee ended, the General Military Party Committee met in Hanoi. Comrade Le Duan, member of the Politburo of the Central Committee, briefed the committee on the spirit of the Resolution of the 15th Plenum.

PREPARATIONS FOR WAR AND THE ESTABLISHMENT OF THE HO CHI MINH TRAIL

In response to the Party Central Committee's assessments of possible future developments in the revolution in the South, the General Military Party Committee discussed such pressing matters as building bases and developing revolutionary armed forces in the South, expanding North Vietnam's role in the revolution in the South, and preparing our armed forces to crush any aggressive scheme the enemy might try to carry out. All this was done so that when armed struggle was needed to unify the nation, our army and our people throughout the nation would be able to fully carry out their duties.

The General Military Party Committee determined that the combat opponents of our army were the American and puppet armed forces, both of which had modern equipment. The equipment of our army was also currently being modernized. Both our situation and the enemy's situation were changing. Combat methods had progressed when compared with the period of the resistance war against the French. The revolutionary war that our population and our armed forces would have to wage, however, was still a people's war, a people's war under modern conditions. It would be necessary for us to arm the entire population and to build an armed force made up of main force soldiers, local troops, and self-defense militia. We had to build our army into a well-equipped, well-trained, modern, regular, appropriately sized revolutionary army with a high level of combat capabilities. We had to combine modern military science and the combat principles of an army made up of many combined-arms branches with the experience we had gained during the recent war against the French in order to decide the kind of training most suited for our new combat missions. We also had to build a politically and economically solid rear area capable of supplying every material requirement for war.

Speaking to the General Military Party Committee conference, Comrade Le Duan stated clearly, "we are not using warfare to unite the nation. If, however, the United States and its puppets start a war, we will also have to resort to war, and the war that the enemy will have started will give us an opportunity to unify the nation."[8] Le Duan affirmed that "the only path open to the United States and Diem is to begin an unjust war, and we will certainly crush them when they take that path."[9]

To implement the Resolution of the 15th Plenum of the Party Central Committee and based on the results of the first military five-year plan (1955–1959), the General Military Party Committee decided to intensify our efforts to build a modern, regular, revolutionary army and to increase the combat strength and the combat readiness of the army. Preparations for sending the army to South Vietnam to join the battle were begun.

The 338th Division, which was composed of Southern regroupees, and a number of our infantry regiments were converted into training groups for cadre and soldiers who would be sent to perform their duties in South Vietnam. Tens of thousands of cadre and soldiers who were natives of South Vietnam or who were familiar with the battlefields of South Vietnam began to be gathered together for training by these units before being sent off to the battlefront. A number of mobile infantry divisions and brigades subordinate to the High Command, to Military Region 4, and to the Northwestern Military Region were brought up to wartime strength. A continuous series of study seminars on the situation and on our revolutionary duties in South Vietnam were held by all units of the army. Many political activities, meetings, readings, and discussions of "Letters from the front lines of the Fatherland," etc., were organized with the aim of teaching our cadre and soldiers to hate the United States and Diem and to properly prepare our troops, in their thoughts and actions, to carry out any duty assigned to them by the Party. From the temporary Demilitarized Zone in Vinh Linh to our northern borders, from the mainland to our offshore islands, all units of our army actively studied and trained to prepare to enter the battle alongside the soldiers and civilians of South Vietnam.

In May 1959, in accordance with instructions from the Party Politburo, a staff agency under the direct control of the General Military Party Committee was formed to study the establishment of a transportation route to send supplies to the South. Comrade Vo Bam, Deputy Director of the Army Agricultural Farms Department, a man who had spent many years working on the battlefields of Interzone 5 and the Central Highlands and who was familiar with the land and sea routes from the North into South Vietnam, was placed in charge of this staff research organization. The Politburo directed that a special military communications group be formed to establish routes to send cadre, weapons, and other needed supplies to South Vietnam. This was a tremendous job of strategic importance that would play a direct role in the liberation of South Vietnam and the unification of our nation.

Military Transportation Group 559 was established on 19 May 1959. Group 559 had an initial strength of two battalions. The 301st Land Transportation Battalion was made up of 500 cadre and soldiers chosen from the ranks of the 305th Brigade. Captains Chu Dang Chu and Nguyen Danh (also known as Chinh) commanded this battalion. The 603rd Sea Transportation Battalion was made up of 107 cadre and soldiers, all natives of South Vietnam with seagoing experience. Comrade Ha Van Xa was appointed 603rd Battalion Commander and Comrade Luu Duc was named Battalion Political Officer.

During the summer of 1959, as Group 559 was urgently preparing troops and weapons for movement to the battlefield, in Military Region 4 the 325th Infantry Division was ordered to build an emergency military road, to be completed within three months, to enable trucks to carry supplies from Dong Hoi city in Quang Binh province to Khe Ho in western Vinh Linh. The 301st Battalion built its launch base at Khe Ho and established its first way station on the Ham Nghi Ridge. From there the battalion crossed the Ben Hai River down to Route 9 and then followed the secret commo-liaison routes used by Huong Hoa district and the Thua Thien Province Party Committee down along the eastern slopes of the Annamite Mountain chain, building a trail and establishing way stations in areas occupied by the Van Kieu, Ta Oi, Pa Co, and Ca Tu tribal peoples, always advancing toward the South.

On 20 August 1959 the 301st Battalion established Way Station 9 at Pa Lin in western Thua Thien province and delivered to this way station its first shipment of supplies (500 kilograms) for passage to Interzone 5. To maintain absolute secrecy all weapons and supplies sent South during this period were manufactured in capitalist countries. The cadre and soldiers at the transshipment stations and the commo-liaison couriers and cadre groups marching to South Vietnam were ordered to avoid clashes with the enemy. They were ordered to "walk without leaving a trace, cook without smoke, and speak without making noise."

By the end of 1959 the human porters of the 301st Battalion had delivered to the Pa Lin Way Station a total of 1,667 infantry weapons, 788 knives, 188 kilograms of explosives, and a number of military maps, compasses, and binoculars.[10] These supplies were delivered to Interzone 5 and a portion of these supplies were transported deeper into the interior to equip armed recently formed self-defense units in the Central Highlands and the western portions of the provinces of Central Vietnam.

By the end of 1959 this route had also been used to send 542 cadre and soldiers, the majority of whom were platoon- and company-level command cadre, sapper training cadre, cryptographic personnel, and weapons repair technicians, into South Vietnam to perform their revolutionary duties. Of these personnel, 515 went to Interzone 5 and 27 traveled all the way to Cochin China. These cadre and soldiers immediately began to form battalions, companies, platoons, and sapper teams in Interzone 5 and Cochin China. Although the numbers of weapons, cadre, and soldiers sent to the battlefield along Group 559's supply network during 1959 were not great, they represented a very valuable capital investment that contributed to the development of our revolutionary armed forces in South Vietnam. They constituted a first step in answering the needs of the Southern revolution following the approval of the Resolution of the 15th Plenum of the Party Central Committee.

To establish a sea infiltration route into South Vietnam, the 603rd Battalion set up a base on the Gianh River in Quang Binh province and stationed a secret radio team high up on the Hai Van Pass in Quang Nam province to broadcast navigation directions. The battalion used wooden boats disguised as local civilian coastal fishing boats. The first trial voyage was scheduled for November 1959 but the trip had to be postponed due to bad weather. On the second trip the boat encountered strong winds that broke the tiller and blew the boat in close to Ly Son Island of Quang Ngai province. The boat's cadre and soldiers, under the command of First Lieutenant Nguyen Bac (who had been proclaimed an "emulation combatant" of the entire army during the resistance war against the French), quickly threw their supplies overboard, thereby preserving the secret of our shipment of weapons to the South. Although these voyages were not successful, they provided valuable lessons for our soldiers to use in our seagoing supply operations in later years.

At the same time our supply routes were beginning to operate by land down the Annamite Mountain range and on the South China Sea from the North to South Vietnam, other transportation routes were also under construction to link our separate base areas. Armed propaganda units from eastern Cochin China began to survey routes to the north. In Central Vietnam the Interzone 5 Party Committee set up communications routes and transportation corridors from the Pa Lin Way Station through the base areas in the western portions of the provinces of Central Vietnam down into the Central Highlands. In Cochin China two armed propaganda units (one belonging to the Cochin China Party Committee and commanded by Comrade Lam Quoc Dang and one belonging to Phuoc Long province under the command of Comrade Pham Thuan, Secretary of the Provincial Party Committee) and the 59th Company of the Eastern Cochin China Inter-provincial Party Committee, under the command of Comrade Nguyen Van Tam, began cutting trails through the jungle, crossing through regions where no human had ever gone in Bu Dang and Bu Gia Map (in Phuoc Long province) and So Nia (in Quang Duc province) to reach the extreme southern regions of Central Vietnam and the southern Central Highlands.

In October 1960, at Kilometer 5 on Route 14B in the triborder area of Cambodia, Laos, and Vietnam, the Phuoc Long province armed propaganda unit established contact with the commo-liaison unit of Interzone 5. At the same time, in the Ro Ti area of Bien Hoa province, the 59th Company established contact with the commo-liaison company of the Party Cadre Affairs Section for the provinces of extreme southern Central Vietnam.

With the establishment of two routes all the way down to eastern Cochin China and the establishment of a transportation route along the Annamite Mountain chain linking our base area in North Vietnam with the South, the Fatherland's front line now began to take shape. The birth of Transportation Group 559 and the strategic North-South transportation route demonstrated the high resolve of the entire Party, the entire population, and the entire army to liberate South Vietnam. It was a very important first step that enabled us to expand our forces and develop a solid strategic position for the cause of the resistance war against the United States to save the nation.

After attending the 15th Plenary Session of the Party Central Committee, the Central Committee ordered the Central Committee members responsible for local areas in South Vietnam and the representatives of the Cochin China and Interzone 5 Party Committees to quickly return to South Vietnam to begin their preparations to elevate the Southern Revolution to a new, higher stage.

THE FIRST UPRISINGS IN THE SOUTH

During the first months of 1959 the situation in South Vietnam became extremely active. Because of the increasingly savage terrorist campaign being waged by the U.S.-Diem clique, the civilian population in many areas, led by our local Party committees, launched uprisings, resolutely combating the enemy and protecting the people's rights to make a living and to enjoy democracy.

In the mountainous regions of Interzone 5 many armed uprisings broke out, conducted by our ethnic minority brethren who opposed enemy efforts to collect them into concentration camps and demanded to be allowed to return to their old villages. On 6 February 1959, the Ba Na tribal people of 11 hamlets of Vinh Hiep and Vinh Hao villages in Vinh Thanh district, Binh Dinh province, moved their hamlets deep into the jungles. By April 1959 most of Vinh Thanh district, consisting of 60 large hamlets (except for four hamlets in Bok Toi village) with a total of 5,000 people, had wrested control away from the government. In Binh Thuan province, on 7 February 1959 the Ra Giai tribal people rose up and destroyed the enemy's concentration areas at Brau and Dong Day in Bac Ai district. In April 1959 they destroyed the Tam Ngan concentration area. Also during 1959 the Cham and Hre ethnic minorities in Tho Lo, Phu Yen province, and the Ede, Gia Rai, Xe Dang, etc., in Ta Booc and Mang Khenh, Kontum province, conducted a series of uprisings, killing tyrants and abandoning their old hamlets to return to the jungles to establish new hamlets where they lived illegally (according to the enemy's law).

Many different ways to organize revolutionary armed forces arose out of these uprisings. These included people's self-defense forces, secret self-defense forces, full-time guerrillas, concentrated armed platoons, etc. In Tra Bong, the 339th Armed Platoon was formed. The platoon was made up of 43 soldiers, 33 of whom were members of the Cor ethnic minority group and ten ethnic Vietnamese. In the contested areas of the lowlands a number of armed propaganda units organized by provincial and district Party committees aggressively eliminated tyrants and traitors and built mass political organizations.

In South Vietnam the elimination of tyrants occurred on a daily basis. Village and hamlet puppets and self-defense forces were terrified. Every night they fled to sleep inside their military outposts and did not dare to arrogantly conduct searches as they had before. Hundreds resigned or were too afraid to carry out their duties. This movement was especially active in areas surrounding the U Minh Forest and the Plain of Reeds. In these areas our armed units, after a period of consolidation during which they had built up a solid base of support among the masses, eliminated many tyrants and repelled many enemy military operations. Supported by our armed operations, the people from a number of villages and hamlets near the U Minh base area moved into the jungle, establishing "youth residences" and "family residences," forming "jungle hamlets," a form of combat hamlet resembling those we had used during the resistance war against the French.

Revolutionary conditions developed in the rural hamlets and villages of the lowlands of Cochin China and the mountains of Central Vietnam. Guided by the correct and timely policies provided by the Party Central Committee and using revolutionary forces we had maintained and developed during the years 1954 through 1959, the people of South Vietnam rose up in a revolutionary struggle that took many rich and creative forms. Many uprisings broke out from mid-1959 through the end of 1960. These uprisings helped South Vietnam's armed self-defense to grow by leaps and bounds, enabling them to provide outstanding support to the mass uprisings.

In the fall of 1959 an armed uprising broke out in Tra Bong. Tra Bong was a district in the mountains of western Quang Ngai province. The Cor, Hre, and Ca Dong tribal people and the ethnic Vietnamese who live in this remote mountain region have a long history of patriotism and a tradition of struggle against oppression and foreign aggressors. During the years of struggle to preserve our revolutionary forces (1954–1959) the Quang Ngai Province Party Committee built a firm organizational base in this area. The committee led the people in struggles against the enemy to preserve their ownership of the agricultural fields of the highland villages. The Party Committee also infiltrated many cadre and revolutionary sympathizers into the puppet governmental apparatus in villages and hamlets in the lowlands. Many "determined-to-die" units were established to eliminate tyrants, and self-defense units were formed to protect the villages.

In August 1959 the people of the villages of Tra Bong district and of the western portion of Quang Ngai province organized enthusiastic meetings to celebrate the 14th anniversary of the victory of the August Revolution, and, in accordance with guidance from the Provincial Party Committee, to boycott the elections for Diem's puppet National Assembly. In a number of villages clashes broke out between our self-defense youth and enemy soldiers. Unit 339 was dispersed into many small cells to key villages to serve as the backbone of the mass struggle. Other armed groups subordinate to the district headquarters intensified their own armed propaganda activities. Everywhere in the district the people blocked roads, planted punji stakes, hid their property, organized guard forces, disseminated information, and built fences for combat hamlets. Some villages withdrew to higher ground.

On 28 August 1959, while enemy troops were searching each hamlet to force the people to go out to vote in the election, the people of Tra Quan, Tra Khe, Tra Nham, Tra Phong, and Tra Lanh villages and people throughout Tra Bong district launched simultaneous uprisings. The soldiers of Unit 339 and self-defense youths ambushed, surrounded, and chased away enemy troops. Each soldier wore a red scarf and carried a pack on his shoulders and a coil of rope on his back. The masses conducting the uprising, wearing red cloth bands on their shirtsleeves, destroyed puppet village offices, pursued and eliminated tyrants and thugs, and dissolved the enemy's apparatus of oppression. Tra Bong's mountain jungles echoed with the sounds of gongs, drums, and horns, interspersed with the shouts of the masses as they conducted their uprisings.

On 29 August enemy troops occupying outposts at Da Lip, Ta Lat, Tam Rung, and Nuoc Vot fled their posts in terror. The revolutionary masses, led by the soldiers of Unit 339, attacked the two remaining large enemy outposts in Tra Bong, located at Eo Chim and Eo Reo. After a two-day siege and after crippling an enemy company from the district capital that tried to come to their rescue, on 31 August the outposts at Eo Chim and Eo Reo were both taken. The remaining enemy troops fled to the district capital. The Tra Bong district chief himself fled to the province capital.

The people of 16 highland villages of Tra Bong district held a people's congress to elect a Revolutionary Committee and established a court to try 63 puppet tyrants within the district. The Tra Bong uprising, and those in the districts of Son Ha, Ba To, and Minh Long in western Quang Ngai province, the first armed uprising mounted by the soldiers and civilians of South Vietnam, was completely victorious.

Formed while preparing for and conducting an armed uprising, Unit 339 expanded into a company and its troops were now fully equipped with weapons. Many village guerrilla units were formed. On 19 August 1959 the Quang Ngai Province Party Committee formed the province's second full-time armed unit[11] in Son Ha district, and the districts of Ba To and Minh Long established the third full-time armed unit.[12]

To deal with this powerful uprising by the people of Quang Ngai province, during the final months of 1959 the Diem puppet government sent a division of regular troops plus provincial and district regional force troops to conduct continuous sweeps through the western districts, with the focus on Tra Bong, aimed at reestablishing their governmental apparatus in the villages and hamlets. Our full-time armed platoons and self-defense guerrilla units relied on defensive systems consisting of punji sticks, mines, and booby traps in the villages to resolutely oppose and repel enemy troop units when they moved into the highland villages. In the lowland villages the Province Party Committees established a policy of exploiting the legal rights of the people to expand the political struggle and to proselytize the enemy's troops. The struggle conducted by people of all ethnic groups in Tra Bong had now taken a new form, one that combined political struggle with armed struggle, to preserve the hold on power the masses had gained during the August 1959 uprisings.

In the base areas of eastern Cochin China and rural areas of the Mekong Delta, after absorbing the essence of the Resolution of the 15th Plenum of the Party Central Committee, our full-time armed units and armed propaganda units intensified their operations and carried out their mission of serving as an assault force to support mass uprisings.

On 25 September 1959, the 502nd Kien Phong Battalion, with a troop strength of over 100 soldiers, gathered to study Resolution 15 at Tan Hoi Co village in Hong Ngu district. After learning that the puppet 42nd Regimental Combat Group, traveling on more than 100 sampans, was conducting a sweep along the An Long Canal, the battalion command section decided to block and attack the enemy in order to capture his weapons, protect the base area, and influence the local population. With combat experience gained during the resistance war against the French and complete familiarity with the terrain of the Plain of Reeds base area, the cadre and soldiers of the 502nd Battalion won two successive victories over the enemy in two ambushes at Giong Thi Dam and Go Quan Cung on 26 September 1959. They wiped out almost an entire battalion of puppet regular troops, captured 105 prisoners (including the entire battalion command staff), and confiscated 365 weapons, 30,000 rounds of ammunition, and 11 radios. The Giong Thi Dam and Go Quan Cung victories created a great impact among the masses, sowed fear in the enemy ranks, and highlighted the traditions of our army: winning victory in the first battle, fighting for a certain victory, and fighting battles that exterminated the enemy.

Using the guns captured in these battles, the Interprovincial Party Committee was able to provide additional armament for the 502nd Battalion and for 23 armed operations units belonging to the districts of Hong Ngu, Cao Lanh, and My An of Kien Phong and Kien Tuong provinces. The population of the areas around the Plain of Reeds, encouraged by this victory and supported by our armed operations units, increased their own efforts to eliminate tyrants and traitors and expanded our revolutionary associations and organizations. In many villages and hamlets the people beat drums and wooden chimes continuously for ten days and nights, terrifying and paralyzing the puppet administrators and puppet militia. In Hau My and Thanh My villages the people rose up, killed puppet administrators, spies, and thugs, and dissolved the village governmental administrative apparatus. In Long An province the 506th Battalion dispersed into squads and armed propaganda teams to work in the eight villages of Duc Hoa district, in the villages along the Vam Co Dong River from Thanh Loi to Binh Duc, and in Thu Thua district. In Rach Gia province the U Minh Battalion, exploiting a moment when the enemy had relaxed his guard, overran the Kien An military headquarters in An Bien district. In Ca Mau province, provincial armed forces destroyed outposts at Vam Cai Tau and on the Doc River, wiped out an enemy platoon at Hon Khoai, and blocked many enemy sweep operations in Nam Can and Cai Nuoc districts. In Tra Vinh province entire enemy platoons were wiped out during battles fought at Lang Nuoc, Dai An, and Long Toan. Beginning with only armed propaganda operations in support of the political struggle of the masses and operations to maintain and develop our forces, the armed self-defense units in the lowlands began to change their methods of operation in accordance with policy guidelines issued by the Cochin China Party Committee. They began to support mass uprisings and insurrections to seize control of villages and hamlets.

EXPLOITING SUCCESS IN COCHIN CHINA

In November 1959 the 4th Conference of the Cochin China Party Committee was held in the Duong Minh Chau War Zone in Tay Ninh province to discuss the implementation of the Resolution of the 15th Party Central Committee's Plenum. Comrade Nguyen Van Linh, Acting Secretary of the Cochin China Party Committee, presided over the conference.

After analyzing the situation in South Vietnam during the final months of 1959, the Party Committee concluded that "the enemy is on the defensive everywhere and can no longer rule the country in the way he wants. At the village and hamlet level the enemy is weak, not strong. Using primarily mass political forces, with our armed self-defense teams serving as the hard core, we are now able to eliminate the enemy's puppet tyrants and his vicious militia forces and take control of the villages and hamlets."[13]

The Party Committee directed the Eastern Cochin China Interprovincial Military Affairs Section to intensify the operations of our full-time troops and to conduct a large attack that would resonate through the entire region to encourage the revolutionary struggle movement of the masses and capture enemy weapons for use to equip our own armed units.

In early January 1960 a conference of military cadre from eastern Cochin China was held in Bau Ra in Tay Ninh province. The conference discussed the work of building up the armed forces of eastern Cochin China and armed operations to implement the resolution of the 15th Plenum of the Party Central Committee and the policies of the Cochin China Party Committee. A plan to attack Tua Hai was presented to this military cadre conference and was subsequently approved by the Cochin China Party Committee.

Tua Hai was an old French fort located seven kilometers northwest of Tay Ninh city. The puppet army had expanded the fort into a regimental headquarters base camp.[14] The puppets had built high walls, dug deep trenches, and constructed many watchtowers. The camp was carefully patrolled and guarded day and night. During mid-1959 our contacts inside the base prepared to mount a mutiny but their plan was exposed. To guard against further mutinies, during the 1960 Tet new year's holiday the enemy allowed only one platoon, the alert platoon, to carry weapons.

This was a very favorable opportunity for our forces. The Eastern Cochin China Military Affairs Section decided to employ three infantry companies (the 59th, 70th, and 80th), the 60th Sapper Company, and three Tay Ninh province armed squads in the attack. A number of weapons that had been cached since 1954 were dug up and distributed to the units. Almost 500 civilian porters were mobilized to support the battle.

On 26 January 1960 (two days before the Tet lunar new year), our units, under the command of Comrade Nguyen Van Xuyen, Chief of the Eastern Cochin China Military Affairs Section,[15] secretly approached the stronghold. In coordination with our agents inside the base who launched an internal mutiny, our units launched a surprise attack that seized control of the entire Tua Hai base, killing or capturing 500 enemy troops and confiscating 1,500 weapons.

The Tua Hai victory achieved the political and military goals set forward by the Cochin China Party Committee. The battle sent shock waves throughout the region, frightening enemy troops, especially the regional forces and militia troops in the villages and hamlets, and giving powerful encouragement to the masses to rise up against the regime.

THE BEN TRE UPRISING

In central Cochin China, in December 1959 the Region 8 Party Committee held an expanded meeting to expedite preparations for uprisings. Comrade Nguyen Minh Duong, Secretary of the Region Party Committee, presided over the conference. The Region Party Committee concluded that "the provinces of central Cochin China have just emerged from a period of ferocious struggle and our revolutionary organizations have suffered losses. In some places these losses have been serious. However, our leadership and our mass organizations still survive. Although their ranks are small, all our members are Party members, cadre, or citizens who are loyal and firm in their resolve to exterminate the enemy."[16]

To implement the resolutions of the Party Central Committee and the Cochin China Party Committee, the Regional Committee decided to mobilize the masses to rise up to break the enemy's grip and seize control of the rural areas. The uprisings had to be widespread to prevent enemy troops from being able to concentrate forces to suppress them. The provinces adjacent to the Plain of Reeds base area would intensify political struggles supported by armed operations. These provinces were directed to break the enemy's grip on the population, assert the people's right to govern themselves, expand our guerrilla bases, attack enemy sweep operations, and protect our bases. Region 8's other provinces would rapidly organize and expand their political forces, at the same time building armed forces to support the masses in preparation for a simultaneous uprising.

The Region Party Committee decided that the time frame for launching mass uprisings would be January 1960. Upon receipt of a guidance cable from the Region Party Committee, Comrade Vo Van Pham, Secretary of the Ben Tre Province Party Committee, held discussions with the members of the Province Party Standing Committee and intensified preparations for uprisings in two areas. Area 1 consisted of the districts of Giong Trom, Binh Dai, and Ba Tri, located on Bao and An Hoa Islands. Area 2 consisted of Mo Cay and Thanh Phu districts on Minh Island. Members of the Province Party Committee were assigned responsibility for individual tasks and sent to these districts to guide preparations for the uprisings.

On 1 January 1960, in Tan Trung village, Mo Cay district, Female Comrade Nguyen Thi Dinh, Deputy Secretary of the Province Party Committee, briefed a number of Province Party Committee members and members of the Mo Cay District Party Committee on the spirit of Resolution 15 and the specific policies of the Region Party Committee.

This meeting reached the following assessment of the situation: Enemy forces in Ben Tre province were numerous and vicious[17] and they had a tight grip on the population. The people were bitter toward the enemy and were ready to rise up. The Provincial Party Chapter's leadership forces had been reduced to only 162 cadre and Party members, but all these individuals had spent many years conducting revolutionary struggle, were experienced at mobilizing the masses, and were trusted by the masses.

The meeting set forward the following requirements for the uprising: To launch powerful, continuous, and widespread mass uprisings aimed at the most dangerous points (which were also the weakest points), that is, the enemy's control apparatus at the village and hamlet level; to seize power and place it in the hands of the masses; to expand our political and armed forces; to consolidate and develop Party organizations; and to seize land for distribution to the peasants.

Since the province had no armed forces, the meeting decided to gather a band of brave youths and arm them with spears, knives, wooden guns, "coconut sprout" guns, etc., and organize them into action teams to eliminate tyrants and support the masses during the uprisings. This group would claim to be North Vietnamese soldiers belonging to the 502nd Battalion[18] to deceive and frighten the enemy. We would combine the launching of our rural uprisings with attacks on a number of locations in the province capital to make a publicity splash in support of the overall movement. The villages of Dinh Thuy, Phuoc Hiep, and Binh Khanh, all in Mo Cay district, were selected as the province's targets. The Standing Committee of the Province Party Committee would directly supervise operations at these target villages. The date for the mass "simultaneous uprising" was set as 17 January 1960. Comrade Pham Tam Cang (alias Hai Thuy), member of the Province Party Committee, was sent to Dinh Thuy village to directly command the uprising.

On 17 January 1960 the people of Dinh Thuy village, with an action team serving as their assault unit, rose up, surrounded, and destroyed a militia group (tong doan) of 12 men and the village militia squad, hunted down and captured vicious puppets and spies, and dismantled the enemy's apparatus of oppression. Using 28 weapons that our forces had captured, the Province Party Committee formed several armed units and sent them to the villages of Phuoc Hiep and Binh Khanh to support mass uprisings there.

On 18 January (in Phuoc Hiep) and 19 January (in Binh Khanh) the people rose up and seized control. The popular uprisings of the three villages of Dinh Thuy, Phuoc Hiep, and Binh Khanh had achieved total victory. This initial assault shook the enemy's ruling apparatus and stimulated a spirit of insurrection throughout the entire province.

In Binh Khanh village, on 19 January the Ben Tre Province Party Committee collected all captured weapons and formed three armed squads, which were sent to perform armed propaganda operations and mobilize the masses in Minh Tan, Thanh Phu, and Mo Cay districts. A number of cadre were given good weapons[19] and formed into the first armed platoon, which was designated the 264th Company [sic]. After beginning their uprising armed only with their bare hands, the people of Ben Tre now had guns and an armed force and could now carry out attacks on the enemy using political forces combined with armed forces and troop proselytizing operations.

During the period from 17 to 24 January 1960, the period called Ben Tre's "week of uprisings by the entire population," the people in 47 villages in the districts of Mo Cay, Giong Trom, Chau Thanh, Ba Tri, and Thanh Phu rose up in a simultaneous wave of insurrection. In 22 villages tyrants were eliminated, outposts were destroyed, the enemy's governing apparatus was crushed, and the entire village and its hamlets were completely liberated. In 25 other villages the people eliminated tyrants, besieged outposts and police stations, and liberated many hamlets. In Ben Tre city, our self-defense forces attacked the Lo Tuong Police Station and eliminated tyrants in the 1st Precinct, at the Thap intersection, and in Phu Khuong. Three hundred puppets, spies, and tyrants were captured, and 37 outposts and police stations were forced to withdraw or surrender. The people of Ben Tre captured 150 guns and a large quantity of ammunition of all types.

In accordance with instructions from the Province Party Committee, the people established courts to try puppet tyrants and vicious landlords and to distribute land to the peasants. Our youth organized guard details, built obstacles, conducted military training, and prepared to fight enemy troops mounting counterattacks. Every village formed one or two armed squads and established "work sites" to produce weapons. The province "work site," located in Binh Khanh village, was able to produce "Pegasus" guns.[20] In February 1960, the Ben Tre Province Party Committee collected the armed units on Bao Island (the districts of Giong Trom, Ba Tri, and Chau Thanh) to form its second full-time armed unit, designated the 269th Company.

Frightened by the uprisings of the people of Ben Tre, on 21 January 1960 the enemy sent in a Marine battalion, stationing it in Phuoc Hiep village with the intention of relieving the besieged outposts of Dinh Thuy and Binh Khanh. Armed Unit 264 and armed squads from three villages blocked the enemy force, killing a number of enemy troops and capturing some weapons.

In an action coordinated with our armed forces opposing the enemy's sweep operation, on 4 February 1960 the Ben Tre Province Party Committee and the Mo Cay District Party Committee organized 200 women from Phuoc Hiep village and 5,000 women from neighboring villages. These women were sent into the district to demonstrate against acts of terror and to demand compensation for damages. The puppet administration of Ben Tre province was forced to withdraw its troops from three villages. The struggle movement of 4 February 1960 in the Mo Cay district capital demonstrated that the people of villages and hamlets that had just revolted and seized control over their own lands were capable of maintaining a position of legal struggle and could conduct a political struggle that directly confronted the enemy and proselytized his troops in coordination with our armed struggle against terrorism and sweep operations. During this struggle a political struggle army, organized from the masses and overwhelmingly made up of women, made its appearance. Our people and armed forces affectionately called these women our "long-haired army."

On 25 March 1960 the Diem puppet government sent almost 10,000 troops, including Marines, paratroopers, Rangers, 70 military vehicles, 17 naval vessels, and 47 105mm howitzers, together with the entire Regional Force strength of the province, to conduct a major operation to encircle and clear the villages of Dinh Thuy, Phuoc Hiep, and Binh Khanh. They viciously shot and killed people, burned and looted, and committed many extremely barbarous crimes. They buried 36 youths alive and murdered 80 others.

The Provincial Party Committee decided to mass the 264th and 269th Companies to take the offensive, win the first battle to destroy the enemy's prestige, and conduct coordinated operations with our village guerrillas in support of the mass struggle. On 26 March our troops mounted an ambush at Hamlet 6 of Phuoc Hiep village, killing 50 enemy troops and capturing a number of weapons. Developing this victory, our two companies dispersed their forces and worked with village armed squads to form sniper teams, set out booby traps, and conduct guerrilla warfare. They fought the enemy for ten straight days, inflicting over 300 casualties on the enemy force. The people of the villages enthusiastically fed and housed our troops and guerrillas and cared for our wounded. Mothers and sisters tried to win over enemy troops or to detain or deceive them, thereby enabling our troops to move forward and attack the enemy.

On 1 April 1960, thousands of people from the villages of Dinh Thuy, Phuoc Hiep, and Binh Khanh, traveling on hundreds of boats and bringing with them old people, children, blankets, mats, pots, skillets, pigs, chickens, etc. . . . mounted an "evacuation in reverse" to Mo Cay city. Over 5,000 people from other villages, the overwhelming majority of whom were women, were mobilized in a "preemptory evacuation" to come to the district capital to avoid the sweep operation. The people of Mo Cay town cooked rice, boiled water, and provided support to their compatriots from the rural villages in support of the struggle. Over 10,000 people, conducting a stubborn struggle lasting 12 days and nights in the town and supported by the combat activities of our armed forces, forced Diem's puppet administration to withdraw all of its Marines from the three villages of Dinh Thuy, Phuoc Hiep, and Binh Khanh.

Because the enemy still maintained its governmental apparatus at the district, province, and national level, and because his armed forces were still too numerous for us, the enemy was able to gradually reestablish 27 Regional Force and militia outposts that had previously been forced to withdraw or surrender. Using the full-time armed units, guerrilla squads, and mass political forces that had been formed and expanded during the uprising, the people of these villages continued to besiege enemy outposts and police stations. Real control of the villages and hamlets remained in the hands of the people.

The victorious uprising of the people of Ben Tre provided a model for uprisings in the lowlands and for the tactic of conducting uprisings to seize governmental authority at the grass-roots level by using mass political forces as our primary weapon with an armed self-defense force element to provide support and serve as the assault spearhead of the uprising. This tactic created a composite power of revolutionary violence made up of two forces: political forces and armed forces. Although our armed forces were still small, their ability to hold their own was very important because they provided a new source of strength for the revolutionary forces of the masses. The tactics of conducting a two-legged attack (political struggle combined with armed struggle) and a three-legged attack (political, military, and military proselytizing) against the enemy were used for the first time in this uprising.

THE 1960 GENERAL UPRISING

During the first months of 1960, while the simultaneous uprising was exploding in Ben Tre, political struggle movements and armed propaganda operations in support of mass revolts to seize control of villages and hamlets were breaking out in many of the provinces of Cochin China. As a direct result of the Tua Hai victory, in Tay Ninh province 30 Regional Force and militia outposts (out of a total of 60 outposts throughout the province) were either abandoned by their occupants or were forced to withdraw by mass uprisings and sieges. Seventy percent of the enemy's governmental apparatus at the village and hamlet level collapsed and disintegrated. The people held real control of 24 villages and had basically liberated another 19 villages (out of a total of 49 villages in the entire province). The armed forces of Tay Ninh province, which had begun as a number of squads responsible for protecting our bases and defending the province and district leadership organs, had now grown to 44 village guerrilla units, one battalion and two engineer-sapper companies at the province level, and the district local force companies.[21]

In Rach Gia province the U Minh Battalion destroyed the Ba The Regional Force outpost and a column of enemy reinforcements sent to rescue the outpost. The battalion also supported popular revolts, eliminated tyrants, and destroyed the Ba The Concentration Area.

In My Tho province the province's full-time armed platoon (which called itself the 514th Battalion), together with the Kien Tuong province armed platoon (which the Region Party Committee had sent as reinforcements) and the armed propaganda units of Cai Be, Cai Lay, and Chau Thanh districts stepped up armed propaganda operations along the Nguyen Van Tiep Canal, forcing the withdrawal of six enemy outposts and capturing 30 weapons. Supported by our armed operations, the population of many of the villages north of Route 4 rose up and held demonstrations, marches, etc. The revolutionary spirit of the people boiled over, resembling the days of the August General Uprising.

In July 1960 the Cochin China Party Committee held its 5th conference in War Zone D. Concluding that the insurrection movement of the masses in the rural areas had reached a new stage of development, the Party Committee decided "to continue the political offensive, to cause the enemy to fail, to put him increasingly on the defensive in all areas, to gradually defeat the enemy's plots and policies, and to create an opportunity for an uprising to overthrow the entire U.S.-Diem regime."[22]

On the 15th anniversary of the Cochin China Resistance Day, 23 September 1960, the Party Committee ordered all provinces to launch a general uprising. From mid-September 1960 to the beginning of 1961, our general uprising swept through the lowlands of Cochin China and the mountains of Central Vietnam.

In Cochin China, taking advantage of the experience gained by the people of Ben Tre province, local Party chapters used action teams and guerrilla squads as assault units to support mass uprisings; eliminate puppets, spies, and tyrants; besiege and force the surrender or withdrawal of militia outposts; shatter the enemy's control apparatus; and seize control of the villages and hamlets. On 14 September 1960 the people of Ca Mau, Rach Gia, Soc Trang, Vinh Long, Chau Doc, Long Xuyen, and Can Tho provinces in western Cochin China conducted simultaneous uprisings. Long An, My Tho, Ben Tre, Kien Phong, and Kien Tuong provinces in central Cochin China conducted simultaneous uprisings on 23 and 24 September 1960. In eastern Cochin China our general uprising spread from Tay Ninh, Ben Cat, Dau Tieng, Cu Chi, and Hoc Mon down to Lai Thieu, Thu Duc, Tan Binh, Di An, Nha Be, and Binh Chanh on the outskirts of Saigon–Gia Dinh. People who had been forced into "new agricultural areas" and "concentration areas" revolted and returned to their old villages. Many demonstrations involving tens of thousands of rural people marched into the cities and towns demanding that the enemy end his acts of terror and his artillery attacks, shattering the calm of the cities. By the end of 1960 the populations of over 800 villages (out of a total of 1,296 villages in all of Cochin China) had risen up and taken control of their areas. Over 100 villages had been completely liberated.

In southern Central Vietnam, beginning in September 1960 the Party Cadre Affairs Section for the provinces of extreme southern Central Vietnam and the Interzone 5 Party Committee launched a wave of armed operations to support people of all ethnic groups in uprisings to seize control of the mountain villages. Massed armed units subordinate to the interzone and to provincial Party committees attacked and forced the withdrawal of 55 enemy outposts, wiping out 40 Regional Force platoons and capturing 400 weapons. People who had been forced into concentration camps and "new agricultural areas" rose up, destroyed the enemy's machinery of oppression, and returned to their old villages. Over 20,000 residents of the mountainous areas, representing all ethnic groups, had been liberated. The Interzone 5–Central Highlands base area expanded from north of Kontum down to Route 21, where it linked up with the base areas of the provinces of extreme southern Central Vietnam and the base areas of eastern Cochin China. A number of armed propaganda units went into the contested areas of the lowlands to build political and armed organizations, eliminate tyrants, and support the masses in their struggles against the enemy. In December 1960 the population of six villages, Hoa Thinh, Hoa My, Hoa Tan, Hoa Tong, Hoa Hiep, and Hoa Xuan in Tuy Hoa district, Phu Yen province, rose up and seized control of their villages, launching the general uprising movement in the rural lowlands of southern Central Vietnam. By the end of 1960 the people had seized control of 3,200 of the total of 5,721 mountain hamlets in the area. Of the 3,289 lowland hamlets, revolutionary organizations had been rebuilt in 904 hamlets, and Party chapters had been rebuilt in 102 villages.

THE EXPANSION OF ARMED FORCES IN THE SOUTH

The enemy's governmental apparatus in the majority of the villages and hamlets in the rural lowlands of Cochin China and in the mountains of southern Central Vietnam had been shattered. Tens of thousands of puppets, spies, tyrants, and enemy armed forces at the grassroots level had been eliminated. Many of the enemy's new agricultural areas, concentration areas, and collective living areas had been destroyed. The general uprising had struck an unexpected and powerful blow against the fascist U.S.-Diem administration. Our liberated zones and areas where the masses had risen up and seized control of their lives had been expanded. Over 70 percent of the farmlands that the enemy had seized had now been returned to the farmers. The organized political struggle forces of the masses had greatly expanded, becoming a sharp and powerful attack force for the revolution. Through the general uprising, the revolution in South Vietnam had progressed from merely trying to preserve its forces to a posture in which it was on the offensive.

Under the leadership of the Party and with the support and nourishment of the people, through long years of struggle to preserve and develop our forces, our armed forces in South Vietnam had fulfilled their duty of serving as an assault unit and supporting the masses in their uprisings. Growing out of the high tide of the general uprising, three different forms of organization for the people's armed forces had appeared: self-defense and guerrilla teams at the village level, armed teams at the province and district level, and full-time troop units at the region level.

In Cochin China, 560 villages had formed guerrilla squads and 190 villages had formed guerrilla platoons, with a total strength of 7,000 personnel. In addition, every village also had dozens of self-defense militia. In Interzone 5 the self-defense guerrillas of the mountain villages totaled around 3,000 personnel. Born out of the political forces of the masses and rapidly expanding during the course of the general uprising, the guerrillas and self-defense troops were the Party's widespread popular armed force at the grassroots level. Their missions were to serve as an assault force to support the masses in their political struggle, to protect our revolutionary administrative apparatus at the village and hamlet levels, and to fight in coordination with our full-time troops during the coming revolutionary war.

Cochin China's province and district armed teams consisted of 123 platoons and 20 squads with a total strength of 7,000 personnel.[23] In Interzone 5 we had 123 platoons and 76 armed operations teams with a total strength of 5,500 personnel. These were full-time armed units born out of the mass uprisings and developed from our self-defense and guerrilla forces. They had been formed into local troop units and served as the backbone of the people's war at the province and district level.

The full-time troops of the regions consisted of the 500th Battalion of the Eastern Cochin China Interprovincial Committee (997 soldiers); the 261st Battalion of the Central Cochin China Interprovincial Committee (266 soldiers); the 306th Battalion of the Western Cochin China Interprovincial Committee (771 soldiers); and two infantry companies and 12 sapper teams in Interzone 5, with a total strength of almost 1,000 soldiers. These were our mobile force at the regional level and were made up of units selected from the full-time armed teams at the district and province level. A large number of the cadre and soldiers of these units were Party members, had served during the resistance war against the French, and had matured and been tested in the general uprising. Among those serving in these first full-time units and in the military command sections of the regions, provinces, districts, and villages were 3,500 military cadre and technical personnel who had received training as regulars in North Vietnam and who had returned to the South during the final months of 1959 and the early months of 1960 down the commo-liaison routes established by Military Transportation Group 559. During this initial period, the weapons and equipment of these full-time troops were mostly items our soldiers and civilians had captured during the general uprising, together with items we had cached in 1954 and some home-made weapons and equipment.[24] The weapons of the guerrillas and self-defense forces consisted primarily of knives, halberds, cross-bows, spears, scythes, etc., together with a few guns captured from the enemy.

Supplies for the full-time armed forces were provided primarily by contributions from the people in the area where the unit was stationed and for which our revolutionary governmental apparatus at the village and hamlet level was responsible. A portion of these supplies were produced by our cadre and soldiers themselves.

All armed units were placed under the direct and total leadership of local Party committees. Party and political tasks were carried out by local-level Party committees. Each unit had a wide base among the people, and these units were loved and nurtured by the people.

THE BIRTH OF THE NATIONAL LIBERATION FRONT

On 20 December 1960 the National Liberation Front for South Vietnam was born. The Central Committee of the National Liberation Front for South Vietnam and the National Liberation Front Committees for the provinces and districts were presented to the people. These organizations served to gather together all the forces of the front and served as our revolutionary governmental administration. Military Command Sections were established at the region, province, district, and village levels to aid Party Committees at these levels in guiding and commanding their armed units; in recruiting youth into the armed forces; and in receiving supplies provided by the people for use by our armed forces.

In accordance with a policy formulated by the Politburo of the Party Central Committee, the revolutionary armed forces in South Vietnam were named the "Liberation Army of South Vietnam." Implementing the Politburo's instructions, in January 1961 the General Military Party Committee stated clearly:

> The Liberation Army of South Vietnam is a part of the People's Army of Vietnam, having been organized, developed, educated, and led by the Party. The Party's political and military policies are the decisive factors in its victories. The Liberation Army of South Vietnam bears the heroic traditions, the indomitable spirit, and the combat solidarity of the heroic people of South Vietnam. It also bears the glorious traditions of service to the people of the People's Army of Vietnam. The combat objectives of the Army are to resolutely implement the programs and policies of the Party, to liberate South Vietnam from the imperialist and feudalist yoke of oppression, to secure national independence, to distribute land to the peasants, and to move forward toward socialism.

> The Liberation Army of South Vietnam is both a combat army and an operational and production army. In order to carry out its duties, the Liberation Army of South Vietnam will organize three types of troops: main-force troops, local force troops, and guerrilla militia. The army will be built on an urgent basis, but this must be done in accordance with the actual situation and with our own practical capabilities, and so that the army is able to deal with any unexpected eventuality. The development of full-time units will be our primary focus, but we must also consider the development of local forces and guerrilla militia as very important.[25]

On 15 February 1961 the Central Committee of the National Liberation Front for South Vietnam announced the unification of all revolutionary armed forces in South Vietnam under the name of the "Liberation Armed Forces of South Vietnam."

By the end of 1960, our people had completed six years of peacetime construction in the North and had survived a fierce period of struggle against the U.S.-Diem clique in the South. Under the leadership of the Party Central Committee, headed by Chairman Ho Chi Minh, our people in North Vietnam had completed the rebuilding of our economy, moved forward with socialist reforms, moved into a transitional period for the building of socialism, gradually strengthened our capabilities in all areas, laid the foundation for consolidating a national defense based on the entire population, and created a solid foundation for supporting the revolution in South Vietnam. In South Vietnam, beginning with a political struggle aimed at preserving our forces, our people had shifted to the offensive, beginning with insurrections launched in individual areas.

This was a transitional period for the revolution and a turning point in the development of our army. During this period our army continued to be hardened like steel through numerous political efforts and through the building of a new society, and its socialist awareness and maturity had progressed to a new level. The successful implementation of our first five-year military plan (1955–1960) had changed our army from an exclusively infantry, inadequately equipped force with an organizational structure that was not uniform into an armed force that had a regular, relatively modern Army, the initial organizational components of a Navy and an Air Force, and that possessed both a strong standing army and a powerful reserve force. This was a new stage of development, a revolution in the organization and technical capability of our armed forces, which in turn created a great improvement in the strength and combat ability of our army. The results of the growth of our armed forces opened the door and provided an important foundation for our army to move forward with further building plans that would, step by step, send forces to the battlefields of South Vietnam and gradually, systematically advance toward large-scale combined arms combat operations to secure a glorious victory in the resistance war against the Americans to save the nation.

In South Vietnam, beginning with the political struggle of the masses and continuing through the general uprising, our armed forces rapidly developed into three types of organizations: self-defense teams and village guerrillas; province and district armed teams; and full-time troop units at the region level. This was an important achievement of the South Vietnamese revolution during the years of struggle to preserve and develop our forces. It provided a foundation our army could use to rapidly expand our local combat forces on the battlefields of South Vietnam and to maintain the initiative as we began the fight against the United States and puppet troops.

The achievements of the building and expansion of our army's forces in the North and the South during the years from 1954 to 1960 were very great and were of major importance in many different areas. Our army was able to learn from the experiences of fraternal socialist countries in building regular, modern forces. Because, however, we had not quickly summarized and reviewed our own experiences during the resistance war against the French, in some areas we were limited and deficient in studying and applying the results of foreign experience to the practical realities of our own army and the battlefield realities of our nation. Also, because we did not adequately anticipate the development of the revolution in South Vietnam, we did not adequately prepare the number of cadre needed to respond to the developing revolutionary war in South Vietnam; this was especially true for local military cadre. Six years of building was a short time, but it provided our army with a great deal of valuable experience.

Together with the entire civilian population, our army simultaneously carried out many tasks, resolving many of our own postwar problems (defeating the enemy's postwar plans, eliminating bandits, consolidating the newly liberated areas, rebuilding and developing our economy, and implementing programs for sick and wounded soldiers, for the families of our martyrs, and for the logistics support of the army). The most vital task that our army had to always keep in mind, however, was to increase our combat strength and our combat readiness. The enemy had new strategic plots. This meant our revolutionary army always had to be alert, keep a close watch on our opponent, and prepare our forces in all aspects to be prepared to deal with any eventuality.

Maturing in an armed uprising and a protracted people's war in which we had to simultaneously build our forces and conduct combat operations, our army had not had an opportunity to develop fully. To increase our combat strength to a new level, our main force troops had to gradually, systematically, build themselves up into a regular, modern force. This was the precise direction that the Party had clearly and in a timely fashion pointed out for this new phase. The building of a regular, modern army constituted a revolution in our thinking, organization, and technical capabilities. During this building process we had to fully absorb the guiding principles of the Party, which emanated from the practical experience of our nation and our armed forces, especially in the area of the military arts. To enable our army to properly serve as the backbone force for a people's war and to utilize the creativity of revolutionary military arts, we had to place heavy emphasis on reviewing and summarizing the combat experience of our own army and our own people, our heritage of the strategic skills of our forefathers, and only then study, on a selected basis, the experiences of the armed forces of fraternal socialist nations.

After its liberation, the northern half of our nation moved into a transitional period of building socialism. Completing the tasks of national liberation and protecting the building of socialism became the combat goals of our army. Combining economic construction with consolidating national defense, army building with strengthening our rear area, combining the strength of our race and the strength of our modern age, from this initial period of 1954–1960 our Party and our people prepared, in our nation and our army, the factors that would lead to the ultimate victory that would be won by our soldiers and civilians in the war against the Americans to save the nation.

Beginning in early 1961, because of the failure of their scheme to commit aggression and enslave the southern half of our nation through a policy of neocolonialist rule, relying primarily on their lackeys to suppress our patriotic movement, the American imperialists were forced to change their strategy. They began to carry out a "special war" aimed at snuffing out the revolutionary struggle movement of our people in South Vietnam.

A new era for our people, the era of revolutionary war to protect the North, liberate the South, and unify our nation, had begun.

PART II

Intensifying the Work of Building a Modern, Regular Army, Expanding Our Massed Forces in South Vietnam, and Defeating the "Special Warfare" Strategy of the American Imperialists, 1961–1965

4
Developing Forces, Building a Battle Posture, and Preparing for a New Struggle

STRATEGIC DECISIONS FOR THE NORTH AND THE SOUTH

In September 1960 the 3rd National Party Congress was held in Hanoi. After five years of work, our people in North Vietnam had completed the plan to rebuild and reform our economy and had begun to implement our five-year plan to build the technical and material structures of socialism. In South Vietnam, uprisings in individual areas had spread throughout the lowlands of Cochin China and the mountain jungles of Central Vietnam. It was becoming increasingly clear that the situation was developing into a revolutionary war as the Party Central Committee had foreseen. In Laos, after the May 1959 incident when the 2nd Battalion opened fire against the American imperialists and their lackeys, the Laotian revolution began to combine political struggle with armed struggle. On the international scene, faced with the growing strength of the socialist camp and the offensive force of the three revolutionary tides, the American imperialists had to alter their worldwide strategy. They shifted from a strategy of "massive retaliation" to a strategy of "flexible response." They also began vigorous preparations for direct armed intervention into South Vietnam and Laos.

The Party's 3rd National Congress analyzed the overall situation and set forward two goals as the overall tasks for our nation's revolution during this new period: Push ahead strongly with the socialist revolution in North Vietnam and complete the popular democratic national revolution in South Vietnam. There was an intimate relationship between the two strategic missions of advancing the socialist revolution in North Vietnam and achieving national unification. Each mission would drive the other forward so that both would develop simultaneously. "The building of socialism in North Vietnam is the most decisive mission for the development of the entire revolution throughout our country and for the goal of reunifying our nation. . . . Our brothers in the South have the mission of participating directly in the fight to break the yoke of oppression of the American imperialists and their puppets in order to liberate South Vietnam."[1]

The Party Congress commended the accomplishments of the People's Army of Vietnam, which had performed so many glorious feats of arms during the resistance war against the French, for making so many major contributions to the work of defending our nation and developing our economy and culture since North Vietnam was first liberated and for continuing to write new pages in their outstanding history. Our Party and our people had boundless pride in the high quality of our army.

Based on the policies and tasks of the revolution, the Party Congress laid out the following military missions for the entire Party, the entire population, and the entire armed forces: To defend North Vietnam as it continued to build socialism, to intensify the revolutionary struggle to liberate South Vietnam, and to perform our international duties. To enable the People's Army to complete its missions during this new period, the Party Congress decided to vigorously build the army into a regular, modern force; to strengthen and expand self-defense militia and develop reserve forces; and to link the work of army building with the strengthening of national defense to enable the army to be constantly ready to fight and to win.

The 3rd National Party Congress was a historic event that marked a new stage in the development of our Party and of the revolution of our nation. The two strategic revolutionary missions laid out by the Party Congress were the goals for which our army would fight and the foundation our army would use to determine the proper directions for its growth and for combat operations during this new phase.

To begin to implement the resolution on military affairs approved by the 3rd National Party Congress, the Politburo of the Party Central Committee, meeting on 31 January and 25 February 1961, issued a resolution on military duties for the five-year period 1961–1965 and on the immediate goals for the revolution in South Vietnam.

The Politburo decided that, for the next five years at least, prospects were good for maintaining peace in North Vietnam. If we could maintain peace in the North our people would be able to successfully complete our first five-year plan for building socialist technical and material structures. Having begun as a backward agricultural economy, North Vietnam would have developed industry, agriculture, and a new culture. These achievements would be vital in our efforts to build our army and strengthen national defense and would be decisive factors for the revolution to liberate South Vietnam. The maintenance of peace in general and peace in North Vietnam in particular would be a major problem. The Politburo declared that for the next few years "the maintenance of peace and ensuring the building of socialism in North Vietnam is our most important task."[2]

The revolutionary struggle in South Vietnam during the coming five years would, the Politburo said, also undergo new stages of development and many great changes that would transform the situation. Our troops and civilians had to be fully prepared, both in spirit and in actual strength, to ensure that the revolution in South Vietnam was able to achieve victory when the opportunity presented itself. We would, however, also have to skillfully "avoid a major armed intervention by the imperialists"[3] and restrain and defeat the Americans in South Vietnam. At the same time, the Politburo said, we would have to make active preparations to deal with the enemy's schemes and actions aimed at expanding the war.

The central problem emphasized by the Politburo and about which it constantly reminded all branches and all localities was the need to make the maximum possible use of the time available to build and strengthen our revolutionary power. With regard to the army, the key task during this period was to "build forces for peacetime, at the same time bringing an element of our forces up to wartime strength."[4]

During the 1955–1960 period, with the implementation of the first five-year military plan, our army had taken a step forward down the road toward building a modern, regular force and had maintained and expanded our revolutionary armed forces in South Vietnam. To continue this building program and successfully implement the strategic missions set forward by the 3rd National Party Congress, the Politburo decided that, concurrent with the first five-year plan to build socialism in North Vietnam, we would carry out our second five-year military plan (1961–1965). This plan was prepared by the Central Military Party Committee and the Ministry of Defense and was approved by the Politburo during its session on 25 February 1961.[5]

The major components of the plan were the following:

1. Build up the armed forces and strengthen the national defense of North Vietnam. Focus on increasing the power of the Army, building up anti-aircraft forces, and expanding the basic structures of the Air Force and Navy. Complete the regularization of the armed forces and take another step forward in our modernization of the armed forces to guarantee the strength of our armed forces. This would entail ensuring that an appropriate proportion of our total force structure was assigned to the specialty branches and the Military Services and that the armed forces possessed the political resolve and the combat strength needed to accomplish their missions of defending North Vietnam, liberating South Vietnam, and performing their international duties in Laos. At the same time we would build a foundation for further modernization of the armed forces to be implemented in future plans.
2. Build up a full-time armed force in South Vietnam that was strong, well equipped, and had good logistics support and a good system of command for combat operations. District local force troops would be organized up to platoon and company level. Full-time provincial-level forces would be organized up to the company and battalion level. Build up a force of 10 to 15 main force

regiments with powerful assault capabilities and firepower, and a number of composite artillery units capable, to a limited extent at least, of destroying fortifications, killing tanks, and shooting down aircraft.

3. Assist the revolutionary armed forces of Laos with military advisors and with the training of their cadre. Build up liberated areas and expand the armed forces of our Lao allies. Whenever our Lao allies request assistance, send Vietnamese volunteer forces to fight alongside the troops of our allies.

4. Strengthen the Party's apparatus for providing guidance to the military and guarantee the united collective leadership of the Party over the army. In North Vietnam, take another step forward in reorganizing the leadership and command agencies of the Ministry of Defense and the military regions in response to the need to build modern, regular armed forces and to our requirements and combat missions in South Vietnam and in Laos. At the same time, make active preparations so that, in case the war widened, we could use the headquarters of our military regions as a foundation for the formation of field headquarters to command large main force units and as local military headquarters. Establish staff agencies and military units to carry out our international duties on the battlefields of Laos. In South Vietnam, organize a military command structure from the Central Office for South Vietnam (COSVN) level down through provincial and district Party committees to village Party chapters. Proceed with the establishment of Military Region Headquarters.

The Central Military Party Committee would be the Party's highest-level leadership agency in the army. Now that the struggle of our people in South Vietnam had developed into a revolutionary war, the Politburo gave the Central Military Party Committee the responsibility for directing military activities in South Vietnam.[6]

With regard to the immediate directions and duties of the revolution in South Vietnam, based on the new growth of the movement the Politburo decided to change our struggle formula, to further intensify the political struggle while at the same time elevating the armed struggle by assigning it equal importance with the political struggle to enable us to attack the enemy with both political and military forces. The duties of the armed forces in South Vietnam were to rapidly expand their forces and step up their attacks to annihilate the enemy so that, in cooperation with the political struggle of the masses, they could cause the disintegration of enemy forces and enemy governmental structures in an ever-expanding area, take control of the mountain jungles, take back the rural lowlands, build organizations and intensify the political struggle in the cities, and create conditions that would provide us an opportunity to launch a general offensive and general uprising to totally overthrow the US.-Diem regime.

During the closing session of the Politburo session on 25 February 1961, Chairman Ho Chi Minh spoke and gave advice to the army. Uncle Ho said, "Our army is a people's army. Our war is a people's war. The army must be tightly linked to the people. Within the army the spirit of mutual endurance and sharing of hardship is very important. We must improve our technical equipment, but the lives of the troops must be kept in line with the lives of the people."[7]

The Politburo of the Party Central Committee set out clear directions and missions for our army building and combat operations during this transition period for the revolution, laying out the decisive factors that would ensure our army would be completely successful in fulfilling these responsibilities. The advice given by Uncle Ho provided profound instruction in revolutionary character and clearly showed us the foundation from which we should build the strength of our army.

Carrying out the missions assigned to them by the Party and Uncle Ho, our armed forces in North and South Vietnam entered a new period of growth and combat.

BUILDING THE ARMED FORCES IN THE NORTH

In North Vietnam, after the 3rd National Party Congress, a socialist emulation campaign directed toward the South grew in strength day by day. The Duy Hai Machinery Factory in Haiphong city, the Dai Phong Cooperative in Quang Binh province, and the Bac Ly Middle School in Nam Ha province set leading examples for the work of building socialism for the sake of our brothers in South Vietnam. Within the army, the "Three Firsts" emulation movement (to be the best, the most uniform, and make the most achievements in training and combat readiness), which began with the 2nd Artillery Battery of the 304th Division, quickly expanded into a mass-based, widespread emulation movement.

The socialist emulation movement in North Vietnam and the high tide of insurrection in South Vietnam signaled the beginning of a new phase in the development of our nation and our revolution. Chairman Ho Chi Minh affirmed his faith in the victory of the revolution in the homey, unpretentious lines of poetry he spoke to the All-Armed Forces Congress of Heroes and Emulation Combatants in 1961:

Workers wave high the Duyen Hai flag
Peasants wave the Dai Phong flag
Heroic soldiers wave the "Three Firsts" flag
Workers, Peasants, Soldiers in great competition, in great solidarity
Socialism is certain to achieve great victory
North and South are certain to be united, our nation unified under one roof.

During the first months of 1961 the Central Military Party Committee held many meetings to discuss the force-building and combat missions of the army for the 1961–1965 period. Determining that the "current situation includes new developments, and the requirements of our revolutionary tasks and military tasks are higher than ever,"[8] the Central Military Party Committee decided to take advantage of this time of peace in North Vietnam to step up the pace and increase the quality of all of our activities by building an army with a high level of political awareness, excellent technical and scientific skills, strict discipline, and that was alert and ready to fight to defend North Vietnam and to fully carry out its mission of serving as the strategic reserve for the revolutionary war in South Vietnam.

For the immediate future, based on the developments of the situation in South Vietnam, on our own actual capabilities, and on the assistance provided by our friends, the Central Military Party Committee laid out a number of concrete requirements and objectives that our army must meet during the 1961–1963 period. With regard to our tables of organization and equipment, we needed to take another step forward in reorganizing our standing army to meet the requirements for regularizing and modernizing our forces; to concentrate on building up our specialty branches and cadre training schools and on expanding our militia self-defense forces; and be prepared to expand the army as required by the demands of war. With regard to combat training, we had to press ahead with the work of reviewing and summarizing our war experiences, of conducting research in military science, and of developing fighting methods suited to our army's level of technical equipment, the battlefield conditions in our nation, and our combat opponent: the U.S. armed forces and their lackeys. With regard to political and ideological affairs, we had to give the army a fuller understanding of its duties of building and defending North Vietnam and of being prepared to fight in South Vietnam whenever the order was given.

With a profound understanding of the strategic significance the mission of building our army into a regular, modern force had for the developmental and combat operations of our army, on 29 May 1961 the Central Military Party Committee launched an armywide campaign to "build the army by advancing quickly, strongly, and surely toward becoming a regular, modern force."

In the spring of 1961, arm in arm with the entire Party and the entire population, our army launched a wave of political activities to study the documents issued by the 3rd National Party Congress.

Our units studied revolutionary policy, military policies and requirements, and the relationship between our two strategic revolutionary missions: 1) building the army and defending North Vietnam and 2) intensifying the revolutionary war in South Vietnam. Following the study sessions conducted during the 1955–1960 period, the spring 1961 political activities campaign raised the level of socialist awareness of cadre and soldiers regarding their duties of army building and fighting in this new phase of the revolution, especially their duty to liberate South Vietnam and to deal with the appearance among our forces of instances of pacifism and a lessening of fighting spirit. This campaign laid a very important foundation for the ideas and ideology our army used to successfully implement the second five-year military plan.

In accordance with the directions and plans for army building that had been laid out, in March 1961 the Central Military Party Committee decided to establish the Strategic Review and Summary Section, which was assigned the mission of reviewing and summarizing our experiences in armed struggle and force building during the resistance war against the French to aid our mission of building our army and conducting combat operations. Lieutenant General Hoang Van Thai, member of the Party Central Committee and Deputy Chief of Staff of the People's Army of Vietnam, was chosen to serve as Chief of this section. The Armed Forces History Office of the General Political Department, the Department for the Study of Military Science of the General Staff, and a network of other staff agencies established and organized by each branch down to the division level, worked to summarize our war experiences, draft unit histories, and study military science. The Military-Political Academy was formed out of the Mid-High-Level Military School and the Mid-High-Level Political School. Our schools for training infantry and other specialty branch officers were reorganized, the number of trainees increased, and the quality of their training and instruction improved. Many cadre with a background in military theory and with experience in combat and training activities were brought together at the General Staff, the General Political Department, and the General Department of Rear Services to work to draft combat regulations, textbooks, and training and instruction programs to meet our requirements for building a regular, modern army.

PREPARING FOR BATTLE IN SOUTH VIETNAM AND LAOS

To implement the Central Military Party Committee's directive to prepare our army to enter combat on the battlefields of South Vietnam and perform its international duties in Laos, the General Staff decided to bring a number of units up to wartime table of organization, strength, and equipment standards in order to have on hand a number of powerful infantry units that, when needed, could be sent to operate on the "B" (South Vietnam) and "C" (Laotian) battlefields. Units brought up to wartime status included the 325th Division, the 341st Brigade, and the 244th Regiment of Military Region 4 and the 316th and 335th Brigades and the 148th Regiment of the Northwest Military Region.

The 338th Division was reorganized into a special training group. All cadre and soldiers being sent to the battlefield were sent to Group 338 for training. This training included the situation and duties of the Southern revolution, supplementary training in technical and tactical matters, training for a long march, and physical training. A number of these cadre and soldiers were organized into framework groups for staff agencies and military units, whereas others were organized into units for their long march. After their arrival these individuals would receive specific assignments based on battlefield requirements. Because the international situation was undergoing a number of complicated developments, because of the limited ability of the battlefield to absorb them, and because of the limited ability of Group 559 to support them and to transport supplies, the initial groups of cadre and soldiers sent to fight in the South during the period 1959–1963 were made up primarily of regroupees from Cochin China and Inter-zone 5 and cadre and soldiers with previous experience fighting on the battle-fields of South Vietnam. Weapons sent to the South consisted mostly of infantry weapons plus a number of mortars and recoilless rifles.

In September 1961, the Politburo and the Central Military Party Committee approved a General Staff proposal for building up our forces on the South Viet-nam battlefield during the 1961–1963 period. According to this proposal, besides the expansion using locally-recruited forces, we would send to South Vietnam 30,000 or 40,000 troops who had received regular military training in North Viet-nam. All cadre and soldiers who were natives of South Vietnam or were familiar with the South Vietnamese battlefields, both those in the armed forces and those working in other sectors, were registered and given supplementary political, mil-itary, and physical training to prepare them to be sent to perform their duties on the battlefield. All national defense enterprises increased the production and repair of rifles, submachine guns, mortars, small arms ammunition, grenades, etc., in response to the immediate requirements of our armed forces in South Viet-nam. Military Transportation Group 559 grew to between 2,000 and 3,000 per-sonnel and used primitive forms of transportation to support the southern march of our soldiers and to increase the supply of material support to the battlefield.

Going to "B" (South Vietnam) became a glorious combat duty, a source of honor and pride for every cadre and soldier in the army. With their eyes always turned toward the South, our army's cadre and soldiers trained day and night, improved their combat skills, and practiced long marches carrying heavy packs to prepare themselves to cross the Annamite Mountains to South Vietnam to fight the Americans.

THE WAR IN THE SOUTH

In South Vietnam, during the last months of 1960 and the early months of 1961 the mass uprising movement, combining political struggle with military struggle, expanded into a number of important areas, the outskirts of the cities, and areas populated by followers of various religions. Face-to-face political struggle became ever more widespread and employed even stronger slogans than those used in the past. Areas in which the people had gained control over their own lives expanded day by day.[9] The development of our political forces and our mil-itary forces took a step forward.

The U.S. policy of aggression and its attempt to impose neocolonialist rule over South Vietnam suffered a serious failure. In May 1961 U.S. Vice President L. Johnson visited Saigon and secretly signed a treaty of cooperation with the

Diem puppet regime, promising to support Diem and to be ready to send U.S. military forces to assist Diem's army. In June 1961 Kennedy dispatched the Stalay delegation to South Vietnam to lay out a plan to crush the revolutionary movement in South Vietnam within 18 months.[10] Three months later General M. Taylor, Chairman of the Joint Chiefs of Staff, visited South Vietnam to study the situation and to supplement the military aspects of Stalay's plan.

On 18 October 1961 the United States and the Diem puppet government signed a mutual defense treaty in Saigon. Ngo Dinh Diem proclaimed a "state of emergency" and assumed "special powers" in South Vietnam. In Washington, President Kennedy announced that "the U.S. armed forces are prepared to participate in an increased allied military effort with the Republic of Vietnam . . . and will participate in military operations with the Army of South Vietnam." In November 1961 President Kennedy and the U.S. National Security Council approved a "special warfare" strategy for South Vietnam and approved the Stalay-Taylor plan to "pacify" South Vietnam within 18 months. In December 1961 two U.S. helicopter companies and 400 "Green Beret" commandos arrived in South Vietnam,[11] marking the beginning of a period of transition from the use of U.S. advisors to the direct participation of U.S. armed forces in combat operations.

Operating under American command and using U.S. dollars and U.S. weapons, the Diem puppet regime worked to draft new soldiers and to upgrade troops. In only one year, 1961, the regular army grew to a strength of 200,000 men. These soldiers were organized into seven infantry divisions and six Marine battalions. Regional Force strength grew to 80,000, organized into one or two battalions per province, Popular Force strength grew to 70,000 soldiers, organized up to company strength at the district or precinct level.[12] The enemy built thousands of new outposts and launched tens of thousands of sweep operations aimed at wiping out our revolutionary armed forces, extinguishing the struggle movement of the masses, and restoring control over the village and hamlet level. The two primary measures used by the enemy in his "special warfare" strategy were: a) to collect the population into areas called "strategic hamlets" in order to control the population, wipe out our cadre, Party members, and guerrillas living among the people, and cut our armed forces off from access to the people; and b) to use puppet soldiers to conduct sweep operations using "helicopter assault" and "armored vehicle assault" tactics to annihilate our revolutionary armed forces and support the collection of the population into "strategic hamlets." With regard to North Vietnam, the United States and its puppets dispatched reconnaissance aircraft and sent commandos to conduct sabotage operations to block the movement of personnel and supplies to South Vietnam. The U.S. Joint Chief of Staff prepared a contingency plan for use if the puppet army and puppet government in South Vietnam was in danger of collapse. This plan called for the dispatch of a portion of the U.S. combat forces stationed in the Pacific region and of a number of infantry and Marine divisions from the United States to South Vietnam to participate in combat operations.[13]

Closely monitoring each step in the development of the revolutionary struggle movement in South Vietnam and the enemy's new schemes and actions, in early 1960 the Politburo foresaw the appearance of a new situation, a vicious and complex struggle between ourselves and the enemy for control of grass-roots governmental authority at the village level. To conduct this struggle the United States and its puppets had no other option than the use of military forces as their primary tool to oppose us. To defend against them and restrict and respond to them in a timely manner, our soldiers and civilians had to monitor the ability of the American imperialists to intervene by force of arms.

To implement our formula of combining armed struggle with political struggle, the Politburo decided to intensify attacks in all three strategic areas. In the mountains, where the military struggle would play the primary role, we would annihilate enemy troops in order to widen our liberated areas, build bases, and expand our armed forces. In the rural lowlands the military and political struggles would play coequal roles. We would have to assess the balance between these two types of struggle, depending on the actual balance of forces between ourselves and the enemy in each area. In urban areas the political struggle would be preeminent and would be conducted in both legal and illegal forms.

During the resistance war against the French, our soldiers and civilians in Cochin China and Central Vietnam had built many solid base areas, places where full-time armed units could be maintained. Many war zones became famous for their achievements in annihilating enemy forces and in building up our own forces. These included War Zone D, the Duong Minh Chau War Zone, and the Rung Sat area in eastern Cochin China; the Plain of Reeds in central Cochin China; the U Minh Forest in western Cochin China; the mountains of the Central Highlands; and the western portions of Central Vietnam. During the years of struggle (1954–1960) to preserve our forces and to develop to a high tide of insurrection, we continued to maintain and expand these bases, and once again, in a new historical context, the bases again became areas where the first full-time armed units in South Vietnam could base themselves and conduct operations. Even though these areas were sparsely populated and were economically backward, the mountain and jungle terrain was very advantageous for the building up of forces and for combat operations, especially at a time when our revolutionary armed forces were still young. People from all ethnic groups in the mountain base areas quickly allied themselves with the revolution. With one heart they looked to the Party and Uncle Ho for leadership. Even when suffering shortages and hardships in their daily lives, our people wholeheartedly supported the revolution and contributed toward "feeding our troops." In areas where we had military supply routes the people enthusiastically served as porters, carrying rice and ammunition for our troops. Relying on favorable terrain and assisted by people of all ethnic groups, our full-time armed forces used these mountain bases as places to rest, consolidate, and grow in strength, systematically building the mountainous areas into battlefields to attack and destroy the enemy.

The rural lowlands were a rich, heavily populated area and a local source of personnel and supplies for our armed forces. In these areas our units relied on "leopard-spot" bases (liberated hamlets and villages), "bases in the bosom of the population" to build and expand their forces. When operating in the rural lowlands our full-time armed units received aid and support from the people and the local guerrillas, enabling us to properly combine our military attacks with the political struggle. In the urban areas our cadre and soldiers actively recruited agents from among the civilian population, within the governmental apparatus, and within the enemy's army, and prepared for armed operations.

The work of building and expanding our bases and armed organizations in all three strategic areas was a great achievement by our soldiers and civilians in South Vietnam during the initial years of the war against the Americans to save the nation. These bases were scattered throughout the enemy's area. The bases had strong points within each area, were linked together, and enjoyed solid backing from our great rear area in North Vietnam. With favorable terrain and the protection of the local population, our bases became resting places for our full-time armed units. They contributed to the creation of a widespread people's war battlefield posture, an offensive posture for our three types of troops that supported the political struggle of the masses in all three strategic areas.

Relying on these bases and the ever-expanding areas in which the masses had seized control, our army in South Vietnam took a new step forward in its development.

By the end of 1961, our self-defense guerrillas had grown to a total strength of 100,000, with 70,000 in Cochin China and 30,000 in Region 5 (including Tri-Thien and the Central Highlands). Many liberated villages were able to form full-time guerrilla platoons using weapons captured from the enemy and homemade weapons.[14] This force was the backbone of the armed struggle combined with the political struggle at the village and hamlet level and was an important force providing combat support and a constant source of reinforcements for our full-time armed units.

Our provincial and district local force troops and regional main force troops had a total strength of 24,500 cadre and soldiers. Each district was able to form a local force platoon, and some districts organized forces up to the company level. Each province had one or two companies. The strength of a provincial local force company was around 100 soldiers, more or less, organized into infantry, engineer, and fire support platoons and support subunits. Province and district local force units were equipped with American automatic rifles, light and medium machine guns, and 60 and 81mm mortars. A number of units, especially in Region 5 and the Central Highlands, began to receive French Mat rifles, 57mm recoilless rifles, and 82mm mortars shipped down from North Vietnam. Many provinces established weapons repair facilities and weapons production factories using the abundant supply of unexploded enemy bombs and shells that the local population collected and gave to our soldiers.

The main force troops of our military regions totaled 11 battalions: six battalions belonging to Military Region 5 and five battalions belonging to Military Region 6 (extreme southern Central Vietnam), Military Region 7 (eastern Cochin China), Military Region 8 (central Cochin China), Military Region 9 (western Cochin China Bo), and the Saigon–Gia Dinh Military Region. Each military region battalion had a strength of 400 to 500 soldiers and was organized into two or three infantry companies, one sapper company, one fire support company or platoon, and support subunits. These battalions were primarily equipped with captured enemy weapons and weapons shipped in from North Vietnam.

On 9 September 1962 the 1st Infantry Regiment was officially formed in the Duong Minh Chau base area in eastern Cochin China.[15] This was the first regiment-sized mobile main force unit to serve on the battlefields of South Vietnam during the resistance war against the Americans to save the nation. This was also the first time we had ever formed a regiment-sized unit in Cochin China. The initial forces of the 1st Regiment consisted of two infantry battalions and one cadre framework battalion. Command cadre from company up to regimental level were primarily individuals who had served during the resistance war against the French and had received regular military training in North Vietnam. A number of the regiment's cadre had been transferred to the regiment from Military Region 7's 500th Main Force Battalion and from provincial local force companies. The enlisted soldiers of the regiment were courageous youths who had matured during the years of political struggle and the period of insurrection. Their weapons and equipment consisted of guns captured from the enemy and a number of Mat carbines and rifles, 75mm recoilless rifles, and radios shipped in from North Vietnam.

The Party Central Committee, COSVN, and the local Party committees devoted a great deal of attention to building and increasing the quality of our armed forces in South Vietnam. Many Party members with experience in combat operations and in force building were chosen by the Party to serve as the backbone for building up our main force and local force units. In 1961 Party members serving in our full-time military units made up 50 percent of all Party members throughout South Vietnam. This factor was decisive in establishing the political strength of our units and guaranteed the growth of our forces and the combat victories of our armed forces in South Vietnam.

To ensure the centralized, united leadership of the Party over our armed forces, the Politburo and the Central Military Party Committee organized a system of military command and guidance under the Regional Party Committees, Provincial Party Committees, District Party Committees, and Village Party Chapters. The Military Affairs Section of COSVN was the staff agency that assisted COSVN in guiding and commanding our armed forces in Cochin China and extreme southern Central Vietnam. Major General Tran Luong, member of the Party Central Committee and Deputy Director of the General Political Department of the People's Army of Vietnam, was appointed as Military Affairs Section Chief. Region 5 (including the entire Central Highlands and the provinces of Ninh

Thuan, Binh Thuan, Quang Tri, and Thua Thien) established a Military Region Party Committee and a Military Region Command. Major General Nguyen Don, alternate member of the Party Central Committee and former Commander of Military Region 4, was appointed Secretary of the Region 5 Party Committee and concurrently Military Region Commander and Political Commissar.

Our network of agencies conducting Party and political work within the full-time armed units was consolidated. From the local force company level up, every unit had a political officer. District local force platoons had a Party chapter. The work of political education and ideological leadership focused on educating our cadre and soldiers in hatred of the United States and Diem and increasing their combat spirit and their resolve to liberate South Vietnam and unify the Fatherland.

Rear services [logistics] support for these units was the responsibility of the rear services offices of the COSVN Military Affairs Section and of the various military regions. Each military region built rear services bases[16] and was responsible for collection and purchasing duties, receiving supplies, establishing stockpiles, transporting supplies to operational theaters to support their troops, increasing their own partial self-sufficiency in food, establishing factories for the production and repair of weapons, etc.[17] Rice provided by the population or collected and purchased by rear services agencies and stored in people's homes was transported by civilian porters and by local means of transportation (boats, vehicles) belonging to the civilian population.

While building up their forces, our armed forces in South Vietnam also intensified their activities, eroding the enemy's strength and killing thousands of enemy troops.[18] Province and district local force troops cooperated with village guerrillas to repel many sweep operations mounted by enemy regular and regional force troops and supported the masses in uprisings to seize and retain control over their own lives. In Region 5, full-time armed units conducted powerful operations in the southern portion of the Central Highlands and in the contested areas of the lowlands. During an action campaign in the Bac Ha–An Khe area in mid-1961 they wiped out ten outposts and eliminated from the field of combat three companies of enemy troops. In eastern Cochin China, on 17 September 1961 the 500th Main Force Battalion of Military Region 7, in cooperation with local force troops of Phu Giao and Tan Uyen districts, attacked and seized the Phuoc Thanh sector headquarters, which was held by one Ranger battalion and one police company. Our forces held control of the city for three days. After the battle, using 600 weapons captured from the enemy and with new reinforcements, the military region formed the 700th Infantry Battalion and the 900th Fire Support Battalion.

Although the scale of operations of our armed forces was still small, these operations nevertheless made a contribution toward advancing the revolutionary movement in South Vietnam, combining armed struggle with political struggle. The armed struggle and the armed forces played an increasingly important role in the overall struggle.

In 1961, a year of transition between the period of uprisings in individual areas and the period of revolutionary warfare, through the efforts of the entire Party, the entire population, and the entire army, the armed forces in South Vietnam grew rapidly. They took the first step toward creating the three types of troops, received firm leadership from the Party, and organized a command system from the top down to the bottom. During this first step in building up its forces, the army in South Vietnam still had a number of weaknesses. These weaknesses included a lack of uniformity in the pace of development of armed forces between regions; a lack of balance between the different types of forces; weaknesses in the equipment and level of technical and tactical skills (especially in tactics for attacking outposts and lines of communications) of our full-time units; problems in logistics support in the mountain base areas; and a great shortage of cadre and technical personnel. The birth and development of the armed forces in South Vietnam was one of the success stories of the heroic long-term revolutionary struggle of the people of South Vietnam, and it marked a new step forward in the maturation of our army during the resistance war against the United States to save the nation. Operating under the name of the "Liberation Army of South Vietnam," our full-time troops in South Vietnam became the local combat force of our army on the battlefield. They had the responsibility, together with the entire nation, of directly fighting against and defeating the U.S. and puppet soldiers, liberating South Vietnam, and unifying the nation.

WAR SPREADS TO LAOS

In Laos, following the defeat of the French colonialists and the forced withdrawal of the French army under the terms of the Geneva Agreement of July 1954, the American imperialists replaced the French. They used the rightist forces as lackeys to carry out their schemes of aggression and to impose their own neocolonialist rule over Laos.

Under the leadership of the Lao People's Revolutionary Party the people of Laos began a new period of struggle to maintain and develop their revolutionary forces, protect the two liberated provinces,[19] and achieve their goal of building a peaceful, neutral, and prosperous Lao nation. In May 1959 the United States and its lackeys blatantly attacked the liberated area, seeking to seize weapons and wipe out the armed forces of the Laotian revolution. Under the leadership of the Lao People's Revolutionary Party the 2nd Pathet Lao Battalion fought heroically, breaking through the enemy encirclement and moving its forces out to launch guerrilla warfare in southeastern Xieng Khoang province. This was an important victory, marking the beginning of a period of political struggle combined with armed struggle in the nation of Laos.

The strength of the revolutionary movement and the growing pacifist, neutralist, and patriotic tendencies of the people of Laos after the August 1960 coup in Vientiane[20] greatly disconcerted the U.S. imperialists and their lackeys, Phoumi Nosovan and Boun Um. In September 1960 the United States, using military forces loyal to the rightists supported by soldiers of the Royal Army of Thailand, attacked Vientiane and sought to destroy the bases of the Lao revolution and encroach into the liberated area.

In response to a request from our Lao friends and in accordance with instructions from the Politburo, elements of the People's Army of Vietnam again marched out to carry out our international duty on the battlefields of Laos.

In November 1960 a number of military advisors and a 105mm artillery battery were sent to reinforce Lao troops fighting to defend Vientiane. In early 1961 a number of infantry, artillery, and engineer battalions from the 316th and 335th Brigades of the Northwest Military Region and from the 325th Infantry Division and the 271st Regiment of Military Region 4 were sent to conduct combat operations in support of the soldiers and civilians of our Lao allies.[21] In addition to combat units, our army also sent military advisors and formed operations teams made up of cadre and soldiers experienced in mass proselytizing work, to be sent to Laos to help our allies expand their armed forces, consolidate their liberated zones, and build up revolutionary forces behind enemy lines. A military cadre training school to assist the Lao revolution was established. Weapons captured from the enemy during the resistance war against the French and a number of other types of technical equipment were shipped to our allies.

Carrying out the words of Chairman Ho Chi Minh, who said, "Helping a friend is helping ourselves," our volunteer cadre and soldiers displayed the revolutionary quality and excellent traditions of the People's Army of Vietnam. They took on hardships for themselves while reserving the best things to our allies, they shared the hardships of the people of this friendly nation, they respected and loved the Lao people like members of their own families, and they stood ready to sacrifice their own lives for the revolutionary cause of our friends.

The combat alliance of the soldiers and people of the nations of Vietnam and Laos against one common enemy, the U.S. imperialists, was a special relationship based on the long-standing close association of our two nations and steeped in the sacred spirit of international proletarianism of our two Parties and our two armies. This alliance created new favorable conditions that enabled the Lao and Vietnamese Revolutions to grow in strength and ensured that our army could successfully carry out its tasks of army building and fighting on all battlefields.

From the end of 1960 until April 1961 the soldiers and civilians of Laos, fighting alongside Vietnamese volunteer troops, liberated the provinces of Sam Nua, Phongsaly, and Xieng Khoang and most of the province of Luang Prabang. The strategically important area of the Plain of Jars and Routes 7, 8, 9, and 12 were included in the Lao liberated zone. In May 1961 the U.S. imperialists and their lackeys were forced to accept a cease-fire and agree to attend the Geneva Conference on Laos.

THE STRATEGIC TRANSPORTATION ROUTE EXPANDS INTO LAOS

In view of the growth of the revolution in the nation of our Lao allies and with the agreement of the Lao Party Central Committee and of our own Party Central Committee, the Central Military Party Committee approved a recommendation from Military Region 4 Headquarters and the Headquarters of Group 559 to launch an offensive campaign against enemy forces in the Route 9–Southern Laos area. This offensive was aimed at enabling the Lao revolution to expand to the south and at transferring Group 559's strategic transportation route to the western side of the Annamite Mountain chain. The window of opportunity for launching this campaign was the period before the date of the cease-fire between the Lao parties that was agreed upon during the Geneva Conference.

The 325th Infantry Division, the 19th Border Defense Battalion of Military Region 4, and the 927th Ha Tinh Province Local Force Battalion were dispatched to Laos to conduct coordinated combat operations with the soldiers and people of Laos. The Commander of the 325th Division and the Commander of Group 559 became part of the campaign command headquarters.

On 11 April 1961, the 19th Border Defense Battalion, working with a number of Pathet Lao units, advanced along Route 8 and liberated Cam Cot and Lat Sao. The 927th Battalion attacked Muong Phin town. The 101st Regiment of the 325th Division attacked and captured the town of Tchepone. Exploiting these victories, the Vietnamese-Lao allied forces advanced along Route 9, expanding to the east as far as the Ka-Ki Bridge (Ban Dong) and to the west as far as Muong Pha Lan. The enemy defensive line was shattered along a stretch of more than 100 kilometers along Route 9. The campaign ended in a clear victory on 3 May 1961, before the cease-fire order in Laos came into effect. The liberated areas in Laos had been expanded in an important strategic region and the Pathet Lao army and our Vietnamese volunteer soldiers had been tempered in battle, raising their combat capabilities to a high level.

As soon as Muong Phin and Tchepone were liberated, Group 559 immediately "flipped" its strategic transportation route and its commo-liaison route from the eastern side to the western side of the Annamite Mountain range. The 301st Battalion was given additional reinforcements and was elevated to regimental status, becoming the 70th Regiment. This regiment built a road through Vit Thu Lu and over High Point 1001 and opened a trail for portering supplies along the western slopes of the Annamite Mountains. The 25th and 26th Engineer Battalions of Military Region 4 and the 927th Ha Tinh Province Local Force Battalion built a transportation route for use by vehicles connecting Route 12 with Route 9.[22] The 98th Engineer Regiment (subordinate to the High Command) was sent to the area south of Route 9 to rebuild the road from Ban Dong to Muong Noong.[23] The 98th Regiment then continued to build a supply road to Bac and a commo-liaison trail to Tang Non. Engineering troops from the 325th Division repaired the Ta Khong airfield at Tchepone, enabling transport aircraft of the

People's Army of Vietnam to land and to make parachute drops of supplies, transporting emergency shipments of weapons and vital supplies to the battlefields of South Vietnam.[24]

On 5 May 1961 a group of military cadre being sent to reinforce the COSVN Military Command and the military regions in South Vietnam departed from Xuan Mai[25] in Hoa Binh province to march down the road along the western side of the Annamite Mountains to Cochin China and extreme southern Central Vietnam. This group was made up of 500 personnel, the majority of whom were mid- and high-ranking cadre, and was led by Major General Tran Van Quang, alternate member of the Party Central Committee and Deputy Chief of Staff of the People's Army of Vietnam. The group departed just after the Soviet Union had successfully launched a space capsule named *Orient,* which carried the first person to fly into space, Hero Yuri Gagarin. To celebrate this momentous historic event the group decided to call itself the "Orient Group." On 28 July 1961, after three months of continuous marching, including many days in which the daily food ration had to be cut and cadre were forced to eat forest vegetables instead of rice because of enemy sweep operations or because the rice stores placed along Group 559's commo-liaison trail were insufficient, the "Orient Group" completed its journey of more than 2,000 kilometers, arriving at an assembly area on Hill 300 in Binh Long province.

Comrade Tran Van Quang was named Deputy Chief of the COSVN Military Affairs Section. The other cadre of the group were assigned to staff agencies of the COSVN Military Affairs Section and to the military staff organs of Military Region 7, Military Region 8, Military Region 9, and the Saigon–Gia Dinh Military Region. These assignments were made in preparation for the establishment of military headquarters organizations at the military region level and for the formation of main force regiments. On 1 June 1961 a second cadre group consisting of 400 personnel led by Comrades Nguyen Hoang Lam (also known as Nguyen Van Bua) and Le Quoc San departed for the battlefield. This group reached its assembly point in the South in early September 1961.

In December 1961 Route 129 was completed. The 3rd Truck Transportation Group of the General Rear Services Department was assigned to transport supplies to South Vietnam down Route 129, delivering their shipments to Na Bo, north of Route 9. Group 559's strategic transportation route had entered a new phase—it was now able to combine the use of primitive transportation methods with motorized transport, building the transportation route and the commo-liaison route up to a point where it was secure, stable, and could support an ever-growing flow of supplies and personnel to the battlefield.[26]

During 1961 a new situation developed on the Indochinese Peninsula. The U.S. imperialists launched their "special war" in South Vietnam and made a direct armed intervention into Laos. The Lao and Vietnamese people moved into a new period of building and fighting, a period of revolutionary warfare against the Americans.

Carrying out the strategic military duties set for it by the 3rd National Party Congress, our army rapidly went to work to turn the army into a more regular, modern force and develop sufficient strength to defend North Vietnam. It also worked to build up local combat forces in South Vietnam, sent volunteer soldiers to Laos, and took its first steps toward creating new forces and a new battlefield posture in preparation for future savage battles with the American imperialists and their lackeys.

5

Increasing the Combat Strength of Our Main Force Mobile Troops and Developing Our Massed Troops on the Battlefields of South Vietnam

PREPARATIONS FOR WAR IN NORTH VIETNAM

The development of simultaneous uprisings into revolutionary warfare in South Vietnam and the transition of the Laotian revolution into an armed struggle combined with a political struggle were important events that profoundly influenced the overall state of the revolutionary struggle on the Indochinese Peninsula. North Vietnam became the great rear area for the war to liberate South Vietnam and a firm base for the revolutionary struggle in Laos. Developing the economic and national defense potential of North Vietnam and increasing the combat power of our mobile main force troops became urgent requirements for the revolution.

To implement the resolution of the 3rd National Party Congress, beginning in early 1961 the people of North Vietnam confidently and enthusiastically launched the first five-year plan to build the technical and material structures needed for socialism. Eleven million working peasants were organized into agricultural production cooperatives. The State initiated irrigation projects, built technical support facilities to serve agriculture, expanded capital resources for cooperatives, and helped farmers find the most efficient ways to farm and increase production. In 1963 agricultural production in North Vietnam increased by 11 percent over the 1960 production level. Comparing the 1963 figures to those achieved in 1939, the year in which our economy reached its highest level of development during the entire French colonial period, food production had more than doubled, animal husbandry had doubled, and the value of our industrial crops was seven times higher. Agricultural growth provided the foundation for socialist industrialization and for the work of army building and consolidating national defense. State food reserves increased[1] and cooperatives provided a continuous flow of personnel, food, and moral support to our armed forces.

Our entire industrial and commercial structure underwent socialist reform.

State industrial and commercial enterprises grew strong, completely dominating all aspects of our national economy. In 1954 North Vietnam had only 41 factories, of which 20 were large factories, but by 1963 we had 1,000 factories, of which 217 were large factories. A number of important foundations for heavy industry, such as machine making, electricity, metallurgy, chemicals, and mining, had been laid. Industrial production increased 52 percent between 1960 and 1963. Light industry and handicrafts produced most of the consumer goods used by our people domestically. Our railroad, waterway, and road networks expanded.[2] A civil aviation industry run by the armed forces was founded. The growing strength of the laboring class, together with the development of our industry, communications, and postal system, provided an important foundation for the systematic development of our national defense industries. With aid from the Soviet Union, China, and other fraternal socialist countries, the economy of North Vietnam was able to provide an ever-increasing portion of our technical and material requirements, further advancing our efforts to modernize our army.

Tens of thousands of people from the heavily populated lowland provinces volunteered to build new economic zones in the piedmont and high up in the mountains. Plans for a new rural countryside and for state farms, lumber enterprises, and economic organizations run by the State or by collectives were developed in strategic areas, resulting in a new distribution of our population and combining economics with national defense.

With regard to social and cultural affairs, 95 percent of the population of North Vietnam were now literate. Compared with 1954 figures, the number of students in schools up through the high school level increased by 3.5 times and the number of university and trade school students grew by 25 times. Improvements were made in sanitation and the prevention and treatment of diseases. Our new soldiers, serving under a system of universal military service, were all healthy youths who had received an excellent education in the socialist school system.

Ten years after its liberation, North Vietnam had made progress that was unprecedented in the history of our nation. From the cities to the countryside, everywhere one looked one saw economic and cultural organizations belonging to the State or to collectives. The lives of the people constantly improved and their cultural and spiritual lives made steady progress. The nation, the society, and the individual all had been transformed. North Vietnam was systematically developing into our national rear area and provided a strong foundation upon which to build our army and increase our combat power.

While implementing the first five-year military plan from 1955 to 1960 our armed forces had grown from a number of isolated, inadequately equipped infantry units into a regular, relatively modern Army and had established the initial structures of our Service and specialty branches. In 1961, however, in the face of a number of new military duties, our armed forces displayed a number of weaknesses in organization, equipment, scientific research, and in the military arts.

The goal of the second five-year military plan (1961–1965) was to build a standing army with an appropriate strength level, containing all the elements of a modern army, with a table of organization and equipment capable of meeting the requirements of combat in our own nation and throughout the Indochinese Peninsula, and an army that could be rapidly expanded through the formation of new units when the war widened.

Our organizational tables had set the strength of the standing army in North Vietnam for the 1961–1965 period at 260,000. As long as North Vietnam still enjoyed peace, however, the Politburo and the Central Military Party Committee decided to keep the strength of the standing army at 170,000 troops[3] and provide excellent training to the troops of the standing army to enable them to be able to perform their combat duties during the initial stages of a new war. It was also decided to greatly expand our militia self-defense forces and our reserve forces to enable us to rapidly expand our forces.

To implement this decision of the Politburo, the General Staff established two table of organization structures for our units. Infantry units on combat-alert status, anti-aircraft units, Air Force units, and Navy units were given their wartime table of organization strength levels. Peacetime table of organization strength levels were established for units that were below wartime strength levels and for "framework" units consisting solely of cadre and technical personnel. Cadre excess to table of organization strength levels were "cached" in the staff agencies and schools of the armed forces. Cadre and soldiers who had been discharged back to their local areas or transferred to work in the economic or cultural sectors were registered for the reserve forces and assigned to reinforce the self-defense militia forces. They could be recalled back into the army whenever necessary.

As the nationwide armed force of the masses and the powerful reserve of our army, self-defense militia forces were organized in all administrative units, production facilities, agencies, and schools. Each village in North Vietnam had approximately 100 guerrilla militia fighters. In cities, towns, and industrial areas, self-defense forces were organized in every agency, enterprise, and city block. In 1963 self-defense militia forces throughout North Vietnam totaled 1.4 million personnel organized into 95 battalions, 4,700 companies, and 32,000 platoons. Twenty percent of these militia troops were armed with rifles, submachine guns, and medium machine guns. A number of self-defense militia companies and battalions were equipped with 12.7mm anti-aircraft machine guns. A total of 1.2 million individuals[4] were registered as members of the reserve forces, of whom 180,000 were category 1 reservists who were kept under tight administrative controls. Each year 25,000 soldiers, discharged after completion of their military service requirements, were registered into the reserve forces. Military training was increased for self-defense militia, category 1 reservists, and students at universities and trade schools. The work of inducting youths into the army to fulfill their national service requirements and of returning youths who had fulfilled their service requirements to their local areas was carried out according to a yearly schedule. A number of local areas, agencies, and enterprises carried out on a trial basis the induction of troops into the army in accordance with wartime induction regulations.

During 1963 North Vietnam continued to maintain the strength of its standing armed forces at 173,500 personnel.[5] With a strong reserve force and an excellent national program of military training, 15 days after mobilization orders were issued North Vietnam could increase its combat forces to 260,000 troops. In the event of a wider war it would be possible to quickly increase the size of the standing army to between 350,000 and 400,000 (during the 1964–1965 period) and to 500,000 during the 1966–1967 period.

STRENGTH AND ORGANIZATION OF THE PEOPLE'S ARMY

Based on the strength of our standing army, during the 1961–1963 period the Central Military Party Committee and the Ministry of Defense made additional adjustments to the tables of organization and upgraded the equipment of the entire armed forces in order to increase the combat power of the Army and to continue to build the basic organization structures of the Anti-Aircraft–Air Force and Navy Service Branches.

The Infantry Branch was organized into six divisions, six brigades, and three independent regiments subordinate to the High Command;[6] the main force battalions and regiments subordinate to the military regions; and the local force provincial and district companies and battalions. An infantry division included many different specialty branch components, had relatively modern equipment, and was capable of moving across all types of terrain. Each division had a table of organization strength of 9,590 personnel organized into three infantry regiments, one artillery regiment, one anti-aircraft artillery battalion, one battalion of anti-tank guns, one engineer battalion, and assorted support units. The division's weapons and equipment consisted of 5,000 automatic rifles, submachine guns, and light machine guns, all firing the same caliber of cartridge;[7] 174 artillery pieces and mortars of different calibers;[8] 40 37mm and 20mm anti-aircraft cannon; 190 trucks and artillery prime movers; a number of sets of light bridging equipment; 250 radios, 36 switchboards, 300 field telephones, and 300 kilometers of telephone wire. The 308th Division was brought up to full table of organization strength in personnel, weapons, and equipment in order to study the organization, equipment, and tactics of regiment- and division-sized combat units on all types of terrain.

The Artillery Branch was organized into 70 battalions and more than 100 separate batteries equipped with more than 1,000 pieces of field artillery and 1,700 mortars and recoilless rifles. Directly subordinate to the Artillery Command were four brigades equipped with long-barreled 85mm and 122mm guns and 152mm howitzers and capable of providing fire support to two different theaters of operations.[9] Each military region was assigned one artillery regiment (equipped with 105mm howitzers and 160mm and 120mm mortars) and one battalion of 75mm anti-tank guns. These forces were capable of providing fire support for one infantry division in combat within the military region's area of operations. Military regions along the coast formed a number of artillery units to defend offshore islands and assumed direct control over coastal defense regiments. The Artillery Command organized two cadre framework brigades and reserved a number of artillery pieces and mortars that could be used when needed to rapidly form new units.

Engineer troops were organized into seven regiments directly subordinate to the Engineer Department and the engineer battalions subordinate to the military regions and infantry divisions. Now equipped with river-crossing equipment, vehicles, and road construction machinery, our engineer troops were able to support the movement of infantry divisions in one theater of operations and to support traffic in the theater rear area.

Armored forces consisted of one regiment (three battalions) equipped with T-34 and T-54 medium tanks, PT-76 amphibious tanks, and CAY-76 76mm self-propelled guns. The armored forces, operating alongside our infantry, were capable of conducting combat assaults in key battles.

Signal troops were organized into regiments and signal centers subordinate to the Signal and Liaison Department and signal battalions and companies subordinate to military regions, infantry divisions and brigades, and to Service and specialty branches. Our signal equipment had grown rapidly in both quantity and quality, ensuring uninterrupted communications between the High Command and all units of our armed forces and with the battlefields in South Vietnam and Laos.[10]

Sapper forces were organized into three mobile sapper training battalions, sappers responsible for the battlefields of South Vietnam,[11] and sapper-reconnaissance cadre framework units of platoon and company size for the entire armed forces. In March 1974, Battalion 74B of the Research Department of the General Staff was formed. This battalion was made up of nine sapper-reconnaissance training teams to support the war in South Vietnam and four sapper training teams to perform international duties.

Chemical troops were organized into companies and battalions equipped with chemical defense equipment. These units were subordinate to the General Staff and to the military regions and infantry divisions.

Transportation troops were organized into three regiments (the 225th, 235th, and 245th) subordinate to the General Rear Services Department and transportation companies subordinate to military regions, Service and specialty branches, and infantry divisions.

By the end of 1963 our Army had grown into a full-fledged Service Branch made up of many separate combined-arms branches. The level of equipment and mobility of our infantry divisions and brigades and of our specialty branch units had been substantially improved. Infantry troops made up 49 percent of the total strength of the armed forces; artillery troops made up 10 percent, and engineer troops were 8.5 percent. This proportion was about right in relationship to the combat missions and level of equipment of our armed forces at that time.

Our anti-aircraft and air force troops continued to expand and to improve their equipment, systematically building themselves into a modern service branch. The Anti-Aircraft Artillery Branch consisted of 12 regiments subordinate to the Anti-Aircraft Command. These regiments were organized into two elements: strategic area defense anti-aircraft forces and field anti-aircraft forces. The strength of each anti-aircraft battery was increased from four to six 37mm or 57mm anti-aircraft guns. A number of older weapons (40mm, 85mm, 88mm) were replaced with new 57mm and 100mm weapons. The Radar Branch formed a new regiment, the 292nd Regiment, and added a number of additional companies and pieces of radar equipment to its 290th and 291st Regiments. The Air Force Branch was organized into three regiments. The 919th Regiment operated various types of transport and support aircraft including IL-14s, Li-2s, AN-2s, and MI-4 helicopters. The 921st Fighter Regiment was equipped with three companies of Mig-17s. The 910th Regiment performed training duties. In October 1963 our first anti-aircraft missile regiment was formed,[12] made up of 243 framework cadre and soldiers but not yet equipped with missiles.

To concentrate our forces, unify command, and increase the combat strength of anti-aircraft troops defending our airspace, on 22 October 1963 the Central Military Party Committee and the High Command decided to combine the Anti-Aircraft Command and the Air Force Department into the Air Defense–Air Force Service Branch. Senior Colonel Phung The Tai was appointed Service Commander, and Senior Colonel Dang Tinh was appointed Service Political Commissar. Beginning with one anti-aircraft artillery division (the 367th Division) formed after our victory in the resistance war against the French and subordinate to the Artillery Command, by the end of 1963 the air defense forces of our armed forces had been formed into an independent service branch, administering modern technical support facilities and made up of the Anti-Aircraft Artillery Branch, the Air Force Branch, the Radar Branch, and various support units such as signal, engineers, search lights, meteorology, etc.

Our naval forces grew rapidly and in the proper directions, developing a battle posture capable of defending the coastal areas and offshore waters of North Vietnam and transporting supplies to South Vietnam. In 1961, the first torpedo-boat group[13] and a company of anti-submarine vessels[14] were formed. With these groups, together with our two patrol boat groups (Groups 130 and 135), the People's Navy of Vietnam's fleet of modern naval vessels was born. Military ports at Bai Chay, Gianh River, Cua Hoi, a number of technical stations and radio transmitters, coastal-defense artillery firing positions, anchorages, caves for storage of torpedoes, ship cranes, etc., were built. On 3 August 1961 the Ministry of Defense established Naval Bases 1 and 2 to administer the territorial waters and offshore islands from the Northeast to Military Region 4. Patrol Zone 1 (on Van Hoa Island), Patrol Zone 2 (on the Gianh River), and the Haiphong Zone were established. In August 1963 the Standing Committee of the Central Military Party Committee assigned the responsibility for transportation of supplies from North Vietnam to the battlefields in the South to the Navy. In January 1963 Sea Transportation Group 759 changed its designation to Naval Group 125.

Beginning with a number of boat teams and a company of mine sweepers formed during the initial years of peace in North Vietnam, by 1964 the Navy had almost 100 surface vessels of different types, including coastal patrol vessels, torpedo boats, submarine chasers, transport vessels, reconnaissance vessels, and a number of service and support vessels. Although their numbers were still small, the Navy was a relatively complete force made up of combat and support vessels able to fight in our coastal waters and to transport supplies to the battlefields in South Vietnam. Major General Ta Xuan Thu was appointed as Navy Commander and concurrently Navy Political Commissar. The Navy had become a full-fledged service branch of our armed forces, the backbone of the effort to defend the territorial waters of the Fatherland.

In this way, during the period of force building covered by the second five-year military plan (1961–1965), our army developed the structure of a modern armed force consisting of three Service Branches: the Army, Air Defense–Air Force, and Navy. The mobile main force units of the High Command and the main force troops of the military regions had become significantly stronger. The organizational structure of the entire armed forces and of each unit ensured that they could carry out their short-term missions of army building and combat readiness. This structure also was capable of rapidly expanding our forces to keep pace with the expansion of the war. With the assistance of the Soviet Union, China, and other fraternal socialist countries, our Party, people, and army had overcome the many difficulties confronting an economically backward nation, had developed a number of technical specialty branches and Service Branches, and had significantly improved the equipment of our different types of armed forces.

In comparison with the goals of the five-year plan, especially in light of the increasingly urgent combat duties of the various battlefields, our army was still weak in field artillery, high-altitude anti-aircraft weapons, tanks and armored vehicles, engineering equipment, communications equipment, and transportation vehicles. The plan, however, represented a step forward on the road to building a regular, modern army. It played a decisive role in developing our forces and in increasing our combat power for the resistance war against the Americans to save the nation.

Along with improvements in organization and equipment, our army pushed forward to create technical facilities to support training and combat readiness. Command networks for the High Command, military regions, and service branches; national defense projects in the key defensive sectors; airfields, military ports, artillery firing ranges, strategic communications networks, etc., were built and provided with increasingly modern equipment. A network of repair and maintenance stations for weapons and vehicles was established at the level of infantry regiments and specialty branch battalions. National defense enterprises, warehouses, hospitals, clinics, etc., were combined into large installations ready to carry out production plans in support of wartime operations. The Small-Arms Department and the Ordnance Department of the General Rear Services Department and the service branches and technical specialty branches operated factories to produce and repair infantry weapons and to repair field artillery, anti-aircraft artillery, communications equipment, optical equipment, vehicles, tractors and towing vehicles, boats, barges, etc. Efforts to study and manufacture ammunition for infantry weapons, mortar shells, mines, and grenades increased. Enterprises subordinate to the Military Medical Department and the Quartermaster Department of the General Rear Services Department manufactured military medicines, uniforms, dry rations, canned goods, etc., fulfilling an important portion of our requirements for daily operations, for the establishment of reserve stocks to prepare for enemy attacks against North Vietnam, and for the support of our armed forces in South Vietnam. Construction troops subordinate to the Military Installations Department and to military regions and units did most of the work in constructing headquarters and base camps, schools, rehabilitation stations, a network of warehouses, factories, and machine shops, vehicle and artillery storage garages, etc. The ranks of our technical cadre and workers increased rapidly in quantity and quality. In 1954 our army had only a very small number of doctors and technical cadre,[15] but by 1964 the number of national defense workers in our nation had grown to more than 10,000, among whom were thousands of highly skilled engineers, doctors, pharmacists, technical cadre, and technical workers. These were important elements of our army building program that enabled our army to implement the organizational systems required by a regular force and to increase our combat power. They also created a reserve for use in time of war.

Cared for and nourished by the Party, the State, and the people, the material and spiritual lives of our troops improved day by day. Almost all units had solid, permanent base camps with electricity and water to support the demands of training and daily activities. Besides the salary system that had been put into effect, other supplementary programs to improve health and to provide workers with insurance, sanitation, disease prevention, etc., were implemented on a uniform basis throughout the armed forces. Culture houses and libraries were built at the company level. Cultural classes, artistic performances, film showings, libraries for books and newspapers, and sports and physical fitness activities all became part of the daily life of all of our units.

The task of ensuring that all regulations were firmly adhered to was carried out by properly educating our cadre and soldiers to understand the importance of obedience and discipline and by regular inspections by cadre at all levels. Procedures for duty watches and combat readiness watches; maintenance procedures for weapons, vehicles, and machinery; and procedures for daily activities, study sessions, and maintenance of internal security were implemented, guaranteeing that each unit and each individual maintained a high state of combat readiness. The phrase "disciplined like a soldier" gave evidence of a new lifestyle, a new source of pride for our younger generation, and our youth and students studied this discipline.

The work of Party building within the army and all areas of political activity received special attention. All companies had a Party chapter, and 60 percent of these Party chapters had enough Party members to elect a Party committee. Thirty percent of the infantry platoons and artillery gun sections had at least one Party member. Tens of thousands of outstanding Youth Group members, including thousands of cadre and technical personnel, were admitted to Party membership. Because the work of Party development was performed properly, the percentage of Party members in the entire standing army was constantly kept at around 30 percent, even though each year we trained about 25,000 new soldier draftees. The implementation of the "Four Goods" Party chapter building campaign,[16] the emphasis on criticism and self-criticism during Party activities, and the development of a Party member's vanguard role in serving as an example to others increased the Party's leadership role in units at the lowest level. The ranks of our political officers increased rapidly in both quantity (making up 24 percent of the total number of cadre in the army) and quality (75 percent of political cadre at all levels had received basic and supplementary professional training).

Under the leadership of the Central Military Party Committee and the guidance of the General Political Department, headed by Comrade Song Hao, work on drafting theoretical study documents and political education documents for cadre at all levels and guidance documents for Party and military activities within the army was completed. Some documents were published as books, such as *Activities of the Secretary of a Party Committee* and *Company-Level Political Activities.* Basic subjects in Marxist-Leninist theory (philosophy, political economics, scientific socialism), Party history, Party building, and political activities within the army were all developed into systematic programs of study at the army's schools and institutes, and study documents on these subjects were prepared for on-the-job training of cadre and soldiers. Political activities during training and during combat were subjects taught at basic and supplementary training schools for both military and political cadre.

With a regular and rather systematic program of education in Marxist-Leninist theory and in the major aspects of the political and military policies of the Party, the level of political awareness and the ideological methods of the cadre and soldiers of our armed forces were improved to a significant extent. This was an important success for our second five-year military plan and was a decisive factor in enabling our army to successfully complete its army building plans and in raising the level of combat readiness and the combat power of our armed forces.

With regard to the work of building up our cadre ranks, the second five-year military plan set forward the goal of building a cadre corps that was absolutely loyal to the Party and the revolution and had a high level of political awareness and a rather high level of education and knowledge of modern science and military technology to enable our cadre to meet our requirements for peacetime army building and to gradually build the quantity and quality of our cadre in response to the requirements of combat and of other duties.

Working to make the most of this time while North Vietnam still enjoyed peace, the Central Military Party Committee emphasized the provision of basic, long-term, and supplementary cadre training in our schools and increased the use of supplementary, on-the-job training, using many rich and varied methods such as short-term training, command staff exercises, and encouraging cadre to study on their own.

The school system of the armed forces was strengthened and expanded. In North Vietnam there were two study institutes,[17] eight officers training schools,[18] one basic education school, and five military-political schools at the military region level. A total of about 15,000 students received basic and supplementary training each year. In South Vietnam we established the military-political schools subordinate to COSVN and to the military regions to train company-, platoon-, and squad-level cadre. Our corps of instructors grew in quantity and quality. Relatively systematic training programs were drafted based on our review of lessons learned during the resistance war against the French, on the combat realities in South Vietnam and Laos, and on a review of training documents used by the Soviet Union's Red Army. School and classroom facilities and instructional equipment were expanded and improved. Tests for candidates for entrance into the schools and to meet national graduation standards were developed and organized into a set of formal procedures. In a ten-year period (1954–1964) our army provided basic and supplementary training to a total of 41,000 cadre of all ranks (58 percent receiving basic training and 42 percent supplementary training), 2.7 times as many as were trained during the resistance war against the French. The highest number of cadre graduating in a single year (1964) was 8,473. During this ten-year period a total of 4,900 cadre received basic training abroad, of whom 3,063 were command cadre and 1,837 were specialized or technical cadre. This was the highest number of cadre who received basic training abroad since the establishment of our army. At a time when our country still faced many difficulties, when our instructor corps and instructional and training equipment was still deficient in many areas, the provision of basic and supplementary training in our own schools to 60 percent of our military cadre represented a major effort on the part of our Party, State, and army. After many years of continuous combat, this was a period when the high-level and mid-level cadre of our army had a chance to study and increase their knowledge of theory, the military arts, and their capacity to organize and command a modern army in preparation for a new war. Almost all platoon-level and company-level cadre received basic training in our officers' schools. Cadre of the newly established Service and specialty branches received conversion training for their new specialties. An enthusiastic movement for all cadre to obtain a basic education developed, providing a good foundation upon which cadre at all levels could study to increase their knowledge of science, technology, and the military arts.[19]

In 1964 our entire armed forces had a total number of 52,041 cadre. Of these, 41,420 cadre, 18 percent of our troop strength, were in North Vietnam and 10,621 cadre, representing 10 percent of the total troop strength, were in the South. The makeup of our cadre corps responded to the mission of building a modern armed force made up of many combined-arms branches. Although in 1954 90 percent of our cadre were infantry cadre, by 1964 50 percent of our cadre were infantry and cadre of other service and specialty branches and specialized cadre made up the other 50 percent.[20] Besides the number of cadre serving in military units and staff agencies, we also had cadre reserves working in agencies and schools and cadre receiving basic and supplementary training in schools both in Vietnam and abroad.[21] Our reserve forces had a total of 123,000 cadre registered as reserve members. We had 320,000 cadre who served as commanders of our militia self-defense forces; of this total 54,000 had received some type of training in military schools.

The growth of our cadre ranks was an important accomplishment of our ten-year program of army building (1954–1964). The cadre corps of our army had grown in response to the need to administer and command an armed force made up of many combined-arms branches. Our Party and our army had seized the initiative by taking the first step in preparing our military cadre corps to be ready to cope with a large-scale, prolonged, and vicious war of aggression conducted by the American imperialists.

DEVELOPING TACTICAL CONCEPTS

In order to increase the quality of training of our troops, especially training of cadre, the Central Military Party Committee set forward a policy:

> On the basis of a review of lessons our army has learned in combat and utilizing the combat experiences of the armies of our fraternal socialist brothers, and based on the tables of organization and equipment that our army has established, urgently study and prepare tactical training documents and strategic campaign training documents for uniform use throughout the armed forces. Increase training activities to allow every military unit and agency of every service and specialty branch to successfully carry out their combat duties in every possible situation.

The goal was to study military science and actual operations of the entire armed forces in order to develop combat principles and tactics for use against our new combat opponent, the U.S. armed forces and their lackeys, on our own terrain in our own country. The principles and tactics chosen would be suitable for use by an armed force made up of many combined-arms branches and operating increasingly modern equipment.

With the direct participation of many leading members of the Party and the army, by 1963 many projects to review and summarize lessons learned in both the armed struggle and the building of the people's armed forces during the resistance war against the French had been completed. Documents were prepared summarizing a number of major campaigns conducted by our main force troops, the guerrilla war behind enemy lines, Party and political activities, and rear services activities of the entire armed forces and of each individual battlefield. All these documents provided many lessons drawn from experience for use by units in carrying out the missions of building up forces and conducting combat operations in the resistance war against the United States. Practical lessons drawn from combat operations currently under way on the battlefields of South Vietnam and Laos provided additional fresh and vivid experiences for these documents. In addition to the strategic review projects conducted by the Ministry, each military region, provincial unit, division, and specialty branch also carried out a review of its experiences in force building and combat operations in its local area and within the confines of the unit itself.

In early 1964, the Central Military Party Committee and the Ministry of Defense held a conference to review lessons learned during the resistance war against the French colonialists. Comrade Truong Chinh, General Secretary of the Party during the resistance war against the French, attended this conference. Based on the experiences of our soldiers and civilians in force building and combat operations, the conference stressed one of the primary lessons learned: Using as our foundation the development of local armed forces and emphasizing guerrilla warfare behind enemy lines to force the enemy to disperse its forces, we would need to aggressively build up and emphasize the importance of the role to be played by our main force mobile troops. If our main force army was equal to or stronger than the enemy's strategic mobile forces, with proper strategic and campaign guidance our soldiers and civilians would be able to win great and continuous victories in campaigns and combat operations, maintain and develop the strategic initiative, and transform the entire character of the war.

After the Ministry's conference to summarize the strategic lessons, staff agencies of the High Command, military regions, service branches, specialty branches, and individual divisions held a number of conferences to summarize and study campaign and tactical subjects.

The Military Science Research Department of the General Staff and the *People's Army* magazine organized a seminar on tactical thinking. Colonel General Van Tien Dung, alternate member of the Party Central Committee and Chief of the General Staff; Major Generals Vuong Thua Vu, Hoang Sam, Chu Huy Man, and Hoang Minh Thao; Senior Colonels Hoang Cam and Doan Tue; and many other high-ranking cadre of our army raised many pressing needs for tactical study, viewing such studies as important work that would help increase the quality of military training and ensure that the army was ready to fight and capable of winning battlefield victories. The conference laid out eight tactical concepts[22] and discussed the application of these tactical concepts to the work of studying and writing training documents, organizational tasks, and tactical training methods.

The lessons drawn from the resistance war against the French and from ten years of force building in peacetime conditions shed light on many of the problems our army faced in force building and combat operations during this new phase. The Politburo and the Central Military Party Committee stressed the idea that the war against the United States to save the nation that our people and our army were now conducting was a people's war, closely combining both guerrilla warfare and conventional warfare methods. The three combat methods suited for this war were maneuver tactics, attacks against bases (by main force and/or local force troops), and guerrilla warfare (by the civilian masses, by self-defense militia, by local forces, and by dispersed elements of our main force troops). These three combat methods were intimately related and mutually supportive. In our war guidance, we had to apply these methods flexibly, depending on the balance of forces between ourselves and the enemy and on the actual situation in each phase of the war and on each battlefield. In building up our army we must firmly grasp practical ideas based on our strategic military responsibilities and on the particular form of warfare and the type of combat method in order to establish the appropriate size and organization for our forces, and we must constantly work to increase the combat power of our three types of troops, with special emphasis on our main force troops.

The Central Military Party Committee set forward 11 tactical principles:

1. Aggressively annihilate enemy troops while preserving our own forces.
2. Fight when victory is certain, fight only after preparations have been completed, fight to win the first battle.
3. Closely coordinate the combat operations of main force troops, local force troops, and self-defense militia.
4. Concentrate forces to annihilate each enemy element.
5. Attack resolutely and continuously, defend actively and stubbornly.
6. Deploy forces with a main focal point and keep a strong reserve force.
7. Exercise independence in battle, take the initiative in cooperating with and supporting friendly units, maintain close coordination.
8. Develop a capacity for close combat, night combat, and continuous combat.
9. Closely link political and military operations, combat and enemy proselytizing operations.
10. Exploit our political and spiritual advantage, fight courageously, defeat an enemy who has a technological advantage.
11. Be aggressive, maintain the initiative, use flexibility and mobility, creativity and cleverness, secrecy and surprise.[23]

These were correct, innovative combat principles derived from actual experience that would be of value in providing guidance for training activities, in increasing the combat power of the army, and especially in the combat operations taking place in South Vietnam and on the battlefields of Laos. Many of these principles were developed into excellent combat traditions and combat behavior that contributed to the glorious feats of arms performed by our soldiers and civilians during the resistance war against the Americans to save the nation.

Based on the review and summary documents and the results of the first phase of research on military science and the military arts, the General Staff supervised the drafting and upgrading of our technical and tactical training programs, placing emphasis on realistic training based on actual combat operations.

With regard to defensive operations, from exclusive reliance on continuous trench lines, our troops now began to train in directional defensive combat operations, firmly holding defensive blocking positions along the enemy's lines of advance in combination with counterattacks against enemy forces landing by air, by sea, or attacking in a number of motorized ground spearhead columns.

With regard to offensive operations, from training in simple attacks against enemy forces occupying continuous trench lines, our troops now began training in deep penetration attacks, continuous attacks from the march, attacking an enemy that had withdrawn into a network of defensive strong points, combining attacks against enemy weak points with envelopment and flanking maneuvers, surrounding and isolating the enemy, and annihilating each separate enemy element.

Each separate specialty branch focused on studying and training in specific tactics suitable for use in specific situations depending on terrain, equipment, and specific opponents. Infantry troops trained in fighting while on the move, in ambushes, and in assaults in various situations, such as while the enemy was conducting a sweep operation, when the enemy temporarily switched over to the defensive, when the enemy was occupying solid defensive fortifications, when he was landing forces by helicopter, when he was conducting a motorized march, etc. Sapper troops trained in tactics for attacking outposts, bridges, ports, airfields, warehouses, command posts, and enemy leadership organizations inside cities and towns. Artillery forces trained in both independent missions and in providing fire support to infantry forces, utilizing such tactics as raids, ambushes, night attacks, secret deep penetrations to attack strong points behind enemy lines, and firing using the "detailed and proper" method[24] in order to meet the requirement for rapid and accurate fire. Anti-aircraft troops trained in different methods of deploying their firing positions, in aircraft recognition, and in the rapid acquisition of targets. Naval troops trained in rapid docking and weighing anchor for vessels and in attack tactics for use against different types of enemy vessels. Self-defense militia trained in tactics for use in defending their areas of responsibility, in firing at low-flying aircraft, and in tactics for use in attacking, surrounding, and capturing enemy commandos, etc.

We made many advances in our technical training, especially in techniques for firing weapons and artillery, techniques for transmitting and receiving communications signals, radar acquisition of targets, naval electronics, and flight techniques for the air force. The combat operations then under way in South Vietnam encouraged our cadre and soldiers to closely link their studies to battlefield realities and to the accomplishment of their combat missions. The phrase "Sweat on the exercise field to lessen bloodshed on the battlefield" became a slogan in our army. Many units immediately applied this training to the conduct of their duties. Our radar troops trained while they turned on their sets to monitor enemy activities. Our engineer troops trained while they built national defense projects.

Based on the realities of combat on the battlefield, all units trained their cadre and troops in the use of different types of weapons and equipment to enable them to support or replace one another during combat. Infantry troops practiced firing every type of rifle, submachine gun, and light machine gun. Artillery gun crew members practiced performing each other's duties. In addition to field artillery, they were also trained in all types of man-portable artillery (57mm and 75mm recoilless rifles, 82mm and 120mm mortars) and practiced firing using field-firing procedures.[25] Sapper soldiers learned to use numerous types of enemy weapons and equipment and learned to drive automobiles, motorcycles, tanks, and ships. Signal troops learned to operate radios and to make reports. All sailors on our naval vessels learned how to operate the vessel's guns, etc.

Units focused on field training on many different types of terrain and in difficult weather conditions in order to enable our cadre and soldiers to make long marches and meet the requirement to be able to march long distances and carry heavy loads along the road from our great rear area to the battlefront. The 308th Division, the unit given the title of "Vanguard Division," conducted a follow-up study of various aspects of march movements. The entire division, carrying its full complement of weapons and equipment, crossed 400 kilometers of mountain trails in 14 days and nights. When it arrived at the assembly point, 93 percent of its troops were in good enough physical condition to immediately begin combat operations. Artillery troops, "legs of bronze and shoulders of iron," practiced carrying 120mm mortars, broken down into component loads, on bicycles and transporting dismantled 75mm mountain guns on modified "wheelbarrows." Signal troops trained in long marches carrying loads of 35 to 40 kilograms (personal equipment, rice for the journey, radios, and enough spare batteries to operate radios for six months). Rear services troops studied and improved different types of quartermaster items and equipment to adapt them to field operations and to reduce the volume and weight of equipment that had to be carried in order to increase the mobility of our troops. Rubber sandals were improved to make them strong and durable. The "frog pack" was produced. This pack was strong enough to carry all necessary personal equipment and had large, thick shoulder straps, which reduced shoulder irritation. Tarps, hammocks, and many different types of personal equipment were fabricated and produced.

The results of this tactical and technical training were reviewed during training exercises and in actual combat operations on the battlefield. Combat exercises conducted at Thanh Oai, Ha Tay province, in 1961 and at Cam Giang, Hai Hung province, in 1963 by the 308th Infantry Division (reinforced by artillery, armored, engineer, and signal elements) demonstrated that the main force mobile units subordinate to the High Command had improved their mobility and combat capabilities. Military region main force units held exercises involving offensive and defensive combat operations in mountain jungle terrain, on low-lying, flat terrain, and practiced opposing "enemy" air and sea landings. The General Staff and headquarters staffs of the military regions, service branches, specialty branches, and divisions drew lessons from these exercises, adapting the organization, equipment, and tactics of their tactical units and adjusting coordination procedures between different forces and between main force and local force units.

THE NAM THA CAMPAIGN IN LAOS

During the spring of 1962, at the suggestion of our Lao allies and pursuant to instructions issued by the Politburo of the Party Central Committee, the Central Military Party Committee and the High Command assigned the Northwest Military Region responsibility for sending seven infantry battalions and a number of specialty branch units from the 316th, 335th, and 330th Brigades to Laos to cooperate with our Lao allies in launching an offensive campaign against enemy forces in the Nam Tha area in order to crush the enemy threat in northern Laos. After eight years of army building under peacetime conditions, our army would launch its first offensive campaign. This campaign provided an excellent opportunity to test combat training, to make further improvements in our organization and equipment, and to gain experience in conducting an offensive campaign in mountain jungles.

In March 1962, two infantry battalions and a number of specialty branch units of the 316th Brigade marched to Nam Tha, where they built defensive positions to block enemy forces. The High Command established a ground transportation route across from the Northwest Military Region and concentrated the entire 919th Air Force Regiment to transport supplies for the campaign. The 2nd and 4th Infantry Battalions of the 335th Brigade, carrying all their own weapons and equipment, marched for 12 days and nights to reach the assembly area. In late April 1962, after receiving additional reinforcements (the 3rd Battalion of the 330th Brigade), the Lao-Vietnamese allied forces opened fire, destroying a number of enemy positions on the outer perimeter and securing an offensive position from which we could attack the enemy's entire defensive area. By massing our forces to destroy individual enemy units and then, when the opportunity arose, launching powerful, continuous attacks that combined assaults with envelopment and flanking maneuvers, the Lao-Vietnamese allied army drove the enemy back until his forces disintegrated. Our forces liberated Muong Sinh and Nam Tha, then developed the attack by launching a pursuit of enemy forces.

The Nam Tha campaign ended in victory on 12 May 1962. A significant portion of the Lao puppet army's elite forces, equipped and trained by the United States, had been destroyed.[26] The liberated zone of our allies in northern Laos expanded by an additional 800 kilometers and 76,000 people. Our troops gained considerable experience in organizing and conducting an offensive campaign, especially in mobile operations; in organizing defensive positions; in fighting enemy counterattacks; in conducting raids and pursuit operations; in assault tactics; in conducting deep penetrations and enveloping and outflanking enemy forces; and in political and logistics operations during an offensive campaign in mountain jungle terrain.

Worries and concerns that "we may train this way but we do not know if these methods will work when we actually go into battle," which had appeared among a number of our cadre and soldiers, were disproven and we proved that "if we train this way and fight this way, we are certain of victory."

THE WAR IN THE SOUTH ENCOUNTERS DIFFICULTIES

In June 1963 the Central Military Party Committee met to assess the results of army building activities during the period 1961–1963 and to discuss a plan for the defense of North Vietnam. Comrade Le Duan, First Secretary of the Party Central Committee, attended the conference. The Central Military Party Committee concluded that substantial progress had been made during this three-year period (1961–1963) in the work of building a modern regular army, strengthening the self-defense militia, and expanding the reserve forces in North Vietnam. There had been significant improvements in the combat power of our main force mobile troops. We had increased the number of reinforcements being sent to fight in South Vietnam and to assist the Laotian revolution. Our army had grown sufficiently to enable it to successfully carry out its three missions of defending North Vietnam, fighting the revolutionary war in South Vietnam, and fulfilling our international duties. Our army could now be quickly expanded to serve as a strategic reserve force for all of Indochina. We had identified a number of weaknesses we should concentrate on correcting during the coming years. These weaknesses included the fact that our technical specialty branches had not developed at the same rate as our combat elements, that we had limited technical and material support facilities, and that a number of our units did not have the requisite combat skills and mobility to carry out their missions.

The Central Military Party Committee reached the following decisions: To intensify efforts to build a modern, regular army; to reach all the target goals of the second five-year military plan; to send additional forces from the North to fight in South Vietnam, at the same time increasing local recruiting in the South;

and to increase the operations of our full-time troops on the battlefields of South Vietnam. To retain the initiative and cope with the ever-increasing acts of provocation by the American imperialists, the Central Military Party Committee approved a program for the defense of North Vietnam. This program consisted of combat planning directives, plans for the mobilization and expansion of the armed forces during the initial outbreak of hostilities, and plans to convert North Vietnam's economy to a wartime production economy.

Speaking to the conference of the Central Military Party Committee, Comrade Le Duan stressed the need to adhere to practical realities when conducting studies, organizing forces, and providing combat guidance to the armed forces. Our army building efforts and our buildup of the rear area of North Vietnam must be based on our strategic revolutionary duties and on the size of our population, our nation's economic capacity, and on the amount of assistance provided by fraternal socialist nations. The issue of combat operations had to be addressed in the following manner: "Based on the enemy's situation and on our own capabilities, we must seek every possible means to defeat the enemy."[27]

During the first few months of 1963 the situation in South Vietnam underwent considerable changes, and North Vietnam no longer enjoyed peaceful conditions for the work of army building in North Vietnam. Our armed forces confronted many new problems in carrying out its army building and combat missions, which included maintaining combat readiness and defending North Vietnam, defeating the U.S. imperialist "special war" in South Vietnam, and performing our international duties.

As part of their "special war" strategy, the American imperialists rapidly increased U.S. economic and military assistance to the Saigon puppet regime.[28] In June 1961 they hurriedly began to carry out "preparatory steps," rapidly increasing the strength and equipment of the puppet army; redeploying their forces throughout the battlefield; training regular troops, Regional Force troops, and Popular Force troops in "counterguerrilla" tactics; and expanding their intelligence networks in order to identify the revolution's armed units, bases, and leadership organs. To support puppet regular troops the United States strengthened its advisory structure and forces that provided the regulars with fire support.[29] American advisors were assigned down to the subsector[30] and the battalion level. American pilots participated in puppet military operations by conducting "tactical bombing" attacks. U.S. troops in South Vietnam were given permission to "fire in self-defense when necessary."[31] A civilian defense force organized and trained by "the Special Forces of the American Army in Vietnam" supported puppet army combat operations as they implemented their "pacification" program. A network of heavily fortified "special forces camps," each with its own airstrip, was established. These camps were built in important locations along the Vietnamese-Lao border where they could conduct reconnaissance, provide fire support, and block the movement of our personnel and supplies from North Vietnam to the battlefront.

In August 1962 the U.S. Department of Defense established the Military Assistance Command (MACV), commanded by General Harkins, to replace the Military Advisory Group (MAAG). The purpose of this change was to "coordinate the American effort in Vietnam."

In late March 1962 the United States and its puppets shifted into an "offensive phase." They mobilized the entire puppet regular army, Regional Forces, Popular Forces, and the police, all under the command of American advisors, to launch thousands of sweep operations. A series of campaigns were conducted in important areas such as the area around Saigon, the Mekong Delta, and the lowlands of Central Vietnam.[32] The enemy's goals were to collect the people into specified areas and institute tight controls over the population; to destroy our revolutionary forces while they were still small and weak; and to seal the borders to block the flow of assistance from the North into South Vietnam.

The principal enemy tactic used to accomplish these goals was the establishment of "strategic hamlets" that would totally control each person, controlling each individual's food and property inside a neighborhood or hamlet surrounded by a network of fences, barriers, and watchtowers manned by police and armed forces. This tactic included the use of deceitful political and social tricks and economic "bribes" to win popular support. As they built these "strategic hamlets" the enemy also organized a network of intelligence agents and informants to expose our followers and employed military forces to mount sweeps and drive our Party organizations and guerrillas away, pushing our armed revolutionary forces back into isolated base areas in the mountain jungles where they could be attacked and destroyed. This was a poisonous American and puppet scheme combining political, economic, and social tactics. The main focus, however, was placed on military schemes aimed at destroying revolutionary armed forces by "filtering the fish out of the water."

The enemy plan called for the establishment of 16,000 "strategic hamlets"[33] throughout South Vietnam by the end of 1962. The enemy believed these hamlets would essentially wipe out our armed forces, crush the revolutionary struggle movement of the people in South Vietnam, and demonstrate the ability of the U.S. "special war" strategy to contain and defeat the revolutionary national liberation movement. These new enemy plots and schemes created many problems for our armed forces and our people.

In Region 5, just as the political struggle combined with armed struggle began to develop in late 1960–early 1961, the enemy launched a vicious counterattack. Using large numbers of troops, superior mobility, and heavy firepower,[34] the United States and its puppets constantly attacked our bases in the mountains, mounted sweeps and blockades of the contested areas, and seized and occupied portions of our liberated areas in the lowlands. In the provinces of Quang Ngai and Quang Tin our bases at Do Xa, Con Ha Nung, and Chu-de-lay-a were hit the hardest. By mid-1963 the enemy had been able to establish 3,520 "strategic hamlets," including 2,750 hamlets in the lowlands and 780 hamlets in the mountains, and gain control over more than two-thirds of the rural population. With a network of outposts and strong points and a web of roads, airfields, and "strategic hamlets," the enemy was able to establish fairly tight control over Region 5. In the rural lowlands our self-defense guerrillas and local force troops were few and weak. They were not strong enough to support the people in the effort to destroy "strategic hamlets." The narrowness of the contested areas and the mountain region combined with enemy attacks designed to split these areas and isolate them made it difficult for our full-time troop units to find bases and operating areas.

In Cochin China and extreme southern Central Vietnam, after the victories of the 1960 uprisings, in 1961 we continued to intensify the political struggle combined with armed struggle. Our liberated zones grew constantly in size and strength, our political and armed forces expanded, and the mass struggle movement became very strong.

During the last months of 1961, using mass political forces and guerrillas to mount "internal attacks" and province and district local force troops to mount "external attacks," the soldiers and civilians of Cochin China destroyed more than 200 newly established "strategic hamlets" and damaged or caused the disintegration of more than 1,000 other "strategic hamlets." A number of our local areas and units underestimated the enemy plot to establish "strategic hamlets." When the United States and its puppets began to implement the "Stalay-Taylor" plan, using larger military forces and more savage terrorist measures, many local areas did not know how to respond to these measures. In Region 9 (western Cochin China) the enemy launched a continuous series of "Binh Tay" and "Wave of Affection" campaigns. They divided the area into many clusters, each cluster not quite ten kilometers apart. In each cluster the enemy used three to five battalions to encircle the area and then sent in troops by helicopter to seek to destroy the armed forces of the revolution and to help their regional and popular forces set up "strategic hamlets." In Region 8 (central Cochin China) the puppet 7th Division launched a series of sweeps through the Plain of Reeds base area, aimed at destroying our full-time troop units and at enabling Ranger battalions and local armed forces to set up "strategic hamlets." In Region 7 (eastern Cochin China) the enemy extended the "Binh Minh" campaign through the entire year of 1962. The goal of this campaign was to destroy our Long Nguyen base, isolate War Zone D from the Duong Minh Chau base, and drive the civilian population of our base area into "strategic hamlets" along Route 13. They destroyed many of our agricultural fields and rice stores. Short of rice, some units were forced to eat rice gruel seven days a week.

By the end of 1962 the enemy had established more than 2,000 "strategic hamlets" throughout Cochin China, controlling three million out of a total of nine million people. Liberated areas and areas where the masses had seized control shrank. Guerrillas from a number of villages and hamlets were forced to move to other areas or flee to our base areas. Cadre and Party members hid in rice paddies and along canal banks to wait for nightfall to enter the hamlets to contact our supporters and rebuild our armed forces.

In February 1962, as the enemy was beginning to implement its "Stalay-Taylor" plan, the Politburo of the Party Central Committee issued a resolution on the immediate responsibilities of the revolution in South Vietnam. The Politburo issued clear orders for our full-time forces in South Vietnam to take the offensive by fighting battles designed to destroy enemy manpower [kill enemy troops], help local forces increase guerrilla warfare operations, destroy enemy "strategic hamlets," and intensify the political struggle. Our operational tactic would be to fight small battles, battles in which victory was certain, against enemy regular troops conducting field operations and against enemy troops and commando teams mounting helicopter assaults. To deal with the enemy's rapid mobility and his air support, it would be necessary to mount surprise and night attacks, quickly dispersing and concentrating our forces as needed. In operations against enemy sweeps and when attacking "strategic hamlets," our best tactic would be to coordinate the use of three types of struggle: political struggle, military struggle, and enemy proselytizing.

To build up our armed forces the Politburo decided to develop widespread guerrilla forces throughout the three strategic areas and to build up local force troops on all battlefields to stretch enemy forces thin and enable us to fight the enemy everywhere. The expansion of our main force troops would be based on the actual situation in each area, on each area's manpower and matériel capacity, and on the status of their bases. In Cochin China, where guerrillas and local forces were rather well developed, we would need to increase the strength of our main force units. In Region 5 emphasis would be placed on building up guerrilla forces and local forces while, to the extent possible, building up main force units. We would work vigorously to develop specialty branch forces and increase the firepower of our main force troops. We would train all of our different types of armed forces [main force, local force, guerrillas] in anti-aircraft tactics.

In June 1962 the Central Military Party Committee informed our armed forces in South Vietnam that their central, most immediate missions were to intensify military operations and coordinate these operations with the political struggle in order to preserve and expand our forces and to disrupt the enemy plan to set up "strategic hamlets." To implement the Politburo resolution and the instructions of the Central Military Party Committee, COSVN, our regional Party committees, and the military affairs sections of the military regions established concrete policies on force building and provided battlefield guidance for use by the three types of armed forces to deal with the new enemy's war plans and schemes.

Region 5 had experience in forming full-time troop units and in massed combat operations during the resistance war against the French. Since the construction of Group 559's strategic transportation route, because the region was close to our great rear area in North Vietnam and because early in the conflict Region 5 had begun to receive military cadre and weapons from the North, the Region Party Committee and the Military Region Command correctly understood that "if we wish to support the masses in the political struggle, if we wish to change the balance of forces in our favor and defeat the war plots and schemes of the enemy, the key to accomplishing these tasks is to build up a strong main force element to enable us to destroy enemy forces."[35] During 1962 Region 5 formed the 1st, 2nd, and 3rd infantry regiments and a number of sapper and fire support battalions. Each regiment operated in one or two provinces where it shared responsibilities with local provincial military units. Between September 1961 and the end of 1962 the soldiers and civilians of Region 5 launched three successive operational campaigns. The region's main force units and provincial and district local force units were organized into two elements. One element formed armed propaganda teams[36] that were sent to operate in areas under enemy control to mobilize the population to form political organizations, expand guerrilla warfare operations, and support the uprisings of the people to destroy the "strategic hamlets." The other element was organized into companies or multicompany groups operating independently. These groups used infantry and sapper forces to attack and overrun outposts and enemy strong points and attack positions deep behind enemy lines. Region 5's soldiers fought bravely during these operational campaigns, destroying dozens of enemy strong points. These attacks included several famous battles, such as the attacks on enemy strong points at Long Lech in Quang Ngai province and Playmo-rong in Pleiku province. Local force troops of Phu Yen, Binh Dinh, Quang Ngai, Quang Nam, and Thua Thien provinces fought resolutely against the enemy's protracted sweep operations. On 30 August 1962 the 90th Quang Ngai Local Force Battalion repelled an attack on the Na Niu base area by one puppet airborne Ranger battalion using "helicopter assault" tactics. The battalion shot down 13 helicopters and successfully protected the base area.

Because our guerrilla forces in the lowlands of Region 5 were still weak and our main force and local force troops were operating in a dispersed fashion, however, they were not strong enough to resist puppet regular units when the enemy launched large sweep operations and when they mounted rapid counterattacks after we attacked enemy "strategic hamlets." Our troops still lacked weapons capable of destroying fortifications, knocking out enemy armored vehicles, and shooting down enemy aircraft. There was still confusion about what methods should be used to deal with the enemy's use of "armored personnel carrier assault tactics." The 2nd Regiment's 95th Battalion fought two enemy infantry regiments and a troop of M-113 armored personnel carriers at Mo Duc in Quang Ngai province in April 1963. One hundred ten of our cadre and soldiers were killed and 60 weapons were lost. Our full-time armed units encountered many difficulties when they tried to operate in the rural lowlands. In the mountains and contested areas our units were forced to move constantly to evade enemy sweeps and commando operations, lowering their combat efficiency. Our soldiers endured many hardships because food production was unreliable and our warehouses, crops, and food stocks were being attacked and destroyed. Rightist and negativistic tendencies began to appear among our soldiers.

In Cochin China and extreme southern Central Vietnam, COSVN and the COSVN Military Affairs Section established a policy of "launching a people's war based on the use of combat villages and hamlets, with the self-defense militia providing the core force for this battle."[37] Regional main force and provincial local force units were dispersed into small subunits to operate in our base areas. A number of these subunits were sent to fight beside our guerrillas and self-defense forces to maintain and develop the mass struggle movement and to build armed forces at the grass-roots level.

As was the case in Region 5, we had few full-time troops operating in Cochin China, and the troops we had were dispersed into small groups. They were not strong enough to defeat enemy mobile forces when they mounted military operations, conducted sweeps, and constructed "strategic hamlets." The enemy's "helicopter assault" tactics were even more effective here, in terrain cut by many canals and streams, and our soldiers had not yet found an effective method for countering this enemy tactic. For this reason some "strategic hamlets" were built by the enemy, destroyed by our forces, rebuilt by the enemy, and destroyed again, etc., and we were never able to finally wipe out the "strategic hamlet."

The problem confronting Region 5 and Cochin China during the 1962–1963 period was as follows: If we wanted to defeat the enemy's principal strategic methods, sweeps, concentrating the population, and the establishment of "strategic hamlets," we had to be capable of defeating puppet mobile troops when they conducted sweeps and to defeat their "helicopter assault" and "armored personnel carrier assault" tactics. This was an urgent requirement that reflected the objective laws of the development of the revolutionary war in South Vietnam and demanded that our army rapidly strengthen our mobile main force elements on the battlefield, that we resolve our technical and tactical problems, and that we elevate the combat capabilities of our armed forces in South Vietnam to a new, higher level.

On 6 December 1962, the Politburo met to assess the situation and formulate concrete policies and measures to overcome our difficulties and advance the cause of the revolution in South Vietnam.

The Politburo's assessment stated that during two years of vicious fighting against the "special warfare" strategy of the United States and its puppets, the revolutionary movement of South Vietnam had gained a number of new victories, but at the same time had also encountered new difficulties and challenges. The political struggle forces of the masses had developed rather well, but not uniformly so. The armed forces had grown rapidly, but the balance between the three types of troops was skewed. The tactical and technical capabilities of our troops had not kept pace with the changes the enemy had made in his own tactics and technical capabilities. Our tactical guidance in many areas was not precise and firm. Our base areas in the liberated zones were still small, and each individual area was experiencing different problems in such areas as obtaining additional manpower, logistical supply, equipment, and terrain.

To overcome this situation, it would be necessary to mobilize the entire Party and the entire population to build up our armed forces and to develop a widespread pattern of guerrilla warfare. The different battlefields and armed units had to carefully study the pattern of the enemy's military operations and the enemy's tactical and technical weaknesses. They needed to review and synthesize lessons learned from our experience in combat during this most recent period in order to defeat the enemy's short-term and long-term military operations by creating conditions in which we could destroy enemy regular troops and commandos attacking overland and landing by helicopter and simultaneously support popular uprisings to destroy the "strategic hamlets."

THE DECISION TO INCREASE SUPPORT
FOR THE SOUTHERN REVOLUTION

The Politburo decided to quickly send combat forces to South Vietnam and to expand our mobile main force troops and our specialty branch units. Military Transportation Group 559 received additional troops and equipment to expand our supply and commo-liaison lines to the battlefield.[38] After building Route 129, Military Region 4's 25th and 27th Engineer Battalions were transferred to Group 559 to carry out road maintenance duties. In response to the enemy's sweep and commando operations, the General Staff assigned a number of units of the 325th Infantry Division the mission of working with Pathet Lao troops to defend the Kaki Bridge, Ban Dong, and Muong Pha Lan areas and to protect our supply line across Route 9. The cadre and soldiers of Group 559 implemented a number of measures to maintain the secrecy of our strategic transportation route. These measures included "going native,"[39] adopting the lifestyle and the eating and working habits of the local population, and actively building political and armed organizations among the local ethnic tribal population. Weapons were issued to a third of our troops stationed along the transportation route.

Following the Ta Khong campaign in April 1961 our movement of supplies and personnel down the route on the western side of the Annamite Mountains grew to new levels. North of Route 9, trucks driven by motor transport troops of the General Department of Rear Services followed Route 12 across to the western side of the Annamite Mountains and down Route 129 to a supply transshipment point at Muong Phin. A regiment of the 325th Infantry Division portered supplies from Ho to Tchepone. The 919th Air Force Transportation Regiment, assisted by Soviet pilots, dropped supplies by parachute to Muong Phin or landed at the Ta Kong airfield. Our aircraft transported tons of supplies to Group 559, including 57mm and 75mm recoilless rifles, 75mm mountain guns, 82mm and 120mm mortars, radio communications equipment, etc. From the area south of Route 9 onward, the 70th Regiment of Group 559 used primitive transportation equipment (bicycles, elephants, horses) and human porters to transfer supplies down to A Tuc. From there transportation troops of Military Region 5 moved the supplies forward to Tang Non in Quang Nam province, Dac Lan in Kontum province, and Bu Gia Map in Phuoc Long province.[40]

By the end of 1963 over 40,000 cadre and soldiers of our armed forces, consisting primarily of regroupees from South Vietnam and including more than 2,000 mid- and high-ranking cadre and technical personnel, had marched down Group 559's commo-liaison route to the battlefield. These troops represented 50 percent of the full-time armed forces in the South and 80 percent of the cadre and technical personnel assigned to the command and staff organizations in South Vietnam in 1963. These reinforcements played an important role in the rapid formation of main force units and allowed the rapid strengthening of military leadership and command organizations from the regional down to the provincial and district levels. Group 559 transported a total of 165,600 weapons to the battlefields in the South during the 1961–1963 period. This total included a number of artillery pieces, mortars, and anti-aircraft machine guns. Hundreds of tons of other types of military equipment were also sent south by Group 559 during this period, increasing the combat power of our full-time troops and enabling our battlefield forces to defeat the new enemy tactics.

In May 1962, Senior Colonel Vo Bam, Commander of Military Transportation Group 559, was given the honor of personally briefing Uncle Ho on our road building, transportation of supplies, and movement of troops to the battlefield and on the great and warm-hearted assistance being provided to Group 559 by our citizens and by the tribal ethnic minorities all along the transportation route. Uncle Ho praised the spirit of service and devotion of the cadre and men of Group 559. Uncle Ho counseled them that they must work well, they must work even harder, they must maintain secrecy and surprise, and must care for the welfare of the civilian population. Uncle Ho gave Comrade Vo Bam salt and flowered cloth to distribute to the local population.

As we expanded our overland transportation and troop movement routes, we also began to reorganize our sea transportation route after two trial voyages by the 603 Battalion during 1960. In February 1961 the Politburo and the Central Military Party Committee ordered the coastal provinces of South Vietnam to send boats to North Vietnam to pick up weapons. The Navy Department was ordered to study a strategic sea transportation route that could be used over the long term. On 23 October 1961 Military Transportation Group 759 was established. Comrade Doan Hong Phuoc was appointed Group Commander and Comrade Vo Huy Phuc was named Group Political Officer.

In late 1961 and early 1962 the provinces of Ca Mau, Tra Vinh, Ben Tre, and Ba Ria sent a number of cadre and soldiers in six motor-powered wooden vessels, which arrived safely in North Vietnam. On 8 April 1962, a vessel commanded by Comrade Bong Van Dia, which had been sent to reconnoiter the sea transportation route and that carried instructions from Hanoi, arrived at the Ghenh Hao pier in Ca Mau province. On 11 October 1962 a motor-powered wooden vessel built by Haiphong's Shipyard 1 and under the command of Comrades Le Van Mot and Bong Van Dia docked and unloaded the first maritime shipment of weapons at the Vam Lung pier in Ca Mau. A strategic sea transportation route from North Vietnam to the battlefield was now open.

From that time until the end of 1963, using secrecy and surprise, with small vessels disguised as civilian fishing boats, the cadre and soldiers of Group 759 crossed the stormy waters of the South China Sea and slipped past the enemy's blockade to deliver 25 shiploads of supplies. These supplies totaled 1,430 tons of weapons, including mortars, recoilless rifles, and 12.7mm machine guns for delivery to Military Regions 7, 8, and 9. For Cochin China, a battlefield far from the great rear area of North Vietnam and which Group 559's overland supply route did not yet reach, the timely arrival of these supplies was a welcome addition to our strength. This supply route provided additional weapons to our troops in Cochin China and extreme southern Central Vietnam for use in expanding their forces, including weapons that were capable of destroying the enemy's amphibious armored personnel carriers, small riverine vessels, and helicopters.

With the ever-increasing flow of reinforcements from the North and with local recruiting in the South, our armed forces in South Vietnam grew rapidly in numbers, in their scale of organization and equipment, and in combat capabilities. Between 1961 and 1963 our full-time army in South Vietnam increased by 250 percent.[41] Our local force troops grew in a rather uniform manner at the province and district level. Each province had one or two companies, and some of these companies had a strength of more than 500 cadre and soldiers.[42] Main force troops subordinate to the COSVN Military Affairs Section were organized into two regiments[43] and Military Region 5 had under its direct control three regiments and a number of specialty branch companies and battalions. In addition to captured enemy weapons, we also began to equip our main force and local force troops with infantry weapons,[44] mortars, recoilless rifles, anti-aircraft machine guns, and other types of technical equipment manufactured by our fraternal socialist allies. The balance of forces between our full-time armed forces and the enemy underwent an important change. In 1961 the balance of forces was one to ten in the enemy's favor; in 1962 the balance was down to one to five. This change represented a major failure for the United States and its puppets, because it meant that one important goal of the "Stalay-Taylor" plan, wiping out our revolutionary armed forces while they were still young and weak, now was unattainable.

Along with the expansion of our forces and the strengthening and improvement of our equipment, all battlefields worked on providing political education, ideological leadership, and technical and tactical training to our troops.

In early 1963 the Regional Party Committee and the Military Region 5 Military Party Committee launched a campaign of political activities for our Party chapters and armed units aimed at combating the appearance of rightist and negative tendencies, at combating fear of the enemy's armored personnel carriers, and at learning from our experiences in implementing the "two legs, three spearheads" formula for combating enemy sweeps and destroying "strategic hamlets." The Regional Party Committee decided that the region's main force units and provincial local force units would be concentrated for use in operational campaigns, supported by guerrillas and mass political struggle forces, to destroy the enemy's "strategic hamlets." The six-month operational campaign in early 1963 focused on the districts of Tien Phuoc and Tam Ky in Quang Nam province and Phu My and Hoai Nhon in Binh Dinh province. A number of members of the Standing Committee of the Regional Party Committee and of the Military Region Military Party Committee were sent to provide direct leadership to the movements in these districts. In other areas our units were ordered to cling to the local population, attack enemy forces conducting sweeps into our territory, expand attacks against lines of communications, destroy armored personnel carriers, shoot down aircraft, and conduct raids deep inside the enemy's rear areas.[45]

The battles fought by the soldiers and civilians of Region 5 in 1963 were ferocious, totaling 4,000 engagements, large and small. More than 20,000 enemy personnel (including 122 Americans) were eliminated from the field of battle and 337 enemy vehicles, including 40 M-113s, were destroyed. During the first six months of 1963 we took 250 hamlets, and the enemy recaptured 179 of them. The armed forces of Region 5 were gradually honed in combat and grew in maturity. The political struggle movement combined with armed struggle began to undergo a transformation, but the pace of change was slow. The achievements of our combat operations, especially armed operations in support of the people's efforts to destroy "strategic hamlets" in the rural lowlands, were limited.[46]

In Cochin China and extreme southern Central Vietnam, COSVN and the COSVN Military Affairs Section told all full-time armed units that they must fully understand that their primary responsibility during this period was to combat enemy sweep operations. "If we do not actively combat enemy sweeps and do not annihilate enemy forces during these sweeps, not only will we not be able to defeat the enemy plot to collect our people and establish 'strategic hamlets,' our own armed forces may also suffer attrition and slip back into a defensive posture."[47] For this reason, no matter where units were located they were required to have a plan to counter sweeps. Their plan was to be coordinated with local guerrillas and to be based on the use of combat villages or preprepared fortifications. Our troops were to commit themselves to wear down and annihilate enemy forces while preserving our own forces. Units were forbidden to engage in combat that would result in the destruction of our own units. On the other hand, units were to aggressively seek the enemy out to fight him, relying principally on such tactics as attacks on lines of communications, ambushing enemy forces while they were on the move, using sapper tactics to attack small outposts, assaulting enemy weak points, etc.

Pursuant to instructions from COSVN and from the COSVN Military Affairs Section, regional-level main force units and provincial- and district-level local force troops conducted timely reviews of each operational campaign and exchanged lessons learned after each battle, meticulously analyzing each and every combat action down to the individual and squad level, the command organization used by each cadre, etc. At the same time, the enemy's new tactical schemes were studied, especially his landing of assault forces by helicopter. Based on these reviews and analyses, our forces and units developed plans and carried out technical and tactical training in accordance with the struggle formula, the particular combat opponent, and the combat duties of each individual force and each unit. Comrade Vo Chi Cong, Deputy Secretary of COSVN, visited the battlefield in central Cochin China. Working with the Region 8 Party Committee and the My Tho Provincial Party Committee to analyze the situation and draw lessons from the combat experiences of our full-time troops, he and the Party Committees laid out the proper tactics for fighting the enemy as follows: besiege and force the surrender or withdrawal of outposts, stand and fight against enemy sweeps, liberate the rural areas.

In November 1962 the first conference of self-defense militia forces in Cochin China was held in the Duong Minh Chau base area. Thirteen localities that had strong guerrilla warfare movements[48] reported on their experiences in mobilizing the entire population to counter enemy sweeps, destroy "strategic hamlets," and build combat village and guerrilla militia forces. Sister Ut Tich (Tra Vinh province), Sister Ta Thi Kieu (Ben Tre province), and hundreds of other outstanding fighters in the guerrilla warfare movement being conducted in Cochin China were honored at the conference.[49]

RECOVERY OF REVOLUTIONARY FORCES IN THE SOUTH

During late 1962 and early 1963, after a period of difficulties, the armed struggle movement combined with political struggle in Cochin China began to recover and grow. On 13 and 23 September 1962 the 1st Company of the 514th My Tho Provincial Battalion, utilizing combat villages, repelled two puppet sweeps at Ca Nai Canal in My Long village, Cai Be district, and at Phu Phong village in Chau Thanh district. On 5 October 1962 the 1st Company drove off another sweep mounted by a puppet Ranger company, shooting down three helicopters in the process. Drawing lessons from these battles, the My Tho Provincial Party Committee instructed all localities to strengthen their combat villages and hamlets, plant wooden stakes in open fields to prevent enemy troops from landing by helicopter, expand guerrilla warfare activities to stretch enemy forces thin, and cooperate with our full-time troops to counter enemy sweep operations.

In Ca Mau, during a battle against enemy troops conducting a sweep, Guerrilla Fighter Nguyen Viet Khai shot down three enemy helicopters with his rifle. In the Plain of Reeds Combatant Doan Van Manh (261st Main Force Battalion of Region 8), who had been cornered by an enemy helicopter, used a submachine gun to fight back, forcing the enemy aircraft to fly away to save itself. This was a new phenomenon that contributed to a growing confidence in our ability to defeat the enemy's "helicopter assault" tactics. A movement to use infantry weapons to fire at helicopters was launched among the armed forces in Cochin China.

On 13 December 1962 the 1st Company of the Region 8's 261st Main Force Battalion and the 1st Company of the 514th My Tho Province Local Force Battalion, two units that often worked together in combating sweep operations, were stationed at Ap Bac [Bac hamlet] in Tan Phu village. This was a liberated village that lay within a contiguous liberated zone linking Cai Lay and Chau Thanh districts in My Tho province.

Discovering that revolutionary armed forces were located at Ap Bac, on 2 January 1963 the headquarters of the puppet 7th Division and the Dinh Tuong Subsector Regional Force Task Force, under the command of two American advisors (both colonels) and of puppet General Huynh Van Cao, Commander of the 4th Tactical Zone, immediately launched a large sweep operation designated "Duc Thanh 1/63."[50] The enemy divided his forces into many separate columns and advanced overland, by water, and by helicopter landings to carry out the tactic of "casting the net and then throwing the spear" with the goal of encircling and wiping out its opponents.

Relying on a network of fortifications and on the irregular banks of irrigation canals connecting to the Ap Bac Canal to establish a battle position blocking the spearheads of the enemy troop columns, and using orchards in the hamlet to move our forces and attack the flanks and rear of the enemy attackers, 1st Company of the 261st Battalion shattered the helicopter assault landing at Ap Bac, shooting down six H-21 helicopters. The company then repelled a ground attack, setting two M-113s on fire. Squad Leader Nguyen Van Dung and two soldiers of his 3rd Squad, 1st Platoon, closed with the enemy vehicles, using handheld explosive charges to knock out one M-113. The 1st Company, 514th Battalion, fought a fierce battle against an airborne battalion that had jumped into battle from 16 Dakota [C-47] aircraft. The Chau Thanh district local force platoon, fighting alongside one platoon of the 1st Company, 261st Battalion, fought off the enemy advance at the Ong Boi Bridge, organizing an enveloping force that attacked the flank and rear of the enemy force. The 261st Battalion's engineer platoon used mines to sink one enemy vessel on the Vam Kenh 3 Canal and shot up two other vessels, shattering an effort by two puppet Ranger companies to outflank our position by water.

The Standing Committee of the Province Party Committee and the My Tho Province Military Affairs Section, closely monitoring the developments on the battlefield, ordered the 2nd and 211th Companies of the 514th Battalion to mount an attack aimed at the Tan Hiep Firing Range and Than Cuu Nghia airfield to draw a portion of the enemy's forces away from Ap Bac. Political struggle forces of the masses were also mobilized to support the struggle. The people of the villages of Tan Phu, Diem Hy, and Tan Hoi surged out onto Route 4, blocking the road and halting the forward movement of enemy forces. One group marched to

Cai Lay town to conduct a face-to-face struggle, demanding that the enemy halt his sweep operation. More than 700 people from the villages of My Hanh Dong, My Hanh Trung, and My Phuoc Tay conducted a "reverse evacuation," moving in small boats to surround the enemy's 105mm artillery firing positions and demand that they stop the artillery barrages, which were destroying the houses and fields of the people.

The battle lasted from dawn until 2000 hours on 2 January 1963. The enemy regulars, outnumbering us by ten to one and using modern weapons and equipment, were forced to concede defeat and withdraw from Ap Bac. Enemy casualties totaled 450, including nine Americans. Sixteen aircraft were shot down or heavily damaged and three M-113s and one combat vessel were destroyed.

The Ap Bac victory proved that our full-time troops on the South Vietnamese battlefield, with appropriate force levels and adequately organized and equipped, with tactical and technical training, relying on a firm People's War battlefield posture and with the support of the political struggle forces of the masses, were capable of defeating sweep operations by the United States and its puppets using large numbers of troops and new tactics and modern weapons and equipment.

In warfare the defeat of your enemy's military strategies begins by defeating his principal tactical measures. The battle of Ap Bac marked the defeat of the tactics of "helicopter assault" and "armored personnel carrier assault" and signaled the bankruptcy of the "special warfare" strategy of the American imperialists.

Beginning with the Ap Bac victory, a "combined campaign" method of operations, combining the operations of our armed forces with those of our political forces, combining the military struggle with the political struggle at the campaign level of operations, began to take shape.

To exploit the Ap Bac victory, COSVN launched a movement throughout South Vietnam to "emulate Ap Bac, kill the pirates, and perform feats of arms." We had solved the problems of fear of enemy helicopters and of armored personnel carriers. Our cadre, soldiers, and the masses of the people became enthusiastic and trusted in our ability to destroy helicopters and M-113s and to defeat the puppet sweep operations.

After the Ap Bac battle the soldiers and civilians of My Tho province, combining armed struggle with political struggle, overran many enemy outposts, destroyed scores of "strategic hamlets" north and south of Route 4 in the districts of Cai Be, Cai Lay, and Chau Thanh, and moved our forces down to establish positions in Cho Gao and Go Cong districts. In Ben Tre, during July 1963 two provincial local force companies ambushed enemy forces at Go Keo in Giong Trom district, inflicting severe casualties on the 3rd Battalion, 12th Regiment, of the puppet 7th Division.

In western Cochin China in August 1963 two regional main force battalions and the Ca Mau province local force battalion, all under the command of Comrade Pham Thai Buong, Chief of the Region 9 Military Affairs Section, wiped out the Dam Doi and Cai Nuoc district military headquarters in one single night. The next day our units ambushed an enemy battalion sent in to relieve the local garrisons, shooting down ten helicopters. The population of Dam Doi and Cai Nuoc districts rose up and destroyed more than 100 "strategic hamlets." The Region 9 Military Affairs Section massed four battalions[51] and, using the tactic of "attacking a target and destroying relief forces," crushed four enemy battalions and shot down 20 helicopters.

In Long An in eastern Cochin China, province local force troops assaulted the Hiep Hoa commando training center in Duc Hoa district, killing 800 enemy and capturing many weapons. They then attacked the Go Den training center, killing hundreds of enemy troops.

In Thu Dau Mot, on 18 October 1963, the 5th Battalion, 2nd Regiment, annihilated an enemy regional forces company at Cay Truong in Ben Cat district. During this battle, Combatant Tru Van Tho used his body to cover the firing port of a bunker, heroically sacrificing his own life to enable his fellow soldiers to wipe out the enemy outpost.

Supported by our armed forces, the people of the lowlands of Cochin China conducted a second uprising campaign during the summer and fall of 1963, shattering the enemy's network of "strategic hamlets." Although the puppet army had many troops, they were stretched thin trying to cover everything and were unable to mass their forces to deal with the widespread attacks and uprisings being conducted by the soldiers and civilians of the lowlands of Cochin China. In 1962, we had destroyed 100 "strategic hamlets" but were only able to retain control of 15 of them. The enemy was able to rebuild the other 85 and to construct 100 additional "strategic hamlets." In 1963 the enemy was no longer able to rebuild the "strategic hamlets" that we destroyed. The liberated area in Cochin China grew back to the size it had reached during the time of insurrection in 1960.

In the cities, because of the effects of our armed operations and our movement to destroy "strategic hamlets," the struggles conducted by workers, laborers, students, Buddhists, etc., became more widespread and ferocious day by day. Some Buddhist bonzes immolated themselves in protest against the terrorist policies of the dictatorial Ngo Dinh Diem government. The contradictions between the Americans and their lackeys and within the puppet army and the puppet government became serious. In June 1963 U.S. Ambassador to Saigon Nolting was recalled. Henry Cabot Lodge was sent to replace Nolton. On 1 November 1963 the United States organized a coup in Saigon. Ngo Dinh Diem and his brother, Ngo Dinh Nhu, were murdered by lackeys of the Americans. The Saigon regime, the main instrument used by the American imperialists to carry out their neocolonialist policies of aggression, collapsed into a state of continual crisis from which it could not recover.

Taking advantage of the convulsions and contradictions within the puppet army and the puppet regime, all our battlefields increased their operations. In November 1963 the soldiers and civilians of Region 5 destroyed 424 "strategic hamlets" and liberated 219 mountain hamlets. In Gia Lai [Pleiku] province alone, 43,000 residents of 289 villages, representing all ethnic groups, rose up, destroyed the resettlement areas where the enemy had relocated them, and returned to their old villages and hamlets. In the lowlands of Cochin China popular uprisings broke out everywhere, destroying more than 1,000 "strategic hamlets" and capturing 1,500 weapons. This was an excellent opportunity for our soldiers to step up their attacks and kill large numbers of enemy troops. During the 1961–1963 period, however, our main force elements on the battlefields of South Vietnam had only recently been formed and had actually only begun to mass forces for combat operations at the battalion level after the Ap Bac victory. The level of training, equipment, and combat capabilities of our soldiers on the battlefield had improved, but not enough to keep pace with the demands of the situation.

By the end of 1963 the "National Strategic Hamlet Policy" of the Americans and their puppets had been bankrupted. This in turn brought about the total failure of the "Stalay-Taylor" plan and signaled the inescapable defeat of the American "special warfare" strategy. The ruling clique in the United States hurriedly prepared a new plan to expand their war of aggression.

With the results we had achieved in building a regular, modern armed force, and on the basis of our victories on the battlefield, beginning in early 1964 our army seized the initiative and firmly began a new period of combat, increasing our massed combat operations in South Vietnam, completely defeating the "special warfare" strategy of the American imperialists, providing a solid defense for the great rear area in North Vietnam, and moving the war against the Americans to save the nation forward into a new phase.

6

Intensifying Massed Combat Operations: Fighting alongside the Entire Population to Defeat the American Imperialist "Special War" Strategy

NEW AMERICAN AGGRESSION

During the final months of 1963, Vietnam became an increasingly difficult problem for the U.S. ruling clique. After the coup that overthrew Ngo Dinh Diem, the political situation in Saigon remained unsettled and "revolutionary forces made very rapid progress . . . controlling a very large percentage of the population in a number of key provinces."[1] Confronted with this problem, Johnson, who had just replaced Kennedy as President of the United States,[2] decided to carry out a secret program called "Switchback," turning the operations of the U.S. Central Intelligence Agency (CIA) in Vietnam over to the military. U.S. Defense Secretary McNamara and Chairman of the Joint Chiefs of Staff Taylor were sent to Vietnam to personally assess the situation and lay out a "stronger and more resolute policy" aimed at preserving the "vital national interests of the United States"[3] in Vietnam and the Southeast Asian region.

In February 1963 Johnson approved a plan prepared by McNamara and the Joint Chiefs of Staff to increase and expand their "special warfare" operations in Vietnam. The objectives of the plan were to "pacify" the rural areas, completely destroy the military and political organizations of the revolution, and gain control of the entire territory of South Vietnam. The plan also called for the use of airpower to attack North Vietnam and Laos to steadily increase the pressure on North Vietnam to force the North to stop sending support to South Vietnam.

In South Vietnam the United States and its puppets drafted more troops, increasing puppet troop strength by 45 percent as compared with 1962.[4] They adjusted their strategic deployments, using tactical areas and corps as strategic units and tactical zones and divisions as their basic campaign and tactical-level units. These changes enabled all levels of command to independently launch large-scale sweep operations in support of their "pacification" program.

123

In addition to the ten divisions of puppet regulars, the United States and its puppets expanded the number of Ranger battalions to serve as assault forces for sweep operations in each tactical area.[5] They also expanded their "special forces" to almost 23,000 soldiers and used them to patrol, detect, and block infiltration from North Vietnam down to the battlefields.[6] American support forces and those of their satellite nations more than doubled in comparison with 1962.[7] In terms of U.S. aircraft alone, aircraft operated by American personnel rose to 955 and the United States assumed primary responsibility for fire support and air transport.[8] Sweep operations from battalion up to division size increased from 2,948 operations backed by 10,336 air support sorties in 1963 to 6,492 sweeps and 14,749 air support sorties in 1964. Americans and puppet "special forces," located in 74 bases and over 100 camps all along the borders of South Vietnam, carried out thousands of military operations, reconnaissance missions, commando raids, and ambushes against our supply corridors from North Vietnam down to the battlefields.

With regard to North Vietnam and Laos, the American imperialists carried out "Operations Plan 34A" and arrogantly sent destroyers into the Gulf of Tonkin to collect intelligence and to perform acts of provocation and sabotage.[9] The United States also launched air attacks against Laos in preparation for deeper attacks against targets in North Vietnam beginning in the summer of 1964.

To carry out this plan, Johnson increased U.S. economic and military aid to the puppet government by $125 million. In April 1964 General Westmoreland was appointed to replace Harkins as Commander of the U.S. Military Assistance Command, and in June 1964 Maxwell Taylor replaced Cabot Lodge as U.S. Ambassador to Saigon.

This was a new war plan, a continuation of the "special warfare" strategy on a larger scale. It represented the high point of the "special war" strategy and the first step in the launching of a "limited war." Like their other plans for a war of aggression, however, the Johnson-McNamara plan was born out of a period of crisis in the puppet government and after they had lost the military initiative on the battlefield.

THE DECISION TO STEP UP INFILTRATION
AND SEEK A QUICK VICTORY

Analyzing the enemy's new war plans and activities, in December 1963 the 9th Plenum of the Party Central Committee again affirmed that the formula for the revolutionary liberation war in South Vietnam was to combine political struggle with armed struggle. Both of these forms of struggle were basic and both would play a decisive role, but the armed struggle would be the direct deciding factor in the annihilation of the armed forces of the enemy. The war would be protracted, but we should strive to take advantage of opportunities to secure a decisive victory in a relatively short period of time. With regard to leadership guidance, the Plenum decided it was necessary to seek every way possible to limit and defeat the enemy's "special war," at the same time preparing to deal with a large-scale U.S. imperialist "limited war."

To implement the above formula, "the key issue at present is for the entire Party and the entire population to make a maximum effort to rapidly strengthen our armed forces in order to achieve a basic shift in the balance of forces between ourselves and the enemy in South Vietnam."[10] With regard to force building, on the foundation laid by the vigorous development of our guerrilla and local force troops, we would place our main focus on expanding our main force troops. With respect to combat operations, we had to intensify mobile attacks in the strategic areas in order to annihilate puppet regulars and assign the decisive role on the battlefield to massed combat operations.

The Party Central Committee stressed that the conduct of our revolutionary war of liberation in South Vietnam was the duty of our entire nation. However, because of our policy of restraining the enemy and defeating him in South Vietnam, the form of participation in this effort by the Northern region of our country would be different from that taken by the South. It would be necessary to educate all cadre, Party members, soldiers of all our armed forces, and our civilian population to clearly understand the situation, to have a firm grasp of our struggle formula, and to increase combat spirit and readiness to perform their duties on any battlefield. The population and the armed forces in North Vietnam would have to increase economic and national defense capacity to even greater levels, supply all types of assistance to South Vietnam, and rapidly prepare to defeat enemy attempts to expand the war of aggression.

The 9th Plenum of the Party Central Committee (elected by the 3rd Party Congress) displayed a new level of maturity in our Party by its understanding of ideological theory and its ability to organize and implement actions for the resistance war against the Americans to save the nation. The resolutions approved by this Plenum on the "International Duties of the Party" and "Efforts to Move Forward to Gain a Great Victory in South Vietnam" laid out correct, timely policies and directions for our army's use in building up its forces, increasing its combat strength devoted to the defense of North Vietnam, sending main force troops to the South, and intensifying massed combat in South Vietnam in order to, shoulder to shoulder with the entire population, defeat the "special war" being conducted by the American imperialists.

Following the 9th Plenum of the Central Committee, both North and South Vietnam seethed with combat activities and combat preparations. The Central Military Party Committee and the Ministry of Defense decided to bring main force units subordinate to the High Command and to the military regions up to wartime strength and equipment levels in order to raise the size of the standing army to almost 300,000 by the end of 1964. Besides those cadre and soldiers being sent off to battle in South Vietnam as individual reinforcements and as "framework units," in 1964 our army began to send to the battlefield complete units at their full authorized strength of personnel and equipment. The General Staff directed units throughout the armed forces to intensify training and readiness activities so that, when the order was given, we could send battalions and regiments with their full authorized strengths in troops, weapons, and equipment to fight on the battlefields of South Vietnam. The 101st, 95th, and 18th Regiments of the 325th Division were the first mobile main force regiments to march south into battle as complete regiments. Each regiment setting off down the Trail left behind a number of officers, noncommissioned officers, and technical personnel to form a core around which, with the addition of more cadre and new recruits, we could establish a new regiment with the same unit designation.[11] The goal of this arrangement was to strengthen our combat forces without increasing the number of unit designations and to maintain and develop the combat traditions of the mobile main force divisions and regiments formed during the resistance war against the French. In later years other mobile main force divisions, including the 308th, 312th, 320th, 316th, 304th, 341st, etc., one after another marched off to fight in the South. Many divisions were cloned into two divisions, and some into three or four divisions, all with the same unit designation and all of which performed outstanding feats of arms in fighting the Americans and annihilating the puppets, adding new pages to the glorious histories of these divisions. This was an innovation in the art of force organization that responded to our need to rapidly expand our forces and to the increasingly heavy combat duties assigned to our army during the resistance war against the Americans to save the nation.

Along with our mobile main force units, our rear services and technical branches also implemented needed changes aimed at satisfying the material and technical needs of the battlefield and at supporting our units during their march to the South. Weapons warehouses, quartermaster warehouses, production facilities, repair stations, and hospitals shifted the direction of their production and support efforts. A number of repair stations for vehicles, machinery, weapons, and artillery, and a number of surgical teams and transit stations for the rearward transfer of wounded soldiers were formed and sent to the battlefield.

Along our strategic transportation route, the use of primitive forms of transportation was unable to provide sufficient capacity to support large-scale combat operations and to move entire battalions and regiments down the Trail. In early 1964, after being reinforced by the General Staff's 83rd and 98th Engineer Regiments and by the 325th Division's engineer battalion, Group 559 focused its personnel and equipment on building a road for use by motor vehicles crossing Route 9 all the way down to Bac and Ta Xeng. Our commo-liaison route was also reorganized, with appropriately configured way stations and the facilities and supplies needed by our troops on their march south. During the 1963–1964 dry season, Group 559 began to employ a method of transportation that combined primitive methods with motorized equipment, but made maximum use of motorized transportation. Because of these efforts, the quantity of supplies shipped to the battlefields in 1964 was four times greater than that transported in 1963. During 1964, almost 9,000 cadre and soldiers marched down our commo-liaison route to fight in the South. Included in this total were a number of full-strength battalions and regiments. A route to transfer wounded soldiers back from the battlefield also was established.

The sea transportation route, which the Navy had taken over in August 1963 and that used steel-hulled vessels capable of carrying over 100 tons, increased the frequency and volume of its supply shipments, sending many shiploads of weapons and a number of mid- and high-level Party and military cadre to the battlefields. Besides the sea transportation route to Cochin China, in late 1964 Navy Group 125 established a sea transportation route to Region 5, delivering supplies to landing docks at Vung Ro (Phu Yen province), Lo Giao (Binh Dinh province), Dam Thuy (Quang Ngai province) and Binh Dao (Quang Nam province). In 1964, using 20 steel-hulled and wooden-hulled vessels, the cadre and sailors of Group 125 delivered 88 shiploads of weapons, a total of over 4,000 tons, to the battlefields of Region 5 and Cochin China. Many of the heavy weapons delivered by sea helped upgrade the equipment of our main force units and supported a number of combat campaigns conducted in various strategic areas.

In South Vietnam, the Politburo of the Party Central Committee and the Central Military Party Committee implemented a number of measures aimed at strengthening our leadership and command arrangements, steadily perfecting our strategic deployment posture, and rapidly building up our mobile main force armies on the various battlefields.

In October 1963 the COSVN Military Party Committee and the COSVN Military Command [Bo Tu Lenh Mien] were established. Comrade Nguyen Van Linh, member of the Party Central Committee and COSVN Party Secretary, personally served as Secretary of the COSVN Military Party Committee. Lieutenant General Tran Van Tra, member of the Party Central Committee and Deputy Chief of the General Staff, was appointed Deputy Military Commander and Major General Tran Do was appointed Deputy Political Commissar of the COSVN Military Command.

The 1st and 2nd Infantry Regiments and Artillery Group 80 (with a total of five battalions), which were stationed in the base areas of eastern Cochin China, received additional troops and equipment and began training in massed combat operations at the battalion and regimental level. Rear Services Bases A, B, C, and E were transformed into the 81st, 82nd, 83rd, and 84th Rear Services Groups with a more mobile form of organization and method of operation. Each rear services group had warehouses for supply stockpiles, ordnance shops, clinics, transportation units, production teams, collection and purchasing teams, reception teams, etc., which were able to generate, receive, and transport supplies to various sectors and capable of supporting forces fighting in one campaign theater of operations. Eastern Cochin China was systematically developing into an offensive battlefield for the annihilation of enemy forces. COSVN's main force army was gradually taking shape.

In Region 5, Comrade Vo Chi Cong, member of the Party Central Committee and Deputy Secretary of COSVN, served as Secretary of the Region Party Committee and Political Commissar of the Military Region. On 1 May 1964 the Central Highlands Front, subordinate to Military Region 5, was established. Senior Colonel Nguyen Chanh, Deputy Commander of the Military Region, and Senior Colonel Doan Khue, Deputy Political Commissar of the Military Region, were assigned to serve as Commander and Political Commissar of the front.

The main force troops of Region 5, consisting of the 1st and 2nd Infantry Regiments[12] and a number of artillery and sapper battalions and engineer and signal companies, were stationed in base areas in the mountains and the contested areas of Quang Nam, Quang Ngai, and Binh Dinh provinces. Region 5, including the Central Highlands Front, became a combat battlefield for main force troops. The main force army of Region 5 had taken shape.

In this way in 1964 our armed forces were able to build up two mobile main force armies in South Vietnam. Although their numbers were small and their scale of organization still had only reached the regimental level, these battlefield main force armies enjoyed the advantage of a widespread people's war, had firm base areas, and had, in the great rear area of North Vietnam, a massive and continuous source of manpower, material supplies, and moral support. While building up their forces and while conducting combat operations, these armies always received firm and precise strategic guidance from the Party. These factors were of decisive importance in the expansion of our forces and the elevation of their combat morale, ensuring that our troops in South Vietnam would be able to overcome every obstacle and challenge to defeat the puppet main force army, which benefited from powerful American support.

PREPARATIONS FOR THE DEFENSE OF NORTH VIETNAM

Along with the strengthening of our forces and preparations for our main force troops on the battlefields of South Vietnam to intensify their concentrated combat operations aimed at annihilating enemy forces, preparations for combat among the armed forces and population of North Vietnam were carried forward in a very vigorous manner.

In March 1964, the Central Military Party Committee and the High Command decided to shift a portion of the armed forces, including the Air Defense–Air Force Service Branch, "from peacetime status to wartime status." Bomb shelters for personnel and fortifications to protect supplies and machinery were built by state agencies, factories, schools, hospitals, and along the city streets. Thousands of militia self-defense anti-aircraft cells and teams were formed, some of them equipped with 12.7mm anti-aircraft machine guns. Self-defense militia and the civilian population of many localities held practice combat alerts, practiced the evacuation of casualties, fighting fires, and rescuing victims from collapsed bunkers. They also practiced working with our soldiers to surround and capture enemy commando forces.

On 27 March 1964, Chairman Ho Chi Minh convened a Special Political Conference. In a report read to the conference, Chairman Ho Chi Minh reviewed the great victories achieved by the soldiers and civilians of both North and South Vietnam during ten years of struggle and construction. He clearly pointed out the plans and actions of the American imperialists in their war of aggression and stressed that the failure of their "special warfare" strategy was now inevitable. The proper method of resolving the Vietnam problem was to "end American intervention and withdraw American forces and weapons from South Vietnam. The internal problems of South Vietnam should be resolved in accordance with the spirit of the program of the National Liberation Front for South Vietnam."[13]

Chairman Ho Chi Minh announced that "if the American imperialists should be so reckless as to take action against North Vietnam, then they are certain to suffer a disastrous defeat, because the people of our entire nation will resolutely fight against them, because the socialist nations and the progressive peoples of the entire world will massively support us, and because even the American people and the peoples of the nations allied with the Americans will oppose them."[14] Uncle Ho appealed to every soldier and civilian in North Vietnam to "do the work of two people for the sake of our brothers and sisters in South Vietnam."[15]

The Special Political Conference was a Dien Hong National Conference held in a new era. Over 300 participants, including veteran revolutionaries, representatives of different occupations and social classes, delegates who had won the title of "Hero," soldiers who had won emulation awards, progressive intellectuals, and patriotic notables representing more than 30 million people of all ethnic groups of our entire nation demonstrated their complete solidarity with the Party Central Committee and with Chairman Ho Chi Minh in the resolve to fight to defend North Vietnam and to press forward with the revolutionary war to liberate South Vietnam and unify the nation.

The Secretariat of the Party Central Committee and the Cabinet of the National Government launched a movement among the entire armed forces and the entire nation to carry out Uncle Ho's wishes with an emulation campaign "for every person to do the work of two people for the sake of our brothers and sisters in South Vietnam."

During the summer of 1964 the acts of provocation and sabotage against North Vietnam committed by the American imperialists and the Saigon puppet regime became increasingly more numerous and more blatant. The "Kitty Hawk" aircraft carrier task force, armed with nuclear-tipped missiles, was sent to the South China Sea. A number of U.S. bomber squadrons were transferred from

American bases in Japan to bases in Southeast Asia. On 27 May a puppet commando vessel captured a civilian fishing vessel from Quang Binh province. During the evening of 26 June a puppet commando team landed on the coast of Tinh Gia district in Thanh Hoa province and destroyed a small wooden bridge along Route 1.

In June 1964 the Politburo of the Party Central Committee issued instructions to "increase combat readiness and smash the schemes of the enemy air force aimed at conducting acts of provocation and aggression against North Vietnam." The Politburo instructions specified that our armed forces in North Vietnam must be combat ready, must resolutely destroy any enemy violating the territory of North Vietnam, and must increase the level of support being sent to South Vietnam. The Politburo said our armed forces in South Vietnam must strike even harder blows against the enemy to support the defense of North Vietnam. We must actively assist revolutionary forces in Laos to consolidate and exploit the victories they have already won and join our Lao allies in intensified operations once the enemy began bombing attacks against North Vietnam.

These Politburo instructions were distributed all the way down to the secretaries of provincial Party committees and Party committee secretaries throughout the armed forces.

Pursuant to these Politburo instructions, on 1 June 1964 Colonel General Van Tien Dung, Chief of Staff of the People's Army of Vietnam, issued a combat readiness alert to all units of our armed forces in North Vietnam. Preparations for battle against the enemy's air force now became the pressing, immediate duty of our armed forces, and especially of the Air Defense–Air Force Service Branch and the Navy Service Branch.

Since early 1964, pursuant to orders from the Central Military Party Committee and the High Command, the Party Committee and the Headquarters of the Air Defense–Air Force Service had changed the missions of the Service from training and combat to combat and training. "Every activity must revolve around combat and take combat as its ultimate goal. When the enemy comes, we must be able to fight and to win. Before the enemy comes we must utilize the time available for training. We must combine training with preparations for combat. Training activities, political and ideological activities, arrangements to provide technical and material support to our units, everything must be tightly linked with combat readiness."[16]

The Air Defense–Air Force Service carried out a program of political activities to instill in our troops a full understanding of the new situation and the responsibilities of the Service in order to build their resolve to shoot down enemy aircraft immediately, during the very first battle. Because the Service's own forces were spread thin and were still using many different types of older weapons (85mm, 88mm, and 90mm guns),[17] the Air Defense–Air Force Command decided to concentrate an appropriate portion of its manpower and its firepower to defend key targets, at the same time organizing a powerful reserve force.[18] Lessons and training programs were updated and supplemented. Time spent in theoretical training was reduced and time spent practicing individual functions and techniques and practicing coordination between gun crews to shoot down the enemy's high-speed jet aircraft was increased. Besides Servicewide basic combat procedures, each unit established a specific set of combat procedures that foresaw different types of enemy attack (air attack, ground attack, naval attack), established proper courses of action, and covered command, supply, and technical support. These were important combat documents that provided a basis for honing the training of our troops and later were developed into official regulations on combat preparations in our air defense units.

Both in firing positions at strategic sites and while on the move, wherever there were air defense–air force troops, Party committees, governmental units at all levels, and the local population wholeheartedly provided assistance to them in manpower and material support by helping to build firing positions, giving these troops priority in receiving food supplies, and bolstering their combat spirit.

To combine training operations with combat operations, in April 1964 the Air Defense–Air Force Service sent the 234th Regiment to work with local air defense forces in Military Region 4 in conducting mobile operations and air-defense ambushes aimed against enemy commando aircraft operating over Nghe An. In June 1964 the 234th Anti-Aircraft Artillery Regiment and Military Region 4's 24th Anti-Aircraft Artillery Battalion were sent to the battlefields of Laos to provide combat support to our Lao allies. There these units shot down six enemy aircraft. Through these combat operations the Air Defense–Air Force Service gained a great deal of experience in command organization, movement of forces, deployment of forces, combat tactics, methods for providing supplies and technical support to units fighting far from their rear areas, and in reconstituting our forces following combat operations.

The Navy was brought up to wartime status on 6 July 1964. To deal with the ever-increasing acts of provocation and sabotage being conducted by the United States and its puppets along the coast of Military Region 4, the Navy Command decided to establish a forward headquarters on the Gianh River under the command of Comrade Nguyen Ba Phat, Deputy Commander of the Navy. A number of patrol boats were sent down from the north to reinforce the Southern area. Patrol boat units stationed along the coast of Military Region 4 left port and proceeded to anchorage areas from which they took turns in sailing out to sea to conduct operations. Our torpedo boats were lowered into the water and torpedoes were readied for combat. Coastal defense artillery units were ordered to Combat Readiness Condition 2. Headquarters staff agencies and military units located ashore hurriedly built trenches, bunkers, bomb shelters, and fighting positions. Cadre and soldiers who were on leave were recalled to their units.

By the end of July 1964 all preparations for combat by our armed forces in North Vietnam, and especially by the Air Defense–Air Force and Navy Service Branches, had essentially been completed.

THE GULF OF TONKIN INCIDENT

On 31 July and 1 August 1964, U.S. destroyers and puppet commando vessels continuously violated the territorial waters of North Vietnam. U.S. aircraft bombed the Nam Can border defense post and Noong De village in the western part of Nghe An province. On 2 August the American destroyer *Maddox* sailed deep into the Gulf of Tonkin. The General Staff and the Navy Headquarters ordered the 135th Torpedo Boat Group to resolutely punish any enemy vessel violating the territorial waters of the Fatherland. The 3rd Squadron, consisting of three torpedo boats under the command of Group Commander Le Duy Khoai, heroically attacked and drove off the *Maddox,* also fighting a fierce battle against modern enemy jet aircraft and shooting down one aircraft.

With only a few small vessels that had many technical weaknesses, fighting alone against both an enemy destroyer and enemy aircraft, our young Navy gained a glorious victory and struck a severe warning blow against the American imperialists. "The battle demonstrated the high fighting spirit and the determination to win of our entire armed forces and our entire population."[19]

On 5 August 1964, after systematic acts of provocation and sabotage and after fabricating the "Gulf of Tonkin incident" to deceive both the people of the world and U.S. domestic public opinion, the American imperialists openly used their air forces to attack North Vietnam, beginning an incredibly savage war of destruction conducted by large air and naval forces against an independent, sovereign nation. The enemy attack, code-named "Dart," sent 64 sorties of naval aircraft to strike four of our naval bases (Gianh River in Quang Binh, Cua Hoi in Nghe An, Lach Truong in Thanh Hoa, and Bai Chay in Quang Ninh) and the Vinh petroleum storage facility. With a high spirit of combat readiness and having been well prepared, our naval units, air defense forces, and local armed forces in the areas under attack opened fire, courageously striking back against the enemy's attack waves. They shot down eight enemy aircraft, both jet and propeller-driven (A4D and AD-6 aircraft), damaged many other aircraft, and captured one enemy pilot. The U.S. imperialists suffered a major defeat and were completely surprised and stunned.[20]

August 5 became Navy Day, marking the first victory of the heroic People's Navy. The victory of 5 August had an important practical significance to our armed forces. In our first battle against a surprise enemy air attack, our anti-aircraft artillery troops, sailors, and local armed forces, using ordinary air defense weapons (including obsolete 88mm and 90mm guns, machine guns, and rifles), shot down a number of modern jet aircraft on the spot and captured a pilot alive. After the battle the morale of our units was very high, and the prestige of the enemy air forces had been damaged. This was an important factor that aided us in building up our forces, boosting combat morale, and winning big victories in the future. Concerns and a lack of confidence in our weapons and equipment and in our ability to shoot down modern jet aircraft, which had previously surfaced among some cadre and soldiers, dissipated. The strengths and weaknesses of the enemy air force were subjected to scientific analysis based on practical experience. Positive lessons learned and weaknesses that surfaced during the battle, such as not accurately evaluating the tactical plans of the enemy air force, not correctly deploying our manpower and firepower, and not fully exploiting our opportunity to annihilate enemy forces, were reviewed and summarized by our units in a timely fashion.

On 7 August 1964, the High Command held a solemn ceremony to honor the units that had won the victory of 5 August. Chairman Ho Chi Minh attended the ceremony. Uncle Ho told the armed forces, "You have won a glorious victory, but don't become self-satisfied. Don't underestimate the enemy because of this victory. We must realize that, with regard to the American imperialists and their puppets, 'even in the face of death these leopards will not change their spots.' They still harbor many evil plots."

After the battle of 5 August, our previous predictions about the enemy's schemes and the forces and tactics he would use to attack North Vietnam now became clearer and more precise. Under the guidance of the General Staff, the Air Defense–Air Force Service quickly completed an overall combat plan clearly laying out the missions of the Service, combat plans, and the proper utilization of forces to deal with each step in the enemy's escalation of the air war.

One day after the victory of 5 August the 921st Air Force Fighter Regiment, after a period of training in a foreign country, returned to the Fatherland secretly and safely. For the first time in the history of our nation, our people's armed forces possessed modern jet aircraft. The organization of the Air Defense–Air Force Service took a step forward. Immediately after their return home the regiment's flight sections began training operations and initiated a combat alert system to maintain constant combat readiness.

Our anti-aircraft artillery and radar forces were reorganized to improve their ability to detect enemy aircraft at long range and to strengthen both our forces defending key targets and our mobile reserve forces.[21] All units analyzed the combat experience gained on 5 August for training purposes. The General Staff sent the anti-aircraft battalions organic to the 308th, 312th, 320th, and 325th Infantry Divisions to operate in the western portion of Military Region 4.

In November 1964 3rd Company, 14th Anti-Aircraft Battalion, 325th Infantry Division, which was defending the strategic transportation route at Cha Lo in western Quang Binh province, fought an outstanding battle, shooting down three enemy aircraft. During the battle Company Political Officer Nguyen Viet Xuan was severely wounded. He ignored his pain and continued to command and encourage his unit to fire directly at the enemy aircraft. The proud spirit, "Aim straight at the enemy—Fire!" of Martyred Hero Nguyen Viet Xuan provided a shining example and a powerful slogan to encourage our air defense–air force troops and our people's armed forces throughout the years of combat against the war of destruction conducted by the American imperialists.

SOUTH VIETNAM DEFEATS THE AMERICAN SPECIAL WAR

In South Vietnam, the armed struggle movement combined with political struggle, which grew powerfully and uniformly after the Ap Bac victory, defeated the objectives in the enemy's Johnson-McNamara plan right from the start.

Local force troops of the provinces of Cochin China, supported by guerrillas and the people's political struggle movement, repelled many sweep operations conducted by puppet regulars and destroyed or forced the abandonment of hundreds of Regional Force and Popular Force outposts. By the end of 1964 the soldiers and civilians of Cochin China and of extreme southern Central Vietnam had destroyed more than 3,000 "strategic hamlets" out of a total of 3,800 "strategic hamlets" built by the enemy. Liberated areas and areas in which the people had seized control expanded up to the very outskirts of the cities and towns. Bac Ai district in Ninh Thuan province and Duc Hue district in Long An province were completely liberated. In many lowland districts the enemy retained control only of the towns, a few surrounding villages, and the lines of communications.

Relying on our people's warfare battle posture and on the expansion of local armed forces, COSVN's main force regiments began to organize battles involving units of battalion and regimental strength. These battles were designed to counter sweeps, destroy outposts, support the masses in destroying "strategic hamlets," and to train and temper our troops. On 31 December 1963, 4th Battalion, 2nd Regiment, blocked enemy forces conducting a sweep in Duong Long hamlet, Thanh Tuyen village, Ben Cat district, Thu Dau Mot province. The 3rd Battalion, which was stationed nearby, immediately marched to the sound of the guns, and, fighting alongside 4th Battalion, inflicted severe casualties on the puppet 32nd Ranger Battalion. Fifty-seven enemy troops were captured along with more than 100 weapons. Developing this victory, the 2nd Regiment conducted a series of ambushes along Route 13, killing or eliminating from the field of combat hundreds of enemy in battles at Can Dam, Lai Khe, Cay Den, and other locations.

The 1st Regiment was operating in the Tay Ninh–Cu Chi area. In May 1964 the regiment ambushed and destroyed a puppet commando company at Bau Coi. In September and October 1964, the regiment launched a number of successful attacks and ambushes at Suoi Cao, Bau Tram, etc., eliminating from the field of combat two battalions of the puppet 9th Regiment from the 5th Division.

In Region 5, pursuant to COSVN's new policy of launching coordinated operations throughout South Vietnam, the Military Region Command initiated an operational campaign by all regional armed forces during the last six months of 1964 with the goals of annihilating enemy troops, strengthening our own forces, building strong units at the grass-roots level, supporting the effort to gain control of additional population, and destroying "strategic hamlets." Our province and district local force troops and guerrillas held onto the lowlands, fighting off enemy sweeps and preserving and expanding the liberated zone. The military region's main force troops concentrated their forces to fight a number of battles aimed at annihilating enemy troops and supporting the population in destroying "strategic hamlets."

To launch this wave of operations, on 1 July 1964 the 93rd Battalion, 2nd Regiment, ambushed 41 enemy military vehicles on Route 19 in Gia Lai [Pleiku] province. The 407th Sapper Battalion, supported by the 200th Fire-Support Battalion, attacked the puppet commando training center at Play-Co-Rong on 4 July. Many independent actions fought by our province and district local force troops and supported by main force elements achieved a high level of combat efficiency. These actions included a raid against the Nam Dong Commando Training Center in Thua Thien province, the annihilation of a Regional Force company at Trang An in Quang Ngai province, the destruction of the Phu Huu strong point in Binh Dinh province, and the destruction of the Chop Chai strong point in Quang Nam province.

On 9 August 1964, 90th Battalion, 1st Regiment, supported by seven recoilless rifles provided by the Military Region Headquarters, attacked the Ky Sanh "strategic hamlet" in Quang Nam province, wiping out the Regional Force and Popular Force troops stationed in the hamlet. The battalion then regrouped and took up battle positions to attack enemy troops coming to relieve the hamlet. The battalion succeeded in eliminating from the field of battle one enemy battalion and destroying eight M-113s. The Ky Sanh "strategic hamlet" was completely destroyed. This was the first battle in which Military Region 5's main force troops were finally able to defeat the enemy's "armored personnel carrier assault" tactics. Fear of M-113s, which had surfaced in a number of our cadre and soldiers, disappeared. The Ky Sanh victory demonstrated an innovative and effective method devised by the armed forces of Region 5 to destroy "strategic hamlets." It also demonstrated the ability of our main force units to stand their ground and defeat enemy regulars conducting sweeps across open low-lying terrain.

In December 1964, the 2nd Infantry Regiment and the 409th Sapper Battalion simultaneously attacked three enemy strong points and 11 enemy outposts in the An Lao Valley of Binh Dinh province, supporting mass uprisings that destroyed 38 "strategic hamlets." In these battles almost 700 enemy troops were killed or captured and 300 weapons were confiscated. An Lao district was completely liberated. This was the first time in Region 5 that our three types of troops, in coordination with political forces of the masses, had conducted operations throughout an entire district, and our attack was similar in nature to a combined offensive campaign.

Region 5's main forces and local forces had matured rapidly and well.[22] The region's self-defense militia had doubled in strength since 1963.[23] Supported by the armed forces, the people of Region 5 rose up and destroyed 1,485 "strategic hamlets" in the lowlands and 292 "strategic hamlets" in the mountains,[24] liberating 23 villages. In many areas the masses gained control of 15 to 20 interconnected villages with a total population of around 100,000. These areas lay along the coast and close to Route 1 and were linked to our bases in the mountains, providing a firm foothold where our main force troops could rest and from which they could move out to fight to destroy the enemy in the lowlands. The armed struggle movement combined with political struggle grew to a new level, keeping pace with the movement in Cochin China.

In Saigon and the cities and towns of South Vietnam the effects of our sapper and commando operations reverbrated throughout the nation and around the world. With only a few personnel and using perfect tactics, our sapper and commando soldiers attacked targets deep behind enemy lines, attacking the Caravelle and Brinks Hotels, the Kinh Do Theater, and the soccer field at the puppet General Staff Headquarters. Large numbers of American officers and technical personnel were gathered at these locations. Attacks were also made against many U.S. and puppet airfields and logistics installations, inflicting heavy damage on enemy equipment and delaying planned sweep operations. The most outstanding of these sapper/commando attacks were the sinking of the aircraft transport vessel *Card* at Saigon Port, the attacks on the airfields at Tan Son Nhat, Da Nang, Pleiku, and Soc Trang, the attack on the Nha Be petroleum storage facility, etc.

On 2 May 1964 Commando Nguyen Van Troi planted a mine under the Cong Ly Bridge in Saigon in an effort to kill U.S. Secretary of Defense McNamara. The attempt was discovered and Nguyen Van Troi was captured and murdered by the enemy. The courageous example of Martyred Hero Nguyen Van Troi, who gave his life in service to the high ideals of the revolution, was studied by our youth throughout the nation.

Working alongside the sappers, our artillery troops developed independent attack tactics, creeping deep behind enemy lines and mounting daring attacks that achieved a high level of combat efficiency. During the night of 31 October 1964, COSVN's 80th Artillery Group, escorted by the 5th Battalion of the 2nd Regiment and guided by guerrillas from the villages of Tuong Lan and Tan Tich in Vinh Cuu district, Bien Hoa province, covertly carried mortars and recoilless rifles across the Dong Nai River and shelled the Bien Hoa airfield, destroying 59 aircraft and killing hundreds of American pilots and technical personnel.

At a time when the Americans and their puppets were increasing their "special war" activities to the very maximum, were building many bases, airfields, military ports, strategic highways, and logistics installations, and were preparing to bring in a large American army to join the fight, these attacks by our sappers, commandos, and artillerymen constituted a sharp slap in the enemy's face. These attacks represented a new type of combat operation with a high level of combat effectiveness. Using elite elements of our three types of troops to attack enemy rear bases, kill valuable personnel, and destroy their implements of war became an effective tactic used by our soldiers and civilians in the resistance war against the United States to save the nation.

THE POLITBURO DECISION TO SEEK
A QUICK VICTORY IN THE SOUTH

In September 1964, the Politburo of the Central Committee met to assess the situation and approve a new policy. According to the Politburo assessment, the American imperialists were faced with major contradictions in their search for a solution that would rescue them from their current failed position in Vietnam. The solution being studied by Johnson and the American ruling clique, which they were making all-out preparations to carry out, was to send an American expeditionary army into South Vietnam and to launch an air war of destruction against North Vietnam. Our soldiers and civilians would have to very carefully guard against this possibility because the American imperialists were by nature aggressors and warmongers, because Vietnam occupied a very important position in the overall American worldwide strategy, and because the United States possessed enormous economic and military power. Neither the international situation nor the domestic situation in the United States, however, would permit the warmongers of the ruling class to immediately and all at once commit the full force of U.S. military might to the Vietnam War. Their biggest problem, and the factor that had led to the bankruptcy of every war plan the Americans had ever devised, was that on the battlefield the Americans and their puppets were gradually sinking deeper and deeper into failure and passivity. The Saigon puppet regime, the key force on which the United States relied, had been seriously weakened. The battle of Ap Bac and a number of other such battles had shown the Americans that it would be very difficult for the puppet regular army, even with powerful American support, to defeat the armed forces of the revolution in South Vietnam. The only reason the Americans and the puppets were able to stand up to us was because they still controlled the puppet army and because we were not yet militarily strong enough. Our main force army in South Vietnam was still weak and was not yet ready to mount massed combat operations to destroy the puppet regular army.

Our army and our people had new opportunities and new advantages on the battlefields of South Vietnam. The Politburo decided to mobilize the entire Party, the entire population, and the entire armed forces to concentrate all our capabilities to bring about a massive change in the direction and pace of expansion of our main force army on the battlefield, to launch strong massed combat operations at the campaign level, and to seek to win a decisive victory within the next few years.

Senior General Nguyen Chi Thanh, member of the Politburo of the Party Central Committee and Deputy Secretary of the Central Military Party Committee, was dispatched to the battlefield by the Politburo. Many high-level cadre with experience in building up main force units and in leading and directing massed combat operations were sent south with Comrade Nguyen Chi Thanh.

In October 1964 the Central Military Party Committee ordered our armed forces in South Vietnam to launch a campaign during the 1964–1965 winter-spring period aimed at destroying a significant number of puppet regular army units and expanding our liberated zones. Eastern Cochin China, the central part of Central Vietnam, and the Central Highlands would be the main battlefronts for this campaign. COSVN's main force units, which were directed to open fire first, would target their portion of the campaign on the Ba Ria–Long Khanh and Binh Long–Phuoc Long areas. The main force units of Region 5 and the Central Highlands were directed to conduct an offensive campaign against enemy forces in southern Quang Ngai province, northern Binh Dinh province, and the area west of Route 14 in Kontum and Gia Lai [Pleiku] provinces. In all other areas our armed forces would launch strong supporting operations designed to stretch enemy forces thin and to allow us to concentrate our main force units in the main theaters of operations.

The 320th Infantry Regiment,[25] the 545th Viet Bac Battalion, and a number of infantry and specialty branch battalions were ordered to set out immediately on a forced march to the battlefields of the South. In early 1965, Regiments 95, 101, and 18 of the 325th Division arrived in the Central Highlands,[26] where they were assigned to operate as independent regiments directly subordinate to the Central Highlands Front.

THE BINH GIA CAMPAIGN

In Cochin China, upon receipt of the Politburo resolution and of instructions from the Central Military Party Committee, COSVN's Military Affairs Party Committee and the COSVN Military Command began urgent preparations for an offensive campaign. One by one, the 1st and 2nd Infantry Regiments and a number of fire-support battalions arrived in War Zone D. Each unit received additional troops and equipment, was given additional tactical and technical training, and worked to increase the combat resolve of its troops and to motivate its personnel to accomplish new feats of arms. A number of cadre groups were sent to Ba Ria and Long Khanh provinces and to the southern districts of Binh Thuan province to study the situation and prepare the battlefield. Because these areas were far from COSVN's base area, close to Saigon and the enemy's strategic road network, and under tight enemy control, we encountered many problems in our efforts to prepare supplies for the campaign. Our plans called for almost 10,000 troops to participate in this offensive campaign, and the campaign was to last for some time, so our food and ammunition requirements were rather large.

COSVN's Rear Services Groups concentrated their forces and equipment to rapidly transport guns, ammunition, and food from COSVN bases to the campaign assembly area. Many rear services cadre went out to local areas to work with province and district supply committees to purchase food from the population. Some cadre traveled deep behind enemy lines and, evading the enemy's outposts and his strict control measures, purchased rice, medicine, and other necessities, which were transported to the designated points by many different means, such as Lambrettas, cars, oxcarts, motorboats, and human porters. Military proselytizing cadre even contacted a number of puppet officers and arranged for the use of enemy military vehicles to transport rice from Ba Ria and Saigon to our liberated areas. A military medical network was organized, based on our local provincial and district clinics. Group K10 and Group 1500 built piers at Phuoc Chi and Loc An to receive weapons being sent from North Vietnam by sea. It could be said that never since the winter-spring campaign of 1953–1954 had the eastern Cochin China battlefield seen such an enthusiastic atmosphere of campaign preparations. In only two months COSVN's rear services forces, with massive and enthusiastic help from the civilian population, shipped hundreds of tons of weapons and food to the campaign area.

In early November 1964 the 1st and 2nd Infantry Regiments, the 80th Artillery Group (with a total of four battalions), and a number of support units left War Zone D, crossed the Dong Nai River, and, dividing up to follow many different routes, marched toward the Ba Ria battlefield. On 20 November all units arrived at their assembly areas safely and in secrecy. Also participating in the campaign were three main force battalions from Military Regions 7 and 6,[27] Ba Ria province's 445th Local Force Company, and a local force platoon from Hoai Duc district in Binh Thuan province.

The COSVN Military Command organized a Campaign Headquarters to control our operations. Comrade Tran Dinh Xu was appointed as Campaign Commander, Comrade Le Van Tuong was appointed Campaign Political Commissar, and Comrade Nguyen Hoa was appointed Deputy Commander and Campaign Chief of Staff.

The campaign's objectives were to annihilate a portion of the enemy's regular forces and his local Regional Force and Popular Force troops; to intensify guerrilla warfare operations; to support the population in destroying "strategic hamlets"; to expand our liberated areas and link the base areas of eastern Cochin China to the coastal areas of Military Region 6; to protect the docking areas where we received supplies by sea; and to hone our main force troops in battle and increase their ability to conduct mobile operations.

On 2 December 1964, Ba Ria province's 445th Local Force Company attacked the Binh Gia "strategic hamlet" in Dat Do district while COSVN artillery shelled the Duc Thanh district military headquarters, kicking off our offensive campaign. These were very "sensitive" positions for the enemy because they were located in open terrain and because many of the families living in the Binh Gia "strategic hamlet" were the wives and children of puppet Marine Corps personnel. When we attacked the enemy would be compelled to send relief forces, and we would be able to mount a mobile attack and destroy the enemy while he was out in the open outside of his defensive fortifications.

Because our attack force was too small and because the enemy mounted a ferocious counterattack, however, our initial attack failed. In spite of this, faced with our growing pressure against Binh Gia, on 9 December the enemy sent the 3rd Armored Troop of the 1st Armored Regiment up Route 2 to relieve Binh Gia. Our 2nd Regiment, which was in hiding on Nghe Mountain [Nui Nghe], eight kilometers from the road, immediately moved out to attack. Arriving just in time, the regiment split the enemy formation and annihilated the entire armored troop, destroying 14 M-113s. Many of our cadre and soldiers fought very bravely. Company Commander Ta Quang Ty leaped on top of an enemy armored vehicle, using his submachine gun to kill the entire enemy crew, and then turning the vehicle's heavy machine gun around to place suppressive fire on the other enemy vehicles. Ty's fellow soldiers gave him the title of "the company commander who blocked the enemy."[28] Soldier Nguyen Van Xon, 20 years old, had his left arm crushed by an enemy vehicle. Ignoring his pain, with his right arm he threw a hand grenade, which blew the track off the enemy vehicle.

Phase one of the campaign ended. Our forces participating in the campaign were still at top strength and their combat spirit was still very high. On the night of 22 December an oceangoing vessel delivered 44 tons of weapons from North Vietnam to the dock at Loc An, providing a timely infusion of equipment to our units participating in the campaign. After more than half a month of combat operations the Campaign Command Section had gained a thorough understanding of the enemy's method of operations, especially the way in which it mounted relief operations by land and by air. This provided the basis for our troops to continue their attack, to develop a correct offensive posture, to lure the enemy to an area that we had chosen, and to fight a number of key battles.

On 27 December the 445th Company, reinforced by an infantry company of the 1st Regiment, launched a second attack on the Binh Gia "strategic hamlet." After occupying the hamlet our forces regrouped, dug fortifications, and prepared for an enemy counterattack. Artillery units, firing 75mm recoilless rifles and 82mm mortars, continued to shell the Duc Thanh district military headquarters.

On 28 December the enemy amassed 24 armed helicopters and 50 transport helicopters to land the 30th Ranger Battalion in an area southwest of Duc Thanh and to land the 33rd Ranger Battalion northeast of the Binh Gia "strategic hamlet." The 1st Regiment quickly attacked, wiping out part of the 30th Battalion and forcing the rest of the battalion to flee to Duc Thanh. Exploiting this success and learning lessons from a battle that had not been a clear-cut victory, that same afternoon the 1st Regiment maneuvered itself into a position that enveloped both flanks of the 33rd Battalion. The regiment pushed the enemy back into unfavorable terrain and wiped out the entire battalion, shooting down six enemy helicopters in the process.

Anticipating that the enemy would continue to send reinforcements, the Campaign Command Section ordered the 1st Regiment to redeploy and prepare to engage the enemy.

On 30 and 31 December, as the 4th Marine Battalion was in the process of landing to join the battle, the 1st Regiment dispatched one company to engage the enemy and lure him deep into a rubber plantation. This gave 2nd Battalion an opportunity to launch a frontal assault while 3rd Battalion swept around to the rear of the enemy formation. The battle grew extremely savage. The soldiers of 1st Regiment lowered the barrels of their heavy machine guns and recoilless rifles to fire directly into the enemy's ranks and used submachine guns and hand grenades to wipe out individual clusters of enemy troops. Combatants Le Van Dap and Hoang Dinh Nghia "ran back and forth, attacking and destroying the enemy wherever they could find him." The puppet Marine battalion was annihilated. We captured eight prisoners, including one American advisor who held the rank of captain, and confiscated all the enemy's weapons. After this campaign 1st Regiment was given the honorary name "Binh Gia Regiment."

Along Route 15 (the road from Saigon to Vung Tau), on 01 January 1965, the 2nd Regiment ambushed and annihilated a convoy consisting of ten vehicles and a company of enemy troops. Two days later the regiment attacked and inflicted severe casualties on the 35th Ranger Battalion, destroying a 16-vehicle military convoy, including two tanks and two M-113s, on Route 2 as they moved up from Ba Ria to Duc Thanh.

In the secondary theaters of operations, the main force battalions of Military Regions 6 and 7, working with local armed forces, overran many enemy outposts in Long Thanh district, besieged the Hoai Duc district military headquarters, supported the local populations in uprisings to destroy "strategic hamlets," and expanded our liberated zone.

On 3 January 1965 the Binh Gia Campaign ended in victory.[29]

In more than one month of combat our soldiers had fought five regiment-level and two battalion-level battles, wiping out two entire battalions of enemy regulars (including one battalion of the enemy's strategic reserve forces) and one armored troop and inflicting severe casualties on three other battalions.[30] Many "strategic hamlets" along Route 2 and Route 15 in Dat Do, Long Thanh, and Nhon Trach districts had been destroyed. Hoai Duc district was liberated. The Hat Dich base area in Ba Ria province and the southern portion of Binh Thuan province was consolidated and expanded, thereby protecting the sea transportation route from North Vietnam to eastern Cochin China and extreme southern Central Vietnam.

This was the first full-fledged campaign to be conducted by COSVN main force units on the battlefields of Cochin China and extreme southern Central Vietnam. During this campaign our soldiers made excellent logistics preparations, correctly selected the operational theater and the targets to be attacked, employed the proper forces and campaign combat tactics, and were able to annihilate entire battalions of enemy regulars, including even a battalion from the enemy's strategic reserve. Although the scale of the operations was small, the campaign was strategically important because it marked the beginning of a new era in our revolutionary war, the era of combining guerrilla warfare with conventional warfare, combining military attacks with uprisings conducted by the masses.

Comrade Le Duan, First Secretary of the Party Central Committee, made the following assessment of this campaign: The liberation war of South Vietnam has progressed by leaps and bounds. After the battle of Ap Bac the enemy knew it would be difficult to defeat us. After the Binh Gia Campaign the enemy realized that he was in the process of being defeated by us.

THE SPRING 1965 CAMPAIGN IN THE
CENTRAL HIGHLANDS AND MR-5

In Region 5, the Military Region Headquarters launched its own wave of operations during the spring of 1965, directing its main force units to fight massed battles using forces of battalion- and regiment-size and supported by local armed forces. These battles were aimed at destroying a portion of the enemy's regular army, supporting the people of the Central Highlands and of the lowlands of Central Vietnam in mounting uprisings to destroy "strategic hamlets," and exploiting the successes of the uprising campaign conducted during the fall of 1964.

The 101st and 320th Regiments overran or forced the withdrawal of a series of enemy outposts along Route 14 in Pleiku and Kontum provinces. The regiments also ambushed and inflicted severe casualties on the 2nd Ranger Battalion and the 1st Battalion of the puppet 42nd Regiment at Dak Long on 30 March 1965. The 409th Sapper Battalion attacked the Pleiku airfield and a U.S. military base called "Camp Holloway" on 7 February 1965, killing 100 enemy soldiers and destroying 20 aircraft. The 1st Regiment attacked the Viet An district military headquarters in Quang Nam, annihilating one enemy company and a battalion command staff and capturing two 155mm artillery pieces. The 2nd and 10th Regiments ambushed enemy forces at Nhong Pass [Deo Nhong]–Duong Lieu in Binh Dinh province, inflicting losses that rendered two infantry battalions and one troop of armored personnel carriers combat ineffective.

After these successes in annihilating or inflicting heavy casualties on a number of enemy regular battalions and wiping out or dispersing a significant portion of the enemy's armed forces at the grass-roots level, the main force troops of Military Region 5 and the Central Highlands worked with local armed forces to support the people in uprisings that destroyed almost all of the enemy's "strategic hamlets" in Central Vietnam, liberating 2.5 million of the three million residents of the rural lowlands. In many areas the puppet governmental structure at the grass-roots level was completely destroyed and a people's government was established. The enemy's "strategic hamlets" now became our own combat hamlets and villages.

Together with the COSVN main force units, the main force troops of Region 5 and the Central Highlands had progressed to the point of being able to conduct massed combat operations at the battalion and regimental level, wiping out companies of enemy regulars on a routine basis and taking the first step toward annihilating entire enemy battalions.

THE WAR ESCALATES IN THE NORTH AND THE SOUTH

The puppet army, "the backbone of the special war," was in danger of annihilation. U.S. Secretary of Defense McNamara, returning from an inspection trip to South Vietnam, was forced to confess that "the U.S. has failed militarily in South Vietnam." General Westmoreland, Commander of the U.S. Military Command in Saigon, said that "if the situation continues to move in this direction, the Government of the Republic of Vietnam (the puppet regime) will not be able to survive for more than six months."

In order to redeem this failure, Johnson and the American ruling clique decided to send U.S. combat forces to South Vietnam, to mount powerful and continuous air attacks against North Vietnam, to elevate their "special war" to the highest possible level, and to make preparations so that, when the situation became desperate, U.S. soldiers could be sent to engage in large-scale combat operations in accordance with the U.S. strategy of "limited war."

On 7 February 1965, American air forces launched an attack called "Flaming Dart," bombing the towns of Ho Xa in Vinh Linh province and Dong Hoi in Quang Binh province. On 2 March they began a series of continuous large-scale attacks, which they called "Rolling Thunder," against many targets throughout the territory of North Vietnam.

On 8 March 1965, following in the footsteps of French colonialist aggressor troops more than 100 years before, the American 3rd Marine Battalion landed in Da Nang.

Faced with this intensified and expanded war of aggression by the American imperialists, a session of the Central Military Party Committee in February 1965 and the subsequent 11th Plenum of the Party Central Committee in March 1965 approved a number of important decisions aimed at expanding our armed forces in accordance with our plan for wartime force development, switching the entire economy of North Vietnam over from peacetime production to wartime production and further expanding the role of North Vietnam as the great rear area for the great front lines in South Vietnam. In this new situation the people and armed forces of North Vietnam would conduct economic production, at the same time fighting to defeat the American imperialist air campaign against North Vietnam and keeping our transportation artery to the battlefield open. The people and armed forces of South Vietnam were directed to maintain the initiative on the battlefield, to maintain a strategic offensive posture, to lure puppet regular troops out to mountain jungle regions and to other selected areas where we could destroy them, to launch strong popular movements to incite the people to rise up and destroy "strategic hamlets," to expand our liberated zones, and to intensify the operations of our sapper and commando troops and the people's political struggle movement in the cities. Our goals were to destroy so much of the enemy's regular army that it could no longer serve as the backbone of the puppet regime; to drive the Saigon puppet regime further into weakness and crisis;

even if the American imperialists sent a flood of expeditionary troops onto the battlefield, to cause the United States and its puppets to sink deeper into a passive and reactive posture.

During the spring of 1965, while resolve to fight and defeat the Americans swept across our entire nation, the 325th Division, the 21st, 22nd, 23rd, 33rd, 42nd, 66th, and 88th Infantry Regiments, and scores of sapper, artillery, and other specialty branch battalions poured down the Annamite Mountain chain, marching to the battlefront. The General Rear Services Department formed truck battalions that drove from Hanoi all the way down to Route 9. Group 559 was directed to increase its use of motorized means of transportation to speed the flow of weapons, rice, and other essential supplies to Region 5, the Central Highlands, and Cochin China. In January 1965 eight supply ships sent by Navy Group 125, each carrying around 50 tons of weapons, unloaded their cargoes in Ca Mau, Ben Tre, Ba Ria, Phu Yen, etc.

THE SUMMER 1965 CAMPAIGN IN SOUTH VIETNAM

In South Vietnam, developing the victory achieved by our 1964–1965 winter-spring campaign, the COSVN Military Party Committee, the COSVN Military Command, and the Headquarters of Military Region 5 launched a new wave of operations during the summer of 1965 aimed at maintaining the initiative, inflicting greater defeats on the puppet regular army, and administering an initial thrashing to the American aggressor army.

The main force regiments of Military Region 5 and the Central Highlands Front overran a series of enemy strong points along strategic Routes 14, 19, 7, and 21 and helped the local population to destroy dozens of "strategic hamlets" and expand the liberated zones in the northern and southern portions of the Central Highlands. On 28 May, Quang Nam province local force troops assaulted positions held by a company of U.S. Marines at Nui Thanh [Thanh Mountain], virtually annihilating the entire company. The Nui Thanh victory greatly stimulated the desire to fight the Americans and built confidence throughout our nation in our ability to defeat the Americans.

In northern Quang Ngai province Military Region 5 Headquarters began preparations for an offensive campaign that would use our main force units to destroy a portion of the puppet 25th Division. Comrade Tran Kien, member of the Standing Committee of the Regional Party Committee and Chief of Military Region Rear Services, was sent to the districts of Son Tinh, Binh Son, and Tra Bong to work with lower-level Party committees to collect food, mobilize civilian porters, and establish supply caches. Comrade Huynh Huu Anh, Deputy Chief of Staff of the Military Region, led a group of cadre to study the battlefield and develop a battle plan.

In May 1965, the Military Region's main force 1st Regiment, under the command of Le Huu Tru, marched from Quang Nam down to northern Quang Ngai to launch an offensive campaign in Ba Gia alongside local armed forces. The campaign began during the evening of 25 May when the Son Thinh district local force platoon attacked the Phuoc Loc Popular Forces outpost. This action lured the puppet 1st Battalion, 51st Regiment, out from the Go Cao outpost in Ba Gia to relieve our pressure on Phuoc Loc and enabled 1st Regiment to surround and destroy this entire battalion.[31]

On 30 May, the puppet 1st Corps hastily ordered the 39th Ranger Battalion, the 3rd Marine Battalion, and 2nd Battalion, 51st Regiment, all organized into a regiment-sized task force, to mount an operation to relieve Ba Gia. The 1st Regiment, reinforced by the Military Region's independent 45th Infantry Battalion, massed its forces to fight the key battle of the campaign, essentially annihilating the puppet task force on the road from Son Tinh to Ba Gia, and then assaulting and destroying the last remnants of the task force as they retreated to positions at Chop Non, Phuoc Loc, High Point 47, and Ma To.

Coordinating their actions with the military attack, on 3 June the Quang Ngai Province Party Committee mobilized 100,000 civilians from all districts of the province to gather at the province capital to demand the return of their husbands and children and creating a great commotion. The puppet army and the puppet administration in Quang Ngai were confused and severely shaken. Seizing this opportunity, our local armed forces and the political forces of the masses coordinated their actions to force dozens of outposts to surrender or withdraw, destroying entire networks of "strategic hamlets" and liberating the bulk of the rural lowlands and mountains in Quang Ngai province.

Between 10 and 25 June, 1st Regiment, working with local armed forces, destroyed the enemy's apparatus of oppression and liberated five villages with a total population of 15,000 civilians. Between 4 and 20 July the regiment overran the Ba Gia outpost and liberated three villages along an 11-kilometer stretch of road from Tra Bong to Ba Lanh.

During 51 days of heroic combat, the 1st Regiment, operating under the direct command of the Military Region Headquarters and supported by our local armed forces and civilian population, had skillfully outmaneuvered the enemy, utilized appropriate fighting methods, destroyed five battalions of puppet regulars,[32] and supported the civilian population of 29 villages in six districts[33] in uprisings to seize power, liberating almost 200,000 people. For the first time in the history of the South Vietnamese battlefield our troops had annihilated an enemy regiment-sized task force, the largest combat formation used by the puppet regulars at that time, thereby defeating their tactic of conducting relief operations using regiment-sized task forces. After this victory the 1st Regiment was given the title of "Ba Gia Regiment."

In eastern Cochin China, after the end of the Binh Gia campaign, COSVN Military Command recalled its main force regiments to War Zone D. Each unit reviewed and drew lessons from its combat experience, received additional personnel and equipment, allowed its troops to rest and recuperate, and conducted technical and tactical training. The 3rd Infantry Regiment was formed and added to COSVN's main force formation. The main force battalions of Military Region 7 were gathered together to form a new mobile main force regiment, 4th Regiment, directly subordinate to the Military Region.

After more than two months of consolidation and training in early May 1965 the bulk of the main force units subordinate to COSVN and Military Region 7, including four infantry regiments,[34] two independent infantry battalions, the 80th Artillery Group, and assorted specialty branch units, marched out to conduct another campaign.

According to the COSVN Military Command's campaign plan, which had been approved by the General Staff, the campaign area was rather large. The main theater of operations would be the provinces of Binh Long and Phuoc Long, and secondary theaters of operations included five provinces: Lam Dong, Binh Thuan, Ba Ria, Long Khanh, and Bien Hoa. This area was a mountainous, jungle-covered region that was sparsely populated and economically very poor. For this reason, in early 1965 the COSVN Rear Services Department established a rear services apparatus for the campaign. The core elements of this apparatus, the 81st and 83rd Rear Services Groups, worked with the rear services organization of Military Region 6 and COSVN's Forward Supply Council to mobilize thousands of civilian porters and assault youth. These porters and assault youth alone contributed 140,000 man-days to support the campaign.

The goals of the campaign were to annihilate a significant portion of the puppet regular army, to intensify guerrilla warfare operations, to support the masses in destroying "strategic hamlets," and to expand the liberated zone and link COSVN's bases with the southern Central Highlands in order to extend our strategic transportation route from North Vietnam down to Cochin China and extreme southern Central Vietnam.

A campaign headquarters was established. Major General Le Trong Tan, Deputy COSVN Military Commander, was named Campaign Military Commander and Major General Tran Do, Deputy COSVN Military Command Political Commissar, was named Campaign Political Commissar. Senior Colonel Hoang Cam was appointed Campaign Chief of Staff.

On the night of 11 May 1965, the 1st Battalion of the 2nd Regiment, supported by the regiment's organic artillery units, opened fire to launch the campaign with an attack against enemy forces holding fortified positions at the Phuoc Binh District military headquarters. The enemy position was completely annihilated within 25 minutes. That same night the 1st Battalion of the 1st Regiment, Military Region 6's main force 840th Battalion, and a sapper platoon launched coordinated attacks that captured many individual targets inside Phuoc Long city. The enemy massed his helicopters to bring in, one at a time, four battalions to relieve the city. Because we had not correctly anticipated where the enemy would land, our units missed an opportunity to annihilate the enemy.

On 9 June, kicking off the second phase of the campaign, 2nd Regiment, reinforced by a battalion of the 3rd Regiment and supported by artillery and flamethrowers, fought the key battle of the campaign, overrunning the Dong Xoai district military headquarters. Following this victory the regiment maintained control of this area, forcing the enemy to send in relief forces. The 1st and 3rd Regiments, launching their attack at the correct moment, annihilated three battalions of puppet regular troops, one of which was the 7th Airborne Battalion from the puppet's strategic reserve forces.

In honor of this glorious victory 2nd Regiment was given the title "Dong Xoai Regiment."

Between 15 and 22 July (phase three of the campaign) our troops continued attacks throughout the campaign area of operations, securing a number of additional victories. The most outstanding of these was an attack by 2nd Regiment that annihilated an entire infantry battalion and an armored troop at Bau Bang and an attack made by Military Region 6's 840th Battalion, reinforced by elements of the 3rd Regiment, which destroyed the Bu Dop commando training center.

In the secondary theaters of operations Military Region 7's main force 4th Regiment, together with provincial and district local force troops, fought many battles along Routes 1, 2, 13, 14, 15, and 20, isolating the battlefield and blocking enemy relief forces trying to move by road. Our forces supported popular uprisings that destroyed scores of "strategic hamlets," liberated 56,000 of the 67,000 residents of Phuoc Long province, and expanded the liberated zone of eastern Cochin China, linking it to the southern Central Highlands. This made it possible to significantly expand the strategic transportation route from North Vietnam to Cochin China and extreme southern Central Vietnam.

The victories won by the soldiers and civilians of eastern Cochin China in the Dong Xoai Campaign exceeded the goals set by the COSVN Military Party Committee and COSVN Military Command. For example, looking just at the number of enemy troops eliminated from the battlefield, this total reached 4,000 enemy troops, including 73 American advisors. Four battalions of enemy regulars, including an airborne battalion from the strategic reserve forces and dozens of enemy Regional Forces companies, were wiped out or suffered heavy casualties. Large quantities of war equipment were destroyed or captured by our forces.[35]

The Binh Gia, Ba Gia, and Dong Xoai Campaigns marked a new step forward in the ability of our main force troops on the South Vietnamese battlefields to conduct massed combat operations.

The puppet army was the enemy's key tool in conducting the "special war." The American imperialists had spared no effort or expense in building, equipping, and training this army. During military sweep operations, U.S. advisors exercised direct command over puppet forces down to the battalion level and provided these troops with air cover, artillery support, and transportation support using both vehicles and helicopters. In spite of this, however, the puppet army could not withstand the overwhelming and ever-increasing attacks of our people and our armed forces. When they encountered our main force troops in the Binh Gia, Ba Gia, and Dong Xoai Campaigns and in many other battles, many battalions of puppet regulars, including even battalions from their strategic reserve forces, were wiped out. The enemy's "helicopter assault" and "armored personnel carrier assault" tactics had been defeated on the campaign level of operations.

The puppet army could no longer fulfill its role as the primary tool for the conduct of the neocolonialist war of aggression being carried out by the American imperialists. The puppet army was now confronted with the prospect of annihilation and disintegration. In the face of this calamitous situation, the American imperialists were forced to send their own expeditionary army to the battlefield to rescue the puppet army. Their "special war" strategy had been bankrupted. Driven into a posture of passivity and defeat, the American imperialists had to switch to a "limited war" strategy. The resistance war against the Americans to save the nation had moved into a new phase.

Following the period of army building under the first five-year military plan (1955–1960), between 1961 and 1965 our army underwent a period of both force building and combat and reached a new level of maturity.

During this period our nation was both at peace and at war. In North Vietnam our people took advantage of the years and months while we still enjoyed peace to concentrate on implementing the first five-year plan to build the technical and material bases of socialism, significantly increasing our economic and military power.

The accomplishments of the five-year plan greatly encouraged our people, engendering among the population and the armed forces of both North and South Vietnam an unshakable spiritual power and an ever-increasing material power for use in the cause of resisting the Americans, liberating South Vietnam, and unifying our nation.

Relying on the great rear area of North Vietnam, our armed forces were built up rapidly in accordance with the second five-year military plan (1961–1965), significantly increasing their level of modernity and professionalism. During the first three years (1961–1963), while North Vietnam was still at peace and needed to concentrate its forces on the work of economic construction, our army successfully resolved problems of force strength and organization, maintained a standing army with an appropriate strength level, vigorously built up a reserve force, expanded our cadre ranks, established a technical and material base, satisfied our immediate combat readiness requirements, and made preparations to expand our forces whenever war broke out. Within the standing army, based on the dual missions of defending North Vietnam and liberating South Vietnam, our army focused on building up mobile main force units and technical specialty branches, with priority given to air defense–air forces, artillery, sappers, etc. After summarizing and drawing lessons from our experiences in force building and combat operations during the resistance war against the French and during the ongoing fighting in South Vietnam and Laos, our army intensified practical training applicable to the realities of combat and increased the command and organizational abilities of our cadre and the technical and tactical skills of our soldiers to enable us to conduct massed combined arms combat operations. In order to fulfill our combat duties in South Vietnam, our armed forces rapidly opened supply transportation routes both on land and at sea, sending an ever-increasing stream of reinforcements, entire units, weapons, and other supplies to the battlefield.

Beginning in mid-1964, after our initial glorious victory over the modern American air force, our armed forces switched all our forces over to wartime status.

During our history of force building and combat, for the first time our army had been able to concentrate on force building for an extended period of time[36] under peacetime conditions. Our army had gained a great deal of experience in building modern, regular forces in accordance with a long-term plan; in resolving issues involving the relationship between force building, combat readiness, and combat operations; and in establishing the relationship between force building and defense in North Vietnam and intensifying the revolutionary war in South Vietnam.

The ten years we spent building a modern, regular force (1954–1964) was a very important period. Using a formula for correctly building up our forces, maintaining a high resolve, and with an excellent organizational system for implementing these measures, our army made clear and significant improvements in its combat power. At the same time the army created organizations that enabled it to expand its forces and successfully accomplish our ever-growing, ever more urgent, and ever more complicated force building and combat missions during subsequent phases.

In South Vietnam, the liberation armed forces were born and grew out of the political forces of the masses. With vigorous support from North Vietnam they developed an ever more complete organizational structure for the three types of troops. With our experience in force building during the period of resistance warfare against the French and relying on reinforcements received from North Vietnam, especially for cadre and technical personnel, elements of our army serving on the battlefields of South Vietnam overcame many difficulties and much confusion with regard to the organizational scale and methods for employing main force troops. Finally, our army in the South developed innovative and effective methods for defeating even the most effective tactics employed by the United States and its puppets. The massed combat operations of our main force troops during operational high points and campaigns destroyed a significant portion of the enemy's regular forces, rapidly shifted the balance of forces in our favor, and contributed, along with the efforts of the entire population, to the defeat of the enemy's "special war."

In conducting a revolutionary war against an economically and militarily powerful enemy aggressor like the American imperialists, our Party, our people, and our army innovatively developed the tactics of political struggle combined with armed struggle, fighting the enemy in all three strategic areas (the mountains, the rural lowlands, and the urban areas), and attacking the enemy with political forces, military forces, and military proselytizing. The three types of troops in the armed forces all had to firmly grasp these struggle tactics and could only achieve victory in combat through their proper utilization. At the same time our troops had to constantly maintain a firm understanding of the laws of warfare, combining guerrilla warfare with conventional warfare and developing the vital role of our main force troops as the core force for use in armed struggle and revolutionary war. This was a valuable, practical lesson for our soldiers and civilians prior to the outbreak of large-scale combat operations against the American expeditionary army.

On 22 December 1964 our armed forces celebrated their 20th birthday. This glorious anniversary was marked by a glorious feat of arms as the armed forces, shoulder to shoulder with the entire population, defeated the "special war" strategy of the American imperialists.

Chairman Ho Chi Minh attended a solemn ceremony celebrating this tradition day of the armed forces. Uncle Ho said,

> Our armed forces are loyal to the Party, true to the people, and prepared to fight and sacrifice their lives for the independence and freedom of the Fatherland and for socialism. They will complete every mission, overcome every adversity, and defeat every foe. . . . Our armed forces have unmatched strength because they are a People's Army, built, led, and educated by the Party.[37]

These sacred words from Uncle Ho were a source of great strength to our army during a period of fierce and pressing challenges as our army entered into a new battle, and, together with our entire population, wrote one of the most glorious pages in the history of our nation and our army.

PART III

The People's Army of Vietnam
Simultaneously Fights and Conducts Force
Building and, Together with the Entire
Population, Defeats the "Limited Warfare"
Strategy of the American Imperialists,
1965–1968

7

Rapidly Expanding Our Forces
and Continuing the Offensive:
Initial Victories over the Americans

GENERAL SITUATION

After the Ap Bac victory in January 1963, our People's War against the Americans to save the nation expanded rapidly. Our great, successive victories at Binh Gia, Ba Gia, and Dong Xoai, the high tide of insurrection that secured and expanded the power of the people in the rural lowlands and in the mountains, and the rising struggle movement of the urban population "caused the three principal pillars supporting the American imperialists in their war of aggression in South Vietnam: the mercenary armed forces and puppet government, the network of 'strategic hamlets,' and the cities and urban areas, to either collapse or be badly shaken."[1]

With their "special warfare" strategy facing the prospect of total defeat, in early 1965 the American imperialists began to send U.S. and allied combat forces to South Vietnam slowly, one unit at a time. They also expanded their air and naval operations, bombing and shelling North Vietnam. In July 1965 Johnson approved General Westmoreland's "search and destroy" strategy and Westmoreland's three-phase plan[2] to use the American expeditionary army to pursue their main objective of "breaking the back of the Viet Cong," using American troops to support the puppet army. According to this plan, the United States would send to South Vietnam 44 battalions and a total of 193,887 troops. With this decision the American war of aggression exceeded the scope of the "special warfare" strategy and became a "limited war."

In July 1965 the U.S. Army Support Command in South Vietnam became the U.S. Army Command. General Westmoreland, who formerly commanded the U.S. 101st Airborne Division and the U.S. Military Academy, was appointed Commander of the U.S. Military Headquarters in Vietnam. The 1st Logistics Command, the 3rd Marine Amphibious Force, and a Field Force Headquarters (equivalent to a corps) were established. The number of U.S. expeditionary troops in South Vietnam increased from 23,000 in January 1965 to 60,000 in June 1965, then exploded to 184,000 in December 1965. Many of the most elite divisions and brigades of the U.S. armed forces, together with a large quantity of war equipment, were committed to the war of aggression against Vietnam.[3] The 1st Air Cavalry Division, which was formed in 1961 and was equipped with 465 helicopters, was sent to Vietnam in September 1965.

Following on the heels of the Americans were 20,000 satellite troops, made up of the South Korean Capital (Tiger) Division, the South Korean 2nd Marine Brigade, the 1st Royal Australian Infantry Battalion, and a New Zealand artillery battery.

All forces subordinate to the U.S. Pacific Command, the U.S. military bases in Guam, the Philippines, Japan, and Thailand, and the U.S. 7th Fleet were mobilized to provide combat and logistics support to this army of aggression.

As for North Vietnam, the American imperialists expanded their war of destruction, using air and naval forces to block the flow of support from North Vietnam to the South, to destroy the economic and military power of North Vietnam, and to suppress the spirit of resistance of our soldiers and civilians. "From a program that was primarily political and psychological" it became "a continuous bombing program with greater military significance,"[4] and this war of destruction became an integral part of the "limited war" being conducted by the American imperialists.

In Laos the Americans expanded their "special war," pushing the rightist army to attack the Pathet Lao army, using airpower to bomb the liberated areas in Laos, and sabotaging the tripartite coalition government. In Cambodia, the Americans used aircraft to strafe and bomb villages along the Vietnamese-Cambodian border and pressured the Royal Cambodian Government to abandon its policy of peace and neutrality.

The armed forces of the American aggressors tramped over the soil of the Southern portion of our Fatherland. American aircraft bombed and destroyed factories, schools, and hospitals, murdering civilians in North and South Vietnam and in the nation of Laos. They used poison gas, napalm, and carpet-bombing B-52s, committing barbarous crimes against the people of the nations of Vietnam and Laos.

The international community was enraged by this savage war of aggression conducted by the American imperialists. Socialist nations and progressive people throughout the world supported Vietnam's fight against the Americans, but they also feared our nation would not be able to withstand the overpowering military might of the Americans.

Facing serious challenges, the fate of the Fatherland and of the socialist system hung in the balance. The urgent, sacred duty of every Vietnamese and the historic goal of our people and our army, fighting on behalf of the world movements for peace and national liberation and for the cause of socialist revolution, now was to resist and defeat the Americans to save the nation.

The battle being waged by our soldiers and civilians against the Americans to save the nation moved into an extremely difficult and ferocious phase. The People's Army of Vietnam now faced a new battle opponent: the American expeditionary army, an aggressor army that possessed modern equipment, heavy firepower, and incredible mobility. The Americans, however, came to South Vietnam in a defensive posture following the defeat of the "special war." In South Vietnam our soldiers and civilians were in an offensive posture. The formation of our three types of armed forces was now complete. These forces were widespread and properly deployed on all the battlefields. Our main force troops now were organized into regiments that controlled the important areas. Local people's war and the political struggle of the masses in the urban areas had developed to a high level. In North Vietnam, our people had completed the first five-year plan (1961–1965) for building socialism, significantly increasing the economic and national defense capacity of the nation. During the past ten years (1954–1964) our army had made significant progress toward becoming a modern, regular force. Our strategic transportation routes, both by land and sea, from North Vietnam to the battlefield had developed, expanding the role of our great rear area in the liberation war in South Vietnam.

During its 11th Plenum in March 1965, the Party Central Committee decided to "mobilize the soldiers and civilians of the entire nation to strengthen our offensive posture and to attack the enemy. Rapidly expand the standing army, strengthen national defense, strive to secure the maximum possible military support from fraternal, allied nations."[5]

On 20 July 1965 Chairman Ho Chi Minh appealed to the citizens and soldiers of the entire nation: "No matter if we have to fight for five years, ten years, twenty years, or even longer, we are resolved to fight on until we achieve complete victory."[6]

THE WAR IN THE SOUTH

In South Vietnam, as early as the first few months of 1965, COSVN had assessed the situation and reached a strategic decision: Based on our defeat of the "special war" waged by the Americans and their lackeys, we would continue to maintain and expand our offensive posture and make preparations to crush the U.S. plan to mount a massive counteroffensive during the 1965–1966 dry season. COSVN decided to launch a wide-ranging political campaign throughout the armed forces and the civilian population to develop to the highest possible level our revolutionary heroism, to build resolve to fight and defeat the Americans, and to maintain firm confidence in our final victory. Party and political activities within our units focused on education, on building resolve to defeat the American expeditionary army, and on seeking tactics to fight the Americans. In May 1965 the Region 5 Party Committee and the Military Region 5 Command directed all armed forces to make all necessary preparations to fight against American troops. On 19 May 1965, on the occasion of the 75th birthday of Chairman Ho Chi Minh, the Military Region launched an emulation movement called "Resolve to defeat the American aggressors." The slogan, "Seek out the Americans to fight them, pursue the puppets to kill them," was promulgated to all units.

Pursuant to policies set by the Party Central Committee and by the Central Military Party Committee, the people's armed forces in North and South Vietnam rapidly expanded in both size and quality.

In South Vietnam, our guerrilla militia at the village and hamlet level underwent a massive expansion based on the victory won by the People's War over the American-puppet "special war." At the end of 1965 guerrilla militia forces totaled 174,000, more than the enemy's Popular Forces and "Combat Youth." Our local force troops totaled 80,000 and were organized into battalions at the province level and companies at the district level. A number of provinces formed two battalions. A number of local force battalions and companies were combined to form four main force regiments. Seven additional full-strength infantry regiments and a number of specialty branch units, including artillery, sappers, engineers, signal, etc., had been sent from North Vietnam to the battle-field. By the end of 1965, our main force army in South Vietnam totaled almost 92,000 soldiers, organized into 18 infantry regiments and a number of specialty branch units.

During the fall and winter of 1965 the Central Military Party Committee and the Ministry of Defense formed five infantry divisions and one artillery division in South Vietnam. On 2 September 1965 the 9th Infantry Division was formed in the base area of Binh Long province in eastern Cochin China. The division was made up of the 1st Regiment (the Binh Gia Regiment), the 2nd Regiment (the Dong Xoai Regiment), and the 3rd Regiment, which had just been organized from a number of local force units drawn from the provinces of the Mekong Delta. In the lowlands of Military Region 5, the 3rd Infantry Division was formed that same day in the Binh Dinh province base area. The division was made up of Military Region 5's main force 2nd Infantry Regiment and the 12th and 22nd Regiments, which had just arrived from North Vietnam. On 20 October 1965, the 2nd Infantry Division was established in the base area of Quang Nam province. It was made up of Military Region 5's 1st Regiment (the Ba Gia Regiment) and the 21st Regiment, which had just arrived from North Vietnam. On 23 October 1965, the 5th Infantry Division was established in the Ba Ria province base area. The division consisted of Military Region 7's 4th Regiment (the Dong Nai regi-ment) and the 5th Regiment, which had just been formed from a number of local force units drawn from the provinces of Cochin China. On 20 December 1965, the 1st Infantry Division was formed in the Central Highlands. The units making up this division were the 320th, 33rd, and 66th Regiments, all of which had arrived from North Vietnam during the last months of 1964 and during 1965. The 80th Artillery Group, subordinate to COSVN Military Command, received additional personnel, weapons, and equipment, and on 15 October 1965 was reorganized into a division-sized unit designated the 69th Artillery Group.[7]

The main force elements of our military regions were organized into regiments and battalions and consisted of the following forces: one regiment subordinate to Military Region 9 (western Cochin China); two battalions subordinate to Military Region 8 (central Cochin China); five battalions subordinate to the Saigon–Gia Dinh Military Region; one battalion subordinate to Military Region 7 (eastern Cochin China); one regiment and one separate battalion subordinate to Region 5's Northern Subregion (Tri-Thien);[8] and one regiment subordinate to Region 5's Southern Subregion (extreme southern Central Vietnam).

Our sapper and commando forces expanded very rapidly. They consisted of four battalions (the 407th, 408th, 487th, and 489th) subordinate to Military Region 5, the 12th Tri-Thien Battalion, and nine combat teams (designated Teams 3 through 11) and two support teams (A-20 and A-30) subordinate to Saigon–Gia Dinh City Committee.

Rear services operations were strengthened to support the force building and combat operations of our main force troops in each area of the battlefield. In eastern Cochin China, the COSVN Military Command established two additional area rear services groups, Groups 85 and 86. Our forces received a rather large number of additional infantry weapons.[9]

All this meant that during the last half of 1965 our armed forces had formed and deployed three mobile main force armies that held firm footholds in the strategic areas: eastern Cochin China, Region 5, and the Central Highlands. For the first time in history we had main force divisions fighting on the battlefields of South Vietnam. Combining the rapid expansion of our local force units and mass political forces with the formation of mobile main force divisions on the battlefield, our army was able to intensify its massed combat operations in combination with guerrilla warfare to gradually defeat the plots and strategic measures being employed by the American, puppet, and satellite troops.

As we built up our forces, our armed forces in South Vietnam also launched combat operations against the American expeditionary army and defeated them in our very first battles.

After the Ba Gia victory, Military Region 5's 1st Regiment (minus one battalion) moved to Van Tuong to rest and regroup. Van Tuong was a liberated hamlet along the coast of Binh Son district, Quang Ngai province, 17 kilometers from the American base at Chu Lai. As soon as they discovered the presence of our main force troops, on 18 August 1965 American soldiers launched "Operation Starlite" to test their "search and destroy" strategy and demonstrate the technical and tactical superiority of the American military. They used 6,000 American troops of the 3rd Marine Division, 2,000 puppet troops, 200 aircraft, 100 tanks and armored personnel carriers, and 40 artillery pieces in this operation. After a heavy bombardment by air and artillery forces, the U.S. and puppet troops advanced in four columns, using amphibious landings, helicopter assaults, and overland marches in an effort to surround and destroy Military Region 5's main force 1st Regiment.

At the time half of the troops of the 1st Regiment were out collecting rice. Battalion and regimental cadre were away preparing battlefields. The balance of forces was against us, 20 enemy troops for every one of our soldiers. Because the regiment was experienced in fighting in the lowlands, as soon as they arrived in this area our cadre and soldiers, utilizing combat villages and local armed forces and assisted by the civilian population, had organized defenses and established a battle plan. When the American troops attacked Van Tuong, the remaining forces of 1st Regiment, working in close coordination with the provincial 21st Local Force Company and local guerrillas, used the trenches and hedgerows of the village and hamlets and the Binh Son "American killing belt" fortifications to resolutely block the advance of the enemy column landing from the sea. They shot down U.S. helicopters, destroyed armored personnel carriers, and repelled the enemy's attack spearheads. After nightfall, the regiment massed its forces and wiped out one group of American troops.

In one day of ferocious counterattacks the 1st Regiment and local armed forces killed or wounded 900 American soldiers, shot down 13 aircraft, and destroyed 22 tanks and armored personnel carriers. The first American "search and destroy" operation, using combined-arms and combined-services tactics, had failed in the face of the "determined to fight, determined to win" will and the outstanding combat tactics of our troops. This was a "Battle of Ap Bac" for the American military. With this battle our troops took their first step toward assessing the true strengths and weaknesses (in both morale and tactics) of the American expeditionary soldiers. We had proven we were capable of defeating the American expeditionary army.

Encouraged by the victory at Van Tuong, during the fall and winter of 1965 our armed forces throughout the battlefields of South Vietnam intensified their operations, retaining and exploiting the offensive initiative we already held.

In the Central Highlands, in order to study the fighting methods of the Americans in actual combat, the Front Command launched the Plei Me Campaign in Gia Lai [Pleiku] province, carrying out a plan to besiege a position and annihilate the relief force. Our objective was to deal a painful blow to the puppet army in order to lure American troops in so that we could kill them.

To launch the campaign, on 19 October 1965 the 33rd Regiment overran the Chu Ho outpost and established positions beseiging the outpost at Plei Me, an important enemy position 30 kilometers southwest of Pleiku city. Enemy troops launched a ferocious counterattack, dropping more than 1,000 tons of bombs on our positions, but they could not loosen our siege of the outpost. On 23 October two puppet infantry battalions and two tank-armor battalions moved down from Pleiku to relieve the outpost. This column blundered into an ambush position established by the 320th Regiment along Route 21 and suffered severe casualties. The 3rd Brigade of the U.S. Air Cavalry Division, which had arrived in Vietnam in September 1965, was immediately sent to Pleiku to rescue the puppet troops and to conduct a "search and destroy" operation against our troops.

The Central Highlands Front Command decided to modify its tactical plan to lure American forces into the Ia Drang Valley 25 kilometers southwest of Pleiku in order to destroy them. During the evening of 11 November, the 952nd Sapper Battalion raided the headquarters of the 3rd Air Cavalry Brigade at Bau Can. Meanwhile, the 33rd Regiment marched swiftly to the Ia Drang Valley. The 66th Regiment, which had just arrived on the battlefield from North Vietnam, was ordered to drop its heavy equipment and, carrying only weapons, ammunition, and a three-day ration of rice, march quickly toward Chu Pong Mountain in order to arrive in time to participate in the battle.

Between 14 and 19 November 1965, the battalions of the 66th Regiment, together with an element of the 33rd Regiment, charged through the enemy's bombs and shells to "grab the enemy's belt and fight him." They attacked as soon as the American helicopters began landing troops and also made surprise attacks against the enemy's artillery fire support bases and his troop encampments. Two soldiers, Le Khac Nga and Le Van Dieu, killed scores of American troops and were recognized as the first "Heroic Killers of Americans" on the Central Highlands battlefield.

To rescue the 3rd Air Cavalry Brigade the U.S. Command was forced to use B-52 strategic bombers in support of ground combat operations. At the same time, the Americans ordered the puppet 1st and 2nd Airborne Task Forces to the area to reinforce the American unit. These task forces were attacked by the 320th Regiment. One element of the task force was annihilated, and the rest of the unit fled in confusion.

On 19 November, the remnants of the U.S. 3rd Air Cavalry Brigade retreated overland from the Ia Drang Valley. Along their line of retreat we attacked and pursued them, inflicting heavy casualties. The Plei Me Campaign was over. Seventeen hundred Americans and 1,270 puppet troops had been eliminated from the field of combat. The 1st Air Cavalry Battalion had been almost completely annihilated, and the 2nd Air Cavalry Battalion had suffered heavy casualties. Fifty-nine helicopters had been shot down and 89 enemy vehicles and many artillery pieces had been destroyed. The Air Cavalry Division, the first helicopter-transported air mobile division in history to engage in combat, a unit the Americans believed would be able to react quickly and conduct rapid envelopment operations, the unit that was the "greatest hope of the American army," together with its combat method of conducting "relief operations to break sieges" and its "leapfrog" tactics, had been defeated in the mountain jungles of Vietnam.

The Plei Me victory demonstrated that our main force troops had high combat morale and a high resolve to defeat the Americans. It also demonstrated the clever and innovative campaign and tactical combat techniques of our main force army. This victory proved our army was capable of annihilating U.S. battalions operating in large formations and that we could disrupt the helicopter-assault tactics and defeat the most elite, most modernly equipped units of the American army even under the most difficult and savage conditions.

In Region 5, the 2nd Regiment of the 3rd Division attacked traffic along Route 1 (the section running through Phu Cat district of Binh Dinh province), forcing the U.S. Air Cavalry Division to mount many operations in the Thuan Ninh and Hoi Son areas to relieve the pressure we were applying there. Hundreds of American air cavalry troopers were killed or wounded in battles with the 2nd Regiment and by the punji sticks, mines, and sniper bullets of our guerrillas. The 1st Regiment of the 2nd Division, in cooperation with Quang Nam local force troops, liberated Hiep Duc district, besieged the Viet An strong point, and repelled the puppet 5th Regimental Task Force at Dong Duong when it tried to conduct a relief operation. The 90th Battalion of the 1st Regiment conducted a mobile ambush in the Cam Khe area on 25 December 1965, killing or wounding almost an entire U.S. Marine battalion as it moved up to rescue the puppet troops.

In eastern Cochin China, the U.S. 1st Infantry Division and the 173rd Airborne Brigade arrived in the Bien Hoa area. To implement their "search and destroy" strategy and to enlarge the security perimeter of the Bien Hoa base, the American troops immediately launched a number of operations to search the area around their bases. On 8 November 1965, a battalion of the U.S. 173rd Airborne Brigade suffered heavy casualties in a battle with the 1st Regiment, 9th Division, at Dat Cuoc, 30 kilometers north of Bien Hoa city.

Having located our main force troops, on 11 November the 3rd Brigade of the U.S. 1st Infantry Division, accompanied by a tank battalion and an artillery battery, moved up Route 13 toward Long Nguyen. That night they stopped at Bau Bang, 25 kilometers north of the Thu Dau Mot province capital, and formed a large defensive position, using tanks and armored personnel carriers as an outer defensive wall. Seizing an opportunity to annihilate enemy forces while they were outside of their fortified positions, the COSVN Military Command ordered the 9th Division to mount a counterattack against the American troops in accordance with a prearranged combat plan. Because time was short, the cadre and soldiers of the division were forced to make their preparations while they were on the march.

At 0500 hours in the morning of 12 November 1965, the 9th Division (minus two battalions), under the command of Senior Colonel Hoang Cam, Division Commander and concurrently Division Political Officer, launched a surprise attack against the American position at Bau Bang. Closely coordinating its various troop columns, the division managed to isolate and divide the American defensive positions at the beginning of the battle, making a deep penetration that reached the enemy's brigade headquarters. Our assault threw the enemy troops into a state of confusion. Hearing the sounds of the battle at Bau Bang, one element of the 9th Division, which had been assigned to tie down the enemy position at Lai Khe, moved rapidly and blocked the enemy's line of retreat. The battle ended after three hours of fighting. In its first battle against our main force troops on the Cochin China battlefield, the 1st Infantry Division, touted by the Americans as the "Big Red One," the division that American generals and field-grade officers boasted was their "most elite combat division, which performed many outstanding feats of arms during World War II and the Korean War," had lost almost 2,000 men and more than 30 tanks and armored personnel carriers. On our side, during the first direct combat between an entire division and American expeditionary troops, the cadre and soldiers of the 9th Division, demonstrating their firm resolve, seized the offensive initiative, deployed their forces and made their combat preparations rapidly, coordinated the battle in an excellent manner, maintained secrecy and surprise, isolated the battlefield, divided the enemy's forces, and fought a very courageous battle in close combat, achieving a high level of combat efficiency.

In the cities and urban areas, our sapper troops and commandos stepped up their attacks against the enemy. During its war of aggression in Vietnam the American expeditionary army relied on a network of bases, warehouse complexes, airfields, and ports. Its technical and logistical support requirements were very heavy and its bases were scattered along the coast from Quang Tri to Saigon. The disruption of this logistics network was one of our strategic goals. In Region 5, on 5 August 1965 two sapper battalions, the 89th and 409th, attacked the Nuoc Man and Chu Lai airfields, killing 750 pilots and technical personnel and destroying 150 aircraft. Commando Groups [Cum] 3, 4, and 5 of the Saigon City Command attacked the puppet Police Headquarters on 15 August 1965, killing 165 enemy personnel, and planted a bomb at the Metropole Hotel on 1 December 1965, wiping out 200 American officers and technical personnel. Our sappers and commandos attacked airfields at Soc Trang, Bien Hoa, Nha Trang, Da Nang, and Pleiku, and attacked enemy petroleum storage facilities, ammunition storage facilities, vessels, vehicle parks, railroad cars, headquarters facilities, and training schools in many locations. During the last months of 1965 some targets were struck two or three times.

In the rural lowlands and the mountains, our local force troops and guerrilla militia seized the initiative by attacking American and puppet troops in their own base areas, maintained excellent coordination with our main force troops, and supported the people in their political struggle to maintain control of the liberated areas. A number of "American killing belts" appeared around Da Nang, Chu Lai, An Khe, and Cu Chi. Using military and political forces and military proselytizing operations to surround and mount attacks to inflict casualties on American forces in their own bases, the "American killing belts" were typical examples of people's warfare in Vietnam. The civilians and guerrillas of Hoa Hai village, Hoa Vang district, Quang Da province, heroically resisted a sweep operation by four U.S. Marine battalions for seven days and seven nights, killing 47 enemy. The civilians and guerrillas of Village A-1 and Bac village in An Khe district, Gia Lai [Pleiku] province, aggressively defended their hamlets and villages with punji sticks, mines, and booby traps, causing many casualties among the troops of the Air Cavalry and restricting their sweep operations. On 3 October 1965 the Dien Ban district local force company of Quang Nam province inflicted severe casualties on an American company southwest of Da Nang. On 31 October 1965, the Quang Da province local force battalion eliminated from the field of battle one U.S. Marine company. The U.S. military combat tactic of "protecting strong points and bases" with a many-layered defense in combination with sweeps to expand the "security perimeter" was defeated by the resolve of our local armed forces to remain at their posts and by their flexible, crafty fighting methods.

Maintaining the strategic initiative and combining massed combat operations by our main force troops with local people's warfare, our army stepped up its attacks and counterattacks in all three strategic areas, utilizing many diverse and innovative fighting methods and preventing U.S. troops from being able to exploit their own strengths. During the fall and winter of 1965, over 30,000 enemy troops, including 9,000 Americans, were eliminated from the field of combat. With respect to enemy units, 16 battalions, of which five were American battalions, 53 companies, of which seven were American, and six armored cavalry troops, of which three were American, were wiped out or suffered severe casualties.

"Seek out the Americans to fight them, pursue the puppets to kill them," became an enthusiastic movement among the people's armed forces in South Vietnam. These first victories over American troops on the battlefield provided powerful encouragement to the determination of the soldiers and civilians of our entire nation to fight the Americans. They provided a firm foundation for our later victories and at the same time were one of the foundations our Party used to mobilize and organize the soldiers and civilians of the entire nation to defeat the American aggressors.

THE WAR IN THE NORTH AND ALONG THE LINES OF SUPPLY

In North Vietnam, on 7 February 1965, the American imperialists launched a bombing campaign they called "Flaming Dart." On 2 March 1965, they began a fiercer, continuous bombing campaign called "Rolling Thunder," attacking almost all cities and towns, lines of communication, and storage complexes from the city of Ho Xa in Vinh Linh to the 20th parallel and attacking a number of islands in the Gulf of Tonkin.

In June 1965, as they began pouring large numbers of troops into South Vietnam, the imperialists escalated their campaign another notch by attacking the important road and rail networks north and south of the Red River, the Hanoi–Lao Cai railroad, Route 5 and the railroad line between Hanoi and Haiphong, and even bombing a number of heavily populated urban areas, hospitals, and schools. The Americans used a total of 360 aircraft, including many different types of modern Air Force and Navy jet aircraft, in their war of destruction against North Vietnam in 1965. On average they launched 100 sorties per day, the highest daily total being 280 sorties. American aircraft dropped a total of 310,000 tons of bombs on North Vietnam during 1965. The naval forces of the 7th Fleet, including aircraft carriers, cruisers, and destroyers, controlled the territorial waters of North Vietnam and used bombardment vessels to shell important shore targets. This was the first time in the history of warfare that such a war of destruction, using air and naval forces on this scale and with this level of ferocity, had been conducted. Our air defense–air force and naval forces were directly responsibile for combating the two most powerful branches of service of the U.S. armed forces.

Responding to the sacred appeal to fight the Americans and save the nation issued by Chairman Ho Chi Minh and the Party Central Committee, the civilian population and the people's armed forces of North Vietnam displayed a spirit of revolutionary courage, carried out economic production while they fought, defeated each step in the escalation of the war of destruction conducted by the American pirates, continued the work of socialist construction during wartime conditions, provided wholehearted support to our brothers in South Vietnam, and performed our international duty of supporting the revolution in Laos.

Carrying out our policy of converting production over to wartime conditions, many factories, warehouse complexes, state agencies, schools, and hospitals were completely or partially evacuated from the cities and urban areas in order to continue their production, teaching, and other operations. We focused especially on the development of local industries. Many agricultural cooperatives raised their output to a high level, producing five tons of paddy per hectare per year. Many lines of communications, docks, ferries, and detours around the enemy's bombing "choke points" were built. Education, cultural, and health activities were expanded. A worker carrying a rifle to his factory; a female collective farmer, with a plow on one shoulder and a rifle over the other, walking out to the fields; children of the "straw hat units" going to class; these were familiar daily images in the lives of the people of North Vietnam.

The Vietnamese Women's Association launched the "Woman of three abilities" movement: able to produce and work; able to handle household chores; able to fight and to provide combat support to replace husbands and children who had gone off to battle. The Vietnam Labor Youth Group launched the "Youth of three readinesses" movement: ready to fight, ready to enlist in the armed forces, ready to go anywhere and do anything that the Fatherland required. The intellectual class had the "three resolves" movement: resolve to properly support production and combat; resolve to step up the scientific-technical revolution and the ideological and cultural revolution; and resolve to build and expand the ranks of socialist intellectuals.

In coping with this fierce war of destruction waged against us by the enemy, our socialist system clearly demonstrated its power. Social conditions remained stable. Production was maintained and in some areas increased, properly supporting the people's living standards, the ever-growing and ever more urgent requirements of battle in both North and South Vietnam, and fulfilling our international duty to the revolution in Laos. During the course of the war the stability and growth of our great rear area of North Vietnam in all areas of endeavor was a vast source of strength for our army. The combat spirit of our army was based on the resolve of the entire Party and the entire population to fight the Americans and save the nation and grew out of the continuous political mobilization activities of the Party Central Committee and of Uncle Ho.

In April 1965 Chairman Ho Chi Minh issued a decree establishing a wartime military service law. The period of military service of soldiers was extended in accordance with the requirements of combat. All previously discharged officers and enlisted men were recalled to the armed forces. Officers were assigned to positions commensurate with their rank following a three-month training course in one of the officers' schools. During 1965 almost 290,000 men were mobilized into the armed forces, of whom 10 percent were Party members, 50 percent were Youth Group members, and 70 percent were in the 18 to 25 age group.[10] May was the month in which the number of personnel mobilized was the highest—that month 150,000 people were inducted into the army. All units were brought up to full personnel strength according to our wartime table of organization standards. Many new units were formed. Many military specialty branches doubled in strength.

Our self-defense militia forces increased from 1.4 million in 1964 to two million in 1965. Over 3,000 self-defense militia cells and units assigned to fire at aircraft and equipped with rifles, light machine guns, heavy machine guns, and anti-aircraft machine guns, were established, forming a complete and potent air defense curtain to protect the skies over North Vietnam. A number of state agencies and enterprises formed militia platoons and companies. A number of coastal villages in Military Region 4 organized militia artillery teams to fire back at U.S. warships.

Our local force troops grew to 28,000 soldiers, organized into 16 infantry battalions, 32 infantry companies, and a number of anti-aircraft, engineer, and coastal defense artillery units.

Our main force troops grew from 195,000 soldiers in early 1965 to 350,000 soldiers in May 1965 and finally to 400,000 soldiers by the end of 1965. Our mobile main force infantry forces were made up of ten divisions (the 308th, 304th, 312th, 320th, 325th, 330th, 350th, 316th, 324th, and 341st), six regiments, and a number of independent battalions. A number of regiments with combat traditions dating back to the resistance war against the French were sent to the battlefields of South Vietnam with their entire authorized complement of troops and equipment. The Artillery Branch doubled in strength over its 1964 troop levels and was issued long-range 130mm guns and DKB rocket launchers. A second armored regiment, the 203rd, was formed. The Signal Branch and reconnaissance and sapper forces tripled in strength.

Most especially, because of their combat duty of combating the war of destruction being waged by the U.S. Air Force and Navy and their responsibility for protecting the flow of supplies to the battlefield, the Air Defense–Air Force Service Branch, the Engineer Branch, and our rear services troops underwent massive, rapid expansion.

Our air-defense artillery grew from 12 regiments and 14 battalions in early 1965 to 21 regiments and 41 battalions, including eight mobile regiments. These forces formed a powerful low- and medium-altitude air defense curtain over strategic areas, at the same time maintaining mobility and forming anti-aircraft artillery concentrations protecting each individual area.

Our anti-aircraft missile forces were formed during this period. On 1 May 1965, after a period of urgent preparations, covertly shipping in weapons and equipment and constructing a training center, our first missile unit, the 236th Air Defense Missile Regiment (the "Song Da Group") was formed. In June 1965 a second regiment, the 238th, was established. Almost all the original cadre of these two regiments had experience in the resistance war against the French and in our initial battles against the U.S. air war of destruction. A number of cadre and technical personnel had received training in the Soviet Union. The enlisted men were chosen from many different service and specialty branches: anti-aircraft artillery, artillery, radar, signal, engineer, Navy, infantry. The majority of these soldiers had been tested in actual combat and during operations. The Party and the State also assigned a number of scientific and technical cadre and university and trade-school students to these two regiments. Under the guidance of Soviet advisors, our missile cadre and soldiers began their training classes. Each regiment conducted as many as 37 separate training classes for command officers, missile-control officers, and technical personnel. Training time was cut from one year to three months because of the need to rapidly move personnel into combat positions. Later these personnel received supplemental training while carrying out their combat duties. With the birth of our air-defense missile force, our army acquired a modern technical specialty branch. New pages in the history of the Air Defense–Air Force Service Branch's force building and combat operations began to be written.

Our Air Force troops grew from one regiment to three Air Force combat regiments equipped with Mig-17 and Mig-21 fighters.[11] For the first time, an air combat force organized into a modern Service Branch was included within the organizational structure of our armed forces.

Our radar troops expanded from two regiments in 1964 to four regiments subordinate to the Air Defense–Air Force Service Branch, five battalions subordinate to the Navy Service Branch, and five air control radar teams for the Air Force. Navy radar units were deployed along the coast and on a number of offshore islands. They included a number of both fixed and mobile radar stations. The radar regiments assigned to the Air Defense–Air Force Service Branch were deployed along three lines with the goal of detecting enemy aircraft at long ranges to support the combat operations of our air defense missile force and our anti-aircraft artillery forces.

The strength of the Air Defense–Air Force Service Branch in 1965 grew to a level 2.5 times larger than its strength in 1964, and the troops of the Service Branch made up 16 percent of the total strength of our armed forces.[12] With the assistance of the Soviet Union and other fraternal socialist nations, our Air Defense–Air Force troops were equipped with many types of modern weapons and combat equipment. Party and political activities within the Service Branch delved deeply into technical and tactical matters, encouraging cadre and soldiers to study enthusiastically to fully understand and to be able to skillfully utilize their weapons and equipment. These activities correctly established the relationship between political and technical matters, between humans and weapons, and taught our troops to understand the importance of coordination and solidarity, to be innovative in their fighting methods, and to obey all regulations and guidelines for the use and maintenance of technical equipment. Although they quickly settled into their new organization and stepped up their training activities, the specialty branches also quickly engaged in actual combat operations.

Between February and June 1965, on the firing lines of Military Region 4 our anti-aircraft artillery troops, sailors, and local air defense forces shot down more than 300 U.S. aircraft. On 26 and 30 March, our anti-aircraft artillery troops in Ru Nai, Ha Tinh province, cleverly lured the enemy into a prearranged trap, shooting down 12 aircraft and initiating the use of ambush tactics by our air defense troops. Our naval vessels conducted mobile battles on the Nhat Le, Gianh, and Lam Rivers and in a number of coastal areas, shooting down scores of American aircraft and sinking or setting on fire a number of puppet commando vessels. The militia of Dien Hung village, Dien Chau district, Nghe An province, used rifles to shoot down an American aircraft, thereby launching an emulation movement among the self-defense militia forces to shoot down modern U.S. jet aircraft using infantry weapons.

The battles of 3 and 4 April 1965 to protect the Ham Rong Bridge in Thanh Hoa city were particularly significant. During these battles our young Air Force troops opened an "air front," working with anti-aircraft artillery troops, naval units on the Ma River, and self-defense militia of the Nam Ngan subsector, to shoot down scores of American aircraft and capture a number of pilots. On 3 April, a flight of Mig-17s commanded by Flight Commander Pham Ngoc Lan shot down two American F-8 aircraft. The next day, 4 April, when the American pirates assembled a force of more than 100 aircraft to continue their efforts to destroy the Ham Rong Bridge, a flight of Mig-17s commanded by Flight Commander Tran Hanh shot down two F-105 aircraft. These initial feats of arms performed by our air force thrilled our compatriots and soldiers throughout the nation. For the first time in our nation's history of armed struggle we had engaged in an air battle. In their first engagement, the young warriors of the Vietnamese Air Force had defeated the modern air forces of the American imperialists. In the skies, where there were no "fortifications," where our air force usually had to use a few aircraft to attack many aircraft, our air force combatants had employed the innovative military thoughts of the Party in air combat, cleverly seizing the initiative, shooting down unsuspecting U.S. aircraft, and then assisting one another to all land safely. An emulation campaign to perform feats of arms using the slogans "whenever we take off we will be victorious" and "shoot down American aircraft right from the initial engagement" spread throughout our Air Force. The 3rd of April became Air Force Day to mark our victory in the very first engagement fought by the heroic People's Air Force of Vietnam. The 24th of July became Missile Day to honor our heroic missile troops.

In July 1965, faced with a new escalation of the war by the American imperialists, our missile forces, formed only two months earlier, were ordered into combat.

At 1553 hours on 24 July 1965, the 63rd and 64th Battalions, located at firing positions at Suoi Hai, Bat Bat district, Ha Tay province, launched their first missiles, shooting down one F-4C aircraft and capturing one pilot. This was the 400th aircraft to be shot down over North Vietnam. Uncle Ho was overjoyed when he heard the report of the results of this first battle victory of our missile troops. He personally wrote a letter of commendation to our air defense missile cadre and soldiers. The official birthday of our heroic missile troops became 24 July. On 25 July the American imperialists halted all operations in the skies over North Vietnam to seek ways to deal with this new threat. Meanwhile, our two missile battalions moved to new firing positions. On 26 July, when U.S. aircraft resumed operations, our missile troops shot down two aircraft, one of which was an unmanned reconnaissance aircraft. At the firing positions that our two missile battalions had occupied during the battle on 24 July, our soldiers, assisted by the local population, constructed fake missiles made of bamboo and mats. Around these "firing positions" we deployed two regiments of 57mm anti-aircraft guns, two battalions of 37mm anti-aircraft guns, and ten militia anti-aircraft teams from Bat Bat district. On 27 July, when the American pirates sent 48 aircraft sorties to "retaliate" against our "missile firing positions," 120 anti-aircraft cannon and hundreds of machine guns and rifles instantly fired back in a fierce barrage, destroying five aircraft, two of which crashed on the spot.

With the Suoi Hai victory, our fighting tactic of combining missiles, anti-aircraft artillery, and a low-level curtain of fire from our militia forces into an air defense combat cluster [cum] was born. During the final months of 1965, the Air Defense–Air Force Command formed three mobile air defense combat clusters made up of missile and anti-aircraft artillery troops defending Routes 1, 2, and 5. Forward headquarters to directly control the combat operations of these air-defense clusters were formed. Within each cluster's area militia forces were on combat alert to coordinate their combat operations with our air defense troops.

By the end of 1965 our air defense–air force troops had, together with the rest of the people's armed forces in North Vietnam, shot down 834 American aircraft. The air defense forces of our three types of troops grew rapidly in both quantity and quality. Many different tactics were employed by our anti-aircraft artillery, missile, and air force troops. A style of air defense combining wide-spread local forces with massed combined-arms forces belonging to our main force air-defense units took shape.

On our lines of communications and transportation the battle being fought by our soldiers and civilians was very fierce. From the very first days of the war of destruction against North Vietnam, the American imperialists focused more than 50 percent of their bombing sorties against lines of communications and transportation targets. They used many different types of bombs, conducted waves of attacks concentrated on choke points in combination with efforts to restrict transportation over a broad area, and attacked all our rail, road, and waterway networks, all types of transport equipment, and the production and repair facilities of North Vietnam's communications and transportation sector. They caused a great many difficulties for our troops and civilian population, sometimes causing great backups and obstructions at a number of Group 559's entry points and crossing points in Military Region 4. The Long Dai, Xuan Son, and Ben Thuy ferry crossing points, the Dong Loc three-way intersection, and the Ham Rong Bridge became the focal points of fierce enemy attacks.

"Guaranteeing a clear, unobstructed line of communications and transportation has become a central task for the entire Party, the entire population, and the entire armed forces. It is a task of strategic importance for the consolidation and defense of the Socialist North, for our support for the war of liberation in the South, and for our assistance to friendly nations."[13] The policy of the Party Central Committee and the Government was to encourage the entire population to work on communications and transportation tasks, using our professional communications and transportation forces as the core for this work and using the engineer, rear services, transportation, and air defense troops of the armed forces as the assault force.

In October 1965, the Cabinet decided to establish the Central Traffic Regulation Commission. Comrade Pham Hung, member of the Politburo and Deputy Prime Minister, was appointed as Chairman of this Commission. Provinces, cities, and a number of important traffic nodes established traffic support sections.

Assault youth teams to fight the Americans and save the nation were established. Tens of thousands of young men and women enthusiastically responded to the call of the Party, leading the way in performing duties in locations of hardship and danger. As soon as they were formed a number of these teams marched off to the Annamite Mountain supply corridor and to a number of key locations in Military Region 4 to carry out the work of road building and maintaining the flow of traffic.

Along the routes that the enemy was attacking, especially those in Military Region 4, the road sections and groups of the Ministry of Communications and Transportation were given additional personnel and were organized into traffic control sections for each individual area. These sections were responsible for repairing roads and bridges, building detours and bypasses, and guaranteeing traffic flow through crossing points and choke points.

The villages and hamlets along the lines of communications all organized assault teams to guarantee traffic flow. These teams were made up of male and female militia members who were responsible for guaranteeing the flow of traffic and supplies along the routes that passed through their hamlets or villages and for helping engineers and drivers repair damage caused by enemy attacks.

With a spirit of ardent patriotism, "Everything for our Southern brothers," our compatriots living along the transportation lines in the rear area of North Vietnam, especially in Nghe An, Ha Tinh, Quang Binh, and Vinh Linh, lived up to the slogan "We will not worry about our houses if the vehicles have not yet gotten through." Many families even donated their doors and wooden beds to cover the roads so the trucks could get through. Many people gave their lives for the sake of the supply shipments to the front. "The battle along the lines of communications throughout North Vietnam is a hymn of praise to our communications and transportation soldiers and to our compatriots living along the supply lines."[14]

Sixty percent of the air defense forces in North Vietnam were assigned to protect the lines of communications and transportation. Many anti-aircraft artillery firing positions located inside bomb craters and adjacent to bridge abutments and ferry crossings conducted a continuous battle against the enemy's fierce waves of attacks. One engineer regiment, four engineer battalions, 53 engineer companies, and 17 engineer platoons were employed to build and repair roads and to locate and destroy bombs in order to guarantee traffic flow through the choke points. Using only crude implements, our engineer soldiers devised many ways to disarm delayed-action bombs and magnetic bombs. They were ready to give their lives to keep our vehicles moving and keep the roads open.

On 26 April 1965, the Central Military Party Committee formed the Transportation Department, subordinate to the General Rear Services Department, with the goal of unifying control over all military transportation forces in North Vietnam. The Transportation Department's mission was to receive aid supplies, provide transportation in support of force building and combat operations being performed by our armed forces in North Vietnam, establish supply transshipment points for Group 559, and to support the Laotian battlefield.[15] Colonel Nguyen Danh Phan was assigned to serve as Chief of this department, and Colonel Tran Minh Chung was appointed as Department Political Commissar. All military transportation forces in North Vietnam were reorganized into six troop stations [binh tram] scattered from the supply reception and transshipment points along our northern border and at Haiphong harbor down to Group 559's transportation entry points in southwestern Military Region 4. Each of these troop stations had one truck transport battalion, one engineer company, warehouses, vehicle repair shops, clinics for treatment of wounded soldiers, and an attached anti-aircraft artillery battalion to defend the transportation route. The mobile transportation forces belonging to the Department of Transportation consisted of three truck transport battalions and river transportation equipment of the Hong Ha Boat

Group with a total capacity of 2,000 tons. These mobile forces were also supported by tens of thousands of tons of cargo capacity provided by the State rail, rail-car, and ground transportation networks.

In June 1965 the General Department of Rear Services established Group 665 to support the transportation of troops to the South and the transfer of wounded soldiers from the battlefields back to the hospitals in the rear area of North Vietnam.

Military Transportation Group 559 was developed into a strategic rear services group responsible for road building and transportation to the battlefields of South Vietnam and Laos, for transporting supplies and guaranteeing the safe passage of units marching down the Trail to the battlefield, and for working with the local population and the Pathet Lao armed forces to consolidate and strengthen the liberated areas on the western side of the Annamite Mountain range. Major General Phan Trong Tue, member of the Central Committee and Minister of Communications and Transportation, was appointed to serve as Commander of Military Transportation Group 559. By the end of 1965 the strength of Group 559 had risen to 24,400 soldiers organized into six truck transport battalions, two bicycle transportation battalions, one transport boat battalion, 18 engineer battalions, four anti-aircraft artillery battalions, 45 commo-liaison stations, and various support units.[16] In addition, an engineer regiment and four anti-aircraft artillery battalions under Group 559's operational control were stationed along the Annamite Mountain transportation route. Starting with the use of primitive forms of transportation combined with a small amount of motor transport, Group 559 had gradually expanded the scale of its activities and employed massed transportation methods using motor vehicles as its principal means of operation. Beginning with the use of secret transportation as its primary method, Group 559 gradually built up an ability to transport supplies using combined-arms combat methods. "Build roads to advance, fight the enemy to travel." Along the supply line from North to South Vietnam we began to organize a form of transportation using combined-arms forces in which our truck transportation soldiers played the central role.

With the help of Party committees at all levels and of the local authorities and population, our transportation troops made the supply route their battlefield. Transportation plans served as their combat orders, traffic levels and transportation times were their disciplinary regulations, and locations of enemy attacks or natural obstacles became the points where they engaged in battle. Many cadre and soldiers fought resolutely, overcoming every enemy trick aimed at blocking our movement, holding open the communications and transportation artery between the rear area and the front lines, linking together the various regions of our nation, and linking our nation to the other fraternal socialist countries. In 1965, the volume of supplies transported to South Vietnam along Group 559's corridor was almost equal to the total volume of supplies transported during the previous five years (1959–1964). In addition, during 1965 almost 50,000 cadre and soldiers, including seven infantry regiments and 20 battalions of infantry, sappers, artillery, etc. (equal to the total number of troops sent to South Vietnam during the entire period from 1959 to 1964), marched south to the battlefield. Carrying weapons and individual light equipment consisting of shelter tarps, hammocks, plastic rain ponchos, helmets, trousers, shirts, and individual medicines all packed neatly in a "frog pack," and with a mountain cane and a will to "cross the Annamite Mountains to save the nation," the cadre and soldiers of our armed forces, group by group, marched off to South Vietnam to fight to fulfill the resolve of the entire Party, the entire population, and of Chairman Ho Chi Minh: defeat the American aggressors, liberate South Vietnam, defend North Vietnam, unify the nation, and move the nation forward toward socialism.

RESOLVE TO CONTINUE THE BATTLE

On 27 December 1965, amid the heroic spirit of the soldiers and civilians of the entire nation to fight against the Americans, the 12th Plenum of the Party Central Committee met in Hanoi. Chairman Ho Chi Minh presided over the session.

Assessing the "limited war" conducted by the American aggressors in the southern half of our nation, the Party Central Committee clearly pointed out that in its objectives and nature, this is still a war of aggression aimed at implementing a neocolonialist policy relying on two strategic forces—the American expeditionary army and the puppet army. The American imperialists are the strongest economic and military power in the imperialist camp. The general world situation and the domestic situation in the United States, however, will not allow them to fully utilize their economic and military power in their war of aggression in Vietnam. Politics has always been the enemy's weak point, and it is still the basic weakness he has not been able to overcome. Meanwhile, the revolutionary forces of our people have grown strong in every aspect. Our armed forces have a firm foothold in the important strategic areas. Even though the American imperialists have poured tens of thousands of expeditionary troops into South Vietnam, the basic balance of forces between ourselves and the enemy is unchanged. Our people have a firm foundation for maintaining the offensive initiative on the battlefield.

The Party Central Committee decided that the strategic formula for our resistance war is still protracted warfare, but we will vigorously strive to "concentrate the forces of both North and South Vietnam and seek an opportunity to secure a decisive victory within a relatively short period of time." North Vietnam must defeat the air war of destruction being conducted by the American imperialist, must protect the cause of building socialism, and must mobilize human and material resources for the war to liberate South Vietnam. We must at the same time make vigorous preparations in all areas to be prepared to defeat the enemy should he be so rash as to expand his "limited war" strategy to the entire nation.

With regard to the work of building our armed forces, the Central Committee session established a policy of increasing quality, expanding quantity, strengthening training programs, and providing additional personnel and ammunition to our main force units. Attention was to be paid to building up local force troops and guerrilla militia forces, especially in vital areas. Our main force units in North Vietnam would serve both to defend North Vietnam and would be a strategic reserve force for South Vietnam.

On 16 January 1966, Chairman Ho Chi Minh spoke to the Conference of High-Level Party, State, and Military Cadre studying the resolution of the 12th Plenum of the Party Central Committee.

Uncle Ho said, "Now the Americans have 200,000 troops in South Vietnam. They may increase this even more, to 300,000, 400,000, or 500,000 troops. We will still win. We are certain of victory."[17] However, "victory will not come automatically. Our entire Party, our entire armed forces, our entire population must be resolved to fight to the end to secure the national independence and the unification of our nation, and at the same time we must completely fulfill our international duties."[18]

Carrying out the strategic resolve of the Party Central Committee, as expressed in Resolution 12 and in Chairman Ho Chi Minh's instructions to resist and defeat the American aggressors, our army in both North and South Vietnam marched forward into a large-scale, ferocious battle against the American expeditionary army and its modern air force and navy.

8

Increasing Our Combat Power: Defeating the American Expeditionary Army in South Vietnam and the American Air Force in North Vietnam

REINFORCEMENTS FOR THE SOUTH

Our army's victories in its initial battles against the American expeditionary army in South Vietnam and against American air forces in North Vietnam during 1965 solidified our confidence in the ability of the soldiers and civilians of our entire nation to defeat the American aggressors. After the 12th Plenum of the Party Central Committee the spirit of enthusiasm for the fight against the Americans grew even stronger. The resolve of the Party Central Committee to resist and defeat the Americans infected every cadre, Party member, soldier, and branch of service.

In late 1965 the Politburo foresaw that, with their increased troop strength and mobility, during the 1965–1966 dry season U.S. forces would launch many attacks into the mountain jungles and contested areas to seize the initiative and drive us back onto the defensive. Our soldiers and civilians had to make immediate, across-the-board preparations and maintain the initiative by mounting attacks and vigorous counterattacks. In our view, enemy attacks during the dry season would provide a good opportunity to kill American troops outside of their defensive fortifications.

Pursuant to the resolution of the Party Central Committee and instructions from the Politburo, in February 1966 the Central Military Party Committee met in Hanoi. Senior General Nguyen Chi Thanh, who had just returned from South Vietnam, briefed the committee on the battlefield situation in the South.

The Central Military Party Committee decided to exploit our offensive posture, gain greater and greater victories, and strive to achieve decisive victory in South Vietnam. Based on an assessment of battlefield developments, the Central Military Party Committee set forward six combat methods:

- Intensify massed combat operations and launch medium-size and large-scale campaigns by our main force units in the important theaters of operations.
- Intensify guerrilla warfare efforts and conduct coordinated combat operations between the guerrilla militia, local force troops, and a portion of our main force troops.
- Attack and destroy enemy rear area installations and enemy leadership organizations.
- Expand attacks against lines of communications.
- Combine armed operations with the political struggle of the masses in the cities and their surrounding areas.
- Maintain close coordination between the military struggle, the political struggle, and troop proselytizing.

With regard to the positions and responsibilities of each battlefield, the Central Military Party Committee decided that eastern Cochin China, the Central Highlands, and Tri-Thien were the key battlefields on which to engage and annihilate enemy forces. On these battlefields we needed to build, in a step-by-step and focused manner, a large transportation and supply warehouse network to prepare for combat operations using our main force troops. In the lowlands of Cochin China and Central Vietnam our three types of armed forces would increase guerrilla operations and small-scale mobile attacks. Our volunteer soldiers in central and lower Laos would work with our allies to step up activities everywhere and to protect our strategic supply corridor. In Cambodia we had to maintain and exploit the political and economic advantages we held in that nation in support of the fight against the American aggressors.

With regard to force building activities, the policy of the Central Military Party Committee was to rapidly expand our total troop strength and increase the quality of our armed forces, especially our main force units. During 1966 the strength of our full-time forces in South Vietnam would be increased to between 270,000 and 300,000 soldiers, organized into 35 main force regiments and 51 local force battalions. At the same time we would expand our guerrilla militia to cover a much broader area. The specialty branch units of our main force army would be strengthened, sapper and commando forces would be greatly expanded, and we would organize both specialist units to attack lines of communications and "assault units" to operate in urban areas. In North Vietnam, we would further expand our air defense, engineer, and transportation forces in order to defeat the enemy's ferocious war of destruction; maintain our strategic lines of communications; fulfill all plans for providing support to South Vietnam; properly prepare units to fight on the battlefront; and be ready to expand our forces when necessary.

To disseminate the resolution of the 12th Plenum of the Party Central Committee and the resolution of the Central Military Party Committee, and at the same time to reinforce the leadership apparatus and military command structure of the various battlefields, the Politburo and the Central Military Party Committee dispatched a large number of high-ranking cadre to South Vietnam. The General Staff, the General Political Department, and the General Department of Rear Services directed the battlefields to quickly consolidate their forces, prepare combat plans for the winter-spring campaign of 1966, and predict which areas might be attacked by the enemy. All battlefield units were to prepare for enemy counterattacks and be ready to shift forces to other theaters of operations when so ordered. Nine infantry regiments, three field artillery regiments, and a number of full-strength artillery, anti-aircraft, engineer, and signal units were ordered to set out rapidly for the southern battlefield to reinforce our mobile main force elements in the Central Highlands, Region 5, and eastern Cochin China.

The 24th Regiment (formerly the 42nd Regiment of the 304th Division), the 88th Regiment (from the 308th Division), Regiments 95B and 101B from the 325B Division, the 68th Artillery Regiment (equipped with 105mm howitzers), and the 95th and 96th Artillery Battalions (equipped with 120mm mortars) were sent to reinforce the Central Highlands Front (B3 Front).

Military Region 5 received the 20th Regiment (formerly designated Regiment 18B), the 31st Regiment (formerly Regiment 64A of the 320th Division), the 368B Artillery Regiment (equipped with DKB rockets), and the 19th Artillery Battalion (equipped with A-12 rockets).

The battlefields of Cochin China and extreme southern Central Vietnam received the 141st and 165th Regiments of the 312th Division, the 52nd Regiment of the 320th Division, the 16th Regiment (transferred south from the Central Highlands Front and formerly designated Regiment 101A), Artillery Regiment 84A (equipped with DKB rockets), and four battalions equipped with 120mm mortars and 12.8mm machine guns.

For the first time in the history of our resistance war against the Americans to save the nation our troops marched in regiment-sized units from North Vietnam across the Annamite Mountain range down to the battlefields of eastern Cochin China. The road was 2,000 kilometers long. Every cadre and soldier carried a load of between 30 and 40 kilograms. The commo-liaison trail from the Central Highlands into Cochin China had only recently been built, and many stretches of the route and many of the way stations had not yet been properly organized. The long distance and heavy loads, the savage sweep operations and bombing attacks conducted by the enemy, and severe weather conditions all combined to extend the time required for the march to five or six months, adversely affecting the health of our troops. On days when rice supplies were exhausted our soldiers had to dig up jungle roots to eat in place of rice. Almost all cadre and soldiers caught malaria, some soldiers died on the march, and a number had to remain behind in our medical clinics along the commo-liaison route. Some units suffered heavily, such as the 52nd Regiment, which had a strength of 2,800 soldiers when it set out but had only 1,200 troops left when it arrived in eastern Cochin China. The march further honed the will, endurance, and love of his comrades-in-arms of every one of our cadre and soldiers. Overcoming all hardships and challenges, our cadre and soldiers strode down the road, following the call of the Party to fight the Americans and save the nation, "following the flame in their hearts."

THE WAR IN THE SOUTH

In South Vietnam, in March 1966 COSVN met and set forward concrete policies to implement the resolution of the 12th Plenum of the Party Central Committee and the February 1966 resolution of the Central Military Party Committee. COSVN directed the three types of armed forces to develop their attack posture, "pull the enemy out of his lair to fight him, stretch his forces thin to fight him, wade into the enemy ranks to fight him, creep deep into the enemy's rear areas to fight him." The Region 5 Party Committee, the Region 5 Military Party Committee, and the Military Region 5 Command also established timely policies aimed at expanding guerrilla warfare to a high overall level to force the enemy to disperse his forces, and, on this basis, launch attacks against the enemy.

Following the 1965–1966 fall-winter campaign, the battlefields immediately began preparing for the 1966 spring-summer combat plan. The civilian population and guerrillas of the liberated villages and hamlets urgently strengthened their combat villages and established cells and teams specializing in attacking enemy communications routes and in firing at enemy aircraft. Many local areas held field exercises to practice countering enemy sweeps. Sapper and commando teams in and around the cities conducted reconnaissance operations day and night to assess the enemy situation and develop plans to attack assigned targets. Main force and local force units received additional troops, equipment, and supplies, and used the time available for political study and military training. Congresses of "Heroic Killers of Americans" were organized in many provinces and military regions to honor units and individuals who had accomplished feats of arms during 1965 and to share experiences in fighting the Americans. Emulation campaigns for the title of "Heroic Killer of Americans," "Heroic Destroyer of Vehicles," "Heroic Destroyer of Aircraft," "Hero Unit for Killing Americans," etc., were enthusiastically launched in all units and battlefields.

In January 1966 the American imperialists used their entire force of American, puppet, and satellite troops to launch their first strategic counteroffensive in South Vietnam. During a five-month period (from January through May 1966) they conducted 450 military sweep operations, of which 20 were large sweep operations.[1] The two principal theaters for the enemy's counteroffensive were eastern Cochin China and the lowlands of Region 5. These were strategic areas containing large liberated zones where our main force troops were mounting strong operations and exerting pressure on the military bases of the Americans and their puppets. The objectives of the enemy's counteroffensive were to defeat our main force units,[2] to support the focused "pacification" program,[3] to strengthen the puppet regime, and to regain the strategic initiative on the battlefield.

In the areas north-northeast and southwest of Saigon, the enemy launched many large operations to destroy the Duong Minh Chau, Boi Loi, Cu Chi, and Long Nguyen base areas; War Zone D, Xuyen Moc, and Hat Dich; and to seek out and destroy COSVN's main force 9th and 5th Divisions.

To deal with the enemy counteroffensive, COSVN Military Command directed all units and localities to launch attacks everywhere using the forces they had on hand to prevent the enemy from concentrating his forces in one theater and to force him to disperse his forces to deal with our attacks. Meanwhile, our main force troops would mass to attack areas the enemy had left exposed and attack important targets. Our troops were to utilize mobile attacks to annihilate enemy forces outside of their defensive positions as the principal tactic, in combination with shelling attacks and raids by sappers. North of Saigon the 9th Division and local armed forces mounted continuous attacks and counterattacks in Nha Do–Bong Trang (Thu Dau Mot province), Phu Hung and Ba Nghia (War Zone D), Bau San (the Duong Minh Chau War Zone), etc. In the Nha Do–Bong Trang battle on 24 February 1966, the 9th Division used one element of its forces to launch an attack to establish our position, while the majority of the division waited until the American troops pulled back to a position adjacent to the Nha Do "strategic hamlet." The division then launched a powerful surprise attack, inflicting severe casualties on one enemy regimental task force (consisting of a headquarters element, two infantry battalions, and one armored battalion).

Coordinating their combat operations with our main force troops, local force troops and guerrillas developed many innovative fighting tactics, which in some locations shattered large enemy sweep operations. In Cu Chi district (30 kilometers northwest of Saigon) the 306th Local Force Company and guerrillas from the various villages skillfully used homemade weapons and a tunnel system hundreds of kilometers long to fight off a large sweep operation conducted by almost 10,000 American troops.[4] During 12 days and nights of combat, the soldiers and civilians of Cu Chi district killed or wounded almost 2,000 American troops, destroyed 100 military vehicles, and shot down and destroyed 50 aircraft of all types. On 7 February 1966, the congress of "Hero Killers of Americans" of Cu Chi district laid out ten possible ways to defeat the enemy in guerrilla warfare[5] and rewarded the American-killing achievements of many local force cadre, local force soldiers, guerrillas, and civilians.

Southeast of Saigon the 4th and 5th Regiments of our 5th Division, working in coordination with local armed forces, mounted strong attacks against Route 15, attacked the American base at Vung Tau on 12 March 1966 (killing 300 enemy and destroying 30 helicopters), and mounted a mobile attack at Nui La north of Binh Gia, inflicting severe casualties on a battalion of the American 173rd Airborne Brigade.

In our theaters north-northeast of Saigon and southwest of Saigon, none of the "search and destroy" operations conducted by the Americans, puppet troops, and satellite troops achieved their objectives. COSVN's main force army maintained a firm foothold in the bases of eastern Cochin China and defeated the American expeditionary army during its first test of strength on the battlefield.

In Region 5, on 16 January 1966 the Military Region Command issued the following order to all armed forces: Wherever the enemy attacks first, mount a vigorous counterattack; wherever the enemy has not yet launched an attack, continue preparations and take the initiative to launch attacks in accordance with the spring 1966 combat plan.

In late January 1966, the Americans and their puppets mobilized 50 battalions[6] to conduct sweep operations in the provinces of the central part of Central Vietnam. They concentrated their forces in three theaters of operations: southern Quang Ngai province, northern Binh Dinh province, and southern Phu Yen province. Their objectives were to "seek out and destroy" the Military Region's main force 2nd and 3rd Divisions, to "pacify" a number of focal point areas in the coastal lowlands, to reopen their strategic lines of communications, and to clear the way for U.S. combat forces to move up into the Central Highlands. Strategic Route 19 (from Quy Nhon to Pleiku) in Binh Dinh province was the primary theater of operations for the enemy counterattack. Twenty-one of the 50 enemy battalions on the Military Region 5 battlefield were concentrated in this theater.

To deal with this massive counterattack, in January 1966, Military Region 5 unified command over the armed forces of the three types of troops in the Binh Dinh province area, establishing a Front Command headed by Senior Colonel Giap Van Cuong, Commander of the 3rd Division, Military Commander, and Comrade Hai Lam, Secretary of the Province Party Committee, Political Commissar. Three regiments of the 3rd Division were ordered to the districts of Hoai Nhon, An Lao, and Kim Son to serve as the core force to fight the enemy alongside our local armed forces.

From 28 January until early March 1966, the 22nd Regiment, together with Hoai Nhon district guerrillas, used our combat villages and hamlets to conduct a ferocious battle against the offensive spearheads of the American air cavalry soldiers at Cho Cat, Gia Huu, Chuong Hoa, Hy The, etc. The 2nd and 12th Regiments, working with guerrillas in Kim Son and An Lao districts, skillfully maneuvered their forces to enemy weak points and launched a number of assaults at Vuong Thom, Hill 304, Sung Stream [Suoi Sung], Da Tuong Stream [Suoi Da Tuong], and Loc Giang. In each battle, our soldiers and the guerrillas killed hundreds of enemy troops.

The specialty branch units of the 3rd Division displayed their independent combat tactics, sneaking deep behind enemy lines to conduct daring attacks against enemy rear bases. The 407th Sapper Battalion conducted a raid against the U.S. Air Cavalry Division base at An Khe, eliminating from the field of combat 520 enemy troops and destroying 97 aircraft. The 3rd Division's artillery units shelled the headquarters of the enemy operation at Bong Son, killing many enemy soldiers and destroying ten aircraft.

On 7 March 1966, the American troops were forced to halt their sweep operation in Binh Dinh province. Combining massed combat operations by our main force troops with local people's warfare and utilizing many innovative fighting methods, the 3rd Division and the local armed forces of Binh Dinh province conducted a heroic battle, shattering the largest counterattack mounted by American and satellite troops in South Vietnam during the 1965–1966 dry season.[7]

In Quang Ngai, on 26 January 1966 the enemy used 13 battalions (including five U.S. battalions) to mount a sweep operation in Duc Pho district aimed at seizing our liberated zone, destroying Military Region 5's 2nd Division, and opening Route 1 for traffic between Quang Ngai city and Sa Huynh. Relying on our people's warfare posture, the province and district local force troops and the guerrillas of Duc Pho blocked the operation and maneuvered their forces to attack enemy weak points. The Pho An village guerrilla team fought off two American companies during a six-hour battle, inflicting 106 casualties on their opponents. The Pho Cuong village guerrilla team organized their forces into two columns that mounted a surprise attack on the headquarters staff of an American battalion, killing 57 enemy. The civilian population of our villages supported combat operations of our soldiers and guerrillas and organized many face-to-face struggle movements to confront the American troops, thereby limiting their acts of murder and their pillaging of the people's property.

During this same period, in accordance with the Military Region Command's combat plan, the 2nd Division, under the command of Comrade Nguyen Nang, attacked a number of strong points held by puppet troops in western Son Tinh district. The enemy hurriedly transferred five battalions of U.S. troops conducting the sweep in Duc Pho over to reinforce the Son Tinh area.

On 4 and 5 March, the 1st and 21st Regiments of the 2nd Division used tactics that combined the use of blocking forces with mobile attacks to repel many assault waves of American troops in the area of High Point 62 and Chua Hill. U.S. Marines stationed at Chu Lai had to be brought in as reinforcements. On 17 and 18 March, the regiments of the 2nd Division mounted continuous assaults against this Marine relief column at Tinh Ha (in western Son Tinh) and An Hoa (in Binh Son district), eliminating from the field of combat hundreds of enemy troops. The counterattack mounted by U.S. and puppet troops in the Quang Ngai province area was a complete failure.

In Phu Yen province, on 18 January 1966 12 battalions of American, puppet, and South Korean troops launched a sweep operation in Tuy Hoa district aimed at locating and destroying the Southern Subregion's 10th Regiment and occupying our liberated zone. Seizing this opportunity to annihilate enemy forces outside their defensive fortifications, the 10th Regiment and provincial local force troops seized the offensive initiative, eliminating from the field of combat two companies of South Korean troops at Hao Son and the Ca Pass during an attack that was launched while the enemy was in the process of deploying his forces along Route 1. Following this battle, combining attrition tactics and small-scale annihilation attacks designed to hold each enemy column in check by concentrating our forces to annihilate individual enemy units in separate battles, the soldiers and civilians of Phu Yen province shattered a number of enemy columns, inflicting heavy losses on them.

The enemy's strategic counteroffensive in all three theaters of Region 5 failed because of our widespread people's war posture, our willingness to attack the enemy, and the innovative fighting methods of the armed forces of our three types of troops throughout the Military Region.

In the Central Highlands, the 1st Division and local armed forces launched two successive waves of operational activity. These were the spring operations, lasting from 15 February to 6 March 1966, northwest of Ban Me Thuot and the summer operations, from 25 March to 15 August 1966, in Pleiku. During these two operations the soldiers and civilians of the Central Highlands eliminated from the field of combat over 3,000 enemy, including over 1,000 American troops.

In Tri-Thien, the province and district local force troops, in cooperation with local village guerrillas, crushed the "Lam Son 325" operation mounted by puppet soldiers between 17 February and 3 March 1966, overran the A Sau commando base, expanded the liberated zone in western Thua Thien province, and protected the strategic transportation corridor.

Our sapper and artillery troops attacked and shelled many bases lying deep behind enemy lines, such as the airfields at Da Nang, Nuoc Man, Chu Lai, Pleiku, Tan Son Nhat, and Tra Noc. Many storage facilities for weapons and petroleum products and many hotels where American officers lived were attacked. Hundreds of pilots, officers, and technical personnel were killed and millions of liters of petroleum products and many aircraft and other implements of war were destroyed.

Units of the armed forces of our three types of troops specializing in attacks on enemy lines of communications, of which our engineer troops served as the core element, destroyed a number of bridges and culverts, built obstacles in the roads, and ambushed and annihilated infantry and mechanized forces, blocking enemy movements along a number of strategic routes for many days at a time and forcing the American and puppet armies to disperse their forces in outposts to protect the roads.

Working in coordination with the military struggle, the political struggle and troop proselytizing efforts conducted by the masses continued to increase. In many locations, the masses maintained their legal status and held power even in areas under enemy control. The "three clings" slogan, "The Party clings to the people, the guerrillas cling to the enemy, the people cling to the land," was put forward and implemented in many areas. In Cochin China, the people held power to at least some extent in 2,600 out of the total of 3,000 hamlets. In extreme southern Central Vietnam, the people destroyed 247 out of 560 "strategic hamlets." The citizens of Saigon, Hue, Da Nang, and many other cities and towns organized continuous struggles against American imperialist aggression, against terrorism, against the military draft, and demanding democracy and people's rights.

By mid-1966, after six months of fierce and difficult fighting, our soldiers and civilians in South Vietnam had defeated the first strategic counteroffensive conducted by 200,000 American and satellite troops and almost 500,000 puppet troops, eliminating from the field of combat 70,000 enemy troops (including 30,000 Americans), crippling 15 enemy battalions (including nine U.S. battalions), and preventing the enemy from successfully achieving the principal objectives of its counteroffensive.[8]

Evaluating this victory, the Politburo of the Party Central Committee pointed out:

> This was an extremely critical period for the resistance war against the Americans to save the nation. We achieved very important successes in strategy, tactics, and in our direction of the war. We won the first round in the limited war being waged by the American imperialists. We were victorious both militarily and politically, but most especially militarily. During the course of the fighting, we learned the strengths and weaknesses of the American expeditionary army and took our first step forward in drawing lessons from this valuable experience and clearly grasping the principles of the national liberation revolution in South Vietnam, thereby giving the entire Party and the entire population the resolve necessary to defeat the American aggressors.[9]

After the failure of their first large counteroffensive during the dry season of 1965–1966, the American imperialists continued to increase their troop strength and made urgent preparations to launch a second counteroffensive. During the summer of 1966 Johnson hastily dispatched an additional 100,000 troops, drawn from bases inside the United States and from American military bases in Europe, to the battlefields of South Vietnam.[10] By August 1966 the number of American troops directly involved in the war of aggression in Vietnam had risen to almost 300,000. The numbers of aircraft and of air strikes launched in the air war against North Vietnam during 1966 were double the 1965 figures: Five hundred tactical aircraft were involved, and the daily sortie average was between 200 and 250 sorties per day, with the maximum figure being almost 400 sorties on one day.

On 29 June 1966 the American imperialists sent their aircraft to bomb the Duc Giang gasoline storage facility in Hanoi and the Thuong Ly gasoline storage facility in Haiphong. This was a very serious new escalation of the war.

In July 1966 the Supreme National Defense Council of the Democratic Republic of Vietnam met in Hanoi. Chairman Ho Chi Minh presided over the meeting. The council was briefed on the combat and economic production situation of the army and civilian population in both North and South Vietnam. The council made an assessment of the enemy's new schemes and reached a number of decisions on major policies aimed at intensifying the war against the Americans to save the nation.

On 17 July 1966 Chairman Ho Chi Minh made an appeal to the soldiers and civilians of the entire nation: "This war may go on for five more years, ten more years, 20 more years, or even more. Hanoi, Haiphong, and a number of our other cities and enterprises may be destroyed, but the people of Vietnam are not afraid. *There is nothing more precious than independence and freedom.* When victory finally comes, our people will rebuild our nation so that it is even better, even more beautiful, than it was before."[11]

The words of Chairman Ho Chi Minh were the sacred voice of the Fatherland and had a powerful effect on the soldiers and civilians of our entire nation, encouraging them to unite as one person, to ignore every hardship and sacrifice, and to fight resolutely until we achieved total victory.

In response to Chairman Ho Chi Minh's words, "There is nothing more precious than independence and freedom," during the summer of 1966 almost 200,000 young people, men and women, in North Vietnam and thousands of youths in the liberated areas of South Vietnam enthusiastically enlisted in the armed forces. By the end of 1966 the total strength of our armed forces was 690,000 soldiers.[12] The number of troops training and fighting in North Vietnam was 460,000, and the number of troops fighting on the battlefields of South Vietnam was 230,000. In comparison with the figures for 1965, the technical and material support facilities of the General Department of Rear Services had increased by six times, equipment used in national defense enterprises increased by 3.3 times, and the storage capacity of our gasoline storage facilities increased by 2.7 times. Many groups specializing in training and dispatching troops to the battlefield were formed. We improved our handling of the movement of our troops, improving provisions for housing and feeding troops and for caring for the sick and wounded along the strategic transportation corridor in order to reduce our personnel losses along the Trail to the maximum extent possible. During the last six months of 1966, in addition to reinforcement troops, the Central Military Party Committee sent to South Vietnam two infantry divisions,[13] four separate infantry regiments, one artillery regiment equipped with DKB rockets, one artillery regiment equipped with A-12 rockets, four battalions of 12.8mm anti-aircraft machine guns, and numerous specialty branch units. The number of replacement troops sent south in 1966 was six times greater than the number sent in 1965. Our combat battalions in South Vietnam increased from 103 battalions (including 65 mobile battalions) in 1965 to 136 battalions (including 98 mobile battalions) in 1966.[14]

CORRECTING PROBLEMS

After more than a year of direct combat against the American expeditionary army in South Vietnam and against the U.S. air forces in North Vietnam, our army, together with our entire population, had demonstrated a very high will to fight and to win and had learned new lessons from our experiences in combat against the Americans. Our army had grown in strength and significantly increased its organizational capabilities and combat power. However, facing a new combat opponent and the ever-increasing demands of a revolutionary war, there appeared among a small number of our cadre and soldiers a number of distorted perceptions and thoughts, such as overestimating the military strength of the enemy, fear of bombing and shelling, and fear of the protracted, ferocious nature of the struggle. Many of the battles fought by our troops did not fulfill our requirements for wiping out entire units and capturing prisoners and weapons. Our losses of personnel and weapons in a number of battles were heavy. Our troops' adherence to disciplinary and other types of regulations and the administration of our troops and our technical and material facilities did not live up to our previous high standards. The material and spiritual lives of our soldiers, especially those serving on the battlefields and along the strategic transportation corridor, were fraught with difficulty.

In order to overcome these shortcomings and weaknesses, and to prepare for an even fiercer battle against the American, puppet, and satellite troops during the 1966–1967 dry season, the Central Military Party Committee decided to organize a wave of political activities called "Resolve to defeat the American aggressors" throughout the people's armed forces. The principal documents studied in this campaign were the resolution of the 12th Plenum of the Party Central Committee and Chairman Ho Chi Minh's 17 July 1966 appeal to the soldiers and citizens of the entire nation. The General Political Department issued directions and guidance plans and prepared education documents to stimulate patriotism, love of socialism, and hatred of the American aggressors in order to build up offensive thinking and determination to fight and to win. The main study methods used were on-the-job training and short-term training, using regular study sessions during combat and operations and reviewing experiences and deriving lessons learned as the primary method. At the same time we emphasized study conducted during Party committee and Party chapter activities and held cadre conferences and short-term political activities during the period between the two waves of combat operations.

In South Vietnam, during August 1966 COSVN and the COSVN Military Party Committee convened the second conference on political activities among the liberation armed forces of South Vietnam. COSVN emphasized that, in the new situation confronting the resistance war against the Americans to save the nation, the work of ideological leadership had to be proactive, flexible, and timely. This work had to ensure that in every possible situation our armed forces would not be confused or hesitant about our combat objectives and that a scientific basis would be used to build confidence and an offensive spirit. The conference honored units that had correctly carried out political work and had made substantial progress in their force building and combat operations. These units included COSVN's 5th and 9th Divisions; Military Region 5's 2nd and 3rd Divisions; the local force troops of Long An, Binh Duong, and Quang Nam provinces; the local force troops and guerrilla militia of the districts of Chu Chi (Saigon–Gia Dinh area); Duc Hoa (Long An province); Ben Cat (Thu Dau Mot province); Chau Thanh (My Tho province); Mo Cay (Ben Tre province); Phung Hiep (Can Tho province); etc.

The campaign to build "four good" Party chapters pursuant to the instructions of the Secretariat of the Party Central Committee was expanded widely and applied as appropriate, consistent with the conditions of combat and operations encountered by the armed forces. The work of educating Party members to increase their quality, knowledge, and operational abilities was carried out vigorously and constantly, combining study with honing their skills during combat and operational activities. A number of new members were admitted to the Party (over 50,000 during the two years 1966–1967) and the number of Party members who were drafted into the armed forces was sufficient to replace combat losses and to raise the leadership percentage of Party members in the army from 30 percent in 1966 to 40 percent in 1967. Because of these efforts, during a period when the number of troops and the number of units was expanding rapidly and there were many disruptions as a result of combat, all companies and units of equivalent size still had a Party chapter. The leadership quality of the Party chapters, and especially of the Party chapters in units directly involved in combat operations, was raised to a high level. Our Party members unceasingly strove to display their vanguard roles both during combat and during operational activities, resolutely putting into practice the revolutionary ideals that Chairman Ho Chi Minh had expressed in concrete terms for use during this era of combat against the Americans to save the nation: "As long as South Vietnam is not yet liberated, our Fatherland is not yet unified, and our people are not yet peaceful and happy, all of us must devote all of our spiritual resources and our energy to strive for and to sacrifice for the cause of the total victory of the revolution."[15]

The work of building Party organizations was directly related to the campaign to build military units that were strong in every respect, consistent with the combat position and operations of each type of unit. Beginning with a number of units that were developed on a trial basis in 1965, the campaign to build strong basic-level units expanded to all companies and company-sized units. Staff, political, and rear services agencies of all levels sent many cadre to assist basic-level units to implement this campaign. Thousands of units and Party chapters achieved the honorary title "Determined to Win Unit" and "Determined to Win Party Chapter."

In May 1966 the first All-Armed Forces Congress of Determined to Win Youth was held in the capital city of Hanoi. The congress reviewed the results of the Determined to Win Emulation Campaign conducted by youths in the armed forces, honored Youth Group chapters and Youth Group members who had made outstanding achievements in combat and combat support activities, and put forward examples of good experiences achieved in the work of educating and mobilizing youth within the army.

Following the first congress of emulation hero fighters of the liberation armed forces of South Vietnam (held in 1965), in late 1966 a congress of emulation hero fighters of the armed forces in North Vietnam was solemnly convened in the Ba Dinh Hall in Hanoi. The congress announced that the Chief of State of the People's Democratic Republic of Vietnam had issued an order awarding the title of "Hero of the People's Armed Forces" to 45 units and 43 individual cadre and soldiers. Good experiences and lessons learned in the work of youth mobilization within the army and heroic examples within the armed forces were used by the army's units and Youth Group chapters for study and to effectively encourage our youth to play the leading role while conducting the unit's force building and combat operations.

Along with the work of political development, military training also changed direction in response to the requirements of our combat missions in this new situation.

Based on the realities of combat operations conducted against the American expeditionary army, the General Staff prepared documents providing guidance to units from platoon up to division level for tactical training in mobile assault operations, ambushes, attacks against enemy forces holding fortified positions, urban combat, the use of measures to preserve secrecy and surprise, sticking close to enemy forces, attacking quickly and withdrawing quickly, and conducting continuous attacks. All these training measures were aimed at our goal of annihilating entire enemy battalions and regiments. After completing their training, a number of divisions held field exercises. A combined-arms combat exercise conducted by the 308th Infantry Division in Dong Trieu, Quang Ninh province, in late 1966 demonstrated that we had taken a new step forward in the combat skills of our troops. Live fire exercises conducted on 17 April 1966 by Regiment 84A, firing DKB rockets,[16] and by the 99th Battalion, firing A-12 rockets,[17] produced excellent results. Chairman Ho Chi Minh and a number of Politburo members personally watched and encouraged these units during this firing exercise. Also in 1966 the General Staff and the headquarters of the various military regions held many training classes for regiment- and division-level cadre, aimed at examining and exploiting good fighting techniques used by the various battlefields that had a high potential for annihilating enemy troops. These training classes helped to raise the capabilities of our cadre in such areas as command organization, deploying in-depth combat formations in a campaign-level operation, securing and maintaining superiority during the conduct of a campaign-level operation, and in organizing to fight key battles.

To carry out the instructions of the Central Military Party Committee and of the High Command, all armed forces schools changed the direction of their training, shifting from long-term training for peacetime conditions to short-term training for wartime. The length of each class was reduced from three years down to one year, and in some cases six months. The students attending these courses were cadre and soldiers who had participated in combat operations on the various battlefields, former military personnel who had been recalled to service, cadre from the various civilian governmental agencies, scientific and technical cadre, and university students. In response to our need to expand our armed forces, and especially our technical specialty branches, all schools increased the number of students attending basic and supplemental training classes, doubling the number of students. All schools placed special emphasis on training students who were transferring from one branch to another. The Army Officers School itself began training 3,500 students per year. The Signal and Chemical Faculties were separated from the Army Officers School to form the Signal Officers School (in mid-1965) and the Chemical Officers School (in late 1966). Using the realities of combat on the battlefield, with the guiding combat principles of the Party serving as a foundation, and drawing on the combat traditions and experience of the army, our schools studied course content and developed training programs that were suited to our various combat opponents and that responded to our ever-increasing need for cadre, especially cadre for low-level units within the army.

In South Vietnam, in August 1966 Lieutenant General Hoang Van Thai, Secretary of the Region 5 Party Committee and concurrently Political Commissar of Military Region 5, presided over a conference to review and learn lessons from the waves of operations conducted by the region's main force troops from the spring of 1965 through the summer of 1966. The conference raised many new issues regarding campaign-level and tactical-level techniques and political activities during combat operations against the new enemy, the American expeditionary army. In Cochin China and extreme southern Central Vietnam, the COSVN Military Command also reviewed and disseminated a number of lessons learned from experiences in command organization, in Party and political activities during combat operations against American infantry and mechanized forces, and in building "American killing belts." In September 1966, COSVN and the Region 5 Party Committee held a conference to summarize guerrilla warfare, to set forward immediate policies aimed at expanding local armed forces, to strengthen our ideological leadership activities, political education, and military training, and to provide military training and additional equipment to guerrilla militia forces.

Movements to make outstanding achievements in military training and to resolve to defeat the American aggressors were launched throughout the people's armed forces. The goals of these campaigns were to increase the combat power of our soldiers, to build combat-ready units, and to enable our troops to expertly employ mobile attack methods, tactics for attacks against fortified positions, independent combat tactics, and coordinated combat tactics on all types of terrain. The Military Region 5 Command and the COSVN Military Command set forward standards for designating "expert" regiments and "expert" battalions in order to provide concrete incentives for our units.[18]

An emulation movement to secure the "Resolved to defeat the American aggressors" flag, a rotating award presented by Uncle Ho, swept through the local areas and the units of the armed forces in North Vietnam. The soldiers and civilians of Military Region 4, Military Region 3, Quang Binh province, and many other localities won the honor of receiving this periodic award from Chairman Ho Chi Minh. On the flag were sewn the combat achievements in shooting down American aircraft that the local soldiers and civilians had attained. Individuals both within and outside the armed forces who had made outstanding achievements in combat or combat support were awarded the personal insignia of Chairman Ho Chi Minh.

Throughout North Vietnam, the task of building and increasing the combat quality of our armed forces, especially those serving in the Air Defense–Air Force Service, was the subject of special attention.

During the early months of 1966, as they were launching their first strategic counteroffensive on the battlefields of South Vietnam, the American imperialists simultaneously escalated their air and naval war of destruction against North Vietnam. They altered their flight formations and increased the number of fighters escorting their bombers and covering and suppressing our airfields, thereby causing many difficulties for our air force when our aircraft took off and attacked the enemy at low and medium altitudes. A number of anti-aircraft artillery units did not properly resolve the question of the relationship between killing the enemy and protecting the target. They emphasized firing to scare off and drive away enemy aircraft, putting up a "curtain of fire." This type of tactic caused the rapid deterioration of gun barrels, used up large quantities of ammunition, and was not effective either in shooting down enemy aircraft or in protecting the target. The enemy's increased use of jamming flight formations and jamming the guidance frequencies of our missile warheads caused 60 percent of the missiles launched by the missile battalions protecting Hanoi to lose guidance and self-destruct (this percentage is from early 1967). Along the coastline of Region 4 and of some provinces in Region 3 the enemy used commando vessels belonging to the puppet Navy and started using American cruisers and destroyers, anchored more than ten kilometers out to sea, to fire 187mm and 203mm guns at a number of onshore targets, primarily at night. Our artillery troops trying to provide counterbattery fire against these vessels ran into many problems. A number of units were confused about how to deal with the enemy's modern technical equipment and new tactics.

Chairman Ho Chi Minh constantly focused his attention on caring for the living standards and the combat situation of our troops. Every day Uncle Ho received a briefing, either in person or by telephone, from the Combat Operations Department on the combat situation in both North and South Vietnam. During these years, although Uncle Ho was growing increasingly old and weak, he still visited many anti-aircraft artillery and missile firing positions and many air force and radar units. When he visited an anti-aircraft artillery position, he would pick up a helmet to see how heavy it was and touch the gunner's seat to see if it was hot. Uncle Ho stressed the need to economize on ammunition, not to fire just to scare off or drive away the enemy but to shoot him down on the spot and capture the pilot. In each gun crew six soldiers must act as one, in a battery six guns must act as one, all firing at one aircraft. When he visited our air force troops, Uncle Ho instructed them, "You boys should take a lesson from the Liberation Army of South Vietnam, you should grab the enemy's belt to fight him." Uncle Ho donated his entire life savings as a gift to the air defense soldiers defending Hanoi.

To carry out Chairman Ho Chi Minh's instructions, the Party Committee of the Air Defense–Air Force Service Branch conducted studies that delved deeply into a number of major problems, such as the leadership and guidance requirements of a technical service branch; determining the relationship between destroying the enemy, protecting targets, and preserving our own forces; the relationship between political and technical matters; the relationship between people and weapons; teaching an understanding of the need to economize and to preserve our technical weapons and equipment; building coordination and solidarity to achieve collective feats of arms; stimulating every unit, every cadre, every soldier to seek good fighting methods and to exploit to the maximum the potential of the technical weapons we currently possessed to create a collective force to defeat the enemy. The Air Defense–Air Force Service Command, headed by Senior Colonel Phung The Tai as Military Commander and Senior Colonel Dang Tinh as Political Commissar, worked with the commands of the Anti-Aircraft Artillery, Missile, Air Force, and Radar Branches to study the operational procedures and attack tactics of enemy aircraft and to determine the strengths and weaknesses of both the enemy and ourselves. These studies were conducted through democratic discussions and were aimed at seeking fighting methods for use against the enemy.

Our anti-aircraft artillery troops held many specialized training programs on how to shoot down low-flying enemy aircraft, conducted supplemental training on combat procedures, held combined exercises with the air force, etc., simultaneously conducting vigorous training and field activities in all weather conditions. After a period of research conducted on the sites of many battles, the instructors from the Air Defense Officers School, with the enthusiastic cooperation of a number of instructor cadre from Hanoi University and the Hanoi University of Arts and Sciences, developed a table of calculations to determine where to site each firing section and each individual anti-aircraft gun to guarantee the placement of a steady and concentrated stream of fire during battles to protect specific targets.

Our missile troops held a conference to summarize combat operations for the year 1965, presenting at the conference many good experiences in moving our forces and constructing battle positions, in methods for firing at low-flying aircraft and in "guerrilla"-type fighting methods used by missile forces. In April

1966 a staff conference of the Missile Branch was convened to standardize the content of training classes, unify command and coordination activities during combat, and to standardize procedures for maintenance of equipment. After the conference, the Missile Branch held a training class for regiment- and battalion-level cadre and for a number of company level cadre and missile-firing team officers. The training class covered the work of studying the enemy and applying the combat leadership thoughts of our armed forces to the special circumstances and combat missions of our missile troops. Our missile battalions employed many types of wide-ranging, mass-type training, such as organizing classes to both teach and study, where good soldiers tutored those who were weak; studying during combat operations; studying while doing repairs and scheduled maintenance, etc. After receiving this excellent training, our missile troops step by step overcame the enemy's jamming tactics, continuing to fire missiles and maintain guidance on them during flight.

Our air force troops focused on improving our pilots' skills, practicing flying during bad weather conditions, low-altitude flying (including flying at low altitude over the ocean), flying at night, and attacking enemy aircraft at medium altitudes. At the same time they trained in the use of air-to-air missiles, in coordinated combat operations between Mig-17s and Mig-21s, in the use of small flight formations, and in the use of surprise and hit-and-run tactics.

Our radar troops focused on providing supplemental specialized training to our guidance operators and radar reporting personnel, combining theoretical training with practical training on actual radar machines to resolve technical problems in order to overcome the enemy's use of active and passive jamming equipment.

Along with these training activities, the organization and deployment of air defense forces in North Vietnam was also studied and adjusted. Because of the ever-increasing scale of combat operations, the use of air defense clusters whose principal organizational component was a regiment or battalion was no longer sufficient. The Air Defense–Air Force Service Command had a decentralized command organization, and we had been forced to establish a number of forward headquarters.

In June 1966 the General Staff decided to concentrate our main force air defense units into five divisions. The 361st, 363rd, 365th, and 369th Strategic Area Defense Divisions were formed, each with an authorized strength of between three and five anti-aircraft artillery regiments equipped with 57mm and 100mm guns. The 367th Mobile Air Defense Division had four anti-aircraft artillery regiments and one missile regiment. The scale of forces used in both static area defense and mobile air defense combat operations was expanded. Command organization and combat coordination between units, between anti-aircraft artillery, missiles, and air force aircraft, and between the air defense forces of our three types of troops was constantly improved. The birth of the air defense divisions was a new step forward in the development of our air defense–air force troops.

As soon as they were formed, our mobile and strategic area defense divisions displayed their coordinated combat power, shooting down many enemy aircraft. In July 1966 the Air Defense–Air Force Service Branch undertook a mobile combat operation in the Thai Nguyen area. The combat forces involved in this operation consisted of three missile regiments and three anti-aircraft artillery regiments. In September 1966, while enemy aircraft were mounting concentrated, continuous attacks on the stretch of Route 1 from Ninh Binh to Thanh Hoa, the 367th Air Defense Division conducted mobile combat operations from Phu Ly to the area north of the Ghep ferry. In one month the division fought 664 engagements (608 engagements using anti-aircraft artillery and 56 engagements involving missile forces), protecting the main targets under attack and shooting down 24 enemy aircraft. These were mobile combat operations at the air defense division level, organized in a relatively complete fashion in one theater of operations. They prepared the way for our air defense–air force troops to mount concentrated combat operations at the campaign level in the future.

With regard to the defense of the coastal areas of North Vietnam, the General Staff and the headquarters of the various military regions employed a number of artillery units from our main force elements as the core of our defenses and greatly expanded the artillery forces assigned to local force units and militia forces in our coastal villages. At the same time we launched a movement for the entire population to fight the enemy, putting into practice the slogan "control the close-in coastal waters and drive enemy ships far out to sea," and "the Party clings to the people, and the people cling to the ocean in order to increase production." The staff research agencies of the Artillery Branch and instructors from the Artillery Officers School drafted a number of documents providing guidance in methods for constructing onshore fighting positions, determining firing times, methods for using survey tables and range-finders out at sea, etc.

Three regiments of towed artillery subordinate to the 324th, 325th, and 341st Infantry Divisions and three batteries of coastal artillery subordinate to the Navy were transformed into local force artillery units subordinate to the coastal provinces. In early 1966, the artillery forces defending the coastline of Military Region 4 consisted of 17 local force batteries, 16 militia artillery units, and a number of artillery subunits attached to the units defending the islands of Con Co, Hon Ngu, Hon Mat, etc. The artillery forces defending the coastline of Military Region 3, which were built around a number of battalions from the 57th and 154th Artillery Regiments, consisted of a number of clusters of firing positions located at Hai Hau in Nam Ha province; Hoang Hoa, Sam Son, and Tinh Gia in Thanh Hoa province; and on the islands of Hon Me, Hon De, and Nghi Son. Besides these forces, there were also the militia "water combat teams" of the coastal villages of Vinh Linh, Quang Binh, and Thanh Hoa provinces. These teams, equipped with recoilless rifles, handheld explosive charges, and submachine guns, regularly took their boats out to sea and, in coordination with our coastal artillery positions, attacked enemy commando vessels.

Between early 1965 and October 1966, the artillery forces of our three types of troops sank 16 puppet commando vessels, set another 19 puppet commando vessels[19] on fire, and sank two seaplanes as they sat on the water. On 3 February 1966, Nghe An province's 15th Artillery Battery made the first counterbattery attack on an American destroyer[20] off the coast at Quynh Luu. On 22 April 1966, Ha Tinh province's 4th Artillery Battery hit and set afire a U.S. destroyer with the hull number "567." After October 1966 the American imperialists began using American cruisers and destroyers in place of puppet commando vessels to shell North Vietnam. The battle fought by our artillery forces to defend our coastlines would continue and change into a new phase.

PREPARATIONS FOR BATTLE IN SOUTH VIETNAM

In South Vietnam, after our defeat of the American imperialists' first strategic counteroffensive, all battlefields rapidly strengthened their forces, consolidated their positions, and prepared for even more ferocious battles during the 1966–1967 dry season.

In its early 1966 resolution on building up armed forces, the COSVN Party Military Committee set forward the following guidance:

> During 1966, we will primarily focus on strengthening, consolidating, and increasing the quality of the units we already have on hand and on receiving and properly handling the new forces we will receive from North Vietnam. With regard to our main force army, we will pay attention to building up divisions, but our main focus will be on ensuring that each individual regiment can truly fight well. We will expand our specialty branch forces, especially sappers and engineers, for attacking enemy lines of communications. With regard to our local force troops and guerrilla militia, the primary focus will also be on strengthening them and increasing their quality. Each separate battlefield may create additional units, depending on the battlefield's own individual capabilities, but we must ensure that any units so created actually have the strength and power they are supposed to have.[21]

Following these guidelines for force building, the COSVN Military Command and the military regions and fronts focused their attention on receiving new forces sent from the North, simultaneously sending cadre to localities to work with local Party committees to encourage the search for new recruits. In spite of many difficulties posed by the enemy's fierce "pacification" operations, the enemy's control over many heavily populated areas, and the heavy attrition still being suffered by our reinforcement troops during the long march down from North Vietnam, the total number of full-time troops on the South Vietnamese battlefield in 1966 grew by 32 percent over the total in 1965 (from 166,248 soldiers up to 219,640 soldiers). The main force troops subordinate to COSVN and to the various military regions made up 68 percent (151,111 soldiers) of the total troop strength, and of that total the number of specialty branch troops had grown rather rapidly (artillery troops grew by 162 percent and sappers by 64 percent).

On 13 June 1966, the COSVN Military Command formed the 7th Infantry Division, consisting of the 141st, 165th, and 52nd Regiments, in our base area in Phuoc Long province in eastern Cochin China. The 5th and 9th Divisions and the various independent regiments were gathered together, consolidated, and underwent a number of adjustments appropriate to their new combat responsibilities.[22] Each division was reorganized to add an additional battalion of 12.8mm anti-aircraft machine guns. Artillery Rocket Regiment 84A (which changed its designation to Regiment 72A), equipped with DKB rockets, and the 20th Composite Artillery Battalion (equipped with 75mm mountain guns and 120mm mortars) were added to the 69th Artillery Group to strengthen it.

In the Central Highlands, after receiving four additional regiments (the 24th, 88th, 101B, and 95B Regiments), the Central Highlands Front Command formed two understrength divisions in early 1966. Because of difficulties in providing these divisions with logistics support, however, in August 1966 both these divisions were disbanded. The main force units of the Central Highlands were organized into two separate elements. The mobile main force element consisted of the 1st Division (made up of the 66th, 320th, and 88th Regiments), Infantry Regiment 101B, and four battalions of mortars and anti-aircraft machine guns. The local main force element consisted of the 24th Regiment in Kontum, the 95B Regiment in Gia Lai [Pleiku], and the 33rd Regiment in Darlac. These regiments were assigned the mission of conducting combat operations behind enemy lines to directly support guerrilla warfare and to conduct combat operations in support of the front's mobile main force element.

In Region 5, the Military Region Command assigned the 31st Regiment, which had just arrived from North Vietnam, to the 2nd Division to bring it up to strength. The Military Region Command also transferred the 20th Regiment down to Khanh Hoa province to work with the 10th Regiment, operating in Phu Yen province, to serve as local main force elements in the Southern Subregion. The artillery forces of the Military Region were reinforced by the 368B Rocket Artillery Regiment, equipped with DKB rockets.

Including the 324th Division, which the High Command dispatched to the Route 9 Front in late 1966, the mobile main force elements of our armed forces in South Vietnam had now grown to eight infantry divisions,[23] one artillery division, a number of separate infantry regiments and battalions, and a number of specialty branch units.

While working to strengthen their forces, the COSVN Military Command and the military region and front commands devoted special attention to the issue of supplying and equipping our main force combat troops. In the Central Highlands, the soldiers and civilians of the various ethnic groups built a new transportation network from our main strategic road across to the east side of Route

14 and down to the provinces of Binh Dinh and Phu Yen. The ordnance, weapons, and military pharmaceuticals workshops and the hospitals of Troop Station [Binh Tram] North, Troop Station Central, and Troop Station South in the Central Highlands were consolidated and strengthened. Medical Treatment Teams 80, 81, 82, and 83 were deployed in our various theaters of operations. In eastern Cochin China, the COSVN Military Command established several new units, including Area Rear Services Groups 86 (Phuoc Long and Quang Duc provinces), 85 (Binh Long province), and 87 (Binh Thuan province) and Hospitals K-77B and K-97.

The rear services agencies of the various battlefields, transportation troop stations [binh tram], and area rear services groups properly handled the receipt of supplies from the supply transfer points belonging to Group 962 [ocean transport], Group 559, and Unit K-20 [ground transport][24] and then rapidly transferred these supplies to points where they could be issued to the units and localities. During 1966 many new types of weapons and implements of war were sent to the battlefield, increasing the equipment of main force and local force units. In Cochin China the number of B-40 anti-tank rocket launchers in each company in an infantry division increased from three launchers per company to nine launchers per company. Every regiment was issued 18 B-41 rocket launchers. The local force units of Tay Ninh and Binh Duong provinces had their allotment of B-40 rocket launchers increased from six per province to 70 per province. AK assault rifles were issued to units down to the local force level. Province local force battalions were issued 75mm recoilless rifles to replace their old 57mm recoilless guns, 82mm mortars to replace their 81mm mortars, and 12.8mm anti-aircraft machine guns to replace their old 12.7mm machine guns. Each main force battalion was equipped with a K-63 radio and a 15-watt transmitter. The artillery power of all of our main force elements was strengthened by the addition of DKB and A-12 rockets.

With regard to battlefield organization, pursuant to a decision of the Politburo, in April 1966 the Central Military Party Committee formed the Tri-Thien Military Region (designation: B4), using as its foundation the former Northern Subregion of Military Region 5. Major General Le Chuong was appointed Military Region Commander and concurrently Military Region Political Commissar. The armed forces in the Military Region's area of operations[25] were assigned the missions of intensifying their operations on all fronts, creating a new battlefield situation in Tri-Thien, and properly coordinating operations with other battlefields to prepare for all possible eventualities (including the possibility that the American imperialists might widen the ground war into central and lower Laos).[26]

In June 1966 the Central Military Party Committee and the High Command decided to form the Route 9–Northern Quang Tri Front (designation: B5). Senior Colonel Vu Nam Long was appointed Front Commander and Major General Nguyen Xuan Hoang was appointed Front Political Commissar. This was a correct strategic decision that forced the American army to further disperse their forces, thereby enabling the soldiers and civilians of the lowlands of Cochin China and of the other battlefields to conduct their own operations. The Route 9–Northern Quang Tri Front became a battlefield of attrition where we could annihilate enemy troops, draw in and tie down a significant portion of the American forces, and prevent the Americans from sending additional forces down to the lowlands of the Mekong Delta. It was a battlefield we used for combat operations, to hone our forces, and to elevate the combined-arms combat capabilities of our strategic mobile main force units.

In Central Vietnam, the Military Region 5 Command directed and commanded the main force elements of Region 5 and the local armed forces of Region 5 and the Central Highlands. The High Command directly controlled the combat operations of the main force units in the Central Highlands.

In Cochin China and extreme southern Central Vietnam, in May 1966 the COSVN Military Party Committee established the Rung Sat Special Military Zone (Group 10) to strengthen control over military and force building activities in the Rung Sat base area. In October 1966 Region 10 was formed, consisting of two provinces from Region 6, Quang Duc and Phuoc Long, and Binh Long province from Region 7. Region 10 was formed to consolidate and strengthen our base areas in the mountains, to develop the transportation corridor, and to support combat operations by main force units.

COMBATING THE 1966–1967 DRY SEASON COUNTEROFFENSIVE

During the summer and fall of 1966, all battlefields stepped up combat operations in order to consolidate our battlefield posture, train and hone our troops, and develop the necessary battlefield posture and strength to enable us to conduct military operations during the 1966–1967 dry season. On the Route 9–Northern Quang Tri Front, sappers, working in cooperation with the 324th Infantry Division, crept deep inside the enemy's defensive system south of the Ben Hai River and assaulted a number of strong points. Vinh Linh local force troops crossed the Ben Hai River and worked with the guerrilla militia there to support people's uprisings that seized control of 22 hamlets in the districts of Gio Linh and Cam Lo. In the Tri-Thien Military Region, the main force 6th Regiment and provincial local force battalions moved down into the lowland districts, wiping out Regional Force and Popular Force outposts and supporting popular uprisings that liberated a large, contiguous area from Hai Lang in Quang Tri to Thanh Huong in Thua Thien. Sappers attacked a number of enemy positions inside Hue city. In the Central Highlands, the armed forces of our three types of soldiers were very active in the area west of Routes 14 and 19. Sappers from Military Region 5 attacked the Nuoc Man airfield, the U.S. military vehicle park at Cam Binh, etc. In eastern Cochin China COSVN's main force 9th and 5th Divisions fought a number of regiment-sized battles at Can Dam, Can Le, Ka Tum, Xa Mat, and Long Khanh.

By the fall of 1966 the second phase of Westmoreland's "three-phase" strategic plan was over. The American imperialists had not been able to reach their goal of "searching out and destroying" our main force units in South Vietnam and had not been able to secure the battlefield initiative. Given their stubborn, aggressive, and warmongering nature, however, they hurriedly increased their forces. By the end of 1966 the number of U.S. and satellite troops stationed in South Vietnam had risen to 360,000 men, and the number of puppet troops had grown to 560,000. These forces included a total of 243 combat battalions (83 U.S. and satellite battalions and 160 puppet battalions). In comparison with 1965, the number of American expeditionary soldiers had doubled, and the number of aircraft, artillery pieces, and armored vehicles used in the war had tripled. They prepared to launch a new counteroffensive during the 1966–1967 dry season.

In October 1966, the Politburo of the Party Central Committee met in the capital city of Hanoi. The Politburo made the following assessment of the situation: "Although they have suffered a continuous string of failures, the American imperialists are now striving to increase their troop strength and their implements of war in order to step up their war of aggression with the objective of settling the Vietnam problem during the 1967–1968 period. The year 1967 will be of extremely great importance to both ourselves and the enemy."[27]

The Politburo decided to intensify the military and the political struggle in South Vietnam, to defeat the second strategic counteroffensive the American imperialists were planning, and to create opportunities and conditions favorable to big operations in the future that would secure a great victory and change the face of the war. The combat operations of our main force units would have to be developed to a new level to meet our requirement to annihilate enemy battalions, to be able to annihilate entire American and satellite brigades, and to drive each individual puppet division to its knees.

In October 1966, the American imperialists launched their second strategic counteroffensive on the battlefields of South Vietnam. They concentrated their forces in the main theater, eastern Cochin China, the focal point of which was to be the Duong Minh Chau base area, simultaneously trying to suppress and tie us down in the other theaters: the 1st Tactical Zone (from Tri-Thien to Quang Ngai), the Central Highlands, the lowlands of Region 5, and the Mekong Delta. On the Route 9 Front the enemy carried out an active defense aimed at blocking our main force units. With regard to North Vietnam, the enemy increased the operations of his air and naval forces aimed at destroying economic and military installations and attacking our land and water transportation networks leading to the battlefield.

After previously using "search and destroy" as their primary tactic, the American imperialists switched to a two-pronged strategy of "search and destroy" and "pacification." The American troops were the primary force used in the "search and destroy" prong aimed against our main force units. The puppet army was the primary force used in the "pacification" prong. The imperialists set out the following targets for the counteroffensive: the destruction of a significant portion of our main force army, the destruction of our resistance bases, "pacification" operations to gain population and greatly expand their area of control, relieving the pressure our forces were applying on them in the area surrounding Saigon, and the achievement of a military victory that would change the character of the war by mid- or late 1967.

The United States believed the annihilation of our resistance command organization in South Vietnam and the annihilation of our main force divisions in eastern Cochin China would be a decisive blow that could end the war. Therefore, for their second strategic counteroffensive the U.S. Command concentrated in this theater of operations a total of three U.S. divisions, four U.S. brigades, two puppet brigades, and one reinforced battalion of Australian troops. This force constituted 52 percent of the U.S. infantry strength and 40 percent of the total U.S. troop strength in South Vietnam.

Correctly assessing the enemy's schemes and actions, in early October 1966 the COSVN Military Party Committee and the COSVN Military Command ordered the 9th division and local armed forces to launch a wave of operations in the Tay Ninh province area to seize the initiative, to deliver a preemptive blow to the enemy as he was in the process of implementing his counteroffensive plan, and to protect the Duong Minh Chau base area. At the same time our forces were ordered to prepare and be ready to switch to launching counterattacks should the enemy mount a sweep into our bases. The 5th Division was ordered to mount supporting operations in the Ba Ria–Long Khanh area.

On 4 November 1966, the United States landed troops by helicopter at Bau Gon, launching their Operation "Attleboro" to sweep through the Duong Minh Chau base area.[28] Utilizing fortifications that had been prepared in advance, the 9th Battalion of the 16th Regiment drove back two successive enemy attacks, eliminating 600 troops from the field of battle. The American general commanding the 196th Brigade was relieved of his command on the battlefield. The regiments of the 9th Division flexibly employed mobile attack tactics, inflicting attrition and, alongside the cadre and personnel of the staff agencies and units in our base area, killed thousands of enemy troops. On 26 November the American forces were forced to withdraw from the Duong Minh Chau base area.

In order to prepare a springboard position for further attacks into our base area, and at the same time to implement their plan to expand the security perimeter on the northern approaches to Saigon, on 8 January 1967 over 30,000 U.S., puppet, and satellite troops[29] launched Operation Cedar Falls to sweep through the Cu Chi–Ben Cat–Ben Suc area, the so-called Iron Triangle. The 2nd Regiment of the 9th Division, together with the local people's armed forces of Saigon–Gia Dinh, used the network of tunnels and fortifications belonging to our combat villages to resolutely block the enemy advance, inflicting more than 3,000 casualties on their forces. On 26 January 1967 the American and puppet troops were forced to halt the sweep operation. The Saigon–Gia Dinh City Party Committee, the Saigon–Gia Dinh Military Command, and COSVN's main force 16th Regiment continued to maintain a firm foothold on the "steel earth" of Cu Chi.

Having been unable to achieve their objectives during two large operations, the American military urgently prepared a new attack against the Duong Minh Chau base area. Beginning in early February 1967, every day the enemy sent thousands of truckloads of ammunition to their assembly areas at Hon Quan, Minh Thanh, Dau Tieng, Suoi Da, and Tay Ninh city. B-52 strategic bombers and tactical aircraft mounted continuous bombing attacks and spread poisonous chemicals to burn off the jungle vegetation along the roadsides and riverbanks in order to prepare their routes of advance and landing zones.

COSVN, the COSVN Military Party Committee, and the COSVN Military Command provided guidance to our units and local areas, directing them to urgently prepare to engage the enemy.

The Duong Minh Chau base area lay in a large, sparsely populated jungle mountain area in Tay Ninh province. First formed during the resistance war against the French and further built up during the resistance war against the Americans, Duong Minh Chau had become a large base area in Tay Ninh, a place where we had concentrated many vital command and staff organizations, such as COSVN, the headquarters of the National Liberation Front for South Vietnam, the COSVN Military Party Committee, and Liberation Radio. In order to utilize the combined strength of people's war in a base area that was almost devoid of civilian population to repel a massive military operation conducted by U.S. troops, the COSVN Military Command decided to divide the base area into many large and small battle areas that were designated "districts," "villages," and "hamlets." The "hamlets" linked together to form combat "villages," and our fortified areas were able to support one another. All cadre and personnel assigned to the staff organizations of the COSVN Military Command and the various Party and National Liberation Front organizations (totaling almost 10,000 personnel) were organized into local armed forces and equipped with infantry weapons and B-40 anti-tank rocket launchers. The 1st, 2nd, and 16th Regiments of the 9th Division and the 3rd Regiment were all given additional artillery and mortars and were deployed in mobile positions west of Route 22 and east of Route 13. All staff organizations and military units were issued a three-month supply of food and ammunition. Combat fortifications were consolidated and extended. A command communications network was extended out to each individual area. Soldiers and self-defense forces of staff agencies trained and conducted field exercises in accordance with the combat plan. Instructions on "crushing the two-pronged attack by the Americans and their puppets" and a document on the "situation and duties for 1967" were prepared by COSVN and the COSVN Military Party Committee and were disseminated to every cadre and soldier. From a virtually unpopulated mountain region, the Duong Minh Chau base area was built up into an interconnected fortified area with numerous combat forces organized into three types of troops. The soldiers and civilians of the provinces of Tay Ninh, Binh Long, Thu Dau Mot, Ba Ria, Long Khanh, and of Saigon–Gia Dinh intensified their activities of all types in support of the armed forces in our base area.

On 22 February 1967, the enemy, using 45,000 soldiers, 11,000 vehicles (including 2,000 tanks and armored personnel carriers), and 600 aircraft[30] launched Operation Junction City to attack and destroy the Duong Minh Chau base area. Combining helicopter assault landings with vehicle-mounted assault columns advancing from many different directions, the American and puppet soldiers surrounded and isolated a campaign area covering a large region (from Bau Co–Dong Pan, west of Route 22, all the way out to the Cambodian border). They then sent many attack spearheads deep into the base area. This was the largest operation of the second strategic counteroffensive, and it also was the largest offensive ever conducted by American forces in South Vietnam.

With preprepared positions, the self-defense units of our staff organizations seized the initiative and attacked the enemy as soon as their troops hit the ground. During the first day our soldiers killed almost 200 American troops, hit and knocked out 16 armored vehicles, and shot down 16 aircraft of all types. Our main force regiments launched mobile assaults on enemy command headquarters, troop concentrations, artillery parks, and vehicle parks at Trang A Lan, Dong Pan, Bau Co, and Trang Bang. After almost one month of sweep operations the American troops still had not attained their objectives. We had fought them everywhere, their forces had suffered attrition,[31] and their soldiers were tired and confused. General Seaman, the commander of the operation, was relieved of command. In mid-March 1967 the American soldiers were forced to pull their forces back into separate defensive clusters to prepare for a new round of attacks.

Phase one of the campaign was over. Our units had all made outstanding combat achievements, but there had not yet been any big battles of annihilation. The COSVN Military Command instructed all units to draw lessons from their combat experiences to combat the problems of being afraid to concentrate troops to fight big battles and of fear of the American tanks. Our rear services groups quickly issued additional weapons and ammunition, especially B-40 rocket launchers and B-40 rockets. Determined to achieve a complete victory in this campaign, the COSVN Military Command decided to concentrate our main force units to fight one or two battles aimed at annihilating entire American battalions and simultaneously using our local forces to mount widespread combat activities.

On 18 March, the enemy launched an attack from two directions, continuing its attack into the northeastern sector of the base area. The self-defense teams of our staff agencies resolutely fought them off, wiping out small, scattered enemy units and enabling our main force troops to mass for battle.

On 19 March, the 3rd Regiment assaulted a troop concentration of the 1st Brigade, U.S. 9th Division, at Bau Bang, eliminating from the field of combat 400 enemy troops and destroying 63 armored vehicles. On 20 March, the 2nd and

16th Regiments, coordinating their actions closely, inflicted heavy casualties on a U.S. troop concentration at Dong Rum. The 3rd Brigade of the U.S. 4th Division was rendered combat ineffective (suffering casualties of over 1,200 men, losing 72 armored vehicles and 19 artillery pieces, and ten aircraft destroyed). On 31 March the 1st Regiment and the 7th Battalion of the 16th Regiment attacked an American troop concentration at Trang Ba Vung, inflicting heavy casualties on one infantry battalion and one artillery battalion of the 2nd Brigade, U.S. 1st Division.

Although they had used a heavy concentration of tanks and armored personnel carriers, creating a powerful and overwhelming assault force for their sweep operation, the American forces were unable to attain their objectives. Having suffered severe casualties, they were finally forced to withdraw from the sweep area. One-third of their troops (14,000 men), half of their artillery (112 artillery pieces), one-third of their tanks and armored personnel carriers (775 vehicles), and 160 aircraft had been eliminated from the field of combat.[32] On our side, 280 cadre and soldiers were killed, including 38 self-defense troops of our staff agencies.

Having correctly assessed the plots and actions of the enemy, actively prepared the battlefield, skillfully organized our staff agencies and main force units into an armed force with three types of troops, employed efficient fighting methods, and launched attacks both within and outside of the area covered by the enemy sweep, our soldiers on the battlefield of eastern Cochin China had inflicted attrition on the enemy, wiping out many enemy troops and implements of war, preserved our own forces, protected our leadership agencies and our bases, and defeated the biggest "search and destroy" operation to be launched by the American imperialists during their 1966–1967 dry season offensive.

In the Central Highlands, implementing the strategic coordination plan for all of South Vietnam, the Front Command launched an offensive campaign against the enemy in northwestern Kontum province. The civilian population of the Central Highlands ethnic minority people transported thousands of tons of rice to our troop assembly areas. The 66th, 32nd, and 88th Regiments of the 1st Division, Regiment 101B, and the 200th and 32nd Artillery Battalions, together with local armed forces, established an in-depth combat position in which the area where we were determined to fight was the area west of the Po-Co and Sa Thay Rivers. The 24th and 33rd Regiments stepped up their activities to lure enemy forces to the areas north of Kontum and north of Ban Me Thuot. Regiment 95B and the engineer and signal units of the Front Command conducted a heavy program of deception operations. The U.S. Command hastily moved a brigade of the Air Cavalry Division up into the Central Highlands, where the brigade, together with puppet troops, launched Operation Paul Revere in the area west of the Po-Co and Sa Thay Rivers, an area they suspected was the rear area for our campaign. Artfully manipulating the enemy and relying on the battle positions that we had prepared beforehand, the main force regiments of the Central Highlands Front eliminated from the field of combat over 2,000 enemy troops. In early 1967, the American and puppet forces were forced to pull their forces back to defend the area east of the Po-Co River. Our armed forces on the Central Highlands battlefield, which had been reinforced by the 174th Regiment of the 316th Division and the newly formed 40th Artillery Regiment[33] maintained the initiative in the campaign by continuing to attack the enemy, forcing the Americans to withdraw their forces from the Sa Thay and Sung Thien areas and retreat to defend Kontum and Pleiku cities.

On the Route 9 Front, the American policy was to conduct an active defense aimed at blocking offensive operations by our main force units. In February 1967 they sent the U.S. 3rd Marine Division and two puppet regimental task forces to the area south of the Demilitarized Zone to build a system of strongly fortified defensive strong points, including a firebase at Hill 241 where seven artillery units (including eight 175mm guns) were stationed. From this firebase their artillery fired continuous barrages, creating an arc of fire from Dong Ha through the villages north of the Demilitarized Zone all the way to the western portion of Route 9.

Rocket Artillery Regiment 84B, equipped with DKB rockets, was ordered to cross the Ben Hai River and, in cooperation with elements of the 164th Artillery Regiment equipped with H-6 rockets and 120mm and 82mm mortars and with artillery belonging to the 324th Infantry Division, to attack the enemy. On 28 February 1967, an ammunition transportation squad of Regiment 84B, consisting of ten soldiers under the command of Deputy Platoon Leader Bui Ngoc Du, unexpectedly encountered enemy troops in the area of Cu Dinh Mountain in Cam Lo district, Quang Tri province. The squad drove off 15 separate assaults launched by 200 American Marines, killing 41 enemy troops, capturing nine weapons, and protecting the secrecy of the coming battle.

During the night of 6–7 March 1967, having chosen the most advantageous time, our artillery poured more than 1,000 rounds of all types onto Base 241, killing 1,490 American troops and destroying 80 percent of this enemy base, including 22 large artillery pieces and 35 military vehicles. This was the first large-scale attack by fire employing DKB rockets to be launched in South Vietnam, and it achieved a high degree of combat effectiveness.

In mid-March 1967, the 164th Artillery Regiment of Military Region 4 sent two of its battalions, the 1st Battalion, equipped with 11 100mm guns, and the 11th Battalion, equipped with nine 105mm howitzers, all the way down to the northern bank of the Ben Hai River to prepare to attack the enemy. A regimental observation post, under the command of Platoon Leader Trinh Van Xuat, was placed at the top of the 32-meter-high flagpole north of the Hien Luong Bridge. The civilian population of Bau hamlet, Vinh Thuy village, used wood and bamboo to line the roads to allow the artillery pieces to move. The Thuy Ba cooperative even used their water buffalo to tow the guns to help our soldiers get through the narrowest sections of the road. At dusk on 20 March 1967 our observation post noted that the enemy had just sent two U.S. Marine Battalions, an artillery battalion, and 30 armored personnel carriers to reinforce the Doc Mieu base (located six kilometers south of Hien Luong). Seizing this opportunity, our artillery fired a barrage of 1,120 rounds of artillery, which we then followed up with 350 rounds of 82mm mortars. During this artillery attack we killed over 1,000 enemy troops and destroyed 17 artillery pieces, 57 military vehicles, and three helicopters.

Also during the night of 20 March, taking advantage of the enemy's pre-occupation with trying to deal with our artillery at Doc Mieu, the 4th Battalion of Regiment 84B, assisted by infantry elements, carried 78 launchers and 258 A-12 rockets across the Ben Hai River. Moving rapidly, our soldiers marched 20 kilometers south to fire a barrage at enemy positions in Dong Ha. Our forces then withdrew safely to Vinh Linh before dawn.

On 13 April 1967, Chairman Ho Chi Minh sent a letter of commendation to our artillery troops. He wrote, "Our artillery has the glorious tradition of having legs of bronze and shoulders of iron, of fighting well and firing accurately." He said, however, "Do not become overconfident because of your victories. You must strive to learn from and emulate the skillful, heroic artillery troops of the Liberation Army of South Vietnam. You must maintain a high 'determined to fight, determined to win' spirit, maintain excellent and close coordination with other friendly units and with the people, economize on the use of ammunition, fight well and fire accurately, and accomplish many more feats of arms."[34] Uncle Ho's words of instruction, "legs of bronze and shoulders of iron, fight well and fire accurately," became the eight golden tradition words and the slogan of the heroic Artillery Branch.

This counterpunch thrown by our artillery troops terrified the American troops. They had to pull back from a number of their strong points, and at the same time they sent many waves of B-52 strategic bombers and attack aircraft to bomb our artillery firing positions. The 238th Anti-Aircraft Missile Regiment was dispatched to Vinh Linh by the High Command to strike back at the enemy. During a 600-kilometer march through many steep passes and across many enemy bombing choke points, the 238th Missile Regiment overcame a great many difficulties, protecting its weapons and equipment. The regiment built its firing positions within range of the enemy artillery south of the Ben Hai River. In May 1967 the regiment shot down one B-52 and a number of enemy attack aircraft.

Exploiting the independent fighting methods of the artillery and missile forces, the main force troops of the Route 9 Front wiped out many enemy troops and implements of war and lured in and tied down a significant element of the American and puppet armies, thereby enabling the other battlefields, and most directly the Tri-Thien battlefield, to step up their own operations.

In Tri-Thien, during the night of 5 April our sapper troops, in coordination with infantry forces, simultaneously attacked a number of targets in Quang Tri

202 VICTORY IN VIETNAM

city, the headquarters of the puppet 1st Regiment, 1st Division, at La Vang, and the headquarters of the puppet 3rd Regiment, 1st Division, at Tu Ha. In these battles we killed almost 2,000 enemy, including a number of puppet tyrants, and helped the people in 30 villages rise up in insurrection. The liberated zone of Quang Tri and Thua Thien provinces was expanded right up to the edges of the towns and cities and even to the edge of Hue city. The guerrilla forces of the lowland districts rose to more than 10,000 soldiers. Each district now had one or two local force companies.

In Region 5 the battle against enemy "pacification" was fierce and vicious. In the contested areas, 27 U.S. battalions and 21 battalions of South Korean troops launched many sweep operations aimed at pushing back our main force units. In the lowlands, 54 puppet battalions conducted "pacification," totally destroying 300 villages and hamlets. Over 200,000 residents of our liberated zones were forced into areas that were under the control of the enemy. The people of the lowlands of Region 5 conducted face-to-face political struggles combined with wide-ranging combat operations by local armed forces, resolutely holding onto our liberated zone. In a number of villages, our guerrillas stayed in place, driving back the enemy troops conducting their sweeps. In the contested areas, the Military Region's main force units fought a number of highly productive battles, supporting local armed forces and population in combating "pacification." The 12th and 22nd Regiments of the 3rd Division ambushed enemy forces at Long Giang in Binh Dinh, annihilating four companies of the U.S. Air Cavalry Division, and attacked a base held by U.S. artillery and one U.S. infantry battalion at Xuan Son. The 1st Regiment, 2nd Division, inflicted heavy casualties on a South Korean battalion holding a fortified position at Quang Thach in Quang Nam province. The 31st Regiment, 2nd Division, which had just arrived from North Vietnam, won a victory in its very first engagement, overrunning the Trung Phuoc strong point held by 600 puppet troops. During an ambush on a stretch of road between Huong An and Ba Ren, the regiment destroyed 200 vehicles. The 99th Rocket Battalion, equipped with A-12 rockets, with the help of the Party committees and civilian population of Da Nang and of Hoa Vang and Dien Ban districts, covertly moved its launchers and rockets right up to the edge of the Da Nang airfield. On 22 February 1967 the battalion fired 160 A-12 rockets at their targets, destroying 94 aircraft and 200 military vehicles and killing many pilots and technical personnel. The airfields at Nha Trang and Chu Lai, as well as many other bases of the Americans, their puppets, and their satellite nations, were also attacked by our sappers, artillerymen, and the other armed forces of the Military Region.

In the lowlands of Cochin China, the People's War spread like wildfire. The local force troops of Long An, My Tho, Ben Tre, Tra Vinh, Can Tho, and Rach Gia provinces wiped out or inflicted heavy casualties on a number of enemy battalions operating outside defensive fortifications. In October 1966, Military Region 9's 1st Regiment, together with local armed forces, attacked and caused a puppet regiment at Go Quao, Rach Gia province, to disintegrate. On 28 March 1967, the 1st Regiment, supported by artillery and sappers, sank eight U.S. vessels on the Ham Luong River, eliminating from the field of battle more than 1,000 enemy soldiers. Sapper and commando troops of Saigon–Cho Lon and of the Rung Sat Sapper Group sank U.S. vessels on the Long Tau River and attacked the Long Binh logistics depot and the Tan Son Nhat airfield, inflicting many losses on the enemy and disrupting his rear area. Of special note was an action on 1 November 1966. Two 75mm recoilless rifle teams from the 6th Binh Tan Battalion and from the Rung Sat Special Zone, with the help of the local population, fired accurately into the grandstands of a parade being put on by the puppet army to celebrate the Saigon puppet government's "National Day," spreading complete panic through the entire gathering.

The 1966–1967 dry season ended. With 400,000 American and satellite troops and 800,000 puppet troops and 895 continuous sweep operations, the enemy still had not achieved the target objectives of his second strategic counteroffensive. His losses in manpower and implements of war were much greater than those incurred during the 1965–1966 dry season.[35]

Our soldiers and civilians on the battlefields of South Vietnam had maintained the strategic initiative, successfully combined force building with combat operations, developed many innovative fighting methods, defeated the enemy's two-pronged ("search and destroy" and "pacification") plan of attack, and enabled the revolutionary war against the Americans to save the nation to develop to a new, higher level.

THE WAR IN NORTH VIETNAM

In North Vietnam, in coordination with their strategic counteroffensive in South Vietnam, the American imperialists further escalated their war of destruction. They increased their total number of aircraft, the number of sorties flown, and the quantity of bombs dropped, launched massive aerial assault waves against Hanoi, Haiphong, and a number of other cities, towns, and industrial installations, and sowed mines in the mouths of a number of our rivers and in our coastal waterways.

On 20 April 1967, over 100 U.S. aircraft bombed many targets in Haiphong city, initiating a continuous bombardment program against the center of the city. The 363rd Air Defense Division, with three regiments and two separate battalions of anti-aircraft artillery, the 285th Missile Regiment, and local anti-aircraft forces, fought heroically, firmly protecting the flow of international aid through the port of Haiphong. In 1967 the soldiers and civilians of the city shot down 142 enemy aircraft and captured many pilots.

Predicting that the enemy would launch large attacks against Hanoi, the General Staff and the Air Defense–Air Force Command transferred forces to strengthen the curtain of anti-aircraft fire protecting the skies over the capital city of Hanoi. During the first months of 1967, half of the anti-aircraft artillery units, including two divisions, four separate regiments, and three separate battalions, and all of the Air Force combat regiments of the Air Defense–Air Force Service Branch, were assigned the mission of defending Hanoi. The City Party Committee, the City People's Committee, and the Capital Military Command mobilized and organized collective farmers and workers, cadre and personnel from governmental agencies, youths, students, and city block committees into cells and teams to fire at enemy aircraft with infantry weapons. They also mobilized thousands of laborers to assist our troops in building firing positions. Hundreds of anti-aircraft artillery firing positions, missile firing positions, and firing positions for the self-defense militia combat teams appeared in the rice and vegetable fields on the city's outskirts, under the pillars of the Long Bien Bridge, and on bamboo rafts floating on the city's Western Lake [Ho Tay]. Over half of the residents of the inner city were evacuated. Thousands of fortifications protected supplies and machinery. Tens of thousands of individual shelter holes and bomb shelters were built in the factories, schools, and along the city streets. Chairman Ho Chi Minh, the Party Central Committee, the Cabinet, and the High Command in Hanoi all directly monitored and provided guidance for the battle to protect the Capital and the entire nation.

On 25 April 1967, the enemy sent over 300 aircraft sorties to bomb Hanoi, initiating the most ferocious bombing campaign of 1967. With a high spirit of combat readiness and a resolve to concentrate our forces to protect the important targets and to attack the enemy when he was still far away on his approach to the target, our missile soldiers and anti-aircraft soldiers, together with the air defense forces of our three types of troops, put up a ferocious resistance. On 25 April Hanoi shot down ten enemy aircraft. On 26 April it shot down eight aircraft. A number of aircraft were shot down and crashed on the spot in the fields of the districts of Dong Anh, Tu Liem, etc., on the city's outskirts. Our air force troops made many flights, coordinating well with our ground air defense forces, and on one occasion shot down three aircraft in a single day (16 July 1967).

On 19 May 1967, in celebration of Chairman Ho Chi Minh's 77th birthday, the soldiers and civilians of Hanoi scored an outstanding feat of arms, shooting down eight enemy aircraft. An American aircraft crashed right on Le Truc Street. An American pilot was captured on Thuy Khue Street.

Having suffered heavy losses in his attacks on Hanoi, in June 1967 the enemy had to shift his attacks to the lines of communications from Haiphong and Lang Son to Hanoi and from Hanoi to Military Region 4. The Air Defense–Air Force Service Command swiftly shifted a number of units to these theaters to combat the enemy, at the same time continuing to maintain an appropriately sized force to protect our strategic sites and to defend our lines of communications and dike system during the rainy season. In August 1967 the enemy again concentrated his attacks on striking Hanoi and mining the port of Haiphong. With increased forces[36] that were properly deployed and with combat coordination between the specialty branches, the air defense forces of our three types of troops and the soldiers and civilians of Hanoi and Haiphong crushed the massive attacks launched by the American air forces. In 1967 Hanoi shot down 191 aircraft and captured many pilots. Among these aircraft was the 2,000th aircraft shot down over all of North Vietnam. On 5 November 1967 Chairman Ho Chi Minh sent a letter of commendation to the soldiers and civilians of the Capital. He wrote, "This achievement is a practical remembrance of the 50th anniversary of the October Revolution."

During the heroic fight to defend Hanoi and Haiphong, our air defense–air force troops reached a new level of maturity in their command organization and their ability to conduct large-scale combined-arms combat, mounting combat operations equivalent to anti-aircraft campaigns to protect area targets and transportation lines.

Alongside Hanoi and Haiphong, the soldiers and civilians of all local areas in North Vietnam continued to increase production, intensify combat operations, and vigorously provide all types of support to South Vietnam. During the last months of 1967, there were many days when we shot down ten enemy aircraft throughout North Vietnam, and the highest one-day total was 19 aircraft (on 19 November). During a battle on 17 October 1967 a 37mm anti-aircraft battalion protecting Dap Cau shot down five aircraft, four of which crashed on the spot. The women's militia platoon of Hoa Loc village, Hau Loc district, Thanh Hoa province, and many other self-defense militia units shot down American jet aircraft using only infantry weapons. Quang Binh province's 85mm artillery battery damaged the U.S. destroyer *O'Brian* (on 23 December 1966) and the U.S. cruiser *Canberra* (on 1 March 1967) while they were shelling the coastal areas of North Vietnam.

The great victory of the soldiers and civilians of North Vietnam in crushing this highest level of escalation of the first war of destruction conducted by the American pirates supported and kept pace with the battles being waged by our soldiers and civilians in South Vietnam, defeating the maximum effort of more than one million U.S., puppet, and satellite troops in their second strategic counteroffensive. The Vietnam People's War and the courageous, innovative fighting methods of the People's Army of Vietnam clearly demonstrated our ability to defeat the large, modernly equipped American imperialist army of aggression. America's "limited war" strategy faced bankruptcy. New capabilities and new opportunities had been opened up for our soldiers and civilians to use to secure even greater victories.

9

The People's Army, Together with the Entire Population, Conducts the General Offensive and Uprising of Tet 1968

ORGANIZATIONAL PREPARATIONS FOR THE TET OFFENSIVE

By defeating two successive counteroffensives by the American imperialists in South Vietnam and defeating their war of destruction against North Vietnam, our soldiers and civilians had, to a significant extent at least, defeated the U.S. "limited war" strategy. In South Vietnam our army continued to hold and exploit the strategic initiative. The armed forces of our three types of soldiers had expanded quickly and had, through the flexible use of a number of different tactics, destroyed a large portion of the enemy's manpower and implements of warfare. When measured against the political and military objectives the Americans had set for themselves, and viewed in the context of America's actual political, economic, and social situation, the U.S. war effort in Vietnam had reached its apex.[1] Because, however, they had not been able to attain the objectives they had set for themselves in Vietnam, from a strategic standpoint the American imperialists were caught "between a rock and a hard place." A number of their key leadership personnel became disillusioned.[2] The campaign for the U.S. presidential elections in 1968 further diverted the U.S. ruling clique. However, because of their stubborn, aggressive nature and their confidence in their own strength, the American imperialists continued to send additional troops into South Vietnam,[3] intensified the air war of destruction against North Vietnam, and made rapid preparations to launch a third strategic counteroffensive during the 1967–1968 dry season.

Assessing the situation from every angle and clearly recognizing the strategic situation and opportunity that had appeared, in April 1967 the Politburo and the Central Military Party Committee discussed a policy for achieving a decisive victory. Pursuant to the Politburo's resolve, the General Staff sent many cadre groups to all our battlefields to assess the situation and to encourage the battlefields to ready forces and supplies for use in a strategic offensive. The Central

Military Party Committee recalled a number of leadership cadre from the battle-fields to report on the situation and to participate in the formulation of a strate-gic combat plan.

In June 1967 the Politburo approved our strategic resolve: Although our fun-damental strategy was still based on the concept of a protracted war, the Polit-buro decreed that we would increase our subjective efforts to the maximum extent possible in order to secure a decisive victory within a relatively short period of time (which we projected to be sometime during the year of 1968). If we wished to achieve this goal, we would have to defeat the Americans militar-ily and change the nature of the war in South Vietnam.

In July 1967 the General Staff briefed the Politburo and the Central Military Party Committee on a plan to intensify revolutionary warfare to the highest level through a general offensive–general uprising. The plan called for us to concen-trate our military and political forces to launch a simultaneous surprise attack against the enemy's weakest point: his urban areas. The principal theaters of operations would be Saigon, Hue, and Da Nang. Using powerful main force units, we would crush every large puppet army unit, at the same time luring away and tying down U.S. mobile forces in the mountain jungle battlefields (Tri-Thien, Central Highlands, and eastern Cochin China). We would coordinate the operations of the three attack spearheads [military, political, and military prose-lytizing] in all three strategic areas to annihilate and crush a significant portion of the military forces of the United States and its puppets, change the basic bal-ance of forces on the battlefield, and crush the American imperialist will to com-mit aggression.

Our strategic intentions and the combat plan were held in strict secrecy. The Central Military Party Committee itself directed and encouraged the various bat-tlefields in carrying out a number of preparatory measures, especially measures to increase the capability of our main force troops to fight large battles of anni-hilation.[4] In late July 1967 the Central Military Party Committee held a study seminar on the new situation, our new responsibilities, and problems related to combined-arms combat aimed at meeting the requirement of annihilating Amer-ican brigades. One hundred fifty mid- and high-level cadre from the general departments, service branches, specialty branches, and large mobile units attended this seminar. After this study seminar, all units held political and mili-tary study seminars for cadre at all levels.

A number of training documents written by the General Staff, such as "Com-pany, battalion, and regimental attacks against enemy forces holding fortified positions," "Company Commanders' Handbook," etc., were used in these study seminars, helping to provide our cadre, especially our basic-level cadre, with a uniform system of tactical thought, a command presence, and the ability to man-age their troops during combined-arms operations.

The organizational structure and equipment of our strategic mobile divi-sions, the 308th, 304th, 320th, and 312th, was strengthened. Training of these divisions was increased to ensure they would be ready for battle when the order was given.

On 19 March 1967, our sapper troops were recognized by the Party, Government, and the High Command as an official specialty branch of the people's armed forces of Vietnam. Chairman Ho Chi Minh, Prime Minister Pham Van Dong, and Senior General Vo Nguyen Giap, the Minister of Defense, came to speak with representatives of our sapper cadre and soldiers during the ceremony officially establishing this specialty branch.

Uncle Ho said, "Sapper [dac cong] means special tasks [cong tac dac biet]. This title is a special honor and requires a special effort."

To a sapper, the word "special" permeates every action, from his training through the time when he sets off for battle to the time when he returns. "Your mind must be especially flexible. Your tactics require special practical training. Your political thinking must be especially firm. Your discipline must be especially strict. Your resolve to fight the enemy, your resolve to destroy the enemy also must be especially high."[5]

During 1967 the Sapper Branch trained 3,835 soldiers, provided basic training to 457 new cadre, and supplemental or branch transfer training to 527 cadre from platoon commanders up through battalion commanders. To implement our Party's strategic resolve to vigorously prepare our forces, the sapper branch sent to the battlefields 2,563 cadre and soldiers. These sapper reinforcements were organized into one battalion, 40 teams, seven battalion cadre framework units, and 30 sapper team cadre framework units.

Along the strategic transportation route, Group 559 reorganized its forces into nine troop stations, using as their standard a two-night trip by truck. The vehicle assets of the Group rose from 3,570 trucks in 1966 to 5,372 trucks in 1967. The number of transportation units in the Group increased by five battalions. Senior Colonel Dong Sy Nguyen, Deputy Director of the General Rear Services Department, was appointed as Commander of Group 559. By the end of 1967 Group 559 had built a solid road network with a total of 2,959 kilometers of vehicle-capable roads (275 kilometers of main road, 445 kilometers of secondary road, 822 kilometers of connector roads, 576 kilometers of bypass roads, and 450 kilometers of entry roads into storage areas). Meanwhile, on the forward route managed by the General Rear Services Department, Troop Stations 9, 12, 14, and 16 stockpiled supplies for shipment to Group 559. By October 1967 the quantity of supplies stockpiled in the warehouses at the western end of Route 12 had risen to 10,000 tons, and the quantity of supplies at Route 20 was 4,000 tons.

On 5 November 1967 the entire 559 corridor began to implement the 1967–1968 dry season plan with a total of 61,000 tons of supplies provided to the Group by higher authority. This quantity was double the tonnage for the 1966–1967 dry season. The objective of the plan was to pre-position the supply requirements for the battlefields.

In September 1967 the Cabinet of the Government convened a conference of the people's air defense in North Vietnam. The conference drew lessons from our experiences in organization, early warning, and constructing shelters, camouflage, dispersion, rescue, and damage repair after enemy attacks. These lessons were aimed at protecting our people, protecting production, and keeping open our logistics transportation artery to the battlefields. The manpower resources of North Vietnam would be mobilized on a massive scale to further strengthen the combat forces of the army and satisfy the need to provide reinforcements to the battlefields.

Shoulder to shoulder with the entire population, our army proceeded to carry out the first step in the preparations for a new combat phase in accordance with the strategic intentions of the Party. In August 1967, the Central Military Party Committee launched a campaign "to improve the quality and increase the combat strength of the people's armed forces and to resolve to defeat the American aggressors."

In South Vietnam, in accordance with the Politburo's plan for a general offensive and uprising, in October 1967 COSVN dissolved Military Region 7 and the Saigon–Gia Dinh Military Region and in their place formed a "Focal Point Region" [khu trong diem], including Saigon and a number of neighboring provinces. Comrade Nguyen Van Linh, member of the Party Central Committee and Deputy Secretary of COSVN, personally assumed the position of Party Secretary of this region. Comrade Vo Van Kiet was appointed Deputy Party Secretary. The "Focal Point Region" consisted of six subregions.[6] Armed forces assigned to each subregion consisted of between two and four battalions, each of which was given a compact organizational structure and light equipment to turn them into "spearhead battalions" to attack into the heart of Saigon to support and relieve the sapper and commando teams that would attack and seize the key targets. Subregion 6 (the precincts of Saigon city) had 11 sapper and commando teams organized into three troop concentrations: east, south, and north. The organizational structure of the military forces of the subregions ensured we would have both a spearhead and an in-depth deployment of forces capable of mounting a simultaneous attack from many different directions into Saigon. COSVN's main force army[7] was reinforced by the 88th Infantry Regiment from the Central Highlands and the 568th Infantry Regiment, six separate infantry battalions, two battalions of DKB rockets (the 96th and 208th Battalions), four battalions of 82mm mortars, and a number of engineer, signal, sapper, and chemical defense units,[8] which had just arrived from North Vietnam. The plan called for the main force units to attack and block American and puppet divisions located north, northwest, and east of Saigon to protect the rear of the subregion forces attacking the city. To strengthen command, COSVN and the COSVN Military Command established the First Forward Command Headquarters, responsible for the eastern and northern wings and for the main force units. The Second Forward Command Headquarters commanded the western and southern wings and forces inside the city.

Military Regions 6, 8, 9, and 10 mobilized their guerrilla troops and drafted new recruits locally to form additional battalions and companies subordinate to the regions and provinces to provide additional forces for the attacks on the cities and towns.

In Region 5 the Military Region's main force army was reinforced with the 577th Rocket Regiment[9] (with DKB rockets). The 401st Sapper Regiment was formed, combining the military region's 406th and 409th Sapper Battalions with the 403rd Sapper Battalion, which had just arrived from North Vietnam. This was the first sapper regiment in our army's history. In July 1967 Military Region 5 formed Front 4 to command the primary point of attack, Da Nang. Armed forces subordinate to this front included three infantry battalions and the 575th Rocket Battalion, equipped with DKB rockets.

To increase the fighting qualities of its main force troops and local armed forces, the Region 5 Party Committee and Military Region 5 held many conferences for military and political cadre to review and summarize experiences. These included a conference to review the combat campaigns of the main force troops, a conference to review political activities by the armed forces (August 1967), and a conference to review guerrilla war in the lowlands and in the mountains (October 1967).

In Tri-Thien, in May 1967 the Party Central Committee approved a reorganization of the leadership and command system to adapt the system to its new combat missions. The province Party committees and province military units were dissolved. The district Party committees were placed under the direct control of the Regional Party Committee. In the individual operational sectors, groups were formed that were directly subordinate to the Military Region Command. Group 4, consisting of Infantry Battalion 804B and two engineer battalions, was to attack lines of communication from southern Phu Loc to the northern end of the Hai Van Pass. Group 5, responsible for Hue city and its three surrounding districts, was made up of three infantry battalions (804A, 810, 845), two sapper battalions (K1 and K2), and 14 commando teams. Group 6, responsible for Phong Dien and Quang Dien districts in Thua Thien province, consisted of the 6th Infantry Regiment. Group 7, responsible for the districts of Trieu Phong and Hai Lang in Quang Tri province, consisted of the 9th Regiment of the 304th Division,[10] the 808th and 814th Infantry Battalions, the K-10 Sapper Battalion, and two district local force companies. Group 31, responsible for the area from Route 9 to the temporary Demilitarized Zone, had two infantry battalions that were placed under the command of the Route 9–Northern Quang Tri Front (B5 Front). The Military Region's main force army was reinforced with three additional infantry regiments.[11]

The cities and towns, especially Saigon, Da Nang, and Hue, were reinforced by hundreds of additional cadre and Party members. Mass political struggle forces, the commando teams of the city military unit, and the commando personnel of the associations and revolutionary organizations were strengthened and expanded. Weapons, food, and medicines were secretly shipped into the cities. As for Saigon itself, the preparatory operations were split up, parceled out, and carried out simultaneously in order to resolve problems caused by the lack of adequate time for preparation[12] and by preparatory requirements that were too large. By the end of 1967, within the city we had formed 19 political organizations made up of 325 families living near key targets and had established 400 concealment points to hide troops and equipment in political "spots," such as in Bac Ai Hamlet, Cau Bong [the Bong Bridge area], the Ban Co area, and Xom Chua in Tan Binh.

On 6 July 1967, Senior General Nguyen Chi Thanh, member of the Politburo and Political Commissar of the COSVN Military Command, died after a sudden heart attack. A talented and energetic cadre, Senior General Nguyen Chi Thanh had made many outstanding contributions in the areas of implementing and explaining the political and military policies of the Party and in building political organizations in the army. He had contributed to the development of our offensive posture and the intensification of combat operations conducted by our massed forces on the battlefields of South Vietnam during the initial phase of the resistance war against the Americans to save the nation. His passing was a great loss to our army. The Politburo and the Central Military Party Committee quickly sent many experienced high-level cadre to assume key positions in the various battlefields in order to strengthen leadership and command in the strategic theaters of operation. Comrade Pham Hung, Politburo member and Deputy Prime Minister, was appointed Secretary of COSVN and concurrently COSVN Military Command Political Commissar. Lieutenant General Hoang Van Thai, member of the Party Central Committee, Deputy Chief of Staff, and former Commander and Political Commissar of Military Region 5, was appointed Commander of the COSVN Military Command. In Region 5, Comrade Vo Chi Cong, member of the Party Central Committee, was appointed Secretary of the Military Region Party Committee and concurrently Military Region Political Commissar. Major General Chu Huy Man, member of the Party Central Committee, was appointed Commander of the Military Region 5 Command. In the Central Highlands, Major General Hoang Minh Thao was appointed Front Military Commander and Senior Colonel Tran The Mon was appointed Front Political Commissar. In Tri-Thien, Major General Tran Van Quang, alternate member of the Party Central Committee, became Region Party Secretary and concurrently Commander of the Military Region Headquarters. Major General Le Chuong was named Military Region Political Commissar.

By the end of 1967 our preparations for the strategic offensive had achieved some important results. Our full-time armed forces on the battlefields of South Vietnam rose from 204,000 (at the end of 1966) to 278,000.[13] Our total number of combat battalions had risen from 126 to 190. Our supply situation, especially in weapons and equipment, had been improved. Cochin China alone received more than 50,000 infantry weapons, including a substantial number of B-40 anti-tank rocket launchers. Our sapper forces had been expanded in all three strategic areas and in all of our three types of troops, and were now organized into ground sappers, water sappers, mobile sappers, specialized sappers, and commando sappers.[14] Preparation of the battlefield, especially in the cities, was proceeding according to plan. Our command system had been adapted to the new situation and to our new conditions, ensuring that the offensive would be capable of opening fire simultaneously and of sending deep thrusts into the cities.

PREPARATORY OPERATIONS LEADING UP TO THE TET OFFENSIVE

During the fall and winter of 1967 the General Staff directed the battlefields to step up their operations in order to kill more enemy soldiers and enable our units and local areas to continue their preparations. At the same time the battlefields were to conduct exercises and gain experience in urban combat methods. This activity period was the first phase of our strategic combat plan.

In the Central Highlands, on 3 November 1967 the Front Military Command launched a campaign at Dak To, in northern Kontum. During this campaign, the soldiers of the Central Highlands seized the initiative, developed a battle position, used deception to lure the enemy into preplanned areas, and launched mobile attacks combined with blocking operations that inflicted heavy casualties on two battalions and six companies of the 1st Brigade of the 4th U.S. Division, the 173rd Airborne Brigade, and one brigade of the U.S. Air Cavalry Division.

In eastern Cochin China the 7th and 9th Infantry Divisions and the 69th Artillery Division, in cooperation with Binh Long and Phuoc Long province local force troops, launched the Loc Ninh–Route 13 campaign, attacking the U.S. 1st Infantry Division and the puppet 5th Division. During two combat phases, from 26 October to 5 December 1967, our units fought 60 battles, two of which were division-sized battles and five of which were regiment-sized battles, eliminating from the field of combat 4,700 enemy (including 3,000 Americans). Our victory in this campaign consolidated our offensive springboard north of Saigon and marked a new step forward in the capacity of COSVN's main force soldiers to fight a concentrated battle.

Coordinating their actions with the main force divisions, the armed forces of our subregions attacked many bases and towns, inflicting heavy casualties on enemy troops and destroying substantial quantities of war equipment. A number of these battles were quite effective, such as a 5 January 1968 attack on an element of the U.S. 101st Airborne Division in Hoc Mon, a 7 January 1968 attack on the Can Giuoc district military headquarters, and an 8 January 1968 assault on the Hau Nghia province capital.

In Region 5, beginning in early September 1967 our local armed forces attacked many provincial towns, including Hoi An, Tam Ky, Quang Ngai, and Tuy Hoa. Our local forces also supported popular uprisings to seize control and consolidated our hold on important springboard positions around the provincial capitals. The Military Region's main force divisions attacked American troops in western Quang Nam, the Phu My district capital, the U.S. artillery firebase and forward airstrip at Nhong Pass in Binh Dinh province, etc. This was the first time the armed forces of Military Region 5, operating under one unified command, had mounted simultaneous attacks against numerous cities and towns, cooperating with the forces of the masses rising up in insurrection. A number of lessons learned during this operational phase helped the Military Region Command and the provinces to address a number of problems in command organization and preparations for the strategic offensive.

In Tri-Thien, local armed forces attacked a number of small targets on the outskirts of Hue city and consolidated their springboard positions. During the evening of 27 May 1967 three sapper and commando companies, supported by recoilless rifles and 82mm mortars, launched simultaneous attacks against 12 targets in Hue city, including the Huong Giang and Thuan Hoa Hotels (where many American officers were quartered), the radio station, and the headquarters of the puppet 1st Division. During this attack our sapper and commando forces gained a great deal of experience in attacking enemy headquarters and leadership installations.

In September 1967, the National Liberation Front for South Vietnam held its second Congress of Heroes of the Armed Forces. The Congress was extremely moved to receive a letter from Chairman Ho Chi Minh. Uncle Ho wrote, "In 1965, the first Congress of Heroes of the Armed Forces was a Congress celebrating victory over the 'special war' conducted by the American pirates. This Heroes Congress is a congress of those people who will defeat the American's 'limited war.' I am confident that the people and soldiers of South Vietnam, with their heroic spirit and wealth of experience, will secure even greater victories, which will bring total victory to the cause of opposition to the Americans to save the nation."

Meanwhile, in Laos the rightist army, operating under the command of American advisors, tried to seize control of the areas under Pathet Lao control, escalating the American "special war" in Laos to a new level. In July 1966 they seized Nam Bac, a district in Udomsai province. A large force of Lao puppet army soldiers, consisting of three infantry regiments, one independent infantry battalion, and one artillery battalion, occupied Nam Bac and established a defensive line north of the royal capital of Luang Prabang, threatening the liberated zone in northern Laos.

Determined to crush the enemy's schemes and to restore and consolidate the liberated zone in northern Laos, in December 1967 the Laotian Party Politburo and the Politburo of our own Party Central Committee decided to launch an offensive against enemy forces in Nam Bac.

The 316th Infantry Division was dispatched to Laos to cooperate with the troops of our Lao allies in mounting combat operations. After more than a month of marching, approaching, and encircling the enemy, on 12 January 1968 the 148th Regiment opened fire to kick off the offensive. The 147th Regiment blocked the enemy's line of retreat and pursued fleeing enemy forces. The campaign ended on 27 January 1967. Two mobile regiments of Laotian puppet army regulars were annihilated. More than 3,000 enemy troops were killed or captured. The Nam Bac area, with a population of almost 10,000 people, was liberated. The Nam Bac victory was important strategically, signaling the growth in the combat capabilities of the Pathet Lao Liberation Army and of our Vietnamese volunteer troops. This was the first campaign in which the Lao-Vietnamese allied forces had killed and captured large numbers of enemy regular soldiers, and the campaign contributed to an important shift in the balance of forces in favor of the Laotian revolution. The Nam Bac victory provided timely and effective support to the South Vietnamese battlefield, launching a victorious winter-spring season.

FINAL STRATEGIC DECISIONS AND PREPARATIONS

In October 1967 the Politburo met and discussed in more concrete detail our policy and plans for conducting a general offensive and simultaneous uprising in South Vietnam. After assessing the situation and basing their conclusions on reports from the various battlefields, the Politburo realized it was possible to carry out the plan earlier than we had initially planned. To achieve the element of surprise, the Politburo decided to launch the General offensive during Tet 1968. Major General Le Trong Tan, Deputy Chief of Staff, and Senior Colonel Le Ngoc Hien, Director of the Combat Operations Department, were dispatched to the individual battlefields to brief them on the Politburo resolution and to encourage and oversee preparations.

In January 1968 the 14th Plenum of the Party Central Committee, meeting in Hanoi, approved a December 1967 resolution of the Politburo on "Moving the revolutionary war into a new era, the era of securing a decisive victory."

Assessing the situation from every angle, the Party Central Committee determined that the current situation allowed us to move our revolutionary war into a new era and to raise our revolution to a new level of development. The strategic objectives of the General Offensive–General Uprising were set forward as follows:

- Annihilate and cause the total disintegration of the bulk of the puppet army, overthrow the puppet regime at all administrative levels, and place all governmental power in the hands of the people.
- Annihilate a significant portion of the American military's troop strength and destroy a significant portion of his war equipment in order to prevent the American forces from being able to carry out their political and military missions.

- On this basis, crush the American will to commit aggression and force the United States to accept defeat in South Vietnam and end all hostile actions against North Vietnam. In addition, using this as our basis, we would achieve the immediate goals of the revolution, which were independence, democracy, peace, and neutrality in South Vietnam, and then move toward achieving peace and national unification.

   The Central Committee declared that, since the General Offensive and General Uprising would be carried out while the enemy still had more than one million troops and a vast war-making potential, this strategic offensive would be a very fierce and complicated battle. The two main blows would be the attack of our large main force units on battlefields where conditions favored our forces and the attack of our assault units supporting popular uprisings in the cities and their surrounding areas. Eastern Cochin China and Saigon–Cho Lon would be the most decisive battlefield. Route 9, Tri-Thien, and Quang Da would be the second most decisive battlefield. The three focal points of the offensive would be Saigon, Hue, and Da Nang. Only if we brought the war into the cities could we completely and effectively strike a strategically significant blow. Only if we maintained total secrecy and surprise could we ensure victory in our first attacks.

   The Party Central Committee projected various scenarios that might develop and approved our strategic combat plan.

   During the fall and winter of 1967 General Westmoreland, the U.S. Commander in South Vietnam, continued to ask for additional troops and continued preparations to launch his third strategic counteroffensive during the 1967–1968 dry season. On 17 November 1967 the U.S. Secretary of Defense ordered an airlift, using 373 C-141 sorties, to transport the 10,000 remaining troops of the 101st Airborne Division to South Vietnam. On 21 October 1967 the 198th Light Infantry Brigade was sent to the 2nd Tactical Zone. On 20 October the 11th Light Infantry Brigade was sent to the 2nd Tactical Zone. As for the Saigon puppet regime, the United States increased the aid being provided to them, pushed them to step up "pacification," increased the size of the puppet army, and modernized their equipment.

   Following the conclusion of Operation "Goldstone" into the Duong Minh Chau War Zone, the United States and its puppets prepared to conduct a large sweep in the Phuoc Long area aimed at totally destroying our rear services bases on the Vietnamese-Cambodian border. At the same time they prepared to launch many sweep operations in western Tri-Thien aimed at retaking control of the Ashau Valley and blocking our strategic supply route through the Annamite Mountains. In late December 1967, after discovering we had strengthened our forces around Khe Sanh, increased the flow of supplies down Group 559's transportation corridor, and moved additional forces into our bases surrounding Saigon, General Westmoreland hastily canceled his planned operations. He pulled a number of U.S. units back to defend Saigon and sent 12 battalions from the Air Cavalry Division, the 101st Airborne Division, and the puppet Marine division to the Route 9 area. The enemy believed our movement of forces into the lowlands and our plan to liberate the cities and seize control of the government were deception operations aimed at enabling us to concentrate our forces to create another "Dien Bien Phu" at Khe Sanh and seize control of Quang Tri and Thua Thien provinces.

According to the strategic combat plan approved by the Politburo and the Party Central Committee, the Route 9–Northern Quang Tri Front was one of our important strategic theaters of operations. Our combat forces assigned to this front in December 1967 included four infantry divisions (the 304th, 320th, 324th, and 325th), one separate infantry regiment (the 270th), five artillery regiments (the 16th, 45th, 84th, 204th, and 675th), three anti-aircraft artillery regiments (the 208th, 214th, and 228th), four tank companies, one engineer regiment plus one separate engineer battalion, one signal battalion, and a number of local force units. On 6 December 1967, the Central Military Party Committee established the Route 9 Front Party Committee and the Route 9 Front Military Command. Major General Tran Quy Hai, alternate member of the Party Central Committee and Deputy Minister of Defense, was appointed Military Commander of the front. Major General Le Quang Dao, Party Central Committee member and Deputy Director of the General Political Department, became Front Political Commissar. This was a combat battlefield for our main force units that was assigned the missions of annihilating enemy forces and of drawing in and tying down a significant portion of the mobile reserve forces of the U.S. and puppet armies, thereby creating favorable conditions for the focal points of our attacks and uprisings, and especially for Tri-Thien and Hue.

In early 1968, in the midst of bustling preparations for our traditional Tet holiday, the soldiers and civilians of our entire nation were immensely encouraged and moved by the words of a poem written by Chairman Ho Chi Minh to celebrate the new year:

> This new year will be better than past new years
> Victory and good news will sweep the nation
> South and North vie with each other in fighting the Americans
> Advance—total victory is ours.

During the night of 20 January 1968, implementing our deception plan to lure in enemy forces, our soldiers opened fire on the Route 9 Front. In the west, the 66th Regiment, 304th Division, assaulted the Huong Hoa district capital. The 2nd Regiment, 325th Division, attacked Hill 832. On 23 January 24th Regiment, 304th Division, overran the Huoi San base. In the east, the 64th and 48th Regiments of the 320th Division and the 47th Battalion of the 270th Regiment launched attacks that cut traffic on Route 9 and advanced to attack the district military headquarters at Cam Lo.

General Westmoreland hurriedly increased defensive forces and sent aircraft to mount a ferocious bombing campaign in the area around Khe Sanh and against suspected assembly areas for our troops. The U.S. Command in South Vietnam, the White House, and the Pentagon were obsessed with the prospect of a new "Dien Bien Phu." Johnson forced the American generals to swear they could hold Khe Sanh and set up a "special situation room" in the White House to follow the fighting on the Route 9 Front. Although the time for preparations was too short and our battlefield preparations for the blow to be struck by our main force troops were inadequate, the units assigned to the Route 9 Front overcame all difficulties and carried out their attack orders on schedule, thereby increasing the strategic surprise achieved by the general offensive throughout South Vietnam.

THE TET OFFENSIVE

On the night of 29–30 January 1968, the night of the Tet New Year,[15] our soldiers and civilians launched a simultaneous strategic offensive against many of the cities and towns of South Vietnam. At 12:30 A.M. on 30 January 1968, the Central Highland Front's 2nd Battalion, 174th Regiment, attacked Tan Canh town. A few minutes later simultaneous attacks struck Ban Me Thuot, Pleiku, and Kontum cities. With the assistance of our armed forces, tens of thousands of our compatriots of all ethnic groups whom the enemy had forced into "concentration areas" and "strategic hamlets" rose up and returned to their old villages.

In Region 5, local armed forces made simultaneous attacks on the cities of Nha Trang, Quy Nhon, Tuy Hoa, Hoi An, and on 40 other district capitals and towns. At Da Nang city the Military Region's main force 2nd Division, sapper battalions, the Quang Da province local force battalion, and mass forces participating in the political struggle had been preparing since October 1967. However, because we did not have a firm grasp on the situation, our preparations had been cursory, the movement of our forces forward to seize attack positions had not been well organized, and because enemy forces were too numerous[16] and responded fiercely when we attacked, the forces that attacked the city on the night of 29–30 January 1968 were unable to seize their assigned objectives.[17]

The Americans and their puppets were shocked by our unexpected simultaneous attacks against many cities and towns. They issued an alert for all of South Vietnam, proclaimed martial law in the cities and towns, and ordered all soldiers on Tet leave to return to their bases, but the order was not issued in time. They mounted a violent campaign of terror to block and push back our armed forces and our unarmed groups of civilians to prevent them from entering the cities. In Ban Me Thuot city, puppet troops fired into a group of civilian demonstrators. In Quang Ngai city, American aircraft bombed our civilians as they were gathering on Route 1.

On the night of 30–31 January 1968, the general offensive exploded into Hue, Saigon, and many other cities and towns.

Hue was one of the three focal point targets of the Tet 1968 strategic offensive. Our armed forces attacking the city totaled eight infantry battalions, one rocket artillery battalion with DKB rockets, three sapper battalions, six commando teams, and a number of local force companies. The northern wing was the primary attack sector. The southern wing was an important assault element and was also the primary sector for responding to enemy counterattacks. Because our plan was detailed and the organization and command of our approach march was properly handled (in spite of the fact that we had a large number of forces and had to divide the approach march into many columns, cross many rivers and streams, and bypass many enemy outposts), all units reached their positions securely and on time. Local Party committees at all levels guided the population in preparing areas and facilities, established supply caches, and arranged for guides to lead units to their assembly areas. The civilian population of the Vien Chinh, Duc Thai, Trang Luu, Muc Tra, and Duong Mong areas prepared food supplies and built hundreds of secret bunkers, enough to conceal an entire sapper battalion right next to the enemy positions.

At 2:33 A.M. on 31 January, the DKB rocket battalion poured a violent barrage into enemy positions at Tam Thai and Phu Bai to kick off the attack on Hue city. From the south, sapper and infantry units simultaneously opened fire, attacking and seizing the puppet 7th Armored Regiment's base at Tam Thai, the puppet engineer battalion at Nam Giao, the Thua Thien province military headquarters, the Thuan Hoa Hotel, and the puppet Combat Police headquarters. The units of our northern wing attacked the puppet 1st Division headquarters at Mang Ca, the Tan Loc airfield, and the Citadel area. After three hours of fighting our troops gained control of the Citadel area, raised the liberation flag to the top of the flagpole at Ngo Mon, and controlled many city blocks on the northern and southern banks of the Perfume River.

By 3 February most of the enemy military targets in the city had been taken by our soldiers. The enemy, however, still held out at the headquarters of the puppet 1st Division at Mang Ca. Thousands of our comrades and compatriots imprisoned by the enemy in his many jails were released. The population of Hue city rose up in insurrection, their uprisings becoming strongest after the fourth day of the attack. In many locations the people provided supplies to our soldiers, cared for our wounded, and helped our soldiers reinforce their fighting positions. Under the leadership of Party organizations the people established a revolutionary governmental apparatus and numerous mass organizations. They organized self-defense forces and eliminated tyrants and traitors. In some locations the masses armed themselves and fought arm-in-arm with our soldiers against the enemy counterattack. Many enthusiastic ceremonies to issue guns to soldiers and to say farewell to youths who were joining our army were held in many wards and city blocks. The population of many hamlets and villages of Huong Tra, Huong Thuy, Phu Vang, Phu Loc, Quang Dien, etc., districts rose up and, together with local armed forces, surrounded and destroyed enemy outposts, captured enemy tyrants, and seized power.

In an effort to retake the city, the enemy sent a number of battalions of the U.S. 1st Marine Division, an airborne task force, and a puppet armored troop to attack from the outside into the city in coordination with a counterattack by the remaining elements of the puppet 1st Division at Mang Ca. On 12 February the enemy added a puppet Marine task force and a U.S. Air Cavalry battalion. Napalm bombs, tear gas bombs, and U.S. artillery shells destroyed many heavily populated residential areas, many historical sites, and killed hundreds of ordinary citizens.

The Tri-Thien Military Region Command ordered 3rd Regiment, 324th Division, and 18th Regiment, 325th Division, into the city to join the fight alongside the people and our remaining forces in the city. Relying on solidly built structures, our soldiers and civilians resolutely held their positions. Many vicious battles were fought at the An Hoa gate, the Chanh Tay gate, the Dong Ba gate, the Thuy Quan drainage ditch, and the Tay Loc airfield. At the Dong Ba gate, a squad fought a fierce battle against an entire American battalion, holding its position for eight days.

On 23 February 1968, after 25 days of combat, our soldiers were ordered to withdraw from the city.

The armed force that we used in the attack on Hue was not a large one. Because, however, of the high resolve of the Region Party Committee, the Military Region Command, our units, and the population; because we had an excellent plan for preparations; because we maintained secrecy and surprise; because we employed our forces properly and used appropriate combat tactics; and because we exploited the combined strength of our political and military forces, the offensive and uprising in the Hue theater of operations fulfilled its duties in an outstanding fashion and achieved its high target goals.[18] This was also a very important strategic supporting theater, directly supporting our Route 9–Khe Sanh, Quang Nam–Da Nang, and Saigon campaigns. The success of the offensive and uprising in Hue city strongly encouraged our soldiers and civilians in the other battlefields and had a powerful impact on the U.S. and puppet leadership cliques. Within the general context of the strategic offensive, putting the attack on Hue city into the overall plan aimed at achieving the strategic goals we had set for ourselves, the fact that our soldiers held control of Hue city for 25 days and nights was of tremendous importance, increasing the military and political impact of the Tet 1968 General Offensive and Uprising.

In Saigon–Gia Dinh, during the days before Tet the sapper teams assigned to attack the primary targets within the city dispersed into cells and, traveling by many different routes, joined the flood of people in the streets doing their Tet shopping, secretly hiding their troops and delivering additional explosives and weapons to cache in the homes of our agents. The spearhead battalions of the subregions also began to march toward their objectives inside the city. However, because orders were received at different times, some units had a long way to travel, the command and leadership capabilities of the units were not uniform, and because the terrain surrounding Saigon was open, contained many swamps, and was covered with enemy outposts, many of the spearhead battalions were unable to reach the assembly areas from which they were to attack to reinforce and relieve the sapper and commando companies.

During the night of 30–31 January 1968, the sound of our guns attacking Saigon rang out simultaneously at the U.S. Embassy, Independence Palace, the puppet General Staff Headquarters, the puppet Navy Headquarters, Tan Son Nhat Airbase, and many other locations. The 11th Commando Team, 17 combatants led by Ngo Thanh Van and disguised as a group of puppet soldiers, drove to the U.S. Embassy by car. After using explosives to blow a hole in the front wall, the team divided into three spearheads to seize the front gate, the back gate, and the residential area for embassy personnel. They then expanded the attack up to the second floor of the main building. U.S. soldiers defending the Embassy counterattacked fiercely, but all their efforts were beaten back. At 9:00 in the morning of 31 January, U.S. military policemen landed by helicopter on the roof of the Embassy, coordinating their attack with an enemy force attacking from the residence of the French Ambassador. Our commandos heroically defended each stairwell, each room, and fought to the last man.

The 3rd Commando Team, consisting of 15 combatants (including one female), advanced to attack Independence Palace, the residence of the puppet President. After being detected by the enemy, our soldiers quickly gunned their vehicle forward and used explosives to destroy the main gate. The cells following them were forced to deploy to fight two battalions of puppet troops on Nguyen Du Street. By 5:00 A.M. eight of our soldiers were dead and four lay seriously wounded. The three remaining combatants resolutely clung to each street corner and each house, continuing to fight the enemy.

The 6th and 9th Commando Teams attacked the puppet General Staff Headquarters. Enemy troops supported by helicopter gunships mounted a fierce counterattack. Our commando troops and an element of the 2nd Quyet Thang [Determined to Win] Battalion, which had just arrived to reinforce them, clung to the positions they had taken, repelling many enemy counterattacks and killing hundreds of enemy troops. After suffering heavy casualties and running low on ammunition, on the morning of 31 January the remnants of our force were forced to fall back to fight the enemy on the outer perimeter.

The 4th Commando Team, with a total of 12 soldiers, hid in the home of commando soldier Tran Phu Cuong at 56 Nguyen Binh Khiem Street. The team was able to capture the Saigon Radio Station and repel many enemy counterattacks. Ten soldiers died a hero's death. Two survivors were cared for and hidden by our agents and taken back to our base area.

On the outer perimeter, the 1st Commando team acted as guides for and supported the attacks of the 101st Infantry Regiment against the Hanh Tong Tay General Supply Warehouse complex, the enemy's Artillery Command at Co Loa, and the headquarters base of the puppet Armored Command at Phu Dong. The 3rd

Infantry Battalion of the Phu Loi Regiment, supported by sapper teams from Di An and Thu Duc districts, attacked and seized the Hang Xanh–Thi Nghe area. The 5th Battalion and the 320th Infantry Regiment, supported by the 7th and 8th Commando Teams, attacked the enemy's large logistics storage facilities at Nha Be and Hung Vinh Loc. COSVN's main force divisions pressed in close to Saigon, attacking a number of enemy bases and blocking and hampering the operations of the U.S. and puppet regular divisions. The 9th Division attacked the Quang Trung Training Center and tied down the U.S. 25th Infantry Division at Dong Du. The 5th Division attacked the Bien Hoa air base, the Long Binh warehouse complex, and the headquarters of the U.S. [2nd] Field Force. The 7th Division attacked and crippled a U.S. battalion at Phu Giao and tied down the U.S. 1st Infantry Division.

The people of Saigon–Gia Dinh, with their tradition of patriotism and having been honed in many years of revolutionary struggle, wholeheartedly protected, fed, and cared for our wounded soldiers, providing our combatants with material and moral support.

The unexpected, simultaneous attacks by our elite units against many important enemy targets inside the city of Saigon and the attacks by our main force units against enemy bases on the city's outskirts constituted a daring, risky combat tactic that sent shock waves racing across our country and around the world, all the way to the United States. We had brought our war of revolution right into the enemy's lair, disrupted his rear areas, and made a deep and profound effect on the puppet army, the puppet government, U.S. troops, and on the American ruling clique.

During the attack on Saigon and the other cities and towns, our sappers and commandos, with an unrivaled spirit of heroism, etched the heroic image of the Vietnamese soldier into the pages of history.

In the other cities and towns of the lowlands of Cochin China, because of differences in the level of preparations by each locality, differences in the combat abilities of our armed units, differences in the balance of forces between ourselves and the enemy in each area, and differences in the enemy's response in each location, the progress and results of the general offensive varied. We attacked 13 out of 14 provincial towns (all except Long Xuyen). In My Tho and Ben Tre cities we attacked and held control of the positions we had occupied for three days and nights. In other cities we were only able to hold for one day and night and then withdrew to fight the enemy on the outer perimeter. The force attacking Tra Vinh encountered difficulties from the very beginning and was unable to enter the city, so it turned around and attacked the enemy on the outside, liberating many rural areas.

In coordination with the spearhead attacks by our armed forces into the cities, the people of the villages and hamlets rose up and eliminated tyrants and traitors, dispersed local Popular Force troops, and seized control of their areas. The political forces of the masses in rural areas were reorganized, placed under tight control, and prepared to join the people of the cities and towns and our armed forces in seizing control of the government. Because our military attack was not powerful enough, because enemy forces were numerous and deployed in depth, and because of fierce enemy counterattacks, the uprising of the masses in the cities did not achieve the results projected in the plan.

On the Route 9 Front, after assaulting and destroying a number of enemy strong points in the west, on 6 February 1968 our troops attacked the Lang Vay strong point, which was held by four puppet commando companies.[19] Because orders had arrived late, the 24th Regiment (304th Division) and the 101st Regiment (325th Division) had to make preparations and deploy their forces into attack formation while they were on the march. Our armored troops were entering battle for the very first time. Supported by infantry and engineers, our armored soldiers secretly swam their amphibious PT-76 tanks down the Sepone River to their assembly positions, arriving right on schedule. Enemy troops were completely surprised and shocked when they saw tanks leading our infantry assault. The battle ended in a complete victory. We killed 400 enemy (including three American advisors), captured 253 prisoners, and seized all the enemy's weapons and military equipment. This was the first combined-arms operation that succeeded in destroying an enemy battalion holding a heavily fortified position in the history of the war in South Vietnam and marked a new step forward in the growth of the combat capabilities of our mobile main force troops.

From 10 February onward our troops switched over to the use of siege tactics against Ta Con, a large concentration of strong points held by American troops on the defensive line at the western end of Route 9 in the Khe Sanh area (in Huong Hoa district, Quang Tri province). Enemy troops holding this defensive concentration consisted of the U.S. 26th Marine Regiment, one U.S. artillery battalion, one U.S. tank company, and eight companies of puppet Rangers and regional forces.

Throughout 50 long days and nights, the 304th and 325th Divisions, supported by artillery, anti-aircraft artillery, sappers, and engineers from the Route 9 Front, built siege positions stretching right up to the perimeter of the enemy base. Our forces defeated many enemy counterattacks and, using sniper weapons and artillery attacks, forced American and puppet troops to endure a living hell. Every day scores of wounded Marines received emergency treatment in bunkers deep in the earth of Khe Sanh. They were forced to use parachute drops and helicopters to supply the enemy troops holding the base. Between mid-February and early April 1968, every day the enemy sent 300 tactical bomber sorties and scores of B-52 sorties to drop thousands of bombs and strafe our siege trenches, but they could not loosen the noose around the Khe Sanh base.[20] Concern about a second "Dien Bien Phu" obsessed the American expeditionary army. American generals were forced to promise Johnson they would "hold Khe Sanh at any cost."

On 1 April the enemy massed 17 American and puppet battalions[21] to launch an operation to relieve Khe Sanh. The fighting on the Khe Sanh Front was vicious. Because of the enemy's powerful air and artillery firepower and because our anti-aircraft defenses were weak, the 304th Division was unable to mount any large daytime attacks. On 16 April the enemy withdrew his relief forces. Our soldiers continued the siege of Ta Con.

In the eastern portion of the front, the 320th Division fought many small engagements in the areas of Dong Ha, Gio Linh, and Cua Viet, attacked traffic on Route 9, and tied down ten American and puppet battalions, threatening the enemy defensive line along the eastern section of Route 9.

EVALUATION OF THE RESULTS OF THE TET OFFENSIVE

The protracted offensive and siege campaign conducted by our main force troops on the Route 9–Khe Sanh Front, together with the simultaneous surprise attacks against the cities, especially against Saigon and Hue, threw the Americans and their puppets into a state of great confusion and fear. On 9 February 1968, General Westmoreland, the commander of American forces in South Vietnam, reported to the White House and the Pentagon that "the opposition has dealt the Government of South Vietnam [the puppet regime] a heavy blow. They have brought the war into the cities, inflicting casualties and damage . . . the entire campaign plan for 1968 has been disrupted." A U.S. public opinion poll agency [the Harris Institute] announced the results of their research on 25 March 1968: 80 percent of the American people believed the Tet offensive had caused the failure of the U.S. effort to achieve its objectives in Vietnam.

The Tet General Offensive and Uprising conducted by our soldiers and civilians dealt a major, unexpected blow to the American and puppet armies. We had attacked their leadership and command organizations, conducted a protracted siege against their forces at Khe Sanh, and simultaneously had attacked them in many rural areas, inflicting severe losses on them and seriously shaking the confidence of the American and puppet forces on the battlefield. The American imperialist will to commit aggression began to waver. On 31 March 1968, U.S. President Johnson rejected General Westmoreland's recommendation that an additional 200,000 soldiers be sent to Vietnam, announced his decision to restrict American operations in Vietnam, ended bombing north of the 20th parallel in North Vietnam, agreed to send a delegation to hold talks with us in Paris, and announced he would not run for a second term as President. General Westmoreland was relieved as battlefield commander and recalled to the United States. The "search and destroy" strategy was abandoned and replaced by the "clear and hold" strategy.

The Tet General Offensive and Uprising conducted by our soldiers and civilians secured a great strategic victory. In a short period of time we had killed or dispersed 150,000 enemy soldiers, including 43,000 Americans, destroyed 34 percent of the American war reserve supplies in Vietnam,[22] destroyed 4,200 "strategic hamlets,"[23] and liberated an additional 1.4 million people. We had struck a decisive blow that bankrupted the "limited war" strategy of the American imperialists, shook their will to commit aggression, forced them to deescalate the war, initiated the strategic decline of the American imperialists in their war of aggression against Vietnam, and created a decisive turning point in the war. In its first large-scale strategic offensive against a network of targets deep behind enemy lines, and in concert with mass uprisings to seize power, our army had accumulated a great deal of experience in the organization of forces and the combat arts for urban warfare.

In March 1968, all battlefields analyzed the reasons for success and the short-comings and limitations of the general offensive and uprising. COSVN and Region 5 concluded that all local areas and units had made efforts, but because the time allotted was short and absolute secrecy had to be maintained, our prepara-tions of supplies, spiritual preparations, and preparation of tactics were all insuf-ficient. We were subjective in our assessment of the situation, especially in assessing the strength of the mass political forces in the urban areas. We had somewhat underestimated the capabilities and reactions of the enemy and had set our goals too high. Our plan for military attacks was too simplistic and our arrangements for carrying out and coordinating combat operations by our forces for coordination between the battlefields and between the military attack and the mass uprisings were disjointed. Our soldiers' morale had been very high when they set off for battle, but because we had made only one-sided preparations, only looking at the possibilities of victory and failing to prepare for adversity, when the battle did not progress favorably for our side and when we suffered casualties, rightist thoughts, pessimism, and hesitancy appeared among our forces.

The Tet General Offensive and simultaneous uprisings by our soldiers and civilians inflicted a serious defeat on the aggressors. In the United States the tide of opposition to the war rose day by day. Johnson was forced to announce that he was "de-Americanizing" the Vietnam War, but he continued the war through the use of new strategic measures. The Americans hastily sent two brigades from U.S. worldwide strategic reserve forces[24] to the battlefields of South Vietnam. At the same time they increased the amount of aid provided to the Saigon puppet regime, raising the 1968 defense budget of the puppet regime to 53 billion South Vietnamese piasters. They drafted 65,000 new troops, raising the strength of the puppet army to 650,000.

In South Vietnam the U.S. and puppet armies concentrated their forces to defend the cities, military bases, and strategic lines of communications,[25] at the same time mobilizing forces to conduct continuous operations to "sweep" our armed forces out of the cities and surrounding areas and stepping up their attacks against our strategic transportation corridor.

THE WAR IN THE NORTH

In North Vietnam the Americans were forced to stop bombing attacks from the 20th parallel northward, but they concentrated all artillery and naval gunfire ships to attack the narrow stretch of land called the "panhandle" of Military Region 4 in order to cut the flow of supplies from North Vietnam to the battlefield.

Between April and October 1968, the enemy devoted 79,000 sorties by tactical and B-52 bomber aircraft and 4,596 naval gunfire missions by cruisers and destroyers (including the battleship *New Jersey,* using its 406mm guns) to the "limited" bombing and shelling campaign in Region 4. They concentrated their forces to make powerful attacks against our traffic nodes, forming a continuous line of bombing choke points, with the area under heaviest attack being the area from north of the Lam River (in Nghe An province) to the southern bank of the Gianh River (Quang Binh province). "In a narrow area representing one quarter of North Vietnam, the number of bombing attacks increased by 2.6 times and the concentration of bombs and shells increased by 20 times."[26] Because the enemy was attacking during the rainy season in terrain cut by many rivers and streams, many routes were blocked,[27] and the quantity of supplies being held at Group 559's delivery points in Region 4 dropped to only 1,000 tons in September 1968.

The soldiers and civilians of Military Region 4, the front line of North Vietnam, proudly withstood these extremely horrendous challenges, suffering great sacrifices and adversity and fighting heroically, and kept our supply artery to the battlefield open.

The Politburo of the Party Central Committee and the Central Military Party Committee decided to establish a Headquarters to ensure the continuous flow of supplies through Military Region 4. This Headquarters worked with the Forward Headquarters of the General Department of Rear Services, provincial Party Committees, and provincial people's committees to mobilize all available forces to fight the enemy and ensure the flow of supplies.

The General Staff sent a large combat force to reinforce Military Region 4. The 367th Air Defense Division, the newly established 377th Air Defense Division (formed around three regiments drawn from the strategic area air defense divisions), and the 368th Air Defense Division one by one were sent to Military Region 4 to join the Military Region's anti-aircraft forces of the three types of troops in fighting the enemy.

When our anti-aircraft artillery and missile soldiers first entered the fight they were inexperienced in many areas and did not select the proper areas to concentrate their combat forces for battle. The Air Defense Service provided guidance to units in changing their fighting tactics, combining blocking forces with mobile forces, massing and dispersing in a flexible manner. They studied the enemy's operational principles and gradually increased their combat efficiency. In six months our air defense forces in Military Region 4 shot down more than 100 enemy aircraft.

Our air force troops also were ordered to fight in the skies over Military Region 4. Operating far from their bases in a narrow combat area with limited ground control, our air force fought bravely and cleverly, utilizing small formations and emphasizing the use of secrecy and surprise. In 50 sorties they shot down ten modern American aircraft.

Our artillery troops built solid firing positions on the coastal sand dunes, heroically retaliating against the American cruisers and destroyers when they shelled the mainland. On 28 October 1968, 25th Battery, 21st Artillery Battalion, using 130mm guns, hit the battleship *New Jersey,* setting it ablaze. The Ngu Thuy village militia artillery battery in Quang Binh province (formed on 20 November 1967 and made up of 37 female soldiers between 16 and 20 years of age equipped with four 85mm long-barreled guns) on four separate occasions hit and set ablaze American destroyers.

The Engineer Command sent two river-crossing regiments and a number of engineer units from the Left Bank and Right Bank Military Regions to Military Region 4 as reinforcements. Alongside assault youths and local civilians, our engineer troops worked night and day repairing stretches of road damaged by the enemy and building many detours around the enemy's bombing choke points. The 249th Regiment supported river crossings at Quan Hau, Ly Hoa, Cau Dai, Xuan Son, and the Gianh River. The 239th Regiment provided river crossing support at Nam Dan, Linh Cam, and Ha Tan. Up and down all the transportation routes and at all the ferry crossings of Region 4, our engineer cadre and soldiers ignored danger and resolutely remained at their choke point positions, guaranteeing the safe passage of our transportation convoys. Some soldiers even volunteered to pilot boats over the enemy's magnetic mines to destroy them. They were prepared to give their lives so that supplies could reach the front.

The troop stations subordinate to the Transportation Department in the Military Region 4 area were reorganized to adapt them to the new situation. Three mobile truck battalions subordinate to the Transportation Department and three truck companies drawn from other military regions, a total of 411 vehicles, were sent to reinforce Military Region 4. In mid-1968 the Transportation Department formed four new truck battalions and increased the transportation forces assigned to Route 15. The 1st Hong Ha Boat Battalion used the Nha Le, Van, and Than Canals in Nghe An and Ha Tinh provinces in an effort to push our supplies forward.

The State-owned transportation resources in Military Region 4 were militarized and organized into traffic troop stations. Primitive forms of transportation, such as river sampans, seagoing sampans, and transportation bicycles were mobilized in large numbers to transfer and transport supplies over short sections to support our motorized transportation resources.

On 28 October 1968, the Central Military Party Committee formed Headquarters 500, with a strength equivalent to Group 559, to replace the Forward Headquarters of the General Department of Rear Services in handling responsibility for ensuring the flow of traffic and supplies in Military Region 4.[28] Major General Nguyen Don was named Headquarters Commander and Major General Le Quang Dao became Political Commissar.

The armed forces of Military Region 4, together with tens of thousands of assault youths and hundreds of thousands of frontline civilian laborers, fought and transported supplies in a spirit of "the entire Military Region goes into battle" and "everyone in the entire Military Region is a hero."

The soldiers and civilians of North Vietnam continued to defeat the war of destruction conducted by the American pirates on the territory of Military Region 4, maintaining the strategic supply line to the battlefield and ensuring that the soldiers and civilians of South Vietnam could sustain the general offensive and simultaneous uprisings. In 1968, the quantity of supplies shipped to the battlefield increased to twice the total for 1967. The number of troops sent south increased by 1.7 times.

Military Region 4 was worthy of its role as the front line of the great socialist rear area and the immediate rear area of the great, heroic combat front line.

THE SECOND WAVE OF THE TET OFFENSIVE AND KHE SANH

In South Vietnam, after the Tet General Offensive the Central Military Party Committee and the High Command instructed all battlefields to hold their positions, consolidate their forces, readjust forces and provide additional troops and weapons to the various theaters of operations, and prepare for a new round of attacks.

The 33rd, 174th, and 320th Regiments marched down from the Central Highlands to reinforce eastern Cochin China. The 174th Regiment was assigned to the 5th Division to strengthen it. The 36th Regiment, 308th Division, and the 141st Regiment, 312th Division, were sent from North Vietnam to reinforce the Quang Da Front, subordinate to Military Region 5. The 325C Division (consisting of two regiments, 95C and 101C) and the 209th Regiment, 312th Division, were sent from North Vietnam to reinforce the Central Highlands Front. The 308th Division (consisting of two regiments, the 102nd and 88th) and the 246th Regiment were sent from North Vietnam to the Route 9 Front. Fifteen full-strength field artillery battalions, with a total of 96 85mm guns and 27 D-74[29] guns, were sent from the north to reinforce the various fronts. Between March and August 1968, the Sapper Branch sent 3,797 cadre and soldiers, including eight complete battalions (at full strength in weapons and personnel)[30] to the battlefield.

Our main force and local force troops studied the April 1968 resolution of the Politburo on our new directions and responsibilities. They strengthened their resolve to fight and received reinforcement troops and additional weapons and equipment. Many units quickly reviewed and drew lessons from their experiences in the Tet offensive. As for our sapper and commando forces, which had suffered heavy losses, all battlefields strove to reinforce them and were able to train locally an additional 4,000 cadre and soldiers for these forces.

During the summer of 1968, pursuant to the resolution of the Politburo of the Party Central Committee, our soldiers and civilians in South Vietnam launched a second wave of attacks against the cities and towns, at the same time combating enemy forces that were conducting a fierce counterattack in the rural areas.

In Saigon, the preparations for our attack into the city had lost the element of surprise that we had during the Tet attacks. Our sapper and commando forces, which had suffered heavy losses, and the spearhead battalions of the subregions, which had lost almost 50 percent of their troops and equipment during the first offensive, had received only a limited quantity of replacement troops and equipment. Beginning on 11 March, the United States and its puppets massed 50 battalions to launch two successive sweep operations called "Quyet Thang" [Determined to Win] and "Toan Thang" [Total Victory] in the region surrounding the city, causing a great many difficulties for our units trying to approach their targets. Because the enemy had discovered our intentions, the Front Command had to switch the primary direction of attack, which was to be carried out by the 9th Division, from the north-northwest of Saigon down to the southwest of Saigon. During their advance toward the city our units were forced to fight as they marched and their forces suffered attrition. The 1st Regiment alone lost over 300 cadre and soldiers. With a firm fighting spirit and a high sense of discipline, our soldiers overcame all difficulties and adversities, resolutely carrying out their combat missions.

At 3:10 A.M. on 5 May 1968, our artillery troops simultaneously opened fire against eight targets within the city, launching the second wave of attacks on Saigon. The commando teams of the sections and branches of the City Command attacked and seized the television station and the Phan Thanh Gian Bridge. Moving out from springboard bases on the outskirts of the city, a number of main force regiments and spearhead battalions of the subregions bypassed the enemy's defensive lines and advanced into the city. Units of the 1st and 3rd Regiments attacked a number of enemy targets in the 5th, 6th, and 11th precincts and then held on, fighting the enemy for periods ranging from three to 17 days. Many ferocious battles were fought on the city streets between our soldiers and American soldiers and puppet Airborne troops. Combatant Nguyen Hong Phuc of the 1st Regiment knocked out four enemy tanks with four B-40 rockets. Combatant Dang Van Tuyet of the 3rd Regiment used a light machine gun and hand grenades to beat back many counterattacks mounted by American troops at the Bay Hien three-way intersection.

On 25 May the sound of our guns again erupted in Saigon as the 3rd Regiment of the 9th Division, the Dong Nai Regiment, and the battalions of our subregions attacked again, fighting battles against the enemy in the 6th Precinct, Go Vap, Phu Lam, etc. The people of Saigon enthusiastically provided supplies to our soldiers and treated our wounded troops. In some areas the people brought food and water to our troops in their fighting positions. On occasion, when U.S. troops arrived just as the rice was finished cooking and our troops had to hold off the enemy as they tried to move to different positions, the people had to hide the rice or carry it along as they moved out with our soldiers. Many families cared for soldiers who had been wounded or separated from their units and sought ways to send these soldiers back to their units.

Carried out in a situation in which the enemy had brought in a large force, had organized a defense in depth, and was striking back at our forces in the outskirts of the city, this second wave of attacks by our armed forces against Saigon, and especially by our main force troops, demonstrated the tremendous resolve of our soldiers and civilians.

In Central Vietnam, Military Region 5's main force divisions fought many battles in the contested areas, blocking and drawing in U.S. and puppet mobile troops, enabling our sapper units and local armed forces to attack and shell a number of cities and town. The main force troops of the Central Highlands used small elements to ambush and wipe out enemy patrols and, together with our civilians, tore up roads and built obstacles, cutting many sections of Routes 14, 18, and 19. The armed forces of the Tri-Thien Military Region defeated a sweep operation conducted by the U.S. Air Cavalry Division in the Ashau Valley, inflicting casualties totaling almost 1,000 U.S. and puppet troops between 19 April and 16 May. Because of enemy sweeps, fierce enemy bombing attacks and artillery barrages, and supply difficulties, our soldiers were not able to carry out the plan to mass forces to mount a second offensive against Hue city. After late May 1968 the Military Region's main force regiments and a portion of our local armed forces were forced to withdraw from the lowlands to our bases in the mountains.

On the Route 9 Front, fierce fighting continued in the Khe Sanh area. In May 1968, the 308th Division (minus one regiment) marched to the battlefield to join two regiments (the 66th and 9th) of the 304th Division in continuing the siege of Khe Sanh. When they discovered our new forces the U.S. Marines hastily launched a relief operation south of Ta Con. The 308th Division made a number of battalion-level attacks against them, eliminating from the field of combat almost 2,000 American troops and maintaining firm control of their positions. To the east, the 320th Division and the 270th Regiment conducted powerful operations in the Tan Lam and Cua Viet areas, attacking and crippling six American battalions. During this period the American and puppet mobile forces were forced to commit most of their strength to hold the cities and could not send additional forces to strengthen the Route 9 Front.

On 26 June 1968, the enemy announced he was withdrawing from Khe Sanh. Our armed forces rapidly tightened their siege ring, mounted shelling attacks, suppressed the enemy's efforts to transport troops by helicopter, and conducted fierce attacks to block the overland route, forcing the enemy to prolong his withdrawal. The withdrawal eventually took 17 days, during which we killed 1,300 enemy troops and shot down 34 aircraft. On 15 July 1968 our soldiers were in complete control of Khe Sanh. We had liberated an important strategic area in the western part of Route 9 in Quang Tri province and expanded our strategic North-South transportation corridor.

During the 170-day siege of Khe Sanh we eliminated from the field of combat 17,000 enemy troops (including 13,000 Americans) and destroyed or shot down 480 aircraft of all types. Our forces at Khe Sanh successfully fulfilled their mission of drawing in and tying down a large enemy force (which at its largest totaled 32 battalions, 26 of which were American, representing one quarter of all the U.S. combat battalions in South Vietnam) and coordinated their operations properly with the other battlefields throughout South Vietnam, thereby contributing to our strategically significant victory in 1968.[31]

The retreat from Khe Sanh represented a serious military and political failure for the American imperialists. This failure demonstrated the impotence of their strategically defensive posture, increased internal contradictions within U.S. ruling circles, and increased U.S. domestic and international opposition to the war of aggression in Vietnam.

The victory of the Route 9–Khe Sanh Front proved our main force troops were capable of conducting a protracted siege against a large complex of enemy defensive strong points even when the enemy had an overwhelming superiority of air and artillery firepower. Although main force divisions were unable to achieve the goal of fighting a battle that annihilated large numbers of American troops because of limitations in our battlefield equipment and weaknesses in our command and supply arrangements, etc., operating under conditions of great hardship and adversity the main force divisions participating in this campaign honed their skills in many different tactics, such as massed combined-arms combat operations, siege and encroachment operations, attacks by fire aimed at inflicting attrition on enemy forces, etc.

On 13 July 1968, Chairman Ho Chi Minh sent a message of commendation to the soldiers and civilians of the Route 9–Khe Sanh Front. In this cable, Uncle Ho affirmed that "our victory at Khe Sanh clearly demonstrates the unsurpassed strength and strategic skill of our soldiers, civilians, and cadres. This victory has made a worthy contribution to the great victory gained by South Vietnam from Tet up till the present. Together with our victories on the other battlefields, it has opened the door for even greater victories."[32]

THE THIRD WAVE OF THE TET OFFENSIVE

In August 1968 the Politburo of the Party Central Committee met to assess the initial success of the general offensive and uprising. The Politburo decided to step up our overall offensive through the use of military and political measures combined with a diplomatic offensive aimed at inflicting greater defeats on the enemy on every front and at achieving at all costs the strategic objectives that we had set forward for ourselves.

On 17 August 1968 our soldiers and civilians in South Vietnam launched a new wave of attacks. This attack wave lasted until 30 September 1968. In Cochin

China, COSVN's main force divisions and our local armed forces fought over 300 engagements, of which 16 were regiment-sized battles, crippling 15 enemy battalions, including 12 composite U.S. battalions in the Tay Ninh–Binh Long area and on the enemy's outer defensive perimeter. We also continued to shell a number of targets inside the city of Saigon. In Region 5 the Military Region's sapper troops attacked the 23rd (Americal) Division's base camp. The Military Region's main force 2nd and 3rd Divisions attacked the enemy in the area west of Tam Ky city and Quang Ngai city, worked with local armed forces to cut traffic along Routes 1 and 19, and attacked and crippled an element of the puppet 2nd Division. In the Central Highlands the front's main force troops intensified attacks against enemy forces in southwestern Darlac province and northwestern Kontum province, eliminating from the field of combat almost 2,000 enemy troops. They also supported compatriots of all ethnic groups in Duc Lap district in an uprising that seized power there.

Because we did not reassess the situation in a timely fashion, especially after the development of a number of unfavorable factors in the balance of forces and the progress of the war, we did not move quickly enough to shift the direction of our attacks. We continued to attack the cities, leaving the rural areas open and undefended. When the enemy shifted over to the defensive and strove to hold the cities and block our main force units in order to mass his forces to carry out rural "pacification," we did not fully appreciate the enemy's new plots and the strength he used in his "clear and hold" strategic measures.[33] The follow-up offensives launched by our soldiers and civilians did not have the strength of our first offensive and did not achieve the results our first wave of attacks had. Beginning in mid-1968, the lowlands of Region 5 and Cochin China encountered problems. After participating in a series of fierce, continuous combat operations, our main force units in South Vietnam had suffered losses and their combat power had declined.

CONCLUSIONS

Launched at a time when the enemy had changed his strategy and altered the deployment of his forces, the summer and fall offensives of 1968, although not achieving their projected political and military goals, had the practical effect of maintaining our continuous offensive posture and dealing added blows to the already-shaken will to commit aggression of the American imperialists.

America's "limited war" strategy, which they had pursued for over three years, had failed. The United States had hoped to use its expeditionary army to "break the back of the Viet Cong" and destroy the headquarters and leadership organizations of the resistance, but our main force troops had seized the initiative by attacking the lair of the Americans and their puppets. The United States had intended to stay on the perimeter and push the war out to the border area in order to rescue the puppet army and the puppet regime. However, our soldiers and civilians had taken war into the cities, disrupting the political and economic centers of the neocolonialist regime. The United States had intended to use its war of destruction to prevent North Vietnam from providing support to South Vietnam. That support instead constantly increased.

On 1 November 1968, U.S. President Johnson was forced to announce the unilateral cessation of all acts of war against North Vietnam and to agree to convene a four-party conference in Paris, France. The parties attending the conference were the government of the Democratic Republic of Vietnam, the National Liberation Front for South Vietnam, the U.S. government, and the Saigon government.

This decision was a public admission of the bankruptcy of the American "limited war" strategy in Vietnam, of the failure of their war of destruction against North Vietnam, and of the impotence of the American Army, Navy, and Air Force. North Vietnam had endured great sacrifices throughout the fiercest challenges of war, but it had clearly demonstrated the powerful strength of our outstanding new regime. Over 3,000 modern jet aircraft, the newest models in the American inventory that were being used for the very first time, had been shot down in the skies over North Vietnam. Hundreds of pilots had been killed. Hundreds of warships, large and small, had been set ablaze or sunk. The soldiers and civilians of North Vietnam fought back, at the same time continuing their missions of building socialism and powerfully expanding their role as the great rear area for our great, heroic front lines.

On 3 November 1968, Chairman Ho Chi Minh issued an appeal to the citizens and soldiers of the entire nation: "We have defeated the American imperialists' war of destruction against North Vietnam. This victory is of great importance to our people's great cause of resisting the Americans to save the nation. This victory, however, is only our first step. The American imperialists are very stubborn and cunning. The sacred duty of our entire nation is now to increase our determination to fight and to win, and we are resolved to liberate South Vietnam, defend North Vietnam, and advance toward peace and unification of the Fatherland."[34]

The four-year period (1965–1968) of combat against more than one million U.S., puppet, and satellite troops in South Vietnam and of defeating the modern American Air Force and Navy in North Vietnam was a period of fierce challenges to our army. The American imperialists had mobilized a high percentage of their military might and utilized their newest achievements in military science and technology (all except for nuclear weapons). With their large numbers of troops, tremendous firepower, high level of mobility, and boundless supplies of combat equipment and logistics support, they thought they could quickly destroy our people's armed forces in South Vietnam and completely destroy North Vietnam. The battles in both North and South Vietnam had been extremely fierce and desperate.

THERE IS NOTHING MORE PRECIOUS
THAN INDEPENDENCE AND FREEDOM!

The great thoughts of Chairman Ho Chi Minh pulled together and amplified the strength of our entire nation, millions of people acting as one, determined to fight and determined to defeat the American aggressors.

Relying on the power of the entire nation and on our people's war posture, our army displayed a strong offensive spirit, rapidly increased our forces, and developed many diverse and effective fighting methods. The victories of Van Tuong, Bau Bang, and Plei Me; the crushing of the enemy's two strategic counteroffensives in 1965–1966 and 1966–1967; the defeat of the American Air Force and Navy's many escalations of the war of destruction against North Vietnam; and the Tet 1968 strategic offensive will live forever in the history of our nation as shining feats of arms by the heroic Vietnamese revolution, of the people, and of the heroic People's Army of Vietnam.

In combat, in victory, and even in adversity and hesitancy, all units, all service branches, and all specialty branches grew in maturity. Our infantry divisions, artillerymen, sappers, air defense and air force troops, engineers, transportation soldiers, main force troops, local force troops, and guerrilla militia soldiers on all our battlefields grew rapidly in both size and in combat ability.

This was a strategic period that was a decisive turning point in the resistance war against the Americans to save the nation. Together with the entire population, our army had defeated the American expeditionary army, dealing a decisive blow that defeated their will to commit aggression and forcing the United States to deescalate the war in both North and South Vietnam. Beginning in late 1968 the American imperialists began first to "de-Americanize" and then to "Vietnamize the war." This was a new change in strategy, a turning point in the downward slide in the American imperialist war of aggression against Vietnam.

PART IV

The People's Army of Vietnam Launches Large-Scale Combined-Arms Operations and, Together with the Entire Population, Partially Defeats the U.S. Imperialists' Strategy to "Vietnamize" the War, 1969–1972

10
Maintaining Our Main Force Elements in South Vietnam, Conducting Counterattacks and Offensives, and Developing a New Strategic Posture

PACIFICATION AND VIETNAMIZATION

The Tet 1968 General Offensive and simultaneous uprising by our soldiers and civilians won a strategic victory, defeated the aggressive plans of the U.S. imperialists, and created a strategic turning point in the war. The U.S. "limited war" had been bankrupted and the U.S. imperialists were forced to deescalate and alter their strategy.

The United States and its puppets were forced to shift from "search and destroy" to "clear and hold" tactics. They moved in additional forces to secure the cities and their important bases and launched savage sweep operations on the outskirts of the cities in response to our offensive attacks.

While carrying out a "trial pacification" program in the provinces of Vinh Long and Tra Vinh during late 1968 the enemy discovered our vulnerability in the rural areas. They immediately mobilized forces to conduct an "accelerated pacification" campaign throughout the region aimed at retaking a number of key areas in the rural lowlands and driving out our main force troops.

After the Tet General Offensive and simultaneous uprisings our armed forces in South Vietnam conducted two follow-up offensives in the summer and fall of 1968, killing a number of enemy troops and destroying additional war equipment. Because we did not fully appreciate the new enemy schemes and the changes the enemy had made in his conduct of the war and because we underestimated the enemy's capabilities and the strength of his counterattack, when the United States and its puppets began to carry out their "clear and hold" strategy our battlefronts were too slow in shifting over to attacking the "pacification" program and we did not concentrate our political and military forces to deal with the enemy's new plots and schemes. Beginning in the latter half of 1968, our offensive posture began to weaken and our three types of armed forces suffered attrition. The political and military struggle in the rural areas declined and our liberated areas shrank. COSVN and military region main force units were able to maintain only a portion of their forces in our scattered lowland base areas, and most of our main force troops were forced back to the border or to bases in the mountains.

In January 1969, after replacing Johnson as President of the United States, Nixon laid out a new worldwide strategy called the "Nixon Doctrine." This doctrine was based on three principles: 1) U.S. power; 2) sharing of responsibility; and 3) negotiating from a position of strength.

With regard to Vietnam, Nixon altered the "De-Americanization of the War" policy that Johnson had approved and replaced it with the strategy of "Vietnamizing the war." The primary goal of the "Vietnamization" strategy, which would be the first test of the Nixon Doctrine, was to repress and control the majority of the population of Vietnam in order to remove the very foundation of our revolutionary war. At the same time the United States would use every means possible to block our strategic transportation route [the Ho Chi Minh Trail]; encircle, isolate, and strangle the resistance war of the people of South Vietnam; and drive our main force units far away from the population, causing the war to deteriorate into an "exclusively guerrilla" war that would "gradually die away."

To achieve these goals the Nixon clique carried out a series of measures, including intensified rural "pacification" and the destruction of our grass-roots organizations in order to gain control of the majority of the population; efforts to develop the Saigon puppet army into a modern force that could serve as their main strategic force in South Vietnam, as an assault force for all of Indochina, and to gradually replace U.S. troops in the ground combat role; strengthening the puppet government at all levels; blockading and destroying our economy and doing everything possible to cut off the support North Vietnam was sending to the South in order to isolate the revolution in the South; and using insidious diplomatic schemes to pressure our people into accepting a political settlement advantageous to the United States. Of all these measures, rural "pacification" was considered key to the success of this strategy.

Nixon planned that "Vietnamization" would be basically completed by 1971 and that the program would be finally completed in 1972.

As for Laos and Cambodia, Nixon sought to expand the war of aggression into these two countries, using appropriate, limited measures, and to coordinate these efforts with "Vietnamization" in South Vietnam to suppress the Lao and Cambodian revolutions.

"Vietnamization" was in fact a plan to continue, prolong, and even intensify the war of aggression waged by the American imperialists. It was, however, also an extremely insidious and dangerous plan. Trapped in a position of defeat, the American imperialists were being forced to "deescalate" the war and gradually withdraw U.S. troops. In spite of this, however, they concentrated their forces and, using military, political, economic, and diplomatic measures, launched a ferocious counteroffensive to drive us back, create a new position of strength for themselves, and keep South Vietnam within America's neocolonialist orbit.

In the second half of 1968, and using the large U.S. expeditionary army as their base, the enemy mobilized the entire puppet army to carry out their rural "pacification" program. U.S. troops were used as the main force to conduct sweep operations in contested areas and liberated zones to erode the strength of our main force units. Meanwhile, part of the U.S. army worked with puppet troops to sweep key areas in the rural lowlands, searching out and eliminating our cadre, Party members, and local armed forces, gathering civilians into concentration areas that used such names as "new life hamlets," "peace zones," etc. The enemy built thousands of new outposts, upgraded puppet forces, drafted new troops, and expanded the puppet army, especially local forces and people's self-defense forces used to oppress the population.[1] They blocked our entry points and attacked our supply routes from the lowlands to our base areas.[2] The enemy also collected and tightly controlled the people's rice crops in order to dry up local sources of supply for our armed forces.

The United States and its puppets burned, destroyed, bombed, and spread defoliants over areas around enemy bases that they were unable to control. Using heavy equipment, they bulldozed the terrain flat to create empty zones covering dozens of square kilometers and eliminate the springboard positions we needed to launch our attacks. U.S. troops used bulldozers and tanks to level six villages in Go Noi (Dien Ban district, Quang Nam province). In the northern part of Cu Chi district many villages were razed, with not one clump of bushes left standing. The enemy perpetrated many bloody acts of terrorism aimed at crushing the morale of our civilians. Examples of these acts were the savage massacre of more than 500 people, most of them old people, women, and children, in Ba Lang An (Quang Ngai province) and the murder of 347 people in Binh Duong (Quang Nam province).

Whenever the United States and its puppets found an area used by our forces, they immediately sent heliborne commando assault forces to locate our forces and then either sent troops to conduct sweeps or used aerial and artillery firepower to destroy the area.

With regard to our supply corridors, besides using bombs, artillery, and poison chemicals, the enemy sent reconnaissance and commando troops to attack our supply warehouses to "cut the lifeline" of our armed forces. In 1969 four times as many B-52 sorties were used to attack Group 559's strategic transportation corridor as had been used in 1968, sorties by attack aircraft were 2.5 times higher, and the tonnage of explosives and shells used against the corridor was three times higher than in 1968. The enemy concentrated ferocious attacks against the entry points for Routes 8, 10, 12, and 20 to cut the supply line from North Vietnam to the battlefield.

In addition to sweep operations and savage bombing and shelling attacks, the enemy greatly expanded his use of psychological warfare and of the chieu hoi [rallier] and defector programs to weaken the ranks of the revolution. The enemy's horrible, insidious pacification program and his acts of destruction created immeasurable difficulties and complications for our armed forces and civilian population.

RENEWED RESOLVE TO CONTINUE THE WAR

To motivate and strengthen the resolve of our armed forces and our civilian population to fight the Americans and save the nation after the Tet 1968 general offensive and simultaneous uprisings, Chairman Ho Chi Minh once again affirmed our goals and clearly spelled out what we needed to do to advance our cause. On 1 January 1969, to mark the new year, Uncle Ho sent this letter to our citizens and combatants:

> In 1968 the soldiers and civilians of the entire nation won glorious victories. . . . It is certain that the American pirates will be completely defeated. The soldiers and civilians of the entire nation, building upon these victories, will certainly win total victory. . . . For the sake of our independence, for the sake of our freedom, fight to make the Americans flee, fight to topple the puppet regime.[3]

In April 1969 the Party Politburo issued a resolution on mobilizing the efforts of the soldiers and civilian population of both North and South Vietnam to develop the strategic offensive, to defeat the enemy's "Vietnamization" policy and his scheme to bring the war to a conclusion from a position of strength, to force the United States to withdraw its troops, to force the collapse of the puppet regime, and to move ahead to secure a decisive victory. The people of North Vietnam, the resolution said, must correctly carry out their duty of supporting South Vietnam and at the same time remain ready to crush any enemy schemes aimed at resuming the war of destruction against North Vietnam or at using infantry troops to mount raids against or invade the southern portion of Military Region 4.

The Central Military Party Committee and the High Command ordered all armed forces to quickly reorganize themselves in light of the assigned combat missions and the manpower and supply capacities of each individual battlefield. Our policy, as enunciated by the Party Committee and the High Command, was to increase the quality of our main force troops, consolidate and expand local forces, guerrilla militia, and elite forces in all three types of armed forces, and to strengthen engineer and anti-aircraft forces in order to defend and expand our strategic supply line.

In North Vietnam, taking advantage of the enemy's forced cessation of his air and naval bombardment campaign, the people worked to repair the ravages of war, rebuild the economy, strengthen national defense, and to increase our support to the front lines. The people's armed forces quickly reorganized, withdrawing 14,300 cadre and soldiers from the force structure to form nine regiments whose assigned duties were to perform production tasks and rebuild the economy. In areas where troops were stationed all main force units, local force units, and guerrilla militia (using army engineers as the core element) worked to destroy or dismantle bombs and mines, fill in bomb craters, develop farmland for the civilian population, and restore land and water communications routes.

Within the armed forces, pursuant to the Politburo resolution of April 1969, the Central Military Party Committee implemented many measures designed to strengthen ideological and organizational activities. In May 1969 the General Political Department held a class for mid- and high-level cadre from the staff agencies of the Ministry of Defense, the military regions, the Service and specialty branches, and the divisions to study and review the situation and their responsibilities.

In a letter sent to this class Chairman Ho Chi Minh directed that

> our first priority is to constantly increase our resolve to defeat the American aggressors and to fight on to final victory. We must have high resolve to overcome all obstacles and carry out our duties. This resolve must be transformed into heroic actions and resolute combat operations, into acceptance of sacrifice and hardship, and into absolute adherence to all instructions and orders. No matter what the situation, you must ensure that your units are determined to fight and determined to win. You must also maintain tight administrative control of your units, maintain strict discipline, and properly carry out all policy measures.
>
> You must use correct combat tactics. In every area of operations, you must learn from experience and study the examples set by those units that fight well to ensure that every unit and every locality fights well. Your spirit of duty must be high. You must truly share in the hardships of your soldiers. You must teach your soldiers to properly maintain their weapons and equipment, to economize on the use of each and every bullet, each and every grain of rice, and allow no wastage.[4]

To celebrate Chairman Ho Chi Minh's 79th birthday, on 11 May 1969 a delegation of representatives from the class, representing the entire armed forces, came to wish Uncle Ho a happy birthday. Uncle Ho asked about the personal welfare of these representatives and praised all cadre and soldiers of our armed forces for their many accomplishments. Uncle Ho said, ". . . it is clear that the American pirates have lost, and it is certain that they will be totally defeated. They are still stubborn, however, and are not yet willing to give up their scheme of aggression against our nation. The soldiers and civilians of our entire nation must overcome many sacrifices and hardships to attain our final victory."

Uncle Ho instructed the armed forces that

> you must build forces that are truly excellent, whose quality is truly high. You must always be alert and ready for combat, and you must fight well to

protect our socialist North Vietnam. Pay attention to conserving our manpower and material resources and to proper maintenance of our weapons and equipment. Troops must wholeheartedly assist the people and participate in the development of our rear area so that it grows in strength and stability each and every day. You must work with state agencies and with organizations to properly carry out our policies toward our sick and wounded soldiers and toward those families that have served the revolution. . . . You must strive to learn and always set an example of revolutionary virtue.[5]

The class representatives were overjoyed at this chance to meet with Uncle Ho and were moved by his solicitous and profound words of advice. On behalf of the entire armed forces Major General Vuong Thua Vu, Deputy Chief of the General Staff, promised to try to carry out Uncle Ho's instructions, to build a powerful army, and, working with the entire population, to fight until total victory over the American aggressors was secured.

In the summer of 1969 our army launched a wave of political training. This training covered the new situation and our new responsibilities; promulgated the instructions of the Central Military Party Committee to "strengthen organizations, raise quality, and readjust the number of troops on active duty to an appropriate level"; to ensure that our units were able to carry out their combat duties in South Vietnam; to defend North Vietnam; to support the revolution in Laos; and to provide for the expansion of our forces when needed. The plan to readjust our force structure developed by the General Staff was approved by the Central Military Party Committee. According to this plan, the main force divisions and regiments under the command of the High Command and of the military regions would all be reinforced with additional troops and equipment to bring them up to full table of organization and equipment [TO&E] strength. The Anti-Aircraft–Air Force Service disbanded its 377 Air Defense Division and 268th and 278th Missile Regiments and sent additional cadre to reinforce its static-defense units defending vital locations and units fighting in southern Military Region 4 and along the Ho Chi Minh Trail. The Navy, the military regions, and other branches and schools reduced the number of troops in headquarters and support units in order to increase the proportion of troops directly involved in combat operations. Transportation Group 559 and technical support units received additional personnel and equipment. Weapons and equipment that had been damaged or were in excess of authorized levels were collected for repair and storage. As a result of the 1969 readjustment of forces we were able to strengthen the TO&E of our units and simultaneously send 13,200 excess cadre and soldiers to the battlefront. Although the total number of troops on active duty declined, the organization and combat ability of our units, especially the main force divisions, grew in response to the requirements of the new situation.

The requirement to increase the flow of personnel and supplies to the battlefield was very great. Since the enemy had amassed a large number of aircraft and was using upgraded weapons and new tactics to attack the transportation corridors, especially the launch points for the corridors, we confronted many new problems in trying to build roads, combat enemy aircraft, and defend our lines of supply.

The General Staff sent two engineer regiments, 12 engineer battalions, and six independent engineer companies to southwestern Military Region 4 to work with the troops of Group 559 to build the "20 July" road from the Thach Ban intersection down to Route 9 and build additional bypass roads and detours around the "choke points" that were under constant enemy attack. The 367th Air Defense Division moved to western Quang Binh–Vinh Linh to combat enemy aircraft and protect the supply routes. Group 500, formerly subordinate to the High Command, and the forces of the General Rear Services Department serving in southern Military Region 4 were now placed under the command of Group 559 to further strengthen the strategic transportation corridor.[6] Group 559's cadre and soldiers overcame many obstacles, endured the enemy's bombs and shells, and fought night and day to keep the roads open. In 1969 170,000 tons of supplies were sent to the battlefield over Group 559's transportation corridor, a 29 percent increase over 1968.[7] Over 80,000 soldiers marched from North Vietnam across the Annamite Mountains to reinforce battlefields throughout South Vietnam.

To increase forces available to attack the enemy, the Central Military Party Committee and the High Command sent many units with full TO&E strength to South Vietnam. At the same time the main force units on the battlefield were reorganized to conform to our supply situation and to the new situation and responsibilities of each local area, especially in the key theater: eastern Cochin China.

After a period of reorganization and refitting, the 324th Infantry Division returned to the Tri-Thien Front; the 28th Infantry Regiment was sent to the Central Highlands; and the 141st Infantry Regiment and the 38th Infantry Regiment (formerly 3rd Regiment, 325th Division) were sent to Military Region 5. A number of main force units from the Central Highlands and Military Region 5 were sent to eastern Cochin China. These were the 1st Division (the 95C, 101C, and 209th Regiments) and the 33rd, 174th, 10th, and 20th Infantry Regiments.

Ten sapper battalions and 100 sapper companies and platoons marched from North Vietnam to the battlefields to strengthen the sapper units of COSVN and of the military regions, divisions, and provinces, all of which suffered heavy losses in 1968. COSVN Military Command selected a number of battalions and companies for conversion into sapper units. By the end of 1969, after a period of constant reinforcement, the sapper forces of our three types of troops in South Vietnam consisted of one brigade (COSVN's 429th Sapper Brigade), three groups (equivalent to regiments), 38 battalions, and 71 companies and more than 100 platoons belonging to the provinces and districts. At the village and hamlet level we had "guerrilla sapper" teams. COSVN and the military regions also organized "special duty" sapper units to cling to and attack specific base camps and rear bases from Tri Thien to the Mekong Delta. Working together with the "special duty" sappers were "special duty artillery" assigned to attack these enemy bases.

244 VICTORY IN VIETNAM

Military Region 5 Headquarters formed two additional artillery battalions to cling to and attack bases in Da Nang, Chu Lai, and Nuoc Man. COSVN sent six battalions of the Bien Hoa Artillery Group to become "special duty artillery" units to cling to and attack six U.S. bases in eastern Cochin China—Phuoc Vinh, Technic, Lai Khe, Dau Tieng, Phuoc Binh, and Phuoc Long. The number of local force artillery units was expanded in Cochin China, and included a number of all-female artillery units at the province and district level. This was an innovative approach to organizing the forces of our army in order to overcome the difficulties facing us after the Tet 68 Offensive and Uprising and to increase the combat capabilities of our armed forces operating in the heart of the enemy zone.

GROWING DIFFICULTIES IN THE SOUTH

Throughout the course of this reorganization our armed forces on the battlefield continued to maintain an offensive posture and to counterattack the enemy. During the first half of 1969 we launched two waves of operations (the 22 February–30 March spring wave and the 11 May–25 June wave), causing a limited amount of damage to the enemy.

COSVN's 5th, 7th, and 9th Divisions, COSVN's 88th, 268th, and Quyet Thang Regiments, the 4th Regiment of Military Region 7, and the 95C, 101C, 174th, 33rd, and 209th Regiments (all newly arrived from the Central Highlands) conducted operations in the Tay Ninh–Binh Long and Bien Hoa–Long Khanh theaters. Combining medium-level and small-unit fighting, coordinating infantry and sapper operations, utilizing raid and ambush tactics to attack gaps in enemy defenses, our troops destroyed a number of companies and crippled two U.S. battalions in the battles of Ben Tranh, Tra Cao, Loc Ninh, Dong Pan, and Hon Quan. . . . We also defeated a number of enemy sweep operations in the Dau Tieng area (Thu Dau Mot province) and southwestern Tay Ninh.

Military Region 5's 2nd and 3rd Divisions operated in An Hoa (Quang Da province), Tien Phuoc (Quang Nam province), Tu Nghia and Duc Pho (Quang Ngai province), etc., wearing down and inflicting casualties on the U.S. 5th Marine Regiment and on the U.S. 196th and 198th Brigades. Supported by main force troops, local armed forces and civilians rose up to destroy "strategic hamlets." Over 90,000 people regained control of their own villages and hamlets.

In May 1969 the Central Highlands Front launched an offensive at Dak To in northern Kontum. After a number of preliminary battles and after deploying our forces to gain a favorable tactical position, we lured ten battalions of the puppet's II Corps out to the decisive battle area. The 28th and 66th Regiments conducted continuous envelopment operations and attacks, slicing up enemy troop concentrations and not allowing them to pull back to high ground to regroup. Four enemy battalions were crippled and 100 prisoners were captured.

The 324th Division and the main force regiments of the Tri-Thien Military

Region blocked and struck back at enemy attacks against our strategic transportation corridor in the areas of Co-ca-va, Tam Tanh, A Luoi, and A Bia, eliminating thousands of American troops from the battlefield. The bloodiest battle, which was fought on A Bia Mountain, so terrified American troops that they called the mountain "Hamburger Hill."

The operations of our armed forces, especially the spring wave of operations, tied down and inflicted casualties on the U.S. 1st, 25th, and Air Cavalry Divisions in Tay Ninh, Binh Long, and Thu Dau Mot; the puppet 18th Division in Long Khanh; and the U.S. Americal Division in Quang Nam. These operations enabled our local forces to attack and disrupt the pacification campaign. Because, however, they had been involved in continuous operations, had suffered casualties in 1968 from which they had not had time to recuperate, and because our flow of reinforcements and supplies from North Vietnam was encountering many difficulties, our main force units were not able to kill large numbers of enemy troops in these battles.

The elite units [sappers and urban commandos] among the three types of troops, with their small, compact organization and equipment, developed appropriate fighting techniques and achieved a high level of effectiveness in a number of battles. During the two 1969 waves of operations these forces fought more than 300 battles, of which 52 were attacks on battalion and division headquarters units and 40 were attacks on airfields and storage warehouses. The enemy suffered almost 20,000 casualties during these attacks, including many American officers and technicians, and our elite units destroyed 250 aircraft, 150 artillery pieces, millions of liters of petroleum products, etc. On 26 January 1969 COSVN's 3rd Sapper Battalion and 7th Division's 28th Sapper Battalion, under the command of Hero Nguyen Cu, Deputy Commander of COSVN Sapper Forces, attacked the base camp of the U.S. 25th Mechanized Infantry Division at Dong Du (Cu Chi), eliminating from the field of battle more than 1,000 troops and destroying 50 aircraft, 176 military vehicles, and 12 artillery pieces.

Operating under conditions of great hardship, our elite artillery forces clung to and attacked enemy base camps. They regularly endured bombing and shelling attacks and search operations conducted by the United States and puppet forces. Some units were so short of rice that they had to reserve cooked rice for soldiers who carried the artillery weapons. During the spring wave of attacks the artillery troops of Binh Duc (My Tho province) twice shelled the base camp of the 9th Division, inflicting more than 300 casualties and destroying 20 pieces of artillery and 30 helicopters. The Da Nang artillery unit hit two enemy ammunition ships on the Han River, causing a chain of explosions that destroyed an entire convoy of 15 vessels. The "special duty artillery" units targeted on six enemy bases in eastern Cochin China fought 260 battles during 1969, eliminating from the battlefield thousands of American troops and destroying more than 100 aircraft. Resolutely clinging to their targets and attacking vital targets deep behind enemy lines, our elite forces inflicted great personnel and equipment losses on the enemy and helped our forces maintain the offensive initiative on all battlefronts.

Alongside the operations of our main force units and our elite forces, our local armed forces also clung to their assigned areas. Working with the civilian population, they eliminated local tyrants, destroyed the enemy's apparatus of oppression, conducted sniper attacks against enemy troops in outposts, destroyed enemy lines of communications, etc. In Region 5 local armed forces wiped out more than 10,000 members of the enemy's apparatus of oppression and supported 200,000 civilians in uprisings demanding the right to control their own destinies. In Cochin China the civilian population of 130 hamlets in the provinces of Ben Tre and Chau Doc mounted uprisings. In the provinces of Can Tho, Vinh Tra, Bac Lieu, Soc Trang, and Ca Mau more than 100 "strategic hamlets" were destroyed, liberating more than 10,000 people.

Because of our difficulties in obtaining supplies and replacements and because the enemy was conducting ferocious counterattacks against us, after the summer campaign of 1969 a major portion of our main force army was forced to withdraw to our base areas to regroup. In the rural areas the strength of our local armed forces was seriously eroded. The enemy exploited his advantage during the rainy season by moving into our areas, carrying out rapid pacification operations in the rural lowlands and attacking our base areas in the mountains and our supply corridors, creating further difficulties for our forces.

In Region 5, in late April 1969 the enemy concentrated its forces to launch many sweep operations through the contested and liberated areas from northern Binh Dinh up to Quang Da province. B-52s dropped bombs and helicopters landed assault teams to destroy our base areas and transportation routes. American and South Korean units dispersed their units down to the company level, operating in support of puppet Regional and Popular Forces to attack and control the people in each individual area. By the end of 1969 the population of our liberated areas had shrunk to 840,000 people and the enemy had gained control over an additional 460,000 people. The strength of our guerrilla forces in the entire region dropped by 4,600 soldiers and our local forces declined by 2,000 soldiers as compared with their 1968 year-end strengths.

In Cochin China the U.S. 1st Air Cavalry, 101st Airborne, and 25th Mechanized Infantry Divisions took turns attacking the Vietnamese-Cambodian border area. The puppet 21st Division and 4th Ranger Group established blocking positions along the borders of western Cochin China from Kien Tuong to the Vinh Te Canal. The COSVN base area was insecure and our supply routes from the lowlands were blocked. In the lowlands the enemy used three puppet regular divisions (the 7th, 9th, and 21st) and the 3rd Brigade of the U.S. 9th Division to conduct repeated sweeps through individual areas. By the end of 1969 the enemy had retaken almost all of our liberated zones in the rural lowlands of Cochin China. We were only able to hold onto our bases in the U Minh Forest, the Plain of Reeds, and a number of isolated liberated base "spots" north of Route 4 and in Cao Lanh district. The enemy established 1,000 new outposts and gained control over an additional one million people. Our forces were being rapidly depleted, especially in western Cochin China. In that area, during the first six months of 1969 our village and hamlet guerrilla forces suffered over 15,000 casualties. Each local force company was down to only 20 to 30 fighters. Because we had lost so much of the civilian population we could not maintain the level of local recruitment we had maintained during previous years. In 1969 we were only able to recruit 1,700 new soldiers in Region 5 (compared with 8,000 new recruits in 1968), and in the lowlands of Cochin China we recruited only 100 new soldiers (compared with 16,000 in 1968). Our liberated areas were shrinking, our bases were under pressure, and both our local and strategic lines of supply were under ferocious enemy attack. We had great difficulty supplying our troops. In the staff units of the Military Region 5 Headquarters on some days eight people had to share a half-measure of rice. The supply situation for COSVN's main force troops was not as bad, but by September they had only 2,000 tons of food in reserve. This amount was not sufficient to feed our troops for one month. Units were forced to begin alternately eating rice for one meal and manioc for the next. Some of our cadre and soldiers became pessimistic and exhibited fear of close combat and of remaining in the battle zone. Some deserted their units to flee to rear areas, and some even defected to the enemy.

In the meantime the enemy gained control of many heavily populated areas. He drafted more than 200,000 youths into the army and built up his local force units, organizing what he called "territorial security" forces. The enemy rapidly expanded his regular armed forces, especially technical branches such as the Air Force, armor, artillery, etc. Because his local forces were able to assume a portion of the responsibility for "pacification" and defending territory, the enemy was able to increase his local and strategic reserve forces to more than twice their previous level. In 1968 the puppet army had only 30 mobile battalions, but in 1969 this number grew to 63 battalions (equivalent to 38 percent of their total troop strength). Nixon began to withdraw a portion of the U.S. expeditionary army back to the United States.[8]

Reviewing this situation, the 18th Plenum of the Party Central Committee stated clearly that

> In 1969 the enemy made some progress because our efforts to counter his actions were not timely, the operations of our main force units and our guerrilla warfare actions were not very effective, and we did not devote a sufficient level of attention to the need to attack the enemy's pacification program. This situation has affected the growth of our armed forces and our ability to retain the initiative on the battlefield.

The problem of how to maintain and employ our main force units became a critical issue for all battlefields. This issue involved a savage struggle between the enemy and ourselves, because one of the enemy's strategic schemes was to force our main force units to disperse and to drive our main force units back across the borders. Internally, many of our cadre had differing opinions on this issue. Faced with a situation in which the enemy was seizing our territory and civilian population, our bases were insecure, and we were encountering difficulties in providing supplies and combat support to our main force units, a number of our cadre believed it was essential for us to disperse a portion of our main force troops down to the local areas to attack the "pacification" program and to resolve at least part of our supply problems.

With a firm grasp of the laws governing the development of warfare, the cadre of the COSVN Military Party Committee, the COSVN Military Command, and the Party committees and military headquarters of the military regions were in unanimous agreement regarding the role of our main force troops. All units were directed to resolutely fight the enemy to protect our bases and to take turns in pulling back to reorganize and retrain to increase their combat abilities. At the same time the units were ordered to increase production, to exploit local sources of supply, and to assist in the defense and development of our transportation routes so we could receive support from our great rear area in North Vietnam. In September 1969 a conference of the Military Party Committee of Military Region 5 stated clearly that the primary, central responsibility of the Military Region was to "wipe out oppression and gain control of the population." The Committee said the combat operations of our full-time military forces must be directly related to the goal of gaining control of the population. The conference directed that, along with developing local forces, the region must focus on consolidating our main force units and on fighting major battles aimed at reversing this situation.

To maintain and expand our local armed forces, intensify guerrilla warfare, and develop the areas and facilities needed by our main force units to build themselves up and conduct combat operations, COSVN and the military regions sent a number of main force units to operate in a number of key areas. The 20th and 1st Regiments opened a new front in An Giang province. The 4th, 16th, 33rd, 88th, 286th, Quyet Thang, and Dong Nai Regiments, all subordinate to COSVN or Military Region 7, were assigned to defend areas north, northwest, and northeast of Saigon. Military Region 9's 1st and 2nd Regiments operated in the upper and lower Mekong Delta, and the Dong Thap Regiment returned to My Tho province. Military Region 5's 36th, 31st, and 12th Regiments defended positions in Quang Da and Binh Dinh provinces. A number of our military regions reassigned some of their main force troops to serve as local force soldiers. Military Region 5 disbanded the 3rd Division's 22nd Regiment and sent its three battalions to reinforce the local forces of Quang Ngai, Binh Dinh, and Phu Yen provinces, each province receiving one battalion. The Tri-Thien Military Region assigned 1,500 main force cadre and soldiers to local areas to serve as a hardcore framework to be used to build up local district units and village guerrillas. Military Regions 7 and 9 sent armed operations teams to villages deep behind enemy lines to work with local cadre to rebuild our organizations.

The main force regiments operating in these local areas endured very harsh conditions. Cut off by the enemy's network of local outposts and faced with the disappearance of the base-area "spots" that had previously been scattered throughout the rural areas, our units were forced to disperse down to the company and platoon levels, and some regiments were even forced to disperse down to the squad level. Our most important work became the education of cadre and soldiers operating deep behind enemy lines in moral character and in the revolutionary traditions of the army, building a will to fight and a spirit of resolution to remain in place, to endure and overcome every sacrifice and hardship. Squeezed by the enemy into "strategic hamlets" and with tight enemy controls over the purchase and sale of rice, the local civilian population where our soldiers were operating cleverly deceived the enemy, putting aside small amounts of rice and salt every day to give to our troops. Cadre, Party members, local force soldiers, and guerrillas at the grass-roots level provided wholehearted support to enable our main force units to remain in place. Heroine Le Thi Hong Gam, deputy platoon commander of Chau Thanh district local forces, and many other cadre and soldiers heroically sacrificed their lives during supply missions supporting our soldiers. Operating among the local population, our cadre and soldiers relied on food provided by the people and planted their own vegetables and caught fish to at least partially resolve their food supply shortage.

In the enemy's "pacification" focal areas our main force regiments encountered even more difficulties. The 16th, 238th, and Quyet Thang Regiments were forced to conduct all their daily activities underground in the Cu Chi tunnel system. Units assigned to stay in Trang Bang and Go Dau in Tay Ninh province spent their days hiding in underground tunnels and at night secretly crept into the hamlets to mobilize the masses and recruit local members. COSVN sent the 320th Regiment to Long An province to fight alongside our local forces to preserve the revolutionary movement of the masses. The regiment's cadre and soldiers suffered heavy casualties, twice having to cross Route 4, which bristled with enemy outposts, to return to the COSVN base area to rebuild the regiment before returning to continue the fight alongside the people of Long An province. The 1st Regiment, operating in Long My, Chuong Thien province, an area covered with enemy outposts, lived by the slogan "cook without smoke, speak softly, cough without noise," in order to secretly remain in their assigned area, recruit local forces, and conduct guerrilla warfare.

Most of the cadre and soldiers of the regiments and armed operations teams operating in the lowlands were natives of North Vietnam. Going out to each hamlet and village to serve as local force troops and guerrilla fighters, living in the bosoms of the people of South Vietnam, wherever they went our cadre and soldiers were supported and protected by the people. Because our armed local forces had suffered severe losses, guerrilla operations had declined. The people were severely oppressed; every unit and each individual cadre and soldier faced many challenges. They had to fight courageously and at the same time build up local organizations so they could maintain themselves behind enemy lines. Although they could not yet reverse the situation, the dispersal of a portion of our main force troops to operate in local areas contributed to the continuation of the people's war at the local level and compelled the enemy to disperse his forces to counter our troops. This effort enabled us to defend our base areas and preserve our main force army. It was also a realistic measure that allowed our main force units to expand and provided a basis from which we could launch future attacks.

Our main force units in the base areas firmly held their positions and rapidly regrouped and consolidated their forces. Cadres and soldiers of all units conducted study sessions and all recognized the great victory the Tet 1968 General Offensive and Uprising represented. They came to fully understand the new situation and their new duties and struggled to overcome rightist thinking and pessimism. Their belief in our cause increased, their combat spirit remained firm, and they resolved to cling to the battlefield and maintain their positions.

Our difficulties, however, were not over. During mid-1969 the enemy increased his attacks on our transportation corridors in an effort to completely cut our supply line to our soldiers. The arrival of the rainy season caused added transportation difficulties. A number of main force units operating in forward areas, the troops of Group 559, and replacement troops traveling down the Trail were reduced to eating only two or three "lang" of rice per day [one "lang" is about 38 grams]. For three solid months, from June through September 1969, Group 559's 6th Engineer Battalion, stationed at Troop Station [binh tram] 35, ate sycamore berries, roots, and weeds in place of rice, and they were forced to burn straw and eat the ashes in place of salt. The tribal minority people of the Annamite Mountains harvested immature rice and ground it into powder to cook soup to save our troops from starvation. A number of areas had to promulgate strict regulations to protect forest vegetables that we used for food. Food production in the base areas became more important because it played a vital role in supplying our forces and helped ensure that our soldiers could maintain a firm hold on their battlefield positions.

In Military Region 5 our troops lived by the slogan "food production is the same as fighting the enemy." Each unit devoted 10 to 15 percent of its strength to food production. Military Region Headquarters cadre worked to produce food during the day and did their regular work at night. The Tri-Thien Military Region Headquarters launched a campaign to plant five million manioc plants. In the Central Highlands every cadre and soldier planted 1,000 manioc plants.

The ethnic minority peoples in our base areas shared our hardships and viewed our soldiers as their own children and younger brothers. When they saw the conditions faced by our troops, even though they themselves were starving, the people ate manioc and forest roots so they could save every container of rice to share with our cadre and soldiers. Every night the people in the contested areas, ignoring fear and danger, slipped past enemy outposts to carry rice, cloth, and medicine to our troops. With the help of local cadres and people along the

Vietnam-Cambodian border, COSVN's rear service groups were able to buy and store thousands of tons of foodstuffs.

In addition to developing their own "local" sources of supply, all battlefronts paid special attention to building roads linking up to our strategic supply corridor in an effort to receive more supplies from the great rear area in North Vietnam. Group 559 worked with Central Highlands troops to expand the road transportation network down to eastern Cochin China. In the triborder area the High Command formed the 470th Rear Services Area Division under the direct command of Group 559 Headquarters to strengthen transportation forces sending supplies to the B2 Battlefront. Using many different transportation techniques (trucks, human porters, bicycles, floating supplies down rivers), our transportation troops made great efforts, overcame terrible obstacles and adversity, and increased the flow of supplies to our forward areas.

By the beginning of 1970, with the great supply efforts of the rear area and the initial results of our efforts to increase production and develop "local" sources of supply, all battlefronts alleviated, to a degree at least, the problem of hunger among our main force units.

The problems of fighting the enemy, protecting our base areas, and securing a foothold on the battlefield for our main force units became the constant and critical responsibility of each of our units. Taking advantage of the rainy season, the enemy launched ferocious air attacks on our base areas, especially with B-52s. They sent commandos to launch searches and infantry and mechanized forces to conduct sweeps aimed at pushing our main force troops back beyond the borders of South Vietnam.

COSVN Military Headquarters and the military regions initiated a people's air defense movement, mobilizing and organizing armed elements of the three types of troops to fire at low-flying aircraft with infantry weapons. Many mobile machine-gun units were formed and aircraft ambushes were organized, limiting the enemy's operations and protecting our base areas.

Main force units coordinated with local armed forces to prepare combat plans to ensure that they were always able to launch determined counterattacks whenever the enemy attacked our bases. In late 1969 our armed forces repelled enemy attacks against the Do Xa area (the base area of Military Region 5), the area north and south of Route 4 (the base area of Military Region 8), the northern border area of eastern Cochin China (the base area of the COSVN Military Command), and the U Minh area (the base area of Military Region 9). We won an outstanding victory by defeating a large operation using puppet forces[9] to attack the Military Region 9's U Minh base area in late 1969. As was the case in the other areas, the question of whether to mass or to disperse our main force units was raised and hotly debated in the Mekong Delta area. Military Region 9 Headquarters, under Military Commander Le Duc Anh and Political Commissar Vo Van Kiet, criticized the desire of a number of cadres to disperse the main force troops in order to conduct small-unit battles. When the enemy moved into the base area the Military Region Headquarters massed the 1st and 2nd Regiments, the self-defense teams protecting the headquarters elements, and guerrilla forces from 18 villages in the base area to organize a people's war posture to engage the enemy. Combining widespread attrition attacks by local forces with massed attacks by main force troops, Military Region 9's soldiers and civilians inflicted heavy casualties on the enemy and forced them to withdraw from our base area.

The U Minh victory provided concrete proof that, if we firmly maintained and expanded the role of the main force troops, if we organized and coordinated the operations of the three types of armed forces, we could defeat the enemy's large-scale sweep operations and defend our bases.

By the beginning of 1970, although we still faced many difficulties, our army was able to maintain our main force elements on the battlefield. This was a very important victory. Our soldiers and people had taken the first step toward defeating the schemes and plots of the enemy's "Vietnamization" strategy. We had held our bases, maintained our foothold on the battlefield, and provided an important basis from which we could shift over to counterattacks and offensives when the opportunity arose, preparing the way for a new strategic posture for our forces.

THE PASSING OF HO CHI MINH

At 9:47 A.M. on 2 September 1969, Chairman Ho Chi Minh, the founder, the leader, the man who forged our Party, the man who had created the Democratic Republic and the United National Front, the beloved father of the people's armed forces of Vietnam, passed away. His passing was an immeasurably great loss for our nation, our Party, and our people's armed forces.

> He was our soul, our shining star. He led our entire Party, our entire population, our entire army, all united as one, in our courageous fight, writing the most glorious pages in the entire history of the Fatherland.[10] . . . He left us a priceless heritage. That heritage is the Ho Chi Minh era, the most brilliant period in the glorious history of our nation, the age when our Fatherland gained its independence and freedom and the era when we began building socialism in our nation.[11]

In a memorial service for Chairman Ho Chi Minh held at Ba Dinh Square on 9 September 1969, on behalf of the entire Party and the entire nation Comrade Le Duan, First Secretary of the Party Central Committee, swore a solemn oath to "follow His path and to pursue His great cause."[12] Comrade Le Duan called on the armed forces and the entire population to "quell your grief, make heroic efforts, enthusiastically surge forward, crush every obstacle, and resolve to totally defeat the American aggressors and successfully build socialism."[13]

As his eternal farewell, Uncle Ho left our entire Party, our entire population, and our entire army his historic Last Will and Testament. In this document Uncle Ho declared:

> Although our people will endure many more hardships and sacrifices in the fight against the United States to save the nation, our fight will inevitably end in total victory. . . . The American imperialists will certainly be forced out of our country. The Fatherland will certainly be unified. Our people, North and South, will certainly be united under one roof. Our nation will have the great honor that, although we are just one small nation, we will have heroically defeated two great imperialist powers, France and the United States, and will have made a glorious contribution to the national liberation movement.

The Politburo of the Party Central Committee launched a major wave of political activity within the Party and among the civilian population and the armed forces to "study and follow Chairman Ho's Last Will and Testament." A revolutionary action movement to achieve merit as a tribute to Uncle Ho swept through the entire armed forces.

On 23 September 1969 the 3rd National Assembly, meeting for its 5th Session, held a memorial service for Chairman Ho Chi Minh. The National Assembly unanimously elected Comrade Ton Duc Thang as State Chairman and Comrade Nguyen Luong Bang as State Vice-Chairman of the Democratic Republic of Vietnam.

THE WAR SPREADS THROUGHOUT INDOCHINA

In January 1970 the 18th Plenum of the Party Central Committee was held in Hanoi. The Party Central Committee assessed the great victories secured by our armed forces and our people during the Tet 1968 general offensive and uprisings and clearly laid out a number of errors in leadership that had occurred after the Tet offensive. Analyzing the enemy's new plots and actions, the Party Central Committee laid out the following goals for the entire Party, the entire armed forces, and the entire population: be resolute and increase our resistance, intensify military and political attacks and combine them with diplomatic attacks to create a new turning point in the war and defeat the "Vietnamization" strategy of the American imperialists.

Because of the ever-increasing importance of the armed struggle and the expansion of a wide-ranging people's war, the Party Central Committee stressed the role of our main force troops. These troops had to maintain a close relationship between their combat and army-building activities to enable our armed forces to overcome every difficulty and challenge, to conduct large-scale massed combined-arms combat operations, and, together with local armed forces and with the entire population, defeat the enemy militarily.

In August 1969, with direct air support from the American air force, over 8,000 Laotian puppet troops (most of whom were "special forces" recruited by the Americans) launched the "Cu Kiet" Campaign to seize the strategic Plain of Jars–Xieng Khoang area. The enemy's goals in this operation were to threaten North Vietnam, to tie down a portion of our main force units, and to reduce the amount of support sent from North Vietnam to the South. This was a major operation that exemplified the "Nixon Doctrine" in Laos, using puppet troops aided by U.S. logistics and air support.[14]

In the face of the enemy's massive assault, Pathet Lao units and the 174th Vietnamese Volunteer Regiment put up staunch resistance to slow their advance. In late September the 174th Regiment left a battalion and a separate company behind to continue the fight behind enemy lines alongside friendly Lao units while the rest of the regiment withdrew to regroup. During this initial phase of the battle the 174th Regiment, in cooperation with Pathet Lao soldiers and civilians, killed more than 1,000 enemy troops and retained control of a number of important bases, such as Ta Lin Noi, Ban Son, Lat Buoc, and High Point 852, thereby providing springboard positions for the deployment of our forces in future attacks against the enemy.

In mid-September the combined Lao-Vietnamese army launched a counteroffensive to smash the enemy land-grabbing operation, recover the Plain of Jars, consolidate and expand our liberated areas in Laos, and support combat operations in South Vietnam. Forces participating in this campaign included the 316th and 312th Infantry Divisions, the 866th Infantry Regiment, the 16th Artillery Regiment, one tank company, six sapper and engineer battalions, one Nghe An province local force battalion, and ten Pathet Lao battalions. On 13 September, Senior General Vo Nguyen Giap, Politburo member, Secretary of the Central Military Party Committee, and Minister of Defense, personally delivered the campaign assignments and orders to the Vietnamese units that would conduct a joint combat operation alongside our Laotian friends. The campaign was designated the "139 Campaign."[15]

After more than three months of road building, completing logistics preparations, and deploying our campaign forces, on 11 February 1970 Vietnamese volunteers and Pathet Lao troops opened fire to launch our offensive. During the first few days, because we did not have a firm grasp of the enemy's defensive deployments, a number of our attacks were unsuccessful. The Campaign Headquarters quickly ordered our units to change tactics and combine attacks on enemy strong points with a loose siege designed to trap and destroy enemy forces in the field. By 20 February 1970 our forces had secured complete control of the Plain of Jars. In the west, meanwhile, Pathet Lao soldiers attacked Sala Phu Khun and forced the enemy to withdraw from Muong Xui. On 25 February the enemy abandoned Xieng Khoang city. Exploiting these victories, on 18 March our troops liberated Xam Thong. The main lair of the Vang Pao "special forces" at Long Tieng was threatened. The Americans and their Lao puppets hurriedly pulled forces back from Military Regions 1, 2, and 3 to defend Long Tieng. They organized a counterattack to retake Xam Thong and conduct savage air attacks against our supply lines. By this time the rainy season in Laos had begun and we began experiencing supply problems. On 25 April 1970 the Vietnamese-Lao combined army ended the campaign. A significant portion of Vang Pao's "special forces," 13 battalions (about 7,800 soldiers), had been either wiped out or had suffered severe casualties. The victory of the Plain of Jars–Xieng Khoang campaign marked a new step forward by our main force troops in their ability to organize and command a campaign and conduct combat operations in mountainous jungle terrain.

After the end of the campaign, a number of Vietnamese volunteer units (the 316th Division, the 866th Regiment, and a number of specialty branch battalions) were ordered to remain behind to work with our Lao friends to defend the liberated areas, assist in transporting supplies, and to conduct training activities to increase their combat capabilities in preparation for operations during the next dry season.

In Cambodia, on 18 March 1970 the U.S. imperialists conducted a coup that overthrew Sihanouk and put Lon Nol into power. This was a U.S. strategic plot aimed at destroying the neutrality of Cambodia, bringing this country into the U.S. orbit, blocking our supply routes to the battlefields of Cochin China and extreme southern Central Vietnam, and supporting the implementation of the "Vietnamization" strategy.

Anticipating the actions the enemy would take after the coup, on 27 March 1970 the Politburo of the Party Central Committee ordered COSVN and the Party Committee of Military Region 5 to intensify our attacks against the enemy, expand our liberated areas along the border, and work with the Cambodian insurrectionist movement opposed to the reactionary Lon Nol government. These actions were designed to help our Cambodian friends expand the position and strength of their revolution and to resolve the supply problems our troops were experiencing. After these orders were issued, on 4 April 1970 the Politburo directed COSVN to assemble forces and put together a combat plan so that, when asked by our Cambodian friends, we could help the Cambodian people seize control of ten provinces along the Vietnamese border.

On 29 April 1970, Nixon sent the U.S. 1st Air Cavalry Division, the U.S. 25th Mechanized Infantry Division, six puppet divisions (the 5th, 18th, 25th, 7th, 9th, and 21st Divisions), three puppet Airborne and Marine brigades, five puppet Ranger Groups, and a large force of artillery, tanks, and aircraft (comprising 33.8 percent of all U.S. and puppet combat forces in South Vietnam) to mount a massive surprise invasion of Cambodia along its entire border with Vietnam. The puppet 3rd Corps (with three divisions) and two U.S. divisions conducted the attack in the primary theater (Routes 7 and 13). The objectives of this enemy operation were to kill the leadership and destroy the headquarters of the resistance in South Vietnam, to destroy our main force units and our rear services facilities, to complete the enemy plan for the "Vietnamization of the war," and to suppress the revolutionary struggle movement of the Cambodian people.

The Politburo of the Party Central Committee issued timely instructions to our troops to work closely with our Cambodian friends to "make strong advances to the west," to seize the initiative by striking rapidly, powerfully, continuously, and without restraint in order to, within a short period of time, create a turning point in the strategic situation that would benefit both ourselves and our Cambodian friends.

Pursuant to the Politburo's instructions our troops launched a counterattack, coordinating with our Cambodian friends in making retaliatory attacks against the American aggressor troops. In the east and the southeast our large troop elements (COSVN's 1st, 5th, 7th, and 9th Divisions) were placed under the direct leadership and command of Comrade Pham Hung, COSVN Secretary and Political Commissar, and Comrade Hoang Van Thai, Commander of the COSVN Military Command. In the Northeast another troop component (the 24th and 95th Regiments and a number of independent battalions) under the command of Comrade Hoang Minh Thao, Commander of the Central Highlands Front, and Comrade Tran The Mon, Political Commissar of the Central Highlands Front, attacked outward from the Central Highlands and down from southern Laos.

In all attack sectors our main force units flexibly employed different tactics, including raids, ambushes, mobile attacks, and independent attacks conducted by sappers and artillery. Because our troops were unfamiliar with the terrain and because we did not have sufficient time to prepare the battlefield, we were not able to destroy any large U.S. or puppet units. We did, however, inflict severe casualties on the enemy forces. From April to July 1970 we eliminated from the field of combat more than 40,000 enemy troops, including thousands of Americans. We destroyed more than 3,000 military vehicles, 400 artillery pieces, and captured more than 5,000 weapons, 400 tons of ammunition, 113 transport vehicles, 1,570 tons of rice, 100 tons of medicine, and great quantities of other types of military supplies. This was a major achievement in destroying enemy manpower and implements of war. The people of Cambodia, rich in patriotic traditions, worked closely with our troops in attacking the enemy, overthrowing the puppet government's administrative structures at the local level, and seizing control of their own destiny. Our troops helped our Cambodian friends to completely liberate five provinces and large areas in northeastern Cambodia with a total population of three million people. This large liberated area on our friends' soil right next to the liberated areas of South Vietnam became a strategic rear area for the Cambodian revolution and the immediate rear area for the B2 Battlefield, providing us with a foothold and a springboard for our attacks as we worked to build up our forces and to conduct combat operations.

In the midst of this battle our troops also helped our Cambodian friends train cadre and expand their armed forces. In just two months the armed forces of our Cambodian allies grew from ten guerrilla teams to nine battalions and 80 companies of full-time troops with a total strength of 20,000 soldiers, plus hundreds of guerrilla squads and platoons in the villages. The Cambodian revolution had taken an important step forward.

Coordinating their operations with the Cambodian battlefield and taking advantage of the enemy's concentration of his military forces in that country, the Laotian-Vietnamese combined army launched an offensive campaign to liberate southern Laos. On 1 May 1970 an element of our Central Highlands main force army (the 28th and 24A Regiments), together with Vietnamese volunteer units in southern Laos and the Lao Liberation Army, attacked and seized Attopeu, destroying two Lao puppet battalions. The liberated zone in Laos was expanded and unified from north to south, linking North Vietnam with the liberated zone in South Vietnam from Tri Thien down through the Central Highlands to eastern Cochin China and with the large liberated zone in Cambodia. This area formed a firm base area for the revolutionary forces of the three Indochinese peoples. The strategic transportation corridor through Indochina was linked up, creating a new strategic posture for the Vietnamese, Laotian, and Cambodian Revolutions.

As for our enemies, because of their great defeat on the battlefield and in the face of strong opposition from the peoples of the world, including the people of the United States, on 30 June 1970 Nixon was forced to announce the withdrawal of troops from Cambodia. The American imperialist invasion of Cambodia had failed. The Saigon puppet army had not become stronger as Nixon had hoped— instead it had suffered casualties and become dispersed and bogged down on a new battlefield.[16] This was a heavy defeat for the Nixon doctrine on the battle-fields of the three Indochinese nations.

This period of almost two years of consolidating our forces and combating the new strategic plots and measures of the enemy, at a time when our position and strength on the South Vietnamese battlefield had declined, was a difficult and challenging period for our troops and civilian population in our resistance strug-gle against the United States. With the wholehearted assistance of the civilian population, the Party chapters, and the local armed forces in South Vietnam, and with ever-growing manpower and material support from the great rear area of North Vietnam, our armed forces overcame horrendous difficulties and firmly maintained our main force army on the battlefield. This was one of the most important achievements of the two-year period from 1969 to 1970. Because of this achievement, when the opportunity arrived our army was able to quickly shift to counterattack and attack the enemy, gradually restoring our position and power on the main battlefield in South Vietnam.

11

Increasing Our Ability to Conduct Combined-Arms Operations and Intensifying Counterattacks and Offensives in the Three Nations of Indochina, 1970–1971

REBUILDING FOR VICTORY

As a result of our new victories on the battlefields of Cambodia and Laos, the nature of the war in all three Indochinese nations underwent important changes. In North Vietnam, taking advantage of the fact that our enemy had been forced to cease his bombing attacks, our people redoubled their efforts to rebuild the economy, consolidate national defense, and carry out their duty of increasing our supply of personnel and material support to the battlefield. In South Vietnam our armed forces steadfastly held their positions, consolidated forces, maintained our main force units, and aggressively attacked the enemy to maintain our foothold on the battlefield. We impeded the pace of the enemy's "pacification" plan. The Cambodian revolution grew rapidly, gaining a number of major victories in a relatively short time. Our victories on the Plain of Jars and Xieng Khoang and in southern Laos signaled a new stage in the maturity of the Laotian revolutionary armed forces. The three nations of Vietnam, Laos, and Cambodia became one single battlefield fighting with one common purpose: resisting the American imperialist aggressors.

During this period the Americans had to withdraw a portion of their combat forces in South Vietnam. Many U.S. and Saigon puppet army mobile units had to cross into Cambodia to fight on an unfamiliar battlefield in support of Lon Nol's extremely weak puppet forces. The failure of the Cambodian incursion caused further embarrassment for the United States and its puppet regime. In spite of this, however, because the American imperialists were extremely stubborn and overconfident, the United States continued to pursue its goal of maintaining a neocolonialist system in Vietnam, Laos, and Cambodia, and of holding onto its strategic position in Southeast Asia.

Based on these new factors, in June 1970 the Party's Politburo decided to mobilize the efforts of the entire Party, the entire armed forces, and the entire population of both North and South Vietnam, fighting in a combat alliance with the peoples and armies of Laos and Cambodia to strive to maintain and intensify the resistance war to save the nation in a systematic pursuit of victory and eventually win a final, decisive victory that would expel the American imperialists from the Indochinese Peninsula.

The Politburo decision stated:

North Vietnam is the great rear area for the great frontline area of South Vietnam, and is also the rear area of the revolutions in Laos and Cambodia. North Vietnam's duty is to strengthen and consolidate itself in all areas and to wholeheartedly support the great frontline area of South Vietnam and the battlefields of our brother nations. North Vietnam must also increase its own vigilance and prepare to defeat any act of aggression by the U.S. imperialists. The duties of the armed forces are to liberate South Vietnam, defend North Vietnam, and carry out our international responsibilities by fighting side by side with the soldiers and civilians of Cambodia and Laos to defeat our common enemy on the battlefields of these two friendly nations. The Politburo has decided to focus our efforts on building a powerful main force army strong enough to fight major battles of annihilation and to serve as a strategic mobile [reserve] force for all battlefields.

In late 1968, as soon as the first war of destruction [air campaign against North Vietnam] by the American imperialists had been defeated, the people of North Vietnam quickly began to rebuild the economy and bind up the wounds of war. By 1970 production of rice was 500,000 tons greater than it had been in 1968. In 1971, in spite of the greatest flood in 100 years, production of paddy reached 5.6 million tons, North Vietnam's largest harvest since 1954. Industrial facilities that the enemy had destroyed were rebuilt. Production of electricity, cement, tools and machinery, fertilizer, automobile tires, cloth, etc., rose to levels almost equal to those in 1965. We continued to make progress in the areas of education, culture, and medicine. Our people were able to resume a normal life. In solidarity with the Party Central Committee the people of North Vietnam increased production, increased the support being sent to South Vietnam, and performed their international duties in Laos and Cambodia, simultaneously increasing their vigilance and preparing for the possible resumption of the enemy's air war of destruction against the North and knowing that the enemy might widen his war of aggression and send ground troops to invade the southern part of Military Region 4.

During the 1969–1971 period the American imperialists continuously sent aircraft on armed reconnaissance and bombing raids against portions of Military Region 4. They even mounted a commando raid on Son Tay in a scheme to rescue U.S. prisoners of war.[1]

Faced with these new enemy plots and schemes, the General Staff focused its guidance on strengthening our organizations and on strengthening and upgrading the equipment of the Air Force, the Missile Branch, the Radar Branch, and of four anti-aircraft divisions. Ten additional anti-aircraft artillery battalions were formed to defend "choke points" being attacked by the enemy. A large number of technical specialty branch units, including ten field artillery batteries, dozens of anti-aircraft artillery battalions and batteries, and ten companies of engineers and sapper-reconnaissance troops, were sent to reinforce Military Region 4. The 367th Air Defense Division defended the road heads of Routes 12, 20, and 18 and prepared to fight as part of a combined-arms formation. The Navy was removed from the control of the Northeast Military Region. Colonel Nguyen Ba Phat, Navy Commander, and Colonel Hoang Tra, Navy Political Commissar, worked with headquarters elements and combat units to strengthen the Navy's organizational structure and increase its responsibilities for the protection of the territorial waters of North Vietnam, the transportation of supplies to the battle-fronts, combat operations in the South, and participation in economic development. The Navy Regions covering the Ma River, Cua Hoi, and the Gianh River were reestablished.[2] Each region controlled its own combat vessels, water sappers, and maritime engineers, had its own signal and radar units, and was fully capable of conducting combat operations to defend its assigned area. The 126th Water Sapper Regiment monitored and attacked enemy vessels and logistics installations at Cua Viet Port (Quang Tri province). Armed fishing boat and coastal patrol units were formed.

Under the direct guidance of the Central Military Party Committee, the military regions, provinces, and cities reviewed and summarized their experiences in local military operations during the air war of destruction and correctly applied the lessons learned to build up armed forces units and turn our provinces and cities into powerful basic strategic units for the conduct of the People's War. From mid-1970 onward, the staffs of the provincial units, the district units, and the village units were turned into military command headquarters and command sections responsible for commanding local armed forces in construction and combat tasks within their local areas. Ten new local force companies were formed and local forces were issued additional weapons and equipment.

The levels of organization and equipment of militia self-defense forces were increased. In 1971 North Vietnam had a total of two million militia self-defense troops, including 870,000 combat self-defense and guerrilla troops. In addition to infantry weapons (50,000 guns), our self-defense militia forces were equipped with 1,400 anti-aircraft machine guns and cannon, 200 pieces of field artillery, and more than 800 mortars and recoilless rifles. A number of self-defense battalions at large factories were equipped with 37mm anti-aircraft guns. Villages and enterprises formed self-defense militia platoons and companies equipped with 12.7mm and 14.5mm anti-aircraft machine guns. Militia units in a number of coastal villages were equipped with 85mm guns and assigned responsibility for combating enemy shore bombardment vessels. The self-defense militia of the provinces of southern Military Region 4 were equipped with 60mm and 82mm mortars, B-40 and B-41 anti-tank rocket launchers, recoilless rifles, etc. Party committees, local governmental administrations, and military staff agencies at all levels stressed the importance of training to increase the political and military capabilities of the self-defense militia and the reserve force. Universities, trade schools, and high schools held military training classes for their students in accordance with a uniform training program.

THE BATTLE ON THE HO CHI MINH TRAIL

In June 1970 the Politburo established the Central Council for Support of the Front Lines to mobilize the soldiers and civilians of the North to strengthen our great rear area and support the needs of the battlefronts. Comrade Do Muoi, alternate member of the Politburo and Deputy Prime Minister, was appointed Chairman of this Council.

During the years 1969 to 1971, savage battles raged along the North-South supply line. To achieve their goal of completely blocking the flow of supplies from our great rear area and to "strangle" revolutionary warfare in South Vietnam, Cambodia, and Laos, the American imperialists increased their reconnaissance and commando operations, launching many infantry sweep operations (using three to four battalions) into areas through which our transportation lines passed. Almost 100 B-52 strategic bombers and thousands of tactical fighter aircraft flew day and night dropping bombs and mines to destroy our transportation routes, warehouses, and supply trucks. AC-130E aircraft, equipped with electronic sensors and 40mm guns, flew over the Ho Chi Minh Trail every night, destroying many of our trucks.[3] Fighting with courage, resolve, and great cleverness, our truck drivers overcame horrendous hardships to transport supplies to the front lines, and some comrades died in the cabs of their trucks as they drove toward the front. In the face of this bloody battle on the supply route to the South, a few drivers wavered, and some even abandoned their vehicles when they heard the sound of the enemy's AC-130E gunships flying overhead.

A conference of the Central Party Military Committee in June 1970 laid out many urgent measures aimed at expanding our forces: consolidating our strategic supply route; combining different methods of transportation (by road, by river, by pipeline); and combining direct combat against the enemy with deception and evasion measures.

Front 968 and the 565th Military Advisory Group in southern Laos were integrated into Group 559, making Group 559 equivalent to a Military Region. Group 559 was placed under the direct command and control of the Central Military Party Committee and the High Command. Comrade Dong Si Nguyen was named Commander of Group 559 and Comrade Dang Tinh became Political Commissar. Directly subordinate to Group 559 were five area headquarters: 470,

471, 472, 473, and 571, each area headquarters being equivalent to a division. Over 40 truck, pipeline, anti-aircraft, and engineer regiments and battalions and a large quantity of weapons and equipment were sent to reinforce Group 559's supply corridor.[4]

To carry out the strategic transportation mission in the face of ferocious enemy attacks and over a wide area with a total of 6,000 kilometers of supply roads (from south of the Gianh River in Quang Binh to eastern Cochin China and through eastern Cambodia and lower Laos), the units of Group 559 were organized into mobile forces and static forces. Mobile forces included four truck transport regiments, two petroleum pipeline regiments, three anti-aircraft artillery regiments, eight engineer regiments, and the 968th Infantry Division. The truck regiments operated over long distances to provide rapid transportation, reaching deep into the theaters that had large supply requirements. The static forces were organized into battalions, separate companies, and 27 troop supply stations [binh tram] under the authority of five regional commands. These forces operated along short, interconnected routes from the road heads down to the supply reception points for the battlefronts. Tens of thousands of assault youth and civilian laborers, drawn from throughout North Vietnam, also worked on Group 559's corridor, carrying supplies on their backs or using crude methods of transportation, building roads, supporting and maintaining traffic flow, loading and unloading supplies, etc. The General Staff sent the 377th Air Defense Division (formed in July 1971), many engineer regiments, and a number of Air Force fighter squadrons to the 559 Corridor to participate in the fight to keep the roads open to support our "transportation campaigns."[5]

Since its formation, Group 559 had always shipped most of its supplies down the road network west of the Annamite Mountain chain during the dry season. To counter enemy attack aircraft, trucks moved primarily at night. Because of the expansion of the battlefield into Cambodia and Laos, our requirements for combined-arms combat operations demanded an ever-increasing quantity of supplies and technical equipment. At this time, however, the enemy's AC-130E aircraft had established control over and successfully suppressed, to a certain extent at least, our nighttime supply operations. Enemy aircraft destroyed 4,000 trucks during the 1970–1971 dry season, of which the AC-130E alone destroyed 2,432 trucks (60.8 percent of the total number of trucks destroyed by the enemy). Our supply effort, conducted during a single season of the year and using a "single supply route," was unable to keep up with our requirements and our night supply operations encountered difficulties.

In response to this situation, Group 559 mobilized all engineer units, assault youth, and civilian labor (at its height 30,000 people) and combined truck transport with crude transport methods. Our forces even used deception operations to entice enemy aircraft to bomb mountainsides in order to make gravel for use in building and maintaining roads. During the two-year period 1970–1971, Group 559 built or upgraded six main north-south roads through the western Annamite

Mountains. It also built or upgraded hundreds of kilometers of connecting roads and thousands of kilometers of bypass roads to avoid the "choke points" that were under constant enemy attack. A number of troop stations [binh tram] came up with the idea of improving a number of dry streambeds covered by tall jungle trees to serve as roads for use by trucks during daylight hours. Linking these road sections together, Group 559 built a secret and quite unique new route that we called the "secret road" or the "green road." Beginning in March 1971 a large force of engineers and assault youth built the "secret road" from north of Lum Bum to lower Laos, a total of 1,000 kilometers. To ensure secrecy our engineers built hundreds of fake battle positions and fake vehicles and warehouses to attract enemy attention to our old transportation route (called Road H). They camouflaged the new route, even building trellises for plants to grow over and camouflage nets over the "secret road" (called Road K), maintaining the green hue of the Annamite forests. The construction of this road was an outstanding achievement and a remarkable innovation by the cadre and soldiers of Group 559. From that time on, in addition to the night transportation operations on Road H, thanks to the green road, the warriors who drove trucks down the Ho Chi Minh Trail had another two-way supply route for use during the day, which enabled us to quickly increase the volume and speed of our supply operations and to effectively counter the enemy's AC-130E aircraft.

Our forces also feverishly built a petroleum pipeline from North Vietnam to the battlefields. This work was very difficult and demanded a high level of technology because the pipeline crossed high mountains, wide rivers, and through areas under ferocious enemy bombardment. The level of professional specialization of our cadre and soldiers in this field was limited, construction workers were few, and we had little equipment and supplies. To resolve some of these difficulties the government sent many cadre and technical workers from the Ministry of Metallurgy and Steel-Making, the Ministry of Materials, and the Ministry of Construction to participate in the building of the pipeline and gave this project priority in supplies and equipment. The local population enthusiastically helped our troops build and protect the pipeline. National defense enterprises worked with state enterprises to develop and produce a number of components for use in assembling and operating the pipeline. The "Truong Son" pump, invented and built by Comrade Nguyen Van Sen, a Grade Seven Worker, and the cadre and workers of the Q-165 Factory (Oil and Gas Department), was a valuable product (from both the economic and technical standpoints) used in pumping operations on the pipeline.

The forces that built the pipeline were Troop Stations [binh tram] 169, 170, 171 (Oil and Gas Department), Group 559's 592nd and 671st Regiments, and hundreds of technical cadre and workers and thousands of civilian laborers from Quang Binh, Ha Tinh, Nghe An, Thanh Hoa, Nam Ha, Ninh Binh, Hai Hung, and Ha Tay provinces. Over a three-year span (1969–1971), a pipeline network almost 1,000 kilometers long was completed. From Hanoi the pipeline crossed the Red, Ma, and Lam Rivers and then split into two branches. One branch crossed the "Sky Gate" to the west of the Annamite Mountains, then followed Route 12 to Ka Vat, Ban Xoi, and Lang Khang in Laos. The other branch crossed the Gianh River and followed Route 10 and Route 18, crossing the Se Banh Hieung River and reaching the area north of Route 9. Our oil and gas cadre and personnel accompanied the pipeline wherever it went to maintain and operate the pipeline. During the 1968–1969 dry season our primary method of transporting fuel was by wheelbarrow, and sometimes our soldiers even had to place nylon bags into their packs, fill them with gasoline, and carry the packs on their backs around bombing "choke points." During that period the General Department of Rear Services was only able to provide a little over 90 tons of gasoline to Group 559, whereas the actual requirement for Group 559's entire truck force was 500 tons. By the 1970–1971 dry season the pipeline had begun operation and the quantity of gasoline sent to Group 559 increased tenfold. Group 559 and the battlefronts now were capable of vastly increasing their motorized supply operations and were able to use different types of technical equipment. Although in 1969 Group 559 shipped 20 thousand tons of supplies to the battlefields, in 1970 this total rose to 40 thousand tons and in 1971 it increased to 60 thousand tons.

A number of improvements in the training of reinforcement troops and in arranging their passage from the North to the battlefields were made in light of the new situation. Implementing a resolution of the Central Military Party Committee and recommendations made by delegates to a conference on building a stronger armed force convened by the Ministry of Defense in April 1970, the General Staff reassigned responsibility for training regimental and division-sized infantry units to the Military Regions. Each individual specialty and service branch became responsible for training reinforcement soldiers in its particular branch or service. The training of technical personnel to be sent to the battlefield as reinforcements became the responsibility of our technical schools, training courses, and supplemental professional technical training facilities. Training content was updated to adapt it to each specialty, and responsibility for training content was delegated to the Military Regions and specialty branches, which replaced the specialist training units that had done this job in the past. These changes enabled us to respond to the ever-increasing requirements for speed, quality, and quantity in sending reinforcements, especially cadre and specialized technical personnel of the specialized branches, to the battlefields.

Improvements were made in the movement of troops down the commo-liaison lines of the General Rear Services Department, through Group 559, and down to the battlefields. These improvements included better supply operations, making maximum use of rail, road, and water transport, and providing motorized transport for each route section. These changes reduced the length of the trip to about 20 days and reduced our losses along the way (losses in 1969, which were 13.5 percent, declined to 3.4 percent in 1970 and 2.07 percent in 1971). During the two-year period 1970–1971, 195,000 reinforcement troops, including many cadres and soldiers from our technical branches, were sent to the battlefields. This total represented a major effort by the army and people of North Vietnam, and most directly by the General Department of Rear Services and Group 559, which helped meet our requirement to strengthen the organization and equipment of our main force divisions and regiments, to rapidly increase the presence of specialty branch forces on the battlefield, and increased the ability of our main force troops in South Vietnam to fight large battles and conduct combined-arms operations.

BUILDING CORPS-SIZED MAIN FORCE UNITS
CAPABLE OF FIGHTING THROUGHOUT INDOCHINA

In February 1970 the Central Military Party Committee held a plenary session in Hanoi to discuss the implementation of the resolution of the 18th Plenary Session of the Central Committee. During this session the committee reached unanimous agreement on the status of the military struggle, the role of main force units, and the need to enable our army to conduct combined-arms operations on every battlefield. The committee said that the primary duties of our army at this time are to build powerful main force corps-sized units to serve as the pillars supporting the entire Indochina battlefield; to build up our main force army in South Vietnam and enable it to fight large-scale battles of annihilation; and to increase the combat power and readiness of our strategic reserve forces in North Vietnam to turn them into mobile main force corps-sized units able to conduct massed combined-arms operations on all battlefields.

To achieve this goal the General Staff, the General Political Department, and the General Rear Services Department focused on building up and increasing the combat power and mobility of four main force infantry divisions: the 308th, 304th, 312th, and 320th Divisions. Two divisions, the 325th and 320B Divisions, were converted from reinforcement training divisions into mobile divisions directly subordinate to the High Command. The 316th Division, which was performing its international duty on the battlefields of Laos, was upgraded by reinforcing it with specialty branch units.

The Artillery Branch formed a number of new field artillery units, increased the mobility, power, and range of the units directly subordinate to the Artillery Command, and strengthened the fire support elements attached to the battlefields and campaign theaters of operations. Reserve artillery subordinate to the Artillery Command was increased from three to five regiments.[6] These regiments were equipped with 130mm, 122mm, and 85mm field guns, BM-14 rocket launchers, and 160mm mortars. A total of seven field artillery regiments were assigned to the military regions and fronts.[7] Two composite artillery regiments were assigned to infantry divisions (the 308th and 304th Divisions).

The Armor Branch upgraded the combat power of its two reserve regiments, the 203rd Tank Regiment (with T-34 and T-54 tanks) and the 202nd Armored Regiment, and sent two battalions to reinforce the northern and southern fronts in Laos.

The Sapper Branch organized a number of mobile battalions and increased the strength and equipment of sapper battalions assigned to military regions and infantry divisions. The branch focused its attention on training troops in tactics for conducting independent sapper attacks on enemy bases and rear support facilities and on training to work with infantry forces in campaign-level combat operations.

The Engineer Branch formed additional specialized regiments and battalions for construction, bridge building, river crossing, and explosive ordnance disposal missions in response to our need to support mobile combat operations by infantry, artillery, anti-aircraft, and armored troops.[8]

In addition to forces included in their table of organization strengths, the military specialty branches all held a number of cadre and technical personnel and a quantity of weapons and equipment in reserve in order to be able to form additional new units when necessary. The specialty branches also sent many units and a large quantity of weapons and equipment to the different battlefronts, helping to increase the combined-arms combat power of our main force units.[9]

The formation of many new units, especially technical specialty branch units, demanded a commensurate increase in the number and quality of our military, political, and professional technical cadre. In March 1970 the Standing Committee of the Central Military Party Committee issued a specialized decision on school operations within the armed forces. The Committee ordered that during the 1970–1971 period the principal mission of our training schools (except for schools responsible for training new technical cadre) should be to conduct supplementary training and to increase cadre capabilities to uniform standards. The schools were also informed that it was very important that training new cadre be systematic and complete. The Ministry of Defense's Military Medical School and Polytechnic University's School Number Two were combined to form the Military Technical University. By 1971 we had seven schools subordinate to the Ministry of Defense and three schools subordinate to the General Departments. The school system and initial and supplementary training teams for cadre and professional technical personnel were reorganized from more than 100 separate units into 16 schools. Training periods for initial training and for supplementary training were increased. The Artillery Officers School reinstituted long-term initial training programs lasting three years for entry-level cadre and 18 months for mid-level cadre.

In 1971 the number of students at our different schools rose to 20,000, including more than 1,000 military and political cadre and 7,000 specialized technical cadre. Every year a total of 7,000 students graduated from the entry-level and the supplementary training school systems. By 1971 the Military Technical University had trained 1,056 new engineers in such specialized fields as radio, radar, missile ordnance, artillery ordnance, vehicles, electronic equipment, engines, etc.

With thousands of technical cadre from ten military universities and mid- and entry-level training schools graduating every year, and with a large number of engineers and technical workers transferred into the armed forces by the Government, by 1971 the total number of cadre and technical workers in our entire armed forces had grown to 30,000. Technical organs of the Service and specialty branches, which had previously been assigned to rear services agencies, were organized into technical departments or offices. Seventy-seven national defense enterprises, 86 large and medium-level repair stations, and hundreds of small repair stations subordinate to divisions and regiments manufactured, serviced, and repaired an important portion of the equipment needs of our units, our Service Branches, and our military specialty branches.

Deeply absorbing Uncle Ho's teaching, ". . . the spirit of the man must be transmitted to the weapon, meaning that we must have an excellent technical capability,"[10] our cadre and soldiers worked to master the technical features and exploit the characteristics and capabilities of their different types of weapons and equipment. They succeeded in a number of efforts to modify some components of our different pieces of equipment to adapt them to the specific battlefield conditions, weather conditions, and combat conditions faced by our armed forces. A number of research projects were put into effective combat use. These included firing tables for use by artillery in mountainous jungle terrain, increasing the range of DKB and H-12 rockets by increasing their propellant charges, lightening the steering rods of T-54 tanks, transistorizing the Type 702 voice communications apparatus, developing more effective explosive systems for clearing barbed-wire fences and obstacles, etc.

By the end of 1971 the overall strength of the standing army in North Vietnam was 433,000 personnel (in 1968 the total had been 390,000 personnel), 46 percent of whom were technical specialty branch troops (in 1965 only 30 percent of our armed forces were specialty branch personnel). We had strengthened our weapons and combat equipment levels and the ranks of our cadre and technical personnel had been rapidly improved in both quantity and quality.

In light of our combat duties and requirements, our armed forces still had many weaknesses, such as the fact that our technical equipment was not standardized, reserve levels and replacement capabilities were still low, and our level of mobility was not yet high enough, especially mobility in difficult terrain, in poor weather, and in situations when we were under enemy attack. In spite of this, however, our achievements in building up our organizations and equipment, especially our specialty branch units, had moved us a step forward in our effort to build a modern, regular force. These achievements increased the mobility and combat power of our Army in response to our need to be able to conduct large-scale combined-arms combat operations during this new phase of the war.

TRAINING AND PARTY-BUILDING OPERATIONS

To implement the Central Military Party Committee's resolution on improving our efforts to review and summarize battle experiences and to study military science, the General Staff laid out a program to draft and update campaign-level and tactical-level training documents. It held many cadre training classes and provided guidance for training and field exercises at the divisional and regimental levels.

The Military Science Institute of Vietnam was established in July 1969 to assist the Central Military Party Committee and the Ministry of Defense in studying strategic and campaign problems and in providing guidance for the work of reviewing experiences and conducting studies in military science throughout the armed forces. After summarizing actual combat experiences for all battlefields, the Military Science Institute and staff agencies of the General Staff drafted two campaign training documents covering:

1. Campaign-level offensives by main force troops on selected mountain jungle battlefields to defeat two of the enemy's basic tactical measures: the construction of defensive strong points and relief operations to repel attacks on these strong points. These offensives would be aimed at annihilating a puppet regiment or regimental task force and liberating a specific area.
2. Combined offensive campaigns to disrupt the enemy's pacification program in rural areas using the combined power of our political forces and of the armed forces of our three types of troops, with the backbone for this campaign being a powerful main force unit (a regiment or division). The target of such campaigns would be to gradually annihilate enemy forces, secure and maintain control of the civilian population, and expand our liberated areas.

With regard to tactics, staff agencies and units focused their tactical studies on destroying enemy defensive forces holding solid fortified positions and supported by air and artillery. After analyzing our experiences in large battles during the resistance war against the French (Dien Bien Phu) and in battles against the Americans and their puppets such as Ta Con [Khe Sanh] in Quang Tri, Ka Te, and Dac Sieng in the Central Highlands, etc., and combining these studies with trials during actual field exercises conducted by the 308th Division, the General Staff drafted a tactical training document for use in mounting an annihilation attack against enemy forces holding solid fortified defensive positions. This document called for the use of "encirclement and siege tactics using light weapons" by infantry units reinforced by tanks, artillery, and anti-aircraft guns. These campaign and tactical-level combat methods were suited to the level of organization, equipment, and tactical skills of our troops during these years. Using these tactics, our armed forces could defeat the enemy's main tactical measures on the battlefield and change the very character of the war.

On 24 August 1970, the Central Military Party Committee and the Ministry of Defense organized an all–armed forces training class. Senior General Vo Nguyen Giap, Politburo member, Secretary of the Central Military Party Committee, and Minister of Defense, personally conducted this class. Over 300 cadre, half of whom were high-level cadre from the military regions, military units, staff agencies, and military schools, attended this class. Class content included a number of problems regarding the military policies of the Party; new fighting methods for campaign- and tactical-level combat; staff operations; party and political operations; and campaign- and tactical-level rear service [logistics] operations. Lessons based on experience and effective fighting methods to defeat the enemy's new tactical schemes were disseminated in this class.

During one month of study the cadre attending this class were given a number of new theoretical and practical ideas and their ability to command campaign- and tactical-level operations was improved. Cadre of all ranks, and especially cadre serving on the battlefield, gained confidence in our ability to use campaign-level large-scale concentrated combined-arms tactics to annihilate large enemy units.

After returning to their units, commanders of military regions, specialty branches, and divisions organized brief training classes or supplementary training using training documents for unit commanders and staff. Low-level cadre and soldiers received training in ten basic technical lessons, with special emphasis placed on combating tanks and mechanized vehicles, firing at aircraft, disposal of bombs and mines, overcoming or bypassing obstacles, and chemical defense. Units were trained in four main tactical methods: raids, ambushes, attacks against fortified positions, and mobile attacks combined with the use of blocking forces. A number of battalions were trained to become expert in one of the tactical methods in order to build up the combat traditions of the unit. Divisions and regiments trained in massed combat, combined-arms combat using encirclement and siege tactics to annihilate an enemy force occupying solid defensive fortifications, and mobile envelopment and continuous attacks aimed at annihilating an enemy regiment or regimental task force operating in the field. The specialty branches trained in technical and tactical aspects of their particular specialties and conducted joint training with infantry divisions in combined-arms battle scenarios. Political activities were closely linked with training duties, and lessons learned in particularly well-fought battles were rapidly disseminated. These activities created an atmosphere of excitement and contributed to the clarification of tactical guidance and thinking and to understanding the content and requirements of the new fighting methods.

At the end of 1970 the General Staff sent many cadre groups to the battlefields to work with COSVN and the military regions to provide guidance to units to train their troops for combat in this new phase. In Cochin China and extreme southern Central Vietnam, in September 1970 the COSVN Military Party Committee and the COSVN Military Command held a conference to review and summarize the counteroffensive campaign conducted by our main force troops on the

Cambodian battlefield. One of the main subjects discussed during this conference was fighting big battles to systematically annihilate entire enemy regimental task forces. The conference raised a number of important matters, such as firmly focusing on fighting annihilation battles, seizing the initiative in attacking and counterattacking the enemy, overcoming reluctance to fight big battles because of fear of suffering casualties, increasing the command capabilities of division-level cadre and staff organizations for key battles, training subunits in campaign-level and tactical-level fighting methods, etc. The General Staff's training documents on fighting methods for use at the campaign and tactical levels were used by the conference and the units as primary study documents for cadre training classes, as study documents at the staff level, and for training troops.

To implement the resolution of the Politburo and the March 1970 resolution of the Central Military Party Committee on conducting a campaign to "increase the quality of Party members and induct members of the Ho Chi Minh class into the Party," the General Political Department prepared a guidance document for use by units to carry out this campaign, directly linking the content of the campaign with the force building and combat tasks of the units. Twenty-three thousand outstanding cadre and soldiers of our armed forces were inducted into the Party in the "Ho Chi Minh Party Member Class."

In November 1970 the Central Military Party Committee convened a conference to review and summarize activities aimed at developing Party branches [chi bo] within the armed forces. Drawing on practical experiences in force building and combat, the conference put forward one lesson as a matter of principle: "Only if the Party branch is strong will the unit have a firm foundation and be able to build strong party chapters and strong regiments and divisions."

The campaign to "increase the quality of Party members and induct into the Party members of the Ho Chi Minh Class" and the work of reviewing and summarizing our experience in building Party branches were major events in the work of army building. During this campaign the number of Party members within the armed forces grew and the leadership role of the Party in the armed forces was strengthened. In 1971 over 90 percent of our Party branches had a branch committee. In infantry companies Party members made up between 25 and 35 percent of the company's total troop strength. In specialty branch companies Party members made up more than 40 percent of the total troop strength. Almost all Party cadre conducting Party and political activities had been tempered in combat and then had received either basic training (three years) or supplementary training (one year) at military training schools.

The program of political activities to study the resolution of the 18th Plenum of the Party Central Committee (January 1970), the campaign to study and carry out the "Last Will and Testament" of Chairman Ho, the one-year review of the implementation of Uncle Ho's "Last Will and Testament," etc., engendered new changes in the thoughts and actions of our cadre and soldiers. We reinstituted a program for cadre to study basic theory, both on the job and at schools, after a number of years during which this program had been temporarily suspended because of the harsh wartime conditions. The revolutionary action slogan of "Live, Fight, Work, and Study in Accordance with the Example Set by the Great Uncle Ho" became the goal of every cadre and soldier, and this program generated a bubbling atmosphere of enthusiasm throughout the entire army.

This was an across-the-board building period: We developed our organizations and equipment, especially the technical specialty branches; we strengthened our technical matériel structures; we developed new fighting methods responsive to our combat responsibilities; we increased troop training, and especially cadre training, focused on actual combat requirements; we strengthened Party and political activities in low-level units, etc. In practical terms, the results of this army building effort increased our combat power and ensured that our armed forces on all battlefronts, and especially our mobile main force troops, could conduct massed combined-arms combat activities on an ever-increasingly greater scale of operations.

THE 1971 INCURSION INTO SOUTHERN LAOS (LAM SON 719)

From the enemy's standpoint, during 1969–1970, by making all-out efforts on all fronts, the United States and its puppets successfully carried out a significant portion of their plan to "pacify" the rural lowlands. They rapidly drafted young men into the army, formed many new units, and increased their strength in equipment, weapons, and implements of war. By the end of 1970 the puppet armed forces in South Vietnam had a total strength of 700,000 soldiers (not counting civilian defense forces). Of this total, 350,000 were regular troops equipped with automatic M-16 rifles. When compared with 1968, the mobile elements of the puppet armed forces had doubled (making up 42 percent of all regular troops). Special attention was paid to expanding their specialty branches. The puppets had 60 battalions of artillery and received 500 new artillery pieces. Their armored force now consisted of 18 squadrons, each squadron having 70 tanks and armored personnel carriers. Total armored strength increased from 1,000 to 1,500 armored vehicles. The puppet Air Force consisted of five air wings with a total of 550 aircraft. Their Navy had over 1,000 ships and combat vessels of all types. In comparison with its situation at the end of the "special war" period, the organizational structure and equipment of the South Vietnamese puppet army had been modernized. The Cambodian puppet army also expanded rapidly, growing from 40,000 in March 1970 to 120,000 soldiers. The Laotian puppet army had 60,000 troops (an increase of 10,000), of which almost half were Vang Pao's "special forces," trained and commanded by the Americans. Ten battalions of Thai troops were operating on the Laotian battlefront alongside the Lao puppet troops.

In spite of their defeat on the Plain of Jars, Nixon still held the erroneous view that the "pacification" program in South Vietnam had been effective and that the Saigon puppet army had become stronger. He believed that it was necessary, while there were still 280,000 U.S. troops fighting in Vietnam, to take action now to achieve the goals of the "Vietnamization" program and to win more votes in the 1972 presidential elections.

Correctly assessing Nixon's reckless and warmongering character, and correctly assessing the new plots and schemes of the Americans and their puppets in their "Vietnamization" strategy, the Politburo rapidly reached the conclusion that the enemy might launch a number of medium-sized and large offensives during the 1970–1971 dry season. The Politburo concluded that these offensives would rely primarily on South Vietnamese puppet forces but would be supported by a contingent of U.S. troops. The enemy's goals would be to attack areas in central and lower Laos and northeastern Cambodia to damage the revolutionary organizations of our allies in these two countries, to destroy our supply facilities, and to cut our strategic transportation corridor in order to cut off and isolate the South Vietnamese battlefield. All our battlefronts, especially the units in the Route 9–Southern Laos area, received orders to rapidly prepare for battle.

During the summer of 1970 the General Staff began drawing up combat plans, deploying forces, and directing the preparation of the battlefield in the Route 9–Southern Laos area. Military Region 5's 2nd Division, consisting of the 1st and 141st Regiments plus subordinate support units, was ordered to leave its heavy equipment behind and move secretly from the Que Son area in Quang Nam province to the Route 9 area. There the division was brought up to full personnel and equipment strength. A cadre group drawn from all the general departments helped the division consolidate and strengthen its organization, conduct political training, and trained it in new fighting methods.

In October 1970 the Central Military Party Committee and the High Command organized the 70th Corps-Sized Group, consisting of the 304th, 308th, and 320th Divisions plus a number of specialty branch regiments and battalions.[11] Senior Colonel Cao Van Khanh was named Commander of the 70th Corps-sized Group, and Senior Colonel Hoang Phuong was named Political Commissar and concurrently Secretary of the Party Committee. The mission of the Group was to serve as the core element, working alongside local forces, in annihilating enemy units in large-scale campaigns. The formation of the 70th Corps-Sized Group responded to the combat requirements of our army in this new phase, and the formation of the Group anticipated the future birth of regular army corps in our armed forces.

In the Route 9 area, troops from the B5 Front, Tri-Thien Military Region (B4 Front), and Group 559 quickly redeployed, established fighting positions, and prepared to coordinate their combat operations with our mobile main force troops.

The General Rear Services Department formed a forward command headquarters to work with units of Group 559 to build a campaign supply network south of the Gianh River. Engineer units and assault youth assigned to the strategic transportation corridor built a number of new roads to ensure that our motorized transport units could increase supply shipments to our troop assembly areas. By January 1971 supplies stored by the troop stations [binh tram] of Group 559 in the campaign area of operations had risen to 6,000 tons, which together with the High Command's supply reserves, was sufficient to support 50,000 to 60,000 troops in combat for four or five months. In addition, more than 30,000 tons of supplies were stored in warehouses along Group 559's strategic transportation corridor. When needed, these supplies could be moved to the campaign area in a period of two to three nights. A military medical network was established using the hospitals and clinics of Group 559 and the B4 and B5 Fronts and treatment and surgical teams sent south by the Military Medical Department. This medical network was capable of receiving and treating thousands of sick and wounded soldiers.

To guard against the possibility that the enemy might expand his offensive to include ground attacks into the southern portion of Military Region 4, the General Staff gave the 70th Corps-Sized Group the added responsibility of preparing combat plans, in coordination with Military Region 4 forces, to enable us to crush any such enemy attack. The General Staff sent ten additional anti-aircraft battalions to Military Region 4 to strengthen the forces defending the strategic supply corridor and protecting vital positions. The General Staff also sent ten companies of local forces to reinforce the coastal districts from Thanh Hoa to Nam Ha and prepare to fight enemy amphibious landing forces.

On 30 January 1971, under the command of the Americans, with U.S. air support and with 10,000 American troops covering their rear, the Saigon puppet regime launched Operation "Lam Son 719," attacking the Route 9–Southern Laos area. Over 30,000 regular puppet soldiers, including their most elite units (the Airborne Division, the Marine Division, and the 1st Infantry Division), and a large force of military technical support equipment including 460 tanks and armored personnel carriers, 250 artillery pieces, and 700 aircraft (including 300 helicopters) were mobilized to participate in this operation.[12] To support the South Vietnamese puppet forces, the Laotian puppet army sent four battalions (GM-30) from Dong Hen to attack the Muong Pha Lan area along the western portion of Route 9. The enemy's overall objective was to completely cut our strategic transportation corridor to deprive our combat forces in the forward battle areas of their source of supply of personnel, supplies, and technical equipment. The enemy believed they could defeat our main force mobile troops, demonstrate the success of the "Vietnamization" strategy, and gain a strong battlefield position they could use to force us to make concessions in the Paris talks. This was Vietnamization's largest operation and exemplified the implementation of the American "Vietnamization" strategy.

The Politburo and the Central Military Party Committee issued an order to launch a counteroffensive campaign to annihilate large numbers of enemy troops in the Route 9–Southern Laos area. Colonel General Van Tien Dung, Politburo member, Deputy Chairman of the Central Military Party Committee, and Chief of the General Staff, was sent to the front to serve as the representative of the Central Military Party Committee and the High Command. A Party Committee and Headquarters for the Route 9 Front (code-named Front 702) was formed. Major General Le Trong Tan, Deputy Commander of the General Staff, was named Front Commander and Major General Le Quang Dao, Deputy Chief of the General Political Department, was named Front Commissar and Secretary of the Party Committee. Many senior cadre from the general departments and specialty branches were sent to reinforce the front's staff agencies. This was a strong command structure with sufficient ability and authority to command all forces participating in the campaign and to coordinate operations with the battlefields involved: Military Region 4, the Headquarters of B4, B5, and Group 559, and with Pathet Lao forces in southern Laos.

On 31 January 1971 the Central Committee issued the following appeal to all cadre and soldiers serving in the Route 9–Southern Laos Front: The coming engagement will be a strategically decisive battle. We will fight not only to retain control of the strategic transportation corridor, but also to annihilate a number of units of the enemy's strategic reserve forces, to enable us to deal a significant defeat to a portion of their "Vietnamization" plot, to advance our resistance effort to liberate South Vietnam and defend North Vietnam, to gloriously fulfill our international duty, and to hone our main force troops in the fires of combat. Our Army must certainly win this battle.

The campaign area was located in the sparsely populated mountain jungles of the provinces of Quang Tri (Vietnam) and Savannakhet (Laos). Route 9, running from Dong Ha City to Savannakhet, was a strategic road for both countries. Route 9 from the Vietnamese-Lao border to the sea was a strongly fortified zone containing many strong points occupied by American soldiers and Saigon puppet troops. To the west were the transportation routes and strategic logistics network operated by Group 559.

On 30 January, as the enemy began his deployment, our combat forces throughout the front area quickly occupied their battle positions. In-place forces consisted of the infantry, sapper, anti-aircraft, and engineer units of Group 559, of the B4 and B5 Fronts, and the 24th Regiment of the 324th Division. These forces engaged and attacked the enemy east and west of Route 9. The 324th Division quickly marched up from the B4 Front (Tri Thien) to an area south of Route 9. The 2nd Division engaged and blocked the enemy west of Ban Dong. The 308th Division (subordinate to Corps-Sized Group 70) was moved in 1,500 truckloads down the 500 kilometers of road from western Nghe An province to the area north of Route 9. By early February 1971 our combat forces in the Route 9–Southern Laos Front had grown to 60,000 troops, consisting of five divisions (308th, 304th, 320th, 324th, and 2nd), two separate infantry regiments (27th and 278th), eight artillery regiments, three engineer regiments, three tank battalions, six anti-aircraft regiments, and eight sapper battalions, plus rear service and transportation units. This campaign represented our army's greatest concentration of combined-arms forces in its history up to that point. The campaign plan for the deployment of forces was carried out, and all front cadre and soldiers had a high resolve to win victory.

On 8 February 1971, supported by American troops, seven Saigon puppet infantry, airborne, and armored regiments split into three columns and crossed the Vietnamese-Laotian border. The main column advanced up Route 9 through Lao Bao, reaching Ban Dong on 10 February. The two other columns landed by helicopter on a number of hill positions north and south of Route 9 to protect the flanks of the main column. With powerful fire support from U.S. aircraft and artillery and using modern, mobile equipment, the Saigon puppet troops advanced rather quickly. The puppet officers and some of their troops were arrogant and overly optimistic.

In accordance with the campaign plan the Party Committee of the Front Headquarters quickly deployed forces to block the advance of each column and to create the necessary conditions to enable us to fight decisive battles.

The 24th Regiment, reinforced by artillery and engineers, was deployed in blocking positions at Hill 351 and the Ka-Ki Bridge on Route 9. The regiment's cadre and soldiers steadfastly blocked and struck back at the enemy's spearhead units, killing nearly 100 enemy troops and destroying dozens of tanks and APCs. Group 599's anti-aircraft forces, with more than 300 anti-aircraft machine guns and cannon, threw up a heavy curtain of fire, shooting down 50 helicopters as the enemy landed troops on 8 and 9 February. The armed forces of the B5 Front launched continuous raids and shelling attacks against American base camps. Ambushes along the lines of communications killed hundreds of enemy troops and B5 forces sank nine military supply vessels on the Cua Viet River. The enemy's supply line was blocked for a week.

The battles fought by our in-place forces slowed the enemy's advance and enabled our main force units to move in and deploy to prepare to launch large-scale annihilation battles. In the key sector (north of Route 9), from 12 February until the beginning of March, units of Corps-Sized Group 70 fought a number of savage battles with the puppet Airborne Brigade and the 1st Ranger Group.

The 64th Infantry Regiment (320th Division) and the 88th Infantry Regiment (308th Division) attacked enemy troops before they had finished digging in on Hills 655 and 456, inflicting heavy casualties on two enemy battalions. The 102nd Infantry Regiment (308th Division), reinforced by an additional infantry battalion and five field artillery batteries, besieged and overran Hill 500, an important position protecting the enemy's northern flank, completely annihilating one puppet Ranger battalion. Between 20 and 25 February, the 64th Infantry Regiment, working with supporting arms units (tanks, artillery, anti-aircraft, engineers), besieged and overran Hill 543, annihilating the 3rd Airborne Battalion, one artillery battalion, and the headquarters of the 3rd Airborne Brigade. Brigade Commander Colonel Nguyen Van Tho and his entire brigade staff were taken prisoner. During this battle the 9th Tank Company, with engineers clearing a path for them, made a deep penetration attack that rolled right over the enemy headquarters, enabling our infantry to launch their assault.

In the face of our strong counterattack, the enemy hastily sent the 17th Armored Squadron (with 70 tanks) and the 8th Airborne Battalion from Ban Dong to launch a counterattack to recapture Hill 543. After six continuous days of combat the 36th Infantry Regiment (308th Division) and an element of the 64th Infantry Regiment, supported by two tank companies and front artillery, continuously blocked the enemy force, crushing his counterattack aimed at protecting the enemy's northern flank. The enemy's main group at Ban Dong was now under heavy pressure.

In the area south of Route 9, on 27 and 28 February the 324th Division wiped out one battalion and inflicted heavy casualties on another battalion of the puppet 3rd Regiment as they moved forward to destroy our supply warehouses. Meanwhile, to the west, the 141st Infantry Regiment (2nd Division) and the 48th Infantry Regiment (320th Division), working with an element of the Lao Liberation Army, attacked and crippled three Lao puppet battalions at Pha Do Tuya and Muong Pha Lan. The remnants of the enemy force fled back to Saravanne and Dong Hen.

Surprised at the early appearance of our main force units, under heavy attack and suffering severe casualties, puppet commanders and troops became confused and frightened. On 28 February the enemy was forced to commit his second echelon force (the 2nd Airborne Brigade, the 4th and 7th Armored Regiments, and the 147th and 258th Marine Brigades) to the battle. The enemy continued his planned advance to Tchepone. Our troops prevented the puppet 1st Infantry Division from reaching Tchepone, bringing it to a halt in the area of Hill 723 and "Horse Saddle" [Yen Ngua] Ridge. The 147th Marine Brigade pulled back and concentrated on Hills 550 and 532.

Our opportunity to shift from counterattacks to the offensive throughout the front area had arrived. The Front Command decided to mass our forces to annihilate units of the puppet 1st Infantry Division south of Route 9, an area with many gaps in the enemy defenses. The front also decided to strengthen our forces holding Tchepone and Na Po to protect the strategic transportation corridor and to prepare for the final, decisive battle. On 8 March the Front Party Committee issued an appeal to our cadre and soldiers to secure total victory.

On Route 9 from Lao Bao to Ban Dong, the 2nd, 24th, and 102nd Infantry Regiments resolutely held their blocking positions, conducted mobile attacks against enemy forces attempting to relieve the pressure of our attacks, and pushed the enemy back into encircled, isolated positions. In the enemy rear B5 Front units attacked enemy bases at Sa Muu, Ai Tu, and Ta Con [Khe Sanh], destroying 40 helicopters, thousands of rounds of ammunition, and one million liters of oil and gas and killing over 100 enemy, most of them pilots and technical personnel.

South of Route 9 the 2nd Division (minus one regiment) besieged Hill 723. The enemy troops, backed into a difficult position, were forced to abandon their fortified positions to flee. Our troops pursued them, destroying the puppet 1st Regiment of the 1st Infantry Division. The 64th, 36th, and 66th Infantry Regiments, supported by tank, field artillery, and anti-aircraft units, encircled the main enemy position at Ban Dong, which was held by the puppet 1st and 2nd Airborne Brigades and two armored regiments. Our troops systematically overran enemy strong points, shelled enemy artillery positions and vehicle parks, and totally cut off their line of resupply by air. On 18 March, faced with the possibility of annihilation, the enemy abandoned Ban Dong and retreated. Our troops surrounded the enemy force, blocked their route of withdrawal, and shifted over to the pursuit, killing 1,726 enemy troops, capturing more than 100 prisoners, capturing or destroying 113 tanks and armored vehicles and 24 artillery pieces, and shooting down 52 aircraft.[13] On 20 March the Ban Dong area was completely liberated. That same day the 2nd Division annihilated a major element of the puppet 2nd Regiment (1st Infantry Division) at Hill 660. Two days later, on 22 March, the 324th Infantry Division, supported by one tank company, inflicted heavy casualties on the 147th Marine Brigade on Hill 550. The enemy fled in confusion. Soldiers pushed and shoved each other, some clinging to the skids of helicopters in order to escape. Many enemy officers had to crawl through the jungles to escape our forces. By the time they reached Lang Vay some of them were left only with a ragged pair of shorts. Because our units did not have a full picture of the enemy situation and because our encirclement was not tight enough, a large portion of the enemy force at Ban Dong managed to escape.

On 23 March 1971 the Route 9–Southern Laos counterattack campaign ended in victory. The Saigon puppet army, the backbone for the implementation of the "Nixon Doctrine" in Indochina, had been dealt a serious blow. Over 20,000 enemy, including six regiments and brigades and 13 infantry and artillery battalions, were eliminated from the battlefield. All three divisions involved, the Airborne, Marine, and 1st Infantry Divisions, had suffered heavy losses. Eleven hundred vehicles (including 528 tanks and APCs) and more than 100 heavy artillery pieces had been destroyed; 505 helicopters were shot down. Our troops captured more than 1,000 prisoners and more than 3,000 weapons (including 57 artillery pieces and heavy mortars), six tanks and APCs, 270 radios, more than 100 tons of ammunition, and a large quantity of other military supplies and equipment.

Using the power of combined arms operations and innovative combat tactics, our army had defeated the new enemy tactics, which included holding battalion and regiment-sized positions on hilltops, helicopter assaults, armored assaults, etc. Our troops began and ended the campaign at the correct times, securing a great victory.

On 31 March 1971, the Politburo of the Central Committee of the Party sent a congratulatory message to the cadre and soldiers of the Route 9–Southern Laos

Front, praising them for "fighting well, securing complete victory, and establishing an outstanding combat record."

For the first time since the beginning of the war against the Americans our army had won victory in a large-scale counteroffensive campaign and had annihilated significant enemy forces. The steadfast resolve of our leadership, our command cadre, and our combatants to annihilate large numbers of enemy regular troops had been achieved. The Route 9–Southern Laos victory marked a new level of maturity for our army and was a concrete demonstration of the fact that our army and people were strong enough to militarily defeat the "Vietnamization" strategy of the American imperialists.

1971 COMBAT OPERATIONS IN SOUTH VIETNAM AND CAMBODIA

On the battlefields of the Central Highlands, on 27 February 1971 the enemy 42nd Infantry Regiment and 2nd Ranger Group launched "Operation Quang Trung 4" to attack the triborder area (western Kontum) in order to destroy our bases and our strategic transportation corridor in support of the "Lam Son 719 Operation."

Our Central Highlands troops, who had been preparing for their own 1971 spring-summer offensive, immediately regrouped and launched a counterattack. Between 27 February and 4 March 1971, the 66th, 28th, and 32nd Infantry Regiments destroyed three enemy battalions in the Ngoc To Ba area, blocking the enemy operation. After this victory these units stepped up their attacks on the enemy defensive line northwest of Kontum. On 1 April 1971, the 7th Infantry Battalion (66th Regiment) and a sapper company annihilated an enemy battalion on Ngoc Rinh Rua Mountain. Our troops then used this mountain position and artillery pieces we had just captured from the enemy to shell the Dak To–Tan Canh base. The puppet 2nd Corps hurriedly launched a relief operation called "Quang Trung 6." Two regiments were used initially but this number gradually increased to a total of nine regiments. Our main force troops in the Central Highlands had a total of only three infantry regiments with no tanks or heavy artillery. Using mobile encirclement and continuous attack tactics, our troops annihilated three puppet battalions and crippled nine other puppet battalions. The Central Military Party Committee sent a cable congratulating our Central Highlands troops for "fighting expertly, accomplishing an outstanding feat of arms, and maturing quickly."

Meanwhile, in the southern Central Highlands, the 95th Infantry Regiment in cooperation with Darlac province armed forces, exploited this period when the enemy had concentrated his forces in northern Kontum to attack the Phu Nhon and Phu Thien district capitals. After these attacks our forces defeated all enemy counterattacks and supported the local population in uprisings to take control of their areas.

In the Region 5 lowlands local armed forces overran or forced the withdrawal of many enemy outposts and supported the local population in uprisings to destroy refugee collection areas and "strategic hamlets." The region's 2nd and 12th Infantry Regiments worked with Binh Dinh province local armed forces in two consecutive action campaigns, wiping out tens of thousands of Regional Force and self-defense soldiers and liberating more than 100,000 people. We were able to rebuild many of our "leopard spot" bases within the enemy-controlled areas. Many areas in the Region 5 lowlands that the enemy had "pacified" during the 1969–1970 period were again liberated.

In Cambodia, after defeating the invasion of Cambodia by U.S. and Saigon puppet troops during the summer of 1970, COSVN's main force divisions were able to consolidate their springboard positions, open a supply line, and alternately regroup their forces and attack the enemy to protect our liberated areas. In June 1970 COSVN and the COSVN Military Party Committee established the Binh Long Front, an organization that provided guidance to units operating in two sectors, the northwest and the southwest, and that was responsible for expanding our attack to the west to assist our Cambodian friends in consolidating their hold on the liberated areas and for the creation of a secure position for the defense of our rear services facilities. Binh Long Front forces included the 1st Regiment of the 1st Division, four separate sapper and infantry battalions, and the regional rear services groups.[14] During the last months of 1970 our troops continued their advance to the west, destroying or dispersing 40 battalions of Lon Nol's puppet army and expanding the liberated zone.[15] Many of our armed operations teams went out into the Cambodian villages to help our friends develop political and armed organizations and establish and consolidate revolutionary local governmental administrative structures. By September 1970 over 600 Cambodian villages had formed guerrilla squads or platoons. Districts and provinces all had local force platoons or companies. Some districts had two or three companies. As for main force units, our Cambodian allies had formed five main force battalions, 36 main force companies, and 127 main force platoons, with a total strength of 9,400 soldiers. Our troops helped the local population to stabilize their lives and protect public order. The people of Cambodia loved and supported Vietnamese troops as if they were their own children.

During these years, because they still were dependent on the assistance of our armed forces and our people, the Pol Pot–Ieng Sary clique had not yet begun to openly oppose us. They did, however, institute policies and actions that caused increasingly serious damage to the spirit of combat solidarity between the soldiers and civilians of our two nations. They restricted contacts between our troops and their lower ranks and civilian population, disbanded a number of armed units that we had helped organize, and ordered the civilian population in a number of areas to refuse to sell us rice, not to allow us to quarter troops in their homes, etc. More serious, they sent their troops out to break into our storage areas to steal weapons and ammunition and murdered a number of our cadre and troops who were conducting solitary missions. These actions by the Pol Pot–Ieng Sary reactionary clique were opposed by the cadre and soldiers of the Cambodian revolutionary army and by the Cambodian civilian population.

During the conduct of their international proletarian duties our troops were extremely restrained. They maintained discipline and strictly carried out Party instructions regarding contacts with our Cambodian friends, thereby maintaining and developing the spirit of combat solidarity between the soldiers and civilians of our two nations. We continued to help our Cambodian friends expand their forces. In spite of the obstacles created by the reactionary clique, the Cambodian people continued their heartfelt support to our troops during day-to-day activities and combat situations.

Our COSVN main force divisions carried out their international duties and worked to consolidate their forces, conduct training in new combat tactics, and gradually increased their combined-arms combat power.

On 4 February 1971 the Saigon puppet 3rd Corps, supported by 15 squadrons of U.S. aircraft, launched "Operation Total Victory 1-71" [Toan Thang 1-71] into northeastern Cambodia.[16] The objective of this enemy operation was to attack our rear area and our strategic transportation route in the provinces of Kompong Cham and Kratie in support of the "Lam Son 719" operation on Route 9 and in southern Laos.

The COSVN Military Party Committee and the COSVN Military Command decided that "this is an opportunity for us to annihilate enemy regular forces on a battlefield where conditions are favorable for our forces and not for the enemy." Our units were ordered to mount a vigorous counterattack and to take the offensive to slow down the enemy's rate of advance and create opportunities for large-scale battles of annihilation.

On 6 and 7 February 1971 the 9th Division's 2nd and 3rd Infantry Regiments made two surprise raids against the Chup airfield, inflicting heavy casualties on three puppet Ranger battalions (the 31st, 38th, and 52nd Battalions) and one puppet armored troop just as they arrived at this position. In other areas our forces combined medium-scale attacks with small attacks, conducted raids and shelling attacks against troop concentrations, vehicle parks, and artillery fire bases, and ambushed enemy forces along his lines of communications. A number of these battles were very effective. These included an ambush that destroyed an armored troop at Wat Thmei, an attack that sank or set afire seven enemy transport vessels on the Mekong River in Kompong Cham, an assault on an enemy battalion at the Snoul Rubber Plantation, etc.

Developing our attack, the COSVN Military Party Committee and the COSVN Military Command massed two divisions (the 7th and the 9th) in a decisive area: Dam Be-Wat Thmei. Because, however, we did not have one single command organization to direct, unify, and coordinate the two divisions participating in this battle, we were unable to annihilate the enemy regimental task force. As we moved into the second phase of the battle the COSVN Military

Party Committee and the COSVN Military Command decided to establish a forward command element, called Group 301, to exercise direct command over the 5th, 7th, and 9th Infantry Divisions, the 28th Artillery Regiment, and the 12th Anti-Aircraft Machine-Gun Battalion. With this decision, a corps-level command organization was formed on the eastern Cochin China battlefield.

On 15 March Group 301 sent two divisions, the 7th and the 9th, to fight a key battle in the Mong Reu area of Kompong Cham. Utilizing mobile attack tactics against enemy forces along Route 22, our troops forced the enemy back to Mong Reau, a location where we had predeployed our forces. Our troops annihilated a large number of enemy troops and destroyed scores of tanks and armored vehicles. However, because we lacked experience in conducting blocking operations and because our units were late in launching their attacks, we missed an opportunity for the large-scale annihilation of enemy forces.

Having suffered heavy losses and severely shaken by the failure of their Route 9–Southern Laos operation, the enemy's troops were frightened and their combat spirit deteriorated. They were forced to shift over to the defensive, attempting to hold onto springboard positions to wait for the rainy season so they could again push outward to destroy our rear areas. The COSVN main force divisions immediately launched an attack. Between 25 and 31 May 1971, the 5th and 7th Divisions, closely coordinating their operations, fought the key, decisive battle in the Snoul area. By surrounding and pressuring enemy forces holed up in strong points and conducting mobile attacks combined with blocking operations, our troops defeated a series of enemy counterattacks. When the enemy finally began to flee our troops launched a pursuit and annihilated the 8th Regimental Task Force of the 5th Division. This task force consisted of three infantry battalions, one artillery battalion, and one armored regiment. We captured 300 prisoners, destroyed 200 vehicles, and captured 500 weapons.

"Operation Total Victory 1-71," a major effort by the Saigon puppet army on the Cambodian battlefield, ended in total victory for our soldiers. Over 20,000 enemy troops (including 6,000 Lon Nol puppet soldiers) were eliminated from the battlefield, and we captured over 700 prisoners. We destroyed one enemy regimental task force and one enemy armored regiment, and five enemy regimental task forces suffered severe casualties. Over 1,500 vehicles (including 369 tanks and armored vehicles) and 169 artillery pieces were destroyed, and 200 enemy aircraft were shot down. We captured 1,800 weapons (including 16 pieces of heavy artillery), over 300 tons of ammunition, 34 military vehicles, etc. This was the third major defeat (occurring at the same time as the defeats on the Route 9–Southern Laos Front and in the Central Highlands) suffered by the Saigon puppet's regular army forces during the winter and spring of 1971. COSVN's main force troops had taken a clear step forward in their ability to conduct massed combat operations at the divisional level.

In the lowlands of Cochin China, taking advantage of the fact that all enemy regular forces had been drawn into the Cambodian battlefield, our local armed forces and civilians launched attacks and uprisings in ten cities and 50 district and province capitals, attacked 40 base camps, supply bases, and airfields, and fought hundreds of battles along the enemy's lines of communications, destroying a large quantity of war equipment and killing many enemy soldiers. The struggle movement to fight the enemy was resurrected, even in the enemy's "pacification focal point" areas such as northwest of Route 4 in My Tho province, in the districts of Mo Cay and Giong Trom in Ben Tre province, along the Mang Thit River in Tra Vinh province, in Chuong Thien in Can Tho province, Dau Tieng and Ben Cat in Thu Dau Mot province, Cu Chi in Saigon city, in Duc Hoa and Chau Thanh in Long An province, etc. Many armed operations teams from the military regions and the provinces slipped deep into enemy-controlled territory and into weak zones to mobilize the masses. Revolutionary organizations were organized in 57 villages in central Cochin China and in 500 hamlets in western Cochin China. Our guerrilla forces at the village and hamlet level grew to 3,000 personnel, and in western Cochin China alone these forces increased from 40 teams in 1969 to 180 teams in 1971. Province and district local forces, reinforced with cadre and soldiers who were natives of North Vietnam or drawn from units at the military region level, again began to work in their assigned areas of operations. The rural areas of Cochin China had survived their most difficult period.

After two years of army building and combat alliance with the people and armed forces of Laos and Cambodia, we and our allies had become stronger than the enemy in terms of our strategic position and in our overall strength. Our army, which had made clear progress in the ability to conduct massed, combined-arms combat operations, had destroyed a significant portion of the Saigon puppet regular army in spite of their powerful American air, artillery, and logistics support. Our victories on the Route 9–Southern Laos Front and on the Cambodian battlefield signaled a tremendous maturation of our main force troops, clearly demonstrating the ability of our main force units to totally defeat puppet regular troops.

However, our main force troops had not yet been able to apply strong, direct pressure on the lowlands and the cities, and their level of command organization for combined-arms combat in key battles, their ability to attack an entrenched enemy occupying large defensive systems, and their ability to attack the enemy while in the process of deploying were all still limited. Although the victories of the 1971 winter-spring period had clearly transformed the battlefields of our two neighboring nations, they had not yet created a significant transformation of the battlefield in our own nation. New combat missions, greater and heavier than before, confronted our armed forces on all battlefields.

12

The People's Army, Local Armed Forces, and the Entire Population Launch the 1972 Strategic Offensive and Defeat the Enemy's Second War of Destruction against North Vietnam

PREPARATIONS FOR THE 1972 STRATEGIC OFFENSIVE

The strategic victories of the armies and peoples of the three nations of Indochina during the spring-summer 1971 period brought about important changes in the character of the war. The American imperialist "Vietnamization" policy had suffered a severe defeat. On the battlefields of South Vietnam the Americans and their puppets were forced to shift to an entirely defensive posture, and the American expeditionary army continued its withdrawal from the battlefield.[1] The combat strength of the Saigon puppet army deteriorated, especially in their combat spirit and firepower, and they were forced to spread their forces thin to occupy areas vacated by the withdrawal of 300,000 U.S. troops, further exacerbating their shortage of mobile reserve forces.

In order to accelerate this trend, in May 1971 the Politburo decided to "develop our strategic offensive posture in South Vietnam to defeat the American 'Vietnamization' policy, gain a decisive victory in 1972, and force the U.S. imperialists to negotiate an end to the war from a position of defeat." The immediate objective was to launch large offensive campaigns using our main force units in the important strategic theaters. We would simultaneously mount wide-ranging military attacks coordinated with mass popular uprisings aimed at destroying the enemy's "pacification" program in the rural lowlands. These actions would totally change the character of the war in South Vietnam.

In June 1971 the Central Military Party Committee approved a combat plan for 1972. The plan designated three main theaters for our strategic attack: eastern Cochin China, the Central Highlands, and Tri Thien. In each theater we would use between three to four infantry divisions plus supporting arms units. Our goals for 1972 were to annihilate a number of enemy regimental task forces and brigades; to render entire puppet regular divisions combat ineffective; to liberate a number of areas; to expand our base areas; to move our main force units back into the various battlefields of South Vietnam and provide them a firm foothold there; and to provide direct support for mass popular movements that would conduct attacks and uprisings to destroy the pacification program in the rural lowlands. In North Vietnam we would continue to consolidate and strengthen the combat capabilities of our armed forces, be prepared to defeat any reckless operation the enemy might launch, and increase the quantity of troops and supplies sent to the battlefield.

In June 1971 the Central Military Party Committee held a conference to review and summarize the Route 9–Southern Laos campaign. Comrade Le Duan, First Secretary of the Central Committee, attended the conference. Comrade Le Duan directed the army to apply the lessons learned from this review in an innovative manner. He also directed that our army rapidly increase the capabilities of our command organization and that we increase the combined-arms combat capabilities of our units.

After the conclusion of this conference the Ministry of Defense held a training seminar for mid- and high-level cadre. This seminar, which covered such subjects as tactics for offensive campaigns and for attacks against enemy forces holding fortified positions, was aimed at enabling our forces to annihilate enemy regiments and battalions. Our experiences in attacking and annihilating large numbers of enemy troops occupying fortified defensive positions and in mobile combat operations during the Route 9–Southern Laos counteroffensive were disseminated during the training seminar.

In November 1971 the Military Science Institute of Vietnam and the Military Training Department of the General Staff ordered the 308th Infantry Division to build a field training area at Xuan Mai (Ha Son Binh province). The training area included a mock-up of an enemy regiment-sized base camp, including a system of blockhouses, trenches, bunkers, obstacles, fallback positions, etc. After the training area was completed the institute and the Military Training Department held a four-day combined-arms exercise using the 308th Infantry Division, supported by tanks, artillery, anti-aircraft, and air force units, to annihilate this "enemy base camp." After completing the field exercise practice live firings were conducted with a number of Soviet-made weapons, including anti-tank missiles and shoulder-fired anti-aircraft missiles, which had just recently been issued to our units. We also test-fired the "FR" obstacle breaching system, that had been developed and produced by our army. Delegates representing the units participating in the exercise all expressed their confidence in the combat strength of our forces and their faith in our ability to defeat the enemy's new tactics on the battlefield. The General Staff training manual on attack tactics to annihilate enemy forces holding prepared defensive positions was updated based on ideas contributed by the cadre who participated in the training and on a number of issues that had surfaced during the field exercise.

In South Vietnam, during the initial months of the 1971–1972 dry season, our units had little time for training because they had to fight to defend our bases and forward assembly areas, simultaneously working to build roads and transport rice and ammunition to the assembly areas. A number of flexible methods to make maximum use of the time available were instituted, including having sub-units take turns at conducting training, mixing training in with regular duties, etc. In addition to the standard training program, each division focused on training in combat tactics appropriate to its own specific combat missions and special apti-tudes. The 7th Infantry Division trained in mobile offensive attacks combined with blocking operations, the 9th Infantry Division trained in combat operations in cities and towns, and the 5th Infantry Division trained in envelopment and siege operations and in destroying enemy forces holding solid defensive posi-tions. Our main force regiments in the Central Highlands trained in two tactics that had already been used effectively on the battlefield: mobile envelopment and continuous attack, and siege operations ending with an assault to overrun enemy positions using combined-arms tactics. The 3rd Infantry Division was reorga-nized and trained in conducting regimental and division-sized attacks. In addi-tion to military training, all units also conducted political activities to provide our troops with a full understanding of the decisions of the Politburo and the Central Military Party Committee, to raise combat morale and increase our troops' resolve to overcome adversity and endure the challenges of savage combat, and to encourage them to fight on until complete victory was secured. In accordance with a directive from the Central Military Party Committee, all units held Party congresses from the lowest level up to division level to strengthen the leadership role of the Party in combined-arms combat.

In late 1971, military units, party committees, local governmental apparatus, and the civilian population began to prepare the battlefield and to stockpile sup-plies for the strategic offensive. On the strategic transportation corridor, Trans-portation Group 559 expanded the use of the "secret road" to transport dry supplies and consolidated and expanded the pipeline for the shipment of oil and gas. After receiving more than 2,000 new trucks, the number of trucks operated by Group 559 during the 1971–1972 dry season rose to 8,000. The volume of supplies sent from North Vietnam to the battlefields by the end of the trans-portation season was twice that shipped during the 1970–1971 dry season and included more than 10,000 tons of oil and gasoline.

Based on our experiences in previous campaigns, especially in the Route 9–Southern Laos campaign, the battlefields paid special attention to the construc-tion of a campaign road network and a network of supply warehouses in every theater of operations. All along our campaign road network, engineer troops, assault youth, civilian labor, and the local population in the different areas worked day and night to upgrade existing roads and to build new supply routes. Radiating out from the strategic road network running south down the Annamite Mountain chain, the campaign road network spread down to the area north of Route 9 to the contested areas of western Tri-Thien and western Quang Nam to northern Kontum province, and all the way down to the area west of the Saigon River in northern Loc Ninh district in eastern Cochin China.

In Military Region 5, responding to the "rice campaign" launched by the Military Region Party Committee, provincial councils for supply of the front lines mobilized thousands of civilian laborers to transport rice from the lowlands to our mountain base areas, avoiding the enemy's stringent rice controls. By the end of 1971 the amount of rice in our warehouses had risen to 2,300 tons, enough to feed all the full-time soldiers in the Military Region for six months. Ethnic minority tribal people living east of Route 14 in Kontum province contributed 200 tons of rice even though they themselves were short of food. In Cochin China and extreme southern Central Vietnam COSVN rear services groups organized a purchasing network in the liberated areas of Cambodia and aggressively collected supplies in the rural areas of Cochin China, stockpiling sufficient food and supplies to allow COSVN's entire main force army to operate through the end of 1972.

During the fall and winter of 1971, Infantry Division 320A, Infantry Regiments 24B, 27, and 271, 20 battalions of tanks, armored vehicles, field artillery, anti-aircraft artillery, and motor transport troops, and nine battalions and 44 separate companies of local force troops set off to march south to the battlefront. To protect these units along their route of march, the General Staff sent eight anti-aircraft artillery regiments to southern Military Region 4 and to the strategic transportation corridor to defend against enemy aircraft. Group 559 strengthened its commo-liaison stations and groups, built additional foot trails for use by the troops, prepared troop "rest areas," and provided adequate supplies along the route. Many vehicles with orders giving them special priority transported green vegetables and salt to the commo-liaison stations to support our soldiers marching down the Trail. There was an excited atmosphere of advancing into battle similar to that during the early days of 1965 and during the spring of 1968.

The 171st Tank Battalion, leaving its base in North Vietnam, drove south to eastern Cochin China. The 1,200-kilometer route of the march crossed many high mountains and deep streams. Along the road the battalion underwent dozens of attacks by enemy aircraft. With high resolve and excellent movement organization, using small, light formations, and traveling when opportunities presented themselves and carrying out low-level maintenance along the route, after two months the 171st Battalion arrived safely at the battlefront with 97 percent of its vehicles and machinery. This was an outstanding battlefield achievement of our army in the long resistance struggle against the Americans, and the unexpected appearance of the battalion on the battlefield shocked the enemy.

By early 1972 the main force units of Tri-Thien, Military Region 5, the Central Highlands, and eastern Cochin China had been reinforced with many technical specialty branch and field artillery units and had received additional weapons and combat equipment, including tanks, anti-tank missiles (B-72), shoulder-fired anti-aircraft missiles (A-72), 122mm and 130mm guns, and 160mm mortars. In eastern Cochin China the COSVN Military Command formed the 75th Artillery Division (consisting of three artillery and anti-aircraft regiments) and the 26th Armored Regiment. In Military Region 5 the Military Region Command brought the 3rd Infantry Division (the 2nd, 12th, and 21st Regiments) back up to full strength and formed the 711 Infantry Division (consisting of two regiments, the 31st and the 38th.).[2] After participating in the Route 9–Southern Laos campaign the 2nd Infantry Division was built back up to strength, regrouped, and returned to the battlefront in Military Region 5.

THE WAR IN LAOS AND CAMBODIA

Aware of our massive dry season activities, the Americans and their puppets massed their air forces to continuously attack our transportation routes and rear base areas. They also sent large portions of the Saigon puppet army, the Lao puppet army, and the Lon Nol puppet army to launch numerous operations aimed at seizing control of the Plain of Jars, lower Laos, and northeastern Cambodia and blocking and disrupting our offensive preparations.

The Politburo and the Central Military Party Committee ordered our battlefields to continue preparations for the strategic attack and to fight resolutely to defeat the enemy's land-grabbing operations and enable our main force units to reach the main battlefronts.

In the Plain of Jars area Vietnamese volunteer forces and Lao Liberation Army troops repelled an offensive launched by 27 enemy battalions, forcing the enemy to pull his troops back into defensive positions. In December 1971, after more than three months of road building, logistics preparations, formulating tactical plans, and troop training, the combined Lao-Vietnamese forces launched an offensive campaign, code-named Campaign Z, to recover the Plain of Jars. Vietnamese volunteer forces participating in the campaign included the 312th and 316th Infantry Divisions, the 335th and 866th Infantry Regiments, and six artillery and tank battalions. Campaign Z was launched on 18 December 1971. After two days of combat, our forces had shattered the main enemy defensive lines at Phu Then Neng, Phu Ton, Na Hin, Ban Sui, and Phu Kheng. We annihilated six Thai Army battalions and inflicted heavy casualties on two regiments and five battalions of Lao puppet and Thai Army troops. Enemy forces abandoned the Plain of Jars and retreated to Xam Thong and Long Tieng. Our army shifted to pursuit operations, seizing Xam Thong and the northern portion of Long Tieng, destroying or severely damaging ten enemy battalions (including three Thai Army battalions) and placing heavy pressure on Vang Pao's headquarters. Supported by our tanks and artillery, Lao Liberation troops attacked and liberated the Muong Xui and Sala Phu Khun areas.

The Plain of Jars was completely liberated. Thai troops, the backbone of the Lao puppet army, were dealt a crushing blow. The Plain of Jars victory marked another step forward in our ability to organize offensive campaign operations and in the combined-arms combat capabilities of our main force units.

In lower Laos, in mid-1971 the 968th Infantry Division, working with Lao armed forces, shattered an operation involving 18 enemy battalions, reclaimed the Tha Teng and Lao Nam areas, drove the enemy out of the Paksoong area, liberated the Boloven Plateau, and protected our strategic transportation route.

In Cambodia, on 25 October 1971 the enemy massed 50 regular battalions of the Lon Nol puppet army to launch Operation "Chenla 2," attacking the Route 6–Kompong Thom area. The 9th Infantry Division, the 205th and 207th Infantry Regiments, and C-40 base area troops, working with the revolutionary armed forces and the patriotic masses of Cambodia, launched a counterattack against this operation. This was the rainy season in Cambodia, and transportation of supplies and movement of troops to the target areas was extremely difficult. To defeat the enemy, COSVN's main force regiments flexibly used such tactics as conducting raids and ambushes, mobile attacks combined with blocking operations, and siege and attrition operations. Large numbers of enemy troops were killed and conditions were created that enabled the 9th Division to mass its forces and mount a number of rather effective attacks at Rum Luong (November 1971), Ba Rai (1 December 1971), and other locations.

We had defeated the enemy's Operation "Chenla 2," killing or dispersing more than 10,000 enemy troops and capturing 4,700 weapons, 100 radios, 50 trucks, and 150 tons of ammunition. The 9th Division and COSVN's main force regiments had taken another step toward developing their ability to conduct massed attacks and destroy enemy forces in the field.

In December 1971, COSVN's 5th and 7th Divisions defeated an operation by the Saigon puppet army in the Dam Be area. During the first seven days the two divisions used small-unit tactics to obstruct the enemy advance and then began to launch massed regiment-sized attacks using envelopment and continuous attack tactics. They either destroyed or inflicted heavy casualties on an armored regiment, an infantry regimental task force, a number of airborne battalions, and a mechanized troop. On 22 December 1971 the Saigon puppet soldiers withdrew from the Dam Be area.

The Saigon puppet army still had over one million soldiers and had received a large quantity of additional weapons, ammunition, and technical equipment. The puppet army's combat strength, however, had seriously deteriorated. They had trouble replacing their losses and the strength of a number of enemy battalions fell to around 300 soldiers. In March 1972, after the sixth round of troop withdrawals, the U.S. expeditionary army still had almost 100,000 soldiers in Vietnam, but in fact the United States was no longer engaging in ground combat operations. After the defeat of the Lon Nol puppet army's Operation "Chenla 2" in Cambodia, the Saigon puppet army was forced to withdraw from its defensive line north of the Vietnamese-Cambodian border to consolidate in defensive positions in Tay Ninh province south of the Cambodia border.

FINALIZING PLANS FOR THE STRATEGIC OFFENSIVE

In March 1972 the Politburo met, evaluated the situation, and affirmed the strategic decision originally laid out in mid-1971. The Politburo noted a number of continuing problems, including the limited ability of our main force units to conduct combined-arms combat operations and to attack solid, fortified defensive positions and the fact that some theaters of operations had been slow at completing supply preparations and road construction. In addition, the quantity and quality of our local political and armed forces had not grown rapidly enough to enable them to carry out their duties in this campaign.

On 11 March 1972, the Central Military Party Committee issued supplemental orders to the different strategic theaters of operations. Eastern Cochin China and the Central Highlands were ordered to prepare to send a main force element (one division) on deep penetrations into the lowlands should the opportunity present itself. Tri-Thien, which had previously been designated a supporting theater, was now designated as the most important theater of operations. The reason for the change was that in Tri-Thien we could mass our forces, centralize command, and provide adequate logistics support for a massive, extended offensive campaign. The Central Military Party Committee established a Party Committee and Campaign Command for the Tri-Thien Campaign. The Committee assigned Major General Le Trong Tan, Deputy Chief of the General Staff, to serve as Campaign Commander and Major General Le Quang Dao, Deputy Chief of the General Political Department, to serve as Political Commissar and Party Secretary. Colonel General Van Tien Dung, member of the Politburo and Chief of the General Staff, was assigned to represent the Central Military Party Committee and to provide direct guidance to this important strategic theater.

During mid-March, units participating in the strategic offensive in the three theaters of operations, Tri-Thien, the Central Highlands, and eastern Cochin China, reached their assembly positions. In Tri-Thien our forces consisted of three infantry divisions and three separate infantry regiments; two composite anti-aircraft divisions (the 367th and the 377th) with a total of eight anti-aircraft artillery and two missile regiments; nine field artillery regiments; two tank and armored regiments; two engineer regiments; and 16 battalions of sapper, signal, and transportation troops. In the Central Highlands our forces included two infantry divisions; four separate infantry regiments; five artillery, engineer, and sapper regiments; six anti-aircraft battalions; and one tank battalion. In eastern Cochin China we had three infantry divisions, four separate infantry regiments, and four regiments and eight separate battalions of specialty branch troops, including two field artillery regiments and one tank battalion.[3] This meant that when we launched our 1972 strategic offensive our army had three large campaign-level groups made up of combined-arms units in the three strategic theaters of operations. This was a new step forward in the level of forces and the combat strength of our army. With regard to our organization and command structure, however, even though we had already organized Corps-Sized Group [Binh Doan] B70 for the Route 9–Southern Laos Campaign and Group 301 for the Northeastern Cambodia Campaign during the spring and summer of 1971, the fact that we still had not formed regular army corps meant we were slow and that we could not keep up with the requirements of large-scale combat targeted on destroying enemy regiments and battalions.

As for the enemy, even though it had learned of our urgent preparations, it held to the erroneous view that we did not have sufficient forces to mount large-scale attacks on many different fronts. The enemy thought we might mount an offensive in the Central Highlands, but not on a major scale. In spite of this belief, to defend against any eventuality, in December 1971 the enemy sent the 47th Infantry Regiment and the 2nd Airborne Brigade to reinforce the northern defenses of the Central Highlands. In other theaters of operations the enemy used local forces to block our attacks and continued to implement the "pacification" plan in the rural lowlands. The enemy's target goal was to finish pacifying 11,000 hamlets throughout South Vietnam by 1975 and by that time to have completely eliminated our isolated lowlands base areas, causing the war to "fade away."

When the 1972 Tet New Year went by without any major military operations the enemy erroneously became even more optimistic. Then, at the time of their greatest optimism, our guns roared out on all fronts. On 30 March we attacked Quang Tri and Kontum and on 1 April eastern Cochin China, Military Region 5, and the Mekong Delta launched offensives and uprisings. The enemy was completely surprised by the timing, the direction, and the size of our offensive.

On 31 March 1972, the Central Committee of the Party issued the following appeal:

The historic 1972 Campaign has begun. All comrades must increase their level of revolutionary courage, their determination to fight, and their determination to win. We must actively, aggressively, resolutely, and flexibly attack the enemy and carry out our combat duties in an outstanding manner. We must resolve ourselves to secure great victories for the cause of resistance to the Americans, of national salvation, and to carry out the sacred Last Will and Testament of our beloved Chairman Ho. In this decisive struggle between ourselves and the enemy our military victory on the battlefield will have a decisive strategic significance. At this time, more than at any other time, the duties of the armed forces are very heavy and very glorious.[4]

THE OFFENSIVE ON THE TRI-THIEN FRONT

At 11:00 A.M. on 30 March 1972 our artillery troops launched the 1972 strategic offensive on the Tri-Thien Front. From the very first minutes of the attack our artillery suppressed all enemy bases on the outer defensive perimeter, including five artillery firebases. After the artillery's destructive barrages, combined-arms forces launched assaults in the main sectors, the west and northwest. We also launched coordinated operations to encircle enemy forces, make deep penetrations to the east, cut supply routes, and isolate the campaign area from the south. During the first two days of combat our troops overran one entire group of strong points (Hill 544, Con Tien, Dau Mau, Toan Ridge, Hill 364, Ngo Ridge), shattered the enemy's strong outer defensive perimeter, and liberated Gio Linh district.

On 2 April the 24th Infantry Regiment (304th Division), supported by a tank company, attacked Base 241, held by the puppet 56th Regiment. The 56th Regiment Headquarters and one entire enemy battalion surrendered. The 48th and 27th Infantry Regiments (320th Division) attacked and crippled an enemy force (an armored regiment and a Marine battalion) as it mounted a counterattack at Cua and aided the civilian population as it rose up and liberated Cam Lo district. On 3 April the 66th Infantry Regiment (304th Division) attacked the headquarters of the 147th Marine Brigade, annihilating the bulk of the enemy battalion defending the brigade headquarters at Mai Loc. The puppet 57th Regiment at Bai Son broke and ran. The 2nd Infantry Battalion (36th Regiment, 308th Division) crossed the Cam Lo River through a curtain of enemy air and artillery bombardment and pursued the puppet 5th Regiment all the way to the northern outskirts of Dong Ha. The regiment's mechanized infantry battalion quickly made a deep penetration attack to the east of the town but was struck by enemy aircraft while they were on the move. Eight armored personnel carriers were knocked out and 29 cadre and soldiers were killed or wounded, forcing the battalion to stop to regroup. Although enemy troops in Dong Ha were terrified, we did not bring our reserves forward quickly enough and missed a chance to capture Dong Ha.

By 4 April, after five days of combat, our troops had shattered the enemy's outer defensive perimeter, destroying four regimental base camps and seven battalion base camps on Route 9. The 56th Regiment had been destroyed, the 2nd Regiment and the 147th Brigade had suffered heavy casualties, and Cam Lo and Gio Linh districts had been liberated.

Faced with the potential loss of Quang Tri province, on 3 April Nguyen Van Thieu convened a meeting of his National Security Council. He sent four infantry regiments and brigades and one armored regiment from Saigon and Da Nang to Tri-Thien. Utilizing preexisting defensive fortifications and their reinforced troop strength, the enemy established a defensive system based on three centers of resistance—Dong Ha, Ai Tu, and La Vang–Quang Tri. Hundreds of tanks and armored personnel carriers formed a barrier of steel around these bases. Artillery firebases and tank guns fired tens of thousands of rounds into our positions. Tactical aircraft and B-52 strategic bombers dropped hundreds of tons of bombs.

Because the enemy had increased his troop strength and fire support and because he had changed his defensive plan, our 9 April wave of assaults were unsuccessful. All units were ordered to prepare additional supplies and equipment and to study tactics to defeat the enemy tactic of contracting his lines and using tanks and armored personnel carriers to form a ring of steel around his positions. Many tank-killer teams equipped with B-40s, B-41s, DKBs, and B-72 anti-tank missiles were formed. Comrade Luc Vinh Tuong, commander of an anti-tank missile team, destroyed six tanks in one day. An enthusiastic movement to destroy enemy tanks swept through all our troop positions.

On 27 April 1972, after 16 days of preparation and fighting to move into position, our troops launched a new assault. In the west three divisions, the 308th, 304th, and 324th, with artillery and tank support combined assaults with enveloping and isolating the enemy and with a campaign-level flank attack. They annihilated each individual enemy strong point and repelled numerous enemy counterattacks. On 28 April the 308th Division liberated Dong Ha and on 1 May the 304th Division captured the Ai Tu base camp. During this battle an infantry platoon commanded by Mai Quoc Ca, that was holding a blocking position at the Quang Tri Bridge, fought to the last man, enabling the division to annihilate the enemy and capture the base.[5]

To the east, the 27th Infantry Regiment and one mechanized infantry battalion captured the Hai Lang district capital. The 324th Infantry Division attacked strong points in the rear of the enemy's defensive network, cutting Route 1 south of Quang Tri city. Surrounded and isolated, the enemy troops in La Vang–Quang Tri broke and ran. Our troops clung to and pursued them. Accurate fire from our long-range artillery positions created added terror among the enemy troops. Abandoning their vehicles and artillery pieces, enemy troops fled on foot. Many enemy units fled the My Chanh River defensive positions and ran all the way back to Hue. Route 1 from Quang Tri to northern Thua Thien province became a "highway of death" for the enemy.[6] Brigadier General Vu Van Giai, commander of the puppet 3rd Division, and his U.S. advisors escaped by helicopter. At 1800 hours on 2 May the province of Quang Tri was totally liberated.

In just six days, using the power of combined-arms combat operations, our troops had destroyed one of the enemy's strongest defensive networks, wiping out more than 8,000 enemy troops and capturing 2,100 prisoners. Five enemy infantry regiments and three armored regiments had been destroyed. We captured or destroyed more than 2,000 vehicles (including 286 tanks and APCs), 175 artillery pieces, and shot down 59 aircraft. Using the artillery guns and artillery ammunition we captured from the enemy (73 large artillery pieces), we formed eight new artillery batteries.

After losing Quang Tri, enemy troops in Thua Thien disintegrated. Tri-Thien Military Region troops shifted from envelopment pressure tactics to pursuit tactics, annihilating two enemy battalions on the Tranh Ridgeline. In Hue city enemy soldiers burned the Dong Ba market and looted civilian property. The enemy defense line north of Hue City was held by four regiments but only two of these regiments were at full strength. This was a great opportunity, but, because we lacked a reserve force and because we had not prepared roads and supplies beforehand, our troops were not able to take advantage of this opportunity to exploit our victory and liberate Thua Thien–Hue.

On 3 May, puppet President Nguyen Van Thieu fired Lieutenant General Hoang Xuan Lam, Commander of the puppet 1st Military Region, replacing him with Lieutenant General Ngo Quang Truong, formerly Commander of the 4th Military Region. The enemy hurriedly sent replacement troops and equipment for units that had suffered losses and reinforced Hue with five additional regiments or brigades from Saigon and Da Nang.[7] This brought enemy forces there up to four divisions. The enemy focused on consolidating his defensive line along the My Chanh River and used this line as a base to strike out to the east and west to disrupt our preparations to attack Hue. The enemy loudly boasted that he would "retake Quang Tri." To rescue the puppet troops the United States, concentrating its shore bombardment ships and increasing B-52 sorties from 11 per day in May to 51 per day in June, continuously attacked our campaign rear areas. Our troops experienced many difficulties in maintaining supply levels and we were able to provide only 30 percent of the supplies called for in our plan. In addition, because we had been slow to change our campaign tactics as the enemy strengthened his forces and solidified his defenses, our assault against the My Chanh defensive line from 20 to 26 June was unsuccessful, and we suffered losses that were twice as high as those we suffered during the two previous attacks. In late June 1972 the fighting on the Tri-Thien Front became very complex, with fierce back-and-forth fighting between our troops and the enemy.

THE OFFENSIVE IN THE CENTRAL HIGHLANDS

The enemy anticipated that the northwestern Central Highlands would be our primary attack theater in 1972. He reinforced the defenses of Kontum city, sending in the 2nd Airborne Brigade from his strategic reserves in Saigon to establish a new defensive line along the ridgelines west of the Po-Co River northwest of Kontum city and establish a solid, unbroken line to block our troops and keep them away from the city.

To prepare for the offensive, beginning on 23 March the Central Highlands Front, commanded by Major General Hoang Minh Thao and with Senior Colonel Tran The Mon serving as Political Commissar, used two of its own regiments, the 28th and the 95th Infantry Regiments, and Military Region 5's 12th Infantry Regiment to attack enemy forces on Routes 14 and 19, to surround and threaten the enemy position, and to isolate the campaign area. Front-level sapper and artillery forces attacked enemy artillery firebases. The 2nd Infantry Division (minus) conducted deception operations to attract the enemy's attention to the area north of Dak To. This enabled the 66th Infantry Regiment to complete preparations to attack the headquarters of the puppet 22nd Division and the 42nd Regiment at Tan Canh. Cadre and soldiers of the 66th Regiment secretly built a new road over 100 kilometers long, bringing rice and ammunition all the way up to the assault assembly areas. They also collected and prepared lumber to build fortifications for use in besieging the enemy position. Front engineering troops built roads to a point only five or six kilometers from enemy positions to ensure that our tanks and artillery could move forward to carry out the planned attack against the enemy's rear.

On 30 March 1972, as our troops were opening fire on the Quang Tri Front, Division 320A attacked the 2nd Airborne Brigade's defensive line west of the Po-Co River, destroying or crippling two enemy battalions and clearing the route of advance to Kontum city. The defensive positions held by the puppet 42nd and 47th Regiments at Dak To and Tan Canh were now isolated.

On 24 April the 66th Infantry Regiment, with tank and artillery support and in coordination with 1st Regiment, 2nd Division, attacked the Dak To–Tan Canh defensive line, inflicting heavy casualties on the enemy's 22nd Division (minus), 4th Armored Regiment, and two enemy artillery battalions. One enemy troop element that broke and ran was caught in a loose net established by the 28th Infantry Regiment and captured en masse. Colonel Le Duc Dat, Commander of the puppet 22nd Division, died on the battlefield and Deputy Division Commander Colonel Vi Van Binh and the entire headquarters staff of the 22nd Division were captured. An area of northern Kontum with a population of more than 25,000 people was liberated. For the first time in the history of the Central Highlands, our forces had destroyed an enemy divisional base camp located behind a fortified line of defenses. Immediately exploiting this victory, during the night of 24 April the 141st Infantry Regiment (2nd Division), supported by tanks, attacked the base at Dien Binh, wiping out two entire Regional Force intergroups [an "inter-group"—Lien Doi—was equivalent to a battalion] and capturing six artillery pieces and two helicopters. Kontum city, 50 kilometers south of Dak To and Tan Canh, was now threatened. Enemy military forces defending the city consisted of only two regular battalions plus a number of Regional Force units. The U.S. advisory team fled to Pleiku. Because road travel was difficult and because our units had no pre-positioned supplies and had not brought additional heavy technical equipment forward, the attack had to be temporarily postponed. Taking advantage of this respite, the enemy moved in the 23rd Division to strengthen the city's defenses. On 14 and 25 May, we launched two assaults into Kontum city, but our forces were unsuccessful and suffered losses. Our units were ordered to pull back to regroup and prepare for a new assault.

THE OFFENSIVE NORTHEAST OF SAIGON

In Cochin China and extreme southern Central Vietnam, following a continuous string of defeats of its operations in Cambodia, the puppet 3rd Corps withdrew and built a defensive line along the border in Binh Long, Phuoc Long, and Tay Ninh provinces. In his primary sector, along the Route 22 line, the enemy deployed ten infantry and four armored regiments.

In accordance with our strategic attack plan, on 1 April 1972 the COSVN Military Command ordered its subordinate units to open fire, launching the "Nguyen Hue Campaign." In the main area of operations the 5th, 7th, and 9th Infantry Divisions, together with supporting arms units, assaulted enemy defenses on Route 13. The secondary area of operations (Route 22) was the responsibility of the 24th and 271st Regiments. A Campaign Headquarters Command was formed. Lieutenant General Tran Van Tra, Deputy Commander of COSVN Military Command, was named Campaign Commander, and Major General Tran Do, Deputy Political Commissar of COSVN Command, was named Political Commissar of the Campaign.

As a ruse to distract the enemy, enable our main force divisions to occupy their jumping-off points, and to isolate the battlefield in the main area of operations, the 24th and 271st Infantry Regiments, supported by tanks and artillery, opened fire first. On 1 April the two regiments attacked the Sa Mat and Bau Dung strong points on Route 22, inflicting heavy casualties on the puppet 49th Regimental Combat Group (25th Division). The soldiers and civilians of Tay Ninh province launched coordinated attacks and uprisings, destroying or forcing the evacuation of 20 outposts and completely liberating Tan Bien District.

On 5 April, while the enemy was dealing with our attacks along Route 22, the 5th Division and the 3rd Infantry Regiment (9th Division), supported by long-range artillery and two tank companies, mounted a surprise attack against the Loc Ninh district Military Headquarters, a strongly fortified defensive position on Route 13, 20 kilometers from the Vietnamese-Cambodian border that was held by the puppet 9th Regimental Task Force (5th Division). The enemy was completely surprised by our attack and was terrified by our long-range artillery bombardment and by the appearance of our tanks. The puppet 3rd Corps ordered the 1st Armored Regiment and two infantry battalions to abandon the border defensive line and pull back to rescue Loc Ninh. The 3rd Regiment, 9th Division, conducted an outstanding ambush attack against this relief column, killing or wounding 1,400 enemy troops, destroying 52 vehicles, and capturing 12 enemy tanks. The relief column was totally defeated. By 8 April our troops were in control of the Loc Ninh headquarters base and we had captured Colonel Nguyen Cong Vinh, Commander of the 9th Regimental Task Force. This was a major victory. We had defeated an enemy regimental task force holding fortified defensive positions and had captured a district military headquarters and district administrative capital. This was a new step forward in the capability of COSVN's main force troops to conduct massed combined-arms combat operations.

With the loss of Loc Ninh, the puppet 52nd Regimental Task Force, which was holding blocking positions at Dong Tam base, abandoned their vehicles and artillery and fled in terror to the Binh Long province capital. The 209th Infantry Regiment, 7th Division, ambushed the enemy force during their retreat, killing or capturing 1,200 enemy troops and capturing 14 pieces of heavy artillery.

During their first eight days of combat operations the main force units of COSVN had split and isolated the enemy, setting the stage for the campaign. Exploiting the power of combined-arms combat operations, our units had destroyed or crippled five enemy regimental task forces or regiments, shattered part of the enemy's border defensive line, captured dozens of tanks and artillery pieces and tens of thousands of rounds of ammunition, and liberated 30,000 civilians.

Exploiting our victory and taking advantage of the fact that the enemy's troops were now frightened and wavering, during the evening of 6 April the Campaign Headquarters sent the 9th Infantry Division, supported by one tank company, to attack Binh Long city (24 kilometers south of Loc Ninh). Because preparations for the attack had taken too long, however, the enemy had time to strengthen the defenses of the city, increasing their total defensive strength from one regiment to five regiments. The enemy also had time to bring the 21st Division up from the Mekong Delta to Chon Thanh, where it prepared to support Binh Long. The enemy concentrated a large number of B-52 sorties to savagely attack our campaign rear areas. Three waves of assaults against Binh Long city (on 13 and 15 April and on 11 May) were all unsuccessful. Our units suffered heavy casualties and over half of the tanks we used in the battle were destroyed. On 15 May, after 32 days of ferocious combat, our troops ended the attack on Binh Long city.

THE OFFENSIVE IN OTHER PARTS OF SOUTH VIETNAM

In coordination with the offensive attacks by our main force units in the main strategic theaters of operations, the armed forces of Military Region 5, under the command of Major General Chu Huy Man, Military Commander, and Comrade Vo Chi Cong, Political Commissar, launched a general offensive campaign in northern Binh Dinh province. The 3rd Infantry Division, two sapper battalions, local armed forces, and mass political forces of Binh Dinh province participated in the campaign.

On 9 April 1972, the 40th Sapper Battalion attacked the strong point at Go Loi (seven kilometers southwest of Hoai An district capital), annihilating one Regional Force battalion and threatening the district capital. The enemy brought in an additional regiment to strengthen their defenses. On 18 April the 2nd and 21st Infantry Regiments, 3rd Division, conducting continuous mobile envelopment and attack operations, annihilated the puppet 40th Regiment and liberated the Hoai An district capital. Developing the attack, from 24 April through 1 May the 3rd Division organized forces to besiege and destroy two enemy bases at Binh Duong (Phu My district) and De Duc (Hoai Nhon district). The division sent an element forward that blocked and then destroyed the puppet 41st Regiment as it moved up as a relief force. Supported by our armed forces, tens of thousands of civilians in the villages and hamlets, beating drums and gongs and carrying knives, sickles, and sticks, worked with local guerrillas to besiege and force the withdrawal of more than 100 Regional Force outposts, capture and induce to surrender the local Popular Force militia, and destroyed the puppet's grass-roots governmental structure. The mobile reserve forces of the puppet 2nd Corps, which had been lured away and tied down in the northern Central Highlands, could not come to the rescue in Binh Dinh. Enemy forces in the Phu My district capital and at the Tra Quang base camp became frightened and wavered. Because our troops were forced to stop, regroup, and prepare additional supplies, however, the enemy had sufficient time to rebuild the 40th and 41st Regiments and to strengthen defensive fortifications. The attacks by the 3rd Division against the Phu My district capital and against Tra Quang base failed. On 2 June the offensive campaign in northern Binh Dinh ended. We had wiped out or dispersed 13,000 enemy, including 4,000 prisoners, and liberated Hoai An and Hoai Nhon districts and portions of Phu My district. The 3rd Division and the armed forces of Binh Dinh province received the following congratulatory cable from the Central Military Party Committee: "You increased your overall strength, conducted continuous attacks, fought well, and won great victories."

In Quang Nam, the 38th and 31st Infantry Regiments, 711 Division, liberated the Hiep Duc district capital and attacked and inflicted heavy casualties on three enemy battalions on Route 105 (Que Son district). In Quang Da province the provincial armed forces destroyed or forced the evacuation of ten enemy outposts, destroyed 12 civilian collection areas [refugee camps] and "strategic hamlets," and expanded the liberated area north of the Thu Bon River. The soldiers and civilians of Quang Ngai province, combining military attacks with civilian uprisings, crippled two Regional Force battalions and four independent Regional Force companies, gaining control over 20 villages in the eastern part of Binh Son and Son Tinh districts and south of the Ve River.

The main force regiments of Military Regions 8 and 9, in coordination with the armed forces of the provinces of the Mekong Delta, crippled ten puppet battalions, supported the masses in uprisings and in eliminating enemy thugs, destroyed the enemy's machinery of oppression, and liberated ten villages and a number of hamlets, expanding the base area north and south of Route 4 in My Tho province, in Ben Tre, in Zone 4 of Kien Tuong and Kien Phong, and in the southwestern portion of Long My district. Our armed forces in this area were unable to launch massed operations as called for in the overall campaign plan, however, so our offensive and uprising movement in the Mekong Delta was unable to make any significant progress.

SUMMARY OF THE INITIAL RESULTS OF THE OFFENSIVE

By mid-June 1972 the strategic offensive by our armed forces and civilians on the South Vietnamese battlefield had lasted almost three months and had won a number of great victories. We had killed or eliminated from the battlefield more than 100,000 enemy troops, more than half of whom were regular troops of the puppet army. We had wiped out or heavily damaged five divisions and 18 regiments, shattered a number of strongly fortified enemy defensive lines and positions, and liberated many large areas with a total population of more than one million people. Our main force troops had secured footholds on a number of important areas of the South Vietnamese battlefield. The balance of forces between ourselves and the enemy had been significantly altered. Nixon's Vietnamization strategy was faced with the prospect of total bankruptcy.

Assessing the results of the first three months of the strategic offensive, a conference of the Central Military Party Committee on 30 May 1972 pointed out that our main force troops had achieved superiority in numbers, firepower, and technical military equipment in their attacks and they correctly selected offensive methods, increased our combined-arms power, and successfully attacked and destroyed strongly fortified enemy defensive positions. Because of deficiencies in our command organization, in our preparation of the battlefield, and in our rear service preparations, when we tried to switch over to develop our offensive attack and conduct mobile attacks against the enemy while he was in the process of withdrawing or when his forces were in disarray, however, we usually missed our opportunities.

RESUMPTION OF THE WAR OF DESTRUCTION AGAINST NORTH VIETNAM

Faced with the danger that the puppet army, the backbone of his "Vietnamization" strategy, might collapse, Nixon was forced to mobilize the bulk of the U.S. armed forces and return them to the war of aggression in Vietnam. He doubled the number of strategic and tactical aircraft and tripled the number of combat ships.[8] Using the U.S. Air Force and Navy to fight in support of puppet forces, the enemy launched a counteroffensive in South Vietnam. The focus of the counterattack was the Quang Tri Front. On 6 April Nixon massed aircraft and warships to strike many heavily populated areas from Quang Binh to Lang Son, starting the second war of destruction against North Vietnam. This second war was different from the first war of destruction: This time the enemy employed larger forces and launched massive attacks that began on the first day of the operation, using many modernized, upgraded technical weapons and equipment. On 10 April, B-52s bombed Vinh city, on 13 April they bombed Thanh Hoa city, and on 16 April Haiphong was bombed. On 9 May, U.S. aircraft dropped more than 1,000 ocean mines to block Haiphong harbor. On succeeding days they continued to sow mines to block all harbors, river mouths, and coastal areas of ten provinces in 43 separate locations in North Vietnam. The enemy dropped a total of 7,963 mines. In Laos, the United States used Lao puppet troops and Royal Thai Army soldiers to launch an operation to retake the Plain of Jars.

In coordination with his military measures, Nixon unilaterally announced the indefinite postponement of the Paris talks. Using devious political and diplomatic schemes, the enemy sought to cut back the amount of aid being supplied to us by socialist nations to force us to accept a settlement favorable to the United States.

The war against the Americans became very complicated in all areas: military, political, and diplomatic. Our armed forces had the mission of continuing to attack enemy forces on the battlefield and also combating and defeating the U.S. Air Force and Navy—the two most powerful, modern armed services of the U.S. imperialists. The fighting during the summer of 1972 was arduous and savage in North and South Vietnam and on the battlefields of Laos.

On 1 May 1972, the Party Central Committee issued an appeal to the soldiers and civilians of the entire nation to increase their resolve and vigilance and to prepare to combat and defeat the enemy in any possible situation. The Central Committee made it clear that no matter what reckless action the enemy might take, he could not reverse the situation on the battlefields.

The Central Committee reached the following decision: To continue the strategic offensive in South Vietnam, to defeat the American imperialist war of destruction against North Vietnam, to firmly defend North Vietnam, and to reach, no matter what the cost, the strategic goals that we had set forward. The Central Committee declared that North Vietnam must urgently switch to a war footing, expand the armed forces, counter the enemy blockade, and focus all efforts on carrying out our most vital responsibility, which was to maintain the flow of supplies to support the forward battlefields. In the South, the Central Committee declared that we must expand the offensive by our main force troops with the main focus now being on the rural areas. This effort must be coordinated with attacks and uprisings aimed at disrupting the enemy's pacification schemes.

In North Vietnam, utilizing experience gained during the first war of destruction, the different levels of the Party and the Government and the civilian population in all areas quickly shifted our production focus and expanded our people's anti-aircraft operations. State-owned warehouses and enterprises and technical rear service facilities of our armed forces were once again evacuated and dispersed into rural areas to continue production, to serve the needs of the population, and to support our combat operations.

In response to their new responsibilities and the enlarged scale of combat operations, we increased the size and quality of our armed forces. The High Command's two mobile reserve divisions, the 325th and 320th Infantry Divisions, six mobile main force regiments subordinate to Military Region 4, the Viet Bac Military Region, and the Left Bank and Right Bank Military Regions (all at full table of organization and equipment strength), and a strong provisional reserve division (designated the 312B Division and made up of cadet officers of the Infantry School and of the officer training schools of the other branches of service) were all readied and placed on alert to move out if needed to fight to defend the northern portion of Military Region 4. Anti-aircraft forces were expanded by forming one new division, three new regiments, and 20 new battalions, and were strengthened with additional anti-aircraft guns, missiles, radar, and many new pieces of equipment. Dozens of new battalions and regiments of artillery, armor, sappers, engineers, and signal troops were formed. In a very short period of time our armed forces in North Vietnam grew to 530,000 soldiers.[9] As part of this increase, the number of main force troops assigned to the subregions almost doubled, and the number of main force troops assigned to Military Region 4 increased to five times its previous level.

Militia self-defense forces to fight enemy aircraft and enemy warships were quickly expanded, issued rather powerful equipment, and were appropriately organized. In 1968 there were 172 direct combat teams among our militia forces equipped with 350 12.7mm and 14.5mm anti-aircraft machine guns. By mid-1972, in addition to self-defense cells and teams, the militia self-defense forces in North Vietnam had organized dozens of anti-aircraft artillery batteries equipped with 37mm, 57mm, and 100mm guns. The militia forces also had 170 anti-aircraft batteries or platoons armed with machine guns and 20 batteries or platoons equipped with 85mm field guns to combat American warships along the coast.

With a spirit of vigilance and with high combat spirit, utilizing experience gained in combating the enemy during the 1965–1968 period, the anti-aircraft forces of our three types of troops (main force, local force, militia and guerrilla) vigorously launched this new battle, shooting down many aircraft and hitting and setting afire many U.S. warships. On 6 April the soldiers and civilians of Quang Binh–Vinh shot down ten aircraft. On 9 April Quang Binh coastal artillery units hit and set afire four warships. On 16 April Hanoi and Haiphong shot down 15 aircraft. On 19 April our combat aircraft attacked and heavily damaged an American destroyer, etc.

Because the enemy had escalated his operations rapidly, was conducting massive bombardments, and was using many new types of weapons and items of technical equipment (laser-guided bombs, guided missiles, various types of jammers, etc.), many of our units and local areas suffered heavy losses. Almost all of the important bridges on the railroad lines and on the road network were knocked out. Ground transportation became difficult. Coastal and river transportation was blocked. The volume of supplies shipped across the Gianh River to the battlefields fell to only a few thousand tons per month. Enemy jamming equipment made it difficult for us to locate targets, especially B-52s. Our low combat efficiency, demonstrated by the ineffectiveness of our efforts to defend targets and by the small number of enemy aircraft shot down, became a source of concern to the Air Defense–Air Force Branch and to all the armed forces in North Vietnam.

The Central Military Party Committee and the High Command directed all units to conduct studies to analyze the new operational procedures and schemes being used by the enemy, to increase their capability to coordinate their combat operations, and to overcome manifestations of subjectivism and of clinging to old procedures and experiences. Each unit studied the problem of how to resolve concrete issues regarding the troops' understanding of the enemy's new plots and schemes and analyzed new technical problems that had to be solved to defeat the enemy. The Air Defense–Air Force Service had some initial success in updating techniques for countering electronic jamming and using new methods to increase the capabilities of our different types of weapons, raising the combat effectiveness of all our branches of service. During more than six months of desperate combat (from 6 April until 22 October 1972), the Air Defense–Air Force troops, together with the other armed forces and people of North Vietnam, shot down 651 U.S. aircraft and sank or set afire 80 U.S. ships.[10]

With regard to the effort to counter the enemy blockade, the Party Central Committee and the Government promulgated a number of urgent solutions, such as readjusting the volume of supplies imported by sea in comparison with the volume imported by rail; developing additional harbors and entry points to receive supplies; combining different transportation methods, including road, pipeline, coastal transport, and river transport. Mine-sweeping and mine-destruction teams were organized on a wide-ranging, national scale. Forming the backbone of these efforts were specialized teams from the Navy Command and from local main force engineer units, the port self-defense militia, the river transport self-defense militia, and from militia units of coastal and riverside villages. The Scientific Institute of Vietnam, the Military Technical University, and the University of Arts and Sciences all worked to analyze the triggering mechanisms of the different types of bombs and mines and to find ways to sweep, destroy, or dismantle them using both technical and crude methods.

Using many different methods, combining courage with intelligence, our armed forces, together with the local civilian population, overcame every sacrifice and challenge, dismantling or destroying thousands of mines and defeating the enemy's blockade and obstruction schemes. We maintained firm control of North Vietnam's traffic and transportation lifeline, increasing the volume of supplies sent to the battlefields by road and by water transport. In comparison with 1968, the year we shipped the largest volume of supplies during the first war of destruction, the volume of supplies transported in North Vietnam during 1972 grew to more than 275,000 tons. The volume of military aid shipped to us by land and sea from fraternal socialist countries and the volume of supplies shipped from the North to South Vietnam in 1972 was almost double that shipped in 1971.

Because of their defeats on the battlefields in the South, because they could not achieve the goals of their war of destruction against North Vietnam, and because of the growing international and U.S. domestic movements against the war of aggression in Vietnam, on 22 October 1972 Nixon was forced to announce a bombing halt north of the 20th parallel. The second war of destruction against North Vietnam by the American imperialists had suffered a serious defeat.

VICTORY ON THE PLAIN OF JARS

In Laos the Plain of Jars was fiercely contested by ourselves and the enemy. Because we were not yet strong enough to hold the Plain of Jars, the enemy regularly took advantage of the rainy season to retake this area. Therefore, after ending the 1971–1972 dry season campaign, we and our allies decided to build defensive positions to enable us to defeat the enemy if he again tried to retake the area. Our objective was to maintain firm control of the liberated area and lure in the enemy's mobile forces in order to enable other battlefields to conduct their own operations. The area to be defended was a rectangle bounded by Muong Xui, Noong Pet, Xieng Khoang city, and Tham Lung. This area, 50 kilometers wide and 60 kilometers long in the center of the Plain of Jars, was our primary defensive area. Vietnamese volunteer troops participating in this campaign included the 316th Infantry Division, three separate infantry regiments (the 866th, the 335th, and the 88th Regiment of the 308B Division), and nine specialty branch battalions (tanks, artillery, anti-aircraft artillery, sappers, engineers). A Campaign Headquarters was established, with Senior Colonel Vu Lap serving as Commander and Senior Colonel Le Linh as Political Commissar. Our allies contributed seven battalions to this campaign. The Lao battalions organized the defenses of two areas, Muong Xui and Xieng Khoang city.

Because time for preparation was short, because we had supply difficulties, and because many units lacked experience in defensive combat, our own troops and those of our Lao friends had to make preparations and simultaneously conduct cadre training and train subunits in combat tactics. In less than two months the Vietnamese-Lao military forces built a continuous, in-depth defensive network made up of many defensive zones, including a number of defensive strong points with fortifications and tunnels with a total length of 658 meters. Supplies to support combat requirements were stockpiled in each defensive area. Based on their individual combat missions, Vietnamese volunteer units were organized into two forces: one force to hold the defensive bases (two regiments) and a mobile force (three regiments). A number of units conducted field exercises in their defensive positions to evaluate plans for combat and coordination between forces.

On 21 May, 40 battalions of Lao puppet and Thai Army soldiers, operating under the command of American officers, launched an operation to seize the Plain of Jars area. Using their preprepared positions, our Vietnamese volunteer troops, fighting side by side with Lao Liberation soldiers, heroically defeated many enemy attacks and firmly held their positions. A number of resounding victories were won, the most outstanding of which was a counterattack in the area of Cha Ho–Ban Hai–Ban Phon (southern Plain of Jars) on 26 October 1972. During this battle the Vietnamese-Laotian allied army, using massed forces of divisional strength, annihilated 1,200 enemy troops and captured 80 prisoners and 1,500 weapons. The battle for the Plain of Jars area lasted 170 days (until 15 November 1972).

The Lao-Vietnamese allied army eliminated 5,600 enemy troops from the field of battle, completely defeating the offensive by the Lao puppet troops and Thai Army troops and effectively supporting our strategic offensive in South Vietnam. This was the first time Vietnamese volunteer troops and Lao Liberation troops in Laos had defeated the enemy in the rainy season and been able to defend the liberated area on the Plain of Jars. This was also the first time our main force troops had victoriously carried out a defensive campaign, and we gained a great deal of experience in the art of organizing and conducting such a campaign.

THE ENEMY COUNTEROFFENSIVE IN SOUTH VIETNAM

In South Vietnam, after the wave of simultaneous attacks achieved complete victory on our various fronts, our forces had to halt temporarily to consolidate, rebuild troop strength, and reequip. Exploiting this respite and with massive U.S. air and naval support, the puppet forces mounted a fierce counteroffensive aimed at retaking the positions they had lost. In late May they launched an operation to reopen Route 13 to Binh Long city, in late June they crossed the My Chanh River, attacking toward Quang Tri city, and in early July they launched an operation to retake the northern Binh Dinh liberated zone.

The Politburo and the Central Military Party Committee ordered the battlefields to shift over to combating the enemy's counterattacks; to conduct attrition operations and annihilation attacks to erode enemy strength; and to tie down and draw in the puppet regular mobile forces to allow us to send a portion of our main force units down to the lowlands to work with local forces in a combined campaign to disrupt pacification.

On 28 June, after two days of preparatory bombardment by aircraft and heavy artillery, the Americans and their puppets used two divisions, the Airborne and the Marines, heavily supported by artillery and armor,[11] to launch "Operation Lam Son 72," aimed at quickly retaking Quang Tri city and gaining an advantage in the Paris talks, which were scheduled to resume on 13 July 1972. Enemy troops divided into two columns: one column advanced overland, and another conducted an air assault. On 5 July, the enemy retook the area north and south of the My Chanh River from Route 1 to the seacoast. They retook the Hai Lang district capital and advanced as far as La Vang. With massive fire support from aircraft, artillery, and naval vessels, the puppet troops advanced rather quickly. They tried to secure jumping-off positions for use in retaking Quang Tri city and the Quang Tri Citadel area.

Our forces along Route 1 from Tan Dien (the northern bank of the My Chanh River) to La Vang–Quang Tri consisted of the 2nd Independent Battalion, the 8th Local Force Battalion, and one battalion of the 48th Regiment. Our main campaign force was concentrated south of the My Chanh River. Because time was so short and because the routes of march were under heavy bombardment, the Campaign Command did not have time to redeploy forces and switch from the offensive to the counterattack. In a situation in which we had fewer troops than the enemy, more than half of our artillery prime movers had been knocked out, some infantry companies were down to less than 20 men, and our artillery had no ammunition reserves, our units in all areas fought courageously, beating back many enemy assaults and maintaining firm control of the city.

On 12 July 1972, the 325th and 312th Infantry Divisions were sent into combat on the Quang Tri Front. The Central Military Party Committee sent them a letter to encourage their cadre and soldiers: "Your mission, to march into combat, is extremely urgent. You must move very quickly and arrive very soon and in full strength and also preserve secrecy and security. When you arrive at the battlefield you must be able to start fighting immediately and must begin winning right from your very first battle. Socialist North Vietnam has given you the heavy responsibility of carrying the strength of our great rear area to the front lines to defeat the enemy's army."

Major General Tran Quy Hai, Deputy Minister of Defense, was appointed Front Commander, and Lieutenant General Song Hao, Chief of the General Political Department, was appointed Front Commissar and Secretary of the Front Party Committee. Each unit held study sessions for cadre and soldiers to help them fully understand the importance of the fight for Quang Tri from the political, military, and diplomatic standpoints and, based on that understanding, to strengthen their combat resolve and overcome any wavering of their will and any fears of hardship and casualties. Troops and fire support were quickly redeployed, a network of blocking positions was built, and fighting methods were changed to defend each separate area.

In the area of the Citadel and Quang Tri city, combat forces under the command of the headquarters of the 325th Division consisted of two infantry regiments, the 95th and the 48th, and two battalions of Quang Tri province local force troops. For two months, July and August, these units repelled five separate enemy assaults. During this same period they launched a number of their own attacks, striking the enemy's flanks and rear and inflicting a great deal of damage on the enemy. Our own forces, however, also suffered heavy attrition, especially in units defending the city. Eighty percent of our casualties were caused by U.S. air attacks and U.S. naval gunfire support.

The strength of each battalion fell to only 50 or 60 combatants. Every day the Front Headquarters sent one company (about 100 fighters) of reinforcements to the units defending the city, but this was not sufficient to replace those troops killed and wounded. On 7 September the enemy launched a coordinated attack with two divisions, the Airborne and the Marines, reinforced by two Ranger Groups, a number of artillery battalions and tank squadrons, and M-125 flamethrower vehicles. This force mounted a large offensive from four directions, all directed at the Citadel. A support plan utilizing the maximum available firepower

of the U.S. Air Force and the U.S. Navy was developed to support this operation.[12] Fighting under conditions of great inferiority in both manpower and firepower, our troops used battle fortifications and the walls of the Citadel to contest
every inch of ground, every piece of wall, every section of trench. Some units
fought to the last man or to the last round of ammunition. During this time there
were heavy rainstorms in Tri-Thien and the rivers rose to a high level. Our fighting positions were all flooded. Efforts to deploy our combat forces and ship in
supplies encountered great difficulties. On 16 September the 18th Infantry Regiment was ordered to cross the Thach Han River to support our forces fighting in
the Citadel. Because the enemy held control of the crossing points and because
all our river-crossing equipment had been destroyed by the enemy's air force and
artillery, the regiment was only able to get a portion of its forces across the river.
The units fighting in the Citadel, which had suffered heavy casualties, were
ordered to withdraw at 1800 hours that day.

From the time the enemy began his counterattack through 16 September, the
fighting in the area of the Quang Tri Citadel and Quang Tri city had lasted almost
three months. To support our political requirements and the requirements of our
diplomatic struggle, the units fighting to defend Quang Tri City and the Citadel
had firmly held their fighting positions for 81 days under a ferocious barrage of
bombs and shells and under conditions of great inferiority in strength in comparison with enemy forces. The cadre and soldiers of the Quang Tri Front had set
a shining example of revolutionary heroism, had completed their combat duties
in an outstanding manner, had tied down a major portion of the enemy's mobile
strategic reserve forces, and had encouraged and created favorable conditions for
our diplomatic struggle and to allow other battlefronts to expand their own
attacks. In this battle our army gained much valuable experience in the defense
of a fortified position.

The puppet army had retaken the city, but they had also suffered heavy losses.
They had to withdraw the 258th Marine Brigade to the rear to regroup and consolidate and bring the 147th Marine Brigade forward to replace it. They also had to
bring in the 1st Ranger Group to serve as a reserve force for the Airborne Division.

With a firm understanding of the orders of the Central Military Party Committee that "clearly, only by using tactics involving the defense of fortified positions can we achieve victory,"[13] beginning in early September 1972 the Front
Command directed its subordinate divisions to develop an "area defense combat
plan" aimed at defeating the enemy's counterattacks and defending our liberated
areas. Overcoming the enemy's hail of bombs and shells and the difficulties caused
by rain and flooding, all units focused their efforts on building a network of in-
depth defensive positions, creating positions that could defend each individual
area. While building up our positions and redeploying our forces, each regiment
was pulled back to the rear to regroup, consolidate, and prepare for new battles.

On 22 September, with strong fire support from U.S. aircraft and warships, the puppet army launched Operation "Lam Son 72A" to retake the entire

liberated zone of Quang Tri province. Using our network of defensive positions, our troops stubbornly repelled every enemy attack and maintained firm control of the liberated area of Quang Tri from the Thach Han River to Dong Ha–Cua Viet.

In the Central Highlands the 66th and 28th Infantry Regiments continued to attack and block road traffic on Route 14, defeating all the enemy 23rd Division's counterattacks on the outskirts of Kontum city. The 320A Infantry Division marched down to western Gia Lai province [Pleiku province], overran the outposts at Tam and Chu Nghe, forced the withdrawal of the Chu Po outpost, and mounted an extended siege of the border defense base at Duc Co, which was held by one puppet commando battalion. Aided by local armed forces and by ethnic minority peoples, the division attacked and crippled four enemy battalions that were moving up to relieve the base and then, on 21 November 1972, attacked and captured the Duc Co base.

On 20 September 1972, with the approval of the Central Military Party Committee and the Ministry of Defense, the Party Committee and Headquarters of the Central Highlands Front formed the 10th Infantry Division. Included in the division structure were the 28th, 66th, and 95th Infantry Regiments plus eight specialty branch battalions. All these units had been built into modern, regular units in North Vietnam, had endured many years of combat, and had matured with the love, support, and combat assistance of the ethnic minority people of the Central Highlands.

On 12 October 1972, the 10th Division conducted its first battle, destroying the Plei Can position held by the puppet 95th Ranger Battalion. During this battle the soldiers of the 40th Artillery Group disassembled their 85mm and 105mm guns and carried them to points close to the enemy's positions, where they could provide direct fire on the enemy, supporting our infantry and tanks during the assault. On 29 October the 10th Division destroyed the base at Duc Xieng during a battle lasting 30 minutes.

After a period of combat on the battlefields of the Central Highlands, the 2nd Division of Military Region 5 and the 52nd Infantry Regiment of the 320A Division were ordered to return to the lowlands of Military Region 5. There these units, together with the 3rd Infantry Division, the 711th Infantry Division, the 459th Sapper Regiment, and local armed forces, launched a general offensive campaign in the three provinces of Quang Da, Quang Nam, and Quang Ngai. On 18 September the 711 Division (minus), with fire support provided by a 130mm artillery unit from the Military Region Command, fought the key battle of the campaign in the Cam Doi–Que Son area, eliminating from the battlefield the puppet 5th Infantry Regiment and 4th Armored Regiment. The Que Son–Lac Son area was completely liberated. The people in a number of villages in the districts of Que Son and Tien Phuoc (in Quang Nam province) and the districts of Ba To, Mo Duc, and Duc Pho (in Quang Ngai province) rose up, surrounding and capturing puppet soldiers as they attempted to flee, eliminating enemy thugs, and liberating their hamlets and villages. During this period it was still raining in the Central Highlands and in Tri-Thien. The scale of activity of our troops on these battlefields declined. The Americans and their puppets brought ten regiments of infantry and armor to the lowlands of Military Region 5 to counter our attacks. Meanwhile, the main force divisions of Military Region 5 had not received timely troop reinforcements, replacements for weapons, or food supplies. The enemy retook a number of areas we had liberated in northern Binh Dinh, southwestern Quang Da, and northwestern Quang Nam.

In eastern Cochin China, after three assaults against An Loc [the province capital of Binh Long] had not succeeded in taking the enemy position, the COSVN Military Command ordered all units to change tactics and surround the city, at the same time organizing forces to hold blocking positions along Route 13 to attract and tie down the enemy in order to allow the soldiers and civilian population of the provinces of the Cochin China lowlands to expand their attacks and uprisings.

The 7th Division was given the mission of blocking a section of Route 13 between the Binh Long provincial capital and Chon Thanh, a distance of almost 25 kilometers. The terrain in this area was very open. To conduct this blocking operation the 7th Division had to build many interlocking defensive positions and organize forces to defend the blocking positions and mobile forces made up of elite infantry and artillery subunits. From the end of May to mid-August 1972, units of the 7th Division held their blocking positions and launched mobile attacks, repelling many attacks by the puppet 21st and 25th Infantry Divisions, by the 1st and 3rd Airborne Brigades, by the 3rd, 4th, and 5th Ranger Groups, and by the 3rd and 9th Armored Regiments. The fighting was savage, especially in the area of the Tau O blocking position. There our troops on many occasions fought hand-to-hand battles with enemy troops, struggling for control of each roadblock, each section of trench, each gun position. In late August the 16th Infantry Regiment and the 429th Sapper Regiment crept deep behind enemy lines to the area of Chon Thanh and Lai Khe and attacked the forward headquarters of the puppet 3rd Corps and the puppet 25th Division. Two enemy battalions moving to relieve the forward headquarters were attacked and suffered heavy casualties at Bau Bang. The northern defenses of Saigon were threatened. The Americans and their puppets were forced to pull the 25th Division back to the rear. The enemy operation to clear Route 13 and relieve Binh Long city, which had lasted for more than three months, ended in total failure. The puppet 21st and 25th Divisions suffered heavy damage, the 9th Armored Regiment was annihilated, and the siege of Binh Long city continued. Route 13 became "Thunder Road" to enemy troops.

In the Mekong Delta, implementing instructions from the Politburo, COSVN and the COSVN Military Party Committee launched an offensive campaign in the area north and south of Route 4 in My Tho province and in part of Kien Phong province. The objective was to "shatter part of the enemy's network of oppression and encourage an offensive and uprising movement by the civilian masses in the provinces of Tra Vinh and Ben Tre."[14] This was an area of strategic importance to the enemy, and he had deployed there one infantry division, two separate infantry regiments, and two armored regiments. The enemy had built three lines of defense: the border defense line, the line through the center of the Plain of Reeds, and the Route 4 line.

Pursuant to instructions of the Central Military Party Committee to "mass troops, weapons, and technical equipment for the campaign,"[15] in early June 1972 the COSVN Military Party Committee and the COSVN Military Command moved the 5th Infantry Division, the 24th, 271st, and 207th Infantry Regiments, and the 28th Artillery Regiment from Loc Ninh and Tay Ninh to assembly areas north of the Vietnamese-Cambodian border. Also participating in the campaign were Military Region 8's 1st, 88th, and 320th Regiments and the armed forces and mass political struggle forces of the provinces and districts in the campaign area. Lieutenant General Hoang Van Thai, COSVN Military Commander, assumed direct command of this campaign.

COSVN's main force units opened fire on 10 June 1972, attacking the Long Khot district military headquarters and the town of Moc Hoa along the enemy's border defensive line. Because the time available for preparations was limited and because the combat strength of our troops had not been rebuilt following their attacks against An Loc, our troops were unable to take their objectives. Our units shifted to siege tactics and attacked enemy forces moving up to relieve the besieged positions, inflicting heavy damage on four battalions of the puppet 7th Division. The main force regiments of Military Region 8 and local force troops of My Tho province launched strong attacks north and south of Route 4, supporting the guerrillas and the civilian population in destroying the enemy's network of oppression and seizing control of local areas. In Cai Lay district (My Tho province), we surrounded and forced the withdrawal of 25 outposts, supporting the local population in uprisings to destroy "strategic hamlets." The enemy hurriedly moved the 9th Division and the 4th Ranger Group (subordinate to 4th Corps) up to strengthen the defenses of Route 4.

Moving into the second phase (beginning on 3 July 1972), the Campaign Command left two regiments behind to tie down enemy forces along the border defense line and moved four main force regiments deep into enemy territory north and south of Route 4 to support local armed forces in stepping up their attacks and uprisings. On this new battlefield COSVN's main force units overcame many difficulties and adversities, working with the main force regiments of Military Region 8 to annihilate, encircle, or threaten many enemy positions, defeat enemy relief operations, and cripple six battalions of the puppet 9th Division.

With the support of our main force troops, local armed forces and political struggle forces of the masses in the provinces of My Tho, Kien Phong, Kien Tuong, and Ben Tre caused attrition to or dispersed dozens of enemy Regional Force battalions and Popular Force companies, surrounded and forced the withdrawal of scores of outposts, captured thousands of enemy spies and thugs, and seized the weapons of and dispersed 50 People's Self-Defense teams. Over 7,000 youths enlisted in our revolutionary armed forces. Many villages organized guerrilla platoons and built combat villages. A number of districts were able to organize two companies of local force troops.

The general offensive campaign to attack the pacification program in Military Region 8 lasted more than three months and secured important victories. For the first time in the history of the lowlands of Cochin China, we were able to combine the offensive and uprising strength of our three types of armed forces and our mass political forces in a large-scale campaign. We eliminated more than 30,000 enemy troops from the battlefield, annihilated ten enemy battalions, attacked and crippled five regiments of the 7th and 9th Divisions, annihilated or forced 500 outposts to surrender, liberated 350,000 people, and gained control over 72 villages in My Tho province and in parts of Ben Tre, Kien Phong, and Kien Tuong provinces. A large main force element (equivalent to two divisions) had gained a foothold in a strategic area of the lowlands of Cochin China.

Taking advantage of this period when the main strength of the puppet 4th Corps was forced to deal with our offensive campaigns in eastern Cochin China and in Military Region 8, the main force regiments of Military Region 9 and the local armed forces of its provinces stepped up their attacks, annihilating or inflicting severe casualties on a number of Regional Force battalions, forcing the surrender or withdrawal of hundreds of outposts, and establishing many liberated "spots" with a population in the tens of thousands in Ca Mau, Long My, Thanh Tri, Giong Rieng, and Vinh Thuan. The provinces of Can Tho, Soc Trang, and Tra Vinh were each able to organize a second local force battalion. Our militia and guerrilla forces in the villages and hamlets grew by more than 4,000 people.

By the end of October 1972, the strategic offensive by our soldiers and civilians on the battlefields of South Vietnam had lasted more than six months. Using the striking power of combined-arms forces, our army had shattered many of the enemy's outer defensive lines and then switched over to attacking enemy counterattack forces to defend our liberated areas. An important element of our main force troops had moved down into the lowlands and coordinated with local armed forces and mass political forces to launch a general offensive campaign to disrupt the enemy's pacification plan. After defeating puppet troops fighting with U.S. fire support, our army fought directly against and defeated the U.S. Air Force and the U.S. Navy. In the North our armed forces, fighting side by side with the entire population, defeated, to a significant extent at least, the war of destruction and the blockade conducted by the U.S. Air Force and the U.S. Navy. At the same time, our army and civilian population continued economic production, increased the supply of manpower and material support provided to the battlefields, and, together with the armed forces and population of the South, expanded our strategic offensive.

Based on our great military victories on the battlefield, on 8 October 1972 our Government submitted a draft treaty entitled "Agreement to End the War and Reestablish Peace in Viet Nam."

Because it was in a posture of failure, the United States was forced to agree to the conditions we set forward in our draft treaty. They dragged the negotiations out, however, and were not yet ready to sign. Nixon's intention was to get past the U.S. presidential elections in November and then prepare for a reckless new military adventure to gain a strong advantage in both the military and diplomatic spheres.

Correctly assessing the new plots and schemes of the American imperialists and on the basis of the victories of the strategic offensive of 1972, our armed forces and our entire population made urgent preparations and readied ourselves for new battles.

13

Air Defense and Air Force Units Conduct an Anti-Aircraft Campaign: Defeating the B-52 Strategic Bombing Raids Conducted by the American Imperialists

THE GENERAL SITUATION

As a result of the enormous victories won by our army and our people during the strategic offensive in South Vietnam and the battle against the American imperialist second war of destruction in the North, the nature of the war changed in many important ways. In South Vietnam our liberated area expanded and linked up with the great rear area in the North. Our main force troops now held secure footholds in the important strategic areas. The interspersion of areas under our control within areas controlled by the enemy was gradually changing the balance of forces in favor of our side. Opposition to the Vietnam War was having a profound effect on the economic and political situation in the United States, especially as the U.S. presidential elections drew nearer. On 17 October 1972, the two sides participating in the Paris talks approved the text of an "Agreement to End the War and Reestablish Peace in Vietnam" and agreed on a date for the signing of the treaty.[1] On 23 October, however, the U.S. government demanded another meeting with our representatives and requested changes in many provisions in the text of the treaty. The American scheme was to prolong the process and delay the signing of the agreement to buy time to strengthen the puppet army and puppet government. Then, once the presidential elections were over, the United States planned to seek a decisive military victory to force us to make concessions and agree to new treaty provisions favorable to the Americans.

Recognizing this new enemy plot, the Politburo of the Central Committee of the Party declared:

> In the immediate future the enemy will be under fewer political constraints because the U.S. presidential elections will be over. We must, therefore, be on guard against the possibility that the United States will increase its mili-

tary operations. We must absolutely avoid becoming negligent and dropping our guard. No matter what kind of reckless action the U.S. imperialists may take, however, they cannot reverse the present situation. We are on the road to victory, time is on our side, and we will certainly defeat the U.S. "Vietnamization" strategy and win even greater victories.

On 26 October 1972 our Government issued a public statement on the "status of the negotiations on the current situation in Vietnam," clearly laying out our just position and our goodwill and exposing the dishonest schemes of the U.S. authorities. Our government appealed to our troops and our people throughout the nation to continue the resistance struggle against the Americans until final victory was achieved. It also appealed to all fraternal nations and to the people of the world to support the just struggle of the people of Vietnam.

The mission of the armed forces in this new situation was to build, redeploy, and expand our forces; to continue the strategic offensive; to defeat enemy schemes and operations aimed at seizing our territory in the South; to defeat an intensified war of destruction in the North; to correctly carry out our duty of supporting the forward battlefields no matter what the situation; and to overcome incorrect thinking and assessment, such as delusions of peace, passively sitting back to await the outcome of the negotiations, negligence, lack of vigilance, etc.

PREPARING FOR BATTLE AGAINST THE B-52s

After winning reelection to a second term, U.S. President Nixon urgently prepared for a new military adventure. In November the United States hurriedly sent additional military aid to the Saigon puppet regime[2] and pushed the puppet army to launch counterattacks to seize our liberated areas. As for North Vietnam, the United States doubled the number of B-52 sorties[3] attacking our supply and communications lines in Military Region 4. They supplemented their armed reconnaissance flights with reconnaissance sorties by SR-71 aircraft and unmanned reconnaissance aircraft to prepare for a major B-52 attack against Hanoi.[4]

On 25 November 1972, the Central Military Party Committee issued instructions on "increasing combat readiness." These instructions clearly stated that we must be on alert against new acts of adventurism by the enemy in the near future. The enemy may resume bombing north of the 20th parallel at a level even more intense than their previous bombing campaign. He might recklessly send B-52s to attack and destroy such targets as Hanoi, Haiphong, storage areas, transportation intersections, and our populated areas, and he might increase his naval bombardment of our coastal areas. All units must be extremely vigilant and must review and perfect combat readiness preparations and combat and defensive dispersal plans.

The Central Military Party Committee ordered our Air Force and missile troops to continue their research studies, update fighting methods, and actively train soldiers in ways to combat B-52s and in measures to counter enemy jamming and to combat the enemy's laser-guided and TV-guided bombs.

The B-52 was a U.S. Air Force strategic bomber capable of operating at night and during difficult weather conditions. It dropped its bombs from altitudes between 9,000 and 11,000 meters. Each aircraft was equipped with 16 active electronic jammers, two anti-radar chaff dispensers, and missiles that, when launched, produced a radar signature similar to a B-52 to deceive hostile radar. The United States had a total of about 450 B-52 aircraft. Ever since its introduction, the B-52 had always been considered the "most flexible" weapon in the U.S. strategic weapons triad (strategic missiles, strategic nuclear submarines, and B-52 strategic bombers).[5]

The American imperialists began using B-52s in mid-1965 to attack a number of our base areas in the South. In 1966 they began using B-52s in attacks against North Vietnam. The scale and intensity of B-52 operations steadily increased, keeping pace with the expansion of the war. After conducting numerous attacks without suffering any losses, especially after the carpet bombing of Haiphong on 16 April 1972, the U.S. military was more certain than ever that "the B-52 can strike any target in North Vietnam." They believed the use of this strategic weapon would crush the fighting spirit of our soldiers and our people and force us to concede defeat.

In July 1965, when the U.S. imperialists began using B-52s in South Vietnam, Chairman Ho Chi Minh affirmed our army's and our people's determination to fight and to win: "Even though the American imperialists have lots of guns and lots of money, even though they have B-57s, B-52s, no matter what other type of 'B' they may have, we will still fight them. No matter how many aircraft and no matter how many troops the Americans use, we will still fight them, and when we fight them we will certainly win."[6]

To carry out Uncle Ho's instructions our armed forces conducted studies and vigorously prepared to shoot down this "Super Flying Fortress." In February 1968, as our troops and people in the South were conducting the General Offensive and simultaneous uprisings, the Central Military Party Committee gave the Air Defense–Air Force Command the mission of developing an anti-aircraft battle plan to defend against B-52 bombing raids on Hanoi. The headquarters staff of the Air Force–Air Defense Service completed a "draft plan for combating B-52 strategic bombers." This document was issued in January 1969 to assist our missile troops in training their combat teams. A number of cadre groups from the Air Defense–Air Force Service, from the 238th, 258th, 274th, and 236th Missile Regiments, and from a number of fighter squadrons were pulled together to conduct study seminars and combat operations in the skies over Military Region 4 to seek ways to attack the enemy's B-52s.

With the start of the 1972 strategic offensive on the battlefields of South Vietnam and the U.S. imperialists' second war of destruction against the North, research in combating B-52s received increased attention. In July 1972 the General

Staff ordered the Air Defense–Air Force Service to carry out an urgent research and development program to combat B-52s, to draft training documents, and to train our troops in tactics for combating B-52s in various different types of complicated situations. Senior General Vo Nguyen Giap, member of the Politburo, Secretary of the Central Military Party Committee, and Minister of Defense, personally worked with the Air Defense–Air Force Service, the Radar Command, the Missile Command, the Air Force Command, and the commanders of the air defense divisions defending Hanoi to establish combat procedures for an anti-aircraft campaign to defend Hanoi from B-52s.

In early September 1972, the General Staff and the Headquarters of the Air Defense–Air Force Service completed an air defense plan to defeat an enemy bombing offensive using B-52s. The plan posed a scenario in which the U.S. imperialists would launch a massive attack using B-52s supported by tactical aircraft. Their primary targets would be Hanoi and Haiphong, with Hanoi being the most important target. The plan established the following as the missions of the Air Defense–Air Force Service in this eventuality: to maintain the initiative and avoid surprise; to concentrate forces for the defense of Hanoi; to increase our combined defensive strength, using missile and air force elements as the primary force to attack the B-52s, with missiles being the key attack element; and to defeat the enemy from the very opening shots of the battle, in the first wave, by shooting down B-52s and capturing their pilots and crew. The plan also laid out a number of key points regarding deployment of forces, tactics for each separate specialty branch, and combat support activities.

Therefore, by late 1972 we had already made a number of basic decisions about our armed forces' anti-aircraft campaign tactics, such as assessing the enemy's schemes and techniques; determining the primary direction and target of the enemy attack; and determining the forces and tactics we would use. After approving the battle plan the General Staff rapidly redeployed forces to create a battle posture utilizing our three types of troops and prepared a people's air defense plan aimed at exploiting to the maximum extent possible the power of People's War to prepare ourselves to defeat the new plots and schemes of the enemy. The 361st Air Defense Division, made up of two missile regiments (the 261st and 257th) and five anti-aircraft artillery regiments, was responsible for the defense of Hanoi. The 274th Missile Regiment, which had just returned from the forward battlefields, served as the reserve force for the primary theater of operations: Hanoi. The 363rd Air Defense Division, consisting of two missile regiments (the 238th and 285th) and two anti-aircraft artillery regiments, defended Haiphong. The 375th Air Defense Division, consisting of one missile regiment (the 268th) and five anti-aircraft artillery regiments, defended Route 1 from Hanoi north to Lang Son. The 365th Air Defense Division, consisting of two missile regiments (the 267th and 275th) and five anti-aircraft artillery regiments, defended our supply lines in Thanh Hoa, Nghe An, and Ha Tinh.

Deployed throughout the different zones and concentrated in the main target areas were the anti-aircraft battalions and companies of the military regions, provinces, and cities. Added to these were our militia self-defense forces, which consisted of 350 direct combat teams and units equipped with more than 100 anti-aircraft cannon (100mm, 85mm, 37mm, 20mm), 550 anti-aircraft machine guns (12.7mm and 14.5mm), and 700 medium and light machine guns. The 921st, 923rd, 925th, and 927th Air Force Fighter Regiments were all given the missions of fighting to defend the key sector: Hanoi. Our radar stations were deployed in an interlocking network. Each tactical zone operated six to nine different types of radar, which worked together to track different types of aircraft approaching from different directions and at different altitudes. By October 1972, our radar warning sites covering the skies of Hanoi were fully deployed. The cadre and soldiers of a number of radar companies carried their equipment over long distances and across difficult terrain to set up their radars atop high mountains and on offshore islands to further extend our warning range.

The need to increase the combat power of the Air Defense–Air Force Service to the level demanded by its new mission received special attention from the Central Military Party Committee and the High Command. Because the enemy had made a number of technical improvements and was now using sophisticated jamming equipment on many different types of aircraft, we had problems identifying and tracking B-52s that were within firing range. Most of our radar guidance trackers were new and had just completed their training. Each air defense division in the North had only two or three experienced radar guidance trackers. Most of our cadre from battalion level on down had only recently been promoted from the enlisted ranks. For this reason, no unit had ever been able to shoot down a B-52 "on the spot." A number of cadre and soldiers were concerned and doubted that we could shoot down this "Super Flying Fortress."

In early October 1972, the Air Defense–Air Force Service Party Committee issued a resolution on strengthening political education and guiding political thought to instill in the cadre and soldiers of the Service a deep understanding of the Central Committee's strategic resolution, to encourage cadre and soldiers to overcome all obstacles and difficulties, to develop a collective spirit and a spirit of innovation, and to instill resolve to shoot down "on the spot" large numbers of aircraft, including even B-52s, and capture their pilots and crews as prisoners. The Service held a conference focusing on ideological activities, on mobilizing cadre and soldiers to actively study and train, and on launching a scientific and technical movement to find effective fighting methods.

Following the conference, the entire Service undertook a round of political activities aimed at raising understanding of the situation and of the Service's duties; at building a high spirit of vigilance and combat readiness; and at achieving a high level of combat effectiveness. Each separate specialty branch and each individual unit held a conference to prepare an initial assessment of its experience in force building and combat during the first six months of the U.S. imperialist's second war of destruction. Cadre conferences were also organized to discuss ways to combat B-52s. A number of issues arising from experience gained in operations were analyzed and presented as a foundation upon which the specialty branches could build to prepare field manuals and train their troops. These issues included countering enemy jamming; distinguishing real B-52 echoes from fake B-52 echoes when the aircraft was within firing range; coordinating combat operations with the transmission of radar signals; using both electronic and optical equipment to track enemy aircraft targets; lessons learned in massed combat; combined combat operations using both mobile and static forces; maintaining the initiative in attacking enemy aircraft all along their approach route, from far away to nearby; achieving secrecy and surprise, etc.

At the end of October 1972 a conference of radar guidance trackers from the entire Air Defense Service was held at Radar Company 18, 291st Regiment. The conference analyzed the special characteristics of B-52 jammers and the ability of each different type of radar to identify targets. The conference produced many practical ideas for use in developing a "model for identifying B-52 targets hidden within jamming interference." After the conference the Service sent a radar guidance tracker group to Military Region 4, an area where enemy B-52s regularly operated, to practice on-site methods of recognizing enemy aircraft targets. With high determination to precisely identify and track B-52s, our radar troops practiced tirelessly, resolving to "pierce the interference to locate the enemy" and "not allow the Fatherland to be taken by surprise."

In early November 1972 the Air Defense–Air Force Headquarters held a conference for missile troops to discuss methods for engaging B-52s. Command cadre of the different battalions, a number of outstanding missile firing teams, and a number of cadre from the General Departments and the Military Science Institute participated in the conference. The conference devoted a great deal of time to discussions about the manual on "methods for fighting B-52s," which had been drafted by the Air Defense Headquarters staff. A number of issues arising from practical combat experience gained by radar trackers and missile control officers serving along strategic transportation corridor 559, in MR-4, in Hai Phong, etc., were reported and carefully discussed. These issues included selecting jamming frequencies, when to turn on radar transmitters, the proper location for firing missiles, firing methods, methods for maintaining contact with the target, ways to counter the enemy's Shrike anti-radar missiles, etc.

After the conference the manual for missile troops on "methods for fighting B-52s" was disseminated.[7] The manual helped units standardize their thinking and their combat tactics and added to the quality of combat training given to our troops. From the initial draft (1969) to the time of its final dissemination, the manual on "methods for fighting B-52s" for missile troops had been systematically supplemented and corrected. This manual was an important scientific and military achievement for our armed forces.

To test our fighting methods, in early November 1972 the Air Defense–Air Force Command sent a cadre group and a number of combat teams to Nghe An to work with the 263rd Missile Regiment in combat engagements against B-52s. During the night of 22 November 1972, the 43rd and 44th Battalions of the 263rd Missile Regiment launched four missiles that destroyed two B-52s, one of which crashed in the Laos-Thailand border area, 200 kilometers from our missile firing position and 64 kilometers [sic] from the Utapao airbase in Thailand. This victory by the 263rd Regiment confirmed that our missile troops were capable of shooting down this American "Super Flying Fortress."

The lessons learned by the 263rd Missile Regiment in engaging B-52s were rapidly disseminated to all units. Our missile battalions reconstructed on their radar screens different jamming patterns and numerous complicated scenarios for use in training our radar trackers. The Air Force trained its combat pilots in day and night flying in all types of difficult weather conditions. They practiced attacking B-52s and engaging and driving away strike aircraft. Pilots also practiced takeoffs and landings from rough combat airfields with short runways. Anti-aircraft artillery troops practiced tactics for engaging tactical aircraft that were escorting and protecting the B-52s and for firing at enemy aircraft flying at low levels and at night to defend our missile firing positions. Divisional and regimental headquarters units organized cadre training and practiced command procedures, the use of radio communications equipment, and achieving the concentrations of fire called for in our battle plans. Support operations, especially technical support to the different specialty branches, were rationalized and made more efficient.

A number of combat airfields were secretly constructed around the outer perimeter to ensure that our aircraft could maintain the initiative and achieve surprise when taking off to attack enemy aircraft approaching from all directions and to allow our aircraft returning from combat to land quickly and safely. We built additional field launch positions for mobile missile units, fake positions to deceive and attract enemy aircraft, and both static and mobile gun positions for our anti-aircraft artillery units. A number of radar stations were deployed on the peaks of tall mountains to increase their range. Combining visual observer stations with technical [radar] observation stations, we built a new warning network with a forward line, a rear line, and with coverage of our flanks, giving us the ability to detect targets in any location and coming from any direction. A reserve communications net and a radio communications system guaranteed unbroken command and control from the top down to the bottom. Technical subunits were assigned the mission of supplying missiles to our missile firing positions. Each subunit set up two production lines that worked 24 hours a day. In addition to our regular production facilities, each subunit also established partial, component missile production lines at field facilities to further disperse our forces and equipment. These measures both ensured the security of our missile production and enabled us to speed up the supply of missiles to our units. All missile battalions conducted regular scheduled maintenance and each missile battalion was issued one complete combat load of missiles.

Local militia and self-defense forces were issued additional anti-aircraft guns.[8] Hanoi itself had eight 100mm anti-aircraft artillery batteries manned by the militia of its four suburban districts and by the self-defense forces of the four precincts of the inner city. Hanoi also organized direct combat and mobile self-defense interunits consisting of a number of anti-aircraft machine guns operated by state enterprises and block committees. Additional rescue equipment, including cranes, bulldozers, etc., were issued to our militia and self-defense emergency aid, rescue, and recovery teams. The network of combat fortifications, fighting positions, and air-raid tunnels and holes was repaired and expanded. Warehouses and supply stockpiles, especially military supplies in the principal target areas and in locations we suspected B-52s might attack, were rapidly evacuated and dispersed. Hundreds of thousands of residents of Hanoi, Haiphong, and other cities were evacuated.

On 24 November 1972, Senior General Van Tien Dung, Politburo member and Chief of Staff of the People's Army, received a final briefing from Senior Colonel Le Van Tri, Commander of the Air Defense–Air Force Service, and Senior Colonel Hoang Phuong, Political Commissar of the Air Defense–Air Force Service, on the air defense campaign plan to combat a strategic bombing offensive by the U.S. imperialists using B-52s against Hanoi and Haiphong. The Chief of Staff approved the plan and ordered the Air Defense–Air Force Headquarters to complete all combat preparations by 3 December 1972.[9]

THE BATTLE BEGINS

By mid-December 1972, the situation had become extremely critical. On 13 December, because of the stubborn, duplicitous attitude of the United States, the Paris talks reached an impasse. On 14 December, Nixon formally approved the plan for a strategic bombing offensive using B-52s against Hanoi. The bombing offensive would begin on 17 December [18 December Hanoi time]. The United States sent two more aircraft carriers, the *Enterprise* and the *Saratoga*, to the Gulf of Tonkin, bringing the total number of U.S. aircraft carriers operating in the waters from east of Ky Anh (Ha Tinh province) to the area east of Thanh Hoa to five. Fifty KC-130 [*sic*] tanker aircraft for refueling B-52s were sent from the United States to the Philippines. A headquarters element for the 57th Provisional Strategic Air Division was formed to command three B-52 wings with a total of 103 aircraft and 250 flight crews based at Anderson Airfield in Guam and Utapao airfield in Thailand. On 16 December, many flights of U.S. aircraft flew reconnaissance missions over Hanoi, Haiphong, and over our network of airfields in North Vietnam. On 17 December, the enemy conducted a provocative naval gunfire attack and sowed mines in the coastal waters off Haiphong from the mouth of the Nam Trieu River to Cat Ba Island. On 18 December, the U.S. Pacific Command canceled all B-52 operational flights throughout the Indochina theater in anticipation of new orders.

Closely monitoring the schemes and activities of the enemy, on 17 December 1972 our High Command placed our Air Defense–Air Force units on the highest combat alert status to guard against possible B-52 night attacks from the 20th parallel northward. The General Staff and the General Political Department, in cooperation with the Air Defense–Air Force Headquarters, inspected and encouraged our troops as they finished their preparations for battle.

At 1830 hours on 18 December 1972, the 16th Radar Company (291st Regiment), and shortly thereafter (at 1910 hours the same day) the 45th Radar Company (291st Regiment), deployed in Nghe An province, detected a number of groups of enemy B-52s flying north along the Mekong River. Closely monitoring the enemy's flight path, Radar Station Commander Nghiem Dinh Tich reported to Air Defense Headquarters that "B-52s are now flying toward Hanoi." The General Staff rapidly relayed this situation report to the Politburo and the Central Military Party Committee and, at 1915 hours, ordered a B-52 alert throughout North Vietnam. Twenty-five minutes later, at 1940 hours, B-52s began bombing Hanoi. Our armed forces and civilian population had received 25 minutes advance warning before the attack began. Our radar troops had lived up to their slogan, "We will not allow the Fatherland to be taken by surprise."

From that time on, for 12 consecutive days and nights, the American imperialists, committing the full strength of their strategic air force and of their Air Force and Navy tactical air arms, carried out a strategic bombing offensive against Hanoi, Haiphong city, and a number of industrial centers in North Vietnam.[10] They carpet-bombed hospitals, schools, and crowded residential areas, committing barbarous crimes against our people.

Because of their modern electronic jamming equipment, because they had mobilized a large force of B-52 bombers and tactical support aircraft to rain bombs on different target areas from the very first day of the operation, and because they sent strategic and tactical aircraft to conduct surprise night attacks to support continuous attacks by tactical aircraft throughout the daylight hours, the U.S. imperialists believed our missiles and our air force would be "neutralized." They thought they would be able to quickly achieve the objectives of their strategic bombing offensive.

This was a reckless new military adventure by the U.S. imperialists in their war of aggression against our nation, an aerial bombing attack using strategic aircraft on a scale unprecedented in the history of warfare.

During the first night's bombing raid (18 December), the U.S. imperialists sent three consecutive attack waves, with a total of 90 B-52 sorties and 135 sorties by tactical aircraft, to strike the airfields around Hanoi (Kep, Noi Bai, Gia Lam, Hoa Lac, Yen Bai), the areas of Dong Anh, Yen Vien, Duc Giang, and the transmitter facilities of the Voice of Vietnam Radio in Me Tri. Their naval aircraft also flew 28 sorties against Haiphong.

Because they had been well prepared, the armed forces and civilian population of Hanoi, Haiphong, and the other local areas in North Vietnam entered the battle with a mood of great self-confidence. Our Air Force units engaged enemy aircraft on the outer perimeter. Our anti-aircraft artillery troops and our low-level wall of fire from the militia and self-defense forces opened fire at the proper time, forcing the enemy's tactical aircraft to climb to higher altitudes. Our radar and missile troops overcame the different types of enemy jamming, countered the enemy's Shrike missiles, and, switching on our radar transmitters, detected the B-52 targets. The night skies over Hanoi grew bright with the bursts of our anti-aircraft shells.

At 2013 hours, operating from a firing position beside the walls of the ancient Loa Citadel, a combat team of the 59th Battalion, 261st Regiment (Missile Control Officer Duong Van Thuan, Missile Guidance Trackers Ngo Van Tu, Le Xuan Linh, and Nguyen Van Do, all under the command of Battalion Commander Nguyen Thang), closely monitored the jamming frequencies and launched a missile at the proper position using the "three-point" targeting method, shooting down the first B-52. The carcass of the B-52 Flying Fortress was strewn across the rice fields of Phu Lo village (Dong Anh district), only three kilometers from the missile launch site. Three pirate crewmen were captured. This was the first B-52 shot down "on the spot" during the campaign, and it was also the first B-52 shot down "on the spot" anywhere on the battlefields of Vietnam. With this victory the 261st Missile Regiment earned the glorious tradition name of the "Loa Citadel Missile Group."

This initial victory encouraged the fighting spirit of the soldiers and of the civilian population of Hanoi. At 0439 hours on 19 December, a combat team of the 77th Battalion, 257th Regiment, under the command of Battalion Commander Dinh The Van, shot down "on the spot" one B-52 at Thanh Oai (Ha Tay province). In Nghe An, at 2016 hours on 18 December, the 52nd Battalion (267th Missile Regiment) shot down a B-52 just after it completed its criminal attack against Hanoi and was returning to its base. This B-52 crashed in the Lao-Thailand border area.

The battle of the night of 18 December ended. Our soldiers and civilians had shot down three B-52s (two of which crashed on the spot) and four tactical aircraft and had captured seven pirate aircrewmen. This glorious victory in our initial battle strongly encouraged the fighting resolve and will to win of the soldiers and civilians of the entire nation. It confirmed that the air defense forces of our three types of troops were fully capable of totally defeating the U.S. imperialist strategic bombing offensive using B-52s.

The Voice of Vietnam Radio Station, after being off the air for nine minutes because of the destruction of its transmission facilities at Me Tri, came back on the air with a strong signal to announce the news of the victory achieved by our soldiers and civilians and to denounce the barbaric crimes of the U.S. imperialists.

The entire nation looked to Hanoi and Haiphong.

A number of our military units in South Vietnam and the commanders of the Tri-Thien Front, of Region 5, and of COSVN, sent cables to the Air Defense–Air Force Command describing their excitement and the confidence they felt when they heard the news that Hanoi had shot down enemy B-52s on the spot.

THE BATTLE CONTINUES

On the morning of 19 December, the Politburo met to receive a briefing from the General Staff on the battle of the night of 18 December. The Politburo proclaimed that the armed forces had fought well, reminded all units to increase their vigilance to even higher levels, cautioned against complacency and satisfaction with our performance, and ordered that further, more complete preparations be made in order to be able to fight continuously and shoot down many B-52s. The Politburo directed local areas to correctly carry out defensive and evasive measures, to totally disperse the civilian population, to ensure that traffic along our lines of transportation and communication continued to flow smoothly, and to exploit this time when the enemy was concentrating his strategic and tactical aircraft to attack our northern provinces to make a strong push to increase the flow of supplies to the battlefields of South Vietnam.

The Standing Committee of the Air Defense–Air Force Party Committee launched a political motivation campaign throughout the Service to encourage cadre and soldiers to fight well and to garner great combat achievements in honor of the three historic dates, the 19th, 20th, and 22nd of December.

Every unit held meetings to compile lessons learned from combat experience, reinforced their fighting positions, and increased their ammunition stocks in preparation for the next battle. Our deployment of forces in several sectors was readjusted to adapt it to the situation. Missile supply teams worked constantly, day and night. The local population, led by our militia and self-defense forces, helped our engineers rapidly repair those airfields the enemy had attacked and strengthen the fortifications of the missile and anti-aircraft artillery firing positions. The civilian populations of Hanoi, Haiphong, and of a number of industrial centers were evacuated and dispersed in a rapid but orderly manner, totally evacuating the inner cities. Hundreds of buses and trucks were mobilized to support the evacuation. Rescue, aid, and recovery teams quickly dealt with the casualties and destruction in the areas that had been bombed. Employees of commercial enterprises carried their wares out to fighting positions and factories to support our soldiers, cadre, and industrial workers. The supply of electricity and water to support combat operations, economic production, and to sustain the daily lives of the people of the city continued uninterrupted.

On our roads through Thanh Hoa, Nghe An, Ha Tinh, and Quang Binh, taking advantage of this time when the enemy was concentrating his forces to attack

Hanoi and the northernmost provinces, our local population was mobilized to use many different types of transport equipment (railroad cars, trucks, bicycles) to carry out Transportation Campaigns "DB1" and "DB2" to rapidly ship a large quantity of supplies to the battlefield.[11] The volume of supplies shipped in one day equaled that shipped during the entire course of one or two of the previous months.

During the afternoon of 19 December the Ministry of Defense held a press conference at the International Club in Hanoi to announce our great victory and to denounce the criminal acts of the U.S. imperialists. Before a crowd of domestic and foreign reporters, six B-52 pirate crewmen confessed to Nixon's dangerous acts of war and to their own failure.

The progressive people of the world angrily denounced Nixon's criminal acts. A number of U.S. allies spoke out in criticism of the U.S. government. The people of the socialist countries, the people of countries fighting for national liberation, and the peace-loving people of the capitalist countries were delighted with the great victory won by our armed forces and our people. Opposition to the U.S. war of aggression and support for Vietnam grew.

On 19 and 20 December, the U.S. imperialists sent a large force of B-52s, in coordination with nighttime low-level F-111 attacks and with daytime raids by tactical aircraft, to continue attacks against targets in Hanoi and its outlying suburbs. Navy attack aircraft continued bombing raids against Haiphong city. During the night of 19 December, our missile troops in Hanoi shot down two B-52s (although they did not crash on the spot). Personnel from the headquarters staff of the Air Defense Service went out to the missile units to work with their cadre and soldiers to gather experiences and find new fighting methods based on the use of the methods used so effectively by the 59th and 77th Missile Battalions during the night of 18 December.

During the evening of 20 December our air force pilots attacked a formation of enemy tactical aircraft, disrupting their plan for jamming and combined operations. This gave our missiles an opportunity to destroy B-52s. At 2000 hours, while the B-52s were flying in to attack Hanoi, the 77th, 78th, 79th, 88th, 93rd, and 94th Missile Battalions concentrated their fire on individual bombing cells, shooting down a total of five B-52s (three of which crashed on the spot). The slogan "one missile fired, one B-52 destroyed" was announced in all the missile battalions. At dawn on 21 December a second wave of B-52s attacked the city. The 77th Battalion fired two missiles, shooting down one B-52, which crashed on the spot.

Firing fewer missiles than had been used during the previous two nights (only 35 missiles were launched), Hanoi missile troops fought an outstanding annihilation battle, shooting down seven B-52s (five of which crashed on the spot) and capturing 12 B-52 crewmen. This was the night during which our troops shot down the most B-52s on the spot of all the 12 nights of the entire campaign.

In Haiphong, drawing on the experience of the previous two nights of combat, during the night of 20 December the anti-aircraft forces defending the city changed their previous tactic of dispersing their forces evenly throughout the city. They instead concentrated their firepower to engage the enemy as he came in from each separate direction, shooting down three tactical aircraft (one of which crashed on the spot) and capturing one pirate pilot.

Drawing on the experience of the initial three days and nights of combat and assessing what the enemy would do in the coming days, the High Command confirmed that the main enemy bombing target would continue to be Hanoi. The enemy would strike deep into the inner city and would bomb our missile firing positions. In order to continue our combat operations and shoot down many more aircraft, every unit was given the duty of protecting our missiles. Our air force pilots were ordered to find ways to close with their targets and shoot down B-52s in coordinated operations with our missile troops.

Pursuant to orders from the High Command, the 71st and 72nd Missile Battalions (285th Regiment) quickly moved from Haiphong to Hanoi and were deployed to cover the east and northeast. The 223rd and 262nd Anti-Aircraft Artillery Regiments marched up from Thanh Hoa to Hanoi, further strengthening the anti-aircraft artillery forces defending our missile launch positions. By 21 December, the anti-aircraft artillery force defending Hanoi had grown to a total of seven regiments. Missile production lines and missile unit repair teams stuck close to our firing positions to fulfill requirements for the rapid supply of missiles and for technical support. The local civilian population in areas where our missile troops were stationed cared for the needs of our cadre and soldiers and helped our troops reinforce their positions and camouflage fortifications and equipment.

Party, State, and military leaders visited our fighting positions to talk with our air defense–air force troops and to discuss different tactics for fighting the enemy. Prime Minister Pham Van Dong and Chief of the General Staff Colonel General Van Tien Dung visited the headquarters of the Service to receive a briefing on the situation from Air Defense Command. The Prime Minister transmitted the Politburo's congratulations to our air defense–air force units, solicitously inquired about the health of our troops, and encouraged our cadre and soldiers to fight to gain even greater victories. Senior General Vo Nguyen Giap, representing the Central Military Party Committee and the High Command, visited the 77th Missile Battalion, a unit that had shot down three B-52s on the spot. The General was personally briefed by the firing teams on their battles and he encouraged our missile troops to achieve many new feats of arms.

The American imperialists were greatly surprised to have lost so many B-52s, one after another, during the initial days of the campaign. They were forced to send additional B-52 aircraft and crews to Guam and Utapao. During the nights from 21 to 24 December they reduced their level of operations. Each night they sent only one attack wave against Hanoi, and each wave consisted of only 24 to 33 B-52 sorties. In an effort to force us to disperse our anti-aircraft forces, and especially our missiles, they spread out their attacks to a number of targets in Haiphong, Thai Nguyen, and Dong Mo (Lang Son province). In Hanoi tactical air force aircraft conducted day and night attacks against a number of targets in the inner city, including the Hang Co railyards, the Yen Phu electrical generating plant, the Bach Mai Hospital, etc. They paid special attention to locating and attacking our missile firing positions.

The anti-aircraft forces of our three types of troops continued to shoot down many enemy aircraft. During the night of 21–22 December, in only four minutes our Hanoi missile troops fired 17 missiles, shooting down on the spot three B-52s out of a total force of 24 B-52s in one bombing raid. We captured eight crewmen. In this battle we attained a high level of efficiency, destroying one-eighth of the enemy aircraft involved and attaining an efficiency of 13 percent, which is a high percentage of kills for air defense combat. During the night of 22 December our missile troops defending Haiphong fired 18 missiles, shooting down two B-52s. During the night of 24 December the 256th Anti-Aircraft Artillery Regiment, which was defending the city of Thai Nguyen with 100mm cannon, shot down one B-52. Fighting in coordination with our anti-aircraft artillery and missile troops, and with guidance provided by our radar troops, on 23 and 24 December our Mig-21 aircraft took off, blocked, and attacked the enemy's attack aircraft, shooting down one F-4. However, our air force pilots were unable to get close to the B-52s.

Our militia and self-defense forces organized a widespread anti-aircraft curtain of fire to ambush and shoot down the enemy on the spot and conducted mobile operations in coordination with our anti-aircraft artillery troops to destroy enemy attack aircraft and protect our missiles. During the night of 22 December the 14.5mm machine-gun unit of the self-defense interunit for the Hoan Kiem and Hai Ba Trung areas of Hanoi, using only 21 rounds of ammunition, shot down an American F-111A on the spot. The militia self-defense force of Lac Son in Hoa Binh province captured both pilots of this aircraft and shot down a helicopter sent in to rescue the pilots. The civilian population of Hanoi, Haiphong, Bac Thai, Tuyen Quang, Vinh Phu, Ha Tay, Hoa Binh, Hai Hung, Thai Binh, etc., saw with their very own eyes U.S. "Flying Fortresses" burning in the sky. The civilian population of a number of areas hunted down and captured many U.S. B-52 crewmen and turned them over to the prison camps in Hanoi.

BOTH SIDES REGROUP TO CONTINUE THE BATTLE

Because of their heavy defeats, and using as an excuse the Christmas holiday, at 2400 hours on 24 December 1972 the enemy temporarily suspended the bombing in order to reorganize its forces, stabilize the morale of its pilots and aircrews, and review their performance to come up with new attack plans.

The first phase of the anti-aircraft campaign to repel the U.S. imperialist strategic aerial offensive was over. In six days and nights, from 18 to 24 December, our soldiers and civilians had shot down 46 aircraft, including 17 B-52 strategic bombers and five F-111s, and had captured many pirate air crewmen.

Concluding that the enemy would make even heavier attacks and use even more cunning schemes during the coming days, and that their primary target would continue to be Hanoi, the General Staff ordered the headquarters of the military regions and the Air Defense–Air Force Command to take advantage of the enemy's temporary suspension of his attacks to strengthen our forces, to make better preparations in all areas, and to resolve to inflict even heavier defeats on the enemy during the second phase of the battle in order to secure total victory for our campaign.

On 25 December the Headquarters Command of the Air Defense–Air Force Service convened a meeting of all commanders of specialty branches, all division commanders, and of headquarters staff cadre to draw lessons from our combat experience during the first phase and to put together a number of principal measures for use by our units in preparation for the second phase of the battle. Our missile battalions reviewed each and every battle. Our air force regiments concentrated on studying the B-52 flight formations and on seeking ways to detect, approach, and attack them.

To strengthen the forces protecting Hanoi, the Air Defense–Air Force Command committed two additional reserve missile battalions (from the 274th Regiment) to the battle, increasing the number of missile units protecting Hanoi from nine battalions at the beginning of the campaign up to 13 battalions. Each missile launch position was protected by an anti-aircraft artillery battery. The most vital launch positions were defended by an entire anti-aircraft artillery battalion. A number of 37mm anti-aircraft batteries were moved into the inner city to protect important targets. Missile production units established additional production lines and worked night and day to provide additional missiles for our troops to use in combat. Military Region 4's missile reserve stockpile was quickly shipped to Hanoi. The local civilian population worked feverishly alongside our troops to reinforce our firing sites and to build new firing sites. The bombing recovery teams quickly packed up, evacuated, and dispersed warehouses, repaired transportation routes, etc. Postal, medical, and commercial enterprise cadre and personnel came out to our firing positions and fortifications to serve our troops and our people.

Hanoi, Haiphong, and the other local areas in the north prepared additional forces and fighting positions to strike even more painful blows against the enemy.

THE BATTLE RESUMES

At 1200 on 26 December 1972, U.S. tactical aircraft returned, bombing the cities of Hanoi, Haiphong, and Thai Nguyen. During the night of 26 December the enemy sent 126 B-52s to bomb Hanoi. They struck simultaneously from three directions and concentrated their attacks in a single wave directed against a number of different targets. This was the biggest and most important attack of the enemy's strategic aerial offensive. Crowded residential areas such as the Kham Thien area, the Tuong Mai and Mai Huong labor areas, the Bach Mai Hospital, etc., were bombed flat. Hundreds of ordinary citizens, including many old people, young children, and hospital patients were viciously murdered.

President Ton Duc Thang visited the Kham Thien area, solicitously talking with the people and encouraging the civilian population and the armed forces to turn their pain and suffering into a resolve to defeat the enemy. The cadre and soldiers of Hanoi's air defense forces turned their missile launchers and gun barrels toward Uy No, An Duong, Kham Thien, Bach Mai, etc., in memory of our fellow countrymen and fellow soldiers who had sacrificed their lives. They then turned their launchers and gun barrels toward the Ba Dinh Conference Hall to pledge to the Party and to Uncle Ho that "we swear our determination to die so that the Fatherland will live," that "we will fight for the independence and freedom of the Fatherland" and "for our beloved Hanoi."

The battle of the night of 26 December lasted for more than one hour. Having been well prepared in terms of their morale, organization, and tactics, the air defense forces of the three types of troops of Hanoi, Haiphong, and Thai Nguyen fought an outstanding battle of annihilation, shooting down 18 aircraft, including eight B-52s (five of which crashed on the spot), and capturing many pirate air crewmen.

This was a heavy defeat for the American imperialists. During the following nights they reduced the number of B-52 sorties, sending only 50 to 60 aircraft each night.

During the night of 27 December our air force and missile troops continued to perform new feats of arms. At 2220 hours Mig-21 pilot Pham Tuan, following guidance transmitted by Air Force Headquarters and by Radar Company 20 in Hanoi and Radar Company 50 in Son La, broke through a "wall" of enemy fighters, achieved a favorable position, and accurately launched a missile, which shot down one B-52 over Moc Chau. This was a glorious combat achievement, shooting down the first U.S. "Flying Fortress" to be destroyed by the People's Air Force of Vietnam. During that same night, 27 December, missile troops defending Hanoi shot down four B-52s. One of these was shot down by the 72nd Missile Battalion, newly arrived from Haiphong. Pieces from disintegrating B-52s fell onto Hoang Hoa Tham Street, around the Bach Thao park, into the Ngoc Ha flower garden. Under the light of exploding anti-aircraft shells and burning enemy B-52s, cheering citizens of Hanoi poured into the streets to capture four pirate air crewmen.

During the night of 28 December our air force troops continued their victories. Combatant Vu Xuan Thieu, flying a Mig-21, flew low, barely skimming the slopes of rugged mountains, then suddenly shot skyward, closed on his target, and shot down one B-52 over Son La. Vu Xuan Thieu then died a hero's death after fulfilling his mission.

During the night of 29 December the 79th Missile Battalion, which was defending Hanoi, fought the final battle of the campaign, shooting down one B-52. At 7:00 A.M. on 30 December 1972, the U.S. government was forced to announce a bombing halt north of the 20th parallel and suggested that a meeting be held with representatives of our Government in Paris to discuss signing a peace treaty. The enemy's massive strategic offensive using B-52s against Hanoi and Haiphong had been crushed. Nixon's dream of negotiating from a position of strength had ended in total failure.

In 12 days and nights of heroic combat, our armed forces, with the help of our entire civilian population, had fought an outstanding battle of annihilation, shooting down 81 enemy planes, including 34 B-52s and five F-111s, and capturing 43 sky pirates, including 33 B-52 crewmen. World opinion called this battle a "Dien Bien Phu in the skies." The soldiers and civilians of Hanoi led in overall victories, shooting down 25 B-52s, most of which were shot down on the spot. Hanoi proved worthy of its title of Heroic Capital, the heart of the entire nation. Our missile troops, the key combat force of the campaign, shot down 30 B-52 strategic bombers, making the most decisive contribution to our defeat of the enemy's air offensive. The anti-aircraft forces of the militia and self-defense forces shot down 11 tactical aircraft.

Already having won a glorious victory over America's tactical air force, our armed forces, with the Air Defense–Air Force Service playing the leading role, recorded an outstanding new feat of arms, a brilliant victory over the enemy's strategic air force. Starting from combat operations in which anti-aircraft artillery was our main force and progressing to the use of combined-arms combat tactics on an ever-increasing scale, we reached a pinnacle with this air defense campaign, which defeated a strategic bombing offensive using B-52s. Our air defense–air force troops had made remarkable progress, going from never previously having shot down a B-52 on the spot to shooting them down on the spot in large numbers.

> The combat plan of the missile troops was correct, and they employed excellent fighting methods. Cadre and soldiers made significant progress in modern military science, sought out innovative solutions, gradually overcame the difficulties created by enemy jamming, and struck their targets accurately. . . . The training conducted by all units was excellent, both basic training and the supplemental training called for in the battle plan. Attention was paid to the need to build a cadre organization that was firm in its political views and skilled in technical matters. The Service's leadership and command pointed the Service in the right direction and produced clear results during the course of their preparations and combat operations.[12]

In January 1973 the Central Committee of the Party, the National Assembly, and the Government approved the award of the title of "Heroes of the People's Armed Forces" to our missile troops. They were the first specialty branch of our armed forces to receive this high honor.

THE WAR IN THE SOUTH

During the final months of 1972, as they prepared for and conducted their strategic air offensive against the North, in South Vietnam the United States and its puppets launched many operations to seize and occupy the liberated areas of Quang Tri, the Central Highlands, the lowlands of Military Region 5, and the Mekong Delta. They quickly prepared a plan called "flooding the territory," aimed at expanding the area under their control.

Since its beginning in late March, the strategic offensive conducted by our troops and our people on the battlefields had gone on continuously for more than nine months. In spite of massive assistance from the North, the effort to maintain our troop strength and supply levels had not kept pace with the requirements of the battlefield. The strength of our main force battalions fell to an average level of around 200 men each. Continuing to develop the offensive, our troops on the different fronts overcame many difficulties to rebuild our forces and to attack and counterattack enemy forces, firmly maintaining control of the liberated areas and supporting the battle being waged by the soldiers and civilians of North Vietnam.

Our armed forces on the Tri Thien battlefield continued to reinforce their defensive positions and blocked an enemy attack across the Thach Han River mounted by the puppet Airborne and Marine Divisions and aimed at retaking the Dong Ha and Ai Tu areas. In late January 1973 units of the 304th, 320th, and 325th Infantry Divisions and the 126th and K5 Navy Regiments, supported by tanks and artillery, carried out an outstanding counterattack in the Cua Viet area, annihilating a puppet brigade task force consisting of more than 2,000 troops and over 100 tanks and armored personnel carriers. Following up this victory, an element of Tri-Thien's main force troops advanced into the lowlands and, supported by local armed forces, attacked the enemy, liberating 50 hamlets in Trieu Hai district, 40 hamlets in Huong Tra and Phu Loc districts, and seizing control of several sections of Route 1.

The main force units of the Central Highlands Front repelled a counterattack by the puppet 23rd Division at Vo Dinh, inflicting heavy casualties to four enemy battalions and forcing the enemy to retreat back to Kontum city (22 to 25 January 1973). Exploiting this success, some of our forces advanced down into northwestern Gia Lai [Pleiku] province, overran enemy strong points at Chu Ho and Duc Co (21 January), and expanded the liberated area from Duc Co to Dit village along both sides of Route 19B.

Military Region 5 main force units beat back many enemy counterattacks and maintained firm control of the liberated area in Hiep Duc district (Quang Nam province), Ba To district (Quang Ngai province), and Hoai An district (Binh Dinh province). In late December 1972 the armed forces of Military Region 5 intensified their military attacks to support civilian mass uprisings, which liberated an additional 95 hamlets with a population of 13,000 people, seized control of portions of Route 1, and created a leopard-spot situation with our forces intermingled into enemy areas in many regions.

COSVN's main force troops continued the siege of An Loc and maintained control of many sections of Route 13. On 6 December our artillery troops conducted a concentrated bombardment of the Tan Son Nhat Airbase, destroying 85 aircraft and killing 200 technical personnel. On 13 December our sappers raided the Tuy Ha warehouse storage area, destroying 70,000 tons of bombs and shells. In mid-January 1973, a COSVN main force element advanced down to Cu Chi district where, working with local armed forces, it expanded the liberated zone, cut Route 1, defeated counterattacks by the puppet 5th Division in the Dau Tieng area, and inflicted heavy casualties on Regimental Task Force 8, capturing almost 500 prisoners.

Main force units of Military Regions 8 and 9, in coordination with local armed forces, continuously defeated the enemy's encroachment operations, maintained firm control of the liberated areas north and south of Route 4 and in the center of the Plain of Reeds, overran or forced the evacuation of hundreds of enemy outposts, and secured more than 1,000 hamlets with a population of more than 100,000. A number of units sent troops all the way to the outskirts of the provincial capitals of My Tho, Ben Tre, Bac Lieu, and Vi Thanh and to the towns of Cai Lay, Hong Ngu, etc., cutting and maintaining control over many sections of Routes 4, 12, 26, 30, etc., and pushing back, to a certain extent at least, the enemy's schemes to "flood our territory."

A CEASE-FIRE IS SIGNED

On 27 January 1973 the "Agreement to End the War and Reestablish Peace in Vietnam" was signed in Paris, the capital of the Republic of France. According to the agreement, the United States was forced to recognize the independence, sovereignty, and territorial integrity of Vietnam; had to promise to end its military involvement and to withdraw all U.S. and satellite troops from South Vietnam; and had to acknowledge that there were two governments, two armies, and two zones of control in South Vietnam.

The 1972 strategic offensive conducted by our soldiers and people on the battlefields of South Viet Nam, which had begun in late March 1972, was now over. Our soldiers and civilian population had attacked and crippled ten puppet divisions and 30 puppet brigades, regiments, or regimental task forces; had destroyed 2,500 aircraft and more than 10,000 military vehicles and 500 artillery pieces; had overrun or forced the withdrawal of more than 2,000 outposts; and had liberated many widespread areas with a total population of more than one million people.

The great victory of the 1972 strategic offensive in South Vietnam and the outstanding combat achievements of the anti-aircraft campaign that defeated the American imperialist strategic bombardment campaign against the North using B-52s marked a new step forward in the maturation of our armed forces. Beginning from a time when our main activity involved concentrated combat on the division level, with coordinated combat involving only infantry and artillery forces, we had now progressed to the point that we were conducting large-scale massed combat operations on the corps level, with coordinated combat involving infantry, field artillery, tanks, and many other specialty branches. With this new step forward we had been able to cripple enemy regimental, brigade, and even divisional formations. Our troops had fought continuously on all battlefields for almost the entire year of 1972 and had carried out many different types of large-scale combined-arms operations, including offensive campaigns, defensive campaigns, combined campaigns, and anti-aircraft campaigns. Maturing both through numerous glorious victories and through times of adversity and faltering, our main force troops on all battlefields had expanded their direct, decisive role in annihilating enemy troops; supported local armed forces and the masses in intensifying their attacks and uprisings; expanded the liberated zone; and defeated the enemy's strategic schemes and measures. This new step forward was in accordance with our nation's laws of revolutionary warfare and people's war.

On 29 March 1973 the last units of the U.S. expeditionary army and the armies of its satellites withdrew from South Vietnam. The U.S. Command in Saigon held a ceremony to lower its flag. The longest, most expensive, most unpopular war of aggression in U.S. history had come to a tragic conclusion.

After 18 years of combat filled with sacrifice and heroism, our soldiers and civilians had driven the U.S. expeditionary army, the most powerful army of aggression of the international imperialists, out of our nation. We had fulfilled our strategic mission of "fighting to force the U.S. to withdraw."

Our nation's anti-American resistance war of national salvation had won an enormous victory. Our soldiers and our people had created conditions that gave us a new opportunity to move forward to "fight to force the puppets to collapse," to totally liberate South Vietnam, to complete the popular democratic nationalist revolution throughout our country, and to move toward the unification of our nation.

PART V

The Formation of Strategic Army Corps:
The Entire Nation Urgently Prepares and
Launches the Spring 1975 General Offensive
and Uprising, Bringing the Resistance War
against the United States to Save the Nation
to a Victorious Conclusion, 1973–1975

14

Developing Mobile Main Force Corps-Sized Units, Combating Enemy Efforts to Capture Our Territory, Creating a New Battlefield Posture, and Preparing for the General Offensive and Uprising

POST–CEASE-FIRE PROBLEMS

The Paris Agreement to "End the War and Reestablish Peace in Vietnam," signed on 27 January 1973, was a great victory for our people and a major defeat for the American imperialists and their lackeys. The agreement forced the U.S. imperialists to end their war of aggression in Vietnam; withdraw all U.S. and satellite troops from South Vietnam; promise to respect the basic national rights of the people of Vietnam: independence, sovereignty, unification, and territorial integrity; promise to respect the right of self-determination of the people of South Vietnam and to end their military involvement and interference in the internal affairs of South Vietnam, etc. On the battlefields of South Vietnam, the entire U.S. army of aggression and all satellite troops were forced to withdraw, whereas units of the People's Army of Vietnam were allowed to maintain their forces and positions in all strategic areas. As for North Vietnam, the American imperialists were forced to totally and unconditionally end their war of destruction using air and naval forces. The people of North Vietnam were able to rebuild and develop their economy and to concentrate manpower and material resources for the final battle to attain our goal of liberating the entire nation. The Paris Agreement allowed us to achieve our objective of keeping our forces and positions in South Vietnam intact so that we could continue to attack the enemy. Because the American expeditionary military forces and all satellite troops were forced to withdraw, our army and civilian population had a tremendous opportunity "to topple the puppets," liberate South Vietnam, and win total victory in our resistance war to oppose the Americans and save the nation.

On 27 January 1973, the Party Central Committee appealed to the soldiers and civilians of the entire nation to "strengthen solidarity, increase vigilance, consolidate the victories we have gained so far, secure full independence and democracy for South Vietnam, and advance toward the goal of peace and unification of the nation."

In addition, in January 1973 the Standing Committee of the Central Military Party Committee met to set forward the new missions of the people's armed forces. These missions were to strengthen our organizational structure and increase our fighting abilities in response to the new requirements of the revolution; participate in building socialism in North Vietnam; participate in the political struggle, in the development of political forces, and in the expansion of base areas and secure liberated areas in South Vietnam; stand ready to defeat all enemy plots to sabotage the peace agreement and resume the war; and build our forces into a powerful, modern, regular revolutionary army.

Even though they had signed the Paris Agreement and withdrawn their expeditionary army of aggression from Vietnam, the U.S. imperialists were not yet ready to abandon their effort to use the "Nixon Doctrine" to maintain their neocolonialist rule in South Vietnam and keep our nation divided. They retained a U.S. military presence in Southeast Asia to serve as a "containment force," increased aid to the puppet regime in Saigon, and, from the moment the Paris Agreement was signed, encouraged the puppet army and governmental administration to systematically sabotage the agreement.

During their withdrawal, the United States and its satellites turned over to the puppets the military facilities, weapons, and military equipment that had been used to support the more than 600,000 troops of the U.S. expeditionary army and its satellite troops that had previously been stationed in the South. The United States also provided additional weapons to South Vietnam, including 625 aircraft, 500 artillery pieces, 400 tanks and armored vehicles, and numerous warships. During 1973 the United States continued to provide military aid, giving the puppet army 124 field artillery pieces and anti-aircraft guns, 98 aircraft, and many other types of military equipment. In 1973 the Saigon puppet regime's stockpile of military supplies rose to a total of two million tons.

Relying on the continuing flow of U.S. aid and operating under the command of U.S. military officers disguised as civilians, the Thieu regime launched a major program to draft additional troops and upgrade and regularize former paramilitary forces. As a result of this effort puppet regular troops increased from 650,000 in 1972 to 720,000 in 1973. Peoples Self-Defense Forces [PSDF] rose from 1.1 million to 1.15 million, including 400,000 armed PSDF troops. The enemy's air force, artillery, and armor forces expanded rapidly. Regional Force [RF] troops were organized into regiment-sized units and given additional equipment and combat capabilities. The enemy rapidly adjusted his strategic deployment of forces and launched a three-year military plan (1973–1975) aimed at pushing our main force units back to the border areas and eliminating the "two-zone" situation—the situation in which our liberated zones and the positions of our troops on the battlefield were interspersed within areas occupied by the United States and its puppets. Sixty percent of the enemy's regular troops and all its Regional Force and Popular Force units were mobilized for use in operations called "flooding the territory," aimed at pacifying our liberated areas.

Because of these enemy schemes, beginning the day the Paris Agreement was signed, 27 January 1973, and continuously thereafter, the sounds of the guns of the United States and its puppets never stopped in Cua Viet, Sa Huynh, the Mekong Delta, and all the battlefields of South Vietnam. In fact, the war continued, but under a new form.

After the Paris Agreement the balance of forces between our side and the enemy changed in our favor. Because of our own mistakes and shortcomings, however, during the first few months of 1973 the enemy was able to seize the initiative in a number of locations. The enemy still obstinately and intentionally sabotaged the agreement. On our side, we were, to some extent at least, deluded by illusions of peace and thought we could passively wait to see what happened. As they traveled around explaining the resolution of the Central Committee, some high-level members of the leadership even advocated dividing up zones of control and establishing clear lines of demarcation between the two sides. A number of units and local areas displayed "nonchalant, careless, and right-wing attitudes toward the enemy."[1] Some areas "reduced the level of armed operations and tried to maintain a unilateral peace" or "conducted passive defense, only taking action in areas where the enemy had first initiated an attack."[2] Because of these mistakes, during the first few months of 1973 the enemy was able to retake many of the areas that we had liberated in 1972. These included areas north and south of Route 4 in Military Region 8, the scattered liberated bases in Quang Da province, the area north of Tam Ky (Quang Nam province), the eastern portions of Binh Son, Son Tinh, and Mo Duc districts (Quang Ngai province), Hoai Nhon and Phu My (Binh Dinh province), etc. By mid-1973 the enemy had made encroachments into a number of our liberated zones, seizing 45 villages and 320 hamlets with a total population of 260,000 in Military Region 5; 308 hamlets with a total population of 290,000 in Regions 6 and 7; 24 villages and 120 hamlets with a population of 100,000 in Region 8, etc.

In a number of areas, however, especially in the provinces of the western Mekong Delta (Region 9), not only was the enemy unable to carry out his encroachment and pacification schemes, our soldiers and civilians struck back against him. During the first few months of 1973 enemy forces in Region 9 outnumbered our forces five or six to one. The enemy launched a series of division- and regiment-sized operations aimed at gaining control of 85 percent of the land area and 95 percent of the population of these rich Delta provinces. Under the leadership of Regional Military Commander Le Duc Anh, Regional Political Commissar Vo Van Kiet, and the other leaders of the Military Region Headquarters, the 1st, 2nd, 3rd, 10th, and 20th Regiments worked with local armed forces to mount vigorous counterattacks and regain the initiative by attacking enemy forces. The enemy operations aimed at encroaching on our liberated zones were defeated, a number of puppet regular battalions were destroyed, and the enemy was forced to withdraw from 67 posts and outposts. Region 9 was able to retain control of essentially all of its liberated areas and maintain its forces in the positions they held during 1972.

REGAINING THE INITIATIVE IN THE SOUTH

Assessing the situation in South Vietnam after the signing of the Paris Agreement, the Central Military Party Committee stated clearly that "the enemy was able to carry out a portion of his plans not because he was strong, but because of our own mistakes."[3] The armed forces in South Vietnam were directed to "firmly maintain the strategic initiative, defeat all enemy pacification and encroachment efforts, gain and retain additional civilian population, and maintain firm control of our liberated zones and revolutionary civil administrative structure. At the same time, we must make preparations so that, if the enemy expands the war and resumes large-scale combat, our forces are combat-ready and are determined to annihilate the enemy."[4]

Under the leadership of the Central Military Party Committee, the COSVN Military Committee, the COSVN Party Committee, and all Military Region headquarters conducted a general review of the situation and of military goals for the first six months of 1973. These headquarters elements laid out timely new policies aimed at strengthening and increasing the combat strength of our different types of armed forces, especially of our main force troops. They also issued guidance to units and local areas on resolutely counterattacking, seizing the offensive initiative to defeat the enemy's plan to take and pacify our liberated zones, and firmly retain our deployment of forces in all areas.

In mid-1973 the situation began to change. In Tri-Thien the Military Region Command used provincial and district local force troops, supported by guerrilla forces, to hold our front lines directly in contact with enemy forces. This enabled the Military Region's main force units to be gradually withdrawn from the defense lines in northern Quang Tri and pulled back to base areas for reorganization and consolidation. Cadre of all staff agencies and units were given political training to increase their understanding of the new situation and their new missions. Training in combined-arms operations was conducted. By alternating training and combat operations, assessing the effectiveness of our training in combat, the Military Region's main force regiments accomplished their mission of building and strengthening their forces. Supported by local armed units, they defeated numerous enemy encroachment operations at Tich Tuong, Tai Luong, Khe Thai, Mo Tau, etc. They strengthened their combat posture and stayed ready to advance into the lowlands when an opportunity presented itself.

The Military Region 5 Headquarters used local force troops to continuously attack the enemy while a portion of its main force units defended its most vital areas. The bulk of the region's main force troops were pulled back and trained in combined-arms combat operations. Utilizing experience gained in fighting "pacification" operations, the provinces sent their local force battalions and companies back to their old areas of operations to work with local guerrillas and civilians to develop an offensive posture vis-à-vis the enemy. They rebuilt the minefields, fields covered with punji sticks, and fences protecting our combat villages, which had been dismantled after the signing of the Paris Agreement. The 2nd Division's 31st Regiment advanced to attack the enemy in Thang Binh and Que Son in Quang Nam province. The 3rd Division's 12th Regiment worked with local armed forces in Binh Dinh province's Hoai Nhon district to block enemy forces trying to gain control of our Tam Quan liberated zone. Combining the operations of our three types of troops, combining armed combat with political struggle by the masses, blocking enemy encroachment operations on the outer perimeter and simultaneously sending part of their forces deep behind enemy lines to launch attacks on his rear, Region 5's armed forces retook a number of liberated zones and guerrilla zones in Duy Xuyen and Dien Ban (Quang Da province), Son Tinh (Quang Ngai province), and Phu My (Binh Dinh province). The puppet army was forced to withdraw some of the forces engaged in encroachment operations against our liberated zones in order to defend their rear areas.

In the Central Highlands, during the 1972 strategic offensive we had liberated almost all of Kontum province and Districts 4 and 5 and the area north of Route 19 in Gia Lai [Pleiku] province, creating an expansive liberated area stretching north to south across the Central Highlands and directly linking this liberated area with the mountain jungles and border areas of the provinces of Quang Da, Quang Nam, Quang Ngai, and Binh Dinh in Region 5 and with the provinces of extreme southern Central Vietnam and eastern Cochin China. During the first months of 1973 puppet forces mounted a series of operations to seize and occupy our liberated zones. They managed to loosen our stranglehold on Kontum city and gained an advantage on the battlefield. The Central Highlands Front's 10th Division mounted a series of fierce counterattacks and offensives, driving the enemy out of their positions in Trung Nghia, Ngo Thanh, Cong Play Plo, etc., and forcing them back to the outskirts of Kontum city. The 320th Division attacked the Chu Nghe outpost, annihilating the puppet 80th Ranger Battalion, and then repelled all enemy counterattacks and maintained firm control of this liberated zone.

In eastern Cochin China, the COSVN Military Headquarters used a number of independent regiments and local armed units to block and repel enemy attacks along our front lines and to surround and contain the enemy positions still holding out deep inside our liberated zone, such as Chon Thanh, An Loc, etc. COSVN sent parts of the 7th and 9th Divisions to the area east and west of Route 13 to strengthen our positions along the enemy's middle line of defense. Here our troops repelled two large operations by the puppet 7th and 9th Regimental Task Forces at Bau Bang and Dong Rum. In November 1973 our units launched a new wave of attacks, striking the Bu Bong Headquarters and the Kien Duc District Military Headquarters and then repelling numerous enemy counterattacks. Our forces killed or captured 1,500 enemy troops and confiscated 300 weapons and 20 armored vehicles. The liberated zone of eastern Cochin China, especially around our supply road heads (where Route 559's strategic supply corridor linked up with campaign supply routes operated by COSVN's rear services groups) was expanded.

Military Region 9's main force regiments and local armed forces continued to maintain the initiative and expanded their attacks against the enemy, developing many new liberated zones in Long My, Go Quao, Vinh Thuan, etc. The enemy had been most successful in encroaching into our areas in central Cochin China, but from mid-1973 on, after receiving instructions from the Central Military Party Committee and the Military Region Party Committee, our three types of armed forces resolutely counterattacked and attacked the enemy, retaking the lost positions and gradually regaining the battlefield position they had held at the end of 1972.

The situation in the South during the first few months of 1973 illustrates an important lesson: When the revolution moves into a new phase and when there is a political solution, new situations will arise and we must be prepared to deal with all possible developments. In addition, we had to make every effort to exploit the legal provisions of the agreement to conduct the struggle against the enemy, simultaneously maintaining our vigilance and increasing the strength of the revolution. In the event the enemy decided to continue the war and refused to implement the peace agreement it had signed, our armed forces had to firmly maintain their belief in the role of revolutionary violence and in our offensive strategy. Only in this way could we maintain our battlefield position and consolidate our forces. For localities that had lost territory and civilian population, units that had been driven from their areas of operations, and forces that had suffered casualties and losses, all these losses were caused by the failure of these forces and local areas to correctly evaluate the enemy's new schemes and acts of war. They were caused by confusion and passivity in finding ways to counter the enemy's pacification and encroachment plans. From mid-1973 onward, when we switched over to the counterattack and attack phase, the enemy's encroachment operations were blocked and gradually pushed back.

While these combat activities were going on, our armed forces in the South were exploiting the advantages we had gained with the signing of the Paris Agreement to consolidate our forces, reinforce our manpower and equipment strength, and conduct training to increase our combat capabilities. The Party Central Committee and the Government directed all sectors and local areas to mobilize personnel and supplies to implement an urgent transportation plan aimed at strengthening our forces on the battlefield. From January to September 1973 the volume of supplies shipped from North Vietnam to the South increased to 140,000 tons, four times the volume shipped in 1972. Included in this total were 80,000 tons of military supplies (including 27,000 tons of weapons and ammunition, 6,000 tons of petroleum products, and 40,000 tons of rice) and 45,000 tons of supplies sent to the civilian population of our newly liberated areas. In addition, 10,000 tons of weapons were stored in the warehouses along the Ho Chi Minh Trail. During 1973 more than 100,000 cadre and soldiers, including two infantry divisions, two artillery regiments, one anti-aircraft division, one armored regiment, one engineer regiment, and numerous replacement units, marched from the North to the battlefields in the South.

With this massive reinforcement from the North and with troops recruited locally in the South, by the end of 1973 our three types of armed forces in South Vietnam had taken another step forward in terms of their size, equipment, and combat capabilities. We now had a total of 310,000 main force soldiers organized into ten divisions, 24 regiments, and 102 battalions of infantry and specialty branch troops. Each of our main force divisions now included three infantry regiments, one artillery regiment, and a number of separate battalions and companies of specialty branch and support troops. Each battalion had an authorized strength of around 400 soldiers, and the table of organization strength of a regiment was 1,800 to 2,000 soldiers. All specialty branch regiments and battalions were brought up to full table of organization and equipment strength. Local force troops totaled 70,000 soldiers organized into battalions at the province level and companies at the district level. A number of provinces were able to organize fire support battalions equipped with 85mm field guns, 75mm recoilless rifles, and 120mm mortars. Our village militia guerrillas totaled approximately 120,000 personnel. A number of hamlets in the rural lowlands began to reorganize and develop their own guerrilla units.

In Saigon and other areas where the Four Party Joint Military Commission[5] was carrying out its mission of monitoring and controlling the implementation of the Paris Agreement, officers of the People's Army of Vietnam, displaying the attitude of soldiers of a victorious army, exploited the legal provisions of the agreement to launch an attack on a new front. Together with our sapper and commando troops operating secretly inside the enemy-held cities, the activities of our military delegation provided our army with a new, public platform for use in conducting a face-to-face struggle against the enemy right in his own lair. The civilian population of the cities and of areas temporarily occupied by the enemy gained a new source of pride, and they had faith in and loved the soldiers of our revolutionary army.

Even though we still had a number of weaknesses, such as "the political struggle movement of the civilian population has still not developed strongly, the liberated areas have still not been firmly consolidated, there is still not a proper balance between the three types of troops, and the revolutionary infrastructure in the cities and in rural areas under enemy control is still weak,"[6] overall the posture and strength of the revolution in South Vietnam in 1973 was stronger than at any time since the beginning of the resistance war against the Americans to save the nation. Our armed forces in South Vietnam were a victorious force and held a firm foothold in all strategic areas.[7] The nature of the battlefield and the balance of forces between ourselves and the enemy was gradually shifting in our favor. Our strategic opportunity, which had appeared with the signing of the Paris Agreement, gradually ripened and our day of harvest came ever closer.

PREPARING FOR THE FINAL OFFENSIVE

In July 1973 the Party Central Committee held its 21st Plenum in Hanoi. At this Plenum the Central Committee passed a resolution on completing the people's democratic revolution in South Vietnam and gaining total victory in the resistance war against the Americans to save the nation. With respect to the duties of our armed forces, the Central Committee of the Party laid out the following combat missions for the army: To maintain a secure hold on the mountain jungles and develop this region into a solid, fully functioning base area, and to maintain a secure grasp on our liberated zones in the lowlands to provide positions we could use to threaten the cities and support the political struggle of the masses in contested areas and in areas under enemy control. Our main force troops, local force troops, and guerrilla militia were ordered to make all necessary preparations and stand constantly ready to attack the enemy and vigorously work to crush the enemy's territorial encroachment operations. The main force units were to mount counterattacks and attacks, fight powerful battles of annihilation that would inflict real damage to the enemy in order to defend our liberated zones and base areas, and to create situations that could be exploited by the political struggle movement of the masses.

With regard to the work of building up our forces and increasing our combat capabilities, the Party Central Committee ordered the army to conduct an overall review of our military activities during the resistance war against the Americans to save the nation. This review would be used to properly resolve a number of new problems involving grand strategy, campaign strategy, and tactics and to work out guidance for force building and combat formulas and tactics to be used by each separate battlefield. With respect to our main force troops, the army was ordered to develop an overall program to increase its combat power and develop into an elite, regular, modern, mobile, and flexible force capable of meeting the demands of combat on the battlefield and of the revolutionary war being fought by the entire population. The army was ordered to focus on building and developing local force troops into tightly organized units with relatively modern equipment but also making full use of various types of primitive weapons. The Party Central Committee directed that the guerrilla militia be transformed into a strong, nationwide force and that we correct the current imbalance between our main force troops, local force troops, and guerrilla militia. The Central Committee also issued specific orders covering the expansion and upgrading of our lines of communication and supply and the protection of our supply corridor and our food and weapons warehouse facilities to meet our army's battlefield requirements for technical equipment and supplies.

The resolution of the 21st Plenum of the Party Central Committee was a historic document that played a decisive role in the victory won by our soldiers and civilians in the final phase of our resistance war against the Americans to save the nation. The resolution summarized the achievements and experiences of the different stages of development of the revolution and laid out clear directions and concrete responsibilities for our people and our armed forces to use in advancing toward our ultimate victory.

To implement this Central Committee resolution, the Central Military Party Committee held a plenary session (March 1974) to review the military situation during 1973. This meeting concluded that the duties of the armed forces were to seize the strategic opportunity; to actively make all necessary preparations for large-scale combat operations; to strengthen our armed forces, especially by strengthening our main force mobile strategic reserve force; to mobilize manpower and matériel strength to support the great front line in South Vietnam; and to prepare the battlefield and be ready to launch a major attack when the opportunity presented itself.

In April 1974 the Central Military Party Committee held a conference of high-ranking cadre from throughout the armed forces to study the resolution of the 21st Plenum of the Party Central Committee and the March 1974 resolution of the Central Military Party Committee. During this conference the Party and the State promoted a number of military cadre to the rank of general. President Ton Duc Thang attended the conference and gave instructions to the participants on the assigned duties of the army. Comrade Le Duan, First Secretary of the Party Central Committee, and Comrade Le Duc Tho, Politburo member, provided the participants with additional insights into a number of issues mentioned in the assessment of the situation included in the Central Committee resolution. The First Secretary laid out various possibilities for the development of the revolution in South Vietnam and discussed the things that must be accomplished in order to gain complete victory during the coming years.

After the conference the staff agencies of the High Command began to formulate a strategic combat plan, a development and training plan for large main force units and for the technical service branches, and a plan to provide logistics and technical support for the entire army and for each individual battlefield. The General Staff prepared a strategic plan called "Combat Directions for 1973–1975." Later, in September 1974, the General Staff completed a draft plan, "Study of a Plan to Secure Victory in South Vietnam." Senior officers of the Ministry of Defense, the General Staff, the General Political Department, the General Rear Services Department, and a number of key leadership cadre from the different battlefields, including Comrades Tran Huu Duc (Tri-Thien), Vo Chi Cong and Chu Huy Man (Region 5); Nguyen Van Linh, Tran Van Tra, Tran Nam

Trung, Hoang Van Thai, Vo Van Kiet, and Nguyen Minh Duong (B2), etc., personally participated in this effort, contributing their opinions and providing guidance for the development of these combat plans prior to their submission to a session of the Politburo for approval. Pursuant to orders from the Central Military Party Committee, staff agencies of the High Command prepared plans to form mobile regular army corps subordinate to the High Command.

The question of organizing and conducting combat operations at the corps level had already been raised during the spring 1971 counteroffensive campaigns against the United States and its puppet troops in northeastern Cambodia and in the Route 9–Southern Laos area, and several corps-level command organizations had been formed, including the Forward Headquarters of the COSVN Military Command (Group 301) and the B70 Corps-Sized Group Command [Bo Tu Lenh Binh Doan B70]. After the Paris Agreement was signed our people's resistance war against the Americans to save the nation moved into its final phase. To end the war, we needed to launch large-scale campaigns to annihilate and disperse puppet troops, topple the puppet civil administration at all levels, liberate all of Vietnam, and completely achieve all of the goals of our revolution. The development of combined-arms corps with a high level of mobility, strong firepower, and powerful assault capabilities to serve as the decisive forces in important strategic campaigns was now an objective requirement for our army and was appropriate to the current level of development of our army. By this time our army possessed all the objective and subjective requirements needed to carry out this task.

Based on a proposal submitted by the Central Military Party Committee and the Ministry of Defense, in October 1973 the Party Politburo approved the formation of main force corps units.

In North Vietnam, on 24 October 1973, 1st Corps, which was given the name of the "Determined to Win Group," was established.[8] Included in 1st Corps were three infantry divisions: the 308th Division, the 312th Division, and the 320B Division. These were among the first divisions formed by our army during our resistance war against the French. The 1st Corps specialty branch units included the 367th Air Defense Division, the 202nd Tank Brigade, the 45th Artillery Brigade, the 299th Engineer Brigade, and the 204th Signal Regiment. These units were among the first specialty branch units formed by our army. Almost all 1st Corps units had participated in the Dien Bien Phu campaign and had been part of Corps-Sized Group 70 during the Route 9–Southern Laos campaign (1971) and of the forces operating under the B5 Front during the Quang Tri Campaign (1972). Major General Le Trong Tan, Deputy Chief of the General Staff, and Major General Le Quang Hoa, Deputy Director of the General Political Department, were named Military Commander and Political Commissar, respectively, of the Corps. The forests of Tam Diep Mountain, on the border between Thanh Hoa and Ninh Binh provinces, where 184 years before national hero Nguyen Hue (Emperor Quang Trung) had assembled his forces prior to advancing on Thang Long [Hanoi] to attack and disperse the more than 300,000-man Chinese army of aggression, was chosen as the base area for 1st Corps.

In South Vietnam, on 17 May 1974, 2nd Corps, which was named the "Perfume River Group," was formed.[9] The units chosen to form 2nd Corps consisted of three infantry divisions (the 304th, 325th, and 324th), the 673rd Air Defense Division, the 164th Artillery Brigade, the 203rd Tank Brigade, the 219th Engineer Brigade, and the 463rd Signal Regiment. Major General Hoang Van Thai was appointed as the first Military Commander and Major General Le Linh was named as the first Political Commissar of 2nd Corps. The infantry divisions in 2nd Corps were all units with extensive combat experience during two wars, the resistance war against France and the resistance war against the United States. All three divisions had established glorious combat records, had a tradition of self-reliance and self-improvement, and a record of solidarity between troops and civilians and of international solidarity. The Corps specialty branch units had been formed during the last years of the resistance war against the French and during the resistance war against the United States and had won many combat and combat-support honors on the battlefields of the South. The Corps was first stationed in Ba Long base camp and the jungle-covered mountains of western Tri-Thien, where many of the units of the Corps had been formed and had spent many years training and fighting, wrapped in the love and support of the people of Binh–Tri–Thien.

The main force element of Central Highlands Front consisted of two infantry divisions (the 10th and 320A Divisions), two independent infantry regiments (the 95th and 25th), two artillery regiments (the 40th and 675th), two anti-aircraft regiments (the 272nd and 232nd), the 198th Sapper Regiment, the 273rd Tank Regiment, two engineer regiments (the 7th and the 545th [minus]), and the 29th Signal Regiment. In June 1974 the Central Highlands Party Committee and the Central Highlands Command formed these main force units into a combined-arms combat group and brought the units up to full table of organization and equipment authorized strength. By reducing the percentage of support personnel the front was able to increase its total number of combat troops by 5.48 percent in comparison with 1973, and the number of infantry and sapper troops increased by 6.08 percent. The main force element of the Central Highlands Front was built into a powerful combat force stationed in a strategic theater. This force placed direct pressure on the puppet 2nd Corps and Military Region 2 and prepared the way for the official formation of 3rd Corps in the future.

On 20 July 1974, 4th Corps, which bore the name "Mekong Group," was formed in the eastern Cochin China base area.[10] Major General Hoang Cam was appointed Military Commander and concurrently Secretary of the Corps Party Committee.[11] The Corps was made up of the 7th Infantry Division, which bore the traditions of the Chien Thang [Victory] Division[12] from the resistance war against the French; the 9th Infantry Division, the first main force unit formed in the South during the resistance war against the United States; and the following specialty branch units: the 24th Artillery Regiment; the 71st Anti-Aircraft Regiment; the 429th Sapper Regiment; three signal battalions, etc. The formation of 4th Corps marked the culmination of many years of determined development of main force elements and of the growth of massed combat operations on the battlefields of Cochin China and extreme southern Central Vietnam. By forming a Corps in this strategic theater, our army had created a powerful main force fist with sufficient strength to apply strong pressure on the enemy in an area right next to the enemy's command center.

The formation of these Corps marked a new step forward in the maturation of our army in terms of the scale of its organization and forces and represented a qualitative change in our army after almost 30 years of force building and combat. With several combined-arms corps with rather powerful equipment and considerable assault power, a high level of mobility, and the ability to conduct continuous, sustained combat operations, our army now was able to launch large-scale offensive campaigns using combined-arms forces in several different strategic theaters in order to bring the war to an end.

Along with the organization and deployment of these Corps in the strategic theaters, the Central Military Party Committee laid out a policy of consolidating and strengthening the combat power of a number of main force divisions and regiments to enable them to serve as mobile forces subordinate to the High Command and to the Military Regions.

After spending some time carrying out our international duties on the battlefields of Laos, the 316th Infantry Division was ordered home and stationed in the western portions of Nghe An and Ha Tinh provinces. The 341st Infantry Division was converted from a unit specializing in training replacement troops to be sent to the battlefield into a mobile division at full table of organization and equipment strength. The 341st was stationed in southern Military Region 4. Both these divisions became part of the High Command's strategic mobile reserve force.[13]

Tri-Thien Military Region's main force units consisted of three infantry regiments (the 4th, 6th, and 271st Regiments) and a number of specialty branch units. Military Region 5's 2nd and 3rd Divisions were brought up to their full authorized table of organization and equipment strengths. Each division now had three infantry regiments, one artillery regiment, and a number of specialty branch battalions. The 52nd Brigade was formed, made up of three infantry battalions, two artillery battalions, one battalion of 37mm anti-aircraft guns, and one sapper battalion. Also directly subordinate to Military Region 5 Headquarters were two artillery regiments (the 572nd and 576th), the 573rd Anti-Aircraft Artillery Regiment, the 574th Armored Regiment; the 575th Signal Regiment, and two engineer regiments (the 83rd and 270th). Region 6's main force troops consisted of the 812th Infantry Regiment, the 130th Fire Support Battalion, and the 200C Sapper Battalion. The main force troops of the military regions in Cochin China were collected together into four infantry divisions and two separate infantry regiments: the 3rd Division subordinate to the COSVN Military Command, the 4th Division of Military Region 9, the 8th Division of Military Region 8, the 6th Division of Military Region 7, and the 1st and 2nd Gia Dinh Provincial Regiments of the Saigon–Gia Dinh Military Command. These divisions and regiments were mobile units, each operating within its own military region, which served as local combat forces and could also coordinate their operations with the strategic Corps during campaign operations of strategic significance.

Along with the infantry, our different branches of service and specialty branches were rapidly expanded and standardized for large-scale combined-arms combat operations and in response to the requirements for building our main force Corps units.

The Artillery Branch was organized on three levels: the strategic reserve artillery subordinate to the Artillery Command;[14] military region and corps artillery; and division-level artillery (organized up to brigade and regiment size). In 1972 only two infantry divisions in our army (the 308th and the 304th) included an artillery regiment in their table of organization. By the end of 1974 the main force artillery of our army consisted of six artillery brigades, 28 artillery regiments, 17 separate artillery battalions, and six separate artillery batteries. Local force artillery consisted of 98 batteries, 15 independent platoons, and 52 separate gun sections. In addition, 16 of our infantry divisions now had an artillery regiment in their table of organization. On the battlefields of South Vietnam alone our artillery forces included three brigades, 21 regiments, 21 battalions, and 91 independent batteries equipped with a total of 1,176 artillery pieces of all types.

The Armored Branch was organized into four brigades (two reserve brigades subordinate to the Armored Branch Headquarters and two brigades subordinate to 1st and 2nd Corps), two regiments subordinate to the Central Highlands Front and Military Region 5, and a tank group subordinate to COSVN Military Command.

The Sapper Branch was organized into four mobile battalions directly subordinate to Sapper Command plus regiments and battalions assigned throughout the different battlefields. COSVN Military Command had six regiments, and in Saigon and its surrounding area alone we had one sapper regiment and 13 sapper-commando groups. The Central Highlands Front had one sapper regiment made up of five battalions. Military Region 5 had five mobile sapper battalions and five battalions targeted against specific enemy bases in Da Nang, Quy Nhon, Cam Ranh, etc. The Tri-Thien Military Region had three sapper battalions and three separate sapper companies specifically assigned to attack enemy forces and installations on the outskirts of Hue city and the Phu Bai military base.

The Engineer Branch was expanded to include a number of new road-building and river-crossing regiments in response to the need to build strategic and campaign roads and to ensure the mobility of our combined-arms units. The High Command's engineer reserve force consisted of five bridge-building and river-crossing regiments. The engineer forces of the military regions, corps, and Group 559 Command were organized up to brigade and regimental strength.

The Signal Branch concentrated its operations on three communications networks: radio, telephone, and the military postal system. Of special importance was the network of telephone cables called "Unification" that ran from Hanoi all the way down to the B2 [COSVN] battlefield and its supporting radio network. Signal forces subordinate to the High Command and to the military regions, corps, service branches, and battlefields were all strengthened.

The Air Defense–Air Force Service realigned its forces and its anti-aircraft posture in North Vietnam. The Service transferred one division and half its anti-aircraft artillery regiments to the newly established corps and to the different battlefields.

The Navy reorganized its deployment of forces and its defensive zones. The Naval Regions and the 172nd Regiment were assigned the mission of patrolling our coastal waters from Vinh Linh up to the Northeastern Zone. Areas farther offshore were assigned to the 128th, 171st, and 125th Regiments. The 125th and 128th Regiments had the dual missions of transporting supplies or fishing and simultaneously patrolling and monitoring the situation. A number of naval infantry units and four water sapper teams totaling 258 cadre and soldiers were trained and sent to reinforce the different battlefields.

All these changes marked a new step forward in the organization and equipment of the specialty branches of our armed forces. The dispatch of many additional specialty branch units to South Vietnam not only increased the combat power of local mobile main force units, it also increased the ability of the battlefields to provide technical and combat support to the High Command's mobile forces during large-scale offensive campaigns.

As we centralized and expanded mobile strategic reserve main force troops and main force elements at the military region level, the Central Military Party Committee, the Ministry of Defense, and the headquarters of the military regions also devoted a great deal of attention to the development of local force and guerrilla militia forces. This was an objective requirement for the battlefield because, after many years of ferocious, continuous combat, especially during 1972, our local armed forces had suffered rather serious attrition. The enemy's efforts to conduct pacification, gain control of the civilian population, draft troops into their army, and force youths to join the People's Self-Defense Force caused us a great many difficulties. On a number of battlefields we were even forced to send main force troops, cadre and soldiers who were natives of North Vietnam, down to serve as local cadre and guerrillas. Even though great efforts were made, the expansion of our local armed forces during the two-year period 1973–1974 reached only 30 percent of its manpower goals. By the end of 1974 our province- and district-level local force troops totaled 56,000, whereas guerrilla militia at the village and hamlet level totaled 140,000. To have forces available to support the combat operations of our large main force units and to directly support the civilian population in carrying out uprisings, and to correct, at least in part, the imbalance in the ratio between the three types of troops, all battlefields implemented a variety of measures to increase the personnel strength and raise the fighting capabilities of local armed forces, and especially of the province-level local force battalions and village guerrilla teams in our key focal-point areas. Many areas organized armed operations teams to move deep into the rural lowlands, areas temporarily under enemy control, to work with local cadres to expand our guerrilla and secret self-defense forces and to strengthen and expand our sapper-commando forces. With additional troops provided by higher levels, a number of provinces organized local force regiments.

Because of the great expansion of our forces and our new requirements for combat operations and organization of the battlefield, the provision of rear service [logistics] and technical support for our armed forces became a very great and pressing requirement. During the 1972 strategic offensive we expended a significant quantity of our army's weapons and equipment. By the end of 1974 the total number of large artillery shells possessed by our entire army had fallen to around 100,000 rounds.[15] Meanwhile, international aid had greatly decreased, especially aid in artillery shells and offensive weapons. By developing a spirit of creative labor and expanding production and economizing on expenditures, our soldiers and civilians overcame many difficulties and shortages. They strove to ensure the provision of vital supplies to our armed forces for their force building and combat operations.

In April 1974 the Central Military Party Committee established the General Technical Department, an agency responsible for directing the provision of technical support and for national defense production for the entire armed forces.[16] Comrade Dinh Duc Thien, Director of the General Rear Services Department, was appointed to serve concurrently as Director of the General Technical Department.

To implement the orders of the Central Military Party Committee, during 1973–1974 all units of the armed forces conducted a general inventory of property and finances and organized the retrieval, collection, and repair of equipment, thereby partially resolving some of our logistics and technical support problems. Battlefield units were ordered to reduce their expenditure of ammunition, especially of large-caliber ammunition. Units were also ordered to repair and improve weapons and equipment captured from the enemy so we could use these weapons and equipment to fight the enemy. Cadre and workers of the national defense factories; of the repair stations and shops of the Ordnance Department, the Military Equipment Department, and the Vehicle Administration Department; and of the military regions and corps worked to overcome many supply and technical difficulties, aggressively studying ways to produce a number of different types of weapons, equipment, and replacement parts. The Artillery Branch established a number of collection teams to retrieve damaged artillery pieces from the battlefields and bring them back to North Vietnam for repair. To partially resolve the shortage of large-caliber artillery ammunition, the branch sent to the frontline battlefields smaller caliber artillery weapons (76.2mm and 57mm) for which we still had a great deal of ammunition in storage.[17] The Armored Branch carried out minor repairs on 246 tanks and armored vehicles, 461 cannon, and 65 pieces of optical equipment, raising the branch's combat availability from 60 percent in 1973 to 98 percent at the end of 1974. The Signal Branch put into service more than 1,000 radios captured from the enemy and repaired 2,300 inoperable radios, 3,000 telephones, and 1,000 generators. The 2nd Corps alone repaired more than 1,000 vehicles and almost 10,000 weapons and other pieces of equipment.

To increase the on-site repair capabilities of the different battlefields the General Technical Department and the specialty branches sent to South Vietnam 200 vehicle and machinery repair stations; 21 small-arms and artillery repair stations and signal equipment repair stations; dozens of regiment- and division-level ordnance repair stations; and 13 mobile teams capable of repairing tanks, armored vehicles, and anti-aircraft artillery pieces. Accompanying these repair stations were hundreds of tool kits with specialized tools and thousands of spare parts for machinery and weapons. These gave the battlefields the ability to make on-site, low-level repairs to weapons and combat equipment. Fifteen thousand technical personnel and mechanics were sent to the battlefields during the 1973–1974 period.

As for rear services [logistics] support, the 21st Plenum of the Party Central Committee laid out clear guidelines and responsibilities to be implemented during 1973–1974, directing that the armed forces build, develop, and improve our lines of communications and transportation; protect the supply corridor and its warehouses; and place in storage sufficient food, weapons, and technical equipment to ensure adequate supplies for our armed forces on the battlefield.

To implement these guidelines the government and the army made a major investment in consolidating and improving the strategic road network on the western side of the Annamite Mountain chain and in basic construction work on a parallel strategic road network on the eastern side of the mountains. More than 30,000 soldiers, cadre, technical personnel, and assault youth were sent to the Ho Chi Minh Trail to work with Group 559 on this large construction project, which was considered the entire nation's number one priority during these years. On the western side of the Annamite chain the engineer regiments of the 470th and 472nd Sector Divisions [su doan khu vuc] maintained and improved the two main North-South roads, which were 1,240 kilometers long. On the eastern side of the mountains the engineer regiments of the 471st and 473rd Sector Divisions and a number of reinforcement units employed more than 1,000 vehicles and specialized machinery to do basic construction work on a new road stretching 1,200 kilometers from Khe Giat to Bu Gia Map in eastern Cochin China. Night and day the entire Ho Chi Minh Trail network seethed with an atmosphere of excitement of "building the road to victory." By early 1975 the forces working on the Ho Chi Minh Trail had built 5,560 kilometers of new roads,[18] bringing the total length of roads used for supply and troop movements along the Annamite

Mountain chain to 16,790 kilometers, of which 6,810 kilometers were main roads, 4,980 kilometers were connector roads, and 5,000 kilometers were bypasses and detours. The battlefields also devoted a large quantity of their own manpower and equipment to the building and repair of campaign-level roads, bringing the total length of these roads to 6,000 kilometers (including a number of main roads and connecting roads) to ensure the movement of forces and supplies from our strategic lines of communications into each combat theater.

Paralleling the strategic transportation and troop movement corridor was a petroleum pipeline network 1,712 kilometers long with 101 pumping stations,[19] of which 1,311 kilometers was built during 1973 and 1974. Overcoming many technical, terrain, and weather difficulties, our POL (petroleum-oil-lubricants) troops brought the gasoline pipeline over mountain peaks over 1,000 meters high and across rugged up-and-down terrain, building flat terraces for our pumps on the steep mountainsides, etc. On 15 January 1975, for the first time gasoline flowed through the pipeline all the way to Bu Gia Map in eastern Cochin China.

The 541st Warehouse Regiment and the warehouse units along Group 559's strategic corridor reorganized their forces and their network of strategic storage warehouses on the main transportation route and at intersections with the supply routes leading to individual battlefields. Many warehouses with storage capacity in excess of 10,000 tons were built in the areas of Cam Lo, A Luoi, Kham Duc, Lang Hoi, Bu Prang, La Ba Khe, Bu Gia Map, etc. This network of warehouses was directly linked with the great rear area in North Vietnam and with the rear services bases and networks of the battlefields of Tri-Thien, Region 5, the Central Highlands, and eastern Cochin China via the strategic and campaign road networks (including both land and sea routes through the ports of Cua Viet and Dong Ha). This created a continuous, solid rear services network with a large supply storage capacity, a relatively complete force of support personnel, and a powerful motorized transport force.

On 12 July 1973 the Central Military Party Committee and the Ministry of Defense issued a decision memorandum designating the Group 559 Command the "Annamite Mountains [Truong Son] Command." The motor transportation battalions and regiments directly subordinate to the command were gathered together and formed into two truck divisions, the 571st and 471st. The sector divisions were reorganized as engineer divisions whose main mission was the building and maintenance of our lines of communications. The network of troop way stations [binh tram] was reorganized into 29 transportation regiments (including four newly formed regiments). With this new organizational structure, Group 559 was capable of carrying out "massed, large-scale motorized transportation operations, covering long distances and of a decisive nature," enabling the Group to support large-scale offensive campaigns. The standard mechanized transport formation was the truck regiment, which used a standard transport leg of six to eight days for one trip. At each end of the transport leg were supply and technical support facilities, large storage warehouses, and specialized loading/unloading personnel with the ability to rapidly handle large truck convoys. POL stations were spread all along the entire route, ensuring the rapid servicing of every truck company and battalion. During the 1973–1974 and the 1974–1975 dry seasons, the volume of motorized truck transport traffic operating along the supply routes on the eastern and western sides of the Annamite Mountain chain during a 24-hour period averaged around 600 vehicles per day. The volume of supplies sent down the strategic transportation route system from the beginning of 1974 until the end of April 1975 totaled 823,146 tons, 1.6 times larger than the total volume shipped during the previous 13 years combined. Of this total, 364,542 tons were delivered to the different battlefields, 2.6 times the total for the previous 13 years.

By the beginning of 1975 the work of building new roads and upgrading the existing roads of the strategic and campaign road networks, the construction of the petroleum products pipeline, and the building of a network of roads, warehouses, and ports along the strategic transportation route and the rear services supply roads of the individual battlefields had been essentially completed. These projects, and the motorized transport force of 6,770 trucks, ensured that our army could conduct large-scale movements of infantry and technical specialty branch troops and equipment and that we could increase the power and the speed of our attacks during large-scale combined-arms combat campaigns. On the battlefields of South Vietnam the quantity of supplies stockpiled by our units and rear services bases had risen to 70,000 tons of ammunition, 107,000 tons of gasoline and petroleum products, 80,000 tons of food and food products, 2,400 tons of medicine for our military medical service, and 5,400 tons of other supplies. This supply stockpile was sufficient for us to support large forces conducting protracted, continuous combat operations as called for in our strategic combat plan.

In North Vietnam, immediately after the signing of the Paris Agreement our armed forces rapidly consolidated their organization, increased their combat capabilities, and actively worked with the civilian population to overcome war damages, contributing to our nation's economic recovery and increasing production.

Many units sent troops to local areas to work with the civilian population to strengthen dikes, build water conservancy projects, etc. The 312th Division of the 1st Corps moved more than 10,000 cubic meters of dirt in the dike project for the Hoang Long River. The Ninh Binh Province Party Committee and the Province People's Committee presented the division with a flag honoring them as "a disciplined, technically skilled, and highly efficient labor unit."

Our Navy, engineer troops, and local armed forces rapidly and completely cleared away enemy mines, guaranteeing the safety of both domestic and foreign vessels using the harbors of Haiphong, Hon Gai, Cam Pha, Ben Thuy, the Gianh River, and Nhat Le. Utilizing our experience in sweeping enemy mines during wartime, with large numbers of personnel using both modern and primitive methods, the units carrying out these duties swept and reswept thousands of square kilometers, especially focusing on the large minefields and key waterways. In locations where minesweepers could not operate, teams of naval engineers, frogmen, and divers dismantled and destroyed individual enemy mines. By the end of June 1973 the mine-clearing work was completed. This was a great political, military, and technical victory for our troops and civilian population.[20] We had defeated the enemy blockade and destroyed all the different types of mines he had sown in our coastal waters and rivers. This victory contributed to our overall victory in the resistance war against the Americans to save the nation and provided timely support for the rebuilding of our economy in the postwar period.

In 1973 total economic production in North Vietnam surpassed that in 1965. Both 1974 rice crops were successful and the quantity of paddy produced for the entire year surpassed the state plan by 18 percent and was 21.4 percent higher than that during 1973. Industrial and handicraft production exceeded the plan by 4 percent and was 15 percent higher than in 1973. Transportation and communications were restored. The lives of average citizens returned to normal. During the two-year period 1973–1974, more than 150,000 North Vietnamese youths joined the army. Many combat units at full authorized personnel strength, 68,000 replacement troops, 8,000 technical cadre and personnel, and tens of thousands of assault youth marched off to the battlefields. A large quantity of weapons, petroleum products, and food, nine times more than in 1972, was shipped to our units and support bases in the forward areas. The quantity of weapons and ammunition shipped was six times higher, rice three times higher, and gasoline and petroleum products 27 times higher than 1972.[21]

TRAINING FOR BATTLE

With a firm understanding that the central mission of the army during this period was training and increasing our combat capabilities, the General Staff directed our units to make use of this time of peace in North Vietnam to conduct a series of training sessions, each session being three or six months long. The mid-level and high-level Military Study Institutes doubled the length of training for their students; basic cadre training was increased from one year to two years; and supplemental training was extended from six months to one year. The infantry divisions implemented a two-phase training plan: basic training for subordinate units in offensive and defensive tactics, and combined training, exercising in various types of coordinated operations from company up to regimental level. Special emphasis was placed on training in urban combat, in conducting annihilation attacks against enemy forces occupying fortified positions, etc.

Based on an overall review of combat operations during the 1972 strategic offensive, the General Staff and the military regions and corps held many cadre training classes in the art of organizing and conducting offensive and defensive campaigns, in urban combat operations, in making attacks to annihilate large numbers of enemy troops operating in the field, etc. At the end of 1973 the General Staff held a training class for high-ranking cadre on attacking enemy forces in strongly fortified positions and in liberating cities. In 1974 units held many staff and command-level exercises at the corps and division level to practice our different combat tactics. The 1st Corps held 380 professional-level training classes for a total of 11,385 command-level cadre and 194 professional supplemental training classes for 5,702 technical cadre and personnel. The 2nd Corps sent its cadre who were in training to visit the 324th Division, which was conducting combat operations in western Thua Thien province, to collect lessons in the application of their training to the realities of combat. Our Military Services and specialty branches held 1,200 supplementary training classes for 40,000 command-level cadre and provided basic and supplementary training for 23,000 technical cadre and personnel.

To wind up the 1974 training year, the General Staff directed the 1st Corps to conduct a field exercise involving an offensive campaign operation aimed at liberating a large city and attacking enemy forces mounting counterattacks on the outskirts of the city. Command and staff cadre at three levels, corps, division, and regiment, participated in the exercise. The exercise field was the city of Thanh Hoa. Here the "enemy" had deployed a large military force with army, air force, and navy bases (the Sam Son beach area). The exercise increased the ability of these cadre to deal with many different tactical problems and campaign command issues. The exercise also assisted staff agencies in better understanding their responsibilities and operational systems in order to assist commanders in dealing with various contingencies in a timely, precise manner.

In South Vietnam, the COSVN Military Party Committee, the COSVN Command, the Region 5 Military Region Party Committee, and the Military Region Command launched a campaign to raise the combat strength and combat readiness of their armed forces, especially of main force units. The goals of the campaign were to improve cadre capabilities and exercise troops to enable them to mount massed combined-arms attacks aimed at annihilating enemy forces both in the field and when occupying heavily fortified positions. This campaign was designed to enable main force divisions and regiments to destroy puppet battalions and regiments, liberate district capitals and district military headquarters, and to enable two or three combined-arms divisions to annihilate a puppet division occupying strong bases and to liberate cities and towns. Command-level cadre of divisions, regiments, provincial military units, and military region staff agencies were pulled together to study the resolution of the 21st Plenum of the Central Committee, our general review of 1972 combat operations, and to review a number of basic issues involving campaign tactics. During the 1973–1974 time period the COSVN Military-Political School and the military-political schools of the military regions held dozens of short supplementary training classes for thousands of company and battalion-level cadre from our main force and local force units.

REGAINING THE INITIATIVE IN SOUTH VIETNAM

Combining training with combat operations, our armed forces in South Vietnam gradually regained the initiative, smashed the enemy's encroachment operations, fought a number of battles of annihilation that destroyed enemy regular units, maintained a firm hold on our liberated and base areas, protected the civilian population, and created the necessary conditions for a political struggle movement.

On 8 March 1973, the 320th Division attacked and overran the Le Ngoc base camp on Pleiku city's outer perimeter. The division then destroyed a number of enemy combined infantry-artillery-armor groups at Base 711, High Point 601, and expanded the liberated zone in western Gia Lai [Pleiku] province. On 30 May 1973, the 25th Regiment attacked and destroyed an enemy force at I-a-zup, expanding the liberated zone northwest of Ban Me Thuot city. The 10th Division, supported by local armed forces, destroyed a group of blocking positions in the enemy's "spider-web" defensive network in the Com Ray area, opening up Route 220 for our use. On 15 May 1974, the 10th Division's 28th Regiment and the 325th Division's 95th Regiment wiped out the Dak Pek base network, the enemy's last position on Route 14 in the liberated zone of northern Kontum province. In September 1974 the armed forces of the Central Highlands Front overran the Mang Den and Mang But district capitals and district military headquarters north and northwest of Kontum. The liberated area of the Central Highlands was expanded and a new battlefield posture now took shape in the northern and southern portions of the Central Highlands.

In Region 5, in early 1974 the Standing Committee of the Military Region Party Committee and the Military Region Command decided to take a step forward toward rearranging the deployment of the armed forces of our three types of troops throughout the region to create a new offensive posture for our forces. The 2nd and 711th Divisions, the 52nd Infantry Brigade, and sapper and artillery battalions, together with local forces from the provinces, were deployed to target areas in Quang Da, Quang Nam, and Quang Ngai. The 3rd Infantry Division and local armed forces were deployed to the southern provinces, Binh Dinh, Phu Yen, and Khanh Hoa. A number of artillery units (including 105mm howitzer units) built roads and moved their guns up to high points so they could provide direct fire to suppress and threaten base camps deep within the enemy zone of control. On 18 July 1974, the 2nd Infantry Division, supported by artillery and anti-aircraft guns from the Military Region, attacked and destroyed the Nong Son–Trung Phuoc network of enemy outposts in Quang Nam province, which was held by two puppet Ranger battalions. After this attack the division defeated a number of counterattacks by the puppet 3rd Division and the 12th Ranger Group, rendering two of the enemy's four regiment-sized units in the provinces of Quang Da and Quang Nam combat-ineffective. The Quang Nam liberated zone expanded from Nong Son–Trung Phuoc through Son Cam Ha on the western side of Thang Binh in northern Tam Ky down to the area near Route 1.

The 711th Division (minus) and Quang Da province forces intensified their attacks, expanding the liberated area from western Duy Xuyen through Go Noi down to the outskirts of Da Nang city. The 52nd Brigade overran 11 enemy outposts in support of Quang Ngai local armed forces and civilians as they increased their attacks and uprisings in Nghia Hanh and Minh Long districts. The liberated area in northern Quang Ngai was unified from Tra Bong down almost to the coast and to the outskirts of the Chu Lai military base and the province capital. The 3rd Division destroyed almost the entire network of enemy outposts that had been scattered across the middle of our liberated area in northern Binh Dinh province. The division also supported local armed forces and the civilian population in destroying or forcing the withdrawal of all enemy positions from eastern Phu My to northern Phu Cat. The rural areas of northern Binh Dinh were essentially completely liberated. The local troops and civilian population of Phu Yen combined military attacks with uprisings to destroy almost all "strategic hamlets" along Route 1. The liberated zone and areas under our control in Tuy An, Song Cau, and Dong Xuan districts regained the territory it had held prior to the signing of the Paris Agreement.

This long-term, large-scale wave of operations during the summer and fall of 1974, which involved close coordination between all Military Region 5 forces, produced good results. In many areas the enemy's defensive system had been shattered. We had taken the first step in defeating the enemy plan to seize our territory and establish clear lines dividing areas controlled by us and areas controlled by the enemy. To build on this victory the General Staff ordered 2nd Corps and Military Region 5 to launch "Campaign 711" to attack and seize the Thuong Duc district military headquarters and district capital. The goal of this operation was to kill enemy forces, liberate Thuong Duc, draw in and tie down a portion of the puppet's regular army, support the expansion of our operations in Region 5, coordinate with our other battlefields nationwide, and hone the fighting abilities of our troops during actual combat operations.

Thuong Duc lies in the western portion of Quang Da province, 40 kilometers from Da Nang city as the crow flies. It was a key outpost on the outer defensive perimeter protecting the Da Nang joint services military base, a base the enemy used to launch numerous encroachment operations. The enemy force defending Thuong Duc was rather strong.[22] Relying on the rugged terrain, the enemy had worked hard to build a strong network of fortified defensive positions. When attacked, enemy troops at Thuong Duc could receive air and artillery support from other positions in the area and from Da Nang.

After more than a month of road building, transporting supplies, and moving our forces, on 29 July 1974 the 304th Division's 66th Regiment and supporting units[23] opened fire to launch the attack. For the first three days the battle did not go well. Because the units involved had taken a subjective view of the situation and had underestimated the enemy's capabilities, they had not dug fortifications in the assault area and had suffered many casualties. The 66th Regiment did not carefully coordinate its operations and the command structure did not pay sufficient attention to details. As a result, three separate assaults against the enemy position all failed. The regimental headquarters decided to temporarily break off the battle. The 66th Regiment shifted to securing the jumping-off positions that it had seized while it prepared for a new wave of attacks. Major General Nguyen Chanh, Deputy Commander of Military Region 5, and Senior Colonel Hoang Dan, Deputy Commander of 2nd Corps, together with the Commander of the 304th Division, personally came down to help the regiment rebuild its organization and morale and draw lessons from the battle. The 304th Division Commander personally ordered that 85mm artillery pieces be hauled to positions one kilometer from enemy lines to provide fire support for the infantry attack, and the Division Chief of Staff assumed direct command of the 66th Regiment.

On 6 August 1974, 66th Regiment launched its second assault. In both the northwestern and southern sectors our troops quickly secured an opening, made their assault, and drove deep into the enemy position. The fighting was savage, going back and forth throughout the night. During the morning of 7 August, after redeploying its forces, the 66th Regiment launched a final assault, captured the entire position, and hoisted the Party's revolutionary flag, which the Quang Nam–Da Nang Party Chapter and the people of the province had presented to the division, over the Thuong Duc district military headquarters. The entire enemy force of 1,600 men was killed or captured, 13 aircraft were shot down, and 1,000 weapons were captured. The Thuong Duc district capital and four villages around the district capital, with a total population of 13,000 people, were liberated. Thuong Duc was 2nd Corps' first major victory.

After their initial victory the cadre and soldiers of the 66th Regiment quickly built defensive positions on the high ground around Thuong Duc. The 2nd Corps Headquarters sent 3rd Regiment, 324th Infantry Division, to join 66th Regiment in preparing to repel an enemy counterattack. During the last four months of 1974 our soldiers drove off a series of "massed counterattacks" and "creeping encroachment" operations by the puppet Airborne Division,[24] rendering three enemy battalions combat-ineffective and killing or capturing almost 5,000 enemy troops. On 20 December 1974 the Airborne Division, which was considered the best combat unit in the puppet's strategic reserve force, was forced to turn tail and flee from Thuong Duc. The Quang Da liberated zone had been expanded and we now had a new offensive springboard directly threatening Da Nang city from the southwest. The combat power of our mobile main force units in South Vietnam was clearly stronger than that of the enemy's regular troops.

In Tri Thien, on 28 August 1974 the 324th Infantry Division from 2nd Corps, the Military Region's 6th Regiment, and local forces attacked the puppet 1st Division's defensive perimeter at La Son and Mo Tau, southwest of Hue city. During more than 40 days and nights of continuous combat, our troops eliminated from the field of battle 2,500 enemy troops, captured or destroyed a large quantity of war equipment, and crippled the puppet 1st Military Region's strongest division. The enemy defensive line southwest of Hue was shattered. The soldiers and civilians of Tri Thien liberated an area of almost 300 square kilometers, creating a springboard for use in attacking Hue city and threatening the line of communications between Hue and Da Nang.

In eastern Cochin China the 9th Infantry Division, 4th Corps, struck a number of positions from Rach Bap to Kien Dien, then developed the attack down to Phu Thu, liberating a large area south of Route 7 and threatening the Binh Duong province capital (Thu Dau Mot) and the puppet 25th Division base camp at Dong Du. The 7th Infantry Division, 4th Corps, supported by Military Region forces, attacked the enemy defensive perimeter north of the Dong Nai River, threatening the puppet 3rd Corps Headquarters at Bien Hoa. Sapper and commando forces subordinate to COSVN and to the Saigon–Gia Dinh city Command attacked dozens of enemy positions on the outskirts of the city. The most successful of these attacks was the destruction of the Nha Be gasoline storage facility on 2 June 1974.

In coordination with the other battlefields in South Vietnam the soldiers and civilians of the provinces of the Mekong Delta now went on the offensive, seized the initiative, retook areas captured by the enemy after the Paris Agreement, and liberated a number of new areas. Between July and October 1974 the soldiers and civilians of Military Region 9 destroyed or forced the withdrawal of hundreds of enemy outposts and police stations, liberating 4,000 hamlets and almost 800,000 people. In Region 8 we expanded our liberated area in the Plain of Reeds, cut Route 4, destroyed many enemy outposts, and liberated more than 200 hamlets and 130,000 civilians.

THE STRATEGIC OFFENSIVE AND THE BATTLE OF PHUOC LONG

During the final months of 1974 the nature of the battlefield in South Vietnam changed very rapidly and in directions increasingly favorable to our side. We had created a new offensive posture from north to south, from Tri Thien to the Central Highlands, Region 5, eastern Cochin China, and the Mekong Delta. Our main force troops on the battlefield were now organized up to the corps level and consisted of 16 infantry divisions and numerous specialty branch brigades and regiments deployed in every strategic area. Our strategic and campaign road network had been expanded and continuously improved and upgraded. Our supply stockpiles in the different battlefields were rather large. Since switching over to the counteroffensive role, our armed forces in South Vietnam had totally blocked the enemy's pacification and encroachment operations. We had regained the initiative, consolidated our offensive springboard positions in all the strategic theaters, and now could apply pressure all the way up to the very perimeter of the enemy's cities, bases, and lines of communication.

Meanwhile, U.S. combat troops had been forced to completely withdraw from South Vietnam. U.S. aid to the Saigon puppet administration had declined. The puppet troops had been forced to begin fighting what they called "a poor man's war." Desertion and disintegration in the ranks of the puppet army increased day by day. After having been accustomed to conducting large-scale encroachment operations, by the final months of 1974 the enemy was forced to fall back onto the defensive and could launch only small-scale sweep operations.[25] Clear changes could be seen in the balance of forces throughout the nation, not just on the battlefields of South Vietnam, and all these changes were in favor of the revolution. We had become stronger than the enemy.

On 30 September 1974, the Politburo met in Hanoi to discuss our military goals for the coming two years, 1975–1976. The Politburo reached the following conclusion: Now that the United States had withdrawn, it would not be easy for it to reverse direction and return. Even if the United States should reintervene to a limited extent, it would not be able to reverse the situation. A number of aggressive, hegemonistic powers harbored dangerous plots against Vietnam and Southeast Asia, but they were not yet ready to act. Our army and our people now had an opportunity to launch the final general offensive and uprising; to develop revolutionary war to its highest level; to annihilate or disperse the entire puppet army; to seize the enemy's main lair—Saigon—and all its other cities; to overthrow the national and local puppet governmental administrations; to seize total control of the reins of government; and to totally liberate South Vietnam, complete the people's democratic nationalist revolution throughout our nation; and unify the nation.

During the last months of 1974 and early 1975 our preparations for the two-year 1975–1976 strategic plan reached a new, higher level. In just the first two months of 1975 North Vietnam mobilized 57,000 new recruits (out of a total of 108,000 troops called for in the recruitment plan for 1975) and quickly trained these troops so they could be dispatched to the battlefield. Many cadre groups from the General Staff, the General Political Department, the General Technical Department, and the military services and specialty branches hurriedly departed for the battlefields to supervise and direct our preparations. Our military regions and corps continued to train cadre in the art of attacking enemy forces in an urban environment, organized troop training in policies toward liberated areas and disciplinary regulations for use when entering newly liberated cities, etc. Thousands of vehicles drove day and night down our strategic transportation routes transporting troops and supplies to the front lines.

As the 1974–1975 dry season began, in South Vietnam all battlefields intensified their operations and continued to strengthen themselves for our strategic offensive. In December 1974 COSVN's 16th and 205th Regiments, working with Tay Ninh provincial forces, overran enemy bases at Ba Den Mountain [Black Virgin Mountain] and Suoi Da. The 5th Infantry Division and local armed forces destroyed a number of enemy positions deep inside our liberated zones in Long An and Kien Tuong provinces. Military Region 7 main force troops attacked the

Tanh Linh and Hoai Duc district military headquarters. The armed forces of Military Regions 8 and 9 expanded their operations, supported local civilians in forcing dozens of enemy outposts to surrender or evacuate, and established many new liberated areas in Tra Vinh, Ben Tre, and My Tho provinces. Sapper and artillery units near Saigon shelled the Long Binh warehouse and logistics complex.

Realizing that the war had entered its final phase and that although the enemy still had large numbers of troops, these troops were stretched thin and tied down, permitting us to increase the size and power of our attacks, the COSVN Military Party Committee and the COSVN Military Command decided to use 4th Corps in an offensive campaign in the Route 14–Phuoc Long area. The objectives of the campaign were to annihilate a portion of the enemy's troop strength, to expand the road head for our strategic supply corridor, and to allow us to move our forces down to the enemy's middle defensive line. In early December 1974, after more than two months of preparations, 4th Corps marched out to begin its campaign. The 271st, 165th, and 201st Regiments slogged through heavy rains to occupy their assault positions. Some units marched more than 100 kilometers and were forced to cut their way through the jungles at night. On 14 December our troops attacked the Bu Dang district military headquarters. During this battle, combatant Doan Duc Thai (11th Company) set off a bangalore torpedo while still holding it in his own hands, destroying the enemy's sixth barrier fence, the final defensive line around the enemy base camp, opening the way for an assault by his regiment's main deep-penetration spearhead.[26] After five days of continuous, vicious combat we overran the Bu Dang district headquarters, the Bu Na strong point headquarters, and more than 60 enemy outposts and police stations. We killed or captured 2,000 enemy troops, captured 900 weapons (including four 105mm howitzers and 7,000 rounds of 105mm ammunition), and liberated an area stretching more than 100 kilometers along Route 14 (from Kilometer 11 to Kien Duc) with a population of 14,000 civilians.

Exploiting our victory and putting to immediate use the newly captured artillery shells, on 26 December 7th Division's 165th Regiment overran the Bu Dop district military headquarters and a number of enemy outposts along Route 311. The 7th Division's other two infantry regiments, the 141st and 209th, attacked the Dong Xoai district military headquarters, killing or capturing the entire enemy garrison, including the district military commander and the commander of a Regional Force battalion.

With the loss of Dong Xoai, Phuoc Long city was now isolated. Expanding its offensive, on 31 December 4th Corps, under the command of 4th Corps Military Commander Major General Hoang Cam and Deputy Commander Senior Colonel Bui Cat Vu and reinforced by the 16th Infantry Regiment and two anti-aircraft artillery battalions from the COSVN Military Command, launched an attack on Phuoc Long city. The 165th Regiment (supported by four tanks), the 141st Regiment, and the 79th Sapper Battalion, working closely together, crushed the enemy's outer defensive perimeter and overran the Phuoc Binh district military headquarters and Ba Ra Mountain. The enemy garrison defending the province headquarters concentrated most of its forces (two battalions) to block the only usable road into the city. The puppet 3rd Corps Headquarters sent as many as 80 tactical fighter sorties a day to bomb our positions on the outskirts of the city to reduce our offensive strength and block our advance. By this time, however, the artillery observation post we had emplaced on top of Ba Ra Mountain was able to accurately adjust the fire of our 130mm guns and suppress the enemy's artillery firebases. Eight battalions of anti-aircraft guns gained complete control of the airspace over the city. On 6 January 1975 our troops launched their final assault. At 10:30 the "Determined to Fight, Determined to Win" flag was planted on top of the Phuoc Long province headquarters by Combatant Nguyen Van Hoan of the 141st Regiment and his comrades. Over 2,000 enemy troops in the city were killed or captured. Our troops captured more than 10,000 rounds of artillery ammunition. Working in coordination with our main force troops, local armed forces and the civilian population launched their own attacks and uprisings, completing the total liberation of Phuoc Long province.

Although the puppet 3rd Corps still had large numbers of troops (including the 18th, 5th, and 25th Infantry Divisions, the 3rd Armored Brigade, and other specialty branch units), these troops were stretched thin and tied down along the defense lines north, northwest, and northeast of Saigon. Thieu's puppet regime trumpeted a promise to "retake" Phuoc Long but, in the end, it was afraid to commit its reserves and simply was not strong enough to retake the province. The U.S. imperialists threatened to send expeditionary troops back to South Vietnam and resume the bombing of the North, but because of the international situation and its own domestic situation, the U.S. ruling clique did not dare take action.

In South Vietnam, for the first time in the history of our resistance war against the United States, we had completely liberated an entire province near Saigon. The Route 14–Phuoc Long victory demonstrated the new capabilities of our troops and our civilian population. Our army had successfully conducted a corps-level campaign, attacking and seizing control of enemy district and province military headquarters and liberating enemy cities and towns. This victory was also a kind of "strategic reconnaissance" for us, strengthening our resolve to carry out the strategic decision reached by the Politburo during its October meeting. The victory exposed the limited ability of the United States to react after the forced withdrawal of their expeditionary army from South Vietnam.

During the final days of 1974, after hearing reports from our battlefield commanders in Tri Thien, the Central Highlands, Region 5, Cochin China, and extreme southern Central Vietnam on new developments on the battlefield since the beginning of the 1974–1975 dry season, the Politburo foresaw that a strategic opportunity might appear earlier than anticipated. For this reason, in addition to the basic two-year plan for 1975–1976, the Politburo ordered that another plan be drafted so we would be ready to seize any opportunity to liberate the South during 1975.

On 6 January 1975, news of the victory in Phuoc Long province elated the soldiers and civilians of our entire nation. In his speech concluding the Politburo session on 7 January, Comrade Le Duan, First Secretary of the Party Central Committee, emphasized the importance of firmly seizing the strategic opportunity by altering our combat plan and urgently mobilizing forces and supplies to ensure that our armed forces could launch the strongest and swiftest attack possible and achieve a complete, total victory when we finally launched our attack against Saigon.

Our nation now entered the spring of a new year. Arm in arm with the entire population, our army had made preparations, increased its combat capabilities, and was ready to launch large-scale campaigns aimed at bringing our resistance war against the Americans to save the nation to a victorious conclusion.

15
Striking with Combined-Arms Power: Seizing the City of Ban Me Thuot, Liberating the Central Highlands, and Opening the Way for the Spring 1975 General Offensive and Uprising

PREPARATIONS FOR BATTLE

In September 1974 the Politburo and the Central Military Party Committee decided to launch an offensive campaign in the southern portion of the Central Highlands and directed the General Staff to prepare a plan for this offensive. Both the Politburo decision and the campaign plan were revised in November 1974. The original plan stated that the primary objective of the campaign was to liberate Duc Lap and totally clear Route 14 to enable us to send supplies and heavy technical equipment down Route 14 to eastern Cochin China.

On 9 January 1975, as soon as the December 1974–January 1975 Politburo session ended, the Current Affairs Committee of the Central Military Party Committee met to discuss the military missions for early 1975 in order to implement phase one of the strategic combat plan. A number of leadership cadre and battlefield commanders from Region 5 and the Central Highlands (including Vo Chi Cong, Chu Huy Man, and Hoang Minh Thao) and Deputy Commander of the General Staff Le Trong Tan were invited to attend this meeting.

The Central Military Party Committee affirmed that during the 1974–1975 dry season our main force units would direct their main offensive thrust against the southern Central Highlands. Our armed forces in that area were assigned the following missions:

- Annihilate a significant portion of the enemy's troop strength.[1]
- Liberate the provinces of Darlac, Phu Bon, and Quang Duc. The key target was to be the city of Ban Me Thuot. If the opportunity presented itself we would either expand our attack to liberate Pleiku and Kontum or drive down to the coast to liberate Phu Yen and Khanh Hoa.
- Support the masses in organizing uprisings to expand the liberated areas,

361

expand our local armed forces, and coordinate with other battlefields throughout South Vietnam.

This campaign would strengthen our ability to organize and command combined-arms combat operations, and in particular would improve the ability of our main force units to conduct mobile operations and to attack and seize enemy cities.

Senior General Van Tien Dung, Politburo member and Chief of the General Staff, was sent to the Central Highlands to oversee the campaign as the personal representative of the Politburo, the Central Military Party Committee, and the High Command. General Dung was responsible for implementing our strategic plan to attack Ban Me Thuot and liberate the Central Highlands. A Central Highlands Campaign Headquarters was established. The Headquarters Commander was Lieutenant General Hoang Minh Thao, and Senior Colonel Dang Vu Hiep served as Political Commissar.

During the last weeks of January 1975, the Campaign Command staff prepared a detailed battle plan and the reconnaissance teams assigned to cover the main target, Ban Me Thuot, set out to carry out their duties.

The Central Highlands covered five provinces: Gia Lai [Pleiku], Kontum, Darlac, Phu Bon, and Quang Duc. It was a immense area of mountains and forests on the highland plateau of western Central Vietnam, bordering on lower Laos and northeastern Cambodia and linked to our great rear area of North Vietnam by strategic roads running down the western and eastern sides of the Annamite Mountain chain. From the Central Highlands it was possible to move down to the south (to eastern Cochin China) on Route 14 and to the east (the lowlands of Central Vietnam) on Routes 19, 7, and 21. Throughout the years of the resistance war against the French and on through the resistance war against the United States, the Central Highlands had always been a strategically important battlefield for both ourselves and the enemy. It was an area suitable for mobile operations and could support combat operations by main force units in Vietnam and throughout the Indochinese Peninsula.

Our armed forces on the Central Highlands battlefield had matured in many different ways during the long years of force building and combat. Our main force troops had been honed in combat and were experienced in massed combat operations, especially in mobile [maneuver] operations. A system of strategic and campaign roads and a rear services supply network had been built and continuously expanded, especially during the two years 1973 and 1974. This infrastructure was sufficient to support main force combat operations in large-scale offensive campaigns.

As the 1974–1975 dry season began, because of their erroneous assessment of the strength, capabilities, and probable attack targets of our forces, enemy forces in South Vietnam were deployed in defensive positions in a "heavy at both ends" posture, having strengthened their forces defending Military Region 1 (Tri-Thien and Quang Da) and Military Region 3 (eastern Cochin China).

Prior to our attack, enemy forces in Military Region 2 consisted of two infantry divisions, seven Ranger Groups, 86 Regional Force battalions, five armored squadrons and 12 separate armored troops, 13 artillery battalions and eight separate artillery batteries (a total of 376 guns), and 16 Air Force squadrons (with a total of 487 aircraft). Although the enemy had a large number of troops and units at his disposal, because Military Region 2 covered such a large area[2] he had to spread his forces thin to cover many different locations and his mobile reserve force was quite limited.[3] Realizing the importance of the Central Highlands, the enemy concentrated the bulk of Military Region 2's forces in this vital area.[4] Since he believed we would attack the Central Highlands from the north, the enemy strengthened his forces defending the provinces of Gia Lai [Pleiku] and Kontum.[5]

Based on our battle plan and on an analysis of the strength and deployment of enemy forces throughout the battlefield, especially in the Central Highlands, the Central Military Party Committee and the High Command rapidly built up the troop strength, supply stockpiles, and technical support of the Central Highlands Front. Meanwhile, the other battlefields were directed to intensify their combat and deception operations and their efforts to attract and tie down the enemy to support the Central Highlands campaign.

Along our strategic and campaign transportation routes, engineers and assault youth rapidly improved 226 kilometers of old roads, constructed 141 kilometers of new roads, and built three river-crossing ferry points and 13 fords from Gia Lai [Pleiku] and Kontum to Duc Lap and Ban Me Thuot. A number of secret river fords and river-crossing points were built in areas temporarily under enemy control. Over 1,000 military vehicles from Group 559, the military regions, and the Ministry of Communications and Transportation operated night and day carrying supplies to the Central Highlands. By the end of February 1975, Group 559 and its supporting elements had fulfilled 110 percent of the transportation plan for the campaign, ensuring that the troops of the Central Highlands would have sufficient supplies to operate through the end of 1975.

On orders from the General Staff, between late December 1974 and early February 1975 reinforcement units for the campaign began arriving at their designated assembly positions. The 968th Infantry Division marched into Gia Lai and Kontum from lower Laos. The 316th Infantry Division, a unit with extensive combat experience in forest-covered mountain areas and a distinguished combat record during the resistance wars against the French and the Americans, was secretly shipped from Nghe An to western Darlac province by the Transportation Department's 525th Truck Regiment. To ensure absolute secrecy the division strictly enforced stringent security measures, maintaining complete radio silence during its journey south and after its arrival in the assembly area. Infantry Regiment 95B of the 325th Infantry Division, the 232nd Anti-Aircraft Artillery Regiment, the 575th Engineer Regiment, five battalions and a number of separate companies of signal and reconnaissance troops and river-crossing engineers, three artillery vehicle repair stations, one medical treatment unit, and 8,000 new recruits sent by the Ministry of Defense arrived at the front.

By February 1975 the forces participating in the Central Highlands campaign had grown to four infantry divisions (10th, 320th, 316th, and 968th), four separate infantry regiments (95A, 95B, 25th, and 271st), five field artillery and anti-aircraft artillery regiments, one tank-armor regiment, one sapper regiment, two engineer regiments, one signal regiment, and numerous rear services and transportation units. The 3rd Infantry Division, subordinate to Military Region 5, was assigned the mission of mounting strong supporting operations along Route 19. All units participating in the campaign had been well prepared and their morale was high. The 320th and 10th Divisions and a number of infantry and specialty branch units were familiar with the battlefield and their opposition. Our cadre and soldiers had little experience in urban combat and large-scale combined-arms combat operations, however, and the combat capabilities of the units was uneven.

To remedy these weaknesses, the Campaign Headquarters devoted a great deal of time to providing supplementary training to the units. Cadre from the battalion level up received training in the art of attacking enemy positions. The battalions and regiments took turns training in tactics for use in attacking enemy forces occupying strong defensive fortifications, attacking urban areas using combined-arms forces, etc. Drawing on the experience it had gained during the 1972 campaign, the 10th Division trained in making coordinated attacks using "pairs" of vehicles, one tank and one armored personnel carrier, along with accompanying infantry, to increase our offensive power. The 320th Division trained in coordinated tactics involving infantry, artillery, and engineers and in moving field artillery guns up close to the objective and providing direct fire on targets to support the infantry. As for the 316th Division, which was new to the Central Highlands, cadre from the staff agencies of the Campaign Headquarters went down to the division's subordinate units to work directly with division cadre and soldiers to set up exercise areas and train the troops in the realities of the battlefield and in how to handle the requirements of their new combat missions.

Campaign political staff agencies provided guidance to all units in leadership and in educating cadre and soldiers to understand the special characteristics of this battlefield and the objectives of the campaign. They helped the units build combat resolve, an aggressive attitude, initiative, flexibility, and mobility and instructed them on the need to create and take advantage of opportunities and on the need to maintain the element of surprise. They encouraged cadre and soldiers to develop a high level of bravery and a dynamic spirit to deal with any eventuality that might surface during an offensive attack, to attack enemy forces holding strong fortified positions, to destroy enemy headquarters, to follow through after assaults, and to win the greatest possible victory for the campaign.

On 17 February 1975, the Campaign Command group met to discuss the battle plan, focusing attention on a number of issues, such as the organization and deployment of forces, campaign deception operations, and how to fight the initial engagement. Based on the missions assigned to the campaign by the Central Military Party Committee and the High Command, and based on the strength and dispositions of the enemy on the battlefield, the Campaign Command developed two plans: one for attacking the enemy when it was alert, prepared, and waiting for our attack in defensive positions, and one for attacking the enemy when it was not ready and did not expect us. During preparations for the attack all units were required to prepare for the possibility that the enemy would be alert and ready for us, but every effort would be made to hit the enemy while his forces were still in their current deployment positions, before any reinforcements were made, or, if there were reinforcements, before they were able to reverse the situation.

The city of Ban Me Thuot is located in Darlac province at the intersection of two strategic roads, Routes 14 and 21. In early 1975 the city, which had a population of 114,035 people, occupied an important military, economic, and political position in the Central Highlands. Because enemy forces were stretched so thin and because their attention had been drawn toward the northern part of the Central Highlands, enemy forces in Ban Me Thuot consisted only of headquarters elements of the 23rd Infantry Division, the 53rd Regiment (minus one battalion), one artillery battalion, one tank-armored squadron (minus), and nine Regional Forces battalions. The enemy believed Ban Me Thuot would not be a major target for attack by our forces. They thought our troops were not yet capable of attacking and occupying a large city like Ban Me Thuot, which had strong defensive fortifications and lay deep inside the enemy's rear area.

From our standpoint, if we liberated Ban Me Thuot we would upset the enemy's entire position in the Central Highlands and create favorable conditions that would enable us to develop our offensive down to the coastal provinces of Central Vietnam and down into eastern Cochin China. According to the Central Highlands campaign plan, the city of Ban Me Thuot was our key objective, and the attack on and occupation of Ban Me Thuot would be our first battle. During this battle our army would use a relatively large combined-arms force to attack and occupy a city with solid defensive fortifications. Many new problems surfaced during the course of our preparations, especially the need to determine appropriate tactics to achieve the maximum results, to secure the element of surprise, and to win a great victory.

After a democratic discussion and analyzing all factors and possible eventualities, the Campaign Command decided to use a number of regiments and divisions to cut the lines of communications—Routes 14, 19, and 21—in order to isolate, both from the strategic and campaign standpoints, the Central Highlands from the lowlands of Region 5 and cut the southern part of the Central Highlands off from the northern part. At the same time we would actively conduct deception operations aimed at tying down enemy troops and drawing their attention to the northern Central Highlands in order to give us the element of surprise when we attacked Ban Me Thuot. We would then fight the key battle of the campaign to seize Ban Me Thuot city by using strong combined-arms assault formations moving in from afar, supported by coordinated attacks launched by a number of sapper and infantry battalions, which had secretly infiltrated into the city and hidden themselves near their objectives. Our assault would rapidly destroy key objectives inside the city and then expand outward to destroy the enemy's outposts and bases on the outskirts of the city. We also prepared a plan for dealing with counterattacks and set aside strong reserve forces to be ready to defeat all enemy counterattacks and maintain a firm grip on our liberated area. This was a risky, daring battle plan that demanded that all units occupy their positions at the precise times specified in the plan, that they maintain secrecy right up to the time they opened fire, that they coordinate their operations precisely with one another, and, most important, that they skillfully implement the deception plan.

On 25 February 1975, Senior General Van Tien Dung, Chief of the General Staff and representative of the High Command at the Central Highlands Front, approved the resolution and battle plan of the Campaign Command. Comrade Van Tien Dung directed all units to further develop their planned use of deep penetration tactics, mechanized units striking in coordination with sapper forces secretly pre-positioned within the city.

During the first days of spring 1975, the ethnic minority tribal people living in the Central Highlands liberated zone noisily and openly went off to build roads, transport rice, transport ammunition, etc., and made preparations to greet our soldiers, who would ostensibly be arriving to liberate Pleiku and Kontum. In Gia Lai [Pleiku] province the 320th Division increased its operations in the area west of Route 19, shelling the outposts at Tam, Thanh An, Thanh Binh, etc. A number of the division's units worked with civilian laborers from the province's 4th and 5th Districts to openly build a road headed toward Bau Can–La Son. The 198th Sapper Regiment conducted a raid against the Pleiku gasoline storage facility. Regiment 95A attacked enemy vehicles traveling on Route 19 east of Pleiku city. In Kontum province, soldiers of the 10th Division worked hard to strengthen trenches, bunkers, and combat fortifications in areas in immediate contact with enemy forces. Provincial local force troops and civilian laborers from the 67th and 80th Districts built a number of supply roads and hauled artillery to areas close to the city. At night, our transportation trucks, with their headlights turned on, drove toward the city.

While the enemy's attention was drawn toward Pleiku and Kontum, the 968th Infantry Division secretly moved in to take over positions held by the 320th and 10th Divisions to allow these two divisions to march off to the south. The 968th kept up all the regular activities of these two divisions. Each day division and Campaign Headquarters deception elements sent out large numbers of fake cables, orders, and reports.

The 10th and 320th Divisions were units with many years of combat experience and many combat victories over the Americans and the puppets in the Central Highlands, and the puppet 2nd Corps paid special attention to the activities of these two divisions. They believed there would be large-scale fighting wherever the 10th and 320th Divisions were operating. At the end of February

1975, having discovered that elements of these two divisions were in the southern Central Highlands, the enemy immediately sent the 53rd Regiment out to check the area northwest of Ban Me Thuot city. They also sent the 45th Regiment down from Pleiku to search the area west of Thuan Man. These enemy operations caused problems for our road-building operations and our movement of troops up close to the city.

The Campaign Headquarters assessed the situation and concluded that the enemy suspected we were preparing to attack Duc Lap, Gia Nghia, Cam Ga, and Ban Me Thuot but that he had not yet learned either the full extent of our campaign plans or our true strength in the area. The enemy's search operations were being sent out in many different directions and appeared to be passive and haphazard. Based on this assessment, the Campaign Headquarters directed all units to steadfastly maintain the secrecy of our true intentions and strength in the main combat theater, Ban Me Thuot, and to actively and skillfully conduct more extensive deception operations in the Pleiku and Kontum areas to draw away the enemy's 45th Regiment and to tie down the 44th Regiment and other enemy forces in the northern Central Highlands to allow our soldiers to continue their preparations in the south. The 320th Division, which had just arrived in the area west of Thuan Man, was ordered to immediately pull its units back and to avoid all contact with enemy forces.

On 1 March 1975, the 968th Division, carrying out its mission of drawing the enemy's attention to the northern part of the Central Highlands, attacked the enemy defensive perimeter southwest of Pleiku, destroying or forcing the withdrawal of a number of enemy outposts and putting pressure on the enemy base at Thanh Binh and on the Thanh An district capital. The 19th Regiment of the 968th Division, along with Kontum province armed forces, attacked the enemy defensive perimeter north of the city, cutting Route 14 south of Tan Phu. The puppet 2nd Corps was forced to pull back the 45th Regiment, which had been conducting search operations in the Cam Ga and Thuan Man areas, in order to defend Thanh An.

Our campaign deception operations had been successful. Enemy forces in Darlac province and around Ban Me Thuot city remained unchanged as of early 1975.[6] We had achieved the necessary conditions and would be able to attack Ban Me Thuot using the version of our plan in which the enemy was not prepared for our attack.

THE OFFENSIVE BEGINS

During the night of 3–4 March 1975, Regiment 95A overran a number of enemy outposts, seizing control over a 20-kilometer-long stretch of Route 19 east of Pleiku city. On 4 March, Military Region 5's 3rd Division, overcoming many problems caused by its low troop strength and continuing supply difficulties, opened fire on schedule, destroying two enemy companies and nine enemy out-posts and seizing control of Route 19 from Dong Pho to Thuong An. The fol-lowing night, 5 March, 25th Regiment captured a section of Route 21 east of Chu Cuc. At Cam Ga the 320th Division attacked a convoy of 14 vehicles from the puppet 45th Regiment, destroying eight vehicles, capturing two 105mm how-itzers, and cutting Route 14 north of Thuan Man.

For the first time in an offensive campaign, our army had devoted one entire division and two separate infantry regiments to the task of cutting lines of com-munications. By cutting the three main roads (Routes 14, 19, and 21) and by the effective use of deception operations to stretch enemy forces thin and draw them away, the armed forces of the Central Highlands and of Military Region 5 had created a very advantageous strategic and campaign position for our forces, iso-lating the Central Highlands from the coastal lowlands of Central Vietnam, cut-ting the northern part of the Central Highlands off from the southern part, surrounding and isolating the city of Ban Me Thuot, and creating favorable con-ditions that enabled our units to complete their preparations and open fire on schedule.

On 6 March, faced with isolation and under ever-increasing pressure because of the cutting of Route 21, enemy forces in Ban Me Thuot sent a Regional Force battalion out to conduct a search north of the city. This created problems for our preparations in this area: road building, preparation of assem-bly positions for our infantry units, hauling artillery into firing positions, etc. Determined to maintain secrecy until the last minute for this key battle, the Cam-paign Command ordered all units north of Ban Me Thuot city to temporarily halt their preparations. Because of this order, if they were to open fire on schedule, the infantry units attacking from the north would have to march in from far away and our artillery would not have preprepared, fortified firing positions for use in the attack. This situation demanded great effort from all units. Viewed from the standpoint of the overall campaign, however, this decision benefited our side because if our intentions were discovered by the enemy he would strengthen the defenses of the city and the battle would become more difficult. To alleviate the problems faced by our units, the Campaign Command directed the 320th Divi-sion to attack and seize the Chu Xe hilltop position, an outpost held by Regional Force troops 15 kilometers south of Cam Ga on Route 15. The 3rd Battalion, 48th Regiment, overran this strong point after 40 minutes of fighting, forcing the enemy to bring the 53rd Regiment up from Ban Me Thuot in response to our attack. The units moving in from the north now were able to continue their prepa-rations and move in closer to their targets.

On 8 March, 48th Regiment, 320th Division, attacked and captured Cam Ga (the capital of Thuan Man district), killing more than 200 enemy troops and cap-turing 120 prisoners and 200 weapons. Route 14 was completely cut between Pleiku and Ban Me Thuot, and the enemy could send reinforcements to Ban Me Thuot only by air.

Southwest of Ban Me Thuot city, on 9 March the 10th Infantry Division attacked Duc Lap, a large district capital on Route 14 that blocked our strategic supply route to eastern Cochin China. According to the campaign plan, the 10th Division, reinforced by one tank company and two 105mm howitzers with 300 rounds of ammunition, was to quickly finish off Duc Lap so that the division could move up quickly to serve as the reserve force for the attack against Ban Me Thuot. When the time came to open fire, however, the only reinforcements received by the division were two 105mm howitzers with only 50 rounds of ammunition. Despite this situation, during the morning of 9 March the division resolutely opened fire on schedule and quickly overran Base 23 and Nui Lua. However, because we did not have a firm grasp of the enemy situation and because of poor coordination between infantry and fire support elements, the division did not take the Duc Lap district capital until 10 March, after it had organized and launched a second assault wave. The entire enemy force at Duc Lap, three battalions, was wiped out. We captured more than 100 prisoners along with 14 artillery pieces and 20 tanks and armored personnel carriers.

THE ATTACK ON BAN ME THUOT

By 9 March 1975, the deployment of our forces had been completed, completely isolating the battlefield and establishing our campaign battle position. The main forces of the puppet 2nd Corps had been drawn away and tied down in the northern portion of the Central Highlands.

In the meantime, during the evening of 8 March the units participating in the attack on Ban Me Thuot (12 infantry and specialty branch regiments), which were divided into three attack sectors, north, northwest, and southwest, arrived at their temporary assembly positions 10 to 15 kilometers from the city. Tank units were farther away, 25 to 30 kilometers. The 198th Sapper Regiment and two infantry battalions had crept in close, hiding their troops near important targets: the headquarters area of the puppet 23rd Division, the city airfield, the Hoa Binh Airfield, the Mai Hac De warehouse complex, etc.

Our combat order had been disseminated to each cadre and combatant. Along the different lines of advance, at intersections and river-crossing points, the Campaign Headquarters set up traffic control stations and line-of-march command stations to ensure that our infantry and heavy technical equipment could move quickly without traffic jams. Front engineers and divisional and regimental engineers quickly began building a river crossing over the Se-Re-Poc River as soon as the units began their attack march. Rapid work was finally begun to build military roads to tie into existing road networks. Large trees along these roads had been cut two-thirds of the way through their trunks. When the time came to open fire our tanks pushed these trees down and engineers hauled them away to clear the way for our troops to move forward.

During the night of 9–10 March we completed the task of moving a large force in from a great distance away and along many different lines of march to occupy attack positions. In all the attack sectors our troops had to overcome minefields and bypass enemy blocking positions, and in some attack sectors rivers had to be crossed. Total secrecy had to be maintained along the lines of march because the enemy had begun to detect our activities. Headquarters staffs at all levels dealt with many complicated developments in a timely fashion. With tremendous efforts by our cadre and soldiers we were able to occupy our attack positions on schedule and according to plan.

At two o'clock in the morning on 10 March 1975, the 198th Sapper Regiment, reinforced by fire-support elements equipped with recoilless rifles and B-72s [AT-3 Sagger anti-tank missiles], opened fire, attacking the city airfield, the Hoa Binh Airfield, and the Mai Hac De warehouse complex and raising the curtain on the Ban Me Thuot attack. At the same time our campaign artillery began to fire powerful suppression barrages against all targets: the 23rd Division Headquarters, the Darlac Province Military Headquarters, the artillery base, the armored base, etc. The city's electricity flickered out. Flames lit the night sky. The artillery bombardment, which lasted until 6:00 in the morning, confused and paralyzed the enemy's command structure and eliminated a portion of the enemy's troop strength in the city.

In coordination with the sappers and artillery, our combined-arms attack formations surged toward the city in the various attack sectors. By five o'clock on the morning of 10 March almost all our units had seized their jumping-off positions and had begun organizing for their assaults.

In the northeastern sector, bypassing the city airfield, which the 198th Sapper Regiment had already captured, Regiment 95B surged forward and took the six-way intersection near the center of the city. After some initial moments of terror and disorder, the enemy regrouped and fought to block our attack in this important sector. Vicious fighting swirled around the six-way intersection, the province administration area, the armored area, and especially at the Darlac Province Military Headquarters. Regiment 95B had to commit its reserve force to the battle and launch three separate assaults before it was finally able to capture the Darlac Province Military Headquarters.

In the northwestern sector, according to the battle plan the 148th Regiment of the 316th Division was to launch its attack to capture the artillery and armored areas at 6:00 in the morning. Because of the difficult terrain, however, the regiment had problems securing its springboard position and did not finish organizing its assault formations until 10:00. The enemy in this sector had time to consolidate and prepare. They sent aircraft to bomb our troops and tanks and infantry to make counterattacks to drive our troops back.

Determined not to allow his unit to get bogged down in front of the breach in the enemy's perimeter, Platoon Leader Nguyen Van Duoc hugged a satchel charge to his chest and charged through a curtain of enemy fire, clearing a way for the tanks and infantry to launch their assault.

At 1530 hours the 148th Regiment seized its objective. An element of the regiment then moved up Phan Boi Chau Street, crushing an enemy pocket of resistance in the Bo De High School, and, continuing on to the six-way intersection, linked up with Regiment 95B.

In the west-southwestern sector, the 174th Regiment of the 316th Division attacked and seized the Mai Hac De warehouse complex. The 4th Battalion of the 24th Regiment, 10th Division, reinforced by a company of tanks and a company of armored personnel carriers, quickly bypassed enemy pockets of resistance on the outer perimeter and launched an attack on the signal and transportation areas immediately adjacent to the headquarters complex of the puppet 23rd Division. Enemy aircraft bombed our troops to block our attack and the enemy organized many successive waves of counterattacks. The enemy retook the Mai Hac De supply complex and the Chu Due strong point. Our forces fought enemy forces for control of each individual area. Nine of our soldiers were killed at the parade ground. Hoang Dinh Thu, Commander of 1st Company, 10th Division, and Doan Sinh Huong, platoon cadre of 9th Company, 273rd Tank Regiment, led their units in driving back many waves of enemy counterattacks. Units of the 232nd and 234th Anti-Aircraft Artillery Regiments stuck close to and protected the infantry and tank assault formations, shooting down six A-37 aircraft and driving enemy aircraft up to higher altitudes. During the afternoon of 10 March the 174th Regiment retook the Mai Hac De storage complex.

By 1730 hours on 10 March, our troops had taken almost all of their objectives within the city. Because we did not have a full understanding of the strength of the puppet 23rd Division Headquarters complex, however, and because the command-level cadre of our units did not react quickly to the developing situation, we still had not been able to seize this important military objective.

To secure total victory in this key first battle the Campaign Command decided to set up defenses to hold the positions we had already captured, and at the same time assemble a powerful force that could rapidly overrun the headquarters complex of the 23rd Division and the other objectives that still remained to be taken.

By the afternoon of 10 March the enemy finally realized that our target was in fact the occupation of Ban Me Thuot, but by then it was too late. The President of the puppet government, Nguyen Van Thieu, and the commander of the puppet 2nd Corps, Pham Van Phu, ordered their troops remaining in the city to "defend Ban Me Thuot to the death" and to await reinforcements. Routes 14, 19, and 21 were all cut, however, and although enemy forces in the northern part of the Central Highlands and along the coast of Central Vietnam were still strong, they had no way to get to Ban Me Thuot to rescue their comrades.

At 6:00 A.M. on 11 March, our combined-arms units, attacking from three directions and supported by artillery fire, launched an assault on the headquarters of the puppet 23rd Division. The enemy fought desperately to resist our attack. Enemy aircraft dropped bombs on the city streets. Enemy M-48 and M-

41 tanks recklessly roared out to block the intersections. To protect our infantry attack formations and the civilian population, our anti-aircraft artillery troops waited until enemy aircraft dove down to a low level before opening fire. Our infantry stuck close to and supported our tanks while they overran enemy pockets of resistance. Our tank drivers utilized their armored assault power to clear the way for the infantry to launch their assault.

At 11:00 A.M. on 11 March, the puppet 23rd Division Headquarters complex was overrun. Colonel Vu The Quang, Deputy Commander of the 23rd Division, and Colonel Nguyen Trong Luat, Darlac province Sector Commander, were captured. After 32 hours of heroic combat our troops had killed or captured the entire enemy garrison and totally liberated Ban Me Thuot city. This was the key, decisive battle of the Central Highlands campaign, a "body blow" that surprised and confounded the enemy, upsetting his strategic guidance, disrupting his defensive system for the Central Highlands, and opening the door onto a very advantageous new situation. With this battle our troops took a step forward in the art of selecting a campaign target and fighting the key battle, in the art of deception, of deploying forces and preparing the battle area, and in the creative and effective use of tactics against enemy troops holding defensive positions in an urban area.

DEFEATING ENEMY COUNTERATTACKS

During the afternoon of 11 March the Politburo and the Central Military Party Committee sent a message to the troops and civilians of the Central Highlands congratulating them for displaying a spirit of heroism and determination to win and for daringly, creatively, and quickly securing a great victory during the first days of the campaign. The Politburo and the Central Military Party Committee ordered our forces to rapidly exploit this opportunity to secure many even greater victories. In Ban Me Thuot, the Politburo and the Party Committee ordered that enemy remnants be rapidly destroyed, that our forces expand their attack to clear the area surrounding the city, and that we prepare for enemy counterattacks.

Acting on the orders of the Politburo and the Central Military Party Committee, the Campaign Command quickly organized forces to round up the enemy remnants still left in the city; to destroy the enemy strong points remaining on the city's outskirts, the key positions being the rear bases of the 45th and the 53rd Regiments, in order to deny the enemy bases for use in their counterattacks; and to consolidate the targets we had already taken. The 10th Division was ordered to move to the northeast of the city to prepare to deal with an enemy counterattack.

Between 11 and 14 March the 198th Sapper Regiment and the 148th Infantry Regiment swept away all enemy forces still holding out in the city. The 25th, 95B, 174th, 149th, and 66th Regiments, supported by tanks, overran or forced to surrender many enemy outposts and strong points (Buon Ho, Chu Pao, Dat Ly,

Chau Nga, and Chau Son) on the outskirts of the city. Group 559's 21st Battalion attacked and took Ban Don.

A Darlac province People's Committee, headed by Senior Colonel Y-Bloc, was formed. The revolutionary masses worked with our troops to pursue and capture escaping soldiers and thugs who owed blood debts to the people. Under the guidance of our troops the civilian population urgently dug anti-aircraft shelters. Many people sought temporary refuge outside the city. Our anti-aircraft regiments deployed into firing positions, prepared to do battle against enemy aircraft. Our troops maintained discipline within the city, correctly implementing the policies toward ethnic minorities established by the Party and the Government. A number of warehouses holding rice, salt, canned goods, etc., which we had captured from the enemy, were opened and the goods distributed to the civilian population.

On 13 March, 10th Division's 66th and 28th Regiments, moving by truck from Duc Lap, arrived in the area northeast of Ban Me Thuot city where they joined the 24th Regiment and other units preparing to fight off an enemy counterattack.

Meanwhile, in the northern Central Highlands and on the battlefields of Tri-Thien and Region 5, our troops intensified their operations in support of Ban Me Thuot, isolating and tying down enemy troops and forcing the puppet 2nd Corps to spread its forces thin to cope with the situation. The 968th Infantry Division overran two enemy outposts southwest of Pleiku, moved up close to the Thanh Binh district capital, and shelled Kontum's Cu Hanh Airfield. Gia Lai and Kontum local force troops conducted strong combat operations southeast of Pleiku city. The 3rd Division and Regiment 95A dug in and held the positions they had seized along Route 19 and expanded their attack toward Mang Giang pass and toward Vuon Xoai. The 25th Infantry Regiment destroyed an enemy relief column coming up from Khanh Duong and kept Route 21 cut. The 271st Infantry Regiment and the 14th Sapper Battalion overran a number of outlying hamlets and pressed in close to Nhon Co Airfield in Quang Duc province.

In Tri-Thien military region armed forces sent a large force down to operate in the contested areas and in the lowlands, putting pressure on Hue city from the west and the north. In Region 5, the 2nd Division, the 52nd Infantry Brigade, and local armed forces overran the Tien Phuoc district military headquarters and forced the abandonment of the Phuoc Lam district capital. They then changed the direction of their attack down to the lowlands, cut Route 1, and put pressure on Quang Ngai city and Tam Ky city.

Our great victory at Ban Me Thuot and the continuing coordinated activities of our other battlefields caused great confusion in the enemy ranks. Although their forces in the northern portion of the Central Highlands and along the coast of Central Vietnam were still strong, all the roads were cut, so if they wanted to retake Ban Me Thuot, their only choice was to land troops by helicopter.

On 12 March, after more than 100 bombing sorties to clear landing zones, using 145 helicopter sorties the enemy landed the 45th Infantry Regiment and the

232nd Artillery Battery northeast of Ban Me Thuot. Two days later they landed the 44th Regiment (minus) and a 23rd Division forward headquarters element. By this time we had surrounded the base camp of the puppet 53rd Regiment and had overrun the 45th Regiment's base camp at 9:30 A.M. on 12 March, so the enemy was forced to land his troops in the Nong Trai–Phuoc An area.

Realizing that we had an excellent opportunity to destroy the enemy in the field outside of defensive positions, our troops rapidly shifted over to attack the enemy counterattack force. Our field artillery laid down accurate fire on the enemy landing zones. The 24th Regiment of the 10th Division, supported by tanks and artillery, launched continuous attacks against the enemy force, destroying and dispersing the 1st and 2nd Battalions of the 45th Regiment and one Regional Force battalion, capturing Hill 581, and liberating a 12-kilometer-long section of Route 21. During the afternoon of 14 March the remnants of the 45th Regiment retreated to the Nong Trai intersection, where they joined the remnants of the 21st Ranger Group in trying to defend the area west of the Phuoc An district capital.

On the morning of 16 March our artillery began to shell Nong Trai. Tanks and armored personnel carriers carried infantry troops of the 24th Regiment and 8th Battalion, 66th Regiment (10th Division), across the assault line, located 300 meters from the enemy's front line, launching an attack on the enemy position. After more than one hour of vicious fighting our troops had secured control of the Nong Trai intersection and destroyed the remnants of the 45th Regiment. The enemy force holding the Phuoc An district capital was shattered by this development, and many troops stripped off their uniforms and deserted. On 17 March, 10th Division's 24th and 28th Regiments massed their forces to launch an assault from the march straight down Route 21, destroying the 44th Regiment (minus) and three Regional Force battalions in the area of Ea Phe and Krong But villages. Five hundred enemy troops fleeing to Chu Cuc were caught between a blocking force from the 28th Regiment in the front and a pursuing unit in their rear and were destroyed. The puppet 2nd Corps counterattack to "retake" Ban Me Thuot was a complete failure, and the 23rd Infantry Division had been completely destroyed.

This second key victory demonstrated the active, aggressive, continuous spirit of attack of our troops and the tremendous maturation of our campaign command skills, of our ability to organize and carry out attacks against the enemy while on the march and to destroy large enemy forces conducting a heliborne counterattack. Following our great, decisive victory in the battle of Ban Me Thuot, our crushing of the enemy counterattack (from the 14th to the 18th of March) sped up the pace of our offensive campaign, isolated enemy forces, and drove the enemy army in the Central Highlands to the brink of collapse, opening the way for a collapse of puppet forces that could not be reversed.

THE ENEMY ABANDONS THE CENTRAL HIGHLANDS

On 14 March the Saigon puppet government decided to abandon the Central Highlands and withdraw their forces rapidly and unexpectedly down Route 7 in order to defend the coastal provinces of Central Vietnam and preserve their forces. The withdrawal plan was drawn up by the puppet 2nd Corps Headquarters and implemented in a detailed, systematic manner. On the morning of 15 March, the 3rd Ranger Group and the 19th Armored Squadron moved down to secure Cheo Reo. The 6th Ranger Group, accompanied by engineers, led the way to open the road and build bridges from east of Cheo Reo to Cung Son, Tuy Hoa province. This road had not been used for a long time. It had not been maintained and was unusable in many places.

On 16 March, supported by dozens of aircraft dropping bombs to clear the way, enemy forces in the provinces of Gia Lai [Pleiku] and Kontum began their withdrawal.[7] For the first time in the history of the Indochina Wars and within an entire campaign area, an enemy corps with modern equipment was forced to withdraw from an important strategic area.

Anticipating the way the situation might develop after the Ban Me Thuot victory, as early as 12 March the Politburo and the Central Military Party Committee directed the Campaign Headquarters to prepare to annihilate enemy forces in two different eventualities: First, the enemy might make a large-scale pullback to Pleiku city to defend it and await reinforcements; second, the enemy might be forced to conduct a strategic withdrawal, abandoning the Central Highlands in order to preserve his forces and to implement a strategic contraction of his positions. If the enemy abandoned the Central Highlands, the Politburo and the Central Military Party Committee concluded, this would be a strategic error on their part and would provide an extremely favorable opportunity for us to annihilate a large enemy force and completely liberate the Central Highlands.

Even though we had foreseen this possibility very early on, the situation developed extremely rapidly. At 1900 hours on 16 March, upon receipt of a cable from the High Command reporting that "the enemy has withdrawn down Route 7," the Campaign Command urgently issued orders to its forces and dealt with many complicated developments. The units participating in the pursuit were the 320A Division (reinforced by Regiment 95B), one armored battalion, one artillery group from the Campaign Command, and two Phu Yen province local force battalions.

When the order to pursue the enemy was received, the units of Division 320A were dispersed on operations in many different locations: 64th Regiment was clearing enemy forces in Phuoc An and Buon Ho; 48th Regiment was building a road east of Thuan Man in the direction of Cheo Reo; and 9th Regiment was pursuing the enemy along Route 17 (north of Thuan Man). The commander of the 320A Division sent 9th Battalion, 64th Regiment, which was the unit closest to

Route 7, to march rapidly to Cheo Reo to block the enemy force. Other units quickly collected their forces, some units running on foot, some moving by vehicle. All along the almost 100-kilometer route between the area north of Ban Me Thuot and Cheo Reo city, our troops surged like a storm toward Route 7 to pursue the enemy.

The cadre and soldiers of the 9th Battalion, burning dried bamboo and rubber sandals as torches to light the way, crossed rugged limestone mountains to arrive four kilometers east of Cheo Reo at 1600 hours on 17 March, where they immediately opened fire to block the enemy retreat. The enemy's "every man for himself" retreat was already in disorder, and when they heard the sounds of our guns blocking their way from the front, the enemy troops fell into even greater disarray. Enemy vehicles drove three and four abreast, trying to pass each other to get to the front—they sideswiped each other, rammed each other, and turned over, blocking dozens of kilometers of roadway. The bulk of the withdrawing enemy force was pushed into the Cheo Reo Valley. On 18 March, the 48th Regiment, with artillery fire support, attacked and destroyed a significant portion of the puppet 2nd Corps headquarters element and liberated Phu Bon city. On 21 March the 64th Regiment, moving in trucks belonging to Division 320A and to the 593rd Artillery Regiment, caught up with the fleeing enemy force, surrounding and destroying them at Phu Tuc. Meanwhile, the 96th and 13th Local Force Battalions, which had received orders from Military Region 5 Headquarters, had captured the Son Hoa Bridge east of Cung Son, blocking the enemy's line of retreat. On 24 March the 64th Regiment and the two Phu Yen province local force battalions attacked and liberated the Cung Son district capital, killing or capturing 6,000 enemy troops and capturing or destroying 40 enemy tanks.

This eight-day (from 17 to 24 March 1975) lightning pursuit by the 320A Division, a number of infantry and specialty branch units, and local armed forces units, ended in a complete victory. The entire 2nd Corps force retreating from the Central Highlands was annihilated. The only enemy elements that managed to reach Tuy Hoa were 11 M-113 APCs and an element of the 6th Ranger Group. The enemy plot to make an unexpected withdrawal to preserve his forces and to consolidate and defend the coastal lowlands of Central Vietnam was completely crushed.

Following the initial battle that liberated Ban Me Thuot and the crushing of the enemy's counterattack, this was the third key battle of the Central Highlands campaign—a battle that annihilated the enemy force withdrawing down Route 7.

While the 320A Division was pursuing the enemy down Route 7, on 18 March the 29th Regiment of the 968th Division and local armed forces moved into and liberated Kontum city. On the same day Regiment 95A and the armed forces of Gia Lai province liberated Pleiku city. Between 9 and 24 March the 19th Regiment, 968th Division, liberated the Thanh Binh district capital. The 271st Regiment liberated Kien Duc and Gia Nghia city, and the 12th Regiment of the 3rd Division (Region 5) and one battalion of Regiment 95A liberated the

An Khe district capital. Along Route 21 the 10th Division and the 25th Regiment destroyed and dispersed the 40th Regiment of the puppet 22nd Division and four Regional Force battalions, liberating the Khanh Duong district military headquarters and district capital.

By 25 March, the entire Central Highlands had been swept clean of enemy troops.

The Central Highlands campaign had achieved complete victory. Our troops had fulfilled their campaign responsibilities in an outstanding manner, destroyed and dispersed the entire enemy military force stationed in the Central Highlands, liberated an important strategic area, and shattered one of the enemy's strategic defensive sectors. Together with the victories on our other battlefields, our resounding victory in the Central Highlands caused the sudden collapse of the morale, forces, and battle posture of the enemy, pushing the Saigon puppet army into a position in which it was being destroyed and dispersed without hope of recovery.

With the Central Highlands campaign our army took a great leap forward toward maturity in its ability to organize and conduct large-scale combined-arms offensive campaigns, in its urban combat tactics, in its ability to combat large-scale enemy counterattacks using troops landed by air, and its ability to pursue and destroy an enemy force retreating through mountainous jungle terrain. The main force troops of the Central Highlands had grown rapidly in strength and were now more powerfully equipped because they had been reinforced by the large quantity of supplies and technical equipment they had captured from the enemy.[8]

The Spring 1975 General Offensive and uprising launched by our soldiers and civilians had begun with a victory of strategic importance. A new situation had been created, and a great opportunity had arrived. Seizing this new strategic opportunity, our army on all fronts, together with our entire population, concentrated all our strength to speed up the attack to gain total victory in the resistance war against the Americans to save the nation.

16

Seizing the Opportunity: The Armed Forces of Military Region Tri-Thien, Military Region 5, and 2nd Corps Coordinate Attacks to Liberate Hue, Danang, and the Provinces of Central Vietnam

THE OFFENSIVE BEGINS

The two-year 1975–1976 combat plan described Tri-Thien and Region 5 as important strategic theaters[1] that were to conduct operations in coordination with the main strategic theater, the Central Highlands.

The Tri-Thien–Region 5 battlefield was long and narrow. It was made up of three regions: forest-covered mountains, foothills, and coastal lowlands, and included two large cities, Danang and Hue. Danang was one of the largest joint-services military bases belonging to the Americans and the puppet regime in South Vietnam.

For enemy forces Military Region 1, lying at the northern end of South Vietnam next to North Vietnam, was an extremely important strategic area.[2] Throughout the war, and especially after the Tet 1968 General Offensive and Uprising and our 1972 strategic offensive, the enemy maintained a large concentration of forces there, including their mobile strategic reserve divisions. These forces were organized into a solid defensive system (turning Military Region 1 into one of the most powerful military concentrations in all of South Vietnam) intended to block any large-scale offensive launched by our main force troops from North Vietnam into the South.[3]

From our standpoint, the annihilation of this large enemy concentration (the puppet 1st Corps) and the destruction of the enemy's defensive system in Military Region 1 would create a new change in the balance of forces and in the strategic situation, creating conditions that would allow the transportation of technical equipment and the movement of large military forces down to the south and result in the complete liberation of Saigon and of all the provinces of Cochin China.

During 1973–1974, and especially once the 1974–1975 dry season began, 2nd Corps and the armed forces of Military Region 5 and the Tri-Thien Military

Region had worked hard to train and expand their forces, build and repair roads, stockpile supplies, and step up military attacks. They had pushed back, partially at least, the progress of the enemy pacification program and had forced the enemy to disperse his forces and pull back to defend his own bases. Our three types of troops, and especially our main force troops, were able to maintain a firm foothold in the contested areas and move forces down into the lowlands and up close to the enemy's lines of communications.

On 4 March 1975, as our armed forces on the Central Highlands battlefield were beginning to occupy their assault positions and preparing to attack Duc Lap and Ban Me Thuot, in the Tri-Thien and Region 5 areas 2nd Corps and the armed forces of these two Military Regions opened fire simultaneously, kicking off their local spring-summer campaign, which was also phase one of the two-year 1975–1976 strategic offensive plan. This was a combined campaign aimed at annihilating a significant portion of the enemy's troop strength, pushing back the enemy's pacification and encroachment plan, cutting lines of communications, tying down the enemy's mobile strategic reserve divisions (the Airborne and Marines), creating a new battlefield posture and new level of strength for the two Military Regions, and supporting the Central Highlands Campaign.

When our operation began, the armed forces of the Tri-Thien Military Region consisted of three infantry regiments, three separate infantry battalions, and one sapper battalion, all subordinate to the Military Region; and six infantry battalions and two sapper battalions subordinate to the provinces of Quang Tri and Thua Thien. At that time one element of 2nd Corps, the 324th Infantry Division (minus one regiment), was stationed in the Military Region. To unify command over all armed elements the Central Military Party Committee formed a Front Party Committee made up of representatives of the Tri Thien Region Party Committee and the 2nd Corps Party Committee. Major General Le Tu Dong was chosen to serve as Secretary of the Front Party Committee.

To carry out our deception program in the North and to gradually shift forces down into the foothills and the lowlands, between 5 and 8 March the local armed forces of Quang Tri and Thua Thien provinces fought a number of small battles along the enemy's lines of communications and surrounded and threatened enemy positions in Hai Lang district, Quang Tri province. Meanwhile, five infantry battalions,[4] two sapper battalions,[5] and almost 100 armed operations teams (totaling almost 3,000 armed combatants) began to move down into the lowland districts to join local cadre and armed forces in preparations to attack the enemy.

On 8 March, 2nd Corps' 324th Division attacked the Nui Bong–Nui Nghe area along the enemy's defensive perimeter southwest of Hue and overran a number of hill positions along Route 14. As this attack directly threatened Hue city, the enemy massed four battalions to launch a counterattack. Savage battles for Hills 224 and 303 raged continuously from 11 to 16 March. Meanwhile, Military Region main force units overran the Chuc Mao outpost, attacked and took Hill 300 along Route 12, and put pressure on the area west of Hue. Armed forces from the Military Region and from the provinces of Thua Thien and Quang Tri worked with local-level Party committees to expand armed propaganda operations over a wide area covering 53 villages in eight lowland districts, captured the Mai Linh district capital, and attacked 30 other district and village military headquarters.

As a result of these actions of our armed forces, and because of the powerful impact of our victory at Ban Me Thuot, on 18 March 1975 enemy forces in Quang Tri city retreated to Hue. The enemy's northern perimeter began to crumble. Enemy troops in Thua Thien–Hue were terrified and command and control broke down. The armed forces of Quang Tri province quickly switched over to the offensive, liberating the remaining enemy-controlled portions of the province on 19 March 1975.

The operations of the armed forces of the Military Region and of 2nd Corps from 5 to 20 March created a new battlefield situation on the Tri-Thien battlefront. We had moved a strong main force element down into the contested areas and the lowlands, placed pressure on Hue city from the west and the north, prepared for our next step forward, and provided excellent support to the Central Highlands campaign. Because our operations had been small and dispersed and had not been concentrated against primary targets, however, we had been unable to cut Route 1 and had failed to tie down the puppet Airborne Division. The enemy was able to withdraw this division to Danang.

In the three southern provinces of Military Region 5 (Quang Da, Quang Nam, and Quang Ngai), at the start of the spring-summer campaign regional main force elements consisted of the 2nd Division, the 3rd Division, the 52nd Infantry Brigade, and a number of specialty branch units. Provincial local armed forces were organized into units up to the battalion and regimental level.[6]

On orders from the High Command, the Military Region sent the 3rd Infantry Division and the 19th Engineer Battalion to cut Route 19 to support the Central Highlands campaign. Beginning on 4 March the 3rd Division systematically attacked and seized enemy outposts from the Thuong An Pass to Vuon Xoai. The division then repelled many counterattacks launched by the 41st, 42nd, and 47th Regiments of the puppet 22nd Division. The 92nd and 93rd Binh Dinh Provincial Battalions and district-level armed forces launched attacks and uprisings throughout the province, destroying or forcing the withdrawal of 48 outposts and surrounding and besieging the Tam Quan, Bong Son, and Phu My district capitals.

In the Nam-Ngai theater of operations,[7] on 10 March 1975 the 2nd Division and the 52nd Brigade, under the Military Region Forward Headquarters headed by Major General Nguyen Chanh, Military Commander, and Major General Doan Khue, Political Commissar, attacked and destroyed enemy positions at Suoi Da, Hill 211, and the Tien Phuoc District Military Headquarters, and forced the withdrawal of enemy forces from the Phuoc Lam district capital.[8] The enemy hastily sent the 5th Regiment, 2nd Division, and a Ranger Group from Quang Ngai to Tam Ky to prepare to retake these areas.

Meanwhile, in Quang Da the 96th Provincial Local Force Regiment, working with local armed forces, overran or forced the withdrawal of 11 outposts and liberated three villages in western Thang Binh. This enabled us to send two battalions across to the eastern side of Route 1 where they liberated four villages in the eastern part of Thang Binh district and a number of villages in Dien Ban and Hoa Vang districts.

In Quang Ngai the 94th Regiment destroyed a cluster of enemy strong points northwest of the Binh Son district capital and cut Route 1 north of Chau O. The people of Binh Son rose up and liberated six villages on both sides of Route 1. The enemy was forced to abandon the district capitals of Tra Bong and Son Ha and pull his forces back to defend the lowlands. The 6th Battalion, 52nd Brigade, together with the 403rd Sapper Battalion (Military Region 5) and provincial local force troops, began to pursue fleeing enemy forces, totally liberating the rural areas of Binh Son and Son Tinh districts.

The enemy's deployments in southern Military Region 1 had been completely disrupted. Military Region 5 main force units and the armed forces of Quang Da, Quang Nam, and Quang Ngai provinces began to shift their attacks down into the lowlands, cutting Route 1 in a number of locations and threatening the cities of Quang Ngai and Tam Ky. To respond to our operations the enemy was forced to gradually withdraw his forces to Route 1 and spread them out along a long defensive line stretching from west of Danang to Quang Ngai.

THE LIBERATION OF HUE

In mid-March 1975, just after Ban Me Thuot was liberated, the Politburo and the Central Military Party Committee anticipated that the enemy might make a strategic withdrawal. For this reason they ordered the Tri-Thien Front to send its forces down to Route 1 as soon as possible to cut off and isolate Hue from Danang. To the south, Military Region 5 was ordered to quickly expand its attacks upward toward Danang.

On 18 March 1975 the Politburo made the following assessment: "Our great victory, which is of strategic importance, signals a new step forward in the overall situation, a step leading toward the collapse of the United States and its puppets. The enemy is now carrying out a strategic withdrawal and they may pull back to Danang and Cam Ranh." The Politburo then resolved to complete the liberation of South Vietnam during 1975. The first task to be carried out to fulfill this resolve was to rapidly destroy the enemy 1st Corps, not allowing it to withdraw to Saigon, and to liberate Hue, Danang, and the provinces of Central Vietnam.

On 20 March the Politburo issued new orders to the Tri-Thien Military Region. The Politburo informed the Military Region that, after the abandonment of Quang Tri, the enemy might also abandon Thua Thien and Hue. All units were ordered to take rapid, daring, and resolute measures to isolate the battle area. The Military Region was ordered to send, not just battalions, but entire regiments down to the lowlands to work with local force troops, guerrilla militia, and our action teams to annihilate enemy thugs and destroy their yoke of oppression. Units were ordered to launch a people's war in the lowlands and close in on and isolate Hue city; to destroy the 1st Division, the Ranger Groups, and Regional Force regiment-sized groups; and to make vigorous, overall preparations to liberate both Hue city and the entire lowland coastal area. As for Military Region 5, the Politburo ordered it to strike immediately to destroy the puppet 2nd Division and advance on Danang in support of the overall plan. The 2nd Corps was ordered to rapidly prepare its artillery for an attack on Danang.

In accordance with the High Command's combat orders, and as an atmosphere of enthusiasm and urgency swept across the entire battlefield, the Tri-Thien Military Region Command, Military Region 5, and 2nd Corps skillfully took stock of the situation and rapidly shifted gears, switching from the basic plan to an opportunistic plan.

On 21 March 1975, our soldiers opened fire throughout the battlefields of Tri-Thien and Nam-Ngai, isolating Hue from Danang, destroying the puppet 1st Infantry Division, liberating Thua Thien–Hue, wiping out the enemy 2nd Infantry Division, and liberating Tam Ky city (Quang Nam province) and Quang Ngai province.

Although 2nd Corps had a total of three infantry divisions (the 304th, 324th, and 325th), when the campaign began 2nd Corps had only four infantry regiments actually available to fight in Tri-Thien.[9] Only one battalion of field artillery was available for use in operations. There was not enough time to bring in tanks. Aside from its own organic units, the Tri-Thien Military Region had received only the 46th Infantry Regiment from the High Command as reinforcements, and the region was only able to employ one field artillery battalion for the attack. Military Region 5 was engaged in redeploying its forces, moving the 52nd Brigade up from Quang Ngai, and deploying armor and artillery in accordance with orders of the High Command.

Faced with possible annihilation, the enemy was hurriedly redeploying his forces and carrying out his scheme of strategic withdrawals and consolidation to block our advance. Between 15 and 20 March the enemy moved two brigades (the 369th and the 258th) of the Marine Division from Tri-Thien down to Quang Da to replace two Airborne Brigades (the 1st and 3rd) that were being withdrawn to Saigon. During the next few days, under increasing pressure from our forces, the enemy prepared to abandon Hue and withdraw his forces south to defend Danang.

Keeping a close eye on the developing situation and aggressively expanding the offensive pursuant to its orders from the High Command, 2nd Corps and units subordinate to the two Military Regions quickly and resolutely moved to surround and isolate the enemy, disrupt his tactical formations, block his line of retreat, and annihilate his forces.

After attacking Hills 294, 520, 560, and Kim Sac Mountain south of Hue, on 22 March the 325th Division pushed forward, cutting a section of Route 1 from

Bai Son to Bach Ma (a distance of three kilometers). Thousands of vehicles belonging to puppet Thua Thien province government agencies that were driving down this road trying to flee to Danang were forced to turn back toward Hue in a state of total disorder and despair. Many enemy soldiers and officers in Hue abandoned their units and ran home to arrange for the evacuation of their families. Determined to annihilate the puppet 1st Division and not allow it to get away, 2nd Corps Headquarters ordered the 324th Division to abandon its assaults on the enemy defensive positions on Bong and Nghe Mountains and on Hill 303 and instead advance rapidly down to Route 1 to support the 325th Division in cutting off and isolating enemy forces. The 84th Artillery Regiment, assisted by engineer units, hauled 85mm and 122mm cannon and dozens of H-12 [107mm] multiple rocket launchers up to the top of the 700-meter-high Luoi Hai Ridge. From there the regiment rained its rockets straight down onto Route 1, cutting the road by fire and supporting our infantry forces.

North of Hue, the 3rd, 14th, and 812th Quang Tri province Local Force Battalions did not finally finish organizing their attack until 23 March. On 24 March our units began their offensive, capturing the Huong Dien district capital, crossing the My Chanh River, and crushing the new defensive line that the enemy had established only two days previously. The puppet 147th Marine Brigade, the 14th Ranger Group, and the 1st Division's 51st Regiment were forced to withdraw to the southern banks of the Bo River. To the west and south, the 15th Ranger Group and the 1st and 54th Regiments of the puppet 1st Division were also forced to fall back to Hon Vuon and the Phu Bai airfield.

On the 22nd and 23rd of March Tri-Thien Military Region's 4th Regiment attacked defensive positions held by the puppet Marines, defeated a number of Marine counterattacks, and advanced to the three-way intersection at Sinh. Meanwhile, the Military Region's 6th and 271st Regiments marched down Route 12 toward the Perfume River. Because they had to fight the enemy along the way and because they did not have the proper equipment, as of the night of 24 March these two regiments still had not been able to cross the river.

In coordination with our main force attacks, Phong Dien and Quang Dien district local force troops overran a number of Regional Force and Popular Force outposts, occupied the Pho Trach district capital, and helped the civilian population launch uprisings that liberated many hamlets and villages in the rural lowlands.

Hue city was completely surrounded and isolated. On 22 March the puppet 1st Corps Forward Headquarters escaped to Danang by air. Having lost its command structure and under the pressure of our attacks, enemy troops in Hue collapsed into disorder. One group tried to escape by road but was forced to turn back because Route 1 to Danang had been cut. The enemy still had large numbers of troops, but these troops had lost their will to fight and could only think about finding a way to escape.[10]

Closely monitoring each stage in the development of the situation, the High Command ordered 2nd Corps and the Tri-Thien Military Region to switch to pursuit tactics; block the routes to the sea, which was the only avenue of escape left to the enemy; destroy the 1st Division and the other remaining forces; and liberate Hue city.

On 22 March a D-74 battery (long-barreled 122mm guns) from 2nd Corps' 164th Artillery Brigade moved quickly down from the De Bay Pass, crossed the minefield on Route 14C, and arrived at the La Son intersection, where the battery prepared to open fire to block enemy troops trying to use the Tu Hien and Thuan An harbors.

On 23 March, 2nd Corps and Tri-Thien Military Region artillery (including 130mm and D-74 guns) began placing heavy fire on 1st Division base camps (the Don Mang outpost), Marine Division positions, Phu Bai airfield, etc., and placed blocking fire on all possible enemy escape routes. Many enemy combat vessels coming up from Danang to pick up troops at Thuan An and Tu Hien ports were deterred by our artillery fire and did not dare approach the beaches. Some vessels were hit by our artillery and the majority of the ships were forced to turn back.

Meanwhile, on 23 March, 18th Regiment, 325th Division, overran Ne Mountain, an important enemy stronghold located on Hill 134. After this victory the regiment followed up its attack by wiping out the Phu Loc district military headquarters and district capital. The 101st Regiment annihilated the puppet 15th Ranger Group, liberated the Luong Dien area, and expanded our hold on Route 1. The 324th Division's 1st and 2nd Regiments, after bypassing the stubborn enemy positions on Bong Mountain, Nghe Mountain, and Hill 300, advanced swiftly into the lowlands east of Route 1, surrounding and killing or capturing thousands of 1st Division troops at Phu Thu during the night of 23 March. Guided by local civilians, 1st Regiment crossed the Tam Giang Lagoon and, marching up a narrow strip of land next to the ocean, overran Ke Sung and Cu Lai, cutting the enemy's avenue of escape as he tried to flee northward toward Tu Hien Harbor. The regiment wiped out the Marines at this location as they waited for ships to pick them up. Part of the regiment continued the attack, capturing the Tan My Port and the southern bank of Thuan An Harbor and then, together with Quang Tri province local force troops, overran the northern side of the harbor. The 2nd Regiment followed the western shoreline of the Tam Giang Lagoon, attacking straight ahead on the eastern side of Hue, and, together with 1st Regiment and Military Region Tri-Thien units, sealed off Thuan An Port.

During the night of 24 March the remaining enemy troops in Hue abandoned the city and fled. Military Region Tri-Thien's 3rd Battery, 1st Battalion, 16th Artillery Regiment (equipped with 130mm guns) hit them with an unexpected barrage, causing a group of enemy troops trying to reach Thuan An Port to disintegrate. Our infantry units were able to move in and wipe these troops out, and thousands of enemy troops were captured or dispersed.

By this time the forces attacking Hue from the south, led by the 101st Regiment of the 325th Division, had arrived at Phu Bai. In order to quickly clear a road for our advance into the city, 2nd Corps Headquarters ordered the 101st Regiment to send one battalion to swing around behind the Phu Bai base and capture the Huong Thuy district capital. Cut off from the rear and under heavy attack from the front, the terrified enemy troops in Phu Bai abandoned their heavy equipment and fled. Among this abandoned equipment was one vehicle convoy that was left with its engines still running. The 101st Regiment rapidly developed its attack onward to An Cuu and marched into Hue city itself. The 203rd Brigade's 4th Tank Company, reinforced by two M-48 tanks and two M-113 armored personnel carriers that we just captured at Phu Bai, led the advance of 3rd Regiment, 324th Division, into the Mang Ca military base. Hue city sapper and commando forces mobilized the populations of the 1st and 2nd Precincts and Phu Vang district to rise up and overthrow the local governmental apparatus, then guided our advancing troops as they attacked and seized targets in the heart of the city.

On 25 March 1975, the 101st Regiment, 325th Division, and 3rd Regiment, 324th Division, coming in from the south, and Tri-Thien Military Region units moving in from the north marched into the downtown area of the city. Hue city and the entire province of Thua Thien had been liberated. The entire enemy force stationed in Tri-Thien, including the 1st Infantry Division (one of the puppet army's strongest divisions), the 147th Marine Brigade, the 14th and 15th Ranger Groups, and numerous tank and armored battalions and companies, artillery battalions, and all Thua Thien province Regional Force and Popular Force troops were either annihilated or dispersed. Out of more than 40,000 soldiers only about 16,000 were able to escape to Danang.

During the campaign to liberate Hue, operating directly under the High Command, 2nd Corps and the armed forces of Military Region Tri-Thien conducted their combat operations with the most urgent and daring attitude possible. Every unit and each and every cadre and combatant understood the opportunity that had presented itself to us. Every man fully understood our goals, which were to annihilate enemy troops; to resolutely strike deep into the enemy-controlled area; to isolate, surround, and cut his route of escape; and to secure the quickest and greatest possible victory for the campaign.

Having annihilated a significant portion of the enemy's manpower and liberated a strategic area consisting of the two provinces of Quang Tri and Thua Thien, our army and our entire population quickly launched a general offensive and uprising, speeding up the disintegration and collapse of the enemy's armed forces and creating a springboard in the north that we could use to attack Danang and complete the destruction of the enemy's 1st Corps and Military Region 1.

THE OFFENSIVE SOUTH OF DANANG

As our attacks started in the northern area, on 21 March 1975 Military Region 5 forces also opened fire, beginning the second phase of the spring-summer campaign.

The 52nd Brigade and 2nd Division's 36th Infantry Regiment attacked enemy strong points at the Cay Xanh market, Hill 132, Duong Hue, Day Tham, Nui Vang, Duong Bo, and Nui My, then followed up by crushing all enemy counterattacks. Our forces severely mauled the enemy 2nd Division's 5th Regiment and one battalion of his 12th Ranger Group and shattered a section of the enemy perimeter west of Tam Ky city. To try to hold the city the enemy was forced to move the 4th Regiment and an additional battalion of the 2nd Infantry Division up from Chu Lai and Quang Ngai to Tam Ky to strengthen the city's defenses.

Meanwhile, in the Central Highlands, our soldiers were conducting a major pursuit operation and destroying the puppet 2nd Corps. Enemy forces were spread thin to try to defend many widely scattered locations. When the enemy moved his forces, most of his movements quickly degenerated into disorganized retreats.

Recognizing this opportunity, on 23 March the Current Affairs Committee of the Regional Party Committee and Military Region 5 Headquarters decided to concentrate all forces and quicken the pace of the attack in order to destroy the puppet 2nd Division, liberate Tam Ky city (Quang Nam province) and Quang Ngai province, strategically isolate Danang city, and create an offensive springboard position for an attack on Danang from the south.

Tam Ky city (the capital of Quang Nam province), which had previously been a large U.S. military base, had a strong system of defensive fortifications. In the face of our attack, and especially after the loss of Hue, enemy troops in Tam Ky focused their attention on defense and reinforced their troops defending the city.[11] Region 5's main force units were not strong enough to capture such a strong position solely through the power of combined-arms tactics. The Military Region Headquarters decided to attack the enemy's outer perimeter, draw the 2nd Division out of its defensive positions so it could be destroyed, then use deep penetration spearheads to strike into the city from many different directions and coordinate with our in-place forces to attack and seize key enemy positions.

On 23 March the Ba Gia Regiment (1st Regiment), reinforced by the 31st Regiment's 5th and 8th Battalions and ten tanks and armored personnel carriers, launched the attack in the primary sector, penetrating the enemy's defensive line from Suoi Da to the northern banks of the Tam Ky River. After only a few minutes of fighting our troops had destroyed many of the puppet 2nd Division's defensive positions and had captured the major entrance points for our advance into the city: the Truong Xuan intersection, the Tam Ky steel bridge, the Chieu Dan intersection, etc. This same attack force also expanded its operations outward toward the Ky Bich airfield. In the secondary sector the 4th and 6th Battalions of the 38th Regiment, 2nd Division, annihilated the puppet 37th and 39th Ranger Battalions and captured Cam Khe 2, Khanh Tho Dong, and Duc Tam 4. The commanders of the puppet 2nd Division, the 12th Ranger Group, and the leadership of the puppet governmental administration (the Quang Tin province

Military Headquarters) fled in panic. Advancing from the springboard positions we had seized, our troops advanced rapidly into the heart of the city. At 10:30 A.M. on 24 March the city of Tam Ky was liberated.

Coordinating its operations with the forces attacking the city, 2nd Division's 36th Regiment captured the Ba Bau Bridge, liberated the Ly Tin district capital, and cut the route of retreat of the puppet troop remnants back to Chu Lai. The 38th Regiment, supported by tanks, cut Route 1 north of Chieu Dan and overran the Tuan Duong military base. To the east, the 70th and 72nd Provincial Local Force Battalions, working with local forces and civilians, combined military attacks with uprisings to liberate the coastal villages.

In Quang Ngai, on 21 March province local force troops attacked and captured a section of Route 1 and helped local civilians mount uprisings to overthrow the enemy's machinery of oppression and to hunt down and capture enemy thugs and villains. Many Regional Force and Popular Force outposts were abandoned by their defenders. Enemy troops in the city began to disintegrate. The enemy was forced to bring in the 6th Infantry Regiment (minus one battalion), the 14th Ranger Group, and the 4th Armored Battalion to defend the northern end of the Tra Khuc Bridge and block our route into the city.

Although our troops moved quickly, marching all day and all night, it was 23 March by the time we were able to move one battalion of the 52nd Brigade up to Quang Ngai. We still had not finished our artillery positions and our tank formations were still being organized. To seize our opportunity the Military Region Headquarters ordered all units to immediately advance into the city without waiting for all our forces to arrive.

At 7:00 A.M. on 24 March, firing from positions that had been built only the previous night, the 576th Artillery Regiment poured heavy fire onto enemy targets. The Military Region's 403rd and 406th Sapper Battalions and the province's 7th Local Force Battalion, supported by tanks and armored personnel carriers from the 574th Regiment, attacked a number of targets on the city's outskirts and advanced into the city itself. The 52nd Brigade's 6th Battalion, followed by the brigade's 7th Battalion, which were both just arriving in the area, immediately charged into battle. To the north, the province's 94th Local Force Regiment and district armed forces attacked defensive positions held by the 11th Ranger Group and cut Route 1 between Son Thinh and Binh Son, blocking the enemy's escape route.

Faced with annihilation, the entire remaining enemy force, over 4,000 soldiers, abandoned Quang Ngai city and fled. Taking advantage of the evening darkness, a convoy of 200 enemy vehicles fled along Route 1 toward Chu Lai. The 94th Regiment and local armed forces set up an ambush and, striking at the correct moment, wiped out this enemy force, killing 500 enemy troops, capturing 3,500 prisoners, and capturing or destroying 206 military vehicles.

Advancing from many directions, our troops marched into the city and occupied their targets. By 2330 hours that night all firing had stopped.

During the afternoon and evening of the night of 24–25 March, the soldiers and civilians of all the districts in the province launched simultaneous attacks and, combining these attacks with uprisings, captured the district capitals and liberated the villages.

At 7:00 A.M. on 25 March, the province of Quang Ngai was completely liberated. After five days and nights of fierce fighting, Military Region 5's armed forces had successfully accomplished the combat missions assigned to them in the spring-summer campaign plan. They had destroyed and dispersed a portion of the enemy's main force army (2nd Division, two Ranger Groups, and numerous specialty branch units) along with two-thirds of the enemy's local force troops and had destroyed a great quantity of the enemy's war equipment in the southern provinces of the enemy's Military Region 1. The enemy defensive line in the coastal lowlands south of Danang had been shattered. Enemy troops stationed at the Chu Lai base had all fled. The Danang joint services military base was surrounded and isolated from three directions, the north, the south, and the west, and was totally cut off from all other areas still under enemy occupation.

Alongside the complete victory achieved by 2nd Corps and the Tri-Thien Military Region in the north, the great victory of Military Region 5 in the south created an extremely advantageous strategic position for us. Our combat forces, both main force and local force troops, had grown stronger and had increased their strength with large quantities of weapons and military equipment captured from the enemy. Our cadre and soldiers had a high spirit of victory. A sense of daring, of speed, and a longing for victory permeated every unit and every combatant. The force of the revolution was overpowering the enemy army.

THE LIBERATION OF DANANG

On 25 March, from our two springboard regions, Tri-Thien in the north and Nam-Ngai in the south, our troops swiftly moved out to attack Danang. Assessing the situation as it developed after the Central Highlands campaign and the campaign to liberate Hue and the Nam-Ngai provinces, the Politburo, meeting on 25 March, decided to liberate Saigon and all of South Vietnam before the rainy season began in May 1975. The Politburo decreed that the first task in achieving this goal was to concentrate 2nd Corps and Military Region 5 forces to destroy the Marine Division and the remnants of the puppet 1st Military Region and to liberate Danang city. The formula laid out by the Politburo to guide our operations was to take the most timely, the swiftest, the most daring, the most unexpected actions, and the actions most certain to achieve victory.

The Politburo and the Central Military Party Committee formed a Campaign Headquarters and a Campaign Party Committee. The Campaign Headquarters was given the code name Front 475. Comrade Le Trong Tan, Deputy Chief of the

General Staff, was appointed Front Commander and Comrade Chu Huy Man, Military Commander of Military Region 5, was appointed Front Political Commissar and Party Secretary. The headquarters staff agencies of the Campaign Headquarters would be drawn primarily from the staff agencies of the High Command, and the Headquarters would direct the operations of 2nd Corps and Military Region 5. On 26 March the Campaign Headquarters personnel set out, arriving on 28 March at the campaign command post on Route 14 west of Danang city. Because the situation was so pressing, the Front Headquarters and the Front Party Committee had not yet been able to meet together. The Military Commander and the Political Commissar exchanged views and agreed on a combat plan via electronic communications, then immediately ordered the deployment of forces to move out and attack Danang from the march.

Analyzing the battlefield situation and the situation in the Danang area, the Central Military Party Committee and the High Command foresaw two possibilities.

First, the enemy withdrawal might be successful, enabling the enemy to establish an organized, rather solid defensive position to hold Danang. In this situation, we would have to use 2nd Corps and would also have to quickly send down 1st Corps so these two units, together with Military Region 5 forces, could mount a large-scale combined-arms attack to capture Danang after full preparations had been made.

Second, if the enemy suffered serious losses, if his forces disintegrated, and if Danang became isolated, we would seize the opportunity and rapidly launch an attack to seize Danang using essentially the forces we currently had in place.

The 2nd Corps and Military Region 5 were ordered to make urgent preparations for an attack based on the first premise but to maintain maximum flexibility and be able to quickly launch an attack based on premise two if the opportunity presented itself.

Under orders from the High Command, 1st Corps 320B Infantry Division and a number of 1st Corps specialty branch units, which had left their base areas in North Vietnam on 19 March to move south to reinforce 2nd Corps for the campaign to liberate Hue, were swiftly transported by vehicle down Route 1 toward Danang. The 18th Regiment of the 325th Division, 2nd Corps, which was clearing enemy remnants south of Phu Loc, changed direction quickly and swiftly launched an attack from the march, marching toward Phuoc Tuong Pass and Lang Co. The 219th Engineer Brigade of 2nd Corps rapidly repaired the Thua Luu Bridge, ensuring that 2nd Corps tanks and field artillery would be able to move up promptly to support the infantry. The 2nd Corps reinforced the 304th Division's 9th Infantry Regiment with one tank battalion, one engineer battalion, one artillery battalion, and one anti-aircraft battalion and placed this combined force under the direct command of the Corps Chief of Staff. This regimental task force left the Con Tien base and arrived at its assembly position east of Truoi on 27 March. On orders from the Corps, 9th Regiment rapidly moved down Route

14, overwhelmed the enemy's defensive positions, and seized a springboard position for an attack on Danang from the northwest.

The 304th Division's 66th and 24th Regiments had been engaged in continuous combat against the enemy's regular mobile reserve forces at Thuong Duc for eight months (from August 1974 to February 1975) and had suffered considerable erosion of their strength. In early March these units finally received the preplanned troop reinforcements to enable them to carry out their 1975 combat missions. Determined to carry out the orders of the High Command and 2nd Corps, the cadre and soldiers of these two regiments rapidly switched tactics and began to attack Danang from the southwest.

To the south and the southeast, 2nd Infantry Division, accompanied by the 572nd Artillery Regiment, the 573rd Anti-Aircraft Regiment, and the 574th Tank-Armor Regiment (all subordinate to Military Region 5), immediately switched their attacks to the north. The 52nd Infantry Brigade, which only a few days earlier had sped south from Quang Nam to participate in the liberation of Quang Ngai, now turned around and quickly moved back to Quang Nam from Quang Ngai. All units made their combat preparations while they were on the move.

Danang was the second largest city in South Vietnam and was the site of a large enemy joint-services military base. Before the attack on the city, enemy combat strength there still totaled almost 100,000 troops equipped with many tanks, aircraft, and heavy artillery pieces.[12] In mid-March 1975, U.S. General Gavin and senior puppet officers outlined a plan for defending Danang relying on the naval, army, and air force bases that had been constructed years before on the outskirts and in the heart of the city.

After the enemy attempt to withdraw from Hue was crushed and after the losses of Hue city and Tam Ky city, the enemy abandoned his plan to withdraw the Marine Division south and use it to defend Cam Ranh and eastern Cochin China. The enemy reorganized his forces and recruited volunteers to "defend Danang to the death." His goal was to tie down our main force units and gain time to redeploy his forces into strategic defensive positions in the south. He believed it would take us at least two weeks to organize our forces for an attack against Danang.

During the last days of March 1975 our forces surrounded Danang city. The United States sent a number of warships to the area off the coast of Danang to "contain" our forces and to pick up puppet troops and transport them to the South, but this was not sufficient to restore the morale of the puppet troops. On 26 March the United States began an airlift to evacuate the U.S. Consulate and the families of a number of puppet officers and civilian government officials to Saigon. Many puppet officers packed their possessions and sought ways to escape. Troops who had escaped from Hue and Tam Ky rioted, looting, shooting, and killing one another and plunging the city deeper into chaos. On 27 March more than 2,000 puppet troops at the Hoa Cam Training Center mutinied and deserted. On their own initiative many units abandoned their positions and withdrew to the rear. All three of the brigades of the Marine Division abandoned their defensive positions. The 468th Marine Brigade withdrew to Phu Loc, the 258th Brigade withdrew to the Nuoc Man airfield, and the 369th Brigade withdrew to Hieu Duc. The 57th Infantry Regiment, 3rd Division, retreated to a position near the Hoa Cam Training Center. Ngo Quang Truong, Commander of 1st Corps and Military Region 1, fled to the Son Tra Peninsula, then escaped to a U.S. ship off the coast.

On 27 March the High Command issued the following order to 2nd Corps and Military Region 5: "The Danang situation is extremely urgent. You must take swift action to attack the enemy, bypass intermediate targets, and make the fastest, the most timely, the most daring attack directly into the city of Danang with those forces that can move out at the earliest possible moment."[13]

To carry out the High Command's orders, the Campaign Command ordered 2nd Corps and Military Region 5 not to wait to mass their forces and instead to immediately order the 575th Regiment, equipped with DKB rockets, to shell Danang airport to further encourage the disintegration of the enemy's forces. The 2nd Corps and Military Region 5 were ordered to quickly move field artillery to forward positions to provide fire support for the infantry.

Because of a shortage of artillery prime movers and because the situation was developing so rapidly, by the evening of 27 March the campaign's artillery forces had only been able to establish one firebase with four 130mm guns, and 2nd Corps had only managed to deploy a total of 14 guns (including six 130mm guns) to the Mui Trau Pass and Lang Co. Because the Thua Luu Bridge had collapsed, the 325th Division's artillery had not yet been able to move to new positions and was not within range of Danang. To the south, Military Region 5 Headquarters had only been able to move two batteries (a total of four 130mm guns) to a firing position at Son Khanh. Fulfilling their glorious traditions, "Legs of Bronze, Shoulders of Iron, Fight Well and Shoot Accurately," our artillery soldiers, overcoming many terrain and weather difficulties, rapidly moved their guns forward and set up firing positions, increasing our firepower and providing a powerful force to suppress enemy forces.

At 5:30 in the morning of 28 March, our troops launched an assault from all directions against the city. Heavy barrages were fired by 130mm and D-74 artillery pieces and DKB rocket-launchers against Hon Bang, Tra Kieu, Vinh Dien, the Danang airfield, the Son Tra port facility, the Nuoc Man airfield, and other military targets. Our artillery concentrations drove the already frightened enemy into further disorder. The enemy could not understand how we could have moved into position to attack the city so quickly. The Danang airfield, although it had not yet suffered heavy damage, was forced to close. Just as in Hue, the enemy's only avenue of escape was the sea. However, it was no longer possible for the enemy to retreat.

From the north, the 18th and 101st Regiments of the 325th Division, 2nd Corps, led by the 4th Tank Company and with infantrymen riding on top of the tanks and in wheeled vehicles, rolled down Route 1, attacking the enemy from the march. After a difficult day spent getting past the Thua Luu Bridge and fighting off four enemy counterattacks at Lang Co, on 29 March our troops advanced up to the Hai Van Pass, crushing defensive positions held by two Marine battalions and capturing the Lien Chieu Petroleum Storage Depot. At 10:00 A.M. our leading elements reached the three-way intersection in the center of Danang. Led by armed self-defense troops of the city Military Unit, 18th Regiment's 8th Battalion, led by Battalion Commander Captain Tran Minh Thiet, swiftly advanced onto the Son Tra Peninsula. At 11:00 A.M. on 29 March our troops raised the flag of the Fatherland over the enemy headquarters complex on the peninsula.

In the northwest, the 9th Regiment of the 304th Division, 2nd Corps, riding in vehicles straight down Route 14, shattered the puppet 3rd Division's line of resistance, crossed Phuoc Tuong and Hoa Khanh Mountains, captured the Danang City Hall at 1300 hours on 29 March, and advanced out onto the Son Tra Peninsula.

From the southwest, the 304th Division's 66th and 24th Regiments crushed enemy resistance at Phu Huong and Dong Lam and then shifted over to the pursuit, seizing the Hoa Cam Training Center at 12:30 P.M. on 29 March and advancing to Danang airfield.

From the south and southeast, Military Region 5's 2nd Infantry Division and Quang Da province's 96th Local Force Regiment quickly seized springboard positions south of the Thu Bon River and launched their attack into the city. At 1400 hours on 28 March, enemy aircraft destroyed the Cau Lau and Ba Ren Bridges to block the advance of our forces. Party committees and the local population along both sides of the river quickly mobilized hundreds of boats to transport our troops across the river, but the speed of our movement was still slow. It was not until 3:00 A.M. on 29 March that the lead elements of the 2nd Division were finally able to cross the river. Our tanks and artillery were still stuck on the southern side of the river.

Comrade Nguyen Chon, Commander of the 2nd Division, decided not to wait for his heavy technical equipment and instead organized an immediate attack that took Vinh Dien town. The Ba Gia Regiment [1st Regiment] and the 31st Regiment swiftly crossed the river and advanced into the center of the city, seizing the headquarters of the puppet Air Force Division and the headquarters complex of the puppet 1st Corps. The 38th Regiment captured Nuoc Man airfield and advanced onto the Son Tra Peninsula, linking up with 2nd Corps on the peninsula at 1500 hours on 29 March. Meanwhile, Quang Da province's 93rd and 96th Regiments advanced and liberated the ancient city of Hoi An, the Non Nuoc area, the An Don area, the puppet naval base, and, together with the 38th Regiment, attacked and seized the Nuoc Man airfield.

Inside the city, on the 26th of March the Quang Da province Party Committee completed its plan and assigned missions to the precincts within the city to incite the population to rise up in support of our military attack. Precinct and block cadre affairs sections, the cadre affairs section of the electrical generating plant, etc., were transformed into revolutionary committees. When our troops advanced into the city from different directions our commando forces and self-defense forces provided them with guides and supported them by capturing a number of political, economic, and military targets such as the Trinh Minh The Bridge, the province police headquarters, and the city hall. Our cadre and citizens being held in the Non Nuoc Prison rose up and destroyed the prison. Workers, government officials, and students took part in the occupation and defense of the docks, the train station, the electrical plant, the water plant, hospitals, schools, etc. Many buses and three-wheeled Lambrettas carrying people fleeing the center of the city turned around when they encountered our troops advancing into the city and transported our soldiers quickly into the city. The people of Danang poured out into the streets to cheer our soldiers, their sons and younger brothers. For these people the image of our militia soldiers, the soldiers of the advance to the South, the liberation troops, the soldiers of Uncle Ho, whom they had last seen decades before, was still deeply etched into their minds and their hearts.

The attack to liberate the joint-services military base and Danang city, that had begun at 5:30 in the morning on 28 March, ended after 33 hours of fighting. Launched from many different directions and encountering very different situations and practical difficulties, all our attack columns met in the center of the city and on the Son Tra Peninsula at the same time: 1530 hours on 29 March 1975. This victory was won because the High Command and the Campaign Headquarters were able to seize the opportunity, take daring and timely action, mobilize the forces that were closest, and swiftly move our units into the fight along the quickest routes possible. The main force units that participated in the liberation of Danang totaled only seven regiments, and of these four regiments were at a low manpower strength as a result of their participation in many previous battles. However, the cadre and soldiers of units demonstrated high resolve, selected the proper targets, and took decisive and timely action. This campaign demonstrated our skill in strategic command guidance and the solidarity, the seriousness, and the keenness of all our units and of all our cadre and soldiers. This very dynamic military capability, this rapid unanimity of thought from the top to the bottom regarding the opportunity we faced and the tactics to be employed—all this was the result of experience garnered through 30 years of training and hard combat, filled with sacrifice, filled with the heroic achievements of our armed forces.

During the liberation of Danang, 2nd Corps and Military Region 5, fighting alongside the local population, destroyed and dispersed a large enemy force and captured or destroyed all their weapons and technical and supply facilities.[14]

The Hue-Danang Campaign, launched on 21 March, ended with the liberation of Danang on 29 March 1975. Beginning as several offensive campaigns intended to support the Central Highlands Front as part of a unified strategic plan, when the great opportunity appeared, 2nd Corps and the armed forces of the Tri-Thien Military Region and Military Region 5, under the command of the

High Command, quickly changed their approach and developed their operations into a large-scale combined-arms campaign. During this campaign our soldiers and civilians exterminated or dispersed the entire enemy 1st Corps and 1st Military Region, crushing the enemy's fortified defensive network and liberating five provinces: Quang Tri, Thua Thien, Quang Da, Quang Nam, and Quang Ngai, and two large cities, Hue and Danang.

Following our great victory in the Central Highlands Campaign, the victory of the Hue-Danang Campaign, a campaign organized during the course of the development of a strategic attack and based on the campaign plans of the corps and military regions, transformed the situation and completely altered the balance of forces between ourselves and the enemy, creating very favorable conditions for the launching of our decisive strategic campaign to liberate Saigon.

With its victory in the Hue-Danang Campaign, our army made new forward strides in its conduct of sudden, opportunistic attacks and gained considerable experience in command, combat tactics, and development of the attack during campaign operations. Almost a year after its formation, 2nd Corps had made rapid progress in its organization and combat capabilities, had equipped itself with large quantities of new equipment and weapons captured from the enemy, and had become a large combined-arms formation able to move rapidly and possessing heavy firepower and a powerful assault capability. The armed forces of the Tri-Thien Military Region and Military Region 5 had made remarkable progress. They took over the defense of the newly liberated area and selected many units and collected large quantities of supplies and technical equipment to send to participate in the campaign to liberate Saigon.

THE DRIVE TO SAIGON BEGINS

On 25 March 1975, after the victorious conclusion of the Central Highlands Campaign and while the Hue-Danang Campaign was continuing, based on the new strategic resolution of the Politburo, the Central Military Party Committee and the High Command ordered 1st Corps to leave behind the 308th Division to serve as our strategic reserve and to defend North Vietnam and to make urgent preparations to send the 312th Division and the rest of the Corps specialty branch units to eastern Cochin China.[15] At the same time the Central Highlands Front was ordered to gather together three main force divisions and technical specialty branch units, quickly reorganize them, and prepare them to move out for the primary target, Saigon. The orders stated supplies and technical support also must be collected to support the effort against that target.

On 27 March 1975, in the newly liberated Central Highlands, 3rd Corps—the fourth strategic mobile corps-sized unit of our army—was formed.[16] Included in the Corps were three infantry divisions (10th, 316th, and 320A) and the following specialty branch units: the 675th Artillery Regiment, the 312th Anti-Aircraft

Regiment, the 198th Sapper Regiment, the 273rd Tank Regiment, the 545th Engineer Regiment, and the 29th Signal Regiment. These units had spent many years on the battlefields of the Central Highlands and had compiled a record of outstanding combat achievements during the resistance wars against the French and against the Americans. Major General Vu Lang was appointed Corps Commander and Senior Colonel Dang Vu Hiep was named as Corps Political Commissar.

As soon as it was formed, 3rd Corps sent a number of its elements on a rapid march down into the lowland provinces, working with Military Region 5 armed forces to exterminate and disperse the remaining forces of the puppet 2nd Corps.

Division 320A marched down Route 7 and, alongside Phu Yen province armed forces, liberated Tuy Hoa city on 1 April 1975. Military Region 5's 3rd Division and the 968th Division moved down Route 19, attacked the enemy from the march, crushed all remaining defensive positions held by the puppet 22nd Division, and cooperated with local armed forces to liberate Quy Nhon city and all of Binh Dinh province on 1 April 1975. The 10th Division and the 25th Infantry Regiment shattered the line held by the 40th Regiment of the puppet 22nd Division, liberated the Khanh Duong district capital, and wiped out the 3rd Airborne Brigade in the Ma Drac [Phuong Hoang] Pass. With the road now open, our forces marched to Ninh Hoa and then followed Route 21 to liberate Nha Trang city and the Cam Ranh military port on 3 April 1975.

At this point, the Spring 1975 General Offensive and uprising launched by our soldiers and civilians had lasted just one month. We had destroyed and dispersed two entire enemy corps, comprising 35 percent of the total manpower of the enemy's armed forces, destroyed 40 percent of the enemy's technical specialty branch forces, captured or destroyed 43 percent of his technical and supply installations, and liberated 12 provinces from Tri Thien down to Khanh Hoa and the entire Central Highlands (the enemy's 1st and 2nd Military Regions).

Our armed forces had rapidly matured in terms of their organizational level, their command capabilities, and their ability to conduct combined-arms combat within the context of large-scale campaigns. Their posture and strength had tremendously improved as compared with their situation when the general offensive was first launched.

The road to Saigon, along two separate strategic directions, down from the Central Highlands and along the coast of Central Vietnam, was wide open. To the north, northeast, and southwest of Saigon, 4th Corps, Group 232, and the armed forces of the various military regions were now, step by step, moving their forces in close to the city. Our army was faced with a great opportunity, together with the entire population, to carry out the final decisive strategic battle to end the war.

17

The Ho Chi Minh Campaign: The People's Army and the Entire Nation Fight the Decisive Battle to Liberate Saigon and the Provinces of Cochin China, Bringing the War against America to Save the Nation to a Glorious Conclusion

MOBILIZING FOR THE FINAL BATTLE

The victories of our Central Highlands and Hue-Danang Campaigns signaled a new level of maturity for our army in all aspects of its operations. Our main force units had gained a great deal of experience in the organization and command of combined-arms operations during large-scale campaigns. The combat strength of our large main force units had increased markedly. Our personnel and matériel losses had been extremely low and we had captured large quantities of weapons and technical equipment from the enemy. Our local armed forces had grown enormously in both numbers and quality and had properly fulfilled their duties of conducting local combat operations and defending newly liberated areas, giving our large main force units an opportunity to expand the offensive in the important strategic theaters of operations. The combat spirit of our cadre and soldiers was high and they were enthusiastic and confident in our ultimate victory.

The enemy, on the other hand, had suffered severe manpower losses, had expended or lost large quantities of supplies and equipment, and the combat spirit of his forces had collapsed. The enemy was now working to regroup the remnants of 1st and 2nd Corps, to strengthen his 3rd and 4th Corps units, and to redeploy his forces along a number of defense lines to block our advance and keep us at bay. Their most vital defensive positions were located in the areas of Tay Ninh, Xuan Loc, and Phan Rang.[1]

On 28 March 1975 General Weyand, Chief of Staff of the U.S. Army, came to Saigon to lay out a defense plan for the puppet army. The United States also established an airlift to bring weapons from Thailand and the United States to Saigon and sent the aircraft carrier *Hancock* and 300 U.S. Marines to the South China Sea. Compared with the period when the United States had poured massive numbers of troops into South Vietnam, however, these reinforcements were just a drop in the bucket. The U.S. reaction confirmed the accuracy of the Politburo's assessment that now that the United States had withdrawn it would be very difficult for it to send troops back in and that, no matter how much additional aid the Americans sent, they could not now salvage the situation. In terms both of our strategic posture and our military and political strength, we now had sufficient strength in South Vietnam to overwhelm the enemy's army.

A 31 March 1975 Politburo meeting reached the following conclusions: The revolutionary war in South Vietnam is now growing by leaps and bounds and the time is now ripe for the launching of a general offensive into the heart of the enemy's lair. Our final strategic battle has begun. Our goal is to complete the people's democratic revolution in the South and to achieve peace and the unification of the Fatherland.

During this session the Politburo decided to launch a general offensive and uprising to liberate Saigon as soon as possible, preferably during the month of April, and insisted that we could not afford to delay. The Politburo laid out a number of clear missions for our army: to rapidly send additional forces to the area west of Saigon; to isolate and strategically encircle the city; to completely cut Route 4; and to move in close to Saigon. In the Saigon area the army was to rapidly concentrate its forces east and southeast of the city, attack and seize important objectives, and surround and isolate Saigon from the Long Khanh, Ba Ria, and Vung Tau areas. After this was accomplished the army was to organize powerful combined-arms units to be ready to launch an immediate attack when the opportunity presented itself to seize key targets in the heart of the city.

The Politburo's guiding concept was "lightning speed, daring, surprise, certain victory." To mobilize the strength of the entire nation and build resolve to gain swift and complete victory in this campaign, the Politburo established a Council for the Support of the Battlefield and appointed two Politburo members, Comrade Pham Van Dong, Prime Minister, and Comrade Le Thanh Nghi, Deputy Prime Minister, to serve as Chairman and Vice-Chairman of this Council. Three Politburo members, Van Tien Dung, Pham Hung, and Le Duc Tho, were appointed to serve as representatives of the Politburo at the front. Senior General Van Tien Dung, Politburo member and Chief of the General Staff, was appointed Military Commander of the Saigon–Gia Dinh Front, and Comrade Pham Hung, Politburo member, was appointed Front Political Commissar. Colonel General Tran Van Tra, Lieutenant General Le Duc Anh, and Lieutenant General Dinh Duc Thien were named Deputy Military Commanders of the front. On 22 April 1975 the Politburo made two additional appointments to Front Headquarters: Lieutenant General Le Trong Tan, Deputy Chief of the General Staff, was also appointed Deputy Military Commander of the front, and Lieutenant General Le Quang Hoa, Deputy Director of the General Political Department, was named Deputy Front Political Commissar.

The Politburo resolution was quickly disseminated throughout the nation and the army. The nation burned with the spirit of battle: "Everything for the front lines, everything for victory!"

The ethnic minority tribal peoples of the Northwest and the Viet Bac regions suggested that the plan for shipping rice and salt to their local areas be postponed and that the entire convoy of vehicles carrying these valuable commodities turn around and be sent south to ensure that the plan for the general offensive could meet its time schedule. Many state enterprises, factories, and government agencies cut their work rosters by 30 to 50 percent and sent the excess manpower to support the campaign. Our entire military transportation system, a total of 120,000 personnel (equal to 80 percent of the campaign rear services force), 6,300 transportation vehicles belonging to Group 559, 2,100 vehicles belonging to the Transportation Department, and hundreds of vehicles belonging to the military regions, the corps, service branches, and specialty branches were pulled together to provide transportation support for the campaign. A massive quantity of transportation equipment belonging to the civilian government, including over 1,000 trucks, 32 oceangoing ships (5,000 tons capacity), 130 railroad cars (9,000 tons capacity), and hundreds of tons of air transport capacity were mobilized to ship supplies and troops to the battlefield.[2]

Trains loaded with troops, weapons, and ammunition ran straight from the Hang Co Train Station in Hanoi to Vinh. From there trucks and ships carried the troops and supplies onward by land and sea down to eastern Cochin China. Transport vessels belonging to our river and ocean transport companies and Navy cargo vessels sailed from river ports and seaports to carry tanks, heavy artillery and troops south to Danang, Quy Nhon, and Cam Ranh. From there they were moved overland down Route 1 to Long Khanh and to COSVN's 814th Rear Services Group assembly area in the Dau Day–Tuc Trung region. Cargo aircraft, helicopters, and a number of civilian passenger aircraft flew from airfields in North Vietnam carrying troops, ammunition, books, newspapers, and movies to the Saigon–Gia Dinh Front and to the newly liberated areas. On our overland supply routes, when our trucks reached Dong Ha in Quang Tri province, they split in two different directions. Some trucks drove straight down Route 1, through the newly liberated cities of Hue, Danang, Quy Nhon, etc. Others turned onto our two roads down the eastern and western sides of the Annamite Mountain chain and followed Route 14 through Duc Lap and Dong Xoai to our assembly points in eastern Cochin China. Our army swept forward like a river. Trucks, trains, aircraft, and ships seemed to be pointed in only one direction: Saigon.

Our military and state transportation resources were not alone in the supply effort—the convoys driving south included 426 trucks and buses belonging to private citizens in the newly liberated areas. Military Region 5 Headquarters organized a number of special convoys under the command of Deputy Military Region Commander Major General Vo Thu. These convoys made a total of 1,800 individual truck trips, transporting troops and 4,000 tons of weapons and ammunition that the Military Region had captured from the enemy to support and strengthen our forces participating in the campaign.

PREPARATIONS FOR BATTLE IN THE SAIGON AREA

In Cochin China and extreme southern Central Vietnam, to carry out the plan to support the Central Highlands Campaign, to prepare the battlefield, and to open additional supply corridors to bring troops, supplies, and technical equipment down from the North and up from the Delta, COSVN Headquarters ordered 4th Corps and Military Regions 6, 7, 8, and 9 to launch phase two of the strategic combat plan on 4 March 1975.

In the North and Northwest, 9th Division, reinforced by the 16th Regiment and coordinating its operations with local armed forces, conducted a series of powerful operations in the Tay Ninh–Route 13 area. The division annihilated or drew in and tied down a significant portion of the forces assigned to the puppet 3rd Corps, liberated the Dau Tieng district capital, Chon Thanh town, and the entire province of Binh Long. This created a new offensive springboard area and opened up Routes 13 and 14 to allow the movement of troops, technical equipment, and weapons down to the enemy's defensive perimeter north of Saigon.

To the East, 7th Division, 341st Division, and Military Region 6 and 7 forces overran the Dinh Quan district military headquarters, opened up Route 20 for our own use, and developed the attack northward, liberating Lam Dong. These actions gave our forces new springboard positions and opened up a new route that our forces could move to attack Saigon from the east.

In the Southwest, COSVN's 3rd and 5th Divisions overran enemy positions at Ben Cau, Moc Bai, An Thanh, Tra Cao, and Queo Ba and opened a route to send troops down to Military Region 8, providing yet another direction from which we could launch an attack on Saigon.

In the South, 8th Division (subordinate to Military Region 8), the 4th Division (subordinate to Military Region 9), and provincial armed forces launched powerful operations in Vinh Tra (Vinh Long–Tra Vinh), destroyed the Nga Sau defensive complex in My Tho province, etc. We moved our forces up to Route 4 and put pressure on all enemy district headquarters, provincial headquarters, and military bases.

Meanwhile, in early March 1975 our military engineers and COSVN rear services troops, assisted by the local civilian population, began quickly repairing bridges and roads, building warehouse areas to receive supplies and preparing assembly positions for use by our corps and our brigades and regiments of technical specialty branch troops. The roads leading to Dong Xoai, Ben Bau, etc., were widened. The bridges and fords crossing the Be River, the Saigon River, and the Vam Co Dong River (including those at Nha Bich, Ma Da, Ben Bau, etc.) were repaired and strengthened to support the passage of tanks and heavy technical equipment. COSVN rear services forces were reorganized into five groups (each group capable of supporting one large troop column in one campaign sector) and eight mobile regiments (responsible for receiving and transporting supplies in the different important sectors and for being ready to take over and administer enemy logistics facilities in newly liberated areas). Included among the COSVN rear services transportation forces supporting the campaign were 4,000 civilian coolies for use on the front lines. Never in the 20 years of war against the Americans had the battlefields of eastern Cochin China seethed in such an atmosphere of preparation for battle. By mid-April 1975 our supply stockpiles to support the campaign had grown to 58,000 tons,[3] including 24,000 tons of weapons and ammunition, 21,000 tons of rice, and 11,000 tons of gasoline and petroleum products.

As for the enemy, even after the loss of Military Regions 1 and 2, the United States and its puppets still misread our intentions. They believed we would have to leave many units behind to secure and defend the newly liberated provinces. Because of this and because we would have to move so far and were so deficient in transportation resources, the enemy believed we could send at most one corps down to eastern Cochin China. Even if we moved at maximum speed, they believed it would take us at least two months to move our troops and prepare our attack.

In the Central Highlands, after the sweeping victories won by the campaigns to liberate the Central Highlands and the southern provinces of Military Region 5, on 4 April 1975 3rd Corps was ordered to move south to eastern Cochin China. The 316th Infantry Division and the Corps Forward Headquarters left Ban Me Thuot and drove south down Route 14. Division 320A, which was consolidating its recent victory (the capture of Tuy Hoa) quickly turned around, returned to the Central Highlands via Route 7, then continued down Route 14. The 10th Division was pursuing enemy forces at Cam Ranh and Nha Trang. After rapidly gathering its forces, the division took Interprovincial Route 2 up to Route 20. The 7th and 375th Engineer Regiments led the way, opening the road and building bridges. Thousands of montagnard tribesmen from the Bac Ai base area, the home of Hero Bi Nang Tac, helped build roads and fords across streams to speed the movement of our troops. Trucks belonging to Group 559's 471st Truck Division and 3rd Corps vehicles made over 3,000 trips to complete the movement of 10th Division. When they heard the Corps was moving into battle, many lightly wounded or ill cadre and soldiers being treated in our aid stations and hospitals asked to be allowed to return to their units. After detecting 10th Division's movement along Route 20, the enemy sent bombers to block our advance. These aircraft struck and set dozens of our trucks ablaze. The 10th Division fought off the enemy attacks, repaired the bomb damage, and continued building and repairing the road. Moving swiftly, the division reached its assembly area at precisely the scheduled time. On 15 April, the 316th Division and the leading elements of 3rd Corps reached the newly liberated Dau Tieng area and occupied jumping-off positions for the attack on Saigon from the northwest in accordance with the front's plan.

In North Vietnam, on 31 March 1975 1st Corps was ordered to quickly move the entire Corps (except the 308th Division, which would remain behind to defend the North) to Dong Xoai in eastern Cochin China. At this time Division 320B and a number of Corps specialty branch units, which had left their home bases on 19 March, were in Danang, and the rest of the Corps was conducting training and repairing dikes on the Hoang Luong River in Ninh Binh province. With a high spirit of readiness for battle, the Corps rapidly completed all necessary preparations. At 11:00 A.M. on 1 April, the 312th Infantry Division, Corps branch specialty units, and the main headquarters elements of the Corps moved out in a road march using 1,053 vehicles from the General Rear Services Department's Transportation Department and Group 559's 571st Truck Division and 893 vehicles organic to the Corps. In Dong Ha, Quang Tri province, the Corps turned off onto Route 9, drove through Lao Bao, and drove south on the road running along the western side of the Annamite Mountain chain. At this time the enemy was focusing his attention on Route 1 and our maritime transportation routes, where vehicles and boats transporting troops and supplies in support of the Hue-Danang Campaign were very active. By moving down the western side of the Annamite chain, even though there were many passes and steep inclines on this route, the Corps could move a large force without causing traffic jams, could maintain secrecy and ensure surprise, and would be able to reach its assembly position quickly and safely.

In the Annamite Mountains April is the end of the dry season. The weather was hot and the wheels of our vehicles sank deep into the sand and dust. Hundreds of vehicles were strung out in a long line like a vast river of dust. Our troops slept in their vehicles. Each vehicle was a small, organic unit, living together and helping one another. When the vehicles stopped, each vehicle became a food kitchen. When they met the enemy, each vehicle became an integral fighting unit. When the route was blocked, each unit on its own initiative took action to overcome the problem and cleared the road as fast as possible. Broken-down vehicles were pushed aside to allow those behind them to pass. Each vehicle had two drivers so they could take turns driving and keep the vehicle moving 18 to 20 hours each day. When there was a shortage of water for the armored vehicles, the entire 299th Engineer Brigade went thirsty so the water in their canteens could be used for the vehicles. When a section of the road at the top of the Nua Pass became a swamp because of a heavy rainstorm and an underground stream, in the middle of the night engineers of the 27th Regiment, led by the Regimental Commander, Hero Nguyen Huy Hieu, built a detour road around the swamp.

On 7 April the Corps received a cable from Senior General Vo Nguyen Giap, Politburo member, Secretary of the Central Party Military Committee, and Minister of Defense:

Speed, ever greater speed
Daring, ever greater daring
Exploit every hour, every minute

Rush to the battlefront, liberate the South,
Resolve to fight to secure total victory.[4]

Short and direct as a combat order, with the rhythm of a poem, easy to remember, easy to memorize and understand, this movement order was immediately passed down to every soldier. Written on the sides of trucks, on helmets, and on tree trunks along the sides of the road, this order became a slogan that encouraged our cadre and soldiers to move even faster toward the battlefront. The speed of the march never slowed, and many days our troops covered 150 kilometers.

On 13 April the 320B Division and the Corps forward headquarters reached Dong Xoai. Two days later, on 15 April, the entire Corps had gathered at the assembly point. The Binh Duong province Party Committee, local armed forces, and the local population had already prepared the assembly area, provided food for the troops, and helped the Corps rapidly consolidate its forces, gain an understanding of the enemy situation and the terrain, and prepare to march into battle.

In only 15 days 1st Corps, with its entire complement of modern combat equipment and weapons, had completed a road march of almost 2,000 kilometers, most of which was along mountain roads, and had occupied jumping-off positions for the attack on Saigon from the north exactly on time as ordered by the High Command.

On 1 April, as 1st Corps was setting out from Tam Diep, 2nd Corps received orders to leave the newly liberated city of Danang and make a swift march down Route 1 to advance toward Saigon from the southeast. At that moment a number of Corps specialty branch units were scattered far afield along Routes 14, 73, and 74. The 164th Artillery Brigade's 3rd Battalion was still at Khe Sanh in Quang Tri province. The transport vehicles of the Corps, together with the trucks of the 571st Truck Division (Group 559), which were sent to the Corps by the High Command as reinforcements, were only sufficient to move two-thirds of the Corps' troops. Route 1 between Danang and Xuan Loc was a good road for vehicular movement but there were 569 bridges and 588 culverts along the way, among which were 14 bridges across large rivers. The bridges at Cao Lau, Ba Ren, Huong An, Ke Xuyen, Ba Bau, and An Tan, and numerous smaller bridges, had been blown up by the enemy. From Phan Rang forward enemy forces were still quite numerous. These forces were deployed in strong defensive fortifications and could use infantry, air, and naval forces to block our advance. To overcome these obstacles Corps Headquarters relied on the assistance of the civilian population in the newly liberated areas, made a maximum effort to collect and put into service captured enemy weapons and vehicles, and issued a policy of moving and fighting at the same time to ensure that the Corps would arrive at the time specified in the High Command's orders and that the Corps would be ready for battle as soon as the Corps arrived at its assembly positions.

With regard to those artillery units still deployed in firebases atop tall mountains, the Corps decided to leave these units' guns behind, turning them over to local authorities for safekeeping, while the artillerymen of these units would take over and use captured enemy artillery pieces.[5] Our drivers and mechanics went out to look for and confiscate enemy vehicles, found spare parts to repair them, and put into service 487 trucks and artillery prime movers. The civilians of Hue and Danang contributed more than 100 transport vehicles and drivers to the Corps. The General Staff sent the 83rd Bridge-Building Engineer Regiment to reinforce the Corps and also sent a number of oceangoing ships to transport troops from Danang to Quy Nhon. With the help of Military Region 5 the Corps Rear Services Department sent an advance team out ahead of the Corps to find, test, and collect gasoline and petroleum products for the Corps to use in its advance.

On 7 April 1975, after leaving the 324th Division behind to protect Hue and Danang and to serve as a reserve force, the Duyen Hai [Coastal] Column,[6] consisting of almost the entire strength of 2nd Corps, reinforced by the 3rd Infantry Division and Military Region 5's 3rd Armored Battalion, began the march down Route 1 toward the South. The march formation was hundreds of kilometers long and consisted of a total of 2,276 vehicles carrying troops and supplies, 89 tanks and armored vehicles, and 223 artillery prime movers towing 87 field artillery pieces and 136 anti-aircraft guns. The civilian population of the newly liberated areas were incredibly overjoyed and confident when they saw with their own eyes the power of our army and the combat spirit, the courage, and the revolutionary virtues of our soldiers.

Putting into practice the slogan, "fight the enemy in order to move, clear the road in order to advance," the entire Corps was deployed in combat formation to move and attack from the march using combined-arms assault power. The forward element had a powerful offensive punch. It was composed of infantry, tanks, artillery, and anti-aircraft artillery capable of shattering enemy defenses and a strong engineer component (the Corps' own engineers plus engineering units from the High Command and Group 559) ready to overcome all obstacles along the route of advance. This forward element contained centralized command and fire-support elements and reinforcing units. Behind the forward element was a powerful reserve component including infantry and specialty branch elements.

With help from local Party committees and local civilians, the Corps repaired eight bridges that the enemy had damaged, built scores of kilometers of new, rough military roads, and steadily increased its rate of march, which at its fastest once covered 185 kilometers in one day. While on the march cadre and soldiers studied and drew lessons from their battle experiences in Hue and Danang. They also spent time learning to use new weapons and equipment captured from the enemy, which now represented a rather substantial percentage of the total number of weapons and equipment of the Corps, fulfilling the slogan, "capture enemy equipment and use it to fight the enemy."

On 11 April 1975 the Corps lead element reached Cam Ranh. On 16 April the entire Corps had reached the approaches to Phan Rang, a place into which the enemy had poured a great deal of resources and effort to establish a defensive line to stop our forces and keep them away from Saigon.

The city of Phan Rang (Ninh Thuan province) is located at the intersection between Route 1 and Route 11 to Da Lat. It occupies an important position linking Central Vietnam with the southern end of the Central Highlands and with eastern Cochin China. Enemy forces there included the 2nd Airborne Brigade, the 2nd Infantry Division (with only two regiments), the 31st Ranger Group, and the 6th Air Division. In early April, using a plan provided by U.S. General Weyand, puppet troops began building a series of strong, mutually supporting defensive positions that were centered on tactically important hill positions and on the Thanh Son Airfield. Lieutenant General Nguyen Vinh Nghi, Commander of the puppet 3rd Corps Forward Headquarters, was in direct command of the forces defending Phan Rang.

On 14 April 1975 Military Region 5's 3rd Infantry Division and the 25th Infantry Regiment, Central Highlands Front, with artillery support, launched an attack on Phan Rang city. Combining assault and deep penetration spearheads with flanking maneuvers, our troops quickly cracked the enemy's defensive network north of the city and closed in on Thanh Son Airfield. Puppet troops, with fire support from their air force and naval gunfire support from ships offshore, fiercely resisted our attack.

To crush enemy resistance and quickly open the road to Saigon, a 2nd Corps element that had just arrived in the Phan Rang area was ordered into battle. On 16 April the 101st Regiment, 325th Division, organized as a deep penetration combined-arms spearhead, moved out from a springboard position held by 3rd Division and advanced down Route 1 straight into the city. Leading the assault formation was the 1st Infantry Battalion, mounted on 20 tanks and armored vehicles. The 2nd and 3rd Battalions, riding in wheeled vehicles, followed behind 1st Battalion. Long-barrelled 85mm artillery pieces and 37mm anti-aircraft guns moved forward with the attack formation, ready to provide direct fire against enemy ground and air targets. The 164th Artillery Brigade followed the assault formation to provide fire support to the deep penetration spearhead. To support the main frontal attack, 3rd Division and the 25th Regiment attacked several targets in the city and at the Thanh Son Airfield. Faced with our powerful attack, enemy troops panicked and were unable to resist us. After two hours of fighting our troops had gained complete control of the city. One of our units, moving rapidly, occupied the Tan Thanh and Ninh Tru port areas, completely sealing off the enemy's escape route out to sea. Another group moved down Route 1 and captured the Dao Long Bridge and the Phu Quy district capital, sealing off the overland route and preventing the enemy from escaping to the south. The enemy sent dozens of aircraft to bomb the rear of our troop formations on Route 1, and enemy paratroopers mounted a counterattack from the Thanh Son Airfield. The 325th Division's 101st Regiment and 3rd Division heroically repelled the enemy counterattacks and captured the Thanh Son Airfield, located ten kilometers outside the city. All enemy forces in Phan Rang, more than 10,000 troops, were annihilated or dispersed. Puppet Generals Nguyen Vinh Nghi and Pham Ngoc Sang (Commander of the 6th Air Division) and many officers and enlisted men were captured. We captured 36 aircraft and 37 pieces of heavy artillery.

The victory at Phan Rang illustrated the growth of our army's strength and tactical skills. We had used a combined-arms formation attacking from the march to overwhelm an enemy defensive complex. On 22 April 1975 Senior General Vo Nguyen Giap, Minister of Defense, sent a message of congratulations to all cadre and soldiers who had taken part in the Phan Rang victory. The General ordered all units to quickly consolidate their forces, continue the advance, and develop the attack with lightning speed, using daring and surprise to gain new victories.

On 18 April, the Region 5 Party Committee and Military Region 5 Military Headquarters sent a letter of commendation to the cadre and soldiers of the 3rd Division encouraging the division to achieve new feats of arms and to live up to the honor the division had been given in representing Military Region 5's main force elements by participating in the campaign to liberate Saigon.

After the loss of Phan Rang the enemy was even more frightened by the strength and speed of advance of our Duyen Hai [Coastal] column. The enemy moved a company of commandos north on naval vessels and landed them in Tuy Phong district in northern Phan Thiet province. They sent attack aircraft to bomb our troop columns and used naval gunfire from warships off the coast in an attempt to block our advance. A combined force of infantry and reconnaissance troops from the 325th Division, which was leading our troop column, conducted a sweep operation, pursuing and completely destroying the enemy commando company. Our field artillery and our tanks and anti-aircraft guns set up a firebase on Route 1 itself to fire back, sinking or setting ablaze four enemy naval vessels, shooting down one F-5 aircraft on the spot and damaging another F-5.

On 18 April the 18th Regiment, 325th Division, supported by specialty branch units, made an assault from the march and, assisted by Military Region 6's main force 812th Regiment and by Binh Thuan province's 15th Sapper Battalion, liberated Phan Thiet city and the rest of Binh Thuan province. On the morning of 19 April, 2nd Corps assault formations roared through Binh Tuy province and moved toward Xuan Loc.

THE BATTLE OF XUAN LOC AND OTHER PRELIMINARY ATTACKS

During the first days of April 1975 the battlefields of eastern Cochin China, including the city of Saigon, were extremely active. During the morning of 8 April, Pilot Nguyen Thanh Trung, one of our agents whom we had infiltrated into the ranks of the puppet air force, flew his F-5 aircraft over Saigon and bombed President Thieu's "Independence Palace." Trung then landed safely at the Phuoc Long airfield. This action spread even greater fear and confusion among the ranks of the Americans and their puppets. They worked to strengthen the defensive lines around Saigon, and especially the key areas: Xuan Loc, Bien Hoa, Tay Ninh, etc.

The city of Xuan Loc in Long Khanh province was located at the intersection of three important roads: Route 1, Route 20 (Saigon–Da Lat), and Route 15 (Saigon–Vung Tau). Xuan Loc was an important gateway to Saigon. The puppet army had built it into a key sector of the basic defensive line connecting Bien Hoa, Ba Ria, and Vung Tau. Enemy forces defending Xuan Loc included the 18th Infantry Division (the strongest division in puppet 3rd Corps), one Ranger Group, one armored regiment, and nine Regional Force battalions subordinate to Long Khanh province. When an attack began the enemy force in Xuan Loc could count on receiving rapid reinforcements from the strategic reserve force (the Airborne and the Marines), artillery support from artillery units throughout 3rd Corps, and air support from two strategic airfields very close to the battlefield: Bien Hoa and Tan Son Nhat.

As the situation continued to develop rapidly, on 7 April 1975 the COSVN Current Affairs Party Committee and the COSVN Military Party Committee approved a plan for a military attack on the Saigon Front. The 4th Corps (minus 9th Division, which had been detached to support Group 232 southwest of the city) and Military Region 7's 6th Division were assigned the mission of attacking and capturing Xuan Loc city.

After a four-day march from Lam Dong to the assembly areas and after quickly organizing its forces for combat, at 5:40 A.M. on 9 April 4th Corps elements opened fire, launching the attack on Xuan Loc city.

The 341st Division was assigned to mount a secondary attack, striking the northwestern sector of the city. Having just arrived from North Vietnam at the end of February 1974, the 341st Division had been incorporated into the ranks of 4th Corps and had participated in attacks against enemy positions along Route 20. Now, as it began a new combat operation, the division's cadre and soldiers sought the help of other units and relied on assistance from the civilian population and local armed forces to reconnoiter the terrain and develop an understanding of the enemy situation. The division quickly completed its combat preparations and opened fire exactly on schedule. After one day of fighting the 341st Division had captured the American advisory compound, the information center, the province police headquarters, and the hotel at the Xuan Loc bus station. The division then beat back a number of counterattacks launched by three enemy battalions and maintained a firm hold on the positions it had captured.

The 7th Division made the main assault from east of the city. In this sector the enemy had rather strong defenses, the terrain was open, and the infantry encountered many obstacles during their approach. Because our artillery was not able to completely suppress the enemy's artillery firebases and because the enemy air force conducted a ferocious bombing campaign,[7] none of the division's assaults against the puppet 18th Division Headquarters base camp and the

52nd Regiment Headquarters were successful. Our troops fought the enemy for control of every section of trench, every house, every city block. Puppet 3rd Corps quickly moved the 1st Airborne Brigade, 5th Division's 8th Infantry Regiment, the 2nd Ranger Group, eight artillery battalions, and two regiment-sized armored task forces up from Saigon and across from Tay Ninh to reinforce the 18th Division and to "defend Xuan Loc to the death."[8] Enemy aircraft, taking off from Bien Hoa, Tan Son Nhat, and Tra Noc [Can Tho] airfields, pounded Xuan Loc with bombs. The battle turned into a hard, vicious struggle. Our units suffered heavy casualties. The 341st Division alone lost 1,100 cadre and soldiers killed or wounded during just the first two days—9 and 10 April. Our artillery ammunition became seriously depleted. More than half of our tanks were knocked out. Our troops had also performed many exemplary acts of heroism. Combatant Pham Van Lai (9th Battalion, 266th Regiment, 341st Division) refused evacuation even after being wounded twice. Lai used a captured enemy weapon against enemy forces, killing 31 enemy soldiers and enabling his unit to shift its forces in time to defeat an enemy counterattack. The battle became protracted, and we could not overrun the enemy because we had not selected the proper tactics or the proper location for our main attack. In addition, the enemy had sent in reinforcements and put up fierce resistance. During early April 1975 the enemy was in a losing position throughout South Vietnam. He was confused and many of his forces had disintegrated. In eastern Cochin China, however, and especially at the gates of Saigon, puppet troops were still numerous and they focused all their efforts on defending Saigon, their final lair.

In this situation, and based on our estimate that Xuan Loc was only of value to the enemy as long as it was linked to Bien Hoa, the COSVN Military Headquarters and 4th Corps decided to change tactics. Our forces shifted from making direct assaults on the city to attacking counterattacking enemy units that had not yet secured a firm foothold on the outer perimeter, isolating Xuan Loc from Bien Hoa, and cutting Route 2 between Xuan Loc to Ba Ria. The 95th Regiment (subordinate to 325th Division, 2nd Corps), which had just arrived from the Central Highlands, and a company of tanks were sent to the front as reinforcements. The 4th Corps artillery covered the positions held by 18th Division's 43rd and 48th Regiments and by the 1st Airborne Brigade with heavy fire, supporting infantry attacks aimed at annihilating individual enemy elements as soon as they tried to move forward to rescue their comrades on the outer perimeter. A field artillery firebase located at Hieu Liem and the man-portable artillery pieces of COSVN's 113rd Sapper Regiment shelled Bien Hoa airbase day and night. Military Region 7's 6th Division and the 95th Regiment attacked and overran the Tuc Trung and Kien Tan district military headquarters, wiped out the 52nd Regiment of the 18th Division, developed their attack down Route 20 to repel the 3rd Cavalry Brigade attacking up from Bien Hoa, and seized the Dau Day intersection. Route 1 from Bien Hoa to Xuan Loc was completely cut, enemy forces in Xuan Loc suffered heavy casualties, and Xuan Loc city was completely surrounded and isolated. On 20 April the leading elements of 2nd Corps, our eastern column, reached Rung La, only 20 kilometers from Xuan Loc.

Faced with complete annihilation, during the night of 20 April the remaining enemy forces in Xuan Loc retreated down Interprovincial Route 2 to Ba Ria. Because we were slow in detecting their movement and had not properly organized our blocking forces, 4th Corps and Military Region 7 forces were able to wipe out only a portion of the retreating enemy troop column.

The city of Xuan Loc was now liberated and the eastern gateway to Saigon stood wide open. The 4th Corps, 2nd Corps, Military Region 5's 3rd Division, and our local armed forces now constituted a dangerous flank attack approaching Saigon from the east and southeast.

Meanwhile, southwest of Saigon our personnel worked vigorously to transport supplies, move troops, and prepare offensive springboard positions for our armed forces. To strategically isolate Saigon from the Mekong Delta and simultaneously create an offensive posture that would enable us to move troops up to the outer approaches of Saigon from this direction, in accordance with policy guidance provided by the Politburo, in early 1975 the Central Military Party Committee and the High Command ordered COSVN to send a main force element down to operate in Military Region 8. The 232nd Group was established, made up of the 5th and 3rd Infantry Divisions, a number of specialty branch units, and reinforced by the 9th Division from 4th Corps. Comrade Le Duc Anh was appointed Group Military Commander and Comrade Le Van Tuong was chosen as Group Political Commissar. In early April 1975, in coordination with our attack on the Xuan Loc Front, 5th Division attacked the enemy defense perimeter at Thu Thua–Ben Luc. Because we had little time for preparations, our fire support was weak, and because enemy forces in this area had not yet suffered the confusion and breakdown that had occurred in the north, after a number of assaults failed to overrun the enemy positions, 5th Division shifted tactics. It consolidated its hold on our springboard position west of Tan An city, destroyed enemy outposts, and built roads for use to move heavy weapons and equipment down to the area north of Route 4. The 3rd and 9th Divisions crossed open terrain, swamps, and canals by splitting up into small groups. They established artillery firing positions on the road itself to support our infantry, and transported artillery ammunition by portering it on their backs or by carrying it in small boats. By the middle of April 1975 these two divisions had expanded into the An Ninh–Loc Giang area and had established a new springboard position in a very advantageous position for an attack on Saigon.

The Region 8 armed forces (the Military Region's main force 8th Division, COSVN's 24th and 88th Regiments that had been sent to the region, and two Long An province local force battalions) increased their operations, destroying 45 outposts and village military headquarters, liberating 12 villages in the districts of Chau Thanh, Can Duoc, Tan Tru, etc., and developing a position from which Saigon could be attacked from the south. In Region 9, the 4th Division moved up close to Can Tho city and sapper forces attacked and threatened the Tra Noc airfield.

In Saigon itself, six sapper regiments and four battalions and 11 teams of commandos secretly deployed their forces in the city's outskirts, moved in close to targets inside the city, and prepared to seize and hold the large bridges leading into the city. The Saigon–Gia Dinh city Committee, under Party Secretary Comrade Vo Van Kiet, sent 1,700 cadre into the precincts of the inner city and the villages of the suburbs to prepare to launch a mass uprising in coordination with the military attack by our main force troops. The city Military Command controlled two local force regiments and five local force battalions, and each district had one or two companies of its own. Hundreds of vehicles were equipped with loudspeakers to call upon the masses to rise up. In many locations the masses printed leaflets, sewed flags, wrote banners, etc. An atmosphere of anticipation and preparation to greet our troops coming to liberate the city swept the area.

In this way, even before the opening shots of the general offensive against Saigon–Gia Dinh, we had developed a posture that isolated the city from many different standpoints. It was a strong and daring offensive posture, a posture that isolated the enemy, a coordinated posture both within and outside enemy lines. This posture provided the foundation for a military attack combined with mass uprisings.

PREPARATIONS FOR THE FINAL "HO CHI MINH" CAMPAIGN

On 13 April 1975, in accordance with the desires of our battlefield cadre and soldiers, the Campaign Headquarters forwarded a unanimous recommendation to the Politburo that the campaign to liberate Saigon be designated the "Ho Chi Minh Campaign." At 1900 hours on 14 April 1975, cable number 37/TK from the Politburo was sent to the front: "We approve the proposal that the Saigon campaign be called the Ho Chi Minh Campaign." The Politburo message said that "the Ho Chi Minh Campaign will be a large-scale combined-arms offensive launched in coordination with mass uprisings and aimed at ending the war. This will be a historic strategic campaign." The Politburo's decision had a powerful emotional impact, increasing the strength of the entire army and the entire civilian population. Everyone was proud of being afforded the honor of participating in a campaign named for our beloved Uncle Ho.

Saigon–Gia Dinh was a large city with a population of almost four million. The city had many tall buildings and many different types of construction. The outskirts of the city was open terrain with many swamps, rivers, and streams. The people of Saigon–Gia Dinh had a tradition of determined revolutionary struggle and had led the way in the fight against the Americans. Saigon–Gia Dinh was the enemy's political, military, and economic center and was the enemy's last stronghold. After their defeats at Phan Rang and Xuan Loc, the enemy plan to hold us at arm's length collapsed, the enemy became terrified, and enemy reactions to our activities became passive and confused. On 23 April the President of the United States announced that "the Vietnam War has ended as far as America is concerned" and issued orders to evacuate Americans from Saigon. The United States had to admit defeat in South Vietnam, the main battlefield of the Indochina War. For this reason, on 17 April 1975 the United States was defeated in Cambodia. On 21 April, Nguyen Van Thieu resigned as President of the puppet government and escaped to seek refuge overseas. Tran Van Huong was promoted to replace him. The enemy's remaining forces tried to hold Saigon–Gia Dinh and the Mekong Delta and plotted to block our attack. If they were successful we would run into problems once the rainy season began and they might be able to force us to prolong the attack. They hoped they then could save themselves through a political solution. The forces defending Saigon were still rather strong and continued to prepare for our general attack. Their officers and men were frightened but had not yet fallen into disorder and disintegration. On the outer perimeter the remaining forces of the 5th, 25th, 18th, and 22nd Divisions were deployed in a defensive line 30 to 50 kilometers from Saigon, extending from Long An through Tay Ninh and Bien Hoa to Long Binh. They relied on their base camps and a number of large mutually supporting strong points to block and repel our attack spearheads. On the outskirts of Saigon enemy forces consisted of three Airborne and Marine brigades and three Ranger Groups deployed in Hoc Mon, Tan Son Nhat, Binh Chanh, Go Vap, and Nha Be to defend these areas and to provide support to the outer perimeter when needed. Within the city the enemy was organized into five interzones, whose main forces consisted of police and people's self-defense units.

Our forces participating in the campaign consisted of four corps, Group 232 (which was equivalent to a corps), almost all the technical specialty branch units of our strategic reserve, and the political and military forces of Military Region 7 and Saigon–Gia Dinh. Our entire combat force totaled 270,000 troops (250,000 main force troops and 20,000 local force troops) and 180,000 strategic and campaign-level rear services troops. The main units participating in the campaign were the powerful main force corps-sized groups that had just won great victories in the Central Highlands, Hue-Danang, and on the battlefields of eastern Cochin China and the local force regiments and battalions, the sapper and commando regiments that had for so many years clung to the battlefield and that were familiar with the terrain inside and outside the city. With lightning speed and a resolve to win, in a very short time we had concentrated large combat and logistics support forces, including many units that had just finished a swift march down from our great rear area. This was a great victory for our side and a great surprise for our enemy.

The Campaign Headquarters decided to attack Saigon from five directions: northwest, north-northeast, east-southeast, west, and southwest. In order to attack and win quickly, to annihilate the enemy, protect the local civilian population, and protect the economic and cultural facilities of the city, our tactics for seizing the city would be to isolate, surround, annihilate, and disperse the enemy divisions defending the outer perimeter and not allow them to withdraw back into the city. At the same time we would seize and hold the large bridges to enable the powerful mechanized assault forces that we had carefully organized to advance rapidly along the major highways and strike directly at the five key targets we had chosen[9] in order to topple the enemy in the shortest possible time. To support our powerful assault units and to create conditions that would enable individual corps to advance rapidly to attack and seize their objectives, Saigon–Gia Dinh's special action, sapper, and self-defense forces and the city's armed security and mass political forces would seize the bridges, capture key jumping-off points to enable our main force troops to launch their attacks, and guide our main force troops to their objectives. A plan to mobilize the masses to rise up in coordination with the launching of our military attack was prepared under the personal direction of Comrade Nguyen Van Linh, Deputy Secretary of COSVN. This was a creative battle plan that made maximum use of the determination to win of the troops and the population of the entire nation, exploited position and power we had created on the battlefield, and ensured that our army would gain complete victory in the shortest possible time.

Between 20 and 25 April, our units, one by one, came to the Campaign Headquarters to receive their orders and targets.

The northwest was assigned to 3rd Corps, led by Major General Vu Lang, Military Commander, and Senior Colonel Dang Vu Hiep, Political Commissar. The 3rd Corps had three infantry divisions and numerous specialty branch units with a total strength of approximately 46,000 soldiers. Also operating under the command of 3rd Corps were two local regiments (the 1st and 2nd Gia Dinh Regiments), the sapper-commando units of the Saigon city Military Unit, and additional artillery and anti-aircraft units provided by the Campaign Command. The 3rd Corps objectives were to overrun the Dong Du base camp, annihilate the puppet 25th Infantry Division, capture Tan Son Nhat Airbase, and, together with 1st Corps, seize the puppet General Staff Headquarters.

The north and northeast was the responsibility of 1st Corps (minus the 308th Division), commanded by Major General Nguyen Hoa, Military Commander, and Major General Hoang Minh Thi, Political Commissar. This Corps had two infantry divisions, a number of specialty branch units, and had a total strength of about 30,000 troops. The Corps was reinforced by the 95th Regiment (325th Division, 2nd Corps) and one regiment of self-propelled anti-aircraft guns. The corps was responsible for attacking and capturing the Phu Loi base camp, annihilating the puppet 5th Division, and seizing the puppet General Staff Headquarters and the puppet service branch headquarters in Go Vap.

Two army corps were assigned to the east and southeast directions. One of these was 4th Corps, commanded by Major General Hoang Cam, Military Commander, and Major General Hoang The Thien, Political Commissar. This corps, with three infantry divisions and specialty branch units, had a total strength of about 30,000 men. It was reinforced by the 52nd Infantry Brigade (Military Region 5), one 130mm artillery battalion, three tank and armored personnel carrier battalions, one composite anti-aircraft regiment, and one separate anti-aircraft battalion. The 4th Corps was responsible for destroying the headquarters of both the puppet 3rd Corps and of the 18th Division at Bien Hoa and then making a deep penetration into Saigon to seize Independence Palace. The other corps assigned to this direction was 2nd Corps, commanded by Major General Nguyen Huu An, Military Commander, and Major General Le Linh, Political Commissar. This corps had three infantry divisions plus combat specialty units with a total strength of about 40,000 troops. The 2nd Corps was responsible for capturing Ba Ria, Nuoc Trong, Long Binh, blocking the Long Tau River, and developing the attack into the center of the city where, in cooperation with 4th Corps, it would capture Independence Palace.

The west and southwest was the responsibility of Group 232, commanded by Lieutenant General Le Duc Anh, Military Commander, and Major General Le Van Tuong, Political Commissar. This Group had three infantry divisions, three tank-armored personnel carrier [APC] battalions and one separate APC company, one 130mm artillery battalion, one regiment and five separate battalions of anti-aircraft guns, and the main force and local force troops of Military Region 8. The total strength of this force was about 42,000 men. The forces along this line of attack were assigned the missions of destroying the puppet 25th Division, cutting Route 4, and launching a deep penetration attack to capture the puppet Capital Special Zone Headquarters and the National Police Headquarters.

On the outskirts of the city, sapper units and local armed forces were assigned to attack and seize the major bridges, provide guides for the main force elements to help them to locate their objectives inside the city, and mobilize the civilian population to rise up and seize control of the governmental apparatus at the local level.

After discussions with the General Staff, the Campaign Command decided to use a number of newly captured aircraft to bomb Tan Son Nhat airbase to shatter the enemy's morale, prevent the puppet gang leaders from escaping, and to prevent the enemy from evacuating its remaining modern aircraft at Tan Son Nhat airbase out of the country. As preparations for the campaign to liberate Saigon–Gia Dinh went forward, in early April 1975 the Central Military Party Committee and the High Command decided to use part of our air force, working with Military Region 5 and our Navy, to liberate the offshore islands and the Spratleys Archipelago.

Instructions on political activities from the Campaign Headquarters were disseminated to all cadre and soldiers. These instructions covered the goals of the Party Central Committee; the historic significance of the campaign; guidance formulas and tactics; building a spirit of solidarity and cooperation between units, between main force and local force troops, and between our soldiers and the civilian population; encouraging our troops to gloriously fulfill each of their responsibilities for the campaign; hoisting the "Determined to Fight, Determined to Win" flag above the city that had been given the honor of bearing the name of Chairman Ho Chi Minh; and securing victories to celebrate Uncle Ho's 85th birthday.

On orders from the Campaign Headquarters all the corps quickly disseminated information about our situation and our combat missions to each unit, built up the combat resolve of our troops, and helped every cadre and soldier understand his responsibilities and the honor he had been given: being allowed to participate in this historic campaign that bore the sacred name of Uncle Ho. Our units also received additional weapons, equipment, and supplies, and all units were quickly moved to their assembly positions.

To fulfill their responsibilities as set forward in the plan and to carry out the prescribed campaign tactics, each corps organized two groups of forces. One group (usually consisting of two infantry divisions and a number of specialty branch units) was to carry out the corps' immediate responsibilities, such as crushing the enemy's outer defensive perimeter and opening the door for our units to advance into the inner city. The second group was a deep penetration formation responsible for attacking and seizing key targets within the city. This force consisted of one or two motorized infantry regiments plus tank, artillery, anti-aircraft, and engineer battalions. Each corps also had a reserve force (usually an infantry brigade or regiment plus a number of specialty branch units).

Only three years previously, during the offensive campaign in Quang Tri in 1972, our army had been able to deploy only one motorized infantry regiment. Now, on the five directions of advance into Saigon, our army had five corps, and each corps had a deep penetration force made up of combined-arms units. This was a new step forward for our army in the scale of its organization, its assault power, its firepower, and its mobility. Now, before the final battle began, our army had overwhelming superiority over the enemy.

THE BATTLES OF THE HO CHI MINH CAMPAIGN

At 1700 hours on the afternoon of 26 April 1975, the general offensive against Saigon began. In the east-southeast, after 45 minutes of artillery preparatory fire, the first echelon of 2nd Corps, consisting of infantry and tanks, began assaulting the enemy defensive sectors located along its line of advance. The 325th Division attacked the Long Thanh district military headquarters, wiped out three enemy battalions, captured 500 prisoners, and then crossed Route 15, liberated Phuoc Tuong, and surrounded Long Tan. The 3rd Division (Military Region 5), under the direct command of 2nd Corps Headquarters, captured the Duc Thanh district capital and Ba Ria city. Coordinating with the main force troops, local armed forces liberated the Xuyen Moc, Long Le, Long Dien, and Dat Do districts. By noon on 27 April, Ba Ria city and the entire province of Phuoc Tuy had been liberated.

The 304th Division attacked the enemy base at Nuoc Trong, an important target located on the Corps' route of advance. At this location enemy armored officer cadets and cadet officers from the Thu Duc Officers Academy who were there conducting training fought alongside the puppet 468th Marine Brigade and the 318th Armored Regiment, putting up fierce resistance throughout the day of 27 April. Over 100 enemy air sorties rained bombs on our fighting positions. Under a blazing sun our soldiers became so thirsty their throats burned. The division had to send vehicles through a hail of bullets to carry water to each individual unit. Corps Headquarters ordered the division to abandon its frontal attacks and instead concentrate its tanks to attack the enemy's flanks and rear. By 1700 hours on the afternoon of 28 April the entire enemy force at the Nuoc Trong base had been wiped out.

The 4th Corps' attack formations advanced down Route 1. Making use of the experience it had gained during the Xuan Loc battle, the 341st Division quickly crushed the enemy's defenses and, at 10:00 A.M. on 27 April, captured the Trang Bom district military headquarters, which had been defended by the puppet 18th Infantry Division and the 5th Armored Regiment. The remnants of the enemy force fled, but when they reached Suoi Da they were attacked by the 270th Regiment. Two thousand enemy troops were killed or captured, and the puppet 18th Division suffered heavy casualties.

Exploiting its victory, 4th Corps attacked Ho Nai on the outskirts of Bien Hoa city. Here the puppet 3rd Armored Cavalry Brigade and the 4th Airborne Brigade had built strong defensive positions, including anti-tank ditches, to block our attack. The lead elements of the corps launched many assaults against these positions, but by the afternoon of 28 April they still had not been able to get past Ho Nai. In the face of our powerful attacks and because our campaign artillery, based at Hieu Liem, had paralyzed operations at the Bien Hoa Airbase, the enemy had to evacuate his aircraft to Tan Son Nhat airfield. The puppet 3rd Corps headquarters abandoned Bien Hoa and fled to Go Vap.

To the west and southwest, Group 232's 5th Division and Military Region 8's 8th Division cut Route 4 from the Ben Luc Bridge to the Truong Luong intersection and from Cai Lay to An Huu, blocking the movement of the puppet 7th, 9th, and 22nd Divisions and creating favorable conditions for our other columns to attack the enemy. The 3rd Division captured a bridgehead, ensuring that our main assault force, the 9th Infantry Division plus supporting heavy weapons and equipment, would be able to cross the Vam Co Dong River. In spite of many problems caused by a shortage of equipment and crossing points, and although the road had been turned into a quagmire after a number of heavy rainstorms, our engineering units, with the enthusiastic assistance of the local population, made an excellent river crossing, moving the 9th Infantry Division and a towed field artillery unit across to occupy the Tay Vinh Loc and My Hanh areas. The 24th and 28th Regiments attacked and expanded our movement corridor and advanced northward.

To the north, the 1st Corps used the 312th Division, assisted by the 2nd Local Force Battalion, to overrun a number of enemy artillery firebases. The 1st Corps gained control of a section of Route 16, surrounded the Phu Loi military base, and occupied an area north of Thu Dau Mot city, preventing the puppet 5th Division from pulling back to Saigon.

To the northwest, the 3rd Corps massed its artillery and wiped out 11 of the 18 enemy artillery firebases in its area, allowing our units to deploy their forces for the attack. The 316th Division blocked Routes 1 and 22 and blocked the puppet 25th Infantry Division, preventing it from withdrawing from Tay Ninh to Dong Du and Hoc Mon. The 320A Division moved in close and prepared to attack the Dong Du military base.

On the outskirts of Saigon our sapper and commando troops quickly attacked and captured the river bridges in preparation for the advance of our combined-arms units into the city. This was a very important task that demanded that our sappers not only attack and take the bridges, but also that they had to hold the bridges and repel all enemy counterattacks. No matter what the cost, the sappers had to maintain control of the bridges on every one of our lines of advance. With the wholehearted support and combat assistance of local armed forces and the local civilian population, all units secretly moved in close to the objectives and awaited the attack. On 27 and 28 April the 113rd Sapper Regiment took the Rach Chiec and Rach Cat Bridges. The 115th Sapper Regiment, working with a battalion of the Gia Dinh Regiment, took the Binh Phuoc Bridge and seized control of a section of the Korean highway from the Binh Phuoc Bridge to Quan Tre. The 116th Sapper Regiment seized the Bien Hoa Highway Bridge. The attacks on and efforts to hold these bridges commanding our lines of advance into the city required extremely fierce fighting. Our sapper forces, with only a small number of troops, drove off dozens of enemy counterattacks and defended the bridges until our large units advanced into the inner city. They made an important contribution to the quick victory of our offensive campaign and the rapid restoration of normal life in the city after the war.

In an operation coordinated with the attacks of our large main force units, our air force also received orders to enter the battle. During the Central Highlands and Hue-Danang Campaigns, our army captured many enemy aircraft, airfields, and support facilities. The Air Force–Air Defense Headquarters did an excellent job of repairing and putting these spoils of war back into operation. A number of enemy pilots and air force personnel were educated by our troops and asked to help our technical cadre and pilots modify and familiarize themselves with the technical and operational characteristics of a number of different types of enemy aircraft, including the F-5 and the A-37.

At 1540 hours on the afternoon of 28 April a flight of aircraft consisting of five A-37 bombers, under the command of Pilot Nguyen Van Luc and guided by

Pilot Nguyen Thanh Trung (the man who bombed Independence Palace on 8 April), took off from the Thanh Son airbase at Phan Rang and flew toward Saigon. Evading the enemy's early warning radars, the flight dropped their bombs with precision on the flight lines and hangars at Tan Son Nhat, destroying 34 enemy aircraft and killing 200 puppet soldiers and combat personnel. The rumble of bombs raining down on Tan Son Nhat shook the entire city of Saigon. Enemy troops were terrified by our unexpected attack, and their anti-aircraft guns and fighters did not have time to react to our attack. The attack paralyzed the U.S. fixed-wing evacuation operation at Tan Son Nhat. The United States was reduced to instituting a "death-defying evacuation operation," using only helicopters. Our heroic air force troops had accomplished another remarkable feat of arms and added further gloss to the brilliant traditions of their service. They had used captured enemy aircraft to deal a blow against the enemy. The aircraft flight that carried out the glorious combat achievement of 28 April was given the honorary title of "the Determined to Win Flight."

By the afternoon of 28 April, after two days and nights of continuous combat, our army shattered the enemy's outer defensive ring, cut Route 4, increased the encirclement and pressure against Saigon from all sides, and surrounded and blocked each of the enemy's regular divisions, preventing them from withdrawing to the city suburbs and to the city itself. The puppet Joint General Staff and the staff and command agencies of the puppet 3rd Corps fled. Having lost their strategic and campaign-level commanders, the enemy's troops became increasingly frightened and undisciplined. Tran Van Huong resigned and turned over the presidency to Duong Van Minh. The new President appealed to his troops "not to lay down your weapons" and "protect our territory." They ran around trying to make deals and to arrange a political solution that might save them.

The opportunity to launch a general offensive throughout the entire front had arrived. During the evening of 28 April, the Campaign Headquarters ordered all our assault columns to launch a simultaneous attack on the next morning, 29 April. At the same time, orders were issued to Military Regions 8 and 9 to mount supporting attacks and uprisings to liberate the Mekong Delta.

At 5:00 in the morning of 29 April, just as our attack columns were about to begin their advance into the heart of Saigon, the Politburo sent a cable warmly congratulating all units for the great victories that had been won over the past several days. The Politburo appealed to all cadre, soldiers, Party members, and Youth Group members to strike swiftly and directly into the enemy's final lair with the powerful confidence of an army that had won victory in every battle it had ever fought. The Politburo called on everyone to crush all enemy resistance and combine military attacks with popular uprisings to completely liberate Saigon and Gia Dinh. Our forces were ordered to maintain strict discipline, carry out all instructions and orders, protect and preserve the lives and property of the civilian population, demonstrate the revolutionary virtues and victorious traditions of our army, and gain total victory for this historic campaign bearing the name of our great Uncle Ho.

The Politburo's appeal was disseminated to every cadre and soldier on the entire front. News of the victories of each of our attack columns was quickly disseminated. Terse, practical slogans to encourage our troops: "Delay is a crime against history" and "opportunity is the order of the day" were promulgated and every unit burned with an offensive spirit, with the desire to advance at lightning speed to seize every assigned target and to plant our flag atop the puppet's Independence Palace.

To the east, 325th Division, 2nd Corps, captured the Nhon Trach district military headquarters, the Thuy Ha warehouse area, and developed its attack forward toward Cat Lai. The Campaign Headquarters ordered 2nd Corps to establish a 130mm artillery position at Nhon Trach to shell Tan Son Nhat. Assisted by local civilians, Corps artillery troops set up an observation post next to the airfield and adjusted our artillery precisely onto our targets. Tan Son Nhat airfield was engulfed in flames and was totally paralyzed.

The 2nd Corps' deep penetration unit (the 66th Infantry Regiment, one tank brigade, one anti-aircraft battalion, and one engineer battalion) surged forward heroically. When the artillery barrage lifted, the deep penetration unit had reached the northeastern end of the Highway Bridge over the Dong Nai River and established contact with the 116th Sapper Regiment, which still held firm control of the bridge after beating off numerous attacks by an enemy battalion. Sapper cadre and soldiers rode on top of our tanks, acted as guides during the advance and, alongside our infantry troops, brushed aside all remaining pockets of enemy resistance, ensuring that our tanks were able to cross the bridge and advance quickly into the heart of the city.

The 341st Division (4th Corps) and the 6th Infantry Division (Military Region 7) circled around past Ho Nai to attack Bien Hoa. The 4th Corps' deep penetration unit (7th Division's 141st and 165 Infantry Regiments plus tank and anti-aircraft battalions) attacked down Route 1. Enemy troops defending Bien Hoa Airbase and the Hoc Ba Thuc military base put up fierce resistance. Because they had to assault many separate enemy lines and defense sectors, by the evening of 29 April 4th Corps still had not moved past Bien Hoa city.

To the north, 1st Corps' 312th Division attacked the Phu Loi military base. The 312th Division's 209th Regiment established blocking positions on Route 13 and Interprovincial Route 14, wiping out an enemy column trying to withdraw from Lai Khe and Ben Cat to Binh Cuong city and capturing 200 enemy troops. The bulk of the puppet 5th Division was forced to turn around and return to their previous positions. The Corps' deep penetration unit, the 320B Division's 27th and 48th Infantry Regiments and supporting specialty branch battalions, swiftly captured the Tan Uyen district military headquarters and the Lai Thieu military camp and opened the road for the advance into Go Vap.

To the northwest, Division 320A of 3rd Corps attacked the puppet 25th Division base at Dong Du. The enemy used tanks parked in fortified bunkers to fire on and block the entrances and sent infantry to conduct a counterattack against the rear of our troop formation. Combining deep penetration and flanking attacks and using the power of combined-arms tactics, Division 320A captured the Dong Du base after six hours of fierce fighting. During this battle our troops killed 560 enemy troops, captured 880 prisoners, and captured 17 heavy artillery pieces (including three 175mm guns) and 439 vehicles. Brigadier General Ly Tong Ba, the Commander of the puppet 25th Division, tried to escape but was captured by Cu Chi district guerrilla troops. Seizing this opportunity, with the enemy frightened and wavering after the loss of the Dong Du base, 316th Division switched from surrounding and blocking the enemy to launch assaults at Phuoc Hiep, Trang Bang, and Go Dau Ha, which destroyed or dispersed the 25th Division's 46th and 49th Regiments. The puppet 25th Division, the key unit defending the northwestern approaches to Saigon, had been destroyed. Our local armed forces and the civilian population combined military attacks with uprisings, liberating Tay Ninh province and the district of Cu Chi. The 3rd Corps' deep penetration unit, the 10th Infantry Division plus supporting specialty branch units, advanced down Route 1, crossed the Bong Bridge (which was still being held by the 198th Sapper Regiment), sped past Hoc Mon, and attacked and destroyed the enemy troops defending the Quang Trung Training Center. At 2400 hours during the night of 29–30 April, the Corps' deep penetration unit reached the Ba Queo intersection and attacked Tan Son Nhat airbase.

To the west and southwest, Group 232's 3rd Division, supported by artillery and tanks, liberated the Hau Nghia province capital. Enemy remnants trying to flee down Interprovincial Route 8 were attacked by the 1st Gia Dinh Regiment and more than 1,000 prisoners were captured. Group 232's deep penetration unit, 9th Division, and a number of specialty branch units reached the outskirts of the city.

Meanwhile, our sapper and commando soldiers, in cooperation with local armed forces, continued to fight off enemy counterattacks, maintained firm control of the bridges, captured district military headquarters at Tan Tuc and Tan Hoa and the Phu Lam radar station, and blocked enemy remnants trying to flee back into the inner city.

In three days of savage fighting our troops had captured many enemy base camps and positions, shattered the enemy's outer defensive perimeter, and destroyed or caused the disintegration of the bulk of the enemy's 5th, 25th, 18th, 22nd, and 7th Divisions. Our deep penetration units had reached the outskirts of the city and were between 10 and 20 kilometers from the center of the city. Our local armed forces were conducting strong operations in all areas and held firm control of the routes leading into the city.

Cao Van Vien, Commander of the puppet Joint General Staff, and many puppet generals and field grade officers fled abroad. U.S. President G. Ford ordered the initiation of a helicopter evacuation called "the Death-Defying Man" [sic]. This evacuation, which began at 11:15 A.M. on 29 April, evacuated almost 5,000 Americans from South Vietnam. During the early morning hours of 30 April, U.S. Ambassador Martin was evacuated from Saigon.

THE FORMATION OF STRATEGIC ARMY CORPS   419

The nation turned its gaze toward Saigon–Gia Dinh. The entire attack force for the assault on Saigon was ready. Our cadre and soldiers burned with resolve to win victory. On their helmets, on their shirtsleeves, on their rifle stocks, on the barrels of their cannons, on the sides of their vehicles, everywhere one could see scrawled the famous words of Uncle Ho's proclamation: "Advance! Total Victory is ours!!"

At 5:00 on the morning of 30 April our troops surged forward into Saigon from all directions. The rumble of tanks and the thunder of the engines of thousands of vehicles echoed from every road leading into the city.

As soon as the last explosions of our artillery preparatory barrage died out, the 3rd Corps' deep penetration unit swiftly pushed past the Bay Hien intersection and entered Tan Son Nhat airbase. Enemy troops holding the airfield put up fierce resistance. A flight of aircraft from Can Tho's Tra Noc airbase bombed our forces in the middle of the city streets, killing a number of our soldiers and setting three tanks on fire. Tank Gunner Nguyen Tran Doan asked a fellow soldier to cut off his injured arm so he could continue to fight. By 11:30 A.M. our troops had captured the Air Force Headquarters complex and the Headquarters of the puppet Airborne Division, had made contact with our military delegation at Davis Station,[10] and had secured control of Tan Son Nhat airfield. The 28th Regiment of the 10th Division advanced toward the puppet Joint General Staff Headquarters, fighting alongside 1st Corps forces. The leading elements of 3rd Corps advanced toward Independence Palace.

The 312th Division, working with local armed forces, killed or forced to surrender the entire enemy force holding the Phu Loi military base, then developed its attack by liberating the Binh Duong province capital. The 1st Corps' blocking force deployed in the An Loi area captured an entire convoy of 36 vehicles and 1,200 troops from the puppet 5th Division trying to escape down Interprovincial Route 14 from Lai Khe to Binh Duong. It then launched a direct assault on the Lai Khe military base. All enemy troops at this base surrendered and Brigadier General Le Nguyen Vy, Commander of the puppet 5th Division, committed suicide.

The 1st Corps' deep penetration group attacked and captured Lai Thieu. As it moved toward the Binh Trieu Bridge, the group caught the puppet 3rd Cavalry Brigade as it was working to try to build a new line of defense. Our troops launched an immediate assault, forcing the entire enemy force to surrender. We captured 140 tanks and armored vehicles. The deep penetration group then forced the prisoners to drive their tanks for us and lead our troops across the Binh Trieu Bridge toward the assigned target, the Headquarters of the puppet Joint General Staff.

Group 232's deep penetration unit advanced along Route 9. After destroying a puppet Airborne battalion at Ba Queo, 9th Division moved quickly past the Bay Hien intersection and captured the Headquarters of the puppet Capital Special Military Region. General Lam Van Phat, Commander of the Capital Special Military Region, was taken prisoner. The 5th Division, meanwhile, advanced up

Route 4 and attacked Tan An city and Thu Thua, eliminating and forcing the surrender of the 22nd Infantry Division and the 6th Ranger Group. The 24th and 28th Infantry Regiments coordinated with the 429th Sapper Regiment in attacking and capturing the National Police Headquarters, the Navy Headquarters, and the Nha Be petroleum storage facility.

The 4th Corps' deep penetration unit liberated Bien Hoa city, the Thu Duc district capital, and captured the Tam Hiep military base. The Ghenh Bridge was too weak for our heavy equipment to cross, however, so the Corps was forced to turn around and cross the Dong Nai River over the main highway bridge (the Xa Lo Bridge) to continue its advance toward Independence Palace.

The 2nd Corps' deep penetration unit, assisted by the 116th Sapper Regiment, crossed the main highway bridge and, after eliminating pockets of enemy resistance along the way, drove rapidly toward Independence Palace. Meanwhile, another 2nd Corps attack column liberated Vung Tau city.

Faced with a hopeless situation, puppet President Duong Van Minh finally requested a cease-fire to "discuss the transfer of governmental authority." His request was part of a scheme to halt our advance and to lessen the significance of our victory.

Our troops and civilians were ordered to "continue the attack on Saigon according to plan. Advance with the strongest possible spirit, liberate and occupy the entire city, disarm the puppet army, dissolve the puppet governmental structure at every level, and totally crush all enemy resistance."[11]

Our troops advanced quickly into the city from every point of the compass. All cadre and soldiers had the same resolve: to crush all resistance and shatter all enemy plots.

Their thoughts and actions were precisely in line with the Politburo's orders and reflected the political sensitivity, the political resolve, and the overwhelming resolve to secure victory of our cadre and soldiers. This was the result of our army's 30 years of fighting, training, and maturation in revolutionary struggle.

Our troops moved swiftly. The people of Saigon poured out into the streets to greet our soldiers. From the Binh Trieu Bridge to Quan Tre the people waved flags, beat drums, hunted down and disarmed enemy troops, eliminated enemy spies and traitors, and provided guides to our troops. In many locations the people used loudspeakers to call on puppet troops to lay down their arms and surrender. They showed our troops where enemy soldiers were hiding so we could pursue and capture them. Factory workers protected their machinery and warehouses until they could be turned over to our troops.

At 9:30 in the morning of 30 April, the deep penetration unit of 2nd Corps split into two columns that drove down Thong Nhat and Hong Thap Tu Boulevards and advanced toward the Presidential Palace of the Saigon puppet regime.

At 10:45 A.M., the lead tank, Tank Number 843, commanded by 1st Lieutenant Bui Quang Than, Commander of the 4th Tank Company, crashed through the palace gates and roared into the grounds of Independence Palace. A number of cadre and soldiers of the 66th Infantry Regiment (304th Division) and the 203rd Tank Brigade (2nd Corps) marched into the Palace conference room and took puppet President Duong Van Minh and his entire Cabinet prisoner. At 11:30 A.M. on 30 April 1975, the flag of the Revolution was raised in front of the main building of the Independence Palace complex. This moment signaled the complete liberation of Saigon. The Ho Chi Minh Campaign had won total victory. The city of Saigon, which our Uncle Ho had left 64 years previously in search of a way to save our nation, now had been returned to the people of an independent, united Vietnam. From the streets of Hanoi to the most distant offshore islands and the most remote villages and hamlets, cheers rang out to celebrate the liberation of Saigon. The entire nation lifted its voice in song, singing, "If only Uncle Ho was with us on this great victory day." Everyone was filled with memories of our beloved Uncle Ho.

During the historic campaign to liberate Saigon, 1,447 cadre and soldiers of the People's Army of Vietnam gave their lives for the cause of independence, freedom, and the unification of our Fatherland.

On 30 April 1975 the Politburo sent a congratulatory cable to the soldiers and civilians of Saigon–Gia Dinh. The cable lauded all cadre, soldiers, Party members, and Youth Group members of our main force units, local force units, elite forces, and self-defense militia who had fought with such extreme heroism, who had performed such glorious feats of arms, who had annihilated and dispersed a huge enemy force and forced the Saigon puppet government to accept an unconditional surrender, who had liberated the city of Saigon–Gia Dinh, and who had won total victory in the campaign bearing the name of our glorious Uncle Ho.

The Politburo ordered the army to maintain its determined-to-win spirit and, in cooperation with the local population, to continue its attacks and uprisings to complete the total liberation of our Fatherland's beloved South.

THE LIBERATION OF THE MEKONG DELTA

The liberation of Saigon–Gia Dinh and the surrender of the puppet government provided the decisive factor that enabled our soldiers and civilians to destroy and disperse the puppet 4th Corps and the enemy's entire apparatus of oppression and to complete the liberation of the Mekong Delta.

Beginning in early March 1975, carrying out phase two of the strategic combat plan throughout the region, the armed forces of Military Regions 7 and 8, in coordination with mass uprisings, launched powerful attacks against the enemy. Our liberated areas grew and our forces moved up close to the enemy's lines of communications and to the cities, towns, and enemy military bases, tying down the puppet regular divisions and supporting the Central Highlands and Hue-Danang Campaigns.

During the preparations for and progress of the Ho Chi Minh Campaign, the soldiers and civilian population of the Mekong Delta had two missions: to conduct local attacks and uprisings to tie down the units of the puppet 4th Corps, and to organize the southern attack on Saigon aimed at capturing the National Police Headquarters.

On 6 April 1975, acting on orders from COSVN, Military Region 8's 8th Division, the 241st Engineer Battalion, and local armed forces cut Route 4 in a number of places. The enemy was forced to send two regiments of the 7th Division and several Ranger battalions to secure the road. In Military Region 9 the Military Region's 4th Division, supported by local armed forces, overran the Ba Cang and Binh Minh district military headquarters in Tra Vinh province, built a number of roadblocks on Route 4, and threatened Can Tho's Tra Noc airfield. Every province worked out a plan to combine armed attacks with popular uprisings according to our formula: Every province will liberate itself, every district will liberate itself, every village will liberate itself. The plans approved by the Military Region Headquarters covered two possibilities:

- If region or province military forces mounted a military attack, the masses would rise up to support them.
- If a great opportunity presented itself and our military forces could not react in time, our political and troop proselytizing spearheads would work with local armed forces to seize enemy targets within the cities.

On 26 April, as our main force corps launched simultaneous attacks on Saigon from the east, north, northwest, and southwest, to the south 8th Division quickly cut Route 4 between Long Dinh and Tan Hiep. A My Tho province local force battalion supported by district-level armed forces captured a section of the road between Long Dinh and Bung Mon. The 263rd Sapper Battalion, the 292nd Engineer Battalion, and Cai Be district guerrillas seized control of a section of Route 4 between Hoa Khanh and the northern portion of My Thuan. Every night thousands of people from Cai Be and Cai Lay districts marched down to Route 4 to build mounds and obstacles to block enemy vehicles trying to get to Saigon. Route 4 was completely cut. The soldiers and civilians of the Mekong Delta had performed their duty in an outstanding fashion, isolating and tying down enemy forces in the southern part of the campaign area, simultaneously sending forces down Route 4 to join our main force divisions in the attack on Saigon. Our local armed forces and political attack forces in the provinces and districts rapidly closed in on the cities and towns.

On 30 April and 1 May military attacks and uprisings to liberate the provinces of the Mekong Delta were launched simultaneously and won quick victories.

In Can Tho, Military Region 9's 4th Division overran the Tra Noc airfield and the headquarters of the puppet 4th Air Force Division. The division followed up this success with a rapid advance into the center of the city, seizing important military targets such as the Headquarters of 4th Corps and Military Region 4, Police Headquarters, and staff agencies and military units subordinate to the puppet Navy Headquarters. Two battalions of provincial local force troops mounted a ferocious attack on Vong Cung and the Cai Son Canal during the night of 29 April, finally capturing the residence of the Phong Dinh Province Chief at 1500 hours on 30 April. City commando forces cooperated with the masses in launching an uprising that burst into the prison, freed almost 1,000 cadre and citizens imprisoned by the enemy, captured the radio station, and took control of the precincts and blocks of the city.

In My Tho, at noon on 30 April the commando unit of our Labor Youth Group, using agents of the revolution, incited the masses in several city precincts to launch an uprising and appealed to puppet soldiers, officers, police, and people's self-defense force members to turn their weapons in to the revolution. Students from the Le Ngoc Han and Nguyen Dinh Chieu Schools rode motorcycles and Lambrettas around the streets using loudspeakers to broadcast the news that Duong Van Minh had surrendered. Enemy troops at the Chuong Duong pier opened fire on these vehicles, killing and wounding a number of people. During the afternoon of 30 April, two province local force battalions advanced into the city and, supported by local armed forces, captured the Province Police Headquarters and the Dinh Tuong Province Military Headquarters. Only after these victories and after 1st Regiment, 8th Division, destroyed the last elements of the puppet 6th Armored Squadron at the Old Market did enemy troops in My Tho city and at the Dong Tam military base finally agree to surrender. My Tho province was totally liberated during the night of 30 April.

In Go Cong, because the province capital was remote, enemy forces were weak, and because in early April our military proselytizing cadre had begun recruiting numerous agents in the province's Regional Force and Popular Force units, when word of Saigon's liberation was received our political and military proselytizing spearhead leapt into action, liberating the city on their own at 1530 hours on 30 April. Our forces then mobilized a group of automobiles and Lambrettas and drove up to Vinh Huu, where they picked up two provincial local force companies and brought them back to the city to take control of the city's political and military installations.

In Tra Vinh, during the afternoon of 29 April, provincial armed forces began to move out from the Cay Me [Tamarind] Orchards. At 6:00 A.M. on 30 April these forces attacked the city from many different directions. Working with local armed forces and the civilian population, they forced many Regional Force outposts to surrender and captured the local airfield and the enemy's artillery base. The remaining enemy elements fled to the headquarters of the province chief, where they mounted a fierce resistance. Faced with the overwhelming strength of the revolution, however, at 10:30 A.M. on 30 April the enemy troops were forced to surrender. Tra Vinh was the first province in the Mekong Delta to be liberated.

On 30 April the armed forces and civilians of Vinh Long, Soc Trang, Bac Lieu, Rach Gia, Sa Dec, and Long An provinces combined military attacks with popular uprisings to liberate their own provinces.

On 1 and 2 May the remaining provinces of the Delta, Chuong Thien, Ca Mau, Long Xuyen, Chau Doc, Kien Tuong, and Ben Tre, were also liberated. Using their own forces, trained and brought to maturity through years of continuous fighting, the main force troops of Military Regions 8 and 9 and the local armed forces of the provinces of the Mekong Delta took advantage of the great opportunity that presented itself when the puppet central government surrendered and enemy troops became frightened and disintegrated. Relying on the revolutionary zeal of the masses, combining military attacks with popular uprisings to annihilate and disperse 4th Corps, Military Region 4, and the enemy's forces of oppression, our forces quickly and completely liberated the entire Mekong Delta. These actions were precisely coordinated with the offensive against Saigon and contributed to the winning of a rapid and complete victory for the Spring 1975 General Offensive and Uprising.

As the provinces on the mainland were being liberated, the strategic plan and operational guidance prepared by the Politburo and the Central Military Party Committee also called for the rapid liberation of our offshore islands.

Right after Danang was liberated, on 4 April 1975 the Politburo and the Central Military Party Committee ordered the Region 5 Party Committee, the Regional Military Party Committee, the Military Region 5 Military Headquarters, and the Navy Headquarters to "study and issue orders directed toward seizing the best opportunity to attack and occupy those islands of the Spratleys Archipelago that are currently occupied by South Vietnamese puppet troops. This is an extremely important mission."[12]

Acting on orders issued by the High Command, on 10 April 1975 the Navy Headquarters sent transport vessels 673, 674, and 675 from the 125th Navy Regiment on a quick voyage from Hai Phong to Danang. At 4:00 A.M. on 11 April our combat force, consisting of Unit 4, 126th Water Sapper Regiment, and a number of sapper teams from Military Region 5 and Khanh Hoa province, all under the command of Lieutenant Colonel Mai Nang, 126th Regiment Commander, boarded these three transport vessels and sailed for the Spratleys Archipelago. After three stormy days at sea, at 1900 hours on 13 April our troops neared Song Tu Tay Island. Comrade Nguyen Ngoc Que, Commander of Team 1, led his troops as they rowed dinghies and rubber rafts ashore to attack and capture the island. In a 30-minute battle we killed or captured the entire enemy force on the island (totaling 36 men) and captured all their weapons. At 5:00 A.M. on 14 April 1975 Combatant Le Xuan Phat raised our red flag with its gold star up the flagpole facing the plaque proclaiming this island as Vietnamese territory.

The puppet armed forces sent extra ships out to strengthen the defenses of the remaining islands. On our side, after a period of preparation, on 25 April a sapper team commanded by 2nd Lieutenant Do Viet Cuong attacked and captured Son Ca Island. Between 27 and 29 April, as our main force corps launched their attacks on Saigon, our sapper and navy troops continued the attack by seizing Nam Yet, Sinh Ton, Spratley, and the other islands held by puppet troops.

With the liberation of the Spratleys Archipelago, the most remote portion of our Fatherland, our armed forces completed the mission assigned to it by the Party and by our people, contributing to the total and complete victory of the resistance war against the Americans to save the nation.

After liberating the provinces of Cochin China, the 171st, 172nd, 125th, and 126th Regiments of the People's Navy, together with elements of the 3rd Division, were ordered to launch an operation to liberate Con Son Island. On 2 May, as our troops were on the way to carry out this operation, we were informed that the revolutionary fighters who had been imprisoned on this island had conducted an uprising and had, on their own, liberated the island during the afternoon of 30 April. When our soldiers arrived, they hunted down and captured enemy remnants, maintained public order and security, and worked with the local population to form a revolutionary governmental administration on the island. A few days later, our naval vessels carried our patriotic fighters who had been held on the island back to the mainland.

On Phu Quoc Island, our revolutionary fighters imprisoned on the island rose up in cooperation with local armed forces and civilians to seize the island and liberate themselves on 30 April.

CONSOLIDATING VICTORY

The 1975 spring general offensive and uprisings, the apex of which was the historic Ho Chi Minh Campaign, ended in a glorious victory. During almost 60 days and nights, using our overwhelming military and political strength, our soldiers and civilians totally destroyed and dispersed a puppet army of more than a million men, crushed the puppet governmental structure, threw off the neocolonialist yoke of oppression imposed by the Americans, and totally liberated the southern half of our country.

On 1 May 1975 the Ho Chi Minh Campaign Headquarters met with the Military Commanders and Political Commissars of 1st, 2nd, 3rd, and 4th Corps and of Groups 232 and 559. The Headquarters assigned concrete responsibilities to each unit for the period of military governmental administration of the city and assigned responsibilities for taking control of and preserving enemy military installations and facilities. This was a new mission, filled with many difficulties and complexities. Relying on the prestige of the revolution following our victory, all units engaged in military governmental tasks won the support of the civilian population; correctly carried out the work of administering their troops; provided constant education, training, and discipline; increased the spirit of revolutionary vigilance among our troops; struggled resolutely against the appearance of subjective attitudes among troops who ignored or played down enemy acts of sabotage; and maintained a proper attitude toward the local population. In Saigon and all the newly liberated cities and towns, public order and security were firmly maintained. Working with Party cadre and the local population, our troops conducted sweeps to arrest enemy remnants and collect and preserve enemy weapons and military equipment. They worked with local Party chapters to develop revolutionary governmental institutions and basic-level armed forces and contributed to economic production and the restoration of a normal life to the local population.

Following its great victory in crushing the puppet army and puppet government and completely liberating South Vietnam, our army immediately launched into its new missions, properly carrying its function as a laboring army and setting a shining example of the revolutionary character of the soldiers of Uncle Ho.

On 13 May 1975, President Ton Duc Thang led a delegation of representatives of the Central Committee of the Vietnamese Labor [Communist] Party, the Government of the Democratic Republic of Vietnam, and the Vietnam Fatherland Front to Ho Chi Minh city to attend a victory celebration. On 15 May 1975, 700,000 citizens of Hanoi attended a rally and parade in honor of our nation's great victory. The same day there was a large parade in Saigon with millions of people coming out into the streets to celebrate our victory. In a speech delivered to the rally in Hanoi, Comrade Le Duan, First Secretary of our Party, said, "This victory was won by our Party, by our Great Chairman Ho Chi Minh, and by the martyrs who gave their lives for the Fatherland." Comrade Le Duan warmly praised the cadre and soldiers of our three types of troops, the Service Branches, and the specialty branches, who throughout these historic days had fought bravely, intelligently, and swiftly, crushing the enemy army and scattering it to the winds, performing glorious new feats of arms and gaining further honors for our army's "determined to fight, determined to win" flag of honor.

On 25 April 1976, a general election for the National Assembly of a unified Vietnam was carried out by the people of the entire nation in a spirit of pride in our victory. On 2 July 1976, the 1st Session of the 6th National Assembly approved renaming the nation the Socialist Republic of Vietnam.

Carrying out the teachings of Uncle Ho: "Be loyal to the Party, be true to the people, be ready to fight and die for the independence and freedom of the Fatherland and for socialism. Complete every task, overcome every difficulty, defeat every foe," our army, side by side with our entire population, fought continuously for 30 years, defeating the modern, well-equipped, professional armies of aggression sent by the French colonialists and the American imperialists, and carried Chairman Ho Chi Minh's flag of 100 battles, 100 victories, forward to our final victory.

The nation was unified. The entire country now advanced toward socialism. The Fourth National Congress of Party Delegates, meeting in December 1976, set forward the two strategic duties of our army and our people: to successfully build socialism and to firmly defend the socialist Vietnamese Fatherland.

An era of new development and combat had dawned, an era in which our army would firmly defend our socialist Vietnamese Fatherland had begun.

Conclusion

With the victory of the 1953–1954 winter-spring strategic offensive, the high point of which was the Dien Bien Phu campaign, our soldiers and civilians brought to an end the resistance war against the French colonialist aggressors and liberated North Vietnam. The struggle to liberate South Vietnam and unify the nation, however, still continued.

As we began this struggle, in half of the nation our people lived under a people's government led by the vanguard Party of the laboring class. Our army was no longer the tiny armed force it had been just after its birth (1944–1945) or when the resistance war was just beginning (1945–1946). It had grown mature and powerful. Our army was the backbone of the war waged by our entire population on all battlefields from the North down to the South and had fought arm in arm with the revolutionary armed forces and the patriotic civilian populations of Laos and Cambodia. By the spring of 1954, with a number of division-sized units that had grown famous for their feats of arms, the People's Army of Vietnam had eminently fulfilled its role as a powerful fist that struck "like a ton of bricks," crushing the enemy's strongest defensive fortified complex at Dien Bien Phu. The Vietnamese people's armed forces had won a glorious victory over the professional soldiers of a large nation.

In spite of this, however, when measured against its new responsibilities and in comparison with the American expeditionary army, at that time our army was still very weak in its strength, weapons and technical equipment, and experience in modern warfare. Our army was still an infantry force only and did not possess the full mix of services and specialty branches. For this reason, although it had matured a great deal, in the face of its new responsibilities and its new opponent in battle, our army still would be forced to use small forces to fight big battles and use small numbers of soldiers to fight large enemy forces. Our army had to expand in response to the requirements of combat and force building, getting stronger and stronger the more it fought. This is what we learned from the experiences of our army in fighting and force building. Knowing how to apply this lesson played a critical role in helping our army successfully carry out its duties in the resistance war against the Americans.

The resistance war against the Americans was fought at a different stage in history from the period of the resistance war against the French.

This time our combat opponents were American troops, puppet troops, and satellite troops whose equipment was more modern than ours and who had been carefully trained to meet the requirements of modern warfare. These armies fought to carry out the extremely reactionary political policies of the American imperialists, the leader of world imperialism, a nation that had tremendous economic and military power, advanced science and technology, and that wielded great influence throughout the world.

Our army, on the other hand, had only just begun to plan to develop the service branches and specialty branches necessary for a regular, modern force. These developmental demands presented innumerable problems that we had to solve. Our greatest problem was to develop command and technical specialist cadre. Our situation was critical. Many brand-new tasks had to be carried out simultaneously to rapidly expand our forces and prepare for combat. Cadre and soldiers, high-ranking and low-ranking personnel, all had to study and train in order to carry out their responsibilities.

The work of preparing our army for a new resistance war was being carried out within a new context. The liberation of North Vietnam provided many basic advantages that would help our armed forces develop their organizational structure and their battle strength. The concentration of our nation's labor force on construction in peacetime conditions provided many advantages that enabled the army to carry out the duties entrusted to it. Within itself the army also possessed many advantages it had not held during the resistance war against the French. Tens of thousands of cadre of all ranks had grown to maturity through the challenges of nine years of war. Large numbers of soldiers who had been hardened in combat were a significant resource for the future expansion of our cadre ranks. Strategic agencies such as the General Staff, the General Political Department, and the General Department of Rear Services, large main force units such as the infantry and specialty branch division-sized units, and local military leadership organizations such as the military regions, provincial units, and district units had all grown and matured. The entire army and the entire population had experience in fighting an all-out people's war involving the entire population to combat an imperialist aggressor. Our will to fight for the independence and freedom of the nation, for the unification of the Fatherland, and for socialism had been strengthened and solidified. These factors provided a solid foundation for the creation of an invincible force that could defeat any opponent, even the American imperialist aggressors.

Through nine years of resistance warfare against the French colonialists, our Party, the leader of the people's war in general, and the leader of every aspect of the combat and force building operations of our armed forces in particular, also had matured tremendously and gained a great deal of valuable experience. Many basic issues had been settled, such as the policy of people's warfare; the organization of the people's armed forces into three types of troops, among whom priority was given to the development of a strong main force element with a powerful punch; and the military art of people's war, including both guerrilla warfare and conventional warfare. The leadership role of the Party within the armed forces, a system of Party and political activities within the armed forces through the establishment and functioning of Party committees and political staff agencies, and a cadre organization composed of command cadre and political cadre (political officers and political commissars) at all levels had been developed and increasingly perfected into a set of principles, regulations, and a way of life. This gave us a basic advantage because it helped our armed forces carry out their duties during this period.

In the international arena, the victory of our people in the resistance war against the French, with its glorious conclusion at Dien Bien Phu, signaled the beginning of the collapse of old-style imperialism and had been applauded by the entire world. The Vietnamese people's resistance war against the French colonialist aggressors was recognized as a just cause by all mankind. Our next struggle, the national salvation resistance war against the Americans, which was being fought to oppose neocolonialist aggression, the enslavement of half of our nation, and to complete the Vietnamese people's mission of liberating our race and unifying our Fatherland, was naturally suited to the morals and aspirations of the entire world and to the laws of social development of mankind. This provided us a great advantage, which we used to isolate the enemy and to win for the Vietnamese people's resistance war the ever-growing and ever more effective approval and support of the fraternal socialist nations, of the working classes of the world, of the national liberation movement, and of progressive, peace-loving, justice-loving peoples of the world, including even the American people. At the same time, the socialist bloc continued to grow in strength and the movement to fight for peace, national independence, democracy, and social progress expanded day by day. Even though differing opinions and policies regarding revolutionary strategy and tactics arose within the Communist and international workers movements, when faced with the just cause of our people and our Party's correct policy of independence, self-determination, and international solidarity, the voice of the entire world rang out with one common theme: solidarity with Vietnam against the American aggressors.

Of special importance was the fact that during the course of the struggle against a common enemy, the spirit of combat solidarity between the peoples and the revolutionary armed forces of the three fraternal nations of Vietnam, Laos, and Cambodia grew ever stronger. This close alliance between the revolutions of the three nations of Indochina in combat and development became our formula for defeating the aggressor army and preserving the independence and freedom of each nation. Understanding of this formula had grown stronger during the years of sacrifice and adversity of the resistance war against the French and now had become a special tradition and a matchless source of strength for the revolutions of the three Indochina nations.

The resistance war against the French colonialists lasted nine years, but the struggle by our soldiers and civilians against the American imperialist aggressors was even longer and more vicious. This time the combat opponents of our army were large, modern, well-trained, and rather well-supplied armies. Relying on their power, their modern weapons, their wealth, and their international position, the American imperialists deviously sought every possible method to force our soldiers and civilians to surrender. Five different Presidents of the United States mobilized over half a million American expeditionary soldiers and over half a million puppet and satellite soldiers, used almost every type of modern weapon and technology they possessed (except for nuclear weapons) and tens of millions of tons of bombs and shells, and expanded the war throughout the entire Indochinese Peninsula in an effort to carry out their aggressive intentions. So many hardships and shortages that our armed forces had to overcome! So many adversities, so much violence that our cadre and combatants had to endure, that they had to give their own lives to overcome.

Our armed forces entered this new battle as the victors at Dien Bien Phu. Under the enlightened leadership of the Party and of Chairman Ho Chi Minh, with the wholehearted support of our people, our army overcame great challenges in many different areas, demonstrating its outstanding revolutionary character and its solid fighting capabilities. The "soldiers of Uncle Ho" always stood on a higher plane than their opponents and always found a way to carry out the policies of the Party and the orders and instructions given them by higher authorities to secure victory. Our army's need to expand rapidly into an army made up of many specialty and service branches presented many difficult and complex problems, which we solved in a correct, timely manner. The three massive expansions of our forces also were three occasions when the strength of our armed forces grew explosively, expanding from 170,000 troops (in 1958) to 300,000 (in 1963) then to 700,000 (in 1966) and up to one million (in 1973). Our three major developmental phases were also three phases marking the tremendous maturation of our combat power: the building of a regular army with upgraded equipment (1954–1964), the rapid development of our service and specialty branches, including air force, anti-aircraft artillery, missiles, radar, armor, sappers, artillery, engineers, signal, etc. (1964–1967), and the creation of large strategic units, 1st, 2nd, 3rd, and 4th Corps (1973–1975). With our nation temporarily divided and a fierce war raging, many questions related to the leadership and command of the entire armed forces as well as the leadership and command of the different battlefields and fronts arose, demanding that we make appropriate changes. One of the most representative of these problems was the creation and increasing perfection of the command and leadership organization of the battlefields of Cochin China, Region 5, the Central Highlands, Tri-Thien, Route 9, the Ho Chi Minh Trail, etc., as well as the command and leadership organization of the important strategic campaigns. Many problems encountered during the resistance war against the Americans mirrored and built upon the valuable lessons we had learned from the resistance war against the French. There were also problems in many different areas that went beyond any of our experiences during the resistance war against the French but that we were ultimately able to successfully resolve. These included issues involving the military arts, the scale of combat, the relationship between the great rear area and the great front lines, and the combat alliance of the three Indochinese nations.

With a steadfast resolve to fight and to win and with remarkable revolutionary fortitude, our cadre and soldiers responded promptly to the Party's and Chairman Ho Chi Minh's appeal to conduct a resistance war against the Americans to save the nation with an all-out effort to hone their skills; to master military science, the military arts, and military scientific technology; to constantly increase their capabilities; and to victoriously complete the great, glorious mission entrusted to them by the Party and the people.

Arm in arm with the entire population, our army defeated "special warfare," "limited war," and "Vietnamization" strategies that the American imperialists formulated and implemented in the southern half of our nation. We brought American airpower to its knees during our people's war against the war of destruction conducted by American imperialist air and naval forces in North Vietnam. We crushed the American plots and actions designed to cripple our main force units in the South and to blockade our sea lanes and destroy our land routes to cut off the flow of international aid to Vietnam and to cut our strategic transportation route from North Vietnam to the South.

Fighting alongside the revolutionary armies and patriotic citizens of Laos and Cambodia, our army contributed to the development of the revolutionary organizations and the people's armed forces of our allies, and our army, together with our allies, systematically escalated the scale of revolutionary warfare. Our army also received tremendous assistance from the peoples of these two friendly countries. Through this mutual assistance and learning from one another, conducted in the pure spirit of international proletarianism, our army was able to develop its own capabilities and gloriously fulfill the international duties that the Party and the people had entrusted to it.

Besides carrying out its combat role, our army devoted time and personnel to participate in the mobilization of the masses to perform basic construction tasks on the borders, the offshore islands, and in strategic areas. The army participated in the restoration and development of our economy and culture and contributed to the construction and consolidation of North Vietnam. Side by side with our guerrilla militia and our civilian population, it built and defended base areas, took over administration of newly liberated areas, contributed to the maintenance of law and order, and built up revolutionary armed forces and governmental structures.

After more than 20 years of simultaneously fighting and building during the resistance war against the Americans to save the nation, our army inscribed another glorious feat of arms into the pages of its history: Working with the entire population, the army defeated the large army of the rash and powerful leader of the imperialist clique, liberated South Vietnam, defended North Vietnam, unified the nation, and completely fulfilled its international duties in the fraternal nations of Laos and Cambodia.

Like jade, which shines more brightly the more you polish it, the revolutionary character of our armed forces and the high moral qualities of the "soldiers of Uncle Ho," which began their development at the time of the birth of the Vietnam Propaganda and Liberation Unit and grew during the time of the August Revolution and the resistance war against the French, shone ever more brightly during the resistance war against the Americans to save the nation. This revolutionary character was reflected and disseminated through the thoughts and actions of great masses of cadre and soldiers, eventually becoming the *noble traditions* of the heroic People's Army of Vietnam.

The loyalty of our army to the revolutionary cause of our Party and to our people is boundless, because it has brought independence and sovereignty to our nation and freedom and happiness to our people. That cause is the goal of the entire nation and the just aspiration of every citizen of Vietnam. The cadre and soldiers of our armed forces have an ever-deepening understanding that loyalty to this revolutionary cause will also satisfy their own personal aspirations. For this reason, even if they must give their lives in combat, our soldiers and cadre are not afraid if their sacrifice brings independence and freedom for the nation and happiness and prosperity for the people.

With faith in their just cause and in the victory of the revolution, our army *strictly followed the lines and policies of the Party,* resolutely fighting to defend the Party and the socialist State. This loyalty to the revolutionary cause and this faith in final victory gave great strength to each of our cadre and soldiers, enabling them to overcome every obstacle and adversity and complete every task assigned to them by the Party and the State.

Because of its devotion to the cause of winning the independence and freedom of our nation, our army, fearing neither hardship nor difficulty, not retreating from danger and violence, built the glorious tradition of *determined to fight, determined to win.* During the resistance struggle against the Americans, overcoming every challenge, our cadre and soldiers steadfastly studied and trained, mastering the intricacies of modern weapons and equipment and constantly improving their fighting strength. With a firm understanding of the people's war policy of the Party, our armed forces constantly developed effective combat methods and tactics. The enemy tried a hundred schemes, a thousand plots to increase his own strength and suppress our forces, but he failed. Our cadre and soldiers resolutely found ways to defeat him. They sought excellent strategies and tactics, they overcame difficulties and endured hardships to develop ways to defeat the enemy and implement our offensive concepts. Because they could not endure the continued division of our nation, because they could not stand to see half of our country languishing under the neocolonialist yoke of the American imperialists, no one was able to sit idly by to allow the enemy to run rampant over us. As our people working the land "squeezed water from the soil, making rain in the place of the gods," our army in combat also knew how to "search out the Americans to fight them, search out the puppets to kill them." No matter how bad the situation, in these new conditions our soldiers fought with the courage, intelligence, innovation, and unique tactical skills of the Vietnamese race.

The power of the people's army during both combat and force building operations was magnified many times by its tradition of *solidarity, democracy, and discipline,* which it constantly displayed. During times of peace and times of war, our cadre and soldiers loved each other like brothers, sharing, from top to bottom, a sincere desire to help one another, to share with each other the best of everything. In every task the army performed, its sense of service to the organization and its strict adherence to every order and directive issued by higher authorities were transformed into the daily actions of every member of the armed forces. Because all were fighting together for one high cause, every person was equal from the political standpoint. Criticism and self-criticism in accordance with the instructions of Uncle Ho were voluntarily carried out by the entire army. Life in the great family of the armed forces, whether on the front lines or in the rear area, was filled with a spirit of comradeship and brotherhood; soldiers helped each other so that, together, they could all progress. The tradition of solidarity, democracy, and discipline was regularly expressed in a pure action slogan: "Take the bitter for yourself and leave the sweet for your friend."

Having grown out of the people, been nourished by the people, and fighting for the people, our army was always taught by the Party and Uncle Ho to *maintain close ties to the people.* This tradition became an immeasurable source of strength for the army. During the resistance war against the Americans this perfidious enemy devoted tremendous efforts to divide our soldiers from the people but their efforts were in vain. On countless occasions they caused difficulties for many units of our armed forces that no one thought we could overcome. With the support and protection of the people these units defeated the enemy's schemes and completed their assigned tasks. Responding to the people's love of country as expressed by their disregard of sacrifice and adversity to feed, shelter, and shield our soldiers in times of danger, our army fought selflessly, enduring every adversity and sacrifice for the sake of the people.

Our devious enemy wanted to isolate the sacred resistance war of the people of Vietnam and divide the peoples of the three Indochinese nations. Our army, on the other hand, always understood, strengthened, and displayed our Party's and our people's tradition of *pure international solidarity.* Viewing the revolutionary cause of the people of fraternal nations as being the same as the cause of our own people, our armed forces always supported the national liberation movement and struggles for peace, democracy, and social progress throughout the world. Our cadre and soldiers noted and studied the valuable experiences of the armies of fraternal socialist nations in order to increase our own capabilities. The People's Army of Vietnam maintained close ties to the revolutionary causes of our allies and fought shoulder to shoulder with the revolutionary armed forces and peoples of our two neighboring nations to secure our common victory.

Chairman Ho Chi Minh summarized the traditions of our armed forces in the following words: *"Our armed forces, which are loyal to the Party and true to the people, are prepared to fight and die for the independence and freedom of the Fatherland and for socialism. They will fulfill any duty, overcome any difficulty, and defeat any enemy."*

The Party's 4th National Congress *"heartily commends the cadre and soldiers of the heroic people's armed forces, who fought with extraordinary heroism for decades, won a string of famous victories from Dien Bien Phu to the Ho Chi Minh Campaign, added to the splendor of the glorious traditions of our army, and, together with the entire population, wrote the miraculous epic hymn of Vietnam's war of revolution."*

The People's Army of Vietnam was worthy of the trust of the Party, the love of the people, and the fellowship of our friends and allies.

Our army attained a powerful maturity and victoriously completed its duties in the resistance war against the Americans because, first of all, *the Party invested great efforts in building up the army and providing it with good leadership.* The Party taught the army patriotism, love of socialism, and how to work toward those beautiful ideals. Following correct policy lines, the Party built the armed forces into three kinds of troops. It built a powerful people's army, developed a main force element with a highly effective combat punch, enabled the armed forces to grow stronger and stronger the more they fought, defeated every strategic, campaign, and tactical scheme devised by the enemy, systematically secured victory, and finally attained our complete victory. Under the leadership of the Party, the People's Army of Vietnam became a sharp, reliable tool, which, side by side with the entire population, put into practice the policy of people's war and defeated the American imperialist war of aggression. The army became a force well versed in the Party's people's warfare strategy and carried out its role in a creative fashion, enabling the people's war to develop flexibly and preventing the enemy from coping with our actions. It can be said that without the Party line there would not be a people's army and, on the other hand, without the people's army, built and led by the Party to serve as the backbone of the battle fought by the entire population, the policy of people's war could not have been brought to fruition and the enemy would not have been defeated.

Our army also attained maturity and gained victory because *the people wholeheartedly supported it and continuously contributed to it.* Moreover—and this is extremely important—*it fought shoulder to shoulder with our compatriots of all ethnic nationalities.* Because of this the enemy had to contend with an entire revolutionary nation that maintained a high level of vigilance and that was armed and trained in an extremely unique manner. The army shared the fires of battle against the aggressors everywhere it fought, whether it was on land, at sea, or in the air. The people took onto their own shoulders some of the heavy responsibilities borne by the army, so that, no matter how heavy the responsibility, with the help of the people it could still be successfully completed. Wherever our people lived was a battlefront in the fight against the enemy. Sometimes by political struggle in different forms, sometimes overt and sometimes covert, sometimes by military struggle conducted on an appropriate scale and with appropriate measures, no matter what the form, our compatriots in South Vietnam worked closely with our army to attack the enemy according to the formula, "two legs, three spearheads, three zones." In the great rear area of North Vietnam, "with one hand on the plow and the other on the rifle," "with a hammer in one hand and a gun in the other," our people enthusiastically engaged in economic production and actively fought beside our soldiers, firing at enemy aircraft and enemy warships, capturing air pirates, ensuring the flow of traffic along our transportation networks, etc. With firm reliance on the people and with the help of the people, our army had unrivaled strength and overcame every challenge to fulfill its enormous responsibilities in the resistance war against the United States.

In our just fight for national liberation and to fulfill our international obligations, our army had *enormous international support and assistance.* The people and the armed forces of the Soviet Union, China, and other fraternal socialist countries helped our army progress rapidly on the road to modernization and made important contributions in logistics and technology to the force building and combat operations of our army. Our brothers and sisters and our friends throughout the world strongly encouraged the struggle of our army and our people to achieve independence and national unification. This sympathy and support provided additional strength to our army and our people, helping us endure our long resistance struggle until final victory. Of special importance, in Laos and Cambodia the people of these two neighboring nations viewed our soldiers as their own flesh and blood—these two peoples shared what they had with our soldiers and gave our men their wholehearted support.

The love and the attention to education, training, and mobilization provided by Chairman Ho Chi Minh had an enormous effect on the maturation and growth of our army, both in the past and during the resistance war against the Americans to save the nation. Chairman Ho Chi Minh affirmed that "our army is a people's army. It was born from the people and it fights for the people!" Uncle Ho taught our armed forces that "loyalty to the nation and to the people is a sacred duty, a heavy responsibility, but it is also the pride of our warriors." He taught, "Our army is loyal to the Party and true to the people, it is ready to fight and die for the independence and freedom of the Fatherland and for the cause of socialism." He proclaimed the truth that "there is nothing so precious as independence and freedom," teaching our soldiers to be steadfast in the fight for our goals and to maintain the revolutionary character of the working class. When our entire nation rose up to resist the French, Uncle Ho said, "As long as one colonialist soldier remains on Vietnamese soil we must fight, fight on until we achieve total victory." During the resistance war against the Americans he taught us to be even more resolute. "As long as there is still one aggressor left on the soil of our nation we must continue to fight, we must sweep them all away." He encouraged our cadre and soldiers to hone themselves in every possible way and especially to carry out training to regularize and modernize our army. He said, "Naturally, political awareness is necessary, but we also must have education and technical skills in order to use machinery in ever more sophisticated ways." Chairman Ho Chi Minh always reminded us of the need for quality in the army. He said, "We must build a truly excellent force with truly high quality."[1] He regularly monitored the activities of our units on the battlefields, encouraging cadre and soldiers to study and follow the examples of "good people, good works." The contribution Uncle Ho made to the army was truly enormous. His love for the army was both boundless and intimate. Uncle Ho always reserved a "boundless affection" for the armed forces, for sick and wounded soldiers, and for the families of our martyred comrades. He set aside time to regularly visit our troops, instruct our cadre, check on the care and feeding of our fighters, and reminded all units to be vigilant and ready for battle. As the head of the Party and the State, as the leader of the revolution and the nation, as the Supreme Commander of the people's armed forces, Chairman Ho Chi Minh received the highest respect and the absolute trust of the entire Party, the entire population, and the entire armed forces. It is rare to have any Supreme Commander who was as close to his soldiers as Uncle Ho was to the fighters of the People's Army of Vietnam. It is also rare to have any army that loves its Supreme Commander as much as the People's Army of Vietnam loved Uncle Ho. This sacred sentiment grew out of Uncle Ho's life work and the exemplary life He led, by His very revolutionary and affectionate concern for and actions toward the army. This sacred sentiment was a powerful motivating factor that caused our cadre and combatants to carry out the policies of the Party and follow the teachings of Uncle Ho. It was because of this that our people gave our army the affectionate title of "the soldiers of Uncle Ho" to affirm the army's noble revolutionary character and to praise Uncle Ho for his teachings, which had turned it into an army that truly belonged to the people.

There was another very important factor that brought about the solid maturation of our army and enabled it to fulfill its role in the resistance struggle against the Americans. That was the fact that our cadre and soldiers—the children and grandchildren of a heroic race—*inherited the steadfast and indomitable traditions of our ancestors and were able to develop these traditions into revolutionary heroism during a new era.* This legacy was displayed in the daily actions of our cadre and soldiers as they fought, trained, and labored. Resolved to defeat the American aggressors, our army took advantage of every hour, every minute, to increase its capabilities, racing against time, wrestling with adversity, combating ignorance, and overcoming outdated customs to develop its forces. The process of training and honing our skills was just as tiring and as difficult as combat. Finding ways to defeat the enemy through the use of the Party's policy of people's war demanded an exceptionally courageous spirit, steadfast revolutionary energy, truly intelligent minds, and great creative talent. Our army was able to fulfill these requirements and for that reason progressed by leaps and bounds, overcoming many difficulties and obstacles to defeat the American aggressors.

The maturation of our army during the resistance war against the Americans came about under very critical circumstances. We had to conduct force building and at the same time stand ready for combat. While we fought, we had to also work ceaselessly to increase our capabilities. The entire Party, the entire population showed great care and concern for the work of building up the army to provide sufficient strength to carry out our primary mission—fighting the aggressors and saving the nation. The entire armed forces made great efforts to be worthy of that care and concern and to successfully carry out every duty assigned to us.

With the lessons we had learned in building our army during the resistance war against the French, our Party *placed great emphasis on continuing to build the army politically*. Because we were fighting for a just cause, our army enjoyed absolute superiority over the enemy in political and spiritual matters. At the same time, our just cause alone would not provide the strength required for victory. The American imperialists tried to use their material advantages over us to steal from us our moral superiority. For this reason, building the army politically was a matter of extraordinary importance. It was the basic principle in building up our army and was a basic method for turning our moral strength into material strength and helped increase the combat power of the people's armed forces.

We began our resistance war against the Americans with the experience we had gained during the resistance war against the French. During the course of this new fight the work of building our army politically was carried out in a more orderly and systematic fashion. We taught our cadre and soldiers to clearly understand the situation and the revolutionary responsibilities of both the northern and southern halves of the nation; we taught them the combat goals of the army in the face of the aggressive schemes of the American imperialists and instructed them in the political duties of each individual. These actions built an important foundation, which enabled the entire armed forces to affirm their determination to resist and their resolve to defeat the American aggressors. Our soldiers studied to gain a firm understanding of the political and military policies of the Party regarding the resistance war against the Americans to save the nation and to eliminate incorrect ideas about the situation and inaccurate assessments of the enemy's and our own forces, and especially incorrect assessments of U.S. strengths. These were the most prominent, important themes in our effort to build the army politically. The army's strength was also built by the willingness of our cadre and soldiers to strive to hone their skills, by a spirit of solidarity and discipline, and by the close relationship between the army and the population. When building the army politically we did not underestimate the importance of nour-ishing these sources of strength. This was an outstanding achievement by our Party in our force building effort during the resistance war against the Americans and was the source of an extremely enthusiastic revolutionary movement throughout the armed forces and the entire population, which resolved to "cross the Annamite Mountains to save the nation," "aim directly at the enemy and fire," "cling to the Americans' belts so we can kill them," etc.

Our apparatus directly involved in building the army politically was constantly strengthened. This apparatus was the Party organization within the army, the sys-tem of political cadre and political staff agencies at all levels, all coordinating their activities under the leadership of the Central Military Party Committee and under the guidance of the General Political Department. If that apparatus had not existed the work of building the army politically would have encountered many difficul-ties and would not have yielded the desired results. This apparatus was responsible for providing effective guidance over the content and methods used in Party and political activities throughout the armed forces. This guidance was very important; it did not end simply with the dissemination of Party resolutions and it was not lim-ited to activities conducted during conferences and conventions. It demanded that we become deeply involved in providing guidance to cadre and soldiers in correct thinking and in taking vigorous action based on those correct thoughts, which meant correctly following the Party line and Party opinions, strategies, and tactics. To accomplish this mission, political cadre and staff organizations at all levels needed a deep understanding of their own individual duties. They had to correctly anticipate both positive and negative issues that might arise during the conduct of these duties in order to be proactive in setting forth positive, correct directions and operational methods for the soldiers. In practical terms, since they fought and trained with the unit, political cadre and agencies had more opportunities to improve their ability to perform their duties. They were able to avoid such short-comings as issuing general, meaningless appeals, making empty statements, or crudely interfering with the work of the other specialized branches. They were able instead to delve deeper into military affairs, including military science, the military arts, and modern military science and technology.

The work of building the army politically was carried out continuously and could not be neglected, no matter what the situation. When the Southern revolu-tion encountered difficulties and when it had great successes, when we were defeated and when we gained great victories, when the enemy carried out new schemes against us and when problems developed in the international situation, all these were times when we had to strengthen our Party and political activities in order to quickly agree on correct thoughts and opinions, determine precise operational directions, and fight on resolutely to secure new victories.

While emphasizing the work of building the army politically, our Party also devoted a great deal of attention to leading our armed forces in *developing and perfecting the military art of people's war* in a manner suited to the actual conditions of our country during the historic struggle between the Vietnamese nation and the American imperialists.

Teaching our cadre and soldiers to fully comprehend the revolutionary and military lines and policies of the Party during the resistance war against the Americans was an issue of decisive importance. Only if they were deeply steeped in the military line of the Party and were closely guided by our ideological line would our army have the proper direction and be able to correctly resolve the relationships between men and weapons; between fighting and force building; between strategy, campaign arts, and tactics; between forces, battle posture, and opportunity; between the great front lines and the great rear area; between national factors and epochal factors, etc., in order to create a combined strength able to bring the war to a victorious conclusion.

With a firm grasp of the military policies and thoughts of the Party, our armed forces patiently studied and honed their skills, learning to correctly evaluate both the enemy's and our own positions from the strategic, tactical, campaign, and individual battle standpoint and to draw correct conclusions from a comparison of the positions and strengths of the two sides. Then, through these evaluations, comparisons, and conclusions, they were able to find ways to resolve problems, expand on our strengths, exploit the enemy's weaknesses, and paralyze the enemy's strengths to defeat him. This was the goal of the work of studying the enemy. Constant education to strengthen our resolve to defeat the American aggressors was a very basic method used to raise the fighting spirit, the "determined to fight, determined to win" spirit of our army in the face of any difficulty, adversity, or challenge. This resolve was a powerful factor that motivated our troops to resolutely continue to fight and develop creative ways to defeat the enemy's new plots and schemes. For this reason our military art, above all else, used the spirit of patriotism, the love of socialism, and the resolve to fight and to win of our armed forces and our population to develop a "determined to win" strength that could defeat the modern army of the American imperialist aggressors.

A firm understanding of and a skillful use of the weapons and technical equipment we possessed and the exploitation of the power of these implements of war to the maximum extent possible were practical requirements that enabled us to fight effective battles and further enrich our military arts. The development of this power was very much dependent on the results of our military training and education, on the honing of our self-discipline, and on a spirit of solidarity and close cooperation between comrades in arms who shared a common ideal and a noble political objective: the liberation of South Vietnam, the defense of North Vietnam, and the unification of the Fatherland. Military training activities were usually tied in closely with Party and political activities in order to constantly increase our army's skills in the military arts. These arts closely combined human power with organizational power, the actions of commanders with the actions of staff, political, and rear services agencies, of cadre with soldiers, etc., working together to carry out their responsibilities in accordance with one unified plan aimed at skillfully developing the combined power of each individual person, of each unit, and of the entire armed forces. During the resistance war against the Americans to save the nation, each individual soldier, each individual unit, each individual specialty branch, each individual service branch, and the entire armed forces simultaneously carried out both combat operations and force building activities during combat in accordance with the military policies of the Party and the military art of people's warfare, constantly using whatever time was available to conduct military training. Command cadre and staff agencies at all levels, and especially at the strategic and campaign levels, worked to study and hone their skills, with special emphasis on reviewing and summarizing operations (including strategic, campaign, and individual battles), to constantly improve their abilities to make plans, devise tactics, organize the battlefield, create opportunities for exploitation, and direct our forces in order to use our offensive blows to force the enemy onto the defensive. In this way our military arts were able to skillfully and effectively resolve many complicated contradictions, such as using a small force to attack a large enemy force, using a little force to win a big victory, destroying the enemy while preserving our own forces, conducting combat and force building operations at the same time, growing stronger as we fought, winning more and more victories the more we fought, defeating the enemy on the front lines and at the same time building a strong rear base area, etc.

Our military arts, already steeped deeply in the masses as a result of our armed struggle during the revolution and during our nation's revolutionary war from the time of the August Revolution and the resistance war against the French, developed to a new, higher level during the resistance war against the Americans. Our people's war was fought not only by the army but also by guerrilla militia and self-defense forces; both the armed forces and our entire population fought this war. This war of necessity used guerrilla warfare methods, conventional warfare methods, and a close combination of both those methods. The war against the Americans in South Vietnam developed onto an even higher plane, as it was conducted both through military attacks and mass uprisings, using both armed forces and political forces, a three-pronged military, political, and troop proselytizing attack, mounted in three strategic areas: the mountain jungles, the rural lowlands, and the cities. We taught and trained our army to rely on the people, to have a firm grasp of the roles, responsibilities, and operational methods of the three types of troops and of the two types of forces. Knowing how to skillfully combine all the diverse, rich fighting methods of each individual force was a very important method that helped our army find and implement daring and effective fighting methods that contributed to the growth of the Vietnamese military arts.

After our victory in the resistance war against the French, building a regular, modern force was the correct direction for the development of our army. Our equipment was constantly upgraded, our forces constantly grew, and the scale of our combat operations constantly expanded, so the capabilities of our cadre and soldiers and of staff agencies and units in all facets of operations also had to be increased to enable us to defeat an enemy who possessed the largest, most modern army in the imperialist camp.

As soon as North Vietnam was liberated, Chairman Ho Chi Minh directed that "we must work to build our army into a powerful people's army, a revolutionary army progressing toward regularization and modernization so we can preserve the peace and defend the Fatherland." This was a new mission for our armed forces. Carrying out this mission was a protracted, difficult, and complex struggle from the standpoint of understanding and thought, organization and attitude, between the old and the new, between the positive and the negative.

This was an issue that closely and skillfully combined two factors, revolution and science, to provide high quality and concrete results in our work to increase the power of the army during this new revolutionary period and during combat against a new combat enemy. A correct understanding of the tremendous significance and effect of the implementation of measures to regularize and modernize the army was our first requirement. During the August Revolution and the resistance war against the French our army had matured, growing from a small force to a large one, progressing from a few scattered guerrilla teams. Although the war against the French involved both guerrilla war and conventional war methods, in fact conventional warfare only developed during the final years of the conflict, and then essentially only on the primary battlefield. When our soldiers began force building activities to become a regular, modern force, the habits of dispersion and of acting as one saw fit and a hesitant attitude toward conducting training according to regulations and to a uniform system became major obstacles, slowing and limiting our ability to successfully complete our force building program. To many people at that time, difficulties encountered in educational and technical studies were harder to overcome than the problems they had previously encountered in combat. With patience we gradually overcame these obstacles during our peacetime force building and training and continued to overcome them during our new combat struggle. Only through these efforts was the level of combat skills of our army able to keep pace with the requirements of our duties during the resistance war against the Americans to save the nation.

The regularization and the modernization of the army were aimed at ensuring that our army would always be combat-ready, at concentrating our political, spiritual, material, and technical power, and at making maximum use of our power (the power of our personnel and of our weapons and equipment) in order to properly carry out our duties. The equipment of the armed forces was systematically upgraded based on our own production capabilities and on the assistance provided by fraternal nations. When the war started we were also able to rely on captured enemy equipment. The upgrading of our equipment raised issues of properly organizing our forces, of providing appropriate training to develop a corps of cadre and technical personnel, of building warehouses and roads, and of training soldiers in the maintenance and use of the new weapons and equipment. All types of problems involving technical matters, tactics, and campaign arts, involving coordination arrangements, involving unity and discipline, and involving training, especially training of command and staff cadre, surfaced and had to be resolved. The activities of those branches involved in Party and political activities and in providing rear services and technical support were organized and carried out in ways suited to the changes in the organization of the armed forces.

In view of the great expansion of our forces during the course of the resistance war against the Americans, from 170,000 up to more than one million, it was necessary for the quality of these troops to keep pace with the expansion in numbers and with the growth of the newly established specialty branches and service branches. Training was carried out in a uniform fashion and was aimed at a number of uniform goals during each phase. During the first phase, when the war had not yet widened and North Vietnam was still at peace, we carried out regular training in all areas: military, political, cultural, and physical fitness. We promulgated military regulations, guard regulations, internal regulations, combat discipline regulations, etc., and instituted standard operating procedures for each individual area (staff, political affairs, rear services) and for each individual specialty branch and service branch.

During regular peacetime training we devoted special attention to cadre training, including training of command cadre, leadership cadre, staff cadre, and technical cadre. When the entire nation entered the fight against the Americans, regular training continued, but it shifted immediately to issues and methods suited to wartime operations. During regular training, in addition to technical and tactical matters military training was absolutely essential and was of immense importance to the work of regularizing and modernizing our forces. These were not just formalities; they provided practical content and methods to hone understanding and actions in accordance with uniform standards and developed the habits of living in an organized and disciplined manner and of maintaining a sense of urgency in carrying out orders.

The regularization and modernization of the army demanded that we strengthen our scientific studies. We could not hope to build a high-quality army and yet remain indifferent toward scientific activities. We had to establish an apparatus that met the requirements of modern warfare. We had to develop cadre to perform scientific tasks suited to our requirements and situation. We needed to focus on military science, military technological science, and pure science.

The role of cadre and agencies at all levels as examples in the building of a regular force was of great significance. As Chairman Ho Chi Minh taught us: "Cadre, from command level down, must make greater efforts in their activities, in training, in the way they walk, in their manner of greeting others. In all these things they must be regulars. Cadre must lead the way and serve as examples for their soldiers."[2]

In order to achieve solid results in building a regular, modern army, the most important requirement was close and constant leadership by Party committees at all levels. Because this was a new subject for an army that had developed out of guerrilla teams, correct understanding and tenacious revolutionary energy were needed. We had to create a high level of uniformity in both thought and action throughout the entire army.

A solid rear area was a factor of decisive strategic importance to the victory of the resistance and was of decisive importance for our army to mature and win victory. Close relationships between the rear area and the front lines, between the rear area and the army, were also relationships between political and economic affairs and military affairs, between the people and the army. The strength of the rear area is created by political, economic, and military factors. All these factors are important, but the most important is the political factor, the sympathy of the people. It is the unanimity of the entire population in political and spiritual matters, united under the leadership of the Party. When the people do not have a profound awareness of the struggle for national independence and socialism and do not have a complete determination to fight and to win against a more numerous and powerful enemy, then it is not possible to launch an all-out resistance war involving the entire population. In that case the work of building a people's army will encounter endless difficulties, the combat operations of the army will lack a source of support, and it will be difficult to defeat an opponent who has more troops and more modern equipment than we do.

During the resistance war against the French, the rear area of the people's war, which was established, organized, and led by our Party, consisted of large liberated areas, guerrilla regions, and guerrilla bases behind enemy lines. By the time of the resistance war against the Americans to save the nation, the rear area of the war, the rear area of our army, was totally different and was much more developed. A liberated North Vietnam that was advancing toward socialism became the great rear area of the entire nation in the effort to defeat the American aggressors. Thanks to this tremendously important revolutionary achievement, even though our economic and technological status was still low, the minds of our cadre and soldiers were at ease as they marched off to battle on the front lines. They knew "we will not lack one ounce of rice and our army will not lack one soldier." The great front lines were supported both materially and spiritually by the great rear area, enabling us to overcome difficulties and to gradually secure victory in South Vietnam and at the same time defend the North.

The role of local rear base areas in South Vietnam was extremely important for the force building and combat operations of our army. The intermingling of our areas within enemy-controlled areas throughout South Vietnam gave our troops solid footholds for their operations. Without operations conducted by local armed forces, without civilians supporting our forces and fighting beside them, there would have been no rear base areas, and without those bases our military units would not have been able to maintain firm footholds, conduct protracted operations, and continually grow in strength. Thanks to those local bases, the vast liberated zones in South Vietnam, and the immediate rear area, our army was able to build and consolidate itself after every battle, after every campaign, and was able to continuously prepare for new battles and new campaigns.

Solidarity between the soldiers and the people was constantly maintained and contributed enormously to mobilization, education, and to combat coordination and mutual assistance between the army and the people. Through our victories the liberated zones and local base areas were expanded and linked together in South Vietnam, and, along with the Annamite Mountain transportation corridor, provided a contiguous position linking North and South and gave our forces an important strategic posture.

The requirements for victory and the practical experiences of combat and of our campaigns (especially the strategic offensives) provided a clearer light that gave us a more correct and profound understanding of the role of the rear area. The struggle to build and protect the rear area was just as intense and ferocious as the fight to destroy the enemy on the front lines. First of all the American imperialists attached a great deal of importance to the destruction of our rear areas, including North Vietnam and the liberated zones and base areas in South Vietnam and the transportation routes from the great rear area to the great front lines. Second, within our Party, governmental organizations, and armed forces there were also some opinions that were not entirely correct on this subject. Third, the development of the rear area demanded the uniform employment of ideological and organizational activities, military and economic activities, and the proper resolution of contradictions between the demands of the front lines and the capabilities of the rear area, between immediate tasks and long-term tasks.

The rear area of the people's war and of the army lay primarily in the hearts of the people. That fact expresses the first requirement for the development and consolidation of a rear area: to make the people realize that our regime is a good regime, that our State government belongs to the people, and that our army fights for the people. The more clearly our cadre, Party members, government, and army demonstrate a spirit of service to the people, the more they carry out the teachings of Uncle Ho: "necessity, frugality, integrity, justice," the closer the people will ally themselves with the regime and the more the people will do everything possible to defend the government, support the army, and be ready to sacrifice for the sake of the victory of our resistance war. During the resistance war against the Americans the soldiers and civilians in North Vietnam vigorously responded to the appeals of the Party and of Chairman Ho Chi Minh with countless sincere, noble acts, such as participating in building Party chapters, governmental agencies, and mass organizations; restoring and developing our economy and culture; strengthening national defense and security; supporting the flow of supplies; and combating the war of destruction waged by the air and naval forces of the American imperialists. Massive numbers of people from all social classes participated in campaigns launched by the Party Central Committee and the Government. These campaigns had a great impact on the consolidation of the great rear area in support of the great front lines and on the difficult, savage battles waged by our army throughout the Indochinese Peninsula. Law and order were constantly maintained, our determined-to-fight, determined-to-win spirit stayed at a high level, and the rear area emulated the front lines, everyone contributing to advancing the struggle for independence and national unification toward total victory.

On the South Vietnamese battlefield the consolidation and strengthening of the liberated zones and the revolution's local bases were also constant tasks that we carried out to enable the resistance to conduct a protracted struggle, gaining in strength as we fought and constantly increasing our support to the armed forces fighting on the battlefield. The development and consolidation of Party organizations (Party committees, Party chapters, Party membership), mass organizations (youth, women, farmers associations), etc., were the foundations for building the rear area as well as for the development of the struggle against the enemy and the expansion of guerrilla warfare.

The work of building rear areas and base areas during the resistance war was the duty of the entire Party, the entire population, and the entire armed forces. Wherever the army was stationed or was fighting, in the North and in the South, it always stressed its duty to help carry out this task. This was a question that involved our concept of people's war, people's armed forces, and a national defense involving the total population. The rear area devoted its efforts to enabling the front lines to be victorious in battle and at the same time constantly produced new strength. Only by doing this could the rear area completely fulfill its role with respect to the front lines. When the army fighting on the battlefields economized on its expenditure of ammunition, on its consumption of food, medicine, and petroleum products, when it attacked the enemy with the highest possible effectiveness and limited its losses in personnel, material, and technical resources to the maximum extent possible, this too was a practical way of contributing to the building and development of the rear area. While conducting training and force building operations in the great rear area, in the liberated zones, or in local bases, all our troop units helped build the rear areas in many ways, such as building up organizations, training guerrilla militia, maintaining law and order, combating spies, helping the people to protect against natural disasters, participating in production, respecting the law, maintaining mass discipline, maintaining solidarity with the agencies of government and with people's organizations, etc. In this way they effectively contributed to the building of the great rear area and local rear areas and helped build this matchless source of strength for the people's army.

During the resistance war against the Americans, which entailed unprecedented difficulties, adversities, hardship, and sacrifice for our army, the issue of whether or not our army's force building and combat actions were correctly carried out, whether or not the strength of the army was solid, whether or not the army maintained its revolutionary character and completed each of its assigned duties, *all these things, from the first to the last, depended primarily on the leadership of the Party.* The role and the duties of the army constantly grew, especially in time of war. The enemy, the leader of the imperialist camp, constantly sought every possible method and tested many poisonous schemes in his effort to gain victory. The difficulties and obstacles confronting us grew day by day because the more the enemy suffered defeat, the more he insanely strove to destroy the revolution. However, the capabilities of our cadre and soldiers had also been raised to a high level by their years of trial and challenges in this resistance war. The organization and equipment of the army became ever more powerful. Because of this, leadership and command also grew and became more complex. All these problems were systematically resolved under the leadership of the Central Committee of the Party. These problems also demanded that the Party organizations within the army constantly increase their own leadership qualities. The capabilities of the army's Party committees at all levels always had to be sufficient to respond to the requirements of providing leadership and guidance during a fierce test of wills, a fierce test of strength against an enemy who was equipped with modern weapons and was stubborn and crafty. During the war's turning points, and especially as the end of the war neared, the struggle became ever more vicious. This was not the only problem, however. The struggle within our own ranks, against mistaken opinions, negative thinking, actions that violated the traditions of the revolutionary army, also demanded that the Party's leadership within the army be both firm and sensitive. The Party had to provide the army with precise methods to overcome problems and raise the quality of the armed forces in order to successfully carry out the Party policy of fighting a resistance war against the Americans to save the nation.

To strengthen the Party's leadership role within the army, both our experience in the two recent resistance wars (especially the resistance war against the Americans) and our ideological theories regarding the creation of a new type of Party that belongs to the working classes demand that we must constantly and correctly carry out the work of building strong, honest Party chapters, and that building Party chapters that function politically, ideologically, and organizationally in accordance with the Party's regulations, resolutions, and directions is the way we will increase the leadership capabilities of the different levels of Party committees within the armed forces.

Strong, effective leadership is the art of combining the firm maintenance of principles and applying them flexibly, combining ideological activities with organizational and policy activities, developing both spiritual strength and material strength, and combining revolutionary factors with scientific factors. It is also the art of developing the role of collective leadership and individual responsibility apportioned to each person according to his own role and function. The leadership skill of the Party committee is also demonstrated in its ability to unite Party members and the masses, cadre, and soldiers, in carrying out the Party line of resistance war to save the nation and to complete every duty assigned to the army and to each unit. Solidarity within each Party committee and among command cadre at every level is of decisive importance in achieving the solidarity of the entire Party chapter and the entire unit. To achieve this requirement, which should be considered a matter of principle, it is necessary to properly organize high-quality leadership activities on the part of the Party committee. A basic measure to achieve this level of quality is to properly conduct criticism and self-criticism in a spirit of comradeship in accordance with the teachings of Uncle Ho Chi Minh and with the pure objective of helping each other progress and of completely fulfilling our responsibilities as Party members and as members of the Party committee.

Solidarity within the Party chapter provides the impetus for strengthening wide-ranging solidarity within the unit and for cementing the relationship between the Party and the masses, developing democracy, and honing self-discipline. The Party committee must concentrate its leadership and mobilize the masses to unite around the Party chapter in order to fight, train, work, and correctly organize their lives in strict accordance with the policies and desires of the Party and the laws of the State. The Party committee must focus on building mass organizations within the armed forces, establishing an intimate relationship with local Party organizations, governmental agencies, and the local population, and strengthening the relationship between the soldiers and the people so that they support each other in building up the local area and building up the military unit.

Every Party committee is responsible for developing and nourishing the cadre within the unit for which it is responsible. This task demands an overall leadership capability: understanding people, correctly assessing and utilizing them, and developing the strengths and overcoming the weaknesses of each cadre. All of these tasks demand that the Party committee must discuss and resolve issues according to the principle of collective democracy. During the 21 years of the resistance war against the Americans to save the nation, the Party guided and successfully developed the Party's military cadre ranks; the number of combined-arms branch cadre increased by 500 percent and service branch and technical specialty branch cadre increased by 1000 percent. These cadre became the framework upon which we built a powerful revolutionary army of more than one million soldiers.

The Party's leadership was the decisive factor in every one of the army's victories. Increasing the quality of leadership provided by the Party committees at all levels was a constant requirement for our Party chapters within the armed forces. Members of the Party committees constantly had to hone their skills, increase their own military and political capacities and capabilities, and strictly follow Party principles regarding leadership and action. Solidarity, self-criticism, and criticism to help one another advance were the first responsibilities of every Party committee member. Studying to increase one's capabilities and keep up with the demands of the resistance war against the Americans was a very practical measure that also demonstrated a spirit of responsibility toward the Party and the people in the fight to liberate South Vietnam, defend North Vietnam, and unify the Fatherland.

Looking back over its historic journey from the date of its formation (December 1944) until it brought a victorious end to the resistance war against the Americans to save the nation (April 1975), from the battles of Phai Khat and Na Ngan to the historic Ho Chi Minh Campaign, our army, under the leadership of the Party, fulfilled every one of its duties toward the nation and fully carried out its international duties toward our friends and neighbors. Our cadre and soldiers are profoundly grateful for the leadership of the Party, the work and the teachings of Uncle Ho, the support of our compatriots throughout the nation, and for the assistance of our international brothers and friends.

The revolutionary character and the noble traditions of our army are the result of constant, persistent efforts and training under the Party's guidance and were achieved through the blood, sweat, and tears of many generations of cadre and soldiers. The constant stability and ever-increasing perfection of the leadership and command organization of the army were decisive factors that constantly strengthened the revolutionary character, the noble traditions, and the combat power of our army. Our army was always under the direct, all-encompassing leadership of the Party Central Committee, the Politburo, and the Central Military Party Committee, and was also led by strategic agencies with a wealth of experience, such as the General Staff, the General Political Department, the General Rear Services Department, and the General Technical Department. During the resistance war against the Americans in South Vietnam, the Party committees of the different battlefields (COSVN, the COSVN Military Party Committee, the Regional Party Committees of Regions 5, 6, 7, 8, 9, Saigon, and Tri-Thien, and the provincial Party Committees) all played a major role in leading and guiding the combat and force building operations of our soldiers. The work of building up our army was carried out continuously, each generation continuing the work of its predecessors, from the August Revolution through the resistance war against the French down to the resistance war against the Americans, each further developing the quality and the traditions of the army. The lessons our Party has learned in building a revolutionary army over the past decades are still of enormous practical value. For this reason, no matter where, no matter when, the basic principles for building an army, the requirements for firmly maintaining and developing the revolutionary character and noble traditions of the army, will always be strictly followed and implemented.

Ever since the day our nation was liberated the Fatherland has been united. The entire army, alongside the entire population, has continued down new roads, inscribing new feats of arms into the glorious pages of its history, defeating a war of aggression along the southwestern frontier and the northern border, and once again fulfilling its international duty on the soil of our Cambodian brothers. Many new issues have confronted and continue to confront our entire army, requiring proper study and resolution by Party committees at all levels and by cadre and soldiers in all areas of operation. The situation develops endlessly, the responsibilities of the army are always heavy, and the enemy is always crafty, seeking ways to sabotage the revolutionary cause of our people. All Party chapters within the armed forces and all the cadre and soldiers of the entire armed forces are united with the entire population in implementing the resolutions of the 6th and 7th National Party Congresses and the resolutions of the Party Central Committee. This is the fundamental requirement needed to overcome every obstacle and challenge in every new situation in order to completely fulfill all our duties in the cause of building and defending our socialist Fatherland of Vietnam.

Notes

CHAPTER 1

1. Quotation from the Pentagon Papers on the Vietnam War. From the files of the Military History Institute of Vietnam.
2. Statement by U.S. Secretary of State Dulles. Citation from the Pentagon Papers. Ibid.
3. Ibid.
4. Ho Chi Minh, closing speech, 6th Plenum of the Party Central Committee (15 July 1954).
5. Ibid.
6. Resolution, 7th Plenum of the Party Central Committee, 2nd Party Congress (March 1955).
7. Figures cover the period from mid-1954 until August 1959.
8. A project providing irrigation water to the provinces of Bac Ninh, Hung Yen, and Hai Duong.
9. According to the figures for 1959 of the Central Department of Statistics, total production of paddy in 1939 was 2,407,000 tons; in 1957 it was 3,947,000 tons. The quantity of electricity produced in 1939 was 122,580,000 kilowatt hours; in 1957 it was 121,230,000 kilowatt hours.
10. "On Armed Struggle and the People's Armed Forces," Ho Chi Minh, People's Army Publishing House, Hanoi, 1970, p. 321.
11. Ibid.
12. Division-sized Units 308, 312, 304, 316, 320, and 325. Regiments 148 (Northwest Zone), 238 and 246 (Viet Bac), 46 and 42 (Interzone 3), and 108, 96, and 803 (Interzone 5).
13. The 351st Engineer-Artillery Division-sized Unit, consisting of two artillery regiments and one engineer regiment. Other specialty branch units included six battalions of 37mm anti-aircraft guns, one rocket battalion, a number of 12.7mm anti-aircraft machine-gun units, three signal battalions, one reconnaissance battalion, and 11 truck transportation companies.

14. Equipped with 105mm howitzers, 120mm mortars, and anti-aircraft artillery.
15. Totaling ten battalions, seven companies, and 15 platoons.
16. Resolution of the 7th Plenum of the Party Central Committee, March 1955.
17. Resolution of the 8th Plenum of the Party Central Committee, August 1955.
18. Ibid.
19. Ho Chi Minh, *Collected Works,* part 7, Su That [Truth] Publishing House, Hanoi, 1987, p. 247.
20. Ho Chi Minh, from a letter sent to Southern regroupees in the North dated 19 June 1956.
21. Resolution of the 12th Plenum of the Party Central Committee, March 1957.

CHAPTER 2

1. Resolution of the 12th Plenum (expanded) of the Party Central Committee, March 1957.
2. Ibid.
3. Ibid.
4. Ibid.
5. Ibid.
6. Ho Chi Minh, instructions to the Mid-Senior Level Cadre Reeducation Class of the Ministry of Defense, May 1957.
7. Ibid.
8. General Political Department, Report to the Conference (expanded) of the General Military Party Committee of March 1959. From the files of the Ministry of Defense, file no. 235/QUTU (File 235/Central Military Party Committee).
9. Ho Chi Minh, Report to the 13th Plenum of the Party Central Committee, December 1957.
10. "The Armed Struggle and the People's Armed Forces," Ho Chi Minh, People's Army Publishing House, Hanoi, 1970, p. 336.
11. The seven divisions were the 308th, 312th, 320th, 304th, 325th, 324th, and 330th. The six brigades were the 316th, 350th, 305th, 338th, 335th, and 341st. The 12 independent regiments were the 19th, 42nd, 46th, 50th, 53rd, 120th, 148th, 238th, 244th, 246th, 248th, and 271st.
12. An infantry division was to be equipped with 6,645 infantry weapons of all types, 200 pieces of field artillery and mortars, 42 anti-aircraft cannon and anti-aircraft machine guns, 281 transport vehicles and artillery prime movers, 37 radios, and many other types of equipment.
13. In 1960 our army had a total of 3,000 mortars and field artillery pieces. The total number of vehicles serving as artillery prime movers was 2,000 vehicles.
14. Later redesignated the 205th Regiment.
15. The Northeast Military Region was given the 248th Regiment; the Northwest Military Region had the 335th Brigade and the 148th Regiment; the Viet Bac Military Region had the 246th Regiment; the Left Bank Military Region had the 320th Division and the 19th and 53rd Regiments; Military Region 4 had the 324th and 325th Divisions and the 271st Regiment; and the Vinh Linh Special Region had the 341st Brigade.

16. From 1956 to 1960, the Party transferred 11,705 military cadres to economic, social, etc. . . . tasks. Included in this figure were 67 high-level cadre, 1,484 medium-level cadre, and 10,154 low-level cadre.

17. The 316th, 350th, 335th, 305th, and 338th Divisions, after they had been downgraded to brigades, and the 269th, 713th, and 242nd Coastal Defense Regiments.

18. Reviewing and summarizing the following areas: political education and ideological guidance activities, Party-building activities, cadre activities, protective [security] activities, civilian proselytizing activities, enemy proselytizing activities, and campaign-level and combat political activities.

19. General Political Department, "Review of the Party and Political Activities of the People's Army of Vietnam," document published in 1960, p. 273.

20. Resolution of the 12th Plenum of the Party Central Committee, March 1957.

21. In early 1955, when our army had finished regrouping to North Vietnam, we had a total of 43,653 cadre from platoon level up, of whom 63.3 percent were under 30 years of age, 87 percent were Party members, and 77.8 percent had direct combat experience. However, 90 percent of our cadre were infantry, 76.9 percent had only a level 1 (third grade) education, and only 10 percent had attended a military school.

22. Directive dated 17 May 1955.

23. Established 12 February 1957, in October 1958 the school name was changed to the Rear Services Officers School.

24. From 1955 through 1960, the Mid- and High-level Military Supplementary Training School held three short-term classes and one long-term class (18 months). A total of 2,786 cadre attended this school during this period.

25. The first rank assignment program (in 1958) included 22 cadre granted ranks from Major General up to Senior General, 37 Senior Colonels, and 75 Colonels.

26. These consisted of determining internal deployments and internal affairs at troop bases; internal matters in areas where mechanized vehicles were parked; internal rules; problems related to administering personnel, equipment, property, and finances; problems relating to internal duty personnel, alerts and alarms, fire prevention, floods, accidents, unexpected problems; and the protection of the health of military personnel.

27. From *The Vanguard Division,* vol. 3, People's Army Publishing House, Hanoi, 1979, p. 19.

28. "Review of 4 Years of Training," files of the Ministry of Defense, file no. 404.

29. "Fully qualified artillerymen" meant that every member of a gun crew was able to replace any other member and perform that person's job.

30. General Political Department, Report of the Conference of Political Commissars and Political Directors of the Entire Armed Forces, November 1958.

31. Resolution No. 64-N of the Politburo of the Party Central Committee, dated 19 June 1956. File no. 7,928.

32. Ibid.

33. Ibid.

34. Document No. 76-N, on file at the Committee to Summarize the War in B-2, file no. 12, p. 123.

35. Resolution of the Cochin China [Nam Bo] Party Committee Conference, December 1956. Files of the Military History Institute of Vietnam.

36. In 1954, the Cochin China Party organization had a total of 60,000 members;

after implementing the categorization of Party members and the policy of "reassignment" and "dieing away," the total number of Party members in 1959 was 5,000.

37. Le Duan, "We are certain to win, and the enemy is certain to lose," Su That [Truth] Publishing House, Hanoi, 1965, p. 7.

38. Types of plants that were abundant in the Plain of Reeds. Our soldiers cut them and sold them to the local population, which used them to make mats and rugs.

39. Resolution of Interzone 5 Party Conference, summer of 1958.

40. Ibid.

CHAPTER 3

1. Le Duan, "We are certain to win, and the enemy is certain to lose," Su That [Truth] Publishing House, Hanoi, 1965, p. 7.

2. Ho Chi Minh, speech to the 15th Plenary Session of the Party Central Committee, January 1959. From the files of the Military History Institute of Vietnam.

3. Resolution of the 15th Plenary Session of the Party Central Committee, January 1959. From the files of the Military History Institute of Vietnam.

4. Ibid.

5. Ibid.

6. Ibid.

7. Ho Chi Minh, speech to the 15th Plenum of the Party Central Committee. From the files of the Military History Institute of Vietnam.

8. Le Duan, speech to the conference of the General Military Party Committee, February 1959. From the files of the Ministry of Defense, file no. 243.

9. Ibid.

10. In addition, 1,174 infantry weapons of all types, along with ammunition, were carried south by units being sent to the Southern battlefield.

11. The 89th Platoon.

12. The 229th Platoon, formed on 2 September 1959.

13. Resolution of the 4th Conference of the Cochin China Party Committee, November 1959.

14. For the puppet 3rd Regiment of the 21st Division.

15. Xuyen had been Chief of Staff of eastern Cochin China during the resistance war against the French and had been assigned by the Party to remain in the South instead of regrouping to the North.

16. Resolution of the conference of the Region 8 Party Committee, December 1959.

17. In 1960, enemy forces in Ben Tre province included 850 Regional Force troops organized into seven companies located in the districts and two companies protecting the province capital; 1,670 militia troops, organized into 24 general groups; 115 militia outposts in 115 villages; 210 Coastal Security troops; and 180 policemen. In the entire province the enemy had 300 outposts and police stations.

18. The unit that won the victories at Giong Thi Dam and Go Quan Cung.

19. "MAT" and "Mi-Tuyn" rifles.

20. The "Pegasus" gun: The barrel of the gun was a long iron pipe and the gun was supported by a bipod. The bullets were pieces of broken glass and scrap iron soaked in

poison. They were fired from the barrel by an explosive. With a range up to 20 meters, individuals struck by these projectiles could die of poison.

21. The Tay Ninh province 14th Battalion and the province's 315A and 315B Engineer-Sapper Companies; 40th Company of Chau Thanh district, Company 31C of Duong Minh Chau district, Company 33A belonging to Go Dau and Trang Bang districts, and 61st Company of Ben Cau district; and the armed propaganda companies of the provincial capital and the Cao Dai Holy See area.

22. Resolution of the 5th Conference of the Cochin China Party Committee, July 1960.

23. Comprising 17 provincial companies and 70 district platoons.

24. The armed forces of western Cochin China had a total of 2,644 guns; those of central Cochin China had 2,338 guns. Ben Tre province alone had a total of 326 guns.

25. Central Military Party Commitee, directions for the establishment of the People's Liberation Army of South Vietnam (January 1961). From the files of the Military History Institute of Vietnam.

CHAPTER 4

1. Political report to the 3rd National Party Congress, September 1960.

2. Resolution of the Politburo of the Party Central Committee, 25 February 1961.

3. Ibid.

4. Central Military Party Committee. Major operational policies for the second five-year military plan (1961–1965). From the files of the Ministry of Defense, file no. 264/QUTU.

5. Following the Politburo session of 25 February 1961, the General Military Party Committee was renamed the Central Military Party Committee.

6. Between 1954 and 1960 the agency that directed the revolution in South Vietnam was the Central Unification Committee.

7. Speech by Chairman Ho Chi Minh at the Politburo session of 25 February 1961.

8. Resolution of the Central Military Party Committee, March 1961.

9. The masses had seized control in 1,100 out of a total of 1,296 villages in Cochin China, and in 4,683 out of 5,721 hamlets in the mountains of Region 5 and the Central Highlands.

10. That is, by the end of 1962.

11. Helicopter Companies 8 and 57.

12. In 1960, the puppet regular army consisted of 150,000 men organized into seven infantry divisions, four Marine battalions, and a number of military specialty units. The Regional Forces had 65,000 soldiers and the Popular Forces 45,000 soldiers.

13. A total of six divisions (about 200,000 men).

14. Rubber-band guns, "Pegasus" guns, acetylene [sic], grenades, mines, punji sticks, etc.

15. When first established the regiment was given the code designation of C-56, and it was also called the Q-761 Regiment.

16. In 1961, on the battlefields of South Vietnam we had formed
  • two rear services bases belonging to the COSVN Military Affairs Section. Base A

(also called U-50) was in War Zone D, and Base B (also called U-60) was in the Duong Minh Chau War Zone.

- two rear services bases belonging to Military Region 7 in the area north and south of the Dong Nai River and in War Zone D.
- five rear services bases (also called "pillars" — "tru") belonging to Military Region 8: the Plain of Reeds, Area 4 of Kien Tuong, north and south of Route 4 in My Tho province (the 20 July Area), the Long An area, and Cho Gao.
- three rear services bases belonging to Military Region 9: Base A in Lower U Minh, Base B in Dam Doi–Nam Can, Base C in Upper U Minh.
- two rear services bases belonging to the Saigon–Gia Dinh Military Region, in An Nhon and Ho Bo.
- Military Region 5 established rear services warehouses at A Sau, A Tuc, built Route 343 to porter supplies through Gio Linh and Cam Lo on the eastern side of the Annamite Mountains, and received supplies brought in from North Vietnam.

17. In the battlefields of Cochin China and extreme southern Central Vietnam, between 1961 and 1964 the quantity of supplies provided by the local population and collected and purchased by rear services agencies (not including those supplies provided by people housing troops and wounded soldiers in their own homes) totaled 22,180 tons, equal to 72.4 percent of the total amount of supplies provided to all the armed forces under COSVN.

18. According to a report of the Central Military Party Committee dated 15 January 1962 and titled "A Number of General Aspects of the Situation of the Revolutionary Movement of South Vietnam during 1961," file no. 294/QUTU: In 1960 our armed forces in South Vietnam fought 1,700 battles, killing 5,430 enemy, wounding 1,800, capturing 5,500 prisoners, and confiscating 5,600 weapons; in 1961 we fought 4,400 battles, killing 11,600 enemy, wounding 5,900 enemy, capturing 2,000 prisoners, and confiscating 3,800 weapons.

19. Sam Nua and Phongsaly provinces.

20. In August 1960, the 2nd Airborne Battalion commanded by Kong Le staged a coup to overthrow the reactionary Xom-xa-nit [sic] government. The Central Committee of the Lao Party viewed this as a spontaneous military coup carried out under the command of a number of patriotic officers of the Royal Lao Army, and believed that in reality it was a patriotic movement. The policy of our Lao friends' Party was to cooperate with the forces that conducted the coup, expand the united front against the United States and its lackies, and create conditions favorable to the growth of revolutionary forces.

21. A total of 12,000 Vietnamese volunteer troops carried out their international duty on the battlefields of Laos during this campaign.

22. The connecting road was called Route 129.

23. French General Navarre built this road during the 1953–1954 dry season, and it was commonly called the Navarre Road.

24. Among these supplies was equipment for our Liberation Radio radio station.

25. Xuan Mai was the location where Group 338 was stationed.

26. In 1961, aside from 91 tons of rice used for its own consumption, Group 559 transported to South Vietnam 317 tons of supplies, consisting primarily of weapons and ammunition. It also supported the safe transit of 7,664 cadre and soldiers to the South. When compared with the plan assigned to the Group by higher authority, the number of

personnel sent south exceeded the plan by 28 percent, and the quantity of supplies transported exceeded the plan by 50 percent. The quantity of goods and number of personnel sent south along the Trail in 1961 were four times higher than the figures for 1960.

CHAPTER 5

1. In 1963 State rice reserves totaled 238,000 tons.

2. The road network (including rural roads) in North Vietnam by the end of 1964 totaled 10,495 kilometers (in 1960 it was only 4,365 kilometers). The Hanoi-Vinh rail line was completed, increasing our total railroad network length to 927 kilometers.

3. The 170,000 soldiers of the standing army represented 1 percent of the total population of North Vietnam, 6 percent of all males between the ages of 18 and 45, and 2 percent of the total number of workers in the economic and cultural fields.

4. In 1963, North Vietnam had 3 million males between the ages of 18 and 45, of whom 1 million were youths between the ages of 18 and 25.

5. Aside from troops in the standing army, there were also 16,000 national defense civilian workers, and People's Armed Public Security forces totaled 21,000 personnel.

6. The six divisions were the 308th, 304th, 312th, 320th, 325th, and 341st. The six brigades were the 316th, 305th, 330th, 324th, 350th, and 335th. The three independent regiments were the 50th, 246th, and 148th.

7. SKS rifles, AK submachine guns, and RPD machine guns.

8. 105mm howitzers, 75mm mountain guns, 75mm anti-tank guns, and 120mm mortars.

9. The four artillery brigades were the 364th, 368th, 374th, and 378th.

10. The signal centers of the military regions and service branches were equipped with 50-watt radios. The radio transmission and reception center of the High Command had radios of between 400- and 1,000-watt output and were equipped with remote control systems and antennae that were up to technical standards. A number of VHF radios had also been put into service.

11. The 30th Battalion of Military Region 4 and the 11th and 12th Battalions of Group 338.

12. Designation: Regiment 228-B3.

13. Group designation D-140, equipped with 12 torpedo boats.

14. Designated Company 200, equipped with four sub chasers.

15. In 1954, our armed forces had a total of 177 doctors, pharmacists, and medical students who had almost finished their university training. We had only five university-trained technical cadre.

16. The "Four Goods" Party chapter building campaign included good leadership in operations, good study, good internal solidarity, and good Party development [recruitment].

17. The Mid- and High-Level Military Study Institute and the Mid- and High-Level Political Study Institute.

18. The Army Officers School, the Artillery Officers School, the Air Force Officers School, the Navy Officers School, the Engineer Officers School, the Rear Services Officers School, the Military Medical Officers School, and the Technical Officers School.

19. The education level of the cadre corps of the armed forces was as follows:

	1954	1964
Level 1 [grades 1–3]	76.9 %	1.8 %
Level 2 [grades 4–7]	20.9 %	58.9 %
Level 3 [grades 8–10] [high school]	2.1 %	34.4 %
University	0.2 %	4.6 %

20. Out of the total number of cadre in the armed forces, artillery cadre represented 13.5 percent, anti-aircraft artillery 8.2 percent, signal 8 percent, engineers 6.8 percent, air force 1.9 percent, armor 0.7 percent, plus navy, chemical, medical, rear services, technical, and financial cadre categories.

21. In 1964, we had 22 general officers in our armed forces; of these, three were in training. That same year, we had 1,065 field-grade officers, 255 of whom were attending schools, and 34,361 company-grade officers, 3,802 of whom were attending schools. Of the total number of cadre who had graduated from training schools, 1,558 cadre, primarily company-grade officers, were in reserve working in governmental agencies and had not yet received an operational assignment.

22. The eight tactical concepts were: 1) exploit our political and spiritual advantage, making maximum use of every type of equipment to be victorious in combat; 2) aggressively annihilate the enemy; 3) fight when you are certain of victory; 4) concentrate a superior force to totally annihilate every enemy element; 5) be resolute when on the attack, active and stubborn when on defense; 6) maintain unity and coordination, reinforce on your own initiative, and emphasize independence during battle; 7) aggression, initiative, mobility, cleverness, flexibility; 8) fight continuously, develop the capacity for close combat and night fighting.

23. Central Military Party Committee, resolution on the situation and the military duties of the Party (November 1964). On file at the Ministry of Defense, file no. 368/QUTU.

24. We now call this the complete preparation method.

25. Firing mortars without base-plates or sights, firing mortars from sampans, etc. These procedures were directly related to the terrain conditions, the many rivers and canals, on the battlefields of South Vietnam.

26. We killed 137 enemy soldiers, and 1,427 prisoners were taken. We captured 400 weapons, 96 tons of ammunition, and 1,500 barrels of gasoline.

27. Le Duan, speech to the conference of the Central Military Party Committee in June 1963. On file at the Ministry of Defense, file no. 349/QUTU.

28. In 1961, U.S. aid to the Saigon puppet regime totaled $311 million. In 1962 this increased to $600 million, including $450 million worth of consumer goods provided to supplement the defense budget and $150 million in weapons.

29. In 1962 U.S. military forces in South Vietnam totaled 10,000 officers and men, 264 aircraft flown by U.S. pilots, and many other implements of war.

30. A subsector was a puppet military organization equivalent to a province-level administrative unit.

31. Statement by U.S. President Kennedy, 14 February 1962.

32. In 1962 the enemy conducted 2,577 sweep operations, 749 of which were large sweeps involving forces totaling more than one battalion. They conducted 164 helicopter

assault landings. Three representative operations on which the enemy concentrated their leadership efforts were the "Binh Minh Campaign" in Binh Duong province, the "Chau Tho Campaign" in the Mekong Delta, and the "Hai Yen Campaign" in the lowlands of Central Vietnam. Forces used in each of these operations consisted of one entire regular division plus all Regional Force and Popular Force troops and all police in the area of the campaign. These campaigns lasted for several months.

33. Out of a total of 17,162 hamlets throughout South Vietnam.

34. In 1962 enemy forces in Region 5 and the Central Highlands consisted of six infantry divisions (the 1st, 2nd, 9th, 22nd, 23rd, and 25th), two separate infantry regiments, four Ranger battalions, and 18 specialty branch battalions. This force represented two-thirds of the enemy's total regular armed forces in all of South Vietnam.

35. Military Region 5 Command, Report on the Situation in Region 5 for 1961. On file at the Ministry of Defense, file no. 295/QUTU.

36. There were more than 100 such teams in the entire region, each team having around ten personnel.

37. COSVN Military Affairs Section, Instructions on a Number of Immediate Tasks, December 1962. On file at the Ministry of Defense, file no. 331/QUTU.

38. In 1962 the total strength of Group 559 was 6,000 personnel organized into two regiments (the 70th and 71st) and a number of engineer, transportation, and commo-liaison companies and battalions. The Group was equipped with over 1,000 transport bicycles plus a number of trucks, elephants, and horses for use in transporting supplies.

39. Dressing like the local population, learning the local language.

40. In 1962 transportation forces assigned to the Military Transportation Office of Military Region 5 totaled 2,000 personnel organized into 60 porter and bicycle supply teams.

41. In 1961 we had a total of 25,000 main force and local force troops in South Vietnam; in 1962 the total was 40,000, and in 1963 the total grew to 70,000.

42. Because they were not yet capable of forming battalions, a number of provinces formed companies with troop strengths that exceeded authorized levels.

43. The 2nd Regiment (designated C-58 and also known as Regiment Q-762) was formed in July 1962.

44. SKS rifles, AK submachine guns, and RPD light machine guns.

45. In 1963 the armed forces of Region 5 attacked the cities of Tam Ky and Quang Ngai, the rear base camps of the puppet 25th and 9th Divisions and of the puppet 40th Regiment, and a number of district capitals.

46. Report of Region 5 Party Committee on the situation for the two-year period 1963–1964 and battlefield prospects for the coming period. From the files of the Ministry of Defense, file no. 417/QUTU.

47. Instructions of the COSVN Military Affairs Section, November 1962.

48. The 13 localities that reported on their model programs were Bac Ai district (Ninh Thuan province); Thoi Hoa and Ben Tuong villages (Binh Duong province); Phuoc Vinh An and Tan Xuan villages (Gia Dinh province); Tan Phu Trung village (My Tho province); Tan Thanh and Khanh Thanh Tan (Ben Tre province); Hau My village (Long An province); An Binh village (Can Tho province); and Vinh Chau and Gia Hoa villages (Soc Trang province).

49. In 1965 Sisters Ut Tich and Ta Thi Kieu were awarded the title of "Heroes of the People's Armed Forces."

50. Enemy forces participating in the sweep consisted of eight battalions (3,000 troops), 35 aircraft, 13 amphibious armored personnel carriers, 13 combat vessels, and ten 105mm howitzers.

51. Two main force regional battalions and two local force battalions belonging to Ca Mau and Rach Gia provinces.

CHAPTER 6

1. Report by McNamara to Johnson, cited in Joseph A. Amter, *Statements on Vietnam*, People's Army Publishing House, Hanoi, 1985.

2. Kennedy was assassinated on 22 November 1963.

3. Statement by Dean Rusk, U.S. Secretary of State, quote by Joseph A. Amter in *Statements on Vietnam.*

4. In 1962 the enemy drafted 7,200 soldiers per month, in 1963 11,000 soldiers per month, and in 1964 14,200 soldiers per month (all figures are monthly averages). The total strength of the puppet army in 1962 was 354,000, consisting of 198,000 regulars and 156,000 Regional Force and Popular Force troops. In 1964 the total strength had grown to 471,000, consisting of 245,000 regulars and 226,000 Regional and Popular Force troops.

5. In the Cochin China area alone the enemy formed 14 Ranger battalions.

6. "Special Forces" were divided into three categories: "strategic operations," "tactical operations," and "local operations."

7. In 1964 American military forces in South Vietnam totaled over 20,000 men.

8. The puppet air force had 375 aircraft.

9. "Operations Plan 34A" included flights by U-2 strategic reconnaissance aircraft, kidnapping North Vietnamese citizens to collect intelligence information, dropping teams by parachute to conduct sabotage operations, and atacks by commandos from the sea. Destroyer patrols (Desoto patrols) were aimed at collecting intelligence, supporting Op Plan 34A attacks, and displaying the military might of the United States.

10. Resolution of the 9th Plenum of the Party Central Committee, December 1963.

11. After the 95th Regiment set off for the battlefield, a new regiment was established, designated the 95B Regiment; this was followed by the 95C and 95D Regiments. The 325th Division's 101st and 18th Regiments and other regiments in other divisions followed the same procedure.

12. Because of supply difficulties and in order to strengthen local armed forces, the Military Region Command disbanded the 3rd Regiment and sent two of its infantry battalions down to serve as provincial local force battalions for the provinces of Phu Yen and Darlac.

13. Ho Chi Minh, *Collected Works,* vol. 2, Su That [Truth] Publishing House, Hanoi, 1980, p. 311.

14. Ibid.

15. Ibid.

16. Resolution of the Party Committee of the Air Defense–Air Force Service Branch, 2nd quarter of 1964.

17. Not until early 1964 did our Air Defense–Air Force Service Branch finally establish the Anti-Aircraft Artillery Branch (with seven regiments) and the Radar Branch (three

regiments). The missile regiment consisted of only a cadre framework and as yet had no weapons. The air force fighter regiment was in training in a foreign country.

18. The forces defending Hanoi and Haiphong amounted to 57 percent of our medium-caliber anti-aircraft batteries (88mm to 100mm) and 34 percent of our 57mm batteries. At the other strategic sites (Thai Nguyen, Noi Bai, Viet Tri, Hon Gai, Nam Dinh, Vinh) we deployed 42 percent of our medium-caliber anti-aircraft batteries (primarily 85mm, 88mm, and 90mm), 28 percent of our 57mm batteries, and 100 percent of our 37mm batteries. The Service's reserve force, consisting of two regiments of 57mm guns (representing 38 percent of the total number of batteries equipped with this caliber weapon), was deployed on the left and right banks of the Red River.

19. Citation issued by Senior General Nguyen Chi Thanh to the 3rd Navy Squadron. Excerpted from *History of the People's Navy,* People's Army Publishing House, Hanoi, 1985, p. 100.

20. Out of 64 aircraft sorties, eight aircraft were shot down (12 percent losses).

21. In August 1964 the 212th Anti-Aircraft Artillery Regiment was formed to serve as the Service's reserve force.

22. By the end of 1964, Region 5 main force troops included three infantry regiments (3rd Regiment had been reestablished), one separate infantry battalion, two sapper battalions, and a number of specialty branch units. Region 5 had a total of 13,793 main force troops (not counting 993 working in headquarters staffs and 2,593 serving on the transportation routes). Province local force troops totaled 17,275 cadre and soldiers and were organized up to the battalion level.

23. In 1963 Region 5 had 40,469 guerrillas and 13,102 self-defense soldiers.

24. Half of the total number of "strategic hamlets" that the enemy had built in Central Vietnam.

25. The 320th Infantry Regiment was made up of three infantry battalions from the 308th, 312th, and 320th Divisions.

26. Upon arrival at the battlefront these three regiments were redesignated as the 10th, 11th, and 12th Regiments.

27. The 800th and 500th Battalions from Military Region 7 and the 186th Battalion from Military Region 6.

28. In 1965 Comrade Ta Quang Ty was awarded the title of "Hero of the People's Armed Forces."

29. After two combat phases (from 2 December 1964 to 3 January 1965) our forces continued to exploit the victories of this campaign until 7 March 1965. The conference to review and summarize phase one of the campaign (held from 25 August to 30 August 1985 and presided over by Senior General Hoang Van Thai) unanimously agreed that we should not consider the exploit-the-victory phase to be phase three of the campaign.

30. We also wiped out seven Regional Force companies and dispersed almost all of the Popular Force troops in the campaign theater of operations. Total enemy losses were 1,755 killed, 293 prisoners captured, 45 vehicles destroyed (most of which were M-113s), and 56 aircraft shot down or damaged. We captured over 1,000 weapons.

31. The 1st Regiment eliminated from the field of combat 270 enemy soldiers (including two Americans) and captured almost 200 weapons. The civilian population, armed with knives and sticks, joined our troops in pursuing the enemy, capturing 100 out of a total of 277 enemy captured.

32. A total of 2,054 enemy troops (1,425 of whom were regulars) were eliminated from the field of combat during the campaign. We captured 973 weapons and destroyed 15 military vehicles.

33. Son Tinh, Binh Son, Tra Bong, Nghia Hanh, Tu Nghia, and Duc Pho districts.

34. COSVN's 1st, 2nd, and 3rd Regiments and Military Region 7's main force 4th Regiment.

35. During the Dong Xoai Campaign our troops captured 1,652 weapons; destroyed 28 armored personnel carriers, five tanks, six locomotives, and 12 railroad cars; and shot down 34 enemy aircraft.

36. Ten years, counting from 1954.

37. Ho Chi Minh, *Collected Works,* vol. 2, Su That [Truth] Publishing House, Hanoi, 1980, p. 345.

CHAPTER 7

1. Resolution of the 11th Plenum of the Party Central Committee, March 1965.

2. Phase one: halt the collapse of the puppet army. Phase two: expand offensive operations during the first six months of 1966 in special priority areas in order to wipe out hostile forces and resume rural construction activities. Phase three: If the enemy stubbornly resists, after the completion of phase two an additional one to one and a half years would be needed to defeat and eliminate remaining enemy forces in the base areas.

3. These included the 3rd Marine Division and the 9th Marine Brigade, the 1st Air Cavalry Division, the 1st Infantry Division (the Big Red One), the 3rd Brigade of the 25th Mechanized Infantry Division, the 1st Brigade of the 101st Airborne Division, the 173rd Airborne Brigade, the 30th Naval Regiment, and 25 Navy Mobile Construction Battalions. Before being sent to Vietnam, each American unit was upgraded in terms of its organization and equipment and was given training appropriate to the special conditions of the battlefield and in tactical fighting methods used by the U.S. armed forces. Infantry divisions were organized into three brigades, but their equipment was considerably lighter than in a standard division. Heavy equipment and weapons, such as heavy artillery, missiles (Honest John), and medium tanks were replaced with self-propelled artillery, light tanks, amphibious armored personnel carriers, and units were given additional air transportation equipment. The manpower and equipment strength of a number of American battalions was two or three times greater than that of a puppet battalion (a U.S. infantry battalion had 850 men, and a Marine battalion had 1,200 men). U.S. infantry battalions were equipped with rapid-fire submachine guns, 40mm grenade launchers, 106mm recoilless rifles and mortars, and anti-tank missiles (Entac). During the last half of 1965, the United States sent to Vietnam 378 artillery pieces, 582 tanks and armored personnel carriers, 350 jet combat aircraft, 1,000 helicopters, and 47 warships.

4. According to Joseph A. Amter, *Statements on Vietnam,* People's Army Publishing House, Hanoi, 1985, "The air war during 1965 began between the 17th and 19th parallels and expanded to the 20th parallel. The strength of the air attacks increased relentlessly, rising from 1,500 sorties in April to 4,000 sorties in October."

5. Resolution of the 11th Plenum of the Party Central Committee, 28 March 1965.

6. Ho Chi Minh, *Collected Works,* vol. 2, Su That [Truth] Publishing House, Hanoi, 1980, p. 376.

7. Also called the Bien Hoa Artillery Group.

8. In 1965 the provinces of Quang Tri and Thua Thien were still subordinate to Military Region 5 and were called the Northern Subregion.

9. During the second half of 1965, 42,906 weapons shipped from North Vietnam arrived in the battlefields of Cochin China and extreme southern Central Vietnam.

10. Military Region 3 alone mobilized more than 200,000 personnel into the armed forces during 1965.

11. The 921st Regiment (the Red Star Group) was equipped with Mig-17 fighters when it was formed on 3 February 1964, but these were later replaced with Mig-21s.

12. In 1964 the strength of the Air Defense–Air Force Branch was 22,500; by the end of 1965 this strength had risen to 52,700.

13. Resolution of the Politiburo of the Party Central Committee, October 1965.

14. Pham Van Dong, report read to the 3rd National Assembly, 4th Session, May 1968.

15. The Transportation Department of the General Department of Logistics was established on 18 June 1949. In 1955 the department was disbanded and reorganized as the Military Traffic and Communications Office of the General Staff.

16. Besides the troops in its table of organization strength, Group 559 also had assigned to it 1,500 workers from the Ministry of Communications and Transportation and 7,600 assault youth.

17. Ho Chi Minh, *Collected Works,* vol. 2, Su That [Truth] Publishing House, Hanoi, 1980, p. 392.

18. Ibid.

CHAPTER 8

1. Employing forces of between three and 21 American battalions with heavy fire support provided by artillery and air forces (on average there were between 450 and 500 air sorties per day, of which there were 321 B-52 sorties).

2. The enemy called this "breaking the back of the Viet Cong."

3. The enemy plan called for strengthening 2,000 "strategic hamlets" and gaining control of an additional 2.5 million people.

4. The 2nd and 3rd Brigades of the U.S. 1st Infantry Division, supported by artillery fire and air support.

5. 1) Anyone can fight the Americans; 2) any weapon can be used to fight the Americans; 3) many can fight, a few can fight, even one person alone can fight the Americans; 4) the Americans can be fought anywhere; 5) the Americans can be fought during daytime and at night; 6) an American counterattack presents a good opportunity to kill them; 7) we can fight the Americans both from the front and from the rear; 8) we can fight the Americans inside villages and outside villages, inside hamlets and outside hamlets; 9) we can defeat all of the American specialty branches: infantry, tanks, air force; 10) we can fight the Americans with weapons, with political means, and with troop proselytizing.

6. Four divisions and three brigades of U.S. and South Korean troops, two divisions and two regimental infantry task forces of puppet troops, and two puppet Marine regiments from the strategic reserve.

7. Between 28 January and 7 March 1966, the soldiers and civilians of Binh Dinh province eliminated from the field of combat almost 8,000 enemy troops (including 500 American and South Korean troops) and shot down and destroyed 236 aircraft.

8. On 30 March 1966, Cabot Lodge, U.S. Ambassador in Saigon, sent a cable to U.S. President Johnson in which he confessed, "The offensive has not been able to cripple the Viet Cong, it has not been able to destroy even one large regular Viet Cong unit, and has not stopped the expansion of the enemy's guerrilla forces. The United States is still on the defensive, and the quality of Saigon's army is rapidly declining."

9. Resolution of the Politburo, October 1966.

10. The two remaining brigades of the 25th Infantry Division, two brigades of the 1st Marine Division, the 9th Infantry Division, the 4th Infantry Division, the 196th and 199th Light Infantry Brigades, and a number of specialty branch units.

11. Ho Chi Minh, *Collected Works,* vol. 2, Su That [Truth] Publishing House, Hanoi, 1980, p. 430.

12. Consisting of 600,000 main force troops and 93,000 local force troops.

13. The 324th Division and the 325C Division, both of which went to the Route 9– Tri Thien Front.

14. The balance of forces in South Vietnam between the enemy and our side at the end of 1966: total troop strength (including guerrillas) was 889,000 to 376,000 (2.36 to 1). For just main force (regulars), 582,000 to 151,000 (3.8 to 1); number of combat battalions, 256 to 136 (1.7 to 1), out of which the number of mobile battalions was 137 to 98 (1.4 to 1).

15. Ho Chi Minh, speech to a class for Party members held by the Hanoi City Party Committee in May 1966.

16. DKB: Actual designation DKZ 66, a small, light, rocket weapon, able to be carried on the shoulders of our artillery gunners, and having considerable power. This rocket had a range of 10,080 meters, was easy to operate, and could be employed in every type of terrain and weather condition. Chairman Ho Chi Minh personally suggested to the Soviet Union that they assist us in producing this type of weapon. The name "DKB" designates it as a DKZ [recoilless] weapon specially adapted for use on Battlefront B (South Vietnam).

17. A-12: A 140mm rocket weighing 36 kilograms and with a range of 800 meters. This rocket was modified by our troops from the Soviet vehicle-mounted BM-14 rocket.

18. The standard for an expert regiment was to fight a regiment-sized battle that destroyed an American or a puppet battalion operating in the open or to overrun a strong point held by two or three puppet companies. The standard for an expert battalion was to destroy a puppet battalion operating in the open or to overrun a strong point held by one puppet company.

19. The "Vo-Det" [*sic*] class of puppet commando vessels was between 22 and 24 meters long, between six and seven meters wide, had a displacement of between 35 and 64 tons, and a top speed of 30 to 40 kilometers per hour. The vessel's hull was made of plywood or light metal. The vessel was equipped with two 40mm cannon, two 20mm cannon, three recoilless rifles, and one 81mm mortar. These vessels carried crews of between 17 and 20 men.

20. Destroyer similar to the Fletcher class, 114.7 meters long, 12 meters wide, mounting six 127.6mm double-barreled guns, and with a crew of 300 sailors.

21. COSVN Party Military Committee, Summary of Force-Building Activities during 1966, file no. 1831/QL.

22. The 16th Independent Regiment was assigned to the 9th Division to ensure that the 9th Division could fulfill its role as COSVN's strong main force fist. The 3rd Regi-

ment was detached from the 9th Division and made directly subordinate to COSVN to enable it to operate deep behind enemy lines.

23. The 9th, 5th, and 7th Divisions subordinate to the COSVN Military Command, the 2nd and 3rd Divisions subordinate to Military Region 5, the 1st Division subordinate to the Central Highlands Front, and the 324th and 325th Divisions subordinate to the Route 9–Tri Thien Front.

24. K-20 was a transportation unit of our army operating in Cambodia under the guise of a commercial company owned by local ethnic Vietnamese.

25. These forces consisted of the 6th Infantry Regiment, a number of specialty branch units, and four local force battalions (the 804th, 808th, 810th, and 814th) belonging to Quang Tri and Thua Thien provinces.

26. Resolution of the Standing Committee of the Central Military Party Committee on the duties of the Tri-Thien battlefield, April 1966.

27. Resolution of the Politiburo of the Party Central Committee, October 1966.

28. American forces participating in the "Attleboro" sweep totaled 22,000 soldiers, including the 196th Light Infantry Brigade, five infantry brigades from the 1st, 4th, and 25th Divisions, the 173rd Airborne Brigade, and the 11th Armored Cavalry Regiment.

29. Consisting of three American brigades and three puppet regiment-sized task forces.

30. Consisting of nine U.S. brigades or regiments and three puppet battalions.

31. Between 22 February and 18 March almost 4,000 American soldiers were killed or wounded, 90 aircraft were shot down, and 33 artillery pieces and 352 tanks and armored personnel carriers were destroyed.

32. Our local forces alone (the self-defense troops of the staff agencies) had killed or wounded 6,000 soldiers, and destroyed 625 tanks, 118 aircraft, and three artillery pieces.

33. The 40th Artillery Regiment was established on 5 February 1967. The regiment was made up of the 34th Battalion, equipped with 75mm pack howitzers, the 20th Composite Artillery Battalion, the 32nd Battalion, equipped with 120mm mortars, and the 30th Anti-Aircraft Machine Gun Battalion.

34. Ho Chi Minh, *Collected Works,* vol. 10, Su That [Truth] Publishing House, Hanoi, 1989, p. 543.

35. According to a public statement issued by the Chairman of the Central Committee of the National Liberation Front of South Vietnam, during the winter and spring of 1966–1967 our soldiers and civilians eliminated from the field of battle 175,000 enemy troops (including 70,000 American troops, 15,000 satellite troops, and 90,000 puppet troops). With regard to units, eight U.S. infantry battalions, 15 U.S. armored troops, and five U.S. artillery battalions had been rendered combat ineffective. As for implements of war, it was announced that we had destroyed 1,800 aircraft of all types, 2,000 military vehicles, 340 artillery pieces, and 100 river vessels.

36. More than in April 1967.

CHAPTER 9

1. In mid-1967, the U.S. troop strength in South Vietnam was 480,000, consisting of nine divisions and three brigades, a high percentage of the total strength of the U.S.

standing army. The reserves set aside for a large-scale limited war had been totally depleted. The military draft was inducting 30,000 soldiers per month, far in excess of initial projections. The budget expenditure for the Vietnam War in the 1966–1967 fiscal year was $24 billion, and the estimate for the 1967–1968 fiscal year was $30 billion.

2. In November 1967, U.S. Secretary of Defense McNamara resigned.

3. In August 1967, Johnson sent an additional 55,000 U.S. soldiers to Vietnam.

4. On 9 September 1967, the General Staff sent Cable No. 98 to COSVN and to the COSVN Party Military Committee, clearly setting forward requirements and problems that must be resolved in order to increase the capability of our main force troops to fight large battles of annihilation.

5. Speech by Ho Chi Minh to representatives of the cadre and soldiers of the Sapper Branch, 19 March 1967.

6. Subregion 1: Trang Bang, Dau Tien, Ben Cat, Cu Chi, Hoc Mon, Go Vap; Subregion 2: Duc Hoa, Duc Hue, Ben Thu, Tan Binh, Binh Chanh; Subregion 3: Chau Thanh, Tan Tru, Can Duoc, Can Giuoc, Nha Be; Subregion 4: Vung Tau, Ba Ria, Nhon Trach; Subregion 5: Tan Uyen, Phu Giao, Lai Thieu, Di An, Thu Duc; Subregion 6 included the precincts of Saigon city itself.

7. In late 1967 COSVN controlled three infantry divisions and one artillery division.

8. Two engineer battalions, one signal battalion and one separate signal company, two sapper regiments, and one flamethrower company.

9. Formerly the 68th Artillery Regiment of the 304th Division.

10. In late 1967 the 9th Regiment was withdrawn to become the Military Region's mobile (reserve) force. The High Command transferred the 2nd Regiment, 324th Division, to Group 7 to replace it.

11. The 9th Regiment/304th Division, 2nd Regiment/324th Division, and 18th Regiment/325th Division.

12. Preparations for the attack on Saigon had begun very early (dating back to the end of 1964), but direct preparations for the 1968 attack did not begin until October 1967, so the preparations were very hasty and rushed.

13. In 1967 North Vietnam sent 81,000 replacement soldiers to the battlefield, and the same year we were able to recruit 7,600 new troops locally in South Vietnam.

14. At the end of 1967 sapper forces in South Vietnam consisted of one sapper regiment, two sapper groups (equivalent to regiments), 21 battalions, 58 teams, and hundreds of sapper platoons and squads.

15. According to the calendar issued by the Saigon regime, the first day of the Tet lunar new year in 1968 was 30 January on the Western calendar, one day later than the date for Tet given on calendars used in North Vietnam. On the afternoon of 29 January 1968, Military Region 5 received a cable postponing the attack until the night of 30–31 January. Military Region 5 only had time to alert the 2nd and 3rd Divisions, the 10th Regiment, and Quang Nam and Quang Ngai provinces of the postponement. The provinces of Quang Da, Phu Yen, Binh Dinh, and Khanh Hoa did not receive the postponement order, so they opened fire during the night of 29–30 January 1968, according to the schedule in our initial plan.

16. Enemy forces defending Da Nang included the puppet 1st Division and one puppet Airborne brigade to the north and 16 U.S. battalions and the 1st Ranger Group to the

west and south. Within the city were numerous American bases and the headquarters of the puppet 1st Corps.

17. Because of delays in crossing the river, only one platoon managed to enter the city. The spearhead force attacking the headquarters of the puppet 1st Corps managed to reach the barbed wire surrounding the base, but the enemy resisted fiercely and most of our cadre and soldiers were killed. A small element of our forces attacking the enemy positions at Phuoc Tuong and Non Nuoc made it into these positions, but the enemy counterattacked and blocked them. Meanwhile, the 2nd Division had received the order postponing the time of the attack and had pulled back to the rear.

18. We attacked and captured 39 important targets inside the city, killed or dispersed 20,000 puppet soldiers, captured or destroyed many implements of war (50 aircraft destroyed, 2,500 weapons captured). The puppet governmental structure at all levels in Hue collapsed and disintegrated. The puppet administration in the villages and hamlets was paralyzed. We liberated 296 hamlets with a population of 227,000, including 240 hamlets where we were able to establish a revolutionary governmental administration, expanded our forces by almost 10,000 guerrillas, and mobilized 2,500 guerrillas to use as replacements in our main force units.

19. Our forces attacking Lang Vay consisted of the 24th Regiment of the 304th Division, the 3rd Battalion of the 101st Regiment (325th Division), one artillery battalion equipped with howitzers, and two companies of PT-76 tanks.

20. Between 10 February and 31 March enemy tactical bombers dropped 35,000 tons of bombs, B-52s dropped 75,000 tons of bombs, and 175mm artillery guns fired more than 100,000 shells into the area surrounding Khe Sanh.

21. Enemy forces in the operation included the entire U.S. Air Cavalry Division, one puppet Airborne task force, one Ranger group, 130 artillery pieces, and 60 tanks.

22. Consisting of 1,368,000 tons, including 200 oil storage facilities, 250 ammunition storage facilities destroyed, 60 airfields attacked, 2,370 aircraft shot down or destroyed, 1,700 tanks and armored personnel carriers, 350 artillery pieces, and 280 ships and vessels destroyed.

23. Out of the total number of 5,400 "strategic hamlets" built by the enemy as of the end of 1967.

24. 1st Brigade/5th Mechanized Division and 3rd Brigade/82nd Airborne Division.

25. Saigon was defended by between 40 and 50 U.S. and puppet battalions; Hue was defended by 25 battalions, and Da Nang was defended by ten to 15 battalions.

26. *U.S. Air Force* magazine, April 1969.

27. The sections of Routes 1 and 15A running through Ha Tinh province were blocked 28 days per month during both the months of August and September 1968.

28. The forces assigned to Headquarters 500 included two regiments and 35 battalions of engineers; one division, three regiments, and 23 battalions of anti-aircraft artillery; 18 truck transportation battalions; and two pipeline battalions. The total troop strength was 33,384 personnel, not counting assault youths and civilian laborers (the strength of Group 559 at that time was 35,108 personnel).

29. D-74: A long-barreled 122mm gun with a range of 24 kilometers.

30. The 3rd Battalion went to Tri-Thien; the 491st Battalion (also known as Thanh Hoa province's Lam Son Battalion) went to Region 5; the 200C Battalion went to Region 6; and five battalions (the 251st, 252nd, 253rd, 254th, and 255th) went to Cochin China.

31. Assessing the defeat of American forces during Tet 1968, Presidential National Security Advisor Kissinger described his analysis of Johnson's and Westmoreland's mistake in placing 94 percent of America's most elite forces in mountain jungle areas, including the Route 9 battlefield, which held only 4 percent of the population of South Vietnam. Kissinger said that Hanoi had "played matador," luring the ferocious American bull to the outer perimeter, and then used their military forces to unexpectedly launch an explosive attack against all the urban areas that the Americans had left unprotected, leaving the U.S. Command no time to react.

32. Ho Chi Minh. From a cable sent to Chairman Nguyen Huu Tho and the other members of the Central Committee of the National Liberation Front for South Vietnam, 13 July 1968.

33. Resolution of the 21st Plenum of the Party Central Committee, July 1973.

34. Ho Chi Minh, *Collected Works,* vol. 2, Su That [Truth] Publishing House, Hanoi, 1980, p. 504.

CHAPTER 10

1. As compared with 1968, in 1969 the puppet regular armed forces increased by 20,000 (to a total of 300,000), local forces increased by 35,000 (to a total of 310,000), and armed people's self-defense forces increased by 200,000 (to a total of 263,000). The puppet regular army established more than 30 new artillery, tank, and armored battalions and four new Air Force squadrons with more than 150 aircraft of all types.

2. In Region 5 we were only able to maintain three or four out of a total of 42 purchasing and collection points that we had previously operated.

3. Ho Chi Minh, *The Collected Writings,* vol. 10, Su That [Truth] Publishing House, Hanoi, 1989, pp. 747–748.

4. Ibid., pp. 789–790.

5. Ibid., pp. 779–780.

6. Group 500 had a strength of 13,000 troops, including five troop supply stations [binh tram], seven truck battalions, eight engineer battalions, two anti-aircraft battalions, two POL pipeline battalions, and five medical aid stations.

7. These supplies included 150,000 infantry weapons, 15,000 B-40 [RPG-2] and B-41 [RPG-7] rocket launchers, 2,300 mortars and recoilless rifles, over 100 million rounds of ammunition of all types, 1,500 radios, etc.

8. Between April 1969 and April 1970 110,000 U.S. combat troops were withdrawn from South Vietnam.

9. Enemy forces participating in the sweep consisted of the 4th Marine Brigade and elements of the puppet 9th and 21st Divisions.

10. Condolences of the Central Committee of the Labor [Communist] Party of Vietnam. From the book, *Ho Chi Minh's Last Will and Testament,* Central Committee of the Communist Party of Vietnam, 1989, p. 53.

11. Ibid.

12. Ibid.

13. Ibid.

14. During this campaign the United States used 120 to 150 tactical aircraft sorties per day and for the first time used B-52 strategic bombers in northern Laos.

15. The number 139 was a combination of the month and the day (13 September).

The High Command itself issued the campaign assignments directly to the units involved.

16. After the invasion, the enemy left 20 battalions of Saigon puppet troops in Cambodia to prop up the Lon Nol puppet government.

CHAPTER 11

1. The enemy effort was unsuccessful because we had moved the prisoners to another camp.

2. A Navy Region was equivalent to a regiment.

3. Equipment to locate our supply trucks included night vision devices and sensors able to detect the electrical systems of our truck engines. The American imperialists called the AC-130E the flying "Saboteur" and the "Electronic Bird." It was capable of firing on and destroying 68 vehicles in one hour (it took less than one minute to destroy each vehicle).

4. Between 1969 and the 1970–1971 dry season, the number of supply trucks operated by Group 559 grew from 3,000 to 6,500 trucks, the number of anti-aircraft guns and mortars increased by over 200 weapons, tractors (used to build roads and destroy mines and bombs) increased by more than 1,000, the number of radios increased from 217 to more than 1,000, and Group 559's troop strength grew to 90,000 soldiers.

5. On 19 July 1971 the Ministry of Defense issued Decision No. 109/QD/QP forming the Road-Head Anti-Aircraft Front, designated as the 377th Air Defense Division.

6. The 38th, 45th, 675th, 204th, and 16th Regiments.

7. The 164th, 166th, 154th, 178th, 368th, 572nd, and 42nd Regiments.

8. In 1971 the Engineer Branch consisted of 41,000 cadre and soldiers organized into 15 regiments, 48 battalions, and 17 companies.

9. During the three years 1969–1971, the Sapper Branch sent 22 battalions, 244 independent companies, and 35 independent platoons, for a total of 22,000 cadre and soldiers, to the battlefront. The Engineer Branch sent to the battlefront 1,000 technical personnel and 700 tons of equipment. The Signal Branch sent to the battlefront 600 cadre, radiomen, and repair technicians and 500 tons of equipment.

10. Ho Chi Minh, *Collected Writings,* vol. 10, Su That [Truth] Publishing House, Hanoi, 1989, p. 125.

11. [Translator's note: The Vietnamese word translated as "corps-size group" is "binh doan," which is different from the word used for a regular army corps, "quan doan," to distinguish it from a full-fledged corps. PAVN did not form its first army corps (quan doan) until 24 October 1973.]

12. By 10 March 1971 the enemy force had grown by an additional 13,000 troops (including 6,000 Americans), 120 tanks and armored personnel carriers, 70 artillery pieces, and 300 helicopters.

13. Included in that total was one B-52, shot down by the 69th Missile Battalion (237th Regiment) on 18 March 1971.

14. These were Rear Service Groups 10, 20, 30, 40, 400, 340, 500, and 770. Each group had a total troop strength equivalent to a regiment. The areas of operations of the rear services groups covered ten provinces in northern, eastern, and southern Cambodia.

15. By the end of 1970, our liberated zones in Cambodia covered most of 14 provinces (out of a total of 18 provinces) and 60 districts (out of a total of 102 districts).

The liberated zones had a population of 4.5 million people (out of a total population of 7 million people).

16. Enemy forces participating in this operation consisted of three infantry divisions (the 5th, 25th, and 18th), one Ranger group, five armored and tank squadrons, and other military specialty branch units.

CHAPTER 12

1. By November 1971, only 184,000 U.S. and satellite troops remained in South Vietnam. These forces included one division (minus), two separate infantry regiments, two armored battalions, 29 artillery battalions, and 30 tactical air squadrons (600 aircraft).

2. In May the division was reinforced by the 97th Regiment.

3. In April the B2 Battlefront received one additional tank battalion and two battalions of shoulder-fired anti-aircraft missiles and 37mm anti-aircraft guns.

4. Document in the files of the Vietnam Military History Institute.

5. In June 1972 the National Assembly awarded the Mai Quoc Ca platoon the title of "Hero Unit of the People's Armed Forces."

6. On 2 May 1972 the Western press and the Saigon press named the section of Route 1 from the Dai Bridge [the "Long" Bridge] to the Ben Da Bridge, which was littered with vehicles, artillery, and the bodies of enemy troops, the "Highway of Death."

7. Three Airborne brigades and the 4th and 51st Infantry Regiments.

8. 1,088 tactical aircraft out of the U.S. total force of 3,400 aircraft (31 percent of all active-duty U.S. tactical aircraft), 150 out of a total of 400 B-52s, 58 out of 89 vessels in the 7th Fleet, and six out of 14 U.S. aircraft carriers.

9. An increase of 100,000 over 1968 levels.

10. During the first war of destruction we shot down an average of 72 aircraft per month; during this period the average was 84 aircraft shot down. During the first war of destruction our artillery on average used 153 rounds to score one hit on an enemy ship; this time, the average was 121 rounds.

11. Usually each infantry battalion was supported by one artillery battalion, and each infantry regiment had one armored squadron to serve as an assault force and provide fire support.

12. This was the highest level of American fire support ever provided for one battle. Between 9 September and 16 September, U.S.warships fired a total of 123,725 rounds into the city (52,573 rounds were fired into the Citadel). The United States provided 2,244 bombing sorties for this operation, including, on some days, more than 100 sorties by U.S. B-52 strategic bombers.

13. Cable number 325-DK from the Central Military Party Committee to the Campaign Command Headquarters. Copy on file at the Vietnam Military History Institute.

14. Excerpted from Cable Number 373/TK dated 25 May 1972 from the Politburo to the COSVN Standing Committee and to the COSVN Military Party Committee.

15. Cable from Comrade Vo Nguyen Giap to the COSVN Military Party Committee dated 8 June 1972.

CHAPTER 13

1. The U.S. side had agreed that the treaty would be initialed in Hanoi on 22 October and that the formal signing would be carried out in Paris on 31 October 1972.

2. During the first 20 days of November 1972 the United States poured more than 600 aircraft, 170 tanks and armored vehicles, and 75 pieces of heavy artillery into South Vietnam.

3. Sorties rose from 366 sorties in September to 408 sorties in October and 786 sorties in November.

4. On 30 November 1972, Nixon met with a number of high-ranking U.S. officials, including Kissinger, Laird, and Haig, and decided to launch a powerful B-52 bombing offensive against Hanoi. The offensive would last from three to six days.

5. The U.S. imperialists believed the B-52 could be used in all four types of warfare: strategic nuclear war, tactical nuclear war, conventional warfare, and limited warfare.

6. Ho Chi Minh, *Collected Writings,* vol. 2, Su That [Truth] Publishing House, Hanoi, 1980, p. 372.

7. The manual consisted of four sections: 1) B-52 operational plans and proceedures used when attacking North Vietnam; 2) combat tactics for missile troops; 3) key problems for command organization and combat support; 4) standard procedures for missile battalions.

8. As of November 1972, the militia and self-defense forces of North Vietnam were equipped with 3,090 guns and cannon of all types, including 1,305 medium and light machine guns, 1,076 12.7mm machine guns, 424 14.5mm machine guns, 17 20mm cannon, 82 85mm cannon, and 70 100mm cannon.

9. This was the date on which Comrade Le Duc Tho, Politburo member and representative of our government, was to meet with Kissinger, the representative of the U.S. government, in Paris.

10. The Americans named the strategic bombing offensive using B-52s against Hanoi and Haiphong the "Linebacker II Campaign."

11. "DB1" and "DB2" were special transportation campaigns to send a large quantity of supplies in a very short period of time to the battlefields of South Vietnam [translator's note: "DB" is the abbreviation of the Vietnamese word "special" —dac biet].

12. Resolution of the Standing Committee of the Central Military Party Committee, disseminated to high-ranking military cadre by the Secretary of the Central Military Party Committee on 31 December 1972.

CHAPTER 14

1. Resolution of the 21st Plenum of the Party Central Committee, July 1973.

2. Headquarters of Military Region 5: Summary of Military Activity during the first six months of 1973.

3. Resolution of the Central Military Party Committee, June 1973.

4. Ibid.

5. The Four Party Joint Military Delegation consisted of the Democratic Republic of Vietnam, the Provisional Revolutionary Government of the Republic of South Vietnam, the United States, and the Saigon puppet regime.

6. Resolution of the 21st Plenum of the Party Central Committee, July 1973.

7. Ibid.

8. Pursuant to a resolution of the Politburo of the Party Central Committee, on 24 October 1973 Senior General Vo Nguyen Giap, Politburo member, Deputy Prime Minister, and Minister of Defense, issued Decision No. 124/QD-QP establishing 1st Corps.

9. Decision No. 67/QF-QD dated 17 May 1974.

10. On 20 July 1974, Comrade Pham Hung, Politburo member and COSVN Secretary, officially announced the formation of 4th Corps.

11. On 5 March 1975, Major General Hoang The Thien, former Political Commissar of Group 559, was appointed as Political Commissar of 4th Corps.

12. [Translator's note: The Chien Thang Division is the 312th Division.]

13. During the Spring 1975 General Offensive and Uprising, the 316th Division was sent to the Central Highlands and added to the ranks of 3rd Corps. The 341st Division was sent to eastern Cochin China and was incorporated into the ranks of 4th Corps.

14. Consisting of the 204th, 38th, and 368th Artillery Brigades equipped with 130mm and D-74 (122mm) guns.

15. In Cochin China and extreme southern Central Vietnam (the B2 Front), COSVN main force units and warehouses were down to only 4,800 120mm mortar rounds; 1,190 160mm mortar rounds; 6,500 122mm howitzer rounds; 300 105mm howitzer rounds; and 7,800 130mm artillery rounds. Military Region 5 had only 1,100 120mm mortar rounds, 80 160mm mortar rounds, 1,000 85mm artillery rounds, 4,500 130mm rounds, and 469 122mm howitzer rounds remaining.

16. On 10 September 1974, the Prime Minister issued an official directive establishing the General Technical Department.

17. During 1974, the Artillery Branch shipped to the battlefields a total of 282,000 rounds of ammunition for man-portable artillery.

18. Almost 50 percent of the total length of road built during the previous eight years combined (1965–1972).

19. If the rear area line (in the North) was also counted the total length of the pipeline was 5,500 kilometers.

20. According to the provisions of the Paris Agreement, the U.S. side was responsible for removing the mines it had sown in the coastal areas and rivers of North Vietnam. To carry out this task the United States mobilized a large force consisting of 44 combat vessels and minesweepers, 45 helicopters, and 5,003 officers and men under the command of Admiral McCauley. During the first five months of 1973 this force was able to destroy only three mines outside of Nam Trieu, a location we had been unable to sweep. U.S. losses were rather heavy: one vessel was set afire, three helicopters crashed, and one sailor was killed and nine were injured.

21. From the 1973–1974 dry season until the beginning of 1975, military transportation forces and those of the Ministry of Communications and Transport sent 200,000 tons of supplies to the battlefields. Cochin China and the extreme southern portion of Central Vietnam, the remotest battlefield, had been able to stockpile 45,000 tons of supplies, enough to support 200,000 troops for six months of operations.

22. The enemy force in Thuong Duc consisted of the 79th Ranger Battalion, two Regional Force companies, one company of Field Combat Police, and 16 armed platoons, totaling about 1,600 soldiers.

23. The 1st Engineer Battalion (219th Engineer Brigade), two missile companies

equipped with A-72 [SA-7] and B-72 [AT-3 Sagger] missiles, two Quang Da province local force battalions, two district local force companies, and one MR-5 sapper battalion.

24. On 16 August 1974 the enemy sent the 2nd Regiment (3rd Infantry Division) and the 1st Airborne Brigade to mount a counterattack to Thuong Duc. In November 1974 they sent the 2nd Airborne Brigade to the Thuong Duc Front.

25. At the end of 1974 the enemy had 690,000 troops (340,000 regulars) but the number who had deserted or otherwise disappeared from the ranks during 1973–1974 was quite large. Puppet regular battalions now only had a strength of 200 men (their table of organization strength was 550). In 1974 fire support by tactical aircraft and artillery decreased 75 percent in comparison with 1972, and there were no more B-52s.

26. Martyr Doan Duc Thai was posthumously awarded the title of Hero of the People's Armed Forces by the National Assembly and the Government. He was the first soldier of the 3rd Division to be awarded this glorious title.

CHAPTER 15

1. The campaign plan set the following concrete goals for the campaign: Annihilate four to five infantry regiments and one to two armored squadrons, and inflict significant damage on the puppet 2nd Corps forces.

2. The puppet Military Region 2 consisted of the Central Highlands and seven other provinces: Binh Dinh, Khanh Hoa, Phu Yen, Ninh Thuan, Binh Thuan, Tuyen Duc, and Lam Dong.

3. In the seven lowland provinces the enemy had two infantry regiments, each province in the Central Highlands had one or two regiments, and the Military Region 2 mobile [reserve] force consisted of five to seven infantry regiments.

4. One of the two infantry divisions, all seven Ranger Groups, 36 out of 86 Regional Force battalions, four out of five of the armored squadrons, eight of the 13 artillery battalions, and seven of the eight separate artillery batteries (with 230 out of their total of 376 cannon), and one Air Force Division (with 150 of their 487 aircraft).

5. In Kontum the enemy deployed four Ranger Groups (the 21st, 22nd, 23rd, and 6th), one artillery battalion, one armored squadron (minus), and six Regional Force battalions. In Gia Lai [Pleiku], enemy forces consisted of the 23rd Infantry Division and two of its regiments (the 43rd and 45th), two Ranger Groups (the 4th and 25th), four artillery battalions, three armored squadrons, and 15 Regional Force battalions.

6. Colonel Vu The Quang, Deputy Commander of the puppet 23rd Division who was captured after the battle of Ban Me Thuot, confessed that as of early March 1975 the puppet General Staff and 2nd Corps believed there was little chance we would use large forces to liberate Ban Me Thuot. Even if we did they believed we would only attack positions on the outer perimeter. They still believed our main target was the northern portion of the Central Highlands.

7. The remaining forces of the puppet 2nd Corps in the Central Highlands consisted of six Ranger Groups, three armored squadrons (the 3rd, 19th, and 21st), six artillery battalions (including 175mm guns), one infantry battalion (44th Regiment), the 89th Ranger Battalion (21st Ranger Group), and engineer, signal, Regional Forces, Air Force, and Corps staff units. In total there were 27 different units.

8. During the Central Highlands campaign, we captured or destroyed 110 aircraft, 17,183 weapons (including twelve 175mm cannon), 767 radios, 1,095 military vehicles (including 72 tanks and armored vehicles), and confiscated the entire system of supply warehouses, command facilities and equipment, and repair facilities belonging to the puppet 2nd Corps in the Central Highlands.

CHAPTER 16

1. Tri-Thien included the provinces of Quang Tri and Thua Thien. Region 5 was made up of six coastal provinces: Quang Nam, Quang Da, Quang Ngai, Binh Dinh, Phu Yen, and Khanh Hoa.

2. The enemy's Military Region 1 consisted of Quang Tri, Thua Thien, Quang Nam, Quang Tin, and Quang Ngai provinces.

3. In early 1975 enemy forces in Military Region 1 included five infantry divisions (the 1st, 2nd, 3rd, Airborne, and Marine); four Ranger Groups (the 11th, 12th, 14th, and 15th); 50 battalions and five separate companies of Regional Forces troops; six Police Field Force companies; five armored squadrons (the 4th, 7th, 11th, 20th, and 17th) and six separate armored troops (totaling 449 armored vehicles); 21 battalions, four separate companies and 14 separate platoons of artillery (a total of 418 guns); one air division (338 aircraft, including 116 combat aircraft); and 165 naval vessels.

4. The 8th Quang Tri Battalion, the 3rd and 10th Thua Thien Battalions, and the Military Region's 5th and 21st Battalions.

5. The 2nd Battalion, Hue City Military Unit, and the Military Region's 3rd Battalion.

6. Quang Ngai province had one regiment, Quang Nam province had three battalions, Quang Da province had one regiment.

7. Quang Nam–Quang Ngai.

8. Tien Phuoc and Phuoc Lam were two districts in the foothills of Quang Nam province, ten kilometers south and southwest of Tam Ky city.

9. The 18th and 101st Regiments of the 325th Division and the 1st and 2nd Regiments of the 324th Division. The 95th Regiment, 325th Division, was on detached duty to the Central Highlands Front. The 3rd Regiment, 324th Division, was in Thuong Duc. The 304th Division had three regiments: the 24th and 66th Regiments at Thuong Duc and the 9th Regiment, which was at the time marching down from Quang Tri.

10. On 21 March enemy forces in Thua Thien–Hue still totaled 46,500 soldiers (27,500 regulars), comprising eight infantry regiments (four regiments of the 1st Division, two Marine Brigades, and two Regional Force Regiment-Sized Groups), three armored squadrons, and seven artillery battalions.

11. On 21 March the enemy sent 4th Regiment, which had been pulled out of Chu Lai, and one battalion of the 6th Regiment from Quang Ngai to Tam Ky.

12. Enemy forces in Da Nang were as follows: the Marine Division, the 3rd Infantry Division, the remnants of the 1st and 2nd Infantry Divisions, the 15th Ranger Group, two armored squadrons, 12 artillery battalions (with a total of 220 artillery pieces), one Air Force Division (with 247 aircraft of all types), 12 Regional Forces battalions, and 157 Popular Forces platoons.

13. Cable No. 3 DB/TK (Special/Most Urgent) dated 27 March 1975.

14. All enemy forces in Da Nang, including 1st Corps Headquarters, the Marine Division, 3rd Infantry Division, 15th Ranger Group, specialty branch units, and the remnants of the 1st, 2nd, 22nd, and 23rd Divisions were killed, captured, or dispersed. We captured or destroyed 69,000 weapons, 109 artillery pieces from 105mm to 175mm, 138 tanks and armored vehicles, 115 aircraft, 47 combat vessels, and great quantities of other technical supplies.

15. The 320B Infantry Division and a number of specialty units had previously left on 19 March 1975.

16. In accordance with a decision by the High Command, on 27 March 1975 Comrade Van Tien Dung, Politburo member, Chief of the General Staff, and representative of the Politburo, the Central Military Party Committee, and the High Command, announced the formation of 3rd Corps.

CHAPTER 17

1. In April 1975 enemy forces totaled seven infantry divisions, five Ranger Groups, 33 artillery battalions, 12 tank squadrons, 1,360 aircraft, and 1,496 combat vessels.

2. The campaign attained the highest transportation capacity ever used in the war against the Americans to save the nation (42,000 tons of total cargo capacity).

3. 28,000 tons held in reserve by COSVN Military Headquarters and 30,000 tons shipped down from North Vietnam.

4. Cable No. 157-H-TK sent to Group 559 Headquarters, Group 559's Forward Headquarters, the divisions and technical heavy equipment units along the route of march (Group 559 to forward the message to these units), 1st Corps, 2nd Corps, and to Comrade Le Trong Tan. The cable was sent at 0930 on 7 April 1975. File number 450-DB, Cryptographic Department, General Staff.

5. Captured enemy artillery made up two-thirds of the artillery pieces employed by the artillery units organic to the Corps.

6. In early April 1975, the Politburo and the Central Military Party Committeee decided to form the Duyen Hai [Coastal] Troop Column. This troop column was assigned the mission of making a lightning movement down Route 1 into eastern Cochin China, rapidly assaulting and taking Ba Ria, O-Cap [Vung Tau], sealing off the Long Tau River, and then assaulting Saigon from the southeast. When it reached the battlefront, this troop column would come under the command of the Headquarters of the Saigon Front.

7. The enemy sent 60 to 70 bombing sorties a day to support this battle.

8. The enemy committed 50 percent of the regular troops, 60 percent of the artillery, and virtually all the tanks of the 3rd Corps, as well as units of the strategic reserve equivalent to one division (both Airborne and Marine units), to the defense of Xuan Loc.

9. The five key targets within the city were the General Staff, Tan Son Nhat Airbase, the Headquarters of the puppet Capital Special Zone, the Police Headquarters, and Independence Palace.

10. Within the boundaries of Tan Son Nhat Airbase.

11. Cable No. 149-TK from the Politburo and the Central Party Military Committee to Headquarters, Ho Chi Minh Campaign. The cable was sent at 10:00 A.M. on 29 April 1975. File no. 215/DB, Cryptographic Department of the General Staff.

12. Cable No. 990B/TK sent at 1730 hours on 4 April 1975 by Comrade Vo Nguyen Giap to Comrades Vo Chi Cong and Chu Huy Man.

CONCLUSION

1. Ho Chi Minh, "On the Armed Struggle and the People's Armed Forces," People's Army Publishing House, Hanoi, 1970, p. 398.
2. Ho Chi Minh, "With the People's Armed Forces," People's Army Publishing House, Hanoi, 1962, p. 171.

Index

South Vietnam, Army
  popular forces, strength, 81, 221, 246
  regional forces, 62, 63, 64, 65, 81, 134,
    246, 294, 297, 308, 365, 385, 406,
    454n17, 473n4n5
  strength, 42, 81, 123–124, 195, 271,
    334, 335, 363, 455n12, 459n34,
    460n4, 468n1, 473n25, 475n1
  1st Division, 202, 218, 219, 273, 276,
    277, 355, 383, 384, 466n16,
    474nn3,10,12, 475n14
  2nd Division, 160, 306, 380, 386, 388,
    404, 474nn3,12, 475n14
  3rd Division, 291, 292, 353, 391,
    473n24, 474nn3,12, 475n14
  5th Division, 134, 212, 255, 281, 295,
    329, 337, 407, 410, 411, 417, 419,
    470n16
  7th Division, 110, 119, 120, 246, 308,
    414, 418, 422
  9th Division, 246, 255, 308, 414,
    459n45, 468n9
  18th Division, 245, 255, 295, 359,
    406–407, 410, 412, 414, 418, 470n16
  21st Division, 246, 255, 307, 454n14,
    468n9
  22nd Division, 57–58, 142, 278,
    293–294, 377, 380, 414, 418, 475n14
  23rd Division, 294, 328, 365, 367–374,
    473nn5,6, 475n14
  25th Division, 144, 255, 307, 356, 359,
    410, 411, 412, 415, 417, 418,
    459n45, 470n16
South Vietnam, communist problems and
  weaknesses, 44–45, 110, 112–113,
  117, 244–252, 335, 338, 339,
  453n36. See also PAVN problems
  and weaknesses, South Vietnam
South Vietnam, Marine Division
  1960–1965, 62, 81, 139, 140, 141, 145
  1965–1968, 216
  1969–1972, 255, 273, 276, 277, 303,
    304, 328, 468n9
  1973, 1975, 384, 390, 391, 392, 406,
    410, 474nn3,10,12, 475n14
  147th Brigade, 276, 277, 291, 305, 383,
    385
  258th Brigade, 276, 305, 382, 391

  369th Brigade, 382
  468th Brigade, 391, 414
South Vietnam, military operations, 47,
  62–63, 109–110, 202
  Cambodia, 255–256, 288
  Lam Son 719, 273–278
  Lam Son 72, 303–306
  Quang Trung, 278
  Quyet Thang, 228
South Vietnam, Rangers
  1960–1965, 62, 118, 119, 135, 140,
    142, 145
  1965–1968, 222, 466n14, 467n21
  1969–1972, 255, 275, 278, 304, 305,
    306, 308
  1973–1975, 353, 375, 376, 380, 383,
    385, 388, 404, 406, 407, 410,
    473nn4,5,7, 474nn3,12, 475n14
Soviet Union
  aid, xii, xvi, 21, 29, 30, 97
  pilots, 114
  training, 36, 165
Spratley Islands, 412, 424–425
Stalay-Taylor plan. See under Strategy,
  U.S.
Strategic hamlets, xii, xiii, 81, 109–110,
  113, 117, 121, 134, 135. See also
  Strategy, U.S., strategic hamlet
  program
Strategic transportation route. See Ho Chi
  Minh Trail
Strategy, Communist, xii, 12, 73–76,
  124–125, 247–248, 299, 312, 340,
  359, 375, 378, 397, 410–411
  armed struggle, 50, 82
  political struggle, x, 4, 14–15, 17–19,
    42–44, 82, 180
  quick victory, 137, 143, 171–172
  Tet offensive, 206–207, 214–215
  See also Politburo Resolutions
Strategy, South Vietnamese
  to eradicate the communists, xi, 20, 42,
    44, 47
  to flood territory, 328
  strategic withdrawal, 375, 390, 396,
    400
Strategy, U.S., 4, 73, 206, 396–397, 410,
  462n2

clear and hold, 237
Collins plan, 15
limited war, 125, 143, 153–154, 231, 232
Nixon Doctrine, 238, 257, 311, 334
pacification, 195, 237, 247, 272
search and destroy, 153, 176–177, 195–196
special warfare, 81, 108, 123–124, 125, 153
Stalay-Taylor plan, 81, 110, 116, 122
strategic hamlet program, xii, 81, 109, 122
Vietnamization, 238, 253, 272, 273, 298

Tan Son Nhat airbase, attacks on, 136, 203, 329, 415–416, 417
Ta Quang Ty, 140, 461n28
Ta Thi Kieu, 118, 459n49
Ta Xuan Thu, 97
Taylor, Maxwell, 81, 123, 124
Tay Ninh, 59, 64, 65, 193, 197–198, 231, 249, 295, 357, 455n21
"Tenets of the Revolution in South Vietnam," 43, 46
Tet Offensive
  August mini-Tet, 230–231
  Central Vietnam, 217
  communist assessment of, 217, 219, 221, 222, 223–224
  Danang, 217
  Hue, 217–219
  May mini-Tet, 227–229
  Mekong Delta, 221–222
  planning, 206–207, 214–215
  Saigon, 219–221
  See also Strategy, Communist
Thailand
  Royal Thai Army, 271, 287, 298, 301, 302
  U.S. airbases in, 317, 318, 323
Thai Nguyen, 11, 190, 324, 325
Thanh Hoa, 6, 132, 166, 190, 205, 321
Thua Thien, 52, 135, 180, 194, 201, 379, 380, 463n8
Thu Dau Mot, 17, 46, 47, 121, 135, 184, 356
Ton Duc Thang, 253, 326, 341, 426

Tonkin Gulf incident, xii, 132
Tra Bong uprising, 54–57
Tran Dang Ninh, 10
Tran Dinh Xu, 139
Tran Do, 127, 146, 295
Tran Hanh, 166
Tran Huu Duc, 341
Tran Kien, 144
Tran Luong, 48, 84
Tran Minh Chung, 169
Tran Minh Thiet, 392
Tran Nam Trung, 341, 342
Tran Phu Cuong, 220
Tran Qui Hai, 216
Tran The Mon, 211, 256, 293
Tran Van Huong, 410, 416
Tran Van Quang, 89, 211
Tran Van Tra, 127, 295, 341, 397
Tra Vinh, 58, 115, 202, 221, 237, 308, 309, 422
Truong Chinh, 18, 102
Tua Hai, battle of, 59, 64
Tuyen Quang, 11

U Minh. See Base areas
U Minh Battalion, 4, 58, 64
U.S. Air Force, 161, 318, 470n8. See also Aircraft, U.S./South Vietnamese; Ho Chi Minh Trail, bombing of; North Vietnam, bombing of
U.S. allies, in Vietnam, 154, 195. See also Australia; New Zealand; South Korea; Thailand
U.S. Army 1st Air Cavalry Division, 154, 160, 178, 199, 212, 216, 229, 245, 246, 255, 467n21
  Ia Drang battle, 158–159
U.S. Army 1st Division, 160–161, 199, 212, 221, 245, 463n4, 465n28
U.S. Army 4th Division, 212, 464n10, 465n28
U.S. Army 9th Division, 245, 246, 464n10
U.S. Army 23rd (Americal) Division, 231, 245
U.S. Army 25th Division, 199, 221, 245, 246, 255, 464n10, 465n28
U.S. Army 101st Division, 212, 215, 216, 246